# TUDOR AND STUART
# BRITAIN

## 1471–1714

Second Edition

Rubens painting of the Union of England and Scotland; end panel of ceiling, Banqueting House, Whitehall.

Reproduced by gracious permission of Her Majesty The Queen.

# TUDOR AND STUART
# BRITAIN
# 1471–1714

*Second Edition*

ROGER LOCKYER

*Reader in History at Royal Holloway College*

*in the University of London*

St. Martin's Press, Inc.
New York

LONGMAN GROUP UK LIMITED
Longman House, Burnt Mill, Harlow, Essex CM20 2JE, England
and Associated Companies throughout the World

Published in the United States of America
by St. Martin's Press, Inc.

First published 1964
Second edition 1985
Fifth impression 1993

ISBN 0 312 82254 5

Produced by Longman Singapore Publishers Pte Ltd
Printed in Singapore

The Publisher's policy is to use paper manufactured from
sustainable forests.

# Contents

# Preface

This book was originally published twenty years ago, and during that time the interpretation of many aspects of Tudor and Stuart history has undergone radical change. My aim in preparing this new edition has been to incorporate the most recent findings, and this has led to such substantial alterations that the book has been completely rewritten. In the Preface to the first edition I described it as an interim report. The same is true of this new version, for there has been no slackening in the pace of historical investigation, and doubtless many hypotheses that now seem not only novel but convincing will in due course be challenged and overthrown. But I hope I have given a comprehensive and accurate summary of current interpretations of Tudor and Stuart history and indicated not only the complexity of the issues but also something of their fascination.

Roger Lockyer                                             London 1984

# I

# The New Monarchy

## The End of the Wars of the Roses

Edward IV, Duke of York, claimed the English throne and began his reign as King Edward IV in 1461. Nine years later he was driven out of his kingdom by a Lancastrian coup, but after only a few months in exile he returned to England, crushed the Lancastrians at the battle of Tewkesbury in May 1471, and thereafter kept a firm hold on power until his death in 1483. He left his throne to his son and namesake, the twelve-year-old Edward V. The real ruler of England, however, was Richard, Duke of Gloucester, the brother of the late King. Richard is traditionally one of the villains of English history, and Tudor historians painted an unforgettable picture of the royal Satan: 'little of stature, ill featured of limbs, crookbacked, his left shoulder much higher than his right, hard-favoured of visage . . . malicious, wrathful, envious'. How true a picture this is, it is now impossible to say, but there is no logical reason for going to the other extreme and believing that Richard was kind-hearted and unambitious. Whether or not he really murdered Edward V and his brother, the Princes in the Tower, there is little doubt that he was capable of it. Yet if Richard was a bad man he was not therefore a bad king. Indeed, by seizing the crown for himself, and ruling with a firmness worthy of his brother, Richard may have prevented England from slipping into anarchy once again, as could so easily happen during a royal minority.

When Henry Tudor, Earl of Richmond and leader of the Lancastrians, defeated and killed Richard III at Bosworth in August 1485 he checked the restoration of royal authority that had been steadily proceeding. It seemed as though the Wars of the Roses were about to break out again, and disorder was widespread. For several years Henry was concerned mainly with establishing himself on the throne, for the Yorkists did not regard their defeat as final. In 1487 they put forward Lambert Simnel, the son of an obscure tradesman, as the Earl of Warwick, Richard III's nephew and therefore the chief Yorkist claimant to the throne. Henry, who had the real Earl of Warwick in the Tower of London, paraded him publicly through the streets, but this gesture alone could not avert the Yorkist threat. Simnel and the Yorkist lords had landed in Lancashire and were marching south. Henry only saved his throne by fighting for it. In June 1487 he met the Yorkist army at Stoke, near Newark, and destroyed it. Simnel was captured and allowed to relapse into obscurity as a turnspit in the royal kitchens.

Although this revolt had been easily crushed, the Yorkists were not defeated. Neither were they reconciled to Tudor rule by Henry's conciliatory gesture of marrying Edward IV's daughter, Elizabeth of York, shortly after his accession to the throne. In 1491 they chose Perkin Warbeck, the son of a Tournai Customs officer, to impersonate Richard, Duke of York, the brother of Edward V and one of the Princes in the Tower. Warbeck learnt his part well, and was accepted by the King of France and by Edward IV's sister, Margaret of Burgundy — who both had good reasons for intriguing against the new King of England. In July 1495 Warbeck appeared off Deal and landed a number of men, while prudently remaining on board himself. The invaders were quickly rounded up by the sheriff of Kent, so Warbeck sailed off first to Ireland and then to Scotland to try his luck. James IV of Scotland, who was suspicious of English power, welcomed the self-styled Duke of York, and in September 1496 a Scottish army poured across the border and invaded the northern counties. Warbeck, who was with the troops, called upon 'his' subjects to rise against the Tudor usurper, but they showed remarkably little inclination to do so. The Scots, who could not plunge deep into England without support from the English, turned their attack into a raiding expedition and returned home. Warbeck had no choice but to go with them. A year later he tried his fortunes in Cornwall, where the inhabitants had just risen against Henry VII because of his demands for taxation. But although a large number of men came in to join Warbeck, he could not capture Exeter, the key to the west country, and as success eluded him his followers slipped away. In the end he abandoned the struggle and his ambitions, and threw himself on Henry's mercy. Henry kept him in prison for two years, until another impostor appeared, claiming to be the Earl of Warwick. The King realised that he would have no peace while the Yorkist claimants remained alive, since their mere existence encouraged rebellion. In November 1499, therefore, Warwick and Warbeck, the real earl and the false duke, were both tried for treason, condemned and executed.

Henry was now well established on the throne. He had been recognised by the princes of Europe, he had sons to succeed him, and the longer he kept the crown the more secure he became. Yet he could never afford to relax his watch, for the Yorkists were still plotting and waiting for their opportunity. As late as 1503, when the King lay sick, it was reported from Calais that a number of important officials assembled there had discussed what would happen after Henry's death. 'Some of them', said the informant, 'spake of my lord of Buckingham, saying that he was a noble man and would be a royal ruler. Other there were that spake . . . of Edmund de la Pole. But none of them spake of my lord prince.' Yet when Henry died in 1509 his son succeeded him without difficulty. This showed that, despite the relapse into disorder which followed the death of Richard III, royal authority had been effectively restored.

## *The Revival of Royal Power. I: The Council*

The revival of royal power was carried out through the household and Council. There had for long been an inner and an outer ring in the administration. In the early Middle Ages the expansion of royal government had led to specialisation, and within the King's household departments emerged to deal with finance and secretarial business. These departments, the Exchequer and Chancery, gradually moved out of court and acquired their own routines, but they were still under royal control. As the barons became more powerful, however, and more politically ambitious, they forced their own nominees into these great offices, so as to take over the administration. But the King's household was perpetually fecund. While the barons were taking over the outer ring, an inner ring of household offices was being created, and the Wardrobe or Chamber by-passed the old-established offices and left them only the trappings of power. In times of emergency a determined king could govern his country through the household offices, They were flexible and informal, not yet hamstrung by the formalisation that made the Exchequer, for instance, so ponderous and long-winded in its functioning. Edward IV and Henry VII found within their own household an efficient machine that only needed to be set to work.

The mainspring of royal government was the King's Council, but from the early fourteenth century onwards the magnates claimed a larger and larger share in this body, and eventually came to dominate it. Asserting that they were the King's natural advisers, they had made him accept them whether he wanted to or not. By the time Edward IV came to the throne the Council was a large, aristocratic body, functioning more or less independently of the crown. Edward, however, had no use for such an institution. He wanted something much more immediately under his control, and he created a Council very similar in its composition to that which Henry VII was later to use.

The names survive of nearly 230 people who were called 'Councillors' in Henry's reign, and they can be divided up, as can

Edward's, into nobles, clerics, and a large 'official' element made up of lawyers and country gentlemen trained in estate management. The similarity between the Yorkist and the Tudor body extends not only to structure but even to individuals, since 29 of Henry's Councillors had served Richard III or Edward IV in the same capacity. Trained and efficient men were not, after all, so easily come by that any monarch could afford to deprive himself of their services simply because they had fought for the other side. Neither were Yorkists and Lancastrians separate and unmixable elements, like oil and water. Many people, particularly of the country gentry and lawyer sections of society, were prepared to serve the crown no matter who was wearing it.

There was not much sign under Henry VII, any more than there had been under Edward IV, of a deliberate attempt to oust nobles from the Council, for individual nobles were still men of great estates, and therefore of great influence. Under Henry, several of the most important positions in the administration were held by men who came from long-ennobled families. The Lord Admiral and Constable of the Tower, for instance, was John de Vere, thirteenth Earl of Oxford; while Thomas Howard, Earl of Surrey, who had actually fought against Henry at Bosworth, emerged from three years' imprisonment to take a leading place in the royal Council and to become one of Henry's best soldiers. But Henry was extremely reluctant to create new peerages, perhaps for fear of building up aristocratic power to the point where it might threaten him and his successors. Giles Daubeny, who had been in exile with Henry, was made a baron in 1486, but the few other peerages that Henry conferred were recreations of dormant titles. Henry preferred to reward his faithful servants by appointing them Knights of the Garter — a great honour, of course, but not one which they could pass on to their heirs.

Clerics outnumbered nobles in the Council, and played as big a part as they had done throughout the Middle Ages. Henry VII's most trusted adviser was John Morton, who became Lord Chancellor in 1487 and was to be a cardinal and Archbishop of Canterbury before his death. Among the others were Richard Fox, the King's Secretary and later Keeper of the Privy Seal, who rose to be Bishop of Winchester; and William Warham, who succeeded Morton as Chancellor and also became Archbishop of Canterbury. The big advantage of these men, from Henry's point of view, was that they were well educated, could be rewarded for service to the state by promotion in the Church (which cost Henry nothing) and left no heirs with a legitimate claim to either their wealth or their offices.

As well as nobles and clerics, the late Yorkist and early Tudor Council included the judges and law officers of the crown. There was nothing new in this. The element of novelty was to be found in the 'official' element in the Council, made up of men who were 'new' only in the sense that they did not belong to the handful of great families which had controlled English life in the preceding century. These were the men whom Warbeck denounced as 'caitiffs', but they were far removed from the ordinary people. The majority were country gentlemen, who had been trained in either civil or common law. Empson was the only prominent member of Henry's Council to come from a bourgeois background — his father was a person of some importance in the town of Towcester — and the idea that Henry VII surrounded himself with 'middle-class men' is very misleading. The gentry, whose numbers and importance in the royal administration were steadily increasing, were close in blood and social assumptions to the aristocracy, and counted themselves among the upper ranks of English society.

Although the potential membership of the Council was over 200, numbers varied in practice from four to forty, with seven as the most frequent. A handful of Councillors were regular attenders and formed, in effect though not in name, an inner circle. They were full-time administrators and attended the King not only during the law-terms, when most of the business was transacted, but during vacations as well. This 'Council attendant' was a skeleton staff which simply merged into the larger body when a full meeting took place. Its members included the great officers of state — the Chancellor, Treasurer and Privy Seal — and such officials as Bray, Daubeny and Guildford, who were among the most trusted of Henry VII's servants. The King himself was the heart of the Council, giving it a cohesion and continuity that it would not otherwise have possessed. Both Edward and Henry were frequently, if not usually, present at meetings, and the Council was an extension of the royal personality.

Because it had the authority of the King behind it the Council's competence was virtually unlimited, at least in the administrative sphere, although in practice it made no distinction between administrative and judicial business. It sat regularly in the term time and used for its meetings the two rooms that made up the Star Chamber. Its advisory and administrative functions were probably the most important part of its work, although much of this can only be inferred, since the Council had no seal of its own and had to use the Signet or Privy Seal to authenticate its decisions. Councillors offered advice to the King on matters of policy, and framed letters, warrants, proclamations and all the other documents necessary to execute the royal will.

Until recently historians took it for granted that Henry VII's Council, sitting to do justice in Star Chamber, summoned overmighty offenders to appear before it and more or less superseded the common-law courts in cases of livery (the keeping of retainers) and maintenance (the supporting of unjust claims in courts by violence or threats). Yet in fact the Council rarely dealt with these offences, and the vast majority of cases which came before it were initiated by private suitors. These cases were nominally concerned with rioting, but more often than not this was just a legal fiction to enable the Council to consider disputes over property, which, according to a statute of Edward III's reign, were to be reserved to the common-law courts. Plaintiffs had a number of reasons for seeking redress through the Council rather than the ordinary law courts. The Council, after all, consisted of the most important men in the kingdom, whose decisions were not lightly to be challenged or ignored, and it acted with a speed and resolution that were far from typical of King's Bench, Common Pleas, and the other courts of common law. Yet the influx of private business meant that the Council could not — as Henry may originally have intended — take the lead in imposing order on a turbulent society.

However, the imposition of order remained a major priority throughout Henry's reign. A typical example of the problems with which he was confronted comes from 1486, when the Prior of Leominster complained that a local Justice of the Peace had attacked his community with 160 armed men, who tore down a large tree which they used as a battering-ram to breach the walls of the priory's gaol and free the prisoners inside. Much of the disorder throughout England sprang from the practice of keeping retainers, but Henry never attempted to outlaw this entirely. Retaining was not always harmful. Much depended upon the character and attitude of the man who was responsible for it; if he chose to employ his followers as a police force to impose discipline upon the local communities he was strengthening the social fabric, not weakening it. And in times of crisis Henry was dependent upon the goodwill of his greater subjects, for in the absence of a standing army they alone could provide the soldiers whom he needed. Henry's aim, therefore, was not to abolish retaining but to make sure, as far as possible, that it was used to the public benefit. He took a big step in this direction with a statute of 1504 requiring all those who had retainers to submit a list of their names to the King and obtain a licence from him. This Act did not put an end to retaining, nor was it designed to do so, but it enabled the practice to be brought under an increasing degree of royal control in the reigns of subsequent Tudor monarchs.

The problem of restoring and maintaining order was not susceptible of any simple solution, Henry used a variety of methods. A statute of 1487 — later, and misleadingly, called the 'Star Chamber Act', though it had no connexion with the court of that name — set up a small tribunal of leading Councillors to enforce the laws relat-

ing to livery and maintenance. It is impossible to estimate the effectiveness of this tribunal, since only a handful of records survives of
cases brought before it. However, the fact that the 1487 statute was
re-enacted in 1529 suggests that it had proved useful.

The Council Learned — so called because the majority of its
twelve or so members were 'learned in law' — was another specialised tribunal, though unlike the 1487 one it was based upon the
royal prerogative and not statute. It acted as a debt collecting
agency for the crown, and undertook prosecutions in which the
crown had an interest — usually financial. The Council Learned
was also involved in the drawing up of bonds and recognisances,
binding the person concerned to good behaviour under threat of
a monetary penalty. Hency used these on an unprecedented scale,
as a means of holding the chief men in his kingdom under restraint,
and more than two-thirds of the English nobility were 'at the
King's mercy' in this way during his reign. Henry, in effect, put
the peerage on probation, and the penalties he imposed for anti-
social behaviour could be substantial. In 1504, to take one example,
the Earl of Northumberland and the Archbishop of York, whose
retainers had been involved in a number of violent clashes, were
both required to give bonds of £2,000 to keep the peace towards
each other, and another nobleman, the Earl of Shrewsbury, was
made to take out so many bonds that by the time of Henry's death
he was 'endangered' for more than £5,000. Bonds and recognisances were probably the most effective of the instruments which
Henry employed to impose order, but the nobles who were brought
under constraint in this arbitrary manner bitterly resented the
King's actions. There was nothing they could do about it while
Henry lived, but Empson and Dudley, who were the two members
of the Council Learned most closely associated with these aspects
of Henry's policy, were made scapegoats by the young Henry VIII
and put to death in 1509 — a sign that the harsh regime of the first
Tudor was over, and that the new King intended to win the love
and affection of his greater subjects rather than hold them at arm's
length.

The areas on the borders of Wales and Scotland were remote
from London and particularly liable to disorder. In 1471 Edward
IV created his baby son Prince of Wales and appointed a council
to look after his estates. This council subsequently acquired judicial
functions and supervised the enforcement of law and order throughout the Principality and the marcher lordships which separated
Wales from England. It lapsed at Edward's death, but Henry VII
appointed a similar council for his son, Prince Arthur. The young
prince was later given most of the crown's marcher lordships, including the great Earldom of March, as well as the Principality,
and thus became direct ruler over a large part of Wales. Even after

his death the council continued its work, and the marcher lords, who had previously been semi-independent magnates, were forced to acknowledge the authority of the crown.

To control the north of England, where the great border families of Percy, Neville and Dacre ruled like independent princes, Edward IV made use of his brother Richard, Duke of Gloucester. Richard ruled the north well, and when he became King he kept a council there under the presidency of his nephew, the Earl of Lincoln. At the beginning of Henry VII's reign control of the north slipped back into the hands of the Percies, but after the death of the head of the Percy family, the Earl of Northumberland — killed in a riot at Thirsk while acting as the King's tax collector — Henry took over the guardianship of his estates, thereby becoming a northern magnate in his own right. He subsequently nominated his eldest son, Prince Arthur, as Warden-General of the Marches (the Scottish borderland area), with Thomas Howard, Earl of Surrey, as his deputy and effective head of the administration. Surrey was also the King's lieutenant in the north, and the council which was appointed to advise him performed many of the functions previously carried out by the Yorkist council. It also provided the basis on which, in Henry VIII's reign, a formally-constituted Council of the North was to be established.

No outline of late Yorkist and early Tudor administration would be complete that left out the personality of the monarch. The institutions of government were old; it was the strong will behind them that was new. Much of the achievement of Edward IV and Henry VII was due simply to their energy and determination. When disorder broke out in East Anglia, Edward appointed one of his household officers as sheriff and publicly declared that, though he could ill spare so valuable a man, he had sent him down 'to set a rule in the country', and in 1464 Edward himself went on a tour of the most disturbed districts to make sure that order was enforced and justice administered. Richard and Henry were also constantly on the move, asserting the royal authority simply by making their presence known.

Henry had none of Edward IV's easy charm, but he shared the same iron determination to hold his throne. He had a shadowy claim by blood, being descended, through his mother, from Edward III, but his real title came from victory in battle. He had killed Richard III and taken his crown; he would remain King as long as he could hold off all challengers. Henry was only twenty-eight when he triumphed at Bosworth, and had spent much of his life in exile. The portraits show a clean-cut face with a Roman nose, but they also suggest what his contemporaries remarked about him — a watchful reserve that allowed little or no intimacy. Bacon, in his *Life of King Henry VII*, commented that if he had been a 'private man he would have been termed proud; but in a wise prince it was but keeping of distance'. Because he was a good judge of men, Henry was not jealous of ability, and was served as well as, if not better than, any other Tudor sovereign. He did not have the streak of vindictiveness that was to emerge in his son, and although he would not shirk killing his enemies, he preferred to take their money and let them live. After the failure of Warbeck's rising in the west country, for instance, Henry appointed commissioners to fine all those who had taken part and eventually added nearly £15,000 to his treasury.

The legend of the miser King obscures the true image of the ruler who deliberately cultivated pomp and ceremony in order to raise the throne above the reach of even the greatest noble. Like most men Henry loved money, and between 1491 and 1503 he spent over £100,000 on jewellery, but this was more than a miser's inexplicable greed. The medieval monarchy had collapsed because it had become so poor. Henry knew that if the crown was to be made strong again, it must first be made rich.

## The Revival of Royal Power. II: Finance

There was nothing new about Henry's financial system, except its thoroughness. Edward IV had revived the Chamber and made it the centre of his financial organisation. The Exchequer was bypassed because its methods were too cumbersome and its traditional routine made it insufficiently flexible to meet the demands of the crown. Edward had removed at least part of his lands from Exchequer control. Henry eventually went further and ordered that all receipts from crown lands were to be paid to the Treasurer of the Chamber. Other items of revenue were gradually transferred until the Exchequer was left with only the 'ancient revenue', made up of the *firma comitatus* and the *firma burgi* (long-established annual payments made by counties and boroughs), and the Customs. The Duchy of Lancaster, a model of estate administration, continued to handle its own revenues. Everything else went to the Chamber.

Since the Exchequer did not handle the bulk of the revenue, it could hardly audit it. Henry VII continued Edward IV's practice of appointing officials to audit specific accounts, but he came increasingly to rely upon the assistance of one of his most trusted advisers, Sir Reginald Bray. Bray developed an informal court of audit — which was to be given formal status in Henry VIII's reign as the 'General Surveyors' — but Henry never relaxed his grip, and regularly inspected and initialled the accounts submitted by the Treasurer of the Chamber.

Henry paid particular attention to land revenues, and made the royal estates the foundation of the crown's wealth. By Act of Par-

liament in 1486 he took back into the crown's possession many of
the lands which had been allowed to slip from its grasp in the preceding thirty years of unrest, and throughout his reign he added
to this endowment by confiscating the estates of his enemies. Land
also contributed to the royal finances in another way. Ever since
the Norman Conquest a great deal of property throughout England
had been held on a feudal tenure by 'tenants-in-chief' in return for
providing knights for use in the royal army. By the late fifteenth
century feudalism as a military and social system was in decay, but
Henry was insistent on exacting the financial dues which were an
integral part of it. He could demand extraordinary 'aids', such as
those which Parliament granted for the knighting of Prince Arthur
and the marriage of Princess Margaret. More important, however,
were the 'incidents' which had to be paid every time a death occurred in a landholding family. If the tenant left no heir, then the
crown exercised the right of escheat and took charge of his estates.
Where an heiress succeeded, the crown either made her pay for
freedom to choose a husband or else married her off to the highest
bidder. If the heir was a boy, he became a royal ward, and the
crown would take over his estates until he became of age, or would
sell the guardianship for a large sum of money. In either case the
unfortunate ward's lands would probably be exploited by those
who, in theory, were responsible for safeguarding them.

   Landholders resented this land tax — since that, in effect, is what
it was — as a threat to the prosperity of their estates, and frequently
concealed information about changes that had taken place. Edward
IV appointed commissions to enquire into feudal tenures and make
sure that he was not being cheated of his rights. Henry VII did the
same, and some idea of the resistance offered by landed families is
given by the fact that out of the last fifty *post-mortem* Inquisitions
calendared for Henry's reign — these were enquiries held after the
death of a landholder, to record the change of tenure — well over
half report that the existence of under-age heirs had been deliberately concealed. As a result of enlarging the royal estates and also
of enforcing fiscal feudalism, Henry pushed up his land revenues
by some 45 per cent from £29,000 to £42,000. He also increased the
yield from Customs — duties on trade, of which the most important
were Tonnage and Poundage, voted to Henry for life by the first
Parliament of his reign. The Book of Rates, upon which the yield
of the Customs dues depended, was revised in 1507, and the restoration of stability in government and society encouraged the expansion of commerce. By 1509 Customs were bringing in some
£40,000 a year, an increase of more than 20 per cent over the course
of Henry's reign.

   Edward and Henry both dabbled in trade on their own account.
Edward's agents bought up wool and tin, and shipped these to con-

tinental markets, while Henry made £15,000 from the sale of alum in 1505–6. They showed the same readiness to exploit every source of income open to them, by levying loans and gifts. Edward borrowed money from an Italian financier and from the City of London, but most of these loans had been repaid by his death. Henry took a forced loan in 1486, but this was likewise repaid, and his credit stood high. 'Benevolences' were another matter. Edward IV's demands for 'voluntary' gifts as a sign of the *benevolentia,* or goodwill, which his richer subjects bore him, had been so bitterly resented that a statute of Richard III's reign declared them to be illegal. Nevertheless, Henry raised Benevolences on the grounds of urgent military need. On the face of it, this was an arbitrary exercise of the royal will, but in fact the tax system was rigged in favour of the richer subjects, and Benevolences were one way — admittedly crude and unsatisfactory — of making the more prosperous section of the population contribute a fairer share towards the King's expenses. Yet it remains true that the 'new monarchy', so efficient in administration and expenditure, clung to antiquated methods of collecting money. Henry VII was perhaps strong enough to have reformed the entire financial system, even at the risk of offending the landowners and merchants whose support he needed. But he never did so, nor did his son, and later monarchs were in no position to take such drastic action.

For extraordinary supplies of money Henry turned to Parliament, but he did this as rarely as possible, preferring to follow the example of Edward IV, who told the Commons in 1467: 'I purpose to live upon mine own, and not to charge my subjects but in great and urgent causes concerning the weal of themselves and also the defence of them, and of this my realm'. Any parliamentary taxation was liable to arouse resentment, or even open rebellion, as in the case of the Cornish rising. This alone would account for the fact that Edward, who reigned for twenty-two years, only met six Parliaments, while Henry, who reigned for twenty-four years, was content with seven.

Parliament was still primarily what it had been in the Middle Ages, a meeting of the King and his Council with the peers of the realm. The Commons sat separately, except on a few ceremonial occasions, when they were technically onlookers. The Lords held their debates in a room in the royal palace of Westminster, where they were grouped around the throne. The King himself was often present, and in his absence the Lord Chancellor presided. The Lords consisted of two estates, spiritual and secular. Only thirteen bishops and seventeen abbots and priors came to the first Parliament of Henry's reign, but in a full House the spiritual peers numbered nearly fifty. There were far fewer lay lords; only eighteen attended the first Parliament. This was in part the consequence of the bitter struggle between York and Lancaster, in which many nobles had lost their lives — not so much on the battlefield as by execution, following their defeat and capture. A number of noble families had died out in the male line. Others had been incorporated into the crown. Henry was Earl of Richmond in his own right, and as King he was heir to the Dukedom of Lancaster and also to the Yorkist titles, the Dukedom of York and the Earldoms of March and Warwick. Those families which not only survived but retained their separate identity were often headed by minors, but as the reign progressed minors came of age, attainders were reversed, and eventually there were some fifty lay lords eligible to sit in the Upper House — though it is not known how many of them actually did so.

While the Lords were meeting in the royal palace the Commons were crammed into the nearby chapter house of the Abbey of Westminster. But although the Commons were lower in status than the Lords they were not without power. Since Edward III's reign their assent had been essential to money Bills, and in 1487 the judges declared that an Act of Parliament was not valid unless the Commons had agreed to it. In the later Middle Ages many constituencies had resented sending a member to Parliament at their expense, but this attitude was slowly changing. The increasing importance of the Commons was shown by the presence there of many of the King's Councillors, who, although technically members of the Lords, preferred to exert their influence in the Lower House.

The main function of Parliament, in Henry VII's reign, was to vote money. The standard parliamentary grant, the Tenth and Fifteenth, had originally been a charge on movable property, but had ossified into a fixed levy of about £30,000. Each county knew how much it would be expected to pay, and the incidence of the tax took little note of changes in the distribution of wealth. Various attempts had been made in the Lancastrian period to make parliamentary taxes a truer reflection of the wealth of the nation, and these were taken up by Henry in 1489. In that year Parliament voted him £100,000 to help hold in check the ambitions of the King of France, and it was decided that the greater part of this sum should be raised by a 10 per cent tax based on a new assessment. Royal commissioners were accordingly despatched into the localities to carry this out, but their activities, and indeed the whole idea of a new and realistic assessment, were deeply resented, and in a number of places anger flared into open violence. After a brawl at Thirsk, for instance, in which the Earl of Northumberland — who was one of the royal commissioners — was killed, the tax rebels laid siege to York, and Henry had to raise an army to restore order. Despite this rebuff he repeated the experiment in 1497 and 1504, and thereby helped prepare public opinion for the 'subsidy', the standard Tudor tax, which was implemented by Wolsey in the following reign.

Edward IV and Henry VII summoned Parliaments not only to get money but also to make statutes, which were binding on the judges and enforceable in the courts of common law. There were some two hundred statutes passed during Henry's reign, but many of these probably originated from the Commons, for one of the functions of members was to promote Bills designed to remedy the grievances of their constituents. A number of statutes, however, were clearly the result of government initiative. They included Acts of attainder, which were designed to cripple the King's enemies by depriving them of their property. Henry made considerable use of attainder, and 138 people suffered in this way during the course of his reign. Statute was also used to reinforce the authority of J.P.s, who were the King's agents for governing the local communities and bringing malefactors to justice. In 1495, for instance, they were authorised to determine a whole range of minor offences without waiting for formal 'presentation' by a grand jury. They were also instructed to supervise and control local officials and to make sure that the sheriffs did not show partiality when they embodied jury panels. Other statutes were designed to bring corporations and franchises under closer royal control, to improve the coinage, and to establish uniform weights and measures. Attempts were also made to stimulate the economy, and to inhibit social change. In 1489 the first general statute against depopulating enclosures was passed, and 1485 and 1489 saw the passage of Navigation Acts designed to promote the shipping industry and thereby increase England's naval strength.

## Foreign Policy

One of the main reasons for the collapse of the medieval monarchy had been the enormous cost of the long war against France. Neither Edward nor Henry could afford to uphold the English Kings' claim to the French throne. Yet kings were expected to fight, and it seemed as if the only alternatives were a bankrupting war or an inglorious peace. Edward IV found a way out of this dilemma. In 1474 he allied with the Duke of Burgundy against France, called on Parliament to vote supplies, and led a fine army across the Channel. The French king, however, had no more desire for war than Edward, and offered terms which Edward accepted. By the Treaty of Picquigny Edward agreed to withdraw his troops from France — while maintaining his theoretical claim to the French throne — in return for a large cash payment and a pension for life. This profitable example was closely followed by Henry VII. He sent an army to Brittany to try to prevent the French king from annexing the strategically important seaboard duchy, but when this failed he invaded France in person. Charles VIII, now that he had secured Brittany, saw no point in further fighting. A treaty was signed at Etaples in 1492, by which Charles bound himself not to assist pretenders to the English throne and to pay Henry an annual pension. Henry returned to England triumphant, and richer than when he had set out.

As the Tudor dynasty became more firmly settled on the throne, it was accepted by the European ruling families, and marriage negotiations were started. As early as 1489 it was agreed, in the Treaty of Medina del Campo, that Henry's eldest son, Prince Arthur, should marry Catherine of Aragon, daughter of the King of Spain. The marriage did not actually take place until 1501, when the young princess landed in England, and it lasted only a few months, for in the following year Arthur died. Ferdinand wanted to keep the English alliance which the marriage had symbolised, and Henry was reluctant to lose the dowry, so negotiations were opened for a second marriage, this time between Catherine and Henry's second son Prince Henry. There were difficulties to be overcome, including the fact that a papal dispensation was needed to set aside the law of the Church that a man might not marry his brother's widow. Agreement was eventually reached, but by the time the marriage took place Henry VII was dead. Before his death he had arranged another alliance of great significance for the future. In an attempt to put an end to the perpetual tension between England and Scotland he married his daughter Margaret to James IV in 1503 and thereby opened the way to the union of the crowns that came about exactly a century later.

## A 'New' Monarchy?

By the time Henry died he was enjoying what Bacon called 'the felicity of full coffers', and this was a major achievement after the breakdown of royal finances in the late Lancastrian period. Henry probably left only a small amount of money, but his plate and jewels, on which he had spent heavily, were worth many thousands of pounds. By English standards — though not by those of the rulers of major states such as France and Spain — Henry was rich, and solvency was one of the most novel aspects of the so-called 'New Monarchy' of the Yorkist and early Tudor period. But from the point of view of institutions there was little that was truly new about the reigns of Edward IV and Henry VII. The Council was medieval in origin; Chamber finance was similar in all essentials to the Wardrobe administration of the fourteenth century; and as for the use of 'new men', this was as old as the monarchy itself. There were elements of despotism in Yorkist and early Tudor government, particularly the prerogative courts and the all-powerful royal Council. But there were other elements, such as the common law and the reliance on country gentlemen for local government, that pulled in the opposite direction. Edward and Henry could conceivably have created — or at least tried to create — a more autocratic monarchy on the French pattern, but instead of remodelling English administration and using the royal Council, as their French and Spanish contemporaries did, to invade and take over all other departments of government, they chose the easier course of pumping new blood and vigour into the existing system. The significance of the 'New Monarchs' in the history of Tudor and Stuart Britain comes mainly from the fact that they preserved so much of the past.

# 2

# King and Cardinal

## Henry VIII

The accession of Henry VIII, a handsome, energetic young man,
not yet eighteen, effectively closed the struggle between rival houses
for the throne. While through his father he was the heir to Lancaster, through his mother he was the descendant of York, and as
John Skelton, his tutor and later laureate, declared:

> The Rose both white and red
> In one Rose now doth grow.

Henry's looks were commented on by many foreign observers.
The Venetian ambassador reported that the new King 'is the hand-
somest potentate I ever set eyes on . . . with auburn hair combed
straight and short in the French fashion, and a round face so very
beautiful that it would become a pretty woman', and others pointed
the contrast between the reserved, calculating Henry VII and his
apparently open-hearted, impulsive son.

Henry's character, however, remains a puzzle. Throughout the
first half of his reign he devoted his days to hunting and his nights
to feasting and love, content to leave routine administration and
the formulation of policy to Wolsey. He was never a mere cipher
and occasionally interfered with Wolsey's arrangements, but in the
late 1520s he suddenly emerged as a controlling figure in English
politics, and remained for the rest of his reign much nearer the
heart of government than he had ever been before. The extent to
which he actually initiated policy has almost certainly been exaggerated. The playboy did not turn into an elder statesman overnight, and because he kept his distaste for the day-to-day business
of government — reading documents, weighing opinions, working
out consistent policies — the initiative rested with his servants,
particularly when they were men of outstanding ability like Wolsey
and Thomas Cromwell.. Yet however secure Henry's ministers
seemed to be in their position, the King was never dependent on
them. Their policies were effective only because he approved of
them, and when, in a dark mood of anger or suspicion, he chose

to seize the initiative himself, he swept his advisers out of his way with a ruthlessness unrestrained by gratitude or fear. While these sporadic outbursts of energy lasted he remained, in fact as well as in title, master of England.

For the first twenty years of his reign this arrogant, imperious young man was content to play the prince and let others govern for him. Having been kept very much in the background by Henry VII he found the business of government unfamiliar and uncongenial and preferred, like many a child of the second generation, to enjoy the magnificent inheritance that his father had handed on to him. Only in one incident did a hint of later attitudes appear. Empson and Dudley had served his father faithfully and had done more than any other of Henry VII's Councillors to build up the wealth of the crown which the young King was now consuming. But their zeal in the royal service had made them very unpopular with the richer and politically influential section of English society. Henry VIII, looking around for some gesture that would win him easy popularity and signal the advent of a new and more relaxed reign, saw his opportunity. Empson and Dudley were tried on a trumped-up charge of treason, and executed. Lack of gratitude was to be one of the most typical of Henry's characteristics.

## *Wolsey. I: The Rise to Power*

For the first few years of the new reign Henry relied on his father's Councillors, but it was not long before Thomas Wolsey worked his way into the King's confidence and established a monopoly of royal favour that was to last for nearly twenty years. Wolsey was born in late 1472 or early 1473, the son of an Ipswich butcher and cattle dealer. For an ambitious and talented boy, not born into the upper ranks of late medieval society, the Church was the only possible opening, and Wolsey soon entered it. By the age of fifteen he was at Magdalen College, Oxford, where his contemporaries called him the 'Boy-Bachelor', and he was befriended by the Marquis of Dorset, whose children he had taught at Magdalen College School. Dorset, a nobleman of high birth, was prominent among Henry VII's Councillors and presumably recommended Wolsey to others of his circle. The ambitious clergyman soon came to the notice of Henry VII, who employed him on several diplomatic missions and was apparently impressed by his intelligence, his ability and his enormous capacity for work.

The death of Henry VII was therefore a blow to Wolsey, since he now had to establish his credentials with a new King, some eighteen years his junior. He did not have long to wait before an opportunity arose for him to prove his worth. Henry VIII, being young and rich, lacked nothing but glory. His father had held aloof from the struggle between France and Spain for control of Italy, since no vital English interests were at stake. Henry, however, was determined to make a name for himself and to reassert the ancient English claim to sovereignty over France. In this he was opposed by the Councillors he had inherited from Henry VII — men like Richard Fox, who regarded war as a plague to be avoided at all costs — but he found support and encouragement from Wolsey, who was eager to demonstrate his willingness to serve the new King as fully and faithfully as he had served the old. Plans were drawn up to join the Holy League which Pope Julius II, fearful for the safety of the papal state in Italy, was building up against France. Julius issued a brief, formally transferring to Henry both the kingdom and the titles of Louis XII, but prudently insisted that it should neither be published nor take effect until the French had actually been defeated. It was in order to achieve this that Henry, in response to pressure from his father-in-law, Ferdinand of Aragon, sent an expedition to south-west France. The idea was that it would link up with a Spanish army trying to wrest Navarre from the French, and that the joint force would then seize the great province of Guienne and restore it to the English crown. But Ferdinand — as the inexperienced Henry discovered to his cost — had no intention of keeping his bargain. He planned to use the English troops merely as a screen behind which his own men could complete the conquest of Navarre, and he had no interest in helping Henry fulfil his grandiose ambitions. The English army found itself, therefore, with no clear role to play, and the bored and frustrated troops quickly succumbed to drunkenness and dysentery. In the end, the remnants of the force had to make an ignominious return to England without accomplishing anything against the enemy.

Henry refused to be disheartened by this initial failure, and Wolsey prepared another, and larger, expedition, sparing no effort to ensure its success. The original plan was to attack Boulogne and thereby strengthen the defences of the main English stronghold at Calais, but Henry again gave way to pressure — this time from the Emperor Maximilian — and allowed his army to be used against Tournai, an isolated French outpost in the middle of Maximilian's Burgundian territories. Henry went over to Calais to take command of a force that now numbered thirty thousand men, and struck south-east towards Tournai. On 15 August 1513 a French relieving force fled so rapidly that the engagement was christened 'The Battle of the Spurs', and Tournai fell into the hands of the English — who, instead of handing it over to Maximilian, as he had hoped and assumed, held on to it for the next six years. This was not the only victory which Henry's forces gained in 1513, for the Scots — who traditionally looked to France for protection against their stronger English neighbour — took advantage of

Henry's absence to plunge across the border. The Earl of Surrey was waiting for them, however, and on 9 September destroyed the Scottish army, leaving James IV and many of his nobles dead on the field.

Henry had good reason to be satisfied. Despite the duplicity of Ferdinand and the fiasco of the first expedition he had demonstrated that his kingdom was once again a power to be reckoned with. His enhanced standing abroad was shown in 1514 when Louis XII not only accepted peace terms which included the doubling of the pension payments made under the terms of the Treaty of Etaples but also agreed to marry Henry's sister, Mary. Now that Henry had won the glory he coveted, he rewarded the man who had enabled him to do so. Wolsey was appointed Bishop of Tournai and shortly afterwards was elevated to the see of Lincoln. In 1514 Henry chose him to be the next Archbishop of York, but as long as William Warham remained alive Wolsey could never achieve the highest post in the Church in England by becoming Archbishop of Canterbury. Only a legate *a latere*, sent 'from the side of' the Pope, could supersede the Archbishop within his own province, and such appointments were made only in exceptional circumstances and for a limited period. Wolsey, however, was determined to become master of the Church in England, and with Henry's encouragement he pressed the Pope to appoint him *Legatus a latere* for life. The Pope, caught between the millstones of France and Spain, could not afford to offend so valuable and loyal an ally as the King of England, and eventually gave way. Wolsey had already been made a cardinal, in 1515; nine years later he was appointed *Legatus a latere* for life.

## Wolsey. II: The Problem of Church Reform

Wolsey had the power, as *Legatus a latere*, to intervene in every diocese, overriding the authority of bishops and archbishops alike. He had demanded this power on the grounds that he wished to reform the Church, and reform was certainly needed. There was a growing volume of complaint from the laity against pluralism and non-residence and against the high fees charged for probate and mortuary. Within the Church itself there was also a reform movement, and this was given new vitality by the Christian Renaissance, spread throughout Europe by Erasmus of Rotterdam.

Desiderius Erasmus, born in 1469, was among the first to realise that the literary treasures of the ancient world included not only the pagan classics but also the fundamental Christian texts — the Bible and the writings of the early fathers. He began collating manuscripts and produced editions of these texts which were soon circulating all over Europe.

Even before Erasmus started his work the new learning had spread to England. In 1478 the first printing press at Oxford was set up, and at about the same time an Italian scholar was brought over to the university to inaugurate the study of Greek, though no formal provision was made for this. Among his pupils was William Grocyn, who in his turn inspired a number of young men, including Thomas Linacre, Thomas More and John Colet. With them the humanist movement in England — the study of man and his relationship to God — came of age. Colet visited Italy, where he studied the early fathers, and returned to Oxford to lecture on St. Paul. It was there that Erasmus met him when, in 1499, he paid his first visit to England. The two men felt an immediate sympathy with each other and Colet introduced Erasmus to his circle of friends. Erasmus was delighted. 'I have lost little', he wrote, 'in not going to Italy. When Colet speaks I might be listening to Plato. Linacre is as deep and acute a thinker as I have ever met with. Grocyn is a mine of knowledge; and nature never formed a sweeter and happier disposition than that of Thomas More.'

Erasmus, Colet, More and their friends were all inspired by love for the Church, which they longed to cleanse of its corruption so that it could meet the challenge of an age in which the revival of antiquity and the bursting of the geographical bounds of the medieval world were dissolving so many established institutions and beliefs. As far as England was concerned, there were encouraging signs, not least among them the humanist inclinations of the young King. It was at Henry's insistence that Thomas More accepted appointment as a Councillor in 1517, and shortly before this More's friend and fellow humanist, Cuthbert Tunstall, had been appointed Master of the Rolls. Another humanist, Richard Pace, became the King's Secretary in 1516. The ecclesiastical hierarchy also included a number of advocates of the new learning. John Longland, Bishop of Lincoln, who became the King's confessor, was one of these, and his scholarly qualities as well as his ascetic mode of life won him the approval of Erasmus, More and the saintly John Fisher, who was already one of the great luminaries of the episcopal bench. In other words, the elements of reform were present in both state and Church. What was needed to combine them into an effective pressure group was a lead from the top, and the humanists would have given their full support to Wolsey if only he had provided this.

Wolsey was not simply a hypocrite, using the language of reform without having any real commitment to it. He showed his sympathies by choosing Colet to preach the sermon at the magnificent ceremony in which he received the red hat of a cardinal, and his genuine interest in education led him to found a major new college at Oxford. But Wolsey was engaged in so many and varied activities — diplomatic, judicial and administrative, as well as ecclesiastical — that he never had time to formulate and carry through a coherent programme of reform. Furthermore he chose to live on such a princely scale that he was perpetually short of money, and his search for new sources of revenue drove him to exploit those very abuses which, as a reformer, he theoretically condemned. He always held one other bishopric as well as the Archbishopric of York, thereby introducing episcopal pluralism to England, and he had non-resident Italians appointed to the sees of Salisbury, Worcester and Llandaff, to whom he paid a fixed salary so that he could pocket the surplus. He had himself elected Abbot of St Albans, one of the richest monasteries in England, although he was not and never had been a monk. He interfered in every diocese, appointing his own protégés, regardless of the rights of patrons, and set up legatine courts to which he summoned men from all over England. He charged large sums for probate and was notoriously greedy for riches. He was non-resident on a princely scale, never even visiting three of his sees and first entering the diocese of York sixteen years after he had been made Archbishop.

In an age when the laxness of clerical morals was under savage criticism, Wolsey set an example by having an illegitimate son, on whom he showered lucrative Church offices, and an illegitimate daughter whom he placed in a nunnery. Colet had complained of 'pride of life', but even he could hardly have envisaged the degree of magnificence attained by Wolsey. George Cavendish, who was one of the Cardinal's gentlemen-ushers and later wrote his biography, spends several pages merely listing the members of his household and estimates that he had at least five hundred persons employed in his service. He lived in state at Hampton Court, which he created, or at York Place, which Henry later took over and turned into Whitehall. Cavendish describes how, when Wolsey made his way to Westminster Hall to do justice, he had 'two great crosses of silver borne before him, with also two great pillars of silver, and his Sergeant-at-Arms with a great mace of silver-gilt. Then his gentlemen-ushers cried and said "On, my lords and masters! Make way for my lord's grace!" '

Wolsey's major contribution to reform consisted in the foundation of Cardinal College (now Christ Church) at Oxford. In order to endow this and a smaller college in his home town of Ipswich, Wolsey dissolved twenty-nine monasteries on the grounds that they were hopelessly decayed. This redistribution of the Church's wealth from sterile into creative activities was very much in tune with the policies of the humanists, and Wolsey made another gesture in their direction when he attached six professors to his new college in order to provide a regular series of public lectures. But Wolsey's humanism was narrowly confined. The public lectures were to be on civil law, the traditional training for clerical administrators, for Wolsey

was not concerned with learning for its own sake but only in order
to provide well-educated men who could simultaneously serve both
Church and state, as he himself was doing — men such as Stephen
Gardiner, who studied civil law at Cambridge, became Wolsey's
secretary, was employed on embassies by the King, and ended his
career in Mary's reign as a bishop and Lord Chancellor. Wolsey,
in short, was working on the assumption that the clerical domination of secular administration would continue indefinitely and
that one of the major tasks of the universities was to prepare gifted
students for this important role. There was nothing ignoble or even
anachronistic about such an assumption — for few, if any, could
have foreseen the break with Rome and the subsequent collapse of
clerical power — but Wolsey's pragmatism was a long way removed from the idealism of the Christian humanists. He was too
much a product of the existing system to be able to view it dis-
passionately, and the hopes that were pinned on him turned to contempt and hatred when it seemed that instead of leading the reform
movement he was becoming the embodiment of all the worst
abuses.

While the Church as a whole was not unpopular, and many parish priests were loved and respected figures in their local communities, there was an undercurrent of anti-clericalism which
occasionally broke through to the surface. In 1514, for instance, a
wealthy London merchant, named Richard Hunne, refused to pay
the mortuary fee which the parson demanded for burying his infant
son, on the grounds that it was excessive. The parson thereupon
sued Hunne in a church court, but Hunne countered this by bringing an action against him in King's Bench for a breach of praemunire (see below, pp. 36–7). The praemunire case collapsed, but
Hunne was by this time in an ecclesiastical prison, charged with
heresy. He confessed to this offence, which he had committed by
giving shelter to a convicted heretic, but before he could be made
to do public penance he was found dead in his cell, hanging from
a beam. Suicide seems the most likely explanation, but a coroner's
jury of London citizens returned a verdict of murder and named
the Bishop's chancellor and his accomplices as the murderers. The
Bishop of London wrote to Wolsey pleading that the case should
be dealt with by the royal Council on the grounds that 'if my chancellor be tried by any twelve men in London, they be so maliciously
set in *favorem haereticae pravitatis* that they will cast and condemn
my clerk though he were as innocent as Abel'. Before the matter
could go further, Parliament met early in 1515. The Commons had
under consideration the renewal of a temporary Act of 1512 which
had been designed to exclude clerics in minor orders from Benefit
of Clergy. However, in 1514 the Pope had reasserted the claim that
clerics were immune from lay jurisdiction, and when the Commons

attempted to extend the operation of the 1512 Act the House of Lords, in which the bishops and abbots were in a majority, stifled their initiative.

At the same time as Parliament met, Convocation also assembled, and the Abbot of Winchcombe, Richard Kidderminster, used the occasion of his opening sermon to insist on clerical immunity. The outraged Commons called upon the temporal lords — a significant conjunction — to join with them in appealing to the King, and a conference was held at Blackfriars, in Henry's presence, at which the case against Kidderminster was argued by a doctor of divinity named Henry Standish. Convocation thereupon summoned Standish before it to answer charges of heresy, but Standish appealed to the King. He was joined in this by the Commons and temporal lords, still smarting under the rejection of the Criminous Clerks Act and with the Hunne scandal alive in their minds. They called upon the King to maintain his temporal jurisdiction, which the clergy were seeking to invade.

A second conference then took place at Blackfriars, at which the judges gave their verdict that the clergy who had taken part in the citation of Standish had derogated the King's rights and infringed the Statute of Praemunire. At a subsequent assembly of the Lords and Commons in the King's presence Wolsey, as representative of the clergy of England, knelt before Henry to plead for royal favour on the grounds that Convocation had never intended to invade his prerogative, and to ask that the case might be sent for final judgment to Rome. Henry refused this, and in a speech full of significance because it represents his own opinion, unprompted by any of those advisers on whom he was sometimes to seem so dependent, he declared that 'by the ordinance and sufferance of God we are King of England, and the Kings of England in time past have never had any superior but God alone. Wherefore know you well that we shall maintain the right of our crown and of our temporal jurisdiction as well in this point as in all others'.

Despite the ominous tone of Henry's declaration the Church leaders could feel reasonably satisfied with the outcome of events. The episcopal bench had closed ranks in defence of clerical liberties, and the Criminous Clerks Act was never, in fact, renewed. It is true that Convocation had to drop its attack on Standish, and that he eventually rose, through royal favour, to the bishopric of St Asaph. But appointment to a minor Welsh see was something less than a triumph, and although the Hunne case continued to be a matter of controversy the ecclesiastical hierarchy could take comfort from the assumption that under Henry VIII, as under his father, the traditional rights and privileges of the Church would be maintained. Only the course of events was to demonstrate that such an assumption was unjustified.

## *Wolsey. III. Judicial and Financial Policies*

While this dispute between lay and clerical power was simmering, Archbishop Warham relinquished the Great Seal and Wolsey took his place as Lord Chancellor in 1515. The Chancellor was, by tradition, the greatest man in the kingdom under the King, and this was certainly true of Wolsey. He had all the powers, and more, of a modern prime minister, without any regular Parliament or press to call him to account. As long as he pleased the King, nothing short of a successful revolution could dislodge him.

Wolsey's predecessors, Warham and Morton, both had degrees in law, but Wolsey did not allow his lack of professional qualifications to inhibit him from doing justice. As Chancellor he presided over his own court of Chancery, in which the formalism and rigidity of the common law were softened by principles derived mainly from common sense. The sharp increase in the volume of Chancery records, as well as the evidence of Wolsey's contemporaries, bear witness to his activities in Chancery. He had the determination and the means to enforce the law against those who assumed that they were influential enough to ignore or override it. But he also used his position to pursue private vendettas, and the very arbitrariness of his decisions tended to alienate the common lawyers (whom he treated with a marked lack of respect) and to undermine their confidence in Chancery as an institution.

Since Wolsey was the King's chief minister he was also closely associated with the royal Council. This remained, as it had done under Henry VII, a large and amorphous body. The total membership was about 120, but the largest recorded attendance at any meeting was 54 and the average was 11–25. The King himself was rarely present, since he relied on Wolsey to look after the routine work of government. The Council would have been a more efficient body if it had been reduced in numbers and limited to ministers and officials. Wolsey recognised this, and in the *Eltham Ordinance* of 1526 he laid the ground plan of just such a smaller Council. But this, like so many of Wolsey's projected reforms, was abortive. It was blocked by the pressure of vested interests and by the fact that Wolsey himself was constantly distracted by the many other matters demanding his attention.

Because Wolsey took so many policy decisions himself, the Council was left with little to discuss. It therefore devoted much of its time to judicial questions, and, as a consequence, the King's Council sitting to do justice in Star Chamber developed into a formal institution — the Court of Star Chamber. As far as membership was concerned, Council and Star Chamber were identical, but whereas the Council met throughout the year, its Star Chamber activities were confined to the law terms.

Wolsey was as active in Star Chamber as in Chancery, and Cavendish describes how the Cardinal, after sitting in Chancery 'until eleven of the clock, hearing suitors and determining of divers matters . . . would divers times go into the Star Chamber, as occasion did serve, where he spared neither high nor low, but judged every estate according to their merits and deserts'. Wolsey made many enemies by the firmness with which he enforced the law, particularly against the magnates, who all too frequently regarded themselves as above it. The Cardinal had to decide himself whether or not a subject was becoming over-mighty, whether he needed teaching the 'new law of the Star Chamber' — which was not, of course, a new law but a new vigour in the application of existing laws. Wolsey liked to pose as the champion of the poor and helpless against their social superiors, which in many ways he was. But in Star Chamber, as in Chancery, he was also concerned to settle private scores, and his victims were quick to complain. Skelton, the poet, was one of their mouthpieces:

> In the Star Chamber he nods and becks
> And beareth him there so stout
> That no man dare rout [riot],
> Duke, earl, baron nor lord,
> But to his sentence must accord;
> Whether he be knight or squire
> All men must follow his desire.

Although Star Chamber would sometimes take the initiative in bringing prosecutions, particularly against powerful offenders, most of the cases that came before it were the result of complaints from private individuals. It was a long-established principle that all those who believed that they had suffered injustice should have the right to appeal to the King for redress, and Wolsey encouraged them to do so. But this simply led to a repetition of what had happened in Henry VII's reign, when the Council became flooded with disputes over property thinly disguised as cases of riot or corruption. Wolsey tried to lessen the burden on Star Chamber by transferring much of this business to conciliar committees, but the court still had more cases than it could cope with, and instead of acting as an arbiter, sorting out the tangle of conflicting jurisdictions, or as a court of appeal, it was increasingly involved in matters that could and should have been dealt with by the courts of common law.

Star Chamber was not confined to judicial business — or perhaps it would be truer to say that no clear distinction was made between judicial and administrative matters. Sheriffs, for instance, were often called before the court to account for their actions, and Justices of the Peace were encouraged to attend upon certain formal occasions, when the Chancellor would harangue them about the need to carry out their responsibilities. In 1526 Wolsey also asked the J.P.s to provide him with information about the way in which the law was being administered in their localities — a typical example of his thirst for information as a prelude to action — and in Kent, and no doubt in other counties, he increased the number of gentry who were appointed to the Commission of the Peace and strengthened the ties that linked them to the central government.

One of the conciliar committees established by Wolsey in an attempt to relieve the pressure on Star Chamber acquired a life of its own. By 1521 the Councillors appointed to give special consideration to the petitions of poor men were meeting regularly during term time at Whitehall and had become established as an autonomous Court of Requests. Wolsey also created a council in the north, under the nominal presidency of Henry's bastard son, the Duke of Richmond, to protect the poor against the effects of enclosure and rack-renting. This was given a criminal and civil jurisdiction similar to that of Star Chamber, but it could not control magnates such as Northumberland and Dacre and its work was, in consequence, confined largely to Yorkshire.

Wolsey's passion was for administration, and he had little time for a body like Parliament, which was time-consuming and did not fit neatly into his autocratic conceptions of government. The principal reason for summoning Parliament was the crown's need for money. The opening years of Henry VIII's reign had seen a deliberate slackening in the grip of the royal administration, in order to diminish the dangerous tensions that had been building up under Henry VII, but one of the consequences of this was a marked reduction in the royal revenue. In 1512, therefore, when Henry was preparing for war against France, he called Parliament and requested supply. Parliament responded by voting a subsidy, thereby confirming its acceptance of this new type of tax which Henry VII had attempted, without much success, to introduce. The subsidy was designed to be newly assessed for every levy. It was therefore much more flexible than the ossified Fifteenth and Tenth and took more account of changes in the distribution of wealth. Parliament was called again in 1515, and the total amount raised by taxation in these four years was about £300,000. This was a large sum, but it represented only a third of the crown's expenditure on war, and Henry therefore agreed that forced loans should be taken from his richer subjects. Before this was done, Wolsey ordered a detailed survey to be carried out, on a county basis, of the military and financial potential of the kingdom. This was a major achievement that only an administrator as skilled and determined as the Cardinal could have carried through, and it provided the basis on which the loans were assessed. They brought in some £250,000, but this still left a deficit, and more money was required for the reopening of hostilities in 1523 (see below, p. 29). Hence the decision to summon another Parliament.

Convocation, which met at the same time as Parliament, was browbeaten by Wolsey into making a substantial grant of £100,000, to be spread over five years — a clear indication of Wolsey's assumption that the needs of the state must take precedence over those of the Church. But Parliament was less malleable, and for the only time in the whole of the sixteenth century the Commons opposed the voting of supply on principle. They had subsidised the campaigns of Henry VII without complaint, because they approved of his policies. Henry VIII's wars, however, were caused by no obvious necessity. They were widely regarded as Wolsey's wars, and there was resentment at the Cardinal's demand for a subsidy of four shillings in the pound. Wolsey went down to the Commons and assured them that he was 'from the King's own person sent hither unto you for the preservation of yourselves and all the realm'. He added that he thought it 'meet you give me a reasonable answer', but all he received by way of reply was 'a marvellous obstinate silence'.

The situation was only saved through the efforts of the Speaker, Sir Thomas More — one of Wolsey's protégés — who persuaded the Commons to vote four subsidies, each to be newly assessed and to be taken at the rate of one a year. The first two brought in £136,000; the third was about to be collected when, in 1525, Wolsey sent out commissioners to raise what he called an 'Amicable Grant', but what was, to all intents and purposes, a Benevolence. Wolsey's action was prompted by his reckoning that if Henry was to take advantage of the situation created by the defeat and capture of Francis I at Pavia (see below, p. 29) he would need money immediately. But this new demand, coming at a time when the third subsidy was still being collected, sparked off hostile demonstrations all over the country. According to one chronicler 'all people cursed the Cardinal and his coadherents as subversor of the laws and liberties of England. For, they said, if men should give their goods by a commission, then were it worse than the taxes in France, and so England should be bond and not free.' Henry — who claimed, with whatever justification, that he had known nothing of Wolsey's initiative — was forced to intervene, cancel the 'Amicable Grant' and pardon all those who had demonstrated their opposition to it. This was Wolsey's first real check. It showed that the co-operation of Parliament could not be taken for granted, particularly where the voting of supply was concerned. It also showed that Henry's ear was tuned to public opinion more finely than Wolsey's, and that he was prepared to sacrifice unpopular measures (even if not, as yet, their proponents) in order to preserve the stability of his throne.

*Wolsey. IV: Foreign Policy*

The opening phase of Henry VIII's foreign policy ended with the
Anglo-French peace treaty of 1514 and a marriage between Louis
XII and Henry's sister Mary. Not long after the marriage, however, Louis died, and the throne of France passed to the youthful,
charming and impetuous Francis I. Francis was no less covetous
of glory than Henry had been at his accession, and it seemed inevitable that the rivalry between France and Spain would become
even more intense. But the Pope was anxious to keep peace among
the major Christian states so that they could join in checking the
advance of the Ottoman Turks into the eastern Mediterranean. In
order to obtain Henry's support for this crusade the Pope despatched Cardinal Campeggio to England as his legate, but Wolsey
kept Campeggio cooling his heels at Calais while he took over the
papal initiative and turned it into one of his major diplomatic
triumphs. He began with a treaty between France and England —
which included the restoration of Tournai in return for increased
pension payments to Henry — and then persuaded the Emperor
Maximilian and Charles, the new King of Spain, to add their
names to it. The Treaty of London, as it was now called, had a
system of collective security built into it to try to deter any of the
signatories from resorting to war to settle their disputes. Wolsey
and his royal master were now the acknowledged peacemakers of
Europe and basked in the acclaim that this novel role brought
them. Wolsey, who had his humanist side, may genuinely have
hoped to preserve peace, particularly in view of the costs of war.
But England was not strong enough to maintain peace by herself.
Everything depended upon the balance of power in Europe, and
this was radically altered by the death of the Emperor Maximilian
in January 1519, for when the German prince-electors met to
choose a successor they picked Maximilian's grandson Charles,
who was already King of Spain and Duke of Burgundy. To Francis
I it seemed as though France was now encircled by imperial power
— on her northern frontier, the Netherlands; on her eastern frontier, Luxemburg and Franche Comté; and in the south, Spain herself. Only by securing French control of Italy could he hope to
break out of this stranglehold.

Both Francis and Charles were eager to secure the support of
England for the forthcoming struggle, but Wolsey was not prepared
to commit himself at this stage. For the time being it suited him to
keep on good terms with both powers. In 1520 Henry and Francis
met amid scenes of unparalleled splendour on the Field of Cloth
of Gold, but this was followed by an unpublicised, but equally significant, meeting between Henry and the new Emperor. By the following year Charles and Francis were at war, and Wolsey assumed,

with good reason, that the Emperor would be the victor, in view of the enormous resources at his disposal. It followed from this that if England was to profit from the conflict she should commit herself to the winning side. In August 1521, therefore, Wolsey went over to Bruges and concluded an agreement with the Emperor which was ratified when he made a state visit to England in 1522. Its terms included a promise by Charles to marry Henry's daughter, Mary, when she came of age, and an English commitment to declare war on France in 1523. In order to enable Henry to raise an army to fulfil his obligations, it was decided to call Parliament and ask for supply of £800,000.

Wolsey's main motive in these complex negotiations was to derive the maximum advantage for his royal master. England could not possibly impose its will on monarchs as powerful as Charles and Francis, but by joining the winning side it could hope to gain a share of the spoils. It may be that Wolsey also favoured an imperial alliance because Charles had promised to support his candidature for the papacy, but it is equally possible that Henry was the driving force behind this proposal. Had Wolsey really wanted the papacy he would surely have taken steps to increase his influence at Rome by building up a following in the papal court, but he made little effort to do so. It was hardly surprising, therefore, that on the death of Pope Leo in December 1521, Wolsey was not elected to succeed him. The Emperor, far from supporting Wolsey's candidature, threw his weight behind his former tutor, Adrian, who was duly elected; in the only scrutiny in which Wolsey's name was put forward he received a mere seven votes out of thirty-nine. Adrian's pontificate was relatively brief, for he died in September 1523, but in the subsequent conclave Wolsey was not even considered, and a member of the Florentine family of Medici was elected as Clement VII.

The refusal of the 1523 Parliament to vote supply on the necessary scale meant that Henry could not carry out his commitment to enter the war on the Emperor's side, and this soured relations between the two rulers. In these circumstances it seemed only prudent to try to heal the rift with France, and in 1524 England moved appreciably closer to the league which Pope Clement, alarmed by the sweeping imperial victories in Italy, was forming against Charles. Unfortunately for Wolsey, this drifting away from the imperial alliance came at a time when the tide was running strongly in Charles's favour. In February 1525 the French army was shattered at the battle of Pavia, and Francis I was taken prisoner by the Emperor. When Henry heard the news he immediately sent envoys to Charles to congratulate him upon his success and press him to restore English sovereignty over France. Charles, however, felt that he owned nothing to Henry. Not only did he reject the demand that France be restored to English suzerainty; he also announced his intention to marry a Portuguese princess instead of waiting for Mary.

Faced with this rebuff, Wolsey had no alternative to an anti-imperial policy, and he spent 1526 knitting together the League of Cognac with France and the Papacy. The aim of this league was to expel imperial forces from Italy, or at least force Charles to negotiate. It was agreed that England should take no immediate part in hostilities but would gradually commit herself if Charles remained intransigent. Charles's response to the league was to strike at Rome itself, and in May 1527 an imperial army took the eternal city by storm, sacked it, and forced the Pope to take refuge in the castle of San Angelo, where he remained a virtual prisoner of the Emperor. In the following year France and England formally declared war on the Emperor, and it seemed, for a time, as though French troops would succeed in regaining much of southern Italy. In June 1529, however, the main French army was routed at Landriano, and Charles became the unchallenged master of Italy. The Pope reluctantly accepted the inevitable and announced that he had decided 'to become an imperialist and to live and die as such'. He concluded the Treaty of Barcelona with the Emperor in June 1529, and this was followed, a month later, by the Peace of Cambrai which brought to an end — for some years at any rate — the long struggle between France and Spain. It was high time, for the Turks were at the gates of Vienna, and in Germany the unity of Christendom was being eroded by the rapid spread of Lutheranism.

## The King's Great Matter

Wolsey was conspicuously absent from all this peacemaking, for England had abandoned Charles too soon to profit from the imperial victory. Wolsey had also made an enemy of the Emperor at the very moment when he most needed his support, for on the same day that Landriano was fought a remarkable scene was taking place at Blackfriars, where Henry and his wife, Queen Catherine, appeared before Wolsey and his fellow legate, Campeggio, to answer charges that their marriage was invalid and that they were therefore living in sin.

There had been difficulties about the marriage from the beginning, for according to *Leviticus* 20, 21, if a man marries his brother's widow, 'it is an unclean thing; he hath uncovered his brother's nakedness; they shall be childless'. A papal dispensation had been necessary before the marriage could take place, but there was some doubt about whether the Pope had authority to dispense with the

law when it had the sanction of holy scripture behind it. Although
the dispensation was eventually issued in late 1504, the marriage
was still delayed — mainly because the dowry had not all been paid
— and in June 1505 Henry, who was not quite fourteen at the time,
made a formal protest against the validity of the proposed union.
He was no doubt prompted in this by his father, who was having
second thoughts on the advisability of a Spanish alliance, but the
only effect was further to postpone the marriage, which did not take
place until June 1509, two months after Henry VII's death.

The marriage seems to have been reasonably happy, but unfortunately for the Queen her children died at birth, or soon after,
except for a daughter, Mary, born in 1516. By 1525 Catherine was
forty, all hope of a male heir had gone, and Henry was in a quan-
dary. As a conventionally devout man he was afraid that his failure
to obtain the longed-for son might be a sign of the punishment
threatened in Leviticus. A male heir seemed vital if the Tudor dynasty was to survive. It was not even certain that a woman had
the right to ascend the throne. The last female ruler of England had
been Matilda, whose reign had been marred by civil war, and the
memory of the Wars of the Roses was still very much alive. Henry
was conscious that he was only the second of his dynasty, and that
several of his subjects had a claim to the throne superior to his own
as far as descent was concerned. For this reason he had Edmund
Stafford, Duke of Buckingham, executed in 1521, and he also considered making his bastard son, the Duke of Richmond, his legitimate heir. It is not clear what would eventually have happened
had not the matter been brought to a head by Henry's falling in
love with Anne Boleyn, whose sister was already his mistress.
Henry's love-letters to Anne show how deeply the King's passions
had been aroused, but Anne refused to become Henry's mistress
and stood firm in the hopes of a crown. In any case the King
needed her as his wife if the children she bore him were to be legitimate. By early 1527 Henry was determined to put an end to his
marriage with Catherine and had made this clear to his chief minister. Wolsey may well have been in favour of annulment, since he
did not yet know whom Henry intended as his second wife. The
divorce of Catherine, who was Charles V's aunt, would hurt the
Emperor's pride, and might lead to a French marriage, which
would fit in nicely with Wolsey's plans.

What one Pope had done only another could undo. Julius II had
issued the original dispensation; Clement VII was now asked to
declare that his predecessor had acted *ultra vires* and that no Pope
could set aside the law of the Church in this particular case. Henry
had no reason to expect difficulties. Popes usually gave a sympathetic hearing to princely petitioners and Henry was an ardent
supporter of the papacy and had been rewarded by the title *Fidei*

*Defensor* for defending it against the attacks of Luther. He was therefore eager for Rome to judge his case, since he was convinced that the verdict would be in his favour.

The first stage of the divorce case centred on the attempt to obtain a favourable papal decision. There was no intention at this stage of breaking with Rome since, as far as Henry could tell, the Pope would fall in with his wishes. He even went so far as to ask the Pope for a dispensation permitting him to marry Anne, whose sister had been his mistress. The theological impediment to such a marriage was precisely the same as that which, Henry claimed, invalidated his union with Catherine of Aragon — if a man may not marry his brother's widow, neither may he marry his mistress's sister — yet while the King denied papal competence in the one case, he was eager to accept it in the other. This suggests that Henry's real aim was to marry Anne Boleyn, and that other considerations, however sincerely held, were secondary. Wolsey can hardly have relished the prospect of having Anne as Queen, since she was the niece of the Duke of Norfolk, his rival and enemy, and was also suspected of Lutheran leanings. But Wolsey, as he later told Campeggio, considered that Henry must be allowed to have his way, since otherwise the Church would be endangered.

Campeggio — who was the titular Bishop of Salisbury — had been sent by Clement VII to join Wolsey in judging 'the King's great matter'. Clement was trying to pursue two irreconcilable courses. To avoid offending Catherine's nephew, Charles V, who was defending the catholic church against Lutherans at home and the Ottoman Turks abroad, he wished to postpone any clear-cut action and reserve the ultimate decision to himself. Yet he also wished to conciliate Henry, the Defender of the Faith, and Henry insisted that the two legates should be authorised to pass final judgment in his case.

Clement's tactics were dictated in large part by the changing military situation in Italy. When French forces were in the ascendent he sent Campeggio a decretal commission empowering him to pronounce final judgment. But Campeggio, who was old and gouty, took a long time over his journey to England, and meanwhile the imperial fortunes in Italy were beginning to revive. Clement therefore instructed him that he should show his decretal commission to Henry and Wolsey, as tangible evidence of papal goodwill, but then destroy it. Furthermore, he told Campeggio that in no circumstances should he pronounce judgment without first obtaining papal approval, for 'if so great an injury be done to the Emperor [by a decision in Henry's favour] all hope is lost of universal peace and the Church cannot escape utter ruin, as it is entirely in the power of the Emperor's servants . . . Delay as much as possible.'

Campeggio did not relish this double-dealing. 'I do not see,' he wrote to the papal secretary, 'supposing the King cannot be got from his opinion, how without scandal we can delay what, by our own commission, we have to proceed with and try. It will easily seem to them that I have been sent to gull them, and they may be furious about it.' When Campeggio eventually reached England, in October 1528, he joined Wolsey in trying to persuade Catherine to resolve the problem by acknowledging the invalidity of her marriage. This, however, Catherine refused to do. A trial was therefore inevitable, and in January 1529 Henry sent Stephen Gardiner to Rome with a warning that unless a speedy and favourable decision was given by the two legates he would renounce his allegiance to the papal see. The legatine court at last opened at Blackfriars in May 1529. Catherine was not expected to be present, but on 21 June, the day on which the Emperor's hold on Italy was confirmed by the rout of the French at Landriano, she appeared and made an impassioned and moving speech asserting the validity of her marriage. She finished her oration by sweeping across the courtroom and kneeling at Henry's feet. The King was moved to tears, and publicly declared that 'she hath been to me as true, obedient and as conformable a wife as I could in my fancy wish or desire.' But he had no intention of abandoning his policy. His passion for Anne and the need to safeguard the succession were more powerful than mere sentiment.

The King confidently expected a favourable judgment when the court reassembled in July 1529. But Campeggio, who was awaiting instructions from Rome, played for time by announcing that no decision could be given until after a three-month summer vacation. The court never, in fact, met again, and Henry's anger was expressed by his brother-in-law, the Duke of Suffolk, who stepped forward and 'spake these words with a stout and hault countenance. "It was never merry in England whilst we had cardinals among us." Which words were set forth with such a vehement countenance that all men marvelled what he intended.'

## Wolsey's Fall from Power

Anger swiftly turned to action. The King had no further use for Wolsey, and Parliament was summoned so that an Act of attainder could be passed against the favourite. But the Act was not needed. Wolsey, when commanded to appear before judges to answer charges that by publishing his Bulls of appointment as papal legate he had infringed the Statute of Praemunire, pleaded guilty. His palaces and colleges were confiscated by the crown as a punishment for his offences, and the fallen legate journeyed slowly towards his province of York, which he entered for the first time since his appointment sixteen years earlier. He could not, however, shake off the habit of power, and was secretly negotiating with Francis I and the Emperor for their support in persuading Henry to restore him to favour. His servant, Thomas Cromwell, wrote to warn him that his enemies were still suspicious of him. 'Some allege you keep too great a house and are continually building ... I think you happy you are now at liberty to serve God and banish all vain desires of the world'. But the vain desires of the world still dazzled Wolsey, and he planned a magnificent enthronement for himself in York Minister. Before the ceremony could take place he was arrested on a charge of high treason, and sent towards London. He got no further than Leicester Abbey, where on 29 November 1530 he died, lamenting that 'if I had served God as diligently as I have done the King, He would not have given me over in my grey hairs'.

Wolsey was a great prince of the Church in a tradition so alien to modern assumptions that it is difficult to comprehend him. Yet he was not without his virtues. He promoted education, and made his household a place where men of intelligence and ability learned how to serve the state. He was also tolerant, preferring to burn heretical books rather than the heretics themselves; and although he rose to power by royal favour he was not unworthy of it, for he had an enormous capacity for work, and knew how to win men:

> Lofty and sour to them that loved him not;
> But to those men that sought him, sweet as summer.[1]

---

1 Shakespeare, *King Henry VIII*: IV, ii.

# 3

# The Break with Rome

## The Reformation Parliament

The Parliament which met in November 1529 had been summoned to deal with Wolsey, but Wolsey had capitulated without a struggle and there was no other obvious work for it to do. Henry was now his own chief minister, and although he had no intention, at this stage, of breaking with Rome, the possibility was not ruled out. By this date, Denmark, Sweden and much of north Germany had already repudiated papal supremacy, and the profits of this had gone to the temporal princes. Henry had an eye to profit, and he regarded himself as certainly the equal, if not the superior, of the northern monarchs. Long before he met Cromwell he believed that he was the wearer of an imperial crown — indeed he not only told Thomas More this, but added the unexpected information that he had received this crown from the Pope.

While Henry had an exalted conception of the power and dignity of his position, he did not see how this could serve his immediate purpose. What he proposed to do was not to break with Rome but to drive the Pope into a satisfactory settlement. For this reason he gave Parliament its head in November 1529 and the Commons passed a number of Bills limiting the fees to be charged for probate and mortuary, restricting abuses of sanctuary, and forbidding pluralities and non-residence. The spiritual lords did not accept these measures with equanimity. Although they had failed to initiate reform themselves, they resented action by the laity, and the Bill to limit probate fees provoked Bishop Fisher to an angry outburst: 'now with the Commons is nothing but "Down with the Church!" and all this me seemeth is for lack of faith only.' It was probably in this session that the Commons started drawing up the list of grievances against the Church which was to take shape in 1532 as the *Supplication against the Ordinaries*.

Henry's next step was prompted by a chance meeting between two of his Councillors and Thomas Cranmer, an obscure Cambridge don. Cranmer pointed out that the real issue was whether the command that a man must not marry his brother's widow was based on canon law, which could be set aside by the Pope, or on

God's law, which was irrevocable. This was a matter for theologians to settle, not lawyers, and it was decided to appeal to the universities of Europe. Should they declare in Henry's favour, as he anticipated, the Pope could then be called on to act. The King was pleased with the idea, and 1530 saw the mounting of a major campaign. Libraries throughout Europe were searched for relevant evidence, and money was distributed on a lavish scale to all those scholars who professed to see merit in Henry's case. As a result of this activity eight universities, including the prestigious Paris and Bologna, came down on the King's side, and thereby — or so Henry hoped — strengthened his bargaining position at Rome. Further pressure on the Pope was applied by the *Appeal of the English Nobility and Clergy* of June 1530. This document acknowledged the Pope's sole right to pass judgment in the case but urged him, for the good of the Church in England, to decide in Henry's favour.

Nothing would have pleased Henry more than a papal pronouncement that his marriage to Catherine was invalid, but he was sufficient of a realist to recognise that this was unlikely to be forthcoming. If he could not look for satisfaction from Rome, however, he might well find it within his own kingdom, for Henry had long believed that as the descendant of King Arthur, who was himself descended from the Emperor Constantine, he exercised an autonomous authority over all his subjects, lay and clerical alike. He may have derived this belief in part from his father, for Henry VII had not only christened his eldest son Arthur but in 1489 had issued a new coin, the golden sovereign, on which he was portrayed wearing an imperial crown, closed over the head with hoops, rather than the traditional open circlet. It is perhaps not without relevance that Henry VIII, who rapidly built up a royal navy, chose the name of *The Henry Imperial* for one of his new ships, and some years later, when he came to the defence of the papacy against the challenge from Luther by writing and publishing the *Assertio Septem Sacramentorum*, he was careful to insist that the duty of obedience to the Pope did not extend to temporal matters; hence the significance of Henry's declaration in 1515 that he intended to maintain 'the right of our crown and of our temporal jurisdiction'.

A great deal depended, of course, upon the definition of what was 'temporal', but 1531 witnessed an important development in this respect. Henry's forays into France had left him desperately short of money, and in order to replenish his coffers he decided to follow the precedent set by Wolsey in 1523 and demand a subsidy of £100,000 from Convocation. He offered the clergy, in return, a pardon for the offence they had unwittingly committed by conniving in the exercise of Wolsey's legatine authority — since, in the view of the crown's legal advisers, this had breached the Statute of Praemunire of 1353 (repeated, in stronger terms, in 1393) which stated that 'anyone drawing the King's subjects out of the realm on pleas, the cognisance whereof belongs to the King's courts . . . shall be put out of the King's protection, his lands and goods forfeited and his body imprisoned at the King's pleasure'.

Convocation agreed to make the grant of £100,000, though it gave as justification Henry's determined suppression of Lutheran heresy, but in the subsequent haggling over details Convocation felt impelled to draw up a list of conditions which included the demand that Henry should confirm all the privileges of the Church as guaranteed in *Magna Carta*. Henry could not possibly accept such a demand, for he would thereby have been acknowledging the virtual independence of the Church at the very moment when he needed to assert his control over it in order to obtain the annulment of his marriage. He had been studying a collection of documents, drawn up under the direction of Cranmer, which demonstrated his right to summon councils of the Church within his own dominions and make their decrees binding on his subjects. He might well have to use such tactics to separate himself from Catherine, so he now called on Convocation explicitly to recognise that he was 'sole protector and supreme head of the English church and clergy'. This demand aroused apprehension and anger among the bishops in the upper house of Convocation, and the royal representatives there had to fight hard to persuade them to accept a compromise whereby the clergy acknowledged the King as 'their singular protector, only and supreme lord, and, as far as the law of Christ allows, even supreme head'. Convocation, in fact, had given nothing of substance away, for a royal supremacy so hedged about with qualifications was virtually unenforceable. But Henry was satisfied that he had achieved his immediate aim of opening up the way to an 'English' solution of his marital problems. He therefore assented to an Act of 1531 giving the clergy formal pardon for their offence in exercising independent spiritual jurisdiction. The Commons were quick to realise that by appearing before Church courts and accepting their verdict they also had offended. This led to the passing of a second Act, in which Henry gave a pardon to his lay subjects. In their case, however, no payment was stipulated.

Although Henry was moving towards a declaration of independence from Rome, he was not clear about the best tactics to use, nor could he be sure of carrying his people with him. As long as he emphasised his role as a godly prince, putting into effect the Erasmian reform programme which the Church under Wolsey had so conspicuously failed to adopt, he could count on the support of informed public opinion. But he had to tread warily, for in 1517 Martin Luther had made his celebrated challenge to the Papacy and had thereby set off a reform movement that threatened to split the Christian church into warring fragments. Henry did not ap-

prove of Luther, and regarded many of his beliefs as heretical. Indeed, his attack upon Luther in the *Assertio* prompted the Pope to
confer upon him and his descendants the title of 'Defender of the
Faith'. Yet Lutheran influences were already at work in England,
and there was a very real possibility that Henry, by undermining
the authority of the ecclesiastical hierarchy, might cripple the
Church at a time when it needed all its strength to combat heresy.
He therefore had to consider his next moves carefully, and it may
be that he had no clear idea of what these moves should be. If this
was the case, however, his period of indecision was short-lived, for
he found, in the person of Thomas Cromwell, not only a brilliant
executant of royal policy but a man with ideas of his own about
the lines along which Henry should proceed.

## Thomas Cromwell

Cromwell, the son of a clothworker and alehouse-keeper, was born
in Putney at about the time that Bosworth was fought. He became
a roving soldier in Italy, entered the service of the Frescobaldi, a
famous banking family, and then went on to the Netherlands,
where he made his living as a business consultant. This early experience was invaluable to him, since through it he acquired first-
hand knowledge of Renaissance Italy — the Italy of Machiavelli
and Cesare Borgia. He also came to know the trading world that
embraced the north Italian city states, Antwerp and London, and
that valued efficiency and good administration as money-making
virtues.

After his return to England, in 1512 or thereabouts, Cromwell
took up the study of common law, and subsequently he entered the
service of Wolsey. When Wolsey decided to suppress twenty-nine
monasteries and use their wealth to endow his new colleges at Oxford and Ipswich, he showed his awareness of Cromwell's ability
by choosing him as his agent. In Wolsey's household Cromwell had
a close view of the way of life of higher ecclesiastics and their immediate entourage. He knew how corrupt the Church was, yet he
was not violently anti-clerical or without faith. In the will which
he drew up in 1529 he left £20 to poor householders to pray for his
soul and £5 to the orders of friars. He also instructed his executors
to arrange for masses to be said for his soul for seven years by 'an
honest and continent priest': the adjectives are significant.

When Wolsey fell, it looked as though Cromwell would fall with
him, so closely had he been identified with his master's policies, but
he told Cavendish that he would go to court, where he would, to
use his favourite phrase, 'either make or mar ere I come again'. In
London he was informed that the King had no objection to his
becoming a burgess, and an old friend found him a seat at Taun-

ton. Cromwell did not desert his former master and was apparently responsible for defeating the proposal to pass a Bill of attainder against Wolsey. But he had to make his own way in the world of politics, and he quickly became a prominent figure in the Reformation Parliament. The King was now his patron, and it was probably during the early months of 1530 that Cromwell took the oath required of those who entered royal service. Before the year was out he had been sworn a member of the Council, and since Wolsey was by this time dead he was now free to look to his own advantage. By the end of 1531 he was recognised in the Commons as one of the King's chief spokesmen and he was gradually entering the inner ring of Henry's advisers.

The third session of the Reformation Parliament opened in January 1532 and the Commons immediately reverted to the question of clerical abuses. The outcome of their debates was a list of grievances, which Cromwell may have helped draw up, called the *Supplication against the Ordinaries* (i.e. the judges in ecclesiastical courts; usually the bishops or their deputies). This called in question the right of the Church to make laws of its own, and Henry therefore passed it to Convocation to consider. The bishops were in no mood to welcome such a document, for they were at last engaged in putting their house in order. New canons were being drafted, dealing with non-residency, simony and other abuses, and the Church leaders clearly envisaged a sweeping programme of reform, carried out under their aegis, which would be abruptly halted if their legislative power was called in question. Warham had already made his attitude plain by formally dissociating himself from any parliamentary statutes that derogated from the authority of the Pope or the liberties of the Church, and it was with his encouragement that Stephen Gardiner drew up a reply to the *Supplication* affirming that the Church's right to make its own laws was 'grounded upon the Scripture of God and determination of Holy Church, which must also be a rule and square to try the justice of all laws, as well spiritual as temporal'.

Gardiner was known to be in the King's favour and had only recently been made Bishop of Winchester. He would hardly have committed himself to such an uncompromising defence of the Church's position unless he had assumed that Henry would approve of it. After all, Henry had protected the Church against the anger of the Commons at the time of the Hunne and Standish affairs, and there was no reason to assume that he would act differently on this occasion. However, Gardiner and his fellow bishops had miscalculated, for by putting so much emphasis upon their independence and autonomy they appeared to be calling in question the King's 'imperial' authority, to which he was now so deeply attached. When Henry received the clergy's reply to the *Submission*, in April 1532, he passed it on to the Commons with a broad hint about his own reaction: 'We think their answer will smally please you, for it seemeth to us very slender. You be a great sort of wise men. I doubt not but you will look circumspectly on the matter, and we will be indifferent between you'.

This indication of royal dissatisfaction set debate going again in Convocation, and Henry now insisted that the Church should abandon its claim to make laws without royal permission and should submit existing canons to a mixed commission of clergy and laymen. This demand was no more acceptable to the bishops than the *Supplication* had been, but there were those among them who realised that they could not hold out against an alliance of King and Commons; indeed, the increasing hostility of the Commons made it essential that they should win the support of the King by timely concessions. Those bishops who regarded concessions as betrayal salved their conscience by staying away from Convocation. The handful who continued to attend signed the *Submission* accepting Henry's demands. It had seemed for a time that Archbishop Warham might give a lead to those who wished to stand firm, for he had talked of following Becket's example. In the end, however, he gave way. He was now an old man, over eighty, lacking in both health and strength, and he died a few months after setting his hand to the *Submission*. In the event, it was left to a layman to make the only challenging gesture. On the day the *Submission* was presented to Henry, Sir Thomas More, who had been appointed to succeed Wolsey as Lord Chancellor, resigned from office.

While the English clergy were being brought to heel, the Pope was being threatened with a cut in his revenues. For many centuries annates — the payments by newly-appointed bishops of their first year's income to the Pope — had been a cause of complaint. Now, in 1532, the Act in Conditional Restraint of Annates forbade the payment of these dues to Rome, but left it to the King to decide when this prohibition should be put into effect. The Act also provided that if the Pope should refuse to issue the Bulls that were necessary before a bishop could be consecrated, the bishop should nonetheless be consecrated; and if the Pope then imposed sentences of excommunication or interdict, these should be of no effect.

Care was taken in the Act to present this action in as conservative a manner as possible — the removal, by an orthodox and devout monarch, of a long-standing abuse — and this conservative presentation of the Henrician reformation partly explains the lack of opposition from the bishops. They could not see at what point or on what grounds to take their stand, and having accepted the early measures they found themselves committed to all that followed. They may have had reservations about certain actions, but they felt bound by the biblical commandment to fear God and honour the King, particularly a King who was such an ardent defender of the established church against heresy. In the early 1530s, for instance, at least half a dozen heretics were burnt at the stake, and in March 1532, at the very moment when Convocation was considering its reply to the *Supplication* the King warned Hugh Latimer, a celebrated preacher who had been accused of heresy, that 'I will not take upon me now to be a suitor to the bishops for you unless you promise to do penance as ye have deserved, and never to preach any such things again. Ye shall else only get from me a faggot to burn you.' William Warham was one of the few who saw that the key issue was the sovereignty of the Pope, and that once this had been abandoned the Church would be at the mercy of the King. But Warham died in August 1532 and the King chose as his successor Thomas Cranmer.

## Thomas Cranmer

Cranmer, born four years after Bosworth, became a fellow of Jesus College, Cambridge, and although he had to give up his fellowship when he married, he was restored to it again after his first wife's death. It was while he was lecturing in divinity at the university that the chance meeting took place with Gardiner and Fox, the King's Secretary and Almoner, from which there eventually emerged the scheme to consult the universities of Europe. This brought Cranmer into royal service, and it was during an embassy to Charles V in 1532 that he met some of the Lutheran leaders and took the niece of one of them as his second wife, in spite of his priest's orders. The Lutherans, who did not regard marriage as a sacrament, saw no reason why a man should not marry his brother's widow, and were therefore unsympathetic to Henry VIII. It may have been because Cranmer shared their views that he found the news of his appointment as Archbishop so unwelcome, and delayed his return to England as long as possible.

But if Cranmer hoped that the King would change his mind, he was mistaken. Cranmer was the ideal man for Henry, since he believed in royal supremacy over the Church and dreaded the disorder that uncontrolled reform might lead to. Henry had secretly married Anne Boleyn, now pregnant, in January 1533, but it was essential that this should be formally confirmed so that the child — which no one doubted would be the longed-for male heir — would be legitimate. To give the new Archbishop's decision the fullest possible authority it was important that nothing should be lacking in the details of his appointment. The Pope issued the necessary Bulls without difficulty. He did not know much about Cranmer and

he was pleased to be able to gratify Henry without giving offence
to the Emperor. He was also aware that Henry had not yet made
permanent the restraint of annates, and that a conciliatory move
on his part might persuade the King to delay such action
indefinitely.

In March 1533 Cranmer was formally consecrated, but immediately before the ceremony he read aloud a protestation, declaring that when he took the customary oaths of allegiance to the
Pope it would be with the reservation that his duty to the King
came first. Meanwhile Convocation was discussing the question of
Henry's marriage to Catherine, and decided that it was invalid.
The way was now open for the Church in England to give a formal
verdict in the King's great matter, and in May 1533 Cranmer obtained a licence from Henry authorising him to try the case. He set
up his court at Dunstable and on 23 May pronounced judgment
that Henry's so-called marriage with Catherine had never been
valid and that the King must stop living in sin with this woman
who was not his wife — a provision that Henry found easy to fulfil,
since he had been living apart from Catherine ever since the divorce
proceedings began. Cranmer subsequently declared that Henry's
marriage with Anne Boleyn was valid, and on Whitsunday 1533
he crowned Anne as Queen in Westminster Abbey. A few months
later, on 7 September, the longed-for child was born. Unfortunately
for Anne it was a daughter, and Henry did not bother to hide his
anger and disappointment. The baby girl was given the name
Elizabeth.

### Royal Supremacy. I: The Achievement

Catherine, who had never for one moment doubted the validity of
her marriage to Henry, had made it plain that she would accept
no judgment given by an English court, but would wait for the
Pope to pronounce a final verdict. Henry could not prevent Catherine from appealing to Rome, but if Cranmer's judgment was to
command the widest possible support it was essential to establish
the principle in law that English courts, like the English King, were
subject to no external power. Cromwell had been working on draft
versions of an Act of Appeals even before Anne's pregnancy was
announced, and the final version was laid before Parliament in
March 1533. The Act was deliberately conservative in form, not
claiming a new authority but restoring an old one and asserting
'that this realm of England is an empire, and so hath been accepted
in the world, governed by one supreme head and King having the
dignity and royal estate of the imperial crown of the same, unto
whom a body politic, compact of all sorts and degrees of people
divided in terms and by names of spiritualty and temporalty, be

bounded and owe to bear next to God a natural and humble obedience'. Since the King had no superior on earth the Act therefore
made arrangements for final judgment in all cases to be given by
courts within his jurisdiction. The unity of all laws, under the co-
ordinating authority of the King, was thereby established: so also
was the confusion between ecclesiastical and secular authority
which was to haunt Tudor and Stuart England.

Now that an open act of defiance had been committed, the Pope
was goaded into action. In July 1533 he quashed Cranmer's verdict
and excommunicated him and the other bishops who had taken
part in the proceedings. Henry was given until September to take
back Catherine, failing which he would be excommunicated. Cromwell immediately set on foot a propaganda campaign against the
papacy, and the *Articles*, published in late 1533, referred to 'the
Bishop of Rome, by some men called the Pope'. This was not simply
an insult; it was a reminder that the Pope was like any other bishop,
and had no authority outside his own diocese.

The denial of papal supremacy left the English church, from an
administrative point of view, without an effective head, and further
legislation was needed to replace the Pope by the King. In 1534
the Act in Absolute Restraint of Annates confirmed Henry's letters
patent (issued in August 1533) cutting off this source of papal revenue. It also laid down that in future bishops and abbots were to
be elected only after the issue of a *congé d'élire* containing the name
of the person the King had chosen. If the chapter failed to elect the
person so named its members would be liable to the penalties prescribed in the Statute of Praemunire. Another Act of 1534, asserting
that the realm had been impoverished by 'intolerable exactions of
great sums of money', forbade the payment to Rome of Peter's
Pence — an annual tribute regularly paid since the reign of the
Conqueror — and prohibited the sale of papal dispensations in
England.

Hope of any reconciliation with Rome had by now been abandoned and in March 1534 Clement at last gave judgment in favour
of Catherine. In November of that year Parliament put the coping-
stone upon the new structure of the Church in England by passing
the Act of Supremacy. This did not grant a parliamentary title to
Henry, since the declared assumption of the Henrician Reformation
was that Kings of England had always held this supremacy, even
though papal usurpations had for some time prevented them from
exercising it. 'The King's Majesty justly and rightfully is', in the
words of the Act, 'supreme head of the Church of England'. A
Treason Act of the same year made it an offence to attempt by any
means, including writing and speaking, to deprive the King and
his heirs of their titles or to accuse them of heresy or tyranny. The
heirs in question were named by the Succession Act of March 1534

as the children of the Boleyn marriage, and all subjects were ordered to take an oath accepting this.

Sir Thomas More, former Lord Chancellor, and John Fisher, Bishop of Rochester, refused to take the oath and were imprisoned. More claimed that he was 'not bound to change my conscience and conform it to the counsel of one realm, against the general counsel of Christendom'. His appeal from the law of the state to 'the law of God and His Holy Church' worried Lord Chancellor Audley, who was presiding at his trial, and he asked the Lord Chief Justice for his opinion. The Lord Chief Justice replied that 'if the Act of Parliament be not unlawful, then is not the indictment in my conscience insufficient'. This reply went to the heart of the matter. More was executed because he denied the sovereignty of statute, upon which Henry and Cromwell built the Tudor state. His idealism and his appeal to conscience, as well as his courage and humanity, make More's execution seem a flagrant example of tyrannical injustice. Yet his opponents were also idealists who saw the way of salvation, in this world and the next, leading through the secular state which acknowledged no earthly superior.

The assumption of Henry and Cromwell that anyone who refused wholeheartedly to accept the royal supremacy was a potential traitor found some confirmation in Fisher's case, for the reports of the imperial ambassador over the previous two years had quoted 'that excellent and holy man, the Bishop of Rochester' as calling for prompt action and strong measures on the part of the Emperor against the King. In May 1535 the Pope created Fisher a cardinal. Henry took this as a personal affront and swore that by the time the red hat arrived Fisher would not have a head to put it on. The following month Fisher, found guilty of treason, was executed. More had to wait until July, when he was executed, appropriately enough, on the eve of the feast of St Thomas Becket.

More and Fisher were the most important victims of the 'Terror', the stage common to every revolution when the leaders or potential leaders of a conservative reaction are struck down. The Henrician terror was a small-scale affair, but Henry made it clear that he would not tolerate open opposition to his will. Elizabeth Barton, 'the Nun of Kent', a visionary whose revelations had given her a great reputation, was executed in 1534, along with her accomplices, for prophesying the King's death. The following year, while More and Fisher were awaiting judgment, a number of monks from the London Charterhouse were hanged, drawn and quartered for denying the royal supremacy. This show of force was apparently sufficient. No leader emerged to challenge the policy of the crown.

## Royal Supremacy. II: The Theoretical Foundations

By the middle of 1535 Henry and Cromwell had accomplished the first stage of their revolution by destroying papal authority in England and making the King supreme head of the English church. There were theoretical as well as legal foundations to the royal supremacy. Most obvious, perhaps was the justification of expediency: intervention by the King was necessary because the Church, under papal leadership, had failed to take effective action against abuses. The only power which could effectively challenge papal claims and set reform on foot without causing chaos was the lay ruler. For this reason the early reformers, including Luther, appealed to the prince.

But there were good grounds for princely intervention, quite apart from expediency. The Bible showed the Jewish kings of the Old Testament exercising authority over the Church, while in the New Testament St Paul had written, 'there is no power but of God: the powers that be are ordained of God. Whosoever therefore resisteth the power resisteth the ordinance of God: and they that resist shall receive to themselves damnation' (*Romans* 13: 1,2).

The evidence of scripture was reinforced by the appeal to history. In the ancient world Constantine's authority had been accepted by the early Christian church, and his position, the reformers claimed, had been inherited by the lay princes of Europe. Until Becket, English rulers, while acknowledging the spiritual leadership of the Pope, had not tolerated any interference in the day-to-day administration of the Church. It was Becket who embodied the full Hildebrandine theory that the Church was a monarchy ruled over by the Pope and that the princes of Europe were his feudal vassals. The rulers of late medieval England had moved a long way from this subordinate position, but Henry VIII consciously took up the struggle where his great namesake and predecessor had abandoned it, and in a symbolic gesture he ordered the destruction of St Thomas's shrine at Canterbury in 1538 and forbade the celebration of his feast, on the grounds that 'there appeareth nothing in his life and exterior or conversation whereby he should be called a saint, but rather a rebel and traitor to his prince'.

The reformers drew a distinction between *Potestas Jurisdictionis*, or the right to exercise jurisdiction over the Church, and the *Potestas Ordinis*, the right to exercise spiritual powers — although in practice this distinction was nothing like so clear-cut as it appeared to be in theory: Henry VIII, in particular, had highly idiosyncratic views about the nature of his position, and acknowledged few, if any, limitations to his authority. The Henrician Reformation was portrayed as the transfer to the crown of the *Potestas Jurisdictionis*:

the *Potestas Ordinis* remained in the hands of the bishops. The appeal to history, and the distinction between the two types of ecclesiastical authority, account for the tone of the statutes which brought about the destruction of papal rule. History and the Bible, it was held, showed that the *Potestas Jurisdictionis* belonged to the lay ruler; all that remained was to remove papal usurpations and to restore to the King his rightful authority. The argument was a strong one and it carried many waverers with it.

Conservatives and radicals both appealed to royal authority. The conservatives were afraid that without royal protection the Church would fall victim to radical attack; better a state Church with catholic doctrine than the heresies of Luther and Zwingli. The radicals, on the other hand, hoped that by destroying papal supremacy the King would open the way to a Church reformed in doctrine as well as government. Gardiner, who belonged to the conservatives, wrote that 'the King, yea, though he be an infidel, representeth the image of God upon earth'. William Tyndale, who stood at the opposite extreme from Gardiner and was eventually to be burnt as a heretic, agreed with him on this point. 'He that judgeth the King', he wrote, 'judgeth God, and he that resisteth the King resisteth God.' For those whose consciences were less scrupulous than More's — that is to say the vast majority — obedience to the prince was sufficient in itself, and largely replaced dependence on relics, indulgences and outward observances which had previously given hope of salvation to men well aware of their wicked ways but unable to abandon them. Now they could take refuge with Shakespeare's soldier: 'we know enough if we know we are the King's subjects. If his cause be wrong, our obedience to the King wipes the crime of it out of us.' It was left in the play to the disguised Henry V to make the rejoinder of the later reformers: 'every subject's duty is the King's. But every subject's soul is his own.' (*King Henry V*: IV, i)

Obedience to the sovereign became a religious duty not only because the sovereign was the head of the Church but also because society as a whole, organised under the King, was assumed to have a spiritual function. It was this belief that explains the otherwise paradoxical combination of worldliness and deep religious feeling in the men and women of early Tudor England. Their worldliness — desire for money, lands, honours, titles and glory — led to the adulation of the monarch from whom such things flowed. Yet at the same time their awareness of God and sin and the need for salvation suffused the secular society and its secular head with a spiritual purpose. This was true not only of England but of other countries, whether they were communities like Calvin's Geneva, where the state was conceived to be an aspect of the Church, or like catholic France and Lutheran Germany, where the Church was subordinate to the lay magistrate. In all these the state, whether it was a city, principality or kingdom, became the unit in which and around which matters spiritual were organised.

In England the new society was mapped out by writers like Thomas Starkey, who were the direct heirs of the early sixteenth-century humanists. These men were products of the Renaissance. They had studied the learning of the ancient world and wished to apply their knowledge to the benefit of Church and state. Cardinal College was a centre of humanist studies, and Thomas Starkey was among those students already at Oxford whom Wolsey persuaded to transfer to his new foundation. In the years following Wolsey's fall many of the scholars who had been at Cardinal College, and would normally have gone on from there to be trained in Wolsey's household, found refuge in the circle of Reginald Pole.

Pole was a member of a great family, connected by blood to the throne itself, and he was to become famous as a scholar and humanist. His household at Padua (where his studies were paid for by Henry VIII) was a centre for English scholars like Starkey and Thomas Lupset — one of the leading figures in the academic world, a friend of Erasmus and lecturer in Greek at Oxford. But the smooth development of English humanist studies was broken up by the divorce question. Pole was too big a name for Henry to ignore and the King put pressure on him to give a favourable opinion. Pole was at first far from clear about his own attitude, but Starkey saw in the rise of Thomas Cromwell an opportunity to reform society on humanist lines, and in 1534 he left Pole at Padua to return permanently to England. Starkey assumed that Pole would eventually take the King's part and that English humanists would continue the tradition of service to the state which Wolsey had encouraged. But in 1536 Pole published his *Pro Ecclesiasticae Defensione* which came out clearly against the King. From then onwards Henry regarded Pole as his enemy.

Starkey, meanwhile, was working for Cromwell. His most famous work, *A Dialogue between Pole and Lupset*, was not published until the nineteenth century, but his *Exhortation to Unity and Obedience*, which grew out of his discussions with Cromwell and reflects the views of both men, was produced in 1536 by the King's printer. For Starkey the state was a means to a better life: 'good policy is nothing else but the order and rule of a multitude of men, as it were conspiring together to live in all virtue and honesty'. The contrast between the humanism of Starkey and that of More is nowhere more striking than in their attitude to the state. Starkey revered it; More despised it, and described it as 'nothing but a conspiracy of rich men procuring their own commodities under the name and title of common wealth'.

For Starkey the Bible was the sole source of authority. What it commanded was, by definition, good; what it condemned was bad. But on those topics about which it was silent — for instance, papal power — society should decide for itself. These topics were the *adiaphora*, 'matters indifferent', which were not essential to salvation and belonged by right, as well as by expediency, to the sphere of authority of the lay ruler. Starkey recommended a middle course between the extremes of total preservation and total rejection, maintaining for instance that ceremonies and traditions, being *adiaphora*, should be permitted in so far as they were 'things convenient to maintain unity' and as long as they were not repugnant to 'God's word nor to good civility'. In this he was sketching out the position that the anglican church was eventually to make its own.

## The Henrician Reformation

Henry VIII broke away from Rome because he saw no other means by which to free himself from his marriage to Catherine; if only the Pope had given him the divorce there is every reason to assume that he and his kingdom would have remained within the papal fold. Henry's actions, however, came at a time when the catholic church throughout Europe was under attack. In a sense, the Christian humanists had prepared the ground, for by exposing the weaknesses of the Church which they loved they had put weapons into the hands of those who hated it. In 1516, for instance, Erasmus published an edition of the New Testament in which the Greek text appeared side by side with the Latin version. Had Erasmus been writing half a century earlier his work would have slowly been disseminated through more or less imperfect manuscript copies, but the invention of printing had changed all that. His New Testament quickly became available to the literate public throughout the Christian world and provided his readers with a source of authority to which they could appeal even against the traditions of the Church and the decrees of the Popes. With one fell blow the Church's monopoly of sacred writings was destroyed and religion ceased to be a mystery which only a minority of initiates could fully comprehend. In this way, as Stephen Gardiner later observed, Erasmus laid the egg which Luther hatched.

The printing press played a key role, once again, in the propagation of Luther's ideas, for in the 1520s he wrote a number of powerfully-argued pamphlets which circulated widely throughout Europe and made him a household name. In these he elaborated the doctrine that human nature was utterly corrupted and enslaved by sin and that the only hope of salvation rested in faith in God. 'Good works', in the accepted sense of pious observances, acts of charity, pilgrimages, etc., could not affect the basic corruption of the soul. Without faith they were of no value: with faith they were unnecessary. The catholic church, with its elaborate hierarchy, its shrines, pilgrimages, relics and indulgences, was irrelevant to the human condition.

Luther's ideas found a responsive audience in England, particularly at Cambridge, where a number of English 'Lutherans' came together at the White Horse Tavern, which acquired the nickname of 'Little Germany'. The leaders were Thomas Bilney and Robert Barnes (who was, like Luther, an Augustinian friar). Yet to describe the members of the White Horse group simply as 'Lutherans' is in some ways misleading. For one thing there was a considerable variation in attitudes and beliefs among them; and, for another, their views were constantly evolving. Luther was only one of the influences on them. Among the others were the Swiss reformers Ulrich Zwingli and Martin Bucer, who on a number of points were in disagreement with Luther. The English 'Lutherans' were also men of independent mind, who developed their own attitudes. Bilney, for instance, had been inspired by Erasmus's New Testament to undertake an intensive study of the scriptures, as a result of which he came to accept Luther's belief in justification by faith alone and the uselessness of rites and ceremonies. He could not see any value in prayers to saints, relic worship or pilgrimages, yet he was traditional in his acceptance of transubstantiation — the doctrine that in the mass the bread and wine are changed, at the moment of consecration, into the 'real presence', the veritable body and blood of Christ. Bilney was the first English 'Lutheran' to suffer death at the stake, in 1531. He was followed by John Frith, one of a number of young Cambridge lecturers whom Wolsey invited to transfer to his new foundation at Oxford, and who took their unorthodox ideas with them. Frith eventually adopted a more extreme position than Bilney, denying transubstantiation and refusing to accept the existence of purgatory. This brought him up against Sir Thomas More, the Lord Chancellor, and he was sent to the stake in July 1533.

Among those who came into contact with Bilney and was strongly influenced by him was Robert Barnes. He was accused of heresy in 1526 and narrowly escaped burning, so he took refuge in Germany, from where he addressed a 'supplication' to Henry VIII, defending the Lutheran position on justification by faith and calling on the King to authorise the production of a vernacular Bible. This came to the attention of Thomas Cromwell, who was now the King's chief minister. Cromwell was probably close to Barnes in his religious opinions, and he also saw the need to recruit not simply Erasmian humanists but also radical reformers to engage in polemics on Henry's behalf. At Cromwell's invitation, therefore, Barnes returned to England, where he worked for the King and was

subsequently employed on a number of diplomatic missions to Lutheran divines and princes in Germany. Yet his defence of the royal
supremacy and his relatively moderate position on disputed points
in religion — he was deeply opposed, for instance, to the 'sacra-
mentarians' who denied that there was any trace of the real presence in the consecrated sacraments — could not save him from the
conservative reaction which set in after Cromwell's fall, and he was
sent to the stake in 1540.

One incident in Barnes's life symbolised the fusion of old and
new heretical movements, for in 1527 he had a meeting with two
Lollards from Essex. The Lollards were the spiritual descendants
of Wycliffe and the forerunners of English puritanism. They maintained that the Bible was the sole source of authority. They rejected
Popes, bishops and all ecclesiastical hierarchy, denied the existence
of purgatory, and did not believe in transubstantiation. Their attitude was far more extreme than that of Luther, and the Church
had persecuted Lollards ever since their first appearance. The two
Lollards who met Barnes went up to London specially to see him.
They told him how they had begun to convert their vicar to
Wycliffe's doctrines. They also showed him some manuscript copies
of parts of the Lollard Bible. But Barnes displayed a tolerant contempt for this old-fashioned version of the scriptures, and before
parting with his visitors he sold them a copy of Tyndale's translation of the New Testament.

William Tyndale was among the leading figures of the the early
Reformation in England. He spent his undergraduate years at Oxford and then transferred to Cambridge, where he became a close
friend of John Frith, who assisted him in preparing an English version of the New Testament. Tyndale had been horrified at the way
in which the externals of worship were accepted without any real
understanding of their meaning, and he described how 'thousands,
while the priest pattereth St John's Gospel in Latin over their
heads, ... cross so much as their heels and the very soles of their
feet, and they believe that if it be done in the time that he readeth
the Gospel (and else not) that there shall no mischance happen to
them that day'. Tyndale felt that the only hope of bringing back
the masses to a true understanding of the fundamentals of religion
lay in giving them a vernacular Bible, and he asked permission
from the Bishop of London to undertake the task of translation.
When this was refused he went into voluntary exile in Germany,
where by 1524 he had completed his translation of the New Testament. Copies were soon circulating in England and were among
the 'Lutheran books' which were burned in public bonfires, such
as that at St Paul's which took place in Wolsey's presence in 1526.

In 1528, Tyndale, who was by then in the Netherlands, published *The Obedience of a Christian Man*, in which he declared that

even the rule of a bad king was preferable to anarchy, for 'it is better to suffer one tyrant than many'. Tyndale was not advocating absolutism, for he insisted that although subjects were bound to obey their ruler they should do so only as long as his commands were consonant with faith and conscience. But *The Obedience of a Christian Man* appealed, for obvious reasons, to Henry VIII, who made repeated attempts to persuade Tyndale to return to England and work for him, in 1531, despite the fact that he did not approve of Tyndale's theological views. But when Cromwell sent an agent to Antwerp to persuade Tyndale to come out openly in support of the King, Tyndale demanded that Henry should first agree to promote radical reform by officially licensing a version of the Bible in English. Henry was not, at that time, prepared to accept such a condition, and angrily broke off the negotiations. A few years later Tyndale's hiding-place was betrayed, and he was burnt at Antwerp as a heretic. He died praying God to open the King of England's eyes.

Cromwell's sympathetic attitude towards the radical reformers, taken in conjunction with the King's willingness to use them for his own purposes, made the Henrician Reformation more extreme than it appeared to be on the surface, and drove it beyond a mere transfer of *Potestas Jurisdictionis*. In 1535, for instance, royal injunctions were issued to the universities, abolishing courses and degrees in canon law, and ordering that all divinity lectures should be 'according to the true sense of the Scriptures' and that all students should study the Bible privately. In July 1536 a meeting of Convocation, presided over by Cromwell as the King's representative, produced the *Ten Articles*, defining the doctrinal position of the Church of England. On the sacraments of the altar, baptism and penance these were relatively orthodox, but prayers to saints and special rites and ceremonies were permitted only on the understanding that they were simply reminders of spiritual truths, and not, as orthodox catholics maintained, means to obtain new graces from God. In general the *Ten Articles* were moderate in tone, but they showed clear signs of Lutheran influence and this was an indication of the way in which the pressure of events was driving Henry and the Henrician church in the direction of radical reform, despite the King's reluctance to go down this path.

Reformers of all shades of opinion agreed on the need for an English version of the Bible. There was nothing particularly revolutionary about such a demand. In many other countries the scriptures had been translated into the vernacular with the blessing of the ecclesiastical hierarchy, but in England the bishops were so frightened of encouraging the spread of Lollardy that they refused to sanction any such undertaking. This was a short-sighted attitude, since it merely meant that the work was undertaken by men of more radical persuasion, who put their own gloss on what they translated. Among the earliest complete versions of the Bible in English to be published in Henry VIII's reign, was that by Miles Coverdale — a friend of Robert Barnes, whom he had come to know when they were Augustinian friars together, and also of Thomas Cromwell. When Coverdale's Bible was printed, in October 1535, Cromwell showed a copy to the King who passed it on to Gardiner and other bishops to examine. When they reluctantly agreed that there were no heresies in it, Henry commanded, 'then in God's name let it go abroad among our people'. This was provided for by the *Injunctions* drawn up by Cromwell and issued in October 1538, which required all the clergy to provide 'on this side the Feast of Easter next coming, one book of the whole Bible of the largest volume in English' to be set up in a convenient place in every parish church, where the people might go and read it.

In spite of the order to provide a copy of the Bible in English, there was still no single authorised version available. Since the Church authorities showed no signs of producing one, the radicals once again took the lead. Cromwell commissioned Coverdale to produce an authoritative edition. This, the Great Bible, appeared after many vicissitudes in 1539 and a royal proclamation of May 1541 ordered that it should be made available in accordance with the *Injunctions* of 1538, except in cases where another version had already been provided. Cranmer wrote the preface, and this particular Bible is often called after him, but it was in fact Coverdale's work. The bishops, however, were far from satisfied with the Great Bible, which was too radical in its language for their taste, and after 1541 no more copies were printed until Edward VI's reign brought the radicals to power. Its appearance and authorisation had been largely due to Thomas Cromwell, and was one of his most enduring contributions to English life.

### The Dissolution of the Monasteries. I: Visitation

The mixture of motives that characterised the Henrician Reformation was nowhere shown more clearly than in the Dissolution of the Monasteries. The monasteries were a temptation to men hungry for money. The heyday of the monks had been in the thirteenth and fourteenth centuries when their studies in divinity and canon law had made them the intellectual leaders of Christendom. But the fifteenth century saw the spread of the new learning with its emphasis on classics and philosophy, and although this did not affect England until the reign of Henry VII, English education had also shifted its emphasis towards the the study of common and civil law. While the pattern of education was changing, so also were assumptions about the Christian life. The place of the Church was held to be in the world, though not of it, and there was no longer any instinctive sympathy with the monastic ideal. This was shown by the decline in the number of novices, and by the drying up of legacies. Colet, for instance, who was both an ascetic and a contemplative, left his money to found a school, and it is a reflection on the monastic life that he and More, who were both in a sense 'natural monks', did not enter the cloister.

In England the intellectual attack on the monks ranged from the rapier thrusts of Erasmus to the bludgeoning tactics of Simon Fish. Erasmus wrote in his *Enchiridion* of 1504: 'do we not see members of the most austere monastic orders maintaining that the essence of perfection lies in ceremonies or in a fixed quantity of psalmody or in manual labour? And if you come to close quarters with these men and question them on spiritual matters you will scarcely find one who does not walk according to the flesh.' Simon Fish's complaint, published in 1528, took the form of a *Supplication for the Beggars* who declared that they were being deprived of their legitimate livelihood by 'another sort, not of impotent but of strong, puissant and counterfeit holy and idle beggars'.

The violence of Fish's attack might be thought to have blunted its impact, but in fact it was so widely circulated that More replied to it with a *Supplication of Souls*, in which he reminded his readers that the prayers of the monks helped to shorten the period which souls had to spend in purgatory. Fish's attack and More's reply show how a criticism of abuses (the laziness of monks) could shift imperceptibly into an attack upon doctrine (the existence of purgatory). But only after they had unleashed their assault on the Church did the reformers turn their attention to what they believed in and wished to preserve. In these early days they were much clearer on what they hated, and they focused the full fury of their invective on the monks and the monastic ideal.

The monasteries of early Tudor England had still not recovered from the Black Death which had halved their population and wiped out some communities altogether. Monastic revenues were now so large, relative to the number of monks, that they encouraged worldliness, and the reports of episcopal visitors in the century preceding the Dissolution show how standards were declining. Feasting had replaced fasting, dress was extravagant, services were poorly attended. Sometimes there were more serious faults. To give one example, in 1514 the Prior of Walsingham was a notoriously dissolute and evil liver, who wore luxurious and ostentatious clothes, kept his own private jester, and paid for all this by stealing monastic plate and jewels. Visitation could be very effective, but visitors varied in quality, and too often the punishments they prescribed were absurdly inadequate for the offence, or else were not enforced. In 1491, for instance, a deacon of Langley Priory cut off another monk's hand in a violent brawl. He was sentenced by the visitor to perpetual exile and imprisonment in another house, but six years later he was back again at Langley, this time as sub-prior.

Richard Redman, abbot of the Premonstratensian house at Shap from 1458 to 1505, is an example of a conscientious visitor. He toured the twenty-nine abbeys under his care at regular intervals of three or four years, taking about three months for each circuit. He did his job well and was obviously concerned to keep up the high quality of the houses for which he was responsible. Another of the outstanding figures in English monasticism of this period was Marmaduke Huby, abbot of the Cistercian house of Fountains from 1494 until 1526. Huby is remembered, among other things, as the builder of the great tower at Fountains, and in this particular aspect of their life the monasteries were far from decadent. Building went on throughout the Wars of the Roses and continued without a break right up to the Dissolution. Peterborough's fan vaulting dates from the period immediately preceding Wolsey's fall, and the last priors of Bath had not finished the magnificent work they had set going when the royal commissioners arrived to take over.

Some monasteries ran a school for the poor children of the neighbourhood, while they trained the sons of the rich in the abbot's household. The education of the monks themselves, however, was frequently neglected, particularly the obligation to send them to university. The failure of the orders to educate their members adequately was a serious weakness in an age that saw an increasing number of learned laymen, for it meant that the monks could not meet the intellectual challenge of the Renaissance. Even the fine libraries which many monasteries possessed were out of date, and the connexion of monasteries with literature and learning waned with the decline of the handwritten book. A high musical tradition was maintained in some big houses where the numbers permitted it. Robert Fayrfax directed the music at St Albans during the first twenty years of the sixteenth century, and at Waltham Abbey Thomas Tallis was organist and choirmaster for some years before the Dissolution. Elsewhere, numbers were usually too small for music to play more than a minor part in the life and worship of the monastery.

In charity and hospitality the same decline is recorded. Almsgiving may have averaged the stipulated one-tenth of monastic revenues, but it was indiscriminate and did little to relieve the genuine problem of poverty. Hospitality was a traditional duty of monasteries and was important, particularly in the north of England where inns were rare. The disadvantage of this was that it brought lay people into the cloister, unless, as at Glastonbury and St Albans, a separate inn was built for guests.

There were, on the eve of the Dissolution, about eight hundred and fifty monastic houses, including friaries, varying enormously in population and wealth. Westminster and Glastonbury, for instance, had incomes of nearly £4,000 a year, but some of the smaller houses were heavily in debt. The total annual income of all the houses was about £165,500, derived mainly from their estates, which amounted to a quarter of all the cultivated land in England. Much of this income went on running the estates and maintaining the worship of God, but it still seems an excessive amount for the eleven thousand monks and nuns who benefited from it, and the wealth of the monasteries made them an easy target for criticism and envy. It is true that moral standards were low and that the frequent instances of rushed or neglected services were a denial of the very purpose for which monasteries had been created. Yet these faults could have been cured. The decision to dissolve the monasteries was taken primarily for financial, not moral, reasons. Henry VIII's wars had left him desperately short of money at a time when the Break with Rome might lead to a coalition of catholic powers against him. He was casting around for new sources of revenue, and the monasteries were an obvious target. Their destruction could be attributed to Erasmian motives, but in fact their fate was determined by their wealth and defencelessness in face of a King who was increasingly willing to exercise his enormous latent power. Hence the appointment of Thomas Cromwell as Vicar-General in 1535, with orders to exercise the King's supremacy over the monasteries.

There were many precedents for dissolution. Edward III and Henry V had suppressed alien priories, and one or two English houses had been put down, but the first systematic dissolution had been carried out by Wolsey. Between Wolsey's fall and the Dissolution no major suppressions took place, but in 1532 the Augustinian canons at Aldgate went bankrupt and handed their house over to the King. This was the first instance of monastic property ceasing to be used for a religious or charitable purpose.

Thomas Cromwell had been Wolsey's agent in dissolving twenty-nine monasteries, and was therefore well fitted for the larger task. The commissioners whom he sent round to collect oaths to the succession and supremacy met little opposition, and by the end of 1535 all except a handful of monks had rejected the Pope and accepted the King as head of the Church. The Observant Franciscans held out until Henry suppressed their seven houses in 1534, while the Bridgettines of Syon gave in only after their head, Richard Reynolds, had been executed. The only other opposition came from members of the London Charterhouse, following the example set by their prior, John Houghton. He and two other Carthusian priors refused to take the oath of supremacy and were executed, and eighteen Carthusians suffered death before the London Charterhouse was effectively subdued.

In 1535 Cromwell, as Vicar-General, ordered an assessment to be made of the wealth of the Church. This was a remarkable administrative feat. Commissioners were appointed for each diocese to record all sources of Church revenue, and their returns were incorporated in the *Valor Ecclesiasticus*, a sixteenth-century Domesday Book of the Church. The same year also saw a general visitation of the monasteries by agents whom Cromwell appointed. Four of them, Richard Layton, Thomas Legh, John Tregonwell and John London, were trained in civil law, while the fifth, John ap Rice, was a common lawyer. The main purpose of their enquiries was to elicit as many examples as they could of superstitious practices and immoral conduct. Where mild measures were of no avail they resorted to threats, and ap Rice described Legh at work: 'at Burton he behaved very insolently . . . at Bradstock and elsewhere he made no less ruffling with the heads than he did at Burton . . . wherever he comes he handles the fathers very roughly'. They travelled at great speed. When Legh and Layton were working in the north they visited at least a hundred and twenty monasteries in two months and covered more than a thousand miles. Even had they wished to make a thorough inquiry into the state of any house they did not have time to do so, in spite of the fact that some districts, including the whole of Lincolnshire, appear to have been left out of the visitation altogether.

### *The Dissolution of the Monasteries.II: Suppression of the Smaller Houses*

Cromwell, whose religious opinions made him sceptical of the spiritual value of monasteries, may well have been hoping for a gradual surrender by all the houses, large and small; certainly the suppression of the smaller houses alone would not have made much sense in financial terms, since their combined wealth was insufficient for Henry's needs. But it looks as though Cromwell had to give way to pressure from those — including Henry? — who wanted quick results, and the decision was therefore taken to destroy the lesser monasteries by statute. The reports from his visitors, though incomplete, had given Cromwell sufficient lurid evidence to shock the Commons, and there may have been a feeling, even among those who wanted the monastic life to continue, that the smaller monasteries had the weakest claim to preservation, and that if the King was allowed to take these he might be willing to leave the remainder alone. In 1536 the Dissolution Act was passed, ordering the suppression of all houses whose incomes fell below £200 a year 'forasmuch as manifest sin, vicious, carnal and abominable living is daily used and committed' among them. They were contrasted with the 'great solemn monasteries of this realm wherein, thanks be to God, religion is right well kept and observed'.

The Act affected some three hundred monastic houses. To enforce it new commissions were appointed in each county, consisting of a mixture of local gentry and officials. Reports from these men make revealing comparison with those of Layton, Legh and their colleagues, since they show that there was no ill-feeling towards the religious and their houses on the part of the local population and that many of the charges of Cromwell's men were either unfounded or else based on a misinterpretation of the facts.

Some indication of the hold of the enclosed life on the religious themselves is given by comparing the number of those who, when they were offered the opportunity, left the cloister altogether, with those who transferred to a larger house. The figures are not entirely satisfactory since many of the weaker members of a community would doubtless have abandoned it after the visit of Cromwell's agents, without waiting for the dissolution commissioners to arrive: in eight Norfolk monasteries, for instance, numbers had dropped during this period from sixty-nine to thirty-two. But Cromwell can hardly have believed that the monks were all itching to leave a life that meant nothing to them, since he made provision for about a quarter of the smaller houses to remain in existence to contain the large number of religious who wished to stay. The number varied from region to region, but for the country as a whole the proportion of men who abandoned the religious life was about forty per cent; for women it was much lower, only about ten per cent. This striking difference between the sexes does not necessarily mean that nuns were more fitted for the monastic life. It is rather the case that they had little to gain from leaving the cloister, since the vow of chastity was regarded as binding on both men and women, and whereas an ex-monk could hope to find employment as a secular priest, an ex-nun, vowed to chastity in a world where the only vocation of women was childbearing, had little prospect of happiness.

The King was not as yet committed to the dissolution of all the monasteries. He actually revived the suppressed house at Bisham as 'King Henry's new monastery of the Holy Trinity', and he also placed some Premonstratensian canonesses in the buildings of Stixwold to pray for the good estate of himself and his late wife, Queen Jane. The total destruction of the monasteries only seems to have been decided on after revolt had come in the shape of the Pilgrimage of Grace, and had been defeated.

## *The Dissolution of the Monasteries. III: The Pilgrimage of Grace and Suppression of the Larger Houses*

The Pilgrimage of Grace was the first big challenge to the policy of Thomas Cromwell and his royal master. In 1536 three commissions were at work in Lincolnshire, of which one was concerned with dissolving the smaller monasteries and another with assessing and collecting the subsidy, while a third was busy enquiring into the state of life of the parish clergy. The rumour spread that this third commission was only the prelude to a general confiscation of Church plate and that no man's property would be safe in future. A popular rising broke out at Louth, where the magnificent spire, erected some twenty years earlier, attested the commitment of the townsmen to their parish church. Soon the whole of Lincolnshire was up in arms, and the gentry promptly asserted their control over the movement, which might otherwise have got dangerously out of hand. Yet the Lincolnshire rising lasted little more than a week, for when the news came that the Earl of Shrewsbury was advancing with a royal army the gentry preferred to capitulate rather than fight. The common people felt betrayed, but having entrusted their cause to their social superiors they had no alternative but to follow their example.

While an uneasy calm was settling on Lincolnshire a far more serious revolt broke out in Yorkshire, where the initiative was taken by Robert Aske, a minor gentleman and lawyer. Aske was an idealist, who gave to the rebellion most of its spiritual quality. He proclaimed in October 1536 at York that 'we have taken [this pilgrimage] for the preservation of Christ's church, of this realm of England, the King our sovereign lord, the nobility and commons of the same' from the King's evil advisers. His loyalty to the King was genuine, and he and Henry probably shared many of the same assumptions about religion. Aske wanted the monasteries preserved because 'in the north parts [they] gave great alms to poor men and laudably served God . . . and by occasion of the said suppression the divine service of Almighty God is much minished'. Yet Aske's enthusiasm does not seem to have been widely shared, for only sixteen of the fifty-five monasteries dissolved in the north were restored by the Pilgrims, and they owed their new lease of life to the actions of former inmates, assisted by local clergy, rather than to any groundswell of popular support.

The common people who joined in the revolt did so largely as a protest against agrarian changes, such as higher entry fines and arbitrary enclosure, which were threatening their livelihood. But they shared with the gentry and clerics the fear that increasing governmental activity in the north would erode the autonomy of the region and subvert the established order. Any change was bound to be for the worse, from their point of view. In general the aristocracy took no part in the rising. The Earl of Northumberland, who was head of the Percy family, remained ostentatiously aloof, although in practice he did nothing to impede the rebellion. Admittedly his brothers joined in — no doubt prompted to do so by the knowledge that the Earl had decided to bequeath his vast estates not to them but to the King — as did a number of Percy tenants. But this did not make the Pilgrimage into a 'feudal' revolt. The Earl of Westmorland and Lord Dacre, who were the other major figures in the north, kept a low profile. As for the Earl of Derby, the leading landowner in Lancashire, he came out firmly in support of the crown.

Two nobles who were caught up in the rebellion were Lord Darcy and Lord Hussey. They were careful to give the impression that they had been dragged into it against their will, but in fact both men had good reason for opposing Henry's policies. They were conservative in religion as well as in their social attitudes; they despised and distrusted upstarts such as Cromwell; and they belonged to the 'Aragonese faction' which supported Queen Catherine and her daughter Mary. A year or so before the Pilgrimage, Darcy had been discussing with the imperial ambassador the possibility of organising a popular rising, to force Henry to change course, and there is evidence to suggest that a number of simultaneous disturbances had been planned for 1536. Aske was taken aback when he heard that Lincolnshire had erupted prematurely, and although he went ahead, and the revolt spread to Westmorland, Cumberland and Lancashire, it never became the general rising which he and his associates had hoped for.

The Pilgrimage was not really a rebellion, for there was never any suggestion that Henry should be deposed and an alternative government set up. It was more in the tradition of the protest of 1525 which had persuaded Henry to abandon the Amicable Grant. The Pilgrims probably believed that the King was secretly in sympathy with them and only needed evidence of their support to shake off the evil men who surrounded him. If only the Pilgrimage could have been contained, as some at least of its leaders hoped, Henry might have come to terms. But the very success of the movement in attracting such widespread support confronted Henry with a massive challenge to his authority, and one that he had to defeat.

The King therefore summoned the Duke of Norfolk out of the sulky semi-retirement into which Cromwell's rise to power had driven him. Norfolk was the King's best soldier, and the Pilgrims could hardly complain about his 'villein blood', nor about that of his colleague, the Earl of Shrewsbury. Norfolk had assembled a large army, but his men were not all reliable and he was short of money. He therefore made offers to the Pilgrims that amounted to free pardon, although he had no intention of keeping his word and asked the King 'to take in good part whatsoever promise I shall make to the rebels . . . for surely I shall observe no part thereof'.

At a meeting with Darcy and other leaders of the rising, held at Doncaster in late October 1536, Norfolk agreed that two gentlemen should be sent to Windsor to carry the Pilgrims' demands to Henry personally, and that in the meantime there should be a truce. Henry returned an uncompromising reply, complaining that he found the aims of the Pilgrims 'general, dark and obscure', but Norfolk persuaded him to buy time by allowing further negotiations to take place. In preparation for these the Pilgrims held an assembly at Pontefract in early December at which they drew up a list of articles that covered the entire spectrum of discontent. Religious demands included the suppression of heretical works — among them those of Luther, Wycliffe, Bucer, Tyndale and Barnes — the acknowledgement of the spiritual headship of the Pope, the restoration of the dissolved monasteries, and the statutory confirmation of the rights of the Church, including sanctuary and benefit of clergy. A number of articles dealt with economic complaints, and called for the limitation of entry fines and the enforcement of the laws against enclosure. Gentry grievances were reflected in the demand that the Statute of Uses (see below, pp. 74–5) should be repealed, and there were also a number of articles which dealt with political issues — among them the legitimation of Princess Mary and the inflicting of 'condign punishment' upon 'the Lord Cromwell, the Lord Chancellor and Sir Richard Rich, Knight[1] . . . as the subverters of the good laws of this realm'. One article which, more than any other, reflected the deep unease felt in the north about the apparent arbitrariness of the royal government, demanded that 'the common laws may have place, as was used in the beginning of your Grace's reign'.

When Aske and his fellow leaders presented these articles to Norfolk at Doncaster, during the first week of December 1536, the Duke offered them, on the King's behalf, a general pardon if only they would lay down their arms, and assured them that a Parliament would be summoned to consider their grievances. Aske was prepared to accept this offer. He was convinced of the King's basic honesty and goodwill; indeed the whole rationale of the Pilgrimage depended upon this assumption. When he made his report to the thousands of Pilgrims assembled at Pontefract he met with a hostile response, but he eventually persuaded them to accept the King's offer and disperse peacefully. Aske then returned to Doncaster, in company with other leaders of the rising, and there, in the presence

---

1. Sir Thomas Audley, the Lord Chancellor, and Sir Richard Rich, Chancellor of the Court of Augmentations, were both protégés of Cromwell.

of the Duke of Norfolk, they solemnly tore off the token of the Five Wounds of Christ which they had assumed as the symbol of the Pilgrimage, and declared that in future they would 'wear no badge nor sign but the badge of our sovereign lord'.

Aske assumed that the Pilgrims had won and could return home safely in the knowledge that the King had understood their intentions and would make an appropriate response. This was indeed the case, but Henry's idea of what was appropriate was far removed from Aske's. While the Pilgrims were dispersing Norfolk was ordered to begin the work of retribution, and in the opening weeks of 1537 he was busy carrying out the King's instructions to 'cause such dreadful execution upon a good number of the inhabitants, hanging them on trees, quartering them, and setting the quarters in every town, as shall be a fearful warning'. Altogether more than two hundred prisoners were put to death: they included Aske and the other leaders who were sent to London, tried in May 1537 on charges of treason, and executed in June.

Now that the threat to their policy had come and gone, Henry and Cromwell were able to develop their plans with much greater freedom. In Yorkshire the big abbeys had stood aloof from the revolt, but in Cumberland and Lancashire the Cistercians had supported it. The dispossessed monks of Sawley, for instance, had returned to their house, which they turned into a propaganda centre for the Pilgrims. Henry showed his anger by ordering 'the said abbot and certain of the chief of the monks to be hanged upon long pieces of timber, or otherwise, out of the steeple', and he used a few isolated examples, of which this was one, to justify the suppression of all the remaining monasteries. In the winter of 1537 Thomas Cromwell's commissioners were again sent out to take surrenders, and they seized on any suspicion of opposition to strike hard and reinforce the lesson of the Pilgrimage. Robert Hobbes, Abbot of Woburn, was charged with treason for denying the royal supremacy, condemned, and hanged outside his own monastery. The heads of three other big houses, Colchester, Reading and Glastonbury, were also executed.

With the great abbeys fell the friaries, though these houses were so poor that they yielded little in the way of movable property. The increasing radicalism of the government was shown by a concurrent attack on the shrines of England. Early in 1538 the tomb of St Edmund at Bury was dismantled. It was followed by the Precious Blood of Hailes, and then the great shrine of St Thomas at Canterbury was stripped of its jewels and precious metals, which were sent off in wagon-loads to the King's treasury. The end of this orgy of destruction and dissolution came in April 1540 when the abbey of Waltham, the last survivor of centuries of English monasticism, surrendered to the commissioners. With the respect for legal forms that characterised the Henrician Reformation, a second Act of Dissolution was passed in 1539, confirming all surrenders that had been and were to take place, and formally vesting the surrendered property in the crown.

### The Dissolution of the Monasteries. IV: The Dispossessed

Movables, such as plate and jewels, were sent up to the royal treasury. The rest was sold on the spot, including the lead from the roofs, which was stripped off and melted down. In some places, such as Lewes and Chertsey, the buildings were razed to the ground, while elsewhere they were left to casual plunder. This work was done so well at Sempringham that the shrine of St Gilbert, with its great tower and two adjoining cloisters, completely disappeared and even the site was forgotten, though it stood in open country; while at Walsingham an Elizabethan poet described how:

> Level, level with the ground
> The towers do lie
> Which with their golden, glittering tops
> Pierced once to the sky.

Where a monastic site was sold, the new owner was in theory bound to dismantle the church and conventual buildings, but this was an expensive business and the non-habitable parts were often pillaged for building material, as at Fountains, then left to picturesque decay. A few were adapted for other purposes, like Malmesbury, where a rich clothier set up a factory; and in some cases, as at Bolton, Pershore and Tewkesbury, the local parish bought the monastic church to use as its own.

Luckiest of all houses were those which survived as cathedral churches, either for established sees, such as Canterbury, Durham and Winchester, or for the six new ones — Westminster, Gloucester, Peterborough, Chester, Oxford and Bristol — which Henry created. In these there was a considerable continuity of personnel. At Winchester, for instance, all except four of the monks became secular canons of the cathedral, while at Durham about half the community stayed on. The six new sees were tokens of a much greater reorganisation of the Church, which was never put into effect. Many of the English dioceses were too big, and Henry had himself sketched out a plan for thirteen new ones, making use of monastic buildings and land. But in the event the fear of invasion and the heavy expenditure on defence works made the need for ready cash overriding.

The dispossessed monks and nuns were provided for by the government. Heads of houses were well treated, particularly if they cooperated with the dissolution commissioners and did not attempt private deals with the property entrusted to them. About thirty ex-abbots became bishops within a few years after the Dissolution, and the rest received pensions which were at worst adequate, at best generous. Some abbots and priors retired to country houses, perhaps near their former home or even on part of its property, and not a few married — at the risk of being called to account later for breaking their vow of chastity — and added their names to the roll of county families.

The monks also were given pensions, except for those who had abandoned the monastic life before the surrender of the larger houses began. These pensions, averaging £5 10s per annum, were enough to exist on in 1539, but they took no account of inflation. By 1550, £5 was the wage of an unskilled labourer, and monks who had no resources other than their pension must have been near starvation level. They did not, in any case, receive the full amount. In most years the King and his successors took an ecclesiastical tenth, which was duly deducted from the pensions, and 4d in the pound was payable to the Court of Augmentations to cover the expenses of administering the grants. The pensioner lost between ten and twelve per cent of his meagre income, and in the case of nuns, whose pensions were minute, this made a big difference: a list of 1573, for instance, shows a number of aged nuns losing 4s out of their meagre grant of £2 6s 8d. Pensions were apparently paid regularly right up to the death of the last pensioner early in the seventeenth century, except for brief periods, as in 1552–3, when the government was desperately short of money.

It is not possible to draw up a balance sheet for the monasteries, putting their prayers and their example of the spiritual life on one side, and their corruption and laxity on the other. Any estimate of profit and loss must be a personal one. Henry and Cromwell, at least, were satisfied, for the minister had fulfilled his promise to make his master the richest King England had ever known, and the threat of bankruptcy had been pushed beyond the immediate horizon. Those who bought monastic property from the crown were also presumably satisfied, since they had added to their land and prestige and were determined that the transfer from religious to lay ownership which had taken place should never be reversed. Only the eleven thousand monks and nuns and their dependants had good reason to be dissatisfied with the sudden blow that had transformed their lives and tumbled them out of the security of the cloister into an indifferent world.

# 4

# King and Minister: the Structure of Government under Henry VIII

## The Privy Council

Under Henry VIII, as under his predecessors, the royal Council was the heart of the administration. Successive attempts from the fifteenth century onwards to give it a definite and permanent pattern had failed, and Wolsey's Council was still, in effect, that of Edward IV and Henry VII — a fluctuating body, with the number of Councillors present varying from meeting to meeting and never representing more than a fraction of those who were eligible. Henry VIII, like his father, had Councillors in permanent attendance on him, but he occasionally complained that he was starved of advisers because the majority were waiting on the Cardinal. In 1522, for instance, he called for more Councillors, so that strangers and visitors should not 'find him so bare, without some noble and wise sage personages about him', but although the *Eltham Ordinance* of 1526 nominated twenty members of the Council who were to be permanently attendant upon the King it does not seem that this reform ever came into effect. Following Wolsey's fall the Council increased in importance, since Henry now preferred a small ring of advisers to a single minister. Yet although the inner ring followed the King wherever he went, while the outer ring remained in London where it met daily, the Council was still one body and was too large and amorphous for convenience.

Thomas Cromwell could have been, like Wolsey, a threat to the Council, but instead he was probably responsible for putting into effect the principle laid down in the *Eltham Ordinance* by turning the inner ring of Councillors attendant upon the King into an institution and making it the real centre of the administration. By 1540 this inner ring, or Privy Council, was sufficiently distinct from the rest of the Council to have its own clerk and minute book. The Privy Council, which numbered about nineteen members, consisted of nobles, clerics and household officials. The noble group included representatives of old families, such as Thomas Howard, Duke of Norfolk, and John de Vere, Earl of Oxford, as well as newly created peers, like Cromwell himself (who became a baron in 1536) and

Sir John Russell, later Earl of Bedford. The clerical group, headed by Archbishop Cranmer, included Cuthbert Tunstall of Durham and Richard Sampson of Chichester. The household was represented by its treasurer, Sir William Fitzwilliam, its controller, Sir William Paulet, and its vice-chamberlain, Sir William Kingston.

The Council had an existence of its own and the King was rarely, if ever, present, at meetings. When Cromwell was at the height of his power he and the King decided matters of policy between them, but the Council continued dealing with a wide range of government business — receiving ambassadors, drafting despatches, discussing foreign affairs and issuing administrative orders. The Council was nicely balanced between autonomy and dependence. It could act on its own initiative, but at the same time it was immediately responsive to the King's will. This dual personality was demonstrated towards the end of the reign, when the more conservative Councillors were plotting Cranmer's downfall. Henry allowed them to go ahead, but at the same time he warned his Archbishop what was afoot, and told him to 'appeal . . . to our person and give to them this ring . . . which ring they well know that I use it to none other purpose but to call matters from the Council unto mine own hands'. The King and his Councillors were obviously used to working at a distance from each other. This was due partly to Henry's laziness, his reluctance to involve himself in the day-to-day work of government, but it would not have been possible unless Cromwell had created an administrative machine capable of operating on its own.

## The Secretaryship

The increasing importance of the Secretaryship was a phenomenon common to all the major states of sixteenth-century Europe, for this was the age of kings, and as monarchs extended their power by cutting down feudal, ecclesiastical and corporate franchises, their personal servants became figures of public significance. In the late Yorkist and early Tudor period the King's Secretary, as his name implies, looked after the King's correspondence, had custody of the seal known as the Signet and was frequently employed on diplomatic missions. The development of the King's Secretary into a Secretary of State came under Thomas Cromwell, for he was quick to spot the advantages of an office that had an indeterminate range of authority and indefinite possibilities of expansion. The Chancellorship had too many judicial and routine duties attached to it for Cromwell's purposes, and it did not give control over the all-important financial administration, which was centred in the household. Cromwell replaced Stephen Gardiner as Secretary in

April 1534, and from then on he dealt with every aspect of royal government.

The increasing prestige of the Secretaryship was shown by its change of status. The *Eltham Ordinance* placed the Secretary, for purposes of precedence, in the fourth group of officials, but by 1539 he came immediately after the great officers of state. Cromwell gave up the Secretaryship in 1540, and it was then shared between two of his clients, Ralph Sadler and Thomas Wriothesley. This division of the office was made necessary because of the continuing importance of the household element and especially the Privy Chamber, in Tudor government. The gentlemen and grooms of the Privy Chamber were personal attendants upon the King and therefore played a key role in keeping open the lines of communication between the monarch and his ministers. Ralph Sadler was a member of the Privy Chamber and acted in effect as the King's Secretary, while Wriothesley maintained close contact with Cromwell. In other words, although the Secretaryship had blossomed under Cromwell into a department of government in its own right, it had not moved out of court altogether, in the way that older offices, such as Chancery and the Exchequer, had done. Moreover, when Cromwell gave up the Secretaryship he was determined to retain virtual control over it. While he was a man of an orderly cast of mind, who enjoyed tidying up the royal administration and creating new institutions where necessary, he never intended that any institution, old or new, should become a barrier to the exercise of his own power. This was shown very clearly in the reconstruction of the financial mechanism, for which he was responsible.

## Financial Administration

Under Henry VII the King's Chamber had become the clearing-house for the crown's moneys, by-passing the Exchequer, and this remained the case while Sir John Heron, the Treasurer of the Chamber, was alive. After his death the office remained vacant for a time because Wolsey, with his omnivorous appetite for power, kept a close watch over financial administration and needed little more than clerks to carry out his will. Following Wolsey's fall, Henry left control over the royal finances in the hands of his Keeper of the Privy Purse, and the Privy Chamber took over the role which the Chamber proper had filled under Heron. Then, in 1532, Cromwell was appointed to the relatively minor office of Master of the King's Jewels, and demonstrated his growing power by making the Jewel-house into the principal royal treasury. The fact that he was able to do so shows that household administration was still as fluid as it had been in Henry VII's day, but reorganisation became essential when, after 1536, money from the dissolved monasteries started pouring in at such a rate that the household offices could not cope with it. An Act of 1536 set up a special department, 'The Court of the Augmentations of the Revenues of the King's Crown', to deal with all the problems arising from the disposal of monastic lands and property. This was a court of record controlled by its own chancellor, treasurer, attorney and solicitor, and issuing documents under its own seal. As a piece of administrative engineering Augmentations was remarkably successful, particularly when contrasted with the makeshift organisation of the older household departments like the Chamber, and its statutory basis, for which Cromwell was responsible, gave it a considerable degree of autonomy.

By the time Cromwell fell from power he had given coherence to the royal finances by channelling them into six main departments. Oldest of these was the Exchequer, which continued to collect and control the ancient revenues of the crown, consisting of the county and borough farms and the Customs, as well as the profits of justice. Next came the Duchy of Lancaster, which survived as an independent unit because its organisation was highly efficient and had provided a model for Augmentations. The Chamber kept its control over all crown lands other than recent acquisitions, but Cromwell merged it with the office of general surveyors, which had been set up to do the auditing that Henry VII had done for himself. Not until 1542, however, after Cromwell's fall, was the final stage reached when an Act was passed setting up a formal Court of General Surveyors, controlled by the Treasurer of the Chamber and the two surveyors of crown lands, and provided with its own clerk and its own seal.

Although the Court of Augmentations handled all the new land revenues of the crown, the ecclesiastical revenues went to a separate department. An Act of 1534 had transferred First Fruits (or Annates) and Tenths to the crown, but no new machinery was created to handle this money until after Cromwell's fall. An Act of that year (1540) created a Court of First Fruits and Tenths on the now familiar lines, and the same development took place with the sixth branch of the King's revenue, that which came from his feudal rights over wards. This old and important source of profit had been particularly exploited under Henry VII, but after his death there was considerable confusion. It was left to Cromwell to restore order and efficiency by creating a formal Court of Wards, and he introduced an Act for this purpose into the House of Lords a week before his fall.

Not a great deal of the superstructure of Cromwell's administration survived unchanged. The Privy Council, for instance, which seemed to have acquired a life of its own, independent of royal initiative, was largely ignored by Protector Somerset when he took over the government after Henry's death. As for the financial courts, these were swallowed up by the revived Exchequer in Mary's reign, and only Wards and the Duchy of Lancaster preserved their independent existence. The reformed Exchequer showed in its internal organisation the ground plan of Cromwell's system, but its very size and complexity made it more of an autonomous department than anything Cromwell had created. Independence of close royal control, either by the King or his favourite, was best achieved by a large organisation with traditions of its own — hence the strength of the Exchequer, which had centuries of existence behind it and had survived many vicissitudes.

Better administration, as well as the confiscation of monastic property, sent the King's revenue soaring. Before Cromwell's rise to power it averaged £100,000 a year, of which the Exchequer and Chamber accounted for £40,000 each, the Duchy of Lancaster for £13,000 and the Master of the Wards for the remaining £7,000. Cromwell trebled this annual revenue by adding to it £140,000 from monastic lands — over half from rents, the rest from outright sales — and £70,000 from First Fruits and clerical subsidies. Even when deductions are made for the sales of lands and goods which, in theory at least, were not recurrent, Henry still received in the 1540s considerably more than twice his pre-Cromwellian revenue. Much of the increase was immediately swallowed up by heavy spending — the cost of the royal household, for instance, rose from £25,000 to £45,000 a year, while the Pilgrimage of Grace cost £50,000 to put down — and in the late 1530s the King was often short of ready cash. But he was living well within his income, in spite of mounting inflation, and the royal revenue was now adequate for everything except war.

## Local Administration

As soon as the Pilgrimage of Grace had been suppressed, the government of the north was reorganised, probably by Cromwell, on a permanent basis. A new council was appointed, which was to deal solely with administration and justice and, unlike its predecessors, was not to be responsible for managing the royal estates in the north. The head of this council was the Lord President — the first being Cuthbert Tunstall, Bishop of Durham — and his colleagues included three or four peers, half a dozen knights and half a dozen common and civil lawyers. The council was given full jurisdiction in civil and criminal matters within the area north of the Humber which it controlled, and in this respect it was more powerful even than the Council in London. This reorganisation of 1537 marks the effective establishment of the Council of the North, and from then until its dissolution a century later, the line of presidents was unbroken. Throughout the Tudor and early Stuart period it was the instrument by which the crown tried to enforce order in the remoter parts of the realm. It did its work well, but the north remained dangerously isolated. Revolt broke out there again in Elizabeth's reign, and the appointment of a strong man like Wentworth in the seventeenth century shows how much of a menace local independence and disorder still were.

The Council in the Marches of Wales was a direct descendant of the body which had administered Edward IV's marcher lands. Wolsey revived and reconstituted this council in 1525, but it was not very effective in putting down disorder. Cromwell therefore set up a formal council, similar to that later developed in the north, and he had his friend, Rowland Lee, Bishop of Coventry, appointed as president of it. One of the problems confronting the royal government in this region was the existence of marcher lordships outside the boundaries of the Principality of Wales. Cromwell dealt with this in 1536 by an Act which effectively united England and Wales. The whole region, including the Principality and the marcher lordships, was now broken into shires, each with its own body of Justices of the Peace, and also with the right to elect members to the Parliament at Westminster, on the English model. This reorganisation did not, however, eliminate the need for a prerogative court, and the Council of Wales, now established at Ludlow, supervised the administration of justice throughout the border region, paying particular attention to the complaints of poor men, and making sure that the rich and powerful were not allowed to do as they pleased. But difficulties arose as the union began to take effect, for the common-law jurisdiction of the Council of Wales came up against that of that of the four Courts of Great Session created by statute in 1543, and quarrels between the two undermined the authority of the council and blunted its effectiveness.

A third, short-lived, council was set up in the west in the 1530s. Henry had earlier relied on his distant relative, Henry Courtenay, whom he created Marquis of Exeter, to watch over this distant part of his dominions, but in the reaction that set in after the Pilgrimage of Grace, Henry ruthlessly eliminated all possible pretenders to the throne, including the Courtenays. Henry could not afford to leave the west country leaderless, however, since it was threatened by a French invasion. He therefore transferred a substantial bloc of lands formerly belonging to Tavistock abbey to his close companion, Sir John Russell, whom he made a baron. He also appointed him as president of the newly-established Council of the West. In other words, the crown was applying two distinct remedies to the particular problems of the west country – one quasi-feudal, the other bureaucratic. In the event it was the quasi-feudal solution which proved durable. The Council of the West lacked direction, particularly after Russell's appointment to the demanding post of Lord Admiral in 1540. It also cost a great deal of money, which the King could have found better use for, and soon after it had been established it lost its greatest patron when Cromwell fell from power. Its shadowy existence was swiftly and painlessly terminated, and thereafter Henry looked to Russell, with his network of informal contacts, to govern the west for him.

## Parliament

By the end of the Tudor period Parliament was a far more integral part of the English political system than it had been at the beginning. Yet there was nothing inevitable about this. In Europe as a whole the sixteenth century saw the decline of representative institutions, because they could not reconcile the two principles that governed their existence — namely, the duty to assist the ruler in carrying out the task of government which God had delegated to him; and the right to make known to the ruler the grievances of his people and to call on him to redress them. As royal power expanded, representative institutions became increasingly concerned with the second of their functions, but that simply encouraged rulers to ignore them and to look for alternative, and more efficient, ways of implementing their policies. In Spain, for instance, the *Cortes* of Castile met only nine times during the thirty-year period from 1529 to 1559, while in France the Estates-General never met at all. In England, on the other hand, parliamentary sessions were becoming far more frequent, and only six years out of the thirty were without one. Such a development could hardly have been foreseen prior to 1529, for under Wolsey relations between the government and Parliament reached their nadir. The Commons, in particular, resented being called on to pay for wars of which they did not approve, and adopted what Wolsey obviously regarded as a negative attitude. Had he stayed longer in power, it is likely that parliamentary sessions would have become less and less frequent.

The big change came about with Thomas Cromwell, for it was he who persuaded Henry that the Break with Rome could not safely be carried out by exercise of the royal prerogative alone. The King needed to win the co-operation of his subjects, and to demonstrate to the world that he had done so. He also needed to give his actions the written confirmation of the highest form of law. For both these purposes Parliament was far and away the best instrument, as Cromwell was quick to realise. Cromwell was the first English statesman to exploit the enormous potentiality of statute, and the number of Acts of Parliament passed during his period of office shows the use he made of it. The twenty-two years from Henry VII's death until Cromwell's accession to power had seen the passing of just under 150 public Acts, but in the brief eight years of Cromwell's ascendancy there were 200: the corresponding figure for Elizabeth I's long reign of forty-five years was not quite 80.

These figures are in part, of course, a reflection of the quantity of legislation needed to carry through the Break with Rome, but they also demonstrate Cromwell's own inclinations. He preferred to use statutes even for purposes such as the regulation of food prices for which proclamations had hitherto been regarded as sufficient. And when he did resort to proclamations it was always for the enforcement of existing laws and not the creation of new ones. It used at one time to be thought that the Proclamations Act of 1539, for which Cromwell was responsible, marked the summit of 'Tudor despotism', since it ordained that royal proclamations should in future be 'obeyed, observed and kept as though they were made by Act of Parliament'. But proclamations had not previously required buttressing by statute, and the 1539 Act was therefore, among other things, an affirmation of the principle that statutes were the highest form of law, and that proclamations were inferior to them.

From 1529 onwards Parliament had so important a role to play in the development of Henry's political strategy that the government exerted all the influence it could bring to bear on both Houses. The Lords presented no great problem, for the spiritual peers had long been among the crown's most loyal servants, while many of the lay ones were Tudor creations or were conscious of the need to retain the King's goodwill. As far as the Commons were concerned, some boroughs were effectively in the crown's gift, and approved men could simply be nominated as their members. Others were under the influence of some landed family, which would usually be amenable to royal pressure. Shire elections were more difficult to influence, but these were usually determined by local interests rather than by national political issues. In Henry VIII's reign, as in that of his father, more and more of the King's Councillors who were eligible for a seat in the Lords preferred to stand for election to the Commons. The 1529 Parliament contained a large number of men specially sworn to the King as Councillors, and the Pilgrims of 1536 complained that 'the old custom was that none of the King's servants should be of the Commons House, yet most of the [present] House were the King's servants'.

Cromwell paid particular attention to elections. In 1534 he was busy revising the list of members of the Commons so that he could get a clear picture of what changes had taken place and decide who to recommend as candidates at by-elections. Two years later he intervened directly at Canterbury, putting forward the names of two men for election as burgesses. The mayor replied that the election had already taken place by the time the minister's letter arrived, but Cromwell refused to accept this rebuff and wrote at once to the mayor, ordering him to 'proceed to a new [election] and elect those other, according to the tenor of the former letters to you directed for that purpose, without failing so to do, as the King's trust and expectation is in you, and as ye intend to avoid his Highness's displeasure, at your peril'. The two government-sponsored candidates were duly elected.

There are no other surviving examples of forceful intervention on the Canterbury pattern, and it may be that Cromwell was reacting to a particular situation in which sectional interests were trying to rig the election. In 1539, however, Cromwell was once again very active, and in March of that year he informed the King that 'I and other of your Grace's council here do study and employ ourselves daily upon those affairs that concern your Grace's Parliament ... to bring all things so to pass that your Majesty had never more tractable Parliament'. Cromwell was not concerned to build up a group of his own within the Commons — indeed it was this very Parliament that passed an Act of Attainder against him — but to use all legitimate means to make sure that the House would co-operate loyally with the King at a time when the complications of foreign and religious policy made the situation extremely delicate. In this aim he was entirely successful.

Cromwell's active interest was not confined to elections. Even before Parliament met he would be busy with memoranda and drafts of Bills, and he had a staff of expert advisers, among them the judges, working for him. His frequent corrections and insertions in the drafts show his infinite capacity for taking pains, and it was by this laborious attention to detail that he, like the Cecils after him, charted a reasonably smooth passage for legislation. His own inside experience of the Commons was no doubt invaluable in this.

The House of Commons was not just a rubber stamp, convenient for validating government measures. Members had a right, which they cherished, to discuss those measures, and at the beginning of every session the Speaker made a formal claim for freedom of speech, though its limits were not clearly defined. In 1523 Sir Thomas More, in his petition as Speaker, requested that members should have 'licence and pardon freely, without doubt of your dreadful displeasure, every man to discharge his conscience and boldly in everything incident among, declare his advice. And whatsoever happeneth any man to say, it may like your noble Majesty of your inestimable goodness to take all in good part, interpreting every man's words (how uncunningly soever they be couched) to proceed yet of a good zeal towards the profit of your realm and honour of your royal person.' On the face of it, More was asking that there should be no limits whatsoever upon the Commons' freedom of discussion, but his speech needs to be read in the context of early Tudor assumptions about the relationship between the King and his subjects. More took it for granted that the initiation of policy belonged to the King; what he wanted Henry to grant was permission for members to speak their minds freely on the issues presented to them. Henry's reply is not recorded, but since he had nothing to fear from the Commons there is no reason to assume that it was negative or particularly restrictive.

Henry was remarkably tolerant of those members who dared oppose him. It did not, after all, very much matter what was said in the Commons. Debates were not publicly reported and there are no private journals surviving for this period. As long as the outcome of a debate was satisfactory the discussion which preceded it had little practical significance. Henry could afford to laugh at isolated examples of individuality. In 1529, for instance, John Petite, a member for London, objected to a Bill cancelling the King's debts, on the grounds that while he was content to accept this himself, he could not speak for his neighbours, who might suffer from it. Henry took no offence, but it was reported that he used occasionally to 'ask in Parliament time, in his weighty affairs, if Petite were of his side'. Similarly, when Sir George Throckmorton opposed the Act of Appeals, the King merely sent for him, made him a speech justifying royal policy, and allowed him to return to the Commons.

Henry enjoyed posing as 'bluff King Hal', but members of both Houses of Parliament knew that his joviality could swiftly turn to anger, and that he would not tolerate any fundamental dissent from the policies to which he was committed. There were a number of occasions, however, on which they showed a stubborn independence of judgment. In 1532 the Bill in Conditional Restraint of Annates ran into a barrage of criticism in the Lords, despite the fact that Henry himself was sometimes present. Although the Bill was eventually passed, the bishops voted unanimously against it. There was opposition, too, in the Commons, and the Bill only completed its passage after the Speaker had taken the unusual step of ordering a division.

The Act in Restraint of Appeals of 1533 was only accepted by the Commons after they had amended it, and in the following year they refused to accept the original version of the Act making spoken words treason. One of the most striking examples of parliamentary independence was the treatment given to the Statute of Proclamations. It may be that the first draft of this Bill provided for the enforcement of proclamations in courts of common law, and that amendments in the Lords removed this provision and substituted a special tribunal instead. Whatever Cromwell's intention, Parliament was suspicious of any measure that had a flavour of despotism about it. A collection of landholders and common lawyers knew very well what protection the law offered to property-rights, and was determined to maintain it. From this, no doubt, came the clause inserted in the Act, forbidding proclamations to interfere with the life or property of the subject.

The same concern over property prompted the Lords, in 1534, to make drastic alterations to a Cromwellian measure designed to put a brake on enclosing and engrossing (see below, p. 112) by limiting the right of landlords to buy up farms. Two years later Cromwell's comprehensive scheme of poor relief was given such a savage mauling by the Commons that he had to withdraw it and submit a much milder version. There was one issue, however, on which the government was not prepared to yield, and this concerned 'Uses'. In theory land held from the crown 'in chief' — i.e. on a feudal tenure — could not be freely bequeathed. On the death of the tenant it reverted to the King, who regranted it to the heir only after the feudal incidents — relief, wardship, marriage, livery — had been met. To avoid these exactions, many landholders made over all or part of their land to a third person to hold in trust for the heir. The nominal owner was not, in fact, the user of the land, and since this device, the 'Use', could be repeated indefinitely, a large amount of land was passing out of the King's control. It was this practice which Henry determined to check. In 1529 he came to an agreement with the Lords whereby he would accept the validity of Uses for part of any estate held 'in chief' as long as he retained his feudal rights over the remainder. However, when a Bill was drawn up to put this into effect and presented to the Commons in 1532, it was thrown out — presumably because the members, whose estates were in general smaller, and therefore less conspicuous, than those of the Lords, hoped to continue evading feudal dues altogether. Henry did not conceal his anger. He told a delegation from the Commons: 'I have sent to you a Bill concerning wards and primer seisin, in the which things I am greatly wronged; wherefore I have offered you reason as I think — yea, and so thinketh all the lords, for they have set their hands to the book . . . I assure you, if you will not take some reasonable end now when it is offered, I will search out the extremity of the law, and then will I not offer you so much again'.

Henry was as good as his word. At this stage he might have been prepared to accept feudal dues on only half, or even a third, of the land involved, and allow the rest to be freely bequeathed. But when stubborn opposition made such a compromise impossible, he brought a test case in the law courts and secured a ruling from the judges that land held on a feudal tenure could not legitimately be bequeathed. By this time the landowners in the Commons were thoroughly alarmed, and realised the extent of their miscalculation. In 1536, therefore, the Bill at last completed its passage through Parliament. The Use was now legalised, but in cases where it had been created for no other purpose than to avoid feudal dues the user of the land was to be treated as though he was the actual owner.

The Statute of Uses is important in many ways. It showed how vigorously the royal will could be opposed in Parliament, particularly when it came up against what were held to be property-rights. It also demonstrated the power of the King, who could force landholders to accept a measure from which they stood to lose. But head-on confrontations of this sort were rare, for both the King and the landowners understood the need for compromise if the social system from which they benefited was not to be undermined. The explosion over the Amicable Grant in 1525 had shown the King how dangerous it was to press his demands beyond a certain point, and he learnt a similar lesson from the way in which the Statute of Uses contributed to the gentry disaffection which found expression in the Pilgrimage of Grace. After the suppression of the rebellion, the crown significantly modified its position over Uses. In 1540 the Statute of Wills confirmed the legal right of all those who held 'in chief' — an increasing number because of the creation of new feudal tenures on former monastic property — to bequeath two-thirds of their land. Feudal obligations were to be strictly enforced only on the remaining one-third.

Because he had no reason to fear the increase of the Commons' power, Henry in fact nourished it by encouraging the Lower House to assert its privileges. As a result of Strode's case in 1512 it was enacted that members of Parliament, being judges of the highest court in the land, should not be subject to suits in inferior courts during the time when Parliament was sitting. Until Henry's reign, if a member of the Commons was arrested during the session the Speaker applied to the Lord Chancellor for a writ ordering his release, but as the Commons felt their strength they began to flex their muscles. In 1542, following the arrest for debt of George Ferrers, member for Plymouth, the House sent its Serjeant-at-Arms to fetch him from the London jail where he was lodged. The jailer and the sheriffs of London refused to recognise this unprecedented authority, and when the Serjeant tried to claim his prisoner there was a brawl in which his mace was broken. The Commons promptly complained to the Lords, who declared that the City authorities had been guilty of contempt. The Chancellor offered to issue a writ for the release of Ferrers, but the Commons were 'in a clear opinion that all commandments and other acts of proceeding from the Nether House were to be done and executed by their Serjeant without writ, only by show of his mace, which was his warrant'. The sheriffs of London had by this time realised the error they had made, in fact if not in law, and when the Serjeant appeared before them again they handed over their prisoner. The Commons made this precedent doubly binding by ordering the imprisonment of the sheriffs and other officers who had resisted the Serjeant.

Henry heard of these proceedings and consulted the judges before summoning a delegation of the Commons to present themselves before him. When they appeared he praised them for the way in which they had asserted their privileges. It may be doubted whether, in reality, he entirely approved of their action, for shortly afterwards he took the unusual step of knighting the sheriff who had been principally involved; he also dissolved Parliament before it could approve a Bill giving statutory confirmation to members' privileges. In public, however, Henry expressed his satisfaction and developed his favourite theme that he and his people formed an organic unity. This had not always been the case, even in theory, for the fifteenth-century assumption was that the King stood outside Parliament, quite separate from the three estates of lords spiritual, lords temporal and Commons who represented his people. In Henry's view, however, the King was an integral part of it, and since he and the two Houses formed one body, any injury offered to a member was an injury to himself. 'We be informed by our judges that we at no time stand so highly in our estate royal as in the time of Parliament, wherein we as head and you as members are conjoined and knit together into one body politic, so as whatsoever offence or injury during that time is offered to the meanest member of the House is to be judged as done against our person and the whole court of Parliament'.

Not only in theory but in practice as well Parliament became in Henry's reign an integral part of the constitution. This is shown by the increased length of sessions. In the twenty-four years of Henry VII's reign there were seven Parliaments, which met for a total length of some twenty-five weeks, but the last eighteen years of Henry VIII's reign saw five Parliaments whose sessions occupied one hundred and thirty-six weeks. Longer sessions were accompanied by an extension of Parliament's competence, for as it demonstrated during the 1530s and '40s, there was nothing, not even matters spiritual, which now fell outside its range.

## The Fall of Cromwell

In January 1536 Catherine of Aragon died, and in the following May Anne Boleyn was executed: she had failed to produce the male heir Henry needed, and accounts of her love affairs with other men had infuriated the possessive and disappointed King. He was now free from all impediments and could make an unchallengeable marriage. His third wife, Jane Seymour, the daughter of a Wiltshire knight, fulfilled Henry's hopes at last by giving him a boy prince, Edward, in October 1537, but she died shortly afterwards. Now that Henry had his heir and was no longer saddled with a doubtful marriage, the original reasons for breaking with Rome had disappeared. But the links with the papacy, so swiftly cut, could not be swiftly reforged, and in any case Henry had no desire to reforge them. His belief that lay princes were responsible not simply for the secular but also for the spiritual wellbeing of their subjects was genuine, and he could not have abandoned it without going against his conscience.

During the traumatic opening years of the Reformation Parliament the supporters of the papacy had kept their heads down. The Roman court had long been notorious for its worldliness, and Lutheranism and other unorthodox movements would never have spread so rapidly if only the Popes had been able and willing to assert·their spiritual leadership. Wolsey's fall was in itself a dramatic demonstration of papal feebleness, for although the Cardinal was hated as the embodiment of Roman arrogance the Pope never lifted a finger to save him. And in the following years, when the Church in England was under attack from all sides, it had no guidance or help from Rome. In these circumstances it is hardly surprising that some of its more prominent members came to prefer an active royal headship to a passive papal supremacy. In the mid-1530s, however, the decline of the papacy was halted and the process of reform was set in motion at Rome. The turning-point came in 1534, with the election as Pope of Paul III, for he appointed a commission to consider what was wrong with the Church and suggest what should be done to put it right. Among the commissioners was the Englishman Reginald Pole, whose household in Italy had become a centre for all those who were working to overthrow Henry. Pole maintained close links with his homeland, where a catholic reaction was slowly gathering way. It was given added strength by the infiltration into England of 'sacramentarian' ideas, propagated by radical reformers such as the Zwinglians and Anabaptists who, although they differed among themselves, agreed in denying the existence of the real presence in the consecrated sacraments. In 1538 Pole was touring the major states of Europe as the Pope's representative, trying to persuade their rulers to sink their differences and combine against Henry. A clear lead was given in the closing months of that year by Paul III, when he formally declared the excommunication and deposition of the heretic King of England.

Henry reacted by imprisoning and executing most of Pole's relatives, including his aged mother, the Countess of Salisbury. He also increased the size of the royal navy, ordered the shire levies to be mustered, and began the building of artillery forts along the south coast — all of which meant heavy expenditure and made the wealth of the greater monasteries even more irresistible. In January 1539, when the war scare was at its height, Henry authorised Cromwell to open negotiations for a marriage between himself and Anne, sister of the Duke of Cleves. The Duke himself was a catholic, but his brother-in-law was the Elector of Saxony, one of the greatest of Lutheran princes, and Henry was clearly hoping to build up some sort of alliance with the German reformers in order to strengthen his own position. In October 1539 agreement was reached upon the articles of marriage, and in the following January Anne of Cleves became the King's fourth wife. This was a triumph for Cromwell, but it had dangerous implications, for it tied the King to a particular course in foreign policy at a time when the kaleidoscope of European diplomacy was constantly changing; even more, it bound Henry to Anne, whom he found repugnant. However, there were no outward indications that Cromwell's days in power were numbered. On the contrary, the King appointed Cromwell to the prestigious office of Lord Great Chamberlain and subsequently, in April 1540, created him Earl of Essex. But Henry was falling under the spell of Catherine Howard, niece of the Duke of Norfolk, and this placed Cromwell in a dilemma. If, as Henry now insisted, he arranged a divorce for the King, the only result would be to put his enemies in a powerful position at the heart of government. Cromwell was caught in the same trap that had ensnared Wolsey, and the features common to both cases were the King's infatuation with a member of the Howard clan and the Howards' hatred of upstarts.

Thomas Howard, third Duke of Norfolk, was by now the leading secular figure among the religious conservatives, and he worked in close association with Stephen Gardiner, Bishop of Winchester. The conservatives, unlike the catholic reactionaries, were prepared to accept the royal supremacy — either because they believed in it or because they thought it prudent not to challenge Henry on so sensitive an issue — but they opposed any further drift away from catholic orthodoxy on the grounds that it would encourage the proliferation of the sacramentaries. They hated Cromwell, whom they regarded as the advocate of reformed ideas — which indeed he was, although these did not extend to sacramentarianism — and they were always searching for an opportunity to turn the King against him. They had to move very cautiously, however, for Henry was highly unpredictable, and although he was basically conservative in his religious views he was far from consistent.

The conservatives achieved a major victory in 1539, when they persuaded the King that the impending threat of invasion by catholic powers made it essential for him to demonstrate his orthodoxy. Henry thereupon chose Norfolk to submit a number of propositions on religion to Parliament. These were the basis for the Act of Six Articles, which defined the catholic doctrines of the non-papal Church of England. The first article was concerned with transubstantiation, and declared 'that in the most blessed sacrament of the altar, by the strength and efficacy of Christ's mighty word, it being spoken by the priest, is present really, under the form of bread and wine, the natural body and blood of our Saviour, Jesus Christ'. The second denied the necessity of communion in two kinds, since both the elements were present in each sacrament. The third and fourth insisted on clerical celibacy and the maintenance of vows of chastity, while the last two articles affirmed the validity of private masses and auricular confession. The English church was now definitely committed to an orthodox position, and anyone denying these articles was to be burnt as a heretic.

By 1540 the invasion threat had receded, but the conservatives kept up their pressure on the King, insisting that Cromwell was a secret sacramentary, intent on destroying the Church that Henry had created in England. Henry was by nature suspicious, and age had not mellowed him. Furthermore his passion for Catherine Howard encouraged him to believe what the conservatives were telling him. He made up his mind with typical suddenness, and on 10 June 1540 Cromwell was arrested. A Bill of attainder was pushed through Parliament, condeming him as a heretic and traitor. The charges were flimsy, but Cromwell could make no effective rebuttal, for, as he told Henry in one of a number of letters in which he pleaded for mercy, 'I have meddled in so many matters under your Highness that I am not able to answer them all'. He was kept alive for six weeks so that he could give evidence in the divorce action between Henry and Anne of Cleves, and then, on 28 July, was led to the scaffold.

## The Closing Years of the Reign

Henry did not appoint another chief minister to replace Cromwell. Gardiner and Norfolk were his principal advisers, but the King took most of the major decisions himself, while routine work was dealt with by the Privy Council. Cromwell's fall marked a triumph for the conservatives, but the situation remained highly volatile, as was shown in July 1540, when Robert Barnes and two other so-called 'sacramentaries' were burned as heretics, while three 'papists' were hanged as traitors. Along with Cromwell, Henry rid himself of the Cleves marriage, which was declared invalid in July 1540, and on the day of Cromwell's execution he secretly wedded Catherine Howard. Henry now seemed to have attained happiness, but in late 1541 Cranmer brought to his attention a paper charging the Queen with sexual impropriety both before and after her marriage. Henry appointed a commission to enquire into these charges, and when this declared them to be well founded his anger overflowed. All those who had been accused of complicity with Catherine were executed, late in 1541, and in February of the following year the Queen herself was condemned by Act of attainder and shortly afterwards beheaded. Not until July 1543 did Henry remarry. His sixth, and last, wife was Catherine Parr, a good-natured widow of reformist inclinations in religion, who succeeded where so many others had failed, in maintaining her hold on the King's affections.

The closing years of the reign were marked by the struggle between reformist and conservative factions for control of the Council. Henry held the balance between the two groups. His sympathies inclined him to the side of the conservatives, but he was a practical politician, who would not endanger the stability of his realm by too violent a reaction. As early as July 1540 he had ordered that there should be no more prosecutions under the Statute of Six Articles, and although there was sporadic enforcement in later years the last purge took place in July 1543, when a number of Windsor men were executed for heresy, and John Marbeck, the composer, was only saved by a royal pardon.

Henry's main concern was to preserve order, and this entailed putting a brake upon the progress of religious reform. Increasing access to the Bible had encouraged arguments about religion at all levels of society, including the lowest, and in many places there had been attacks upon 'superstitious images', leading to the widespread destruction of statues, rood screens and stained glass. Henry was not above indulging in iconoclasm himself — as evinced in his destruction of Becket's shrine — but if he let religious radicalism get out of hand among the masses it would endanger the social order. In 1543, therefore, an Act of Parliament condemned all unauthorised translations of the Bible and forbade persons below the degree of gentleman to study it at home, even in the approved version. The Act also promised that some definition of doctrine would be forthcoming. *The Institution of a Christian Man*, usually called *The Bishops' Book*, had appeared in 1537, and Henry had licensed it for three years, though he was careful not to give it his official blessing. *The Bishops' Book* was a relatively moderate statement, but it was apparently not to the liking of Gardiner and the conservative element in Henry's Council. They may have been responsible for the publication in 1543 of *The Necessary Doctrine and Erudition of any Christian Man*, which received Henry's approval and is therefore known as *The King's Book*. This was not without Lutheran traces, but on the key issues of predestination and justification by faith alone it took an orthodox position — much as Henry himself did.

1543 marked the climax of the conservative reaction and culminated in Gardiner's open attack upon Cranmer, who had been introducing many reforms, particularly the removal of images, into his diocese. From this year dates the incident of the ring, referred to earlier, in which Cranmer was saved by the King. Henry seems to have had a genuine affection for Cranmer, whose simple goodness he appreciated. Cromwell once said to the Archbishop: 'you were born in a happy hour, I suppose, for do or say what you will, the King will always well take it at your hand. And I must needs confess that in some things I have complained of you unto his Majesty, but all in vain, for he will never give credit against you, whatsover is laid to your charge'. Cranmer survived this latest attack, and at Henry's command he began work on a major reform of the liturgy. The first instalment of this was the English *Litany* of May 1544. The *Litany* could be regarded as in one sense merely the fulfilment of Erasmus's programme for encouraging vernacular worship, but it went beyond Erasmus, in the direction of more radical reformers, in its suppression of prayers to the saints. Cranmer's *Litany* has been adopted, virtually unchanged, in all succeeding forms of service, and survives today in the Prayer Book — a wonderful example, in its balanced cadences and majestic rhythms, of the English language as it came to flower.

Religion was not Henry's only, or even major, preoccupation during 1544, for that year saw a renewal of the war against France which had been in cold storage ever since the downfall of Wolsey. It may be that Henry's attack on France was dictated by his concern for the succession. A year earlier he had concluded the Treaty of Greenwich with James V of Scotland, whereby James's only child, Mary, would in due course marry Henry's only son, Prince Edward, thereby uniting the two kingdoms. The French, who were the traditional allies of Scotland, stood to lose by this, and their growing influence was demonstrated in December 1543, when the Scots annulled the treaty. Henry showed his anger at this cavalier treatment by sending the Earl of Hertford on a marauding expedition across the border in the spring of 1544, and it could be that his decision to invade France in person in the summer was part of the same reaction. But it is at least as likely that France came first in Henry's list of priorities, and that he was eager to use the wealth he had acquired from the Dissolution to accomplish in late middle age what he had been unable to achieve in the salad days of his youth. Whatever the motivation, Henry crossed over to France in July 1544 and assumed command of an army of nearly 50,000 men — the largest force at that date ever to leave English shores.

His principal objective was Boulogne, to which he laid siege, and by September the town was his. The war dragged on in a desultory fashion for another two years, but in June 1546 Francis I agreed that Boulogne should remain in English hands until 1554, and that if the French then wanted it back they would have to pay for it.

The campaign in France, and the big expansion of the navy which accompanied it, were enormously expensive. The total cost came to some £2 million — a scale of expenditure which was far beyond the resources of an English King even when he had the wealth of the monasteries at his disposal. Henry had already called on Parliament for supply, and in the period 1542–46 the yield from parliamentary taxation was well over £400,000. This vast sum was apparently collected without difficulty, which is in itself evidence of the popularity of the King and his policies, but it could not solve the crown's financial problems. Forced loans were also levied, bringing in about a quarter of a million pounds, and a similar amount was raised on the money market at Antwerp. The clergy were taxed as well as the laity, but the total from all sources still fell short of the crown's needs. In August 1545 Lord Chancellor Wriothesley wrote despairingly to the Council: 'this year and last year the King has spent about £1,300,000. His subsidy and ben-evolence ministering scant £300,000, and the lands being consumed and the plate of the realm molten and coined, I lament the danger of the time to come . . . And yet you write to me still Pay! Pay! Prepare for this and for that!'

Crown lands were sold to meet the deficit, and before his death Henry VIII had parted with two-thirds of the monastic estates, most of them sold to raise capital for his war. The currency was debased, outstanding debts were gathered in, and there was even a plan to unload accumulated reserves of lead — mainly from melted-down monastic roofs — on the European market. In spite of all these expedients the royal finances were crippled and Henry left his son an empty treasury and a diminishing revenue. The an-nexation of monastic property had completed the work begun by Edward IV and Henry VII of making land revenues the basis of royal wealth, and had restored to the crown the flexibility that late-medieval rulers had lost. The end of Henry VIII's reign saw the process reversed. As land was sold off and income declined it be-came necessary to tap other sources, and this immediately involved problems of precedent and consent. Tudor despotism — if, indeed, it had ever been more than a possibility — became increasingly un-likely after the 1540s.

During the last two or three years of his life Henry's attention was focused on the problem of maintaining the unity of his realm and thereby ensuring a peaceful succession for his son. He valued unity above all things and in a speech to his last Parliament in November 1545 he pleaded for an end to discord. 'Behold then what love and charity is amongst you, when the one calleth the other "Heretic!" and "Anabaptist!", and he calleth him again "Papist!", "Hypocrite!" and "Pharisee!". Be these tokens of charity amongst you? Are these signs of fraternal love between you?' He had not, he said, given them the English Bible in order to encourage them to discord. 'I am very sorry to know and hear how unreverently that most precious jewel, the Word of God, is disputed, rhymed, sung and jangled in every alehouse and tavern, contrary to the true meaning and doctrine of the same. And yet I am even as much sorry that the readers of the same follow it, in doing, so faintly and coldly: for of this I am sure, that charity was never so faint among you . . . Love, dread and serve God (to the which I as your supreme head and sovereign lord require you) and then I doubt not but that love and league that I spoke of in the beginning shall never be dissolved or broken between us.'

It was a masterly speech, for Henry, like his daughter, knew how to move men's hearts by the power of words. His genuine concern for harmony in the body politic, and his fear of a possible catholic reaction after his death, drove him closer to the reformers. The ablest man in his Council, and one who would probably have influence over the young prince, was Edward Seymour, Earl of Hertford, the prince's uncle and a known reformer. His influence and that of John Dudley, Viscount Lisle (son of Henry VII's notorious minister), were pushing Norfolk, Gardiner and the conservative element into the background. By the end of 1546 Gardiner was absent from court, in virtual disgrace, and rumours were afoot that bishops were to become salaried officials of the state and have their property confiscated. An Act of 1545 had already ordered the dissolution of the chantries, and commissioners were being appointed to carry it out.

Against this background counter-revolutionary plotting took place, which led, in December 1546, to the arrest of the Duke of Norfolk and his son, the Earl of Surrey — a fine poet, but an arrogant and unstable young aristocrat. Henry was a sick man, so huge with dropsy that he had to be carried upstairs, bloated, suspicious (as he always had been) and in constant pain. He was determined to strike down anybody who stood in the way of his son's inheritance, and when Parliament reassembled in January 1547 Acts of attainder were passed against the two Howards. Surrey was executed on 19 January, and Norfolk's execution was fixed for the 28th. But the Duke was saved by the luckiest of chances, for on the night of the 27th Henry died, his hand in Cranmer's. Not only Norfolk's fate but that of the state and dynasty which Henry had struggled so forcefully to preserve, now depended upon the uncertain future of a nine-year-old boy. It was an ironic comment on all Henry's efforts that in the end he had to bequeath his throne to a minor. But he had not laboured in vain, for Edward's authority was never challenged, nor was the crown ever seriously endangered by the subsequent accession of two women rulers. This did not prove that Henry's fears had been groundless; only that he had underestimated the degree of his own success.

# 5

# Edward VI and Mary I

## Edward VI

Edward VI, born in October 1537, grew up to be a robust, quick-witted boy, and was carefully groomed for the part he was to play. He lived in state, surrounded by the magnificent but impersonal ceremonial of the Tudor court, and not surprisingly he learned to conceal his private feelings behind a mask of regality that observers mistook for a chilly reserve. He was quickly set to work to acquire the learning expected of a Renaissance prince, and by the time that excellent scholar John Cheke was appointed his tutor in 1544 Edward was well grounded in Latin and Greek and, of course, in the Bible — for the future head of the Church would need a knowledge of theology at least equal to that of his bishops.

Parliament had given Henry VIII authority to bequeath the crown as he wished, and in his will he made Edward his heir, with Mary and Elizabeth, in that order, next in line. He also appointed a regency Council from which Gardiner and Norfolk were excluded. The leadership of the conservatives therefore rested with Wriothesley and Tunstall, neither of them very powerful. Against them were ranged the reformers, led by Edward's uncle, Edward Seymour, Earl of Hertford, and his friend, Archbishop Cranmer.

## Protector Somerset

Henry made no provision for a protectorate, although he did not specifically exclude this, but he could not control events from the grave. Even before he was dead the Earl of Hertford was scheming to take effective power into his own hands, and his accomplice, Sir William Paget, one of the King's Secretaries, was later to remind him of the plotting that had taken place 'in the gallery at Westminster, before the breath was out of the body of the King that dead is'. Hertford quickly took possession of Edward and rode with him to London. By the time the Councillors assembled Hertford and Paget had done their work, and the first official act of the Council was to ignore the spirit if not the letter of Henry's will by appointing Hertford 'Protector of all the realms and dominions of the King's Majesty that now is, and . . . governor of his most royal person'. The new Protector immediately paid his debt to those who had made his bid for power successful. Paget announced that Henry had drawn up an honours list before his death and that this would now be put into effect. Hertford was created Duke of Somerset; Wriothesley, who had protested against the setting aside of Henry's will, was persuaded to drop his opposition in return for the Earldom of Southampton; while John Dudley, one of the strongest characters on the Council, was made Earl of Warwick.

For the next three years Protector Somerset was in control of the destinies of England. He carefully cultivated the image of himself as the patron of all those who wanted reformation in Church and state, and he showed his inclinations by appointing a leading English humanist, Sir Thomas Smith, as one of his private secretaries. But the humanism which Somerset adopted was far removed from that of Erasmus and More. The Christian humanists of the early sixteenth century took their stand upon the Bible and the early fathers, and felt it their duty to criticise the state, which they regarded as the transitory, imperfect work of man. In the mid-Tudor period, however, a new type of humanism appeared, which had its roots in the principalities of Renaissance Italy. It was propagated by Castiglione's enormously influential *Il Cortegiano*, which inspired a number of English imitations, among them Sir Thomas Elyot's *Book named the Governor*, published in 1531. This new humanism — as might be expected, given its source — put the emphasis upon the role of the ruler rather than the rights of the ruled, and worked on the assumption that the state was a God-given and positive way of organising human society.

Somerset, then, while sincerely wishing to act as a 'virtuous ruler', took an essentially pragmatic approach to political problems and confined his idealism largely to rhetoric; as he told the imperial ambassador, his aim was to give the people of England 'a little more reasonable liberty without in any way releasing them from the restraints of proper order and obedience'. For this reason, gestures like the repeal of the heresy laws, the treason legislation of Henry VIII, and the Statute of Proclamations, cannot be taken entirely at face value. It might be thought, for instance, that the repeal of the Proclamations Act would have left the government dependent solely upon statute, but this was far from the case. In practice proclamations merely reverted to their earlier prerogative basis, and Somerset used them on an unprecedented scale.

Somerset was a proud, indeed an arrogant, man, and he displayed a love of money and of outward magnificence that were typical of the age in which he lived. The most obvious example of this was the great palace which he built for himself by the riverside, not

far from Whitehall, and christened Somerset House. Although he
had been named in Henry's will simply as one member of the regency Council among others, he took it for granted that his elevation to the dignity of Protector gave him a quasi-regal status, and
he acted accordingly. He left the Privy Council to deal with routine
business, and reserved decisions on all major matters to himself:
consequently, during the first year of the Protectorate his own secretaries, Sir Thomas Smith and William Cecil, were far more important than the Secretaries of State. Somerset no doubt enjoyed
power, but he became a remote, isolated figure, and this was to
prove his undoing when the Edwardian regime ran into trouble.

### Religion. I: The Moderate Settlement

Although the religious reformers came to power with Edward VI,
they were split between moderates and radicals. The moderates
thought it best to move by gradual steps, carrying the people with
them as they did so. The radicals, on the other hand, saw no reason
to compromise with truth. They wanted to use all the powers of
government to impose a radically reformed Church along the lines
of those established in a number of Swiss cities by Zwingli, Bucer
and Calvin. Somerset's religious views were probably close to those
of the radicals, but his attitude was affected by considerations other
than religion. He intended to solve the Scottish problem once and
for all by annexing that kingdom to England, and he realised that
his chances of doing so would be lessened if England were to be
plunged into anarchy through over-hasty action on the part of the
radicals. Somerset also had to take the attitude of Charles V into
account, for the Scots were bound to call on France for help, and
if the Emperor joined in as well, Somerset would be faced with a
formidable threat. However, if the pace of religious change in England was kept moderate, and if Princess Mary — who had never
wavered in her commitment to the Roman Catholic faith — was
allowed freedom of private worship, the probability was that the
Emperor would remain neutral.

Somerset began his Protectorate by putting into effect the plan
drawn up at the end of Henry VIII's reign for dissolving all chantries and transferring their endowments to the crown. This was justified in the Dissolution Act of 1547 on the grounds that chantries,
which existed only to provide prayers for the dead, were no longer
necessary now that belief in the existence of purgatory had been
abandoned. In fact the destruction of the chantries owed as much
to financial as to religious considerations, but Somerset did have
to take account of the radicals and give them at least part of what
they wanted. The accession of Edward VI had been a signal for
the printing presses to produce quantities of religious literature,

much of it violently anti-catholic and anti-clerical in tone. The works of the major continental reformers also appeared in English translations, and the effect of all this was to build up popular pressure to accelerate the pace of change. London was subjected to a wave of iconoclasm in the autumn of 1547, and similar outbreaks were reported from many other places. The government tried to contain this pressure, but it did not dare screw the lid down too tightly for fear of causing an explosion. It therefore lagged in the wake of the radicals, rather than giving a lead, and the order to remove images, issued early in 1548, was little more, in fact, than the granting of official sanction to what was already happening.

The doctrine of the Church of England was still, in law and in theory, that set out in the *King's Book*, but this was no longer acceptable even to moderate reformers. Somerset looked to Cranmer to produce a new formulary, and the Archbishop was already at work on this. He had taken advantage of the change of climate created by Henry's death to invite a number of distinguished European reformers to England. He did so partly because he wanted their advice and guidance while he was drawing up his statement of faith and doctrine, but also because he recognised the need to raise the level of theological learning at the universities and among the clergy in general. In late 1547 Peter Martyr Vermigli, Bucer's friend, arrived in England and was subsequently appointed Professor of Divinity at Oxford. After the defeat of the German protestants by the Emperor Charles V many more refugees found their way to England. John à Lasco, who was largely responsible for arguing Cranmer out of his belief in the real presence, arrived in September 1548, and in the spring of the following year came two of the leading Strasburg reformers, Martin Bucer and Paul Fagius. Cranmer had also invited to England Philip Melancthon, Luther's friend and one of the most influential reformers of his day. But Melancthon was unwilling to leave Germany at a time when the protestant cause was threatened, and this, combined with Luther's death in 1546 and the success of the imperial armies in checking protestantism, accounts for the decline of the influence of Lutheranism in England. The early English reformers had looked to Luther, but their heirs in the mid-1540s took Zwingli and Calvin as their masters.

Before producing the final draft of his formulary Cranmer tested opinion among the bishops and clergy, and also consulted Somerset. His own position was constantly evolving, and he was moving steadily towards the radicals, but the Prayer Book, as it eventually emerged, was a relatively moderate document. This was because of Somerset's desire, which was shared by the Privy Council, to appeal to as wide a range of opinion as possible. Cranmer would have liked to eliminate from the communion service any wording which could be held to imply the real presence, but in the event the rubrics referred to the 'sacrament of the body' and the 'sacrament of the blood' and instructed the priest to say, as he administered them, 'the body (blood) of our Lord Jesus Christ which was given (shed) for thee, preserve thy body and soul unto everlasting life'.

Under Henry VIII statements of doctrine had been issued on the authority of the King, as supreme head, but the first Prayer Book of Edward VI's reign was authorised by Parliament. The Act of Uniformity of January 1549 ordered that the Book should be adopted from the following Whitsunday by churches throughout England, and provided penalties for any clergyman who refused to use it. The radicals found the Book a big disappointment. John Hooper, who was shortly to be made Bishop of Gloucester, declared that he was 'so much offended with that Book that if it be not corrected I neither can nor will communicate with the Church in the administration of the [Lord's] supper'.

## The Western Rising and Kett's Rebellion

Although the first Prayer Book was too moderate for the radicals, it was deeply offensive to many conservatives, who had also been outraged by an Act authorising the clergy to marry if they so wished. Trouble had been brewing in Cornwall ever since the commissioners arrived to take inventories of the chantries, prior to dissolving them, for rumours were soon circulating — just as in Lincolnshire on the eve of the Pilgrimage of Grace — that the treasures of parish churches, the gift of generations of local people, were also to be confiscated. When another group of officials, headed by the Archdeacon of Cornwall, appeared at Helston in 1548 to supervise the destruction of images, riots broke out, and in April the unpopular Archdeacon was assassinated. The final straw, as far as the Cornishmen were concerned, was the imposition of the new English Prayer Book. It had, they asserted, no basis in law, for changes in doctrine could only be made by virtue of the royal supremacy, and this, in turn, could only be exercised by an adult monarch, not by a minor or by those acting in his name.

In June the Cornish rebels moved into Devon. There a spontaneous revolt had broken out in the village of Sampford Courtenay, for although the local priest obeyed orders by using the new service on Whitsunday this so infuriated his parishioners that they forced him to revert to the traditional rites on the following day and came out in open defiance of the government. When the Cornishmen arrived, the combined rebel force moved on to besiege Exeter and drew up a list of articles which they sent to the Protector. These were concerned almost exclusively with religious grievances, possibly because they were drafted in large part by clergymen, but there is no reason to doubt the religious conservatism of the west country. Admittedly, there were some economic causes for the rising, particularly resentment against the tax on sheep which had been imposed by Parliament to check enclosure and pay for the war against Scotland. Enclosures were not a problem in Devon, for if open fields had ever existed there they had long ago disappeared. Sheep, on the other hand, were kept by rich and poor alike, and all stood to suffer from the new measure. One other factor which may have contributed to the rising was continuing loyalty to the Courtenay family and its connexions, for the articles included a demand that Reginald Pole should be invited to return to England and take his place on the Privy Council. The main concern of the rebels, however, was to put an end to religious change. They wanted the Statute of Six Articles to be reimposed, along with images, ceremonies and the Latin Bible. As for the Prayer Book, 'we will not', they announced, 'receive the new service, because it is but like a Christmas game; but we will have our old service of mattins, mass, evensong and procession in Latin, not in English, as it was before'.

Somerset, in his reply to the articles, insisted that the new Prayer Book was 'none other but the old: the selfsame words in English which were in Latin, saving a few things taken out'. But the insurgents were in no mood to engage in theological debate, and the Protector therefore called on Lord Russell, the King's representative in the west, to suppress the rising by force. Russell moved slowly, however, because he found it difficult to raise levies locally for service against their fellow-countrymen, and Somerset could send him only token support. Fortunately for the government, Exeter held out, despite tension between conservative and radical factions among the citizens, and in early August Russell at last relieved the town. The besiegers retreated, but the rebellion smouldered on until the arrival of more royal forces, under the command of the Earl of Warwick. The end came in mid-August, when the rebels were finally routed at Sampford Courtenay, where the rising had started. The usual process of retribution was soon under way. The leaders of the rebellion were sent to London to be hanged. Lesser men were strung up all over the west country as a warning to any who felt inclined to follow their example.

Somerset had not been able to despatch reinforcements to Russell because a major rebellion had broken out in Norfolk. This was, like the Western Rising, a conservative revolt, but the rebels in this case were protesting not against the religious changes, which they welcomed, but against the less easily identifiable economic forces which were transforming their lives. The twin economic evils with which Tudor governments had constantly to contend were inflation and enclosure (using this term, as contemporaries did, to embrace a wide diversity of agrarian changes). Inflation, which prompted landowners to increase rents and bore very heavily upon the poor, had complex causes, but it was made worse in England by the debasement of the coinage to which Henry VIII had resorted and which continued under his successor. Sir Thomas Smith urged Somerset to put an end to debasement and restore a stable currency, but Somerset was in desperate need of money to finance the war against Scotland, which was now costing some £200,000 a year, and could not bring himself to abandon a practice which, however ruinous in the long term, brought the government an immediate profit.

There were other voices, notably that of John Hales, which put the responsibility for inflation and its attendant social ills not upon anything so impersonal as the government's financial policy but on the selfishness and greed of private individuals. This was in tune with Somerset's own conventionally moralist presumptions, and it offered him an alternative to Sir Thomas Smith's austere prescription. In June 1548, therefore, he issued a proclamation against enclosure and he followed the example of Wolsey by setting up commissions to tour those counties that had suffered badly from it. The only commission which really got going was that under John Hales which was concerned with the midland counties, but it came up against sustained opposition from the landowners, who effectively frustrated all its efforts. Somerset, however, was not deterred. He was convinced that his policy was correct and he was prepared to force it through. 'Maugre the devil, private profit, self-love, money, and such-like the devil's instruments', he declared, 'it shall go forward'. In May 1549 he issued a second proclamation against enclosure, and in June, four days after the outbreak of the Western Rising, he announced a general pardon for all those who had taken the law into their own hands and thrown down fences.

Somerset's championship of the common people won him their acclaim. It also prompted them to demonstrations which were designed to show their support for him, but which quickly developed into massive protest movements that no government could have tolerated or ignored. In June 1549 there were a number of risings in Norfolk and Suffolk, which led to the setting up of camps outside Norwich, Ipswich and Bury St. Edmund's. The Suffolk protests fizzled out, largely through the influence of Sir Anthony Wingfield, who as well as being a member of the royal household was also the head of an old-established and widely respected Suffolk landowning family. Norfolk, however, was without any dominating figure since the fall of the Howards, and the leadership of the rising was assumed by yeomen and lesser landowners who would normally have taken little or no part in the government of their local communities: indeed, the revolt was in large part a protest by such men against the traditional gentry rulers of the region, who cared too much for their own interests and too little for those of the people at large.

The Norfolk insurgents had assembled first at Wymondham, where they called on Robert Kett, a local landowner, to be their head. They then advanced on Norwich, throwing down fences as they went, and set up their camp to the north of the city, on Mousehold Heath. By the end of July they had made themselves masters of Norwich, but the bulk of the rebel forces remained in the camp, where Kett, with the help of an elected council, kept good order and discipline. It was a remarkable demonstration of self-government, and it showed the quality of the rebels. They were not a motiveless rabble but a company of small farmers, peasant cultivators, gathered together in defence of what they regarded as their traditional rights.

The main grievance of the rebels, as shown in the articles they drew up, was the excessive number of sheep being pastured by the landowners. Much of the country was well suited to sheep-farming, and the peasants, who had little land of their own, were dependent upon their right of common pasture. A few sheep could make a big difference to a man's income, and when a lord increased the number of animals he turned out to graze he threatened the peasants' livelihood — hence the demand 'that no lord of no manor shall common [i.e. put his sheep to pasture] upon the commons'. Inflated rents were another grievance, as was shown in the request 'that copyhold land that is unreasonably rented may go as it did in the first year of King Henry VII, and that at the death of a tenant or sale the same lands . . . be charged with an easy fine, [such] as a capon or a reasonable sum of money'.

Significantly absent from the list of grievances was any demand for a return to the old ways in religion. The rebels used the new Prayer Book for public services, and among those who were summoned to preach to the thousands assembled on Mousehold Heath was Matthew Parker, the future Archbishop. Moreover, one of the articles in the Norfolk list pointed in a very radical direction by suggesting that any priest who was 'not able to preach and set forth the word of God to his parishioners may be thereby put from his benefice, and the parishioners there to choose another, or else the patron or lord of the town'.

Kett and his followers were convinced — much as Robert Aske and the 'Pilgrims' had been twelve years earlier — that their action was not only morally justified but also lawful, and that they would therefore win the approval of the government. But Somerset was alarmed at the evidence of a widespread breakdown of public order throughout the kingdom and called on the Norfolk men to abandon their violent protest and return peacefully to their homes. He of-

fered them a free pardon if they did so, but warned them that if
they did not accept his offer he would use force. Somerset had already sent a detachment of mercenaries to William Parr, Marquess
of Northampton, with instructions that he should use them as he
thought fit, but Northampton's half-hearted attempt to capture
Norwich was easily beaten off. By this time, however, John Dudley,
Earl of Warwick, had returned from the west country, and he raised
an army of some twelve thousand men — a mixture of mercenaries
and local levies. In late August he seized Norwich, after several
days of fierce street fighting. He then turned on the encampment
at Mousehold Heath and encircled it. Kett gave the order to move
out rather than face starvation, but this merely provided Warwick
with the opportunity he was looking for. He sent his cavalry in
among the rebels and turned their retreat into a rout in which
many hundreds of them were slaughtered.

The rebellion was now all but over. A special commission was
set up to deal with the prisoners, of whom forty-nine were executed.
Kett and his brother William were sent up to London to be tried
on a charge of treason. They were then returned to Norfolk to be
executed. Kett was hanged at Norwich castle. His brother was
strung up from the steeple of Wymondham church. Whatever sympathy Somerset might have felt for the Norfolk peasants, he behaved like any other Tudor ruler when it came to dealing with
rebels.

## The Fall of Somerset

Although Somerset had managed to restore a semblance of order
to England there were many people in the upper levels of society
who blamed him for not taking a firmer stand before popular disturbances got out of hand. The Earl of Warwick was numbered
among these critics, and now that he had command of the only
army in England he was in a position to dictate terms. Somerset
was with the King at Hampton Court in October 1549 when he
became aware that Warwick was plotting against him. He seems
to have contemplated resistance, for he hurried the King away to
Windsor, which was easier to defend. But Somerset had alienated
many of the Council by his combination of arrogance and ineffec-
tiveness, and his popularity with the common people — who called
him 'the good Duke' — was hardly calculated to improve his standing with the landowners, on whose co-operation any government
ultimately depended. Somerset had no choice, in practice, but capitulation. He therefore gave himself up to Warwick without a
fight, and was sent to the Tower. There he remained until the following February, when he was released. This gesture of conciliation
on Warwick's part served its turn by giving him time to gain the

young King's confidence and to establish himself more firmly in power. But Somerset was too dangerous to be left at large. He was actively plotting to restore his supremacy, and he could now count on considerable support from the religious conservatives on the Council, who were alarmed by the increasing evidence of War-wick's radicalism. In October 1551, therefore, Warwick had So-merset arrested and tried for treason. In January of the following year he was executed on Tower Hill, showing no sign of fear and publicly affirming that he had been 'ever glad of the furtherance and helping forward of the common wealth of this realm'.

## *Religion II: Northumberland and the Radical Settlement*

Somerset had been associated with a policy of moderate protes-tantism, and it seemed at first as though his fall might be the signal for a catholic reaction. Cranmer had, after all, been Somerset's sup-porter, while Warwick had allied with Wriothesley, the leader of the catholic group in the Council. But whatever hopes the catholics had, they were not destined to be fulfilled. Although later, on the scaffold, Warwick proclaimed his adherence to the Roman church, he gave no evidence of this attachment during his lifetime. The advocates of rapid and fundamental reform had accepted him as one of their number. Hooper, for instance, who had such scruples about wearing vestments that he tried to evade appointment to the see of Gloucester, called Warwick 'that most faithful and intrepid soldier of Christ'. Another admirer was the young King. Edward had developed, under the tutorship of Richard Cox and John Cheke, into a committed protestant, and he gave a sympathetic ear when Warwick outlined his plans for removing all remaining traces of popery from the English church. The Earl did not proclaim him-self Protector: that title had too many associations with Somerset. He preferred to bring the King forward and use him as a shield behind which he could effectively control policy.

With Warwick in power the pace of the religious reformation quickened. In November 1550 the Council ordered that all re-maining altars were to be destroyed and replaced by a simple wooden table, on the grounds that 'the use of an altar is to make sacrifice upon', while 'the use of a table is to serve for men to eat upon'. Just over a year later, in 1552, Cranmer produced his second Prayer Book. This was a much more uncompromisingly protestant formulary than its predecessor. The first Book had referred to the 'sacrament of the body' and the 'sacrament of the blood', but these savoured too much of the doctrine of transubstantiation which Cranmer had now completely rejected. He replaced them by 'the bread' and 'the cup', and instructed the priest to say 'Take and eat this, in remembrance that Christ died for thee, and feed on him in

thy heart by faith, with thanksgiving'. Albs, vestments and copes
were no longer to be worn by the officiating priest, and although
communicants were still required to kneel when receiving the sacrament, the Council inserted the notorious *Black Rubric* declaring
that 'it is not meant thereby, that any adoration is done, or ought
to be done . . . For as concerning the sacramental bread and wine,
they remain still in their very natural substances, and therefore
may not be adored, for that were idolatry to be abhorred of all
faithful Christians'.

The new Prayer Book was enforced by the second Act of Uniformity, which commanded everyone to attend church on Sundays,
where the Prayer Book, and no other service, should be used. The
doctrines of the Church of England were further defined by the
publication of the *Forty-Two Articles* in 1553, which contained a
statement on predestination of which Calvin would probably have
approved, and dismissed all belief in 'purgatory, pardons, worship-
ping and adoration as well of images as of relics, and also invo-
cation of saints' as 'a fond thing, vainly feigned, and grounded upon
no warrant of Scripture, but rather repugnant to the word of God'.

The Prayer Book and *Articles* represented the positive side of the
Edwardian Reformation, but the ordinary man and woman would
have been more aware of the negative side. In hundreds of parish
churches stained glass windows were smashed, tombs were broken
up and statues removed or decapitated, on the grounds that they
encouraged idolatry. In 1551 the confiscation of Church plate was
ordered, except for the minimum required for carrying out services.
At the universities, libraries were searched for heretical books,
which were then destroyed, and the marked decline in the number
of degrees awarded at Oxford in Edward VI's reign — an average
of just over 30 a year compared with nearly 130 in the opening
three decades of the century — suggests that education was suffering. The impact of these measures varied widely from one part
of the country to another. In places such as Lancashire, where the
authority of the central government was weak and conservative
attitudes deeply embedded, the changes were superficial. Elsewhere, and particularly in the south and east, protestantism began
to take root, and the pressure for change came as much from below
as from above.

In October 1551 Warwick was created Duke of Northumberland.
He suffered much at the time, and has done so since, by being
unfavourably compared with Somerset. But Northumberland was
not without his virtues. For one thing, he was far less aloof than
the Protector, and worked in close co-operation with the Privy
Council. He also began the political education of Edward VI by
encouraging him to attend Council meetings — though the King
was still too young to do more than listen to what was said and

signify his approval. Somerset had proclaimed himself the champion of the poor and oppressed, and had thereby unleashed the forces of disorder. Northumberland avoided rhetorical gestures, and acquired a reputation for harshness, but in fact there was no sharp reversal of the government's social policies, and enclosure was still officially frowned upon. Northumberland's sympathies were with the landowners, of whom he was one, yet he was determined that they should not evade their fiscal obligations, and his success was shown by a substantial rise in receipts from the Court of Wards, in contrast to the decline under Somerset. Northumberland also stimulated the development of English trade by revoking the privileges of the Hanseatic League in 1552 and giving active encouragement to English explorers such as Willoughby and Chancellor (see below, p. 117).

Northumberland was not, of course, a free agent. His hold on power was uncertain, and he had to buy support by allowing his adherents to enrich themselves at the state's expense. The members of the Privy Council, for example, voted themselves royal estates worth £30,000 a year, and the rule that all former Church lands sold by the crown were to be held on feudal tenure, to preserve the valuable financial incidents, was relaxed. The effect of this was further to diminish the royal revenues, but Northumberland now embarked upon a number of policies which were designed to put the crown's finances on a sound footing. He began by abandoning Somerset's military occupation of Scotland, which instead of breaking the union between the Scots and the French had driven them into even closer alliance, and had imposed an intolerable financial burden upon England. He also brought the French war to a close, in March 1550, by allowing Henri II to buy back Boulogne (which had, in any case, proved to be virtually indefensible).

The end of military operations eased the strain upon the Exchequer, but by this time the government was well nigh bankrupt. In 1551 its total net income amounted to a little under £170,000, but ordinary expenditure consumed the greater part of this, and the £36,500 that was left over could not possibly provide for extraordinaries, when garrisons alone cost £80,000 a year and the foreign debt amounted to a quarter of a million pounds. Northumberland dealt with the immediate crisis by suspending government payments — including monastic pensions — and selling crown lands to the value of £150,000. He also melted down confiscated Church plate and turned it into coin, at the same time as he raised further loans at home and abroad. Yet he was not content with these short-term palliative measures, for he recognised, unlike Somerset, that English public finances would never be soundly based until the coinage was restored. After one final orgy of debasement, therefore, in May 1551, new coins of better quality were issued from the mint, and the precipitous decline in the value of the English currency was halted. In a further effort to increase the royal income Northumberland appointed commissioners in March 1552 to enquire into the system of revenue courts and to make recommendations to improve its efficiency. By the time the commissioners' reports were ready, Northumberland's tenure of power was nearing its end, but he had laid the foundations for the financial recovery which took place in Mary's reign.

Northumberland, like most of his contemporaries, regarded the holding of public office as a means to personal enrichment, and his radical religious policies enabled him to strip the Church of much of its remaining wealth. John Ponet, who succeeded Gardiner as Bishop of Winchester in 1551, was persuaded to hand over all the endowments of his see to Northumberland in return for a pension of two thousand marks, and Hooper — who eventually accepted both vestments and the Bishopric of Gloucester — came to a similar arrangement. The new diocese of Westminster was suppressed as unnecessary, and in the last months of his rule Northumberland was preparing to suppress the rich see of Durham and transfer the greater part of its revenues to the crown and himself. Much of the money plundered from the Church did, in fact, go into the crown's coffers, but Northumberland was so identified with the government that it was impossible to say whether his exploitation of all available resources was directed to public or to private ends. The only obvious truth was that the Duke and his cronies were making big profits at a time when they were pleading national bankruptcy, and Northumberland knew what the attitude of the Commons was likely to be when they met. He told Cecil to be careful not 'to seem to make account to the Commons of his Majesty's liberality and bountifulness in augmenting or advancing of his nobles, or of his benevolence showed to any his good servants, lest you might thereby make them wanton and give them occasion to take hold of your own arguments'.

### Edward VI's Death and Northumberland's Fall

Northumberland ruled in the name of Edward VI, but by early 1553 it was plain that the fifteen-year-old King had not much longer to live, for he no longer enjoyed good health, and a cold which he caught turned into congestion of the lungs. Northumberland knew that the King's death would leave him dangerously exposed, for the heir to the throne was Edward's half-sister, Mary, who had refused to abandon her mother's faith. There seemed little reason to doubt that when she ascended the throne she would remove the protestant ministers and restore England to communion with Rome. The only means of avoiding this fate was to change the order of succession. Henry had been empowered to do this by will, and Edward gladly assented to Northumberland's suggestion that in order to ensure the continuance of the Reformation in England he should bequeath the crown to a protestant.

The person chosen to succeed Edward was the fifteen-year-old Lady Jane Grey, descended from Henry VII through the second marriage of his daughter Mary with Charles Brandon, Duke of Suffolk. The nearest protestant claimant was, in fact, Elizabeth, but she was ruled out on the nominal grounds that she might take as husband a foreign and papist prince. To avoid the same fate befalling Lady Jane she was ordered to marry Northumberland's fourth son, Lord Guilford Dudley. The marriage took place, much against Jane's will, on 25 May 1553. At about the same time Edward drew up his 'device' in which he left the throne to Lady Jane and her male descendants: Mary and Elizabeth were both ruled out as illegitimate. The leading figures in the government – Councillors, judges and bishops — were called on to add their signature to the 'device'. Some tried to withhold their assent, but Northumberland and the King would not permit this.

Edward died on 6 July 1553, but the news was kept secret for three days until the Lady Jane could be proclaimed Queen. Mary was at Framlingham, in Norfolk, but no sooner did the news reach her than she raised her standard and called on all loyal subjects to rally to her. The eastern counties rose in support of Mary, and the Councillors at London, quick to scent the changing wind, proclaimed her Queen. The Duke, who had left the capital with a small force to bar Mary's progress, followed suit, for his army melted away. By the end of July he was a prisoner in the Tower, and on 3 August Mary entered London in triumph. The next day the Duke of Norfolk and bishop Gardiner were released from imprisonment in the Tower. The catholic reaction had begun.

## *Mary I*

Queen Mary was thirty-seven when the death of her half-brother brought her to the throne, and the catholics rejoiced at the prospect of a reign in which the old faith would be restored. Success seemed certain, for the Queen herself was popular. She had shown her courage by raising her standard in the face of what must have seemed formidable odds, and for years before that she had resisted all the efforts of Edward VI's ministers to persuade her to abandon her faith. When a deputation of Councillors waited on her in August 1551 and urged her to change her attitude, she proudly refused, and took the opportunity to remind them that her father had 'made the more part of you out of nothing'. Her courage, her pride, and her stubbornness were typically Tudor, but Charles V's am-

bassador thought she was too accessible and too innocent of the arts
and subterfuges of politics. 'I know the Queen to be good', he
wrote, 'easily influenced, inexpert in worldly matters, and a novice
all round', and the years that followed were in many ways to confirm this judgment. For Mary politics were an aspect of religion and
morality. Principle came first and she could see no virtue in compromise. The simplicity of her approach, combined with her natural stubbornness, explains why this well-intentioned woman
became a symbol of intolerance and cruelty.

As far as her administration was concerned, Mary did not make
an abrupt break with the past. She retained the services of a number of Edward VI's advisers in her Privy Council as well as appointing new members more in sympathy with her own aspirations.
Aware of the difficulties confronting her, and of the weaknesses of
her position, she was generous in her welcome to supporters and
frequently added them to her Council. As a consequence, this institution swelled to double its former size, but the number of regular attenders was much smaller, and as a working body the
Marian Council resembled that of Henry VIII or Elizabeth I. The
major impediment to its efficient functioning came from the rivalry
between Stephen Gardiner, who was appointed Lord Chancellor,
and William Paget, a former friend and associate of Protector Somerset who had fallen from favour under Northumberland. The
disagreement between these two leading Councillors was not just
a matter of personalities. Paget stood for a moderate and relatively
tolerant approach, particularly towards the problem of religion.
Gardiner, on the other hand, wanted a speedy and total restoration
of the authority and privileges of the catholic church.

Mary opened her reign with a remarkable display of leniency.
Northumberland was executed, along with two of his accomplices,
but otherwise there were no reprisals against those who had tried
to bar Mary from the throne. Lady Jane Grey and her husband
were condemned to death, as was Archbishop Cranmer, but Mary
intervened to save them from execution, and they were held prisoner in the Tower. Cranmer could have fled abroad rather than
face the accession of a catholic monarch, but he chose not to do so.
He was typical of the early reformers in his reverence for royal
authority, and to have fled out of Mary's jurisdiction would have
meant abandoning one of the main articles of his faith.

### Religion. III: Protestant Exile and Catholic Reaction

The foreign reformers who had come to England in the reign of
Edward VI were encouraged to leave the country, and no obstacle
was put in the way of English protestants who wished to go into
exile rather than live under a catholic ruler. Peter Martyr made his

way to Strasburg, from where he reported that 'English youths have come over to us in great numbers within a few days, partly from Oxford and partly from Cambridge; whom many godly merchants are bringing up to learning, that should it please God to restore religion to its former state in that kingdom, they may be of some benefit to the Church of England'. Other groups of exiles settled at Frankfurt, and elsewhere in France, Germany, Switzerland and Italy. In all, some eight hundred people, mostly from the upper levels of English society, left their native country. Mary's accession had been foreseen, of course, and no doubt many of those who fled had made the necessary arrangements beforehand. But it seems unlikely that the exile as a whole was carefully planned and directed. It was a spontaneous reaction from those who put religious considerations first and preferred the uncertainties of life in a foreign country to acceptance of the mass and all that went with it.

Although Mary had a Council composed largely of men who had demonstrated their loyalty to her, she did not always turn to it for advice. On matters that affected her personally she preferred to consult the imperial ambassador, for she was half Spanish by birth, and ties of blood as well as religion made her desire an alliance with the Habsburgs. Charles V was strongly in favour of this, and proposed a marriage between Mary and his son Philip, the future ruler of Spain. For this reason he did his best to keep out of England Reginald Pole, whom the Pope had appointed as legate and who might persuade Mary to retain her freedom of manoeuvre by remaining unwed. Pole was therefore left kicking his heels in Europe more than a year after he should have been in London.

Meanwhile Mary was going ahead with her plans to restore England to the catholic faith. Of Edward VI's bishops, four, including Miles Coverdale, fled to the Continent; another four, including Cranmer, Ridley and Hooper, were imprisoned; and four more were deprived. Five Henrician bishops, who had been expelled from their sees under Northumberland, were now restored: they included Gardiner, who returned to Winchester, Tunstall, who went back to Durham, and Bonner, who became Bishop of London. These actions were carried out by virtue of the royal supremacy, even though this particular dignity was repugnant to Mary, but more fundamental changes in the structure of the English church needed a greater authority. Accordingly, in October 1553 the first Parliament of the reign was summoned to undo the work of its predecessors under Edward VI. By the first Statute of Repeal it wiped out much of Cranmer's work. The reformed liturgy, the two Books of Common Prayer, the administration of the sacrament in both kinds and the existence of a married clergy were all declared to be illegal, and the clock was turned back to the closing years of Henry VIII.

## The Spanish Match

The Act of Repeal had a difficult passage through Parliament, and on the final reading in the Commons just under a third of those present voted against it. This opposition did not spring from disloyalty to Mary. It was caused rather by fear that the next step would be the restoration to the Church of former monastic property — which would have been anathema to those many members of both Lords and Commons who held Church lands and had no intention of parting with them. It also sprang from a deep-seated hostility towards papal claims, and it is significant that in all the legislation of this Parliament, no mention was made of the Pope. The basic loyalty on which Mary could, in the last resort, rely was weakened by her desire for a Spanish marriage. For her the advantages of such a match outweighed all its disadvantages. It would give her the support of a catholic husband and link her kingdom with the greatest catholic power on the Continent, and when a deputation from the Lords and Commons pleaded with her to take an English husband she brushed them aside with the proud reply that 'Parliament was not accustomed to use such language to the Kings of England, nor was it suitable or respectful that it should do so . . . She would choose according as God inspired her'.

The news of the projected Spanish marriage caused dismay. The first two Tudors had unified their realm by stressing the common allegiance that all Englishmen had towards their sovereign and by asserting the independence of their kingdom from all foreign jurisdictions. Now it seemed as though this work would be undone. England would be subjected to a Spanish king, and, what was worse, would almost certainly be dragged into the conflict between the Habsburgs and the Valois rulers of France, from which she had nothing to gain. The effect of Henry VIII's policy had been to cut England off from the Continent and encourage the growth of xenophobia. Mary failed to appreciate this and to see that her popularity and her strength depended upon the degree to which she could identify herself with this pronounced sense of Englishness.

The terms of marriage were agreed upon in January 1554. Philip was to be called King and was to assist Mary in the government of the country, but the Queen alone was to appoint to all offices in Church and state, and was to choose only Englishmen: there was to be no Spanish take-over. While these terms were being drawn up, a group of conspirators was plotting to make sure that they would never come into effect. Sir Thomas Wyatt, son of one of the finest poets of early Tudor England, planned a revolt against Mary, with simultaneous risings throughout England. He had assurances of support from France, and it may be that Mary's half-sister, Princess Elizabeth, was also in the secret. Although Wyatt counted a number of protestants among his supporters, they were not in the majority, nor was the rebellion primarily religious in its motivation. It was probably provoked rather by fear that the influence of the 'Spanish party' would become dominant, despite the provisions of the marriage treaty, thereby depriving native-born gentlemen of the places at court and in local administration to which they felt they had a prescriptive right. The ultimate aims of the rebels were not clear, nor were they ever to become so, for the government learnt that something was afoot and this left them with little choice but to act at once, even though their plans had not been fully worked out. Partly as a result of this, the attempted risings in the west and midlands went off at half cock and were easily suppressed. The Kentish rising, under Wyatt, was the only one to achieve any success, for several thousand men rallied to his standard, and this enabled him to march on London. The situation was serious, and the City might have fallen to the rebels had not Mary, with her accustomed courage, ridden to the Guildhall, where she appealed to the citizens to remain loyal. Her bold move succeeded. The bridges were held against Wyatt and when he forced his way into the City from the Surrey side he found no one to support him. In the end he surrendered without fighting, and was immediately sent to the Tower.

Although Wyatt's rebellion had been defeated it had come dangerously near success, and about ninety of the rank and file were sent to the gallows, forty-six of them being hanged in London in a single day. Wyatt himself was executed and so were Lady Jane Grey and her husband, even though they had not taken part in the rebellion.

The failure of Wyatt's rebellion cleared the way for the Spanish marriage. Parliament accepted the proposed terms in April 1554, and in the following July Gardiner married Mary and Philip in the cathedral church of his diocese of Winchester. On personal grounds the marriage was a failure. Philip had little love for his wife, whom he found unattractive, and although at first Mary could blind herself to this, she could not ignore her husband's increasingly prolonged absences. She longed for a child, but even this was denied her. The failure of her marriage gradually soured Mary. She who had devoted her life to the restoration of the true Church in England had to accept the fact that her work would be in vain, for she would be succeeded by the protestant Elizabeth.

## Persecution

In November 1554, Reginald Pole at last arrived in England. Not since Wolsey's fall had a legate *a latere* controlled English affairs, and Pole was a very different man from Wolsey. He shared Mary's devotion to the catholic church and wished to see England restored to full communion with Rome. This would not be possible, however, until the nation had expressed publicly its desire for forgiveness. Parliament, which was held to epitomise the nation and which had shared the responsibility for schism, would have to take the initiative in pleading for absolution. On the last day of November 1554 a joint session of both Houses took place at which Mary and Philip, as well as the legate, were present. Gardiner, as Lord Chancellor, read aloud a petition asking for pardon and reconciliation, which Pole accepted. Then, while all present knelt, the cardinal legate pronounced absolution and declared the kingdom of England restored to the unity of Christ's church.

Pole had originally assumed that the restored catholic church in England would take possession once again of all its property, including the former monastic estates, for it ran against his conscience to condone what he regarded as an act of sacrilege as well as robbery. However, the Pope, under pressure from Philip II, came to the conclusion that it would be better to leave the new owners in possession of their ill-gotten gains rather than risk 'the shipwreck of this undertaking'; hence Pole's assurance to Parliament that his commission was 'not to pull down, but to build; to reconcile, not to censure; to invite, but without compulsion. My business is not to proceed by way of retrospection or to question things already settled'.

The Second Statute of Repeal confirmed this implicit bargain. It started by repealing all those statutes passed against Rome since the fall of Wolsey, but it also declared that the holders of monastic lands might 'without scruple of conscience enjoy them, without impeachment or trouble by pretence of any General Council, canons, or ecclesiastical laws, and clear from all dangers of the censures of the Church'.

The Second Statute of Repeal was preceded by an Act reviving the heresy laws. It is not clear who advised Mary to begin the persecution of heretics, but much of the responsibility for this must rest on her alone. There was nothing new, of course, about the burning of heretics, and intolerance was not confined to catholics. Heresy was regarded as a crime against society, and like all crimes it was punishable. Just as a man's predatory instincts had to be restrained by fear of the hangman's knot, so his susceptibility to the devil's wiles had to be restrained by the stake. Between February 1555 and November 1558 just under three hundred men and women were burnt for heresy. The punishment of death by burning was an appallingly cruel one, but it was not this that shocked contemporaries — after all, in an age that knew nothing of anaesthetics, a great deal of pain had to be endured by everybody at one time or another, and the taste for public executions, bear-baiting and cock-fighting suggests a callousness that blunted susceptibilities. What made the Marian persecution so unpopular was the way in which it struck down the small offender while letting most of the big ones go scot-free. The lead in searching out heretics was taken by the lay authorities, and all too often the accused would find himself judged by a man who had been an active propagator of protestant doctrines under Edward VI. When Thomas Watts, a linen draper of a small Essex town, was brought before a Justice of the Peace who asked him 'who hath been thy schoolmaster to teach thee this gear, or where didst thou first learn this religion?', Watts replied: 'forsooth, even of you sir. You taught it me, and none more than you. For in King Edward's days in open session you spoke against this religion now used; no preacher more'.

The overwhelming majority of Marian martyrs came from the lower levels of English society, and included weavers, fullers, shearmen, tailors, hosiers, cappers, husbandmen, labourers, brewers and butchers. Some fifty women were also burnt. Not all of those who suffered were 'conventional' protestants: in Kent, for example, many came from areas where Lollardy was still a living force and they often held opinions that would have been regarded as dangerously heterodox even in Edward's reign. One striking thing about the list of martyrs is the high proportion of rural labourers recorded. It is often assumed, and with reason, that towns were the seedbed of extremism in politics and religion, but it is apparent that by the middle decades of the sixteenth century parts of the countryside had also become radicalised, particularly in southeast England. This impression is confirmed by the story of a small farmer from Cambridgeshire who, in 1555, travelled to Colchester for the sole purpose of taking part in spiritual exercises, and seriously considered going on from there to Oxford, as he had doubts about Christ's divinity and wished to consult Ridley and Latimer.

The executions can hardly have advanced the catholic cause. Henry VIII had found it necessary to martyr a few heretics in order to maintain orthodoxy, and on the whole he had been successful. The far greater persecution of Mary's brief reign is a sign of failure: if thirty fires would not burn out heresy it was unlikely that three hundred would do so. Mary repeated Northumberland's mistake of trying to do too much too quickly and putting the emphasis on the negative, destructive aspects of reform rather than the positive. Protestant pamphleteers at home and abroad were swift to take advantage of this error, and the accession of Elizabeth was followed by the publication of John Foxe's *Book of Martyrs*, which recorded in loving and gruesome detail the lives and deaths of all those who had been put to death by the Queen. Foxe's *Book* came to be almost as widely read in England as the Bible. Mary had given the

English protestant church its martyrs; Foxe made sure that their deeds would be an inspiration to generations of those who came after.

The government hoped that the threat of execution would be enough to drive protestants to recant, and one big success would have made this far more likely. This is why it put so much pressure on Cranmer to make public confession of his errors. Cranmer, Ridley, Hooper and Latimer had all been imprisoned. Hooper was burnt in the early days of the persecution, and Latimer and Ridley went to the flames at Oxford in October 1555. Cranmer was left alone to decide what to do. He was in a genuine dilemma since royal supremacy was for him an article of faith, yet by accepting the commands of his sovereign lady Mary he would be going against what his own conscience told him to be true. It was doubts about his own position, as much as fear, that led him to recant, but at the last moment he changed his mind. Led out to die at Oxford in March 1556, he denounced his recantation as 'things written with my hand, contrary to the truth which I thought in my heart, and written for fear of death and to save my life if it might be', and he plunged his hand into the flames so that it might never again betray him.

Cranmer's dilemma was shared by many protestants. The early reformers in England and on the Continent had transferred to the King the reverence that Roman Catholics gave to the Pope, and had elevated royal authority because it seemed the best possible security against papal claims. Now, however, the royal supremacy which had been employed to destroy the Roman church in England was being used to rebuild it, and protestants had to reconsider their attitude. The first of the Marian martyrs had shown the way when he appealed from the monarch to the word of God, unto which, he said, 'must all men — king and queen, emperor, parliament and general councils — obey. The Word obeyeth no man. It cannot be changed nor altered'. In this way the Marian martyrs, along with the Marian exiles, prepared the ground for Elizabethan puritanism.

It is not possible to plot the religious map of Marian England with any certainty, but the fact that most of the exiles, as well as most of the martyrs, came from the south-east suggests that this was the region in which protestantism had taken firmest hold. The figures for married priests provide further confirmation. Some Suffolk clergy had taken wives in the mid-1530s, long before the legal authorisation of clerical marriage in 1549, and by the time Mary came to the throne probably a quarter of all the clergy in East Anglia were married. In London the proportion was nearer a third. This was in marked contrast to the north of England, where only one out of every ten priests, on average, had a wife. Married priests were not necessarily protestant, of course, but they were certainly more numerous in protestant areas.

In London, during Mary's reign, there was an underground prot-estant church, with a total membership of some two hundred, which held its meetings in different places, to avoid detection. It kept in close touch with the exiles and also with the reformed churches on the Continent, and it had links with another under-ground congregation in Colchester. This sort of active defiance of the Marian regime required great courage and was relatively rare. Passive resistance, however, appears to have been widespread, and took the form of refusing to rebuild altars or to attend mass.

It may be that the nature of the surviving evidence about popular attitudes towards Mary's religious policies distorts the truth, for where the restoration of catholic worship was accepted without difficulty there was nothing to report. The general picture is of a conservative north and west, with some places where catholic prac-tices had never died out, and a protestant south-east. Within this broad framework, however, there was a wide range of variation. In parts of Lancashire, which was generally speaking a catholic stronghold, the evangelising activities of young graduates of radical persuasion stimulated the emergence of protestant cells; while in parts of the south midlands, which were on the whole protestant, the commitment of a number of catholic gentry families ensured the survival of enclaves of orthodoxy.

Although Mary's determination to make England a truly catholic country once again may have been the driving force behind the burnings, she left the constructive aspects of reform largely in the hands of Pole, who was already acting as Archbishop of Canter-bury, even though he could not be formally appointed until after the execution of Cranmer in March 1556. It was by virtue of his legatine authority, however, that Pole summoned a national synod, which met in London in December 1555 and drew up twelve de-crees designed to set the Church on its new course. One of them tackled the long-standing problem of pluralism and non-residency by forbidding the holding of more than one benefice and insisting that all priests should be resident. But this was a statement of in-tent rather than a practical proposition. Mary had returned First Fruits to the Church, and in due course she relieved the clergy of the burden of taxation, but a great deal of Church wealth remained in lay hands and many parishes were so poorly endowed that they could not possibly maintain a priest of their own. Nevertheless, Pole scrutinised all applications for dispensations very carefully, and envisaged a redistribution of resources which would gradually eliminate what he rightly regarded as a major defect.

Another decree required all clergy, including bishops, to carry out their obligation to preach, and Pole broke with tradition by choosing as bishops men who were trained in theology and pastoral care rather than civil law. Some indication of the quality of the episcopal bench is given by the fact that when Elizabeth came to the throne and turned the Church back in a protestant direction, all but one of the bishops preferred to give up their livings rather than conform.

Perhaps the most important of the decrees, for the long-term health of the Church, was the eleventh, which dealt with the education of the clergy. Pole hoped to see the establishment of seminaries for training priests in every diocese, but although some progress was made he came up against the obstacle that there were too few clergy of sufficient quality to staff them. To remedy this situation he needed to increase the flow of graduates from the universities, and he was able to take the initiative since both Oxford and Cambridge had elected him as their chancellor. He therefore carried out formal visitations of the two universities and appointed new, catholic masters to many of the colleges. He did not undertake any new foundations himself, but encouraged others to do so. In 1555 Sir Thomas Pope, a member of Mary's Privy Council who had made a fortune out of monastic property, returned much of this wealth to the Church by founding the college 'of the Holy and Undivided Trinity' at Oxford, while his friend, Sir Thomas White, established another college dedicated to St John the Baptist. These measures bore fruit in Elizabeth's reign, when Oxford provided a significant proportion of the catholic priests who went on the 'English mission'.

The shortage of good priests, which affected the operation of the Church at all levels and throughout the entire kingdom, was not something that could be overcome in a few months or even years, and Pole was working on the assumption that God would provide him with the time that was needed to re-establish the true faith in England upon firm foundations. The same long-term view dictated his response to suggestions that a campaign of catholic evangelisation should be launched in order to eliminate heresy. The Jesuits offered to send members of their Society over to England to take the lead in this, but Pole gave a negative response. In his view England had suffered from an excess of evangelism, and although preaching was an essential part of the clergy's functions, it should be carefully controlled and directed. The sending out of missionaries to combat heresy might stir up religious passions at a time when they needed dampening down. In Pole's own words, 'I think that it is better to check the preaching of the Word rather than proclaim it, unless the discipline of the Church has been fully restored'.

Pole was an aristocrat by temperament, as well as by birth, and he shied away from mass movements. He was also an autocrat, who took it for granted that leadership belonged only to the chosen few, and that the duty of the many was to obey. Eventual success depended, in Pole's view, upon restoring the full functioning of the catholic church in England, so that its rituals, its ceremonies, and its discipline could exert their benign spiritual influence. But many parish churches were in a state of decay, and vestments and plate, essential for catholic worship, had been stolen, lost, or destroyed. These losses could not be made good overnight. Indeed, little effective could be done until the scale of the damage had been accurately assessed. This was one of the reasons that led Pole to adjourn the national synod in February 1556. He hoped that by the time it reassembled he would be able to put before it a detailed statement of the situation, which would form the basis for a coherent programme of renovation. Meanwhile he encouraged the revival of monasticism, to provide a source of spirituality on which the Church could draw. The Observant Franciscans returned to Greenwich, the Carthusians to Sheen, and the Dominicans to Smithfield. And in the capital itself, the Benedictines took over once again the great Abbey of Westminster.

Pole, like Wolsey before him, derived his legatine authority from the Pope, and he looked to Rome as a source of inspiration and a symbol of catholic unity. In May 1555, however, Cardinal Caraffa was elected Pope as Paul IV. Caraffa was a hard-line reactionary, who suspected that all liberals — among whom he included Pole — were potential heretics. He was also violently anti-Spanish, since he wanted to free Italy from the Habsburg yoke. Charles V had abdicated in October 1555, and papal fury was concentrated on his son, Philip, who was now King of Spain, Italy and England. While Pole was addressing the synod that seemed to promise a new era for the catholic church in England, Paul IV was negotiating a treaty of alliance with France. Philip II, in reply, sent the Spanish general, the Duke of Alva, to occupy the papal states. Paul promptly excommunicated Philip and withdrew all his representatives from the King's dominions. He also deprived Pole of his legateship, and ordered him to return to Rome to answer charges of heresy.

Mary, a devout daughter of the catholic church, was in the invidious position of being married to an excommunicate husband and having as her chief adviser a suspected heretic. The situation would have been comic had it not been so full of tragic implications, and even had Mary lived it is at least possible that England would again have seceded from the Roman church. Rather than lose Pole, Mary forbade him to return to Rome, and petitioned the Pope to restore him to his legateship. Her support of Philip was made clear when in June 1557 she declared war on his enemy, France. The war was a failure. Calais, the last English stronghold on the Continent, had poor defences and an insufficient garrison, and when French troops made an unexpected mid-winter assault in January 1558, the city was forced to surrender. Calais had been a symbol, even though a hollow one, of English greatness, and its loss was one more nail in Mary's coffin. She and her Church were now identified not only with persecution and foreign domination but with inglorious failure as well.

## Financial Reorganisation and the Closing Years of the Reign

Mary inherited a debt of over £185,000, while her annual revenue was about £130,000. She depended for advice in financial matters upon the aged William Paulet, Marquis of Winchester, whom she confirmed in office as Lord Treasurer — a post to which he had first been appointed by Protector Somerset in 1550. Winchester began by putting into effect the report of the commission on courts of revenue set up by Northumberland. The Court of Augmentations, established by Cromwell to deal with the revenues arising from the Dissolution, was dissolved, along with the Court of First Fruits and Tenths. Control over the royal finances was restored to the Exchequer, except for the Court of Wards and the Duchy of Lancaster, which preserved their separate identities. No doubt Winchester hoped that this measure of rationalisation would in due course diminish the costs of financial administration, but in the short term something more substantial was needed; hence the decision to summon Parliament in 1555. After the opening ceremonies were over, Privy Councillors took the initiative in pressing for supply, but they made no attempt to justify this on grounds of national defence, as had been the practice hitherto. The crown's needs were the only reason that they put forward, and although there were some dissentient voices the Commons accepted this as valid and voted a subsidy which eventually brought in over £180,000. Even so, the government was still short of ready cash, and in 1556 it resorted to forced loans. More of these were levied in the following year, and the crown made a net profit of some £65,000.

In 1557, at Winchester's suggestion, a commission was appointed to enquire into the reasons 'why Customs and subsidies be greatly diminished and decayed'. It recommended, among other things, that the Book of Rates — which listed the official prices of customable articles, upon which the actual amount of duty to be paid was based — should be brought up to date. This was done, and in May 1558 a new Book of Rates was issued, taking full account of the impact of inflation. As a consequence, the yield from Customs substantially increased. The level of rents and entry fines on crown lands was also raised, and attempts were made to reduce expenditure on the royal household. If Mary could have kept her country at peace, the state of the royal finances would have gradually improved, but involvement in the war against France put an end to this prospect. Crown lands had to be sold, and the government was forced, once more, to raise loans on the Antwerp money market. By the time Mary died, therefore, the annual deficit was running at £100,000, and the total debt which she bequeathed Elizabeth was not far short of £300,000.

Financial reorganisation and religious reformation had this in common – they both needed time for their full effect to be felt. But time was not granted to Mary. By the autumn of 1558 she was very ill and spent long periods in a coma, during which, so she told her attendants, she had good dreams and saw 'many little children like angels play before her, singing pleasing notes'. Early on the morning of 17 November she died in her palace of St James. On the other side of the river, Reginald Pole was also lying ill in his palace at Lambeth. He survived Mary by only a few hours. The catholic reaction ended as abruptly as it had begun.

# 6

# Tudor England

## *Population and the Price Rise*

An increase in population and a steep rise in prices determined
much of the course of English history — political and religious, as
well as economic — in the Tudor and Stuart period. The hundred
years preceding Bosworth had seen recurrent attacks of plague
which wiped out about a third of the population and produced an
acute labour shortage. Land was abundant, demand was small, and
prices and rents were consequently low. This situation was already
changing by the time Henry VII came to the throne, for economic
security and growing immunity to plague had halted the decline
in population, and although there are no reliable figures it seems
likely that by 1600 there were about four million people living in
England — perhaps twice as many as there had been at the time
of Bosworth.

As the population increased, so did the demand for food, and this
put pressure upon agricultural prices, which began rising steeply
from about 1510. By the middle of the sixteenth century they were
twice as high as they had been at the beginning, and by the end
of the century more than six times. Industrial prices also went up
from the 1540s, as demand increased. If population pressure had
been the only cause of inflation, then prices would have moved
steadily upwards. In practice, however, inflation went in fits and
starts, and other factors clearly contributed to it. Increased government expenditure in the 1540s was one of these factors, as was
the scarcity of grain created by a run of poor harvests in the 1590s.
But the most important contributory cause was the debasement of
the coinage which began in 1542 and lasted until 1551. During this
period the quantity of pure metal in silver coins was cut by 75 per
cent and in gold coins by 25 per cent. The crown made an immediate profit, but in the absence of that public confidence which
enables currency to be taken at its face value the true worth of new
coins was determined by their pure metal content. Since this was
so low, more coins were demanded for goods, the value of money
dropped even further and the rise in prices accelerated.

Mary put an end to debasement and Elizabeth issued a new coinage, but money continued to decline in value. One of the reasons for this was the influx of Spanish silver from the New World, which was affecting price levels throughout Europe. Until the mid-1580s this silver came into England by way of normal commercial transactions, mainly with the Spanish Netherlands. The outbreak of war with Spain disrupted this trade, but privateering expeditions, such as the one which Drake led so successfully in 1577–80, resulted in the delivery of large quantities of bullion to the Mint, which turned them into coin. This had much the same effect as debasement, for although there was more money in circulation there was little or no increase in the amount of goods available, and inflationary pressures therefore persisted.

## Agriculture and Enclosures

Although agriculture was the main occupation of Tudor England, its practice varied from one region to another, and there was a broad distinction between the highland zone of the north and west and the lowland zone of the south and east. The highland zone included extensive areas of mountains and moorlands, whose thin soils were best suited to pasture farming. The population of this zone tended to be dispersed in isolated farmsteads or tiny hamlets, and the communal regulation of agricultural activities, as well as manorial supervision, were difficult to enforce. The lowland zone, on the other hand, had richer soils suitable for both arable and pasture. Its inhabitants were generally settled in tight-knit nuclear villages under close manorial control, and the cultivated area was divided into open fields which were broken into individual strips. Around them were the commons and wastes which were for the use of the whole community.

These common lands were essential to the cottagers who constituted about a third of the rural population. The luckier ones might hold a few acres of land, but these smallholdings would not provide them with a living. They made money by selling their labour to the yeomen farmers and gentry, but they were dependent upon the commons for pasturing any sheep or cattle they might possess and upon the wastes for supplies of winter fuel. Yet the expansion of population was putting pressure on these communal lands, particularly in the midland region of England, for the most obvious way in which to provide more work as well as more food for the increasing number of inhabitants was by encroaching on the commons and wastes and bringing them under cultivation. Even where they were allowed to remain they were often so diminished in size that they could no longer serve the needs of the community, particularly since the more enterprising yeomen and husbandmen were increasing the number of sheep and cattle they put out to pasture in order to meet the ever growing demand from urban markets.

In areas suitable for mixed cultivation the open fields also were being eroded by the practice of enclosure. During the first half of the sixteenth century the cloth industry was booming and the demand for wool sent prices soaring. Landowners reacted to this by increasing the number of sheep on their estates and turning arable into pasture. It made more sense, from their point of view, to abandon the strip system and instead create enclosed fields in which their sheep and cattle could be kept and tended. Even if they did not give up arable farming there was still much to be said for enclosure, since it made it easier for them to try out new crops and new techniques. Outside the midland area a great deal of enclosure, either of arable strips in the open fields or of common and waste ground, had already taken place by 1500, much of it by agreement. During the course of the sixteenth century problems arose when no agreement could be reached and landlords acted alone, evicting tenants-at-will and buying out freeholders. Sir Thomas More spoke of sheep devouring men, and Sir Thomas Smith, in the *Discourse of the Common Weal of this Realm of England*, written in 1549, made the husbandman say: 'these enclosures do undo us all, for they make us pay dearer for our land that we occupy . . . all is taken up for pastures, either for sheep or for grazing of cattle. So that I have known of late a dozen ploughs within less compass than six miles about me laid down within these seven years; and where forty persons had their livings, now one man and his shepherd hath all'.

Although the outcry against enclosures became intense in the mid-sixteenth century, the actual amount which took place in Henry VIII's reign was limited, and largely confined to the midland region. Even where landlords were as ruthless and covetous as the pamphleteers held them to be, they were restrained by the fact that their freehold and copyhold tenants enjoyed security of tenure. It was the cottagers and landless labourers who suffered most from enclosure. If they held a few acres they would be compensated, but the small parcel of land they received would not make up for the loss of the commons and wastes. If they had nothing but their cottage they would get no compensation, nor could they easily find work to keep body and soul together if the estate on which they lived was being turned over to pasture. They had little alternative but to take to the road and seek a livelihood elsewhere. By doing so they added to the numbers of the migrant poor who were on the move throughout England, creating big problems for the local authorities, particularly in the towns where so many of the poor took refuge.

Tudor governments, with their lack of any police force or standing army, were sensitive to symptoms of unrest and tried to check depopulation and enclosures in general. They valued the peasant as a tax-payer and potential soldier, and they were afraid that enclosures for sheep would so reduce the area available for corn growing that England would become dependent for food supplies on the goodwill of other powers. A statute of 1489 recited how 'great inconveniences daily doth increase by desolation and pulling down and wilful waste of houses and towns within this ... realm, and laying to pasture lands which customably have been used in tilth', but merely ordained that similar decay should not be allowed to take place in future. In 1515 Wolsey turned his attention to the matter and showed his usual determination and administrative capacity. He persuaded Parliament to pass a Bill requiring the restoration to tillage of all lands that had recently been converted to pasture, and then appointed commissioners who toured the country, gathering an enormous mass of information which they passed on to Chancery. The commissioners did their task thoroughly, but it was often difficult to prove that an enclosure was recent, within the terms of the Act. A royal proclamation of 1526 therefore ordered the pulling down of any enclosure that had been made since the accession of Henry VII, but this was no more effective in practice than the statute had been. The crown was up against the difficulty that the enforcement of government policy depended on the men of property in the localities, but these were often the very people who were doing the enclosing.

Thomas Cromwell attacked the problem from another direction by attempting to limit the number of sheep which owners were allowed to keep, but the Bill which he introduced to this effect in 1533 was gravely weakened during its passage through the Lords and had little or no effect. However, the late 1540s saw an economic crisis brought about by debasement and successive harvest failures, and the desperate need to do something revived interest in Cromwell's approach. In March 1549 Parliament passed a Bill which imposed a poll tax upon sheep, on the assumption that farmers would hardly convert their land from arable to pasture if, by so doing, they made themselves liable to heavy taxation. This Act, which caused widespread resentment among farmers and wool merchants, marked the climax of the attempt to hold back agrarian change by legislation, but it was as ineffective as its predecessors. Peasant unrest, which had been stimulated by the government's appointment of commissioners in 1548 to enquire into agrarian grievances, brought down Protector Somerset, whom the peasants regarded as their champion, and opened the way to Northumberland. The change of ruler did not bring about a *volte-face* in government policy, for although Northumberland was more sympathetic to sheep-owners than to peasant cultivators, and quickly secured the repeal of the poll tax, an Act passed by his second Parliament made it an offence for anyone to convert to pasture land that had been under the plough since 1509, and prosecution of enclosure continued, though at a declining rate. The significance of Somerset's fall is that it coincided with the collapse of the overseas market for English cloth, and it was this which succeeded where government action had failed, and checked the spread of enclosures for sheep.

Enclosure did not cease altogether, however, nor did conversion from arable to pasture, though much of this was now for the fattening up of cattle to supply urban markets, particularly London. In the early years of Elizabeth's reign there was an attempt to reinvigorate the anti-enclosure legislation, and commissioners were once again appointed in 1565 to carry out a detailed investigation. But this was a short-lived initiative, for Parliament was losing interest in the question of enclosure now that grain supplies seemed assured. In 1593 it signalled a complete change of course by repealing all the legislation forbidding the conversion of arable to pasture, but this was followed by the worst harvests of the century, which caused such a shortage of grain that maintenance of arable cultivation became once more a major priority. In 1597, therefore, Parliament passed an Act requiring that any land which had been converted to pasture since the beginning of Elizabeth's reign should be put back under the plough. It also ordered 'that all lands which now are used in tillage, having been tillable lands . . . by the space of twelve years together at the least . . . shall not be converted to any sheep-pasture or to the grazing or fatting of cattle . . . but shall . . . continue to be used in tillage for corn and grain'.

In many ways it was fortunate for England that the attempts made by successive Tudor governments to perpetuate traditional patterns of land use and occupation failed, for a growing population could only be fed by increasing the amount of land under cultivation and making the best possible use of it. Open field farming was not necessarily inefficient, nor was it incompatible with experimentation, but enclosure gave farmers a greater degree of freedom to adapt to market conditions. There were some improvements in agricultural techniques, of which the two most important were the flooding of meadows in order to improve the quantity and quality of the grasses, and the switch to 'up-and-down husbandry', which meant ploughing up land for a number of years and then putting it down to grass for a time, thereby allowing the soil to recover and enrich itself. But improved techniques alone would not have enabled agricultural production to expand as the population was doing, at around one per cent every year. Bigger supplies of home-produced grain and livestock could only be obtained by extending the cultivated area, and this was done so successfully that the expanding population was fed. Admittedly the poorer elements in society lived dangerously close to the famine level, but only when there were repeated harvest failures, as in the late 1540s and the 1590s, did starvation become a reality. Generally speaking English agriculture met the challenge of a rising population, and by the end of the Tudor period it was producing more grain than was needed for home consumption in normal circumstances.

Abnormal circumstances were brought about by harvest failure. A long spell of bad weather would cut grain yields and send prices rising. Small cultivators operating on narrow margins would have to choose between eating the seed corn which they needed for their next year's crop or going hungry. One bad harvest caused suffering, but where there were several in a row the results could be catastrophic, particularly for the poor. In 1549 the harvest was bad, in 1550 it was no better, and in 1551 it was even worse. This, coming on top of the collapse of the Antwerp cloth market and the climax of debasement, produced what is sometimes referred to as the mid-Tudor crisis. For the greater part of Elizabeth's reign harvests were reasonably good, with occasional years of abundance, but 1594–97 saw four successive years of crop failure which produced such an acute shortage of grain that there were food riots in many counties.

Bubonic plague was another scourge which struck without warning and caused not only suffering but acute social dislocation. Plague attacks were nothing like as frequent as they had been in the fourteenth and fifteenth centuries, however. The last of those regular outbreaks occurred in 1479–80; thereafter they became more sporadic. Henry VII's accession coincided with the outbreak of a form of influenza, known by the graphic name of sweating sickness, but this was not a killer on the scale of bubonic plague. The late 1470s and the 1480s therefore mark a watershed in English demographic history, for as the incidence of plague declined so the population increased.

Although outbreaks of the dreaded disease became rarer in the sixteenth century, they did still occur. London was hit by plague in the mid 1540s, as were many other parts of England, and further attacks in 1549–51 intensified the suffering already produced by harvest failure. In 1555–56 incessant rain caused the harvest to fail once more, and this coincided with an influenza epidemic which sent the death rate soaring. In 1563 London was struck by plague again, to be followed two years later by Bristol, and there was a further severe outbreak in the capital in 1593. Plague attacks in big cities, where large populations were huddled together in insanitary conditions, could kill off as much as 20 per cent of the inhabitants. This figure would have been even higher had not the wealthier citizens fled into the country as soon as the first signs manifested themselves.

## Trade and Industry

'It is not our conquests', said one seventeenth-century writer, 'but our commerce; it is not our swords, but our sails, that first spread the English name in Barbary, and thence came into Turkey, Armenia, Muscovy, Arabia, Persia, India, China, and indeed over and about the world.' For the first half of the sixteenth century, however, there was little to suggest that the English would eventually take a leading part in the phenomenal expansion of western Europe over the oceans. English commercial energies were fully occupied in the lucrative cloth trade with the Netherlands. Raw wool was exported to Calais by the Company of the Staple, but heavy taxation had depressed this trade, and as the century wore on more and more English wool went to native manufacturers. The production of cloth was the big business of Tudor England, and the chief exporters were the Merchant Adventurers of London, who were granted a charter by Henry VII. Their overseas headquarters was Antwerp, from where English cloth found its way all over Europe, and as long as trade flourished between England and the Netherlands there was no capital to spare for oceanic ventures, nor was there any incentive to engage in them.

Henry VII, however, was concerned to expand English trade, since Customs duties gave him a share of the profits. By commercial treaties with the Baltic states he tried to break the stranglehold of the Hanseatic League of merchants, who had a big depot — the Steelyard — in London and enjoyed privileges greater even than those granted to English merchants. In this attempt he failed, because the Hanseatic League was well entrenched in the valuable Baltic trade, and without its goodwill the essential supply of naval stores would have been interrupted. The Hanse merchants remained important in English commerce until after 1550, when the increase in English shipping and the growth of continental rivals to the Hanse gradually eroded the profits and the privileged position of the League. Henry VII was more successful in breaking the monopoly of Venice in Mediterranean trade, and English merchants were building up a flourishing commerce with Italy when they, like the Venetians, were checked by the westward expansion of Turkish power.

Shortage of shipping was a hindrance to the growth of English commerce, and Henry attempted to remedy this at the very beginning of his reign by a Navigation Act which forbade merchants to use foreign ships when English ones were available. By encouraging the building of merchant ships, by creating the nucleus of a royal navy, and by claiming for his subjects a greater share of European trade, Henry VII set the pattern which the commercial development of England was to follow in the next two centuries. His prescience was also shown by his patronage of the Cabots, who in 1496 were granted letters patent 'to sail to all parts, regions and coasts of the eastern, western and northern sea' in the hope of finding a short sea route to those oriental lands in which spices and precious metals were to be found. John Cabot sighted Newfoundland and came back with glowing reports of the cod fisheries there, but he still believed that Asia lay on the far side of the Atlantic, and set out on a second expedition from which he never returned.

Under Henry VIII there was little exploring activity, for the cloth trade continued to flourish and Henry's money and energy were consumed in the vain dream of rebuilding an English empire in France. By 1550, however, the quality of English cloth was declining and over-production had glutted the European market. New outlets were needed, and the initiative was taken by the Duke of Northumberland, who claimed, at this late date, a share for England in the great adventure of overseas exploration that had so far been left largely to Portugal and Spain. Since the two catholic powers controlled the southern approaches to the orient, English attention was concentrated on finding northern passages, particularly as the cold climate of these regions offered good prospects for the sale of woollen cloth. In 1554 Willoughby and Chancellor set sail to find a north-east passage to Cathay. They did not succeed, and Willoughby died in the attempt, but Chancellor made his way into the White Sea and from there journeyed to Moscow, where he appeared at the court of Ivan the Terrible. This epic journey inaugurated a flourishing trade between England and Russia, and led to the formation of the Muscovy Company.

The cloth trade picked up again, particularly after the recoinage carried out by Cecil in 1560 at the suggestion of Sir Thomas Gresham — a prominent London merchant and the Queen's financial adviser — but the Netherlands market was far from stable even before the outbreak of rebellion in 1572. Elizabeth's accession took place at a time when the price rise and unemployment had so seriously upset the English economy that Parliament authorised the drastic measures embodied in the Statute of Artificers (see below, p. 125). It also coincided with the emergence of Spain as the strongest power in Europe and an increasing threat to Britain. It was this which prompted English seamen to challenge the Spanish monopoly of trade with the New World.

In 1562 John Hawkins set out on the first of three voyages in which he collected slaves from the West African coast and shipped them to the Spanish colonies in America. The Spanish government resented this heretic invasion of the New World, even though it was a peaceful one, and on his third voyage Hawkins only just escaped alive from a surprise attack made on his ships while he was sheltering in the harbour of San Juan de Ulloa. This news reached England at a time when Elizabeth was putting pressure on Philip in hopes of persuading him to moderate his aggressive policy in the

Netherlands. The only effective way in which she could show Philip that her wishes must not be lightly disregarded was by attacks on Spanish shipping, and she encouraged — and sometimes contributed money to — the many expeditions which set out for the New World. Most famous of these was Drake's expedition of 1577. He passed through the Magellan Straits, sailed up the west coast of America where he captured a heavily laden treasure-ship, and returned to England by way of the Indian Ocean and Cape of Good Hope. Not only did he have the glory of being the first English circumnavigator; he also gave the shareholders in the expedition a profit estimated at nearly five thousand per cent.

English seamen were short of bases in the New World, and the first attempts at colonisation were designed to provide these. Sir Walter Ralegh obtained a patent for an American colony in 1584, and in the following year a settlement was established on Roanoke Island in the area that Ralegh christened, in honour of his Queen, Virginia. The colony managed to survive, short of supplies, only until the following year, when Drake, returning from one of his voyages, took the settlers home with him. A second attempt in 1587 was no more successful, for although the colonists were once again established on Roanoke they were then deserted for several years, since all English shipping was needed in home waters to face the threat of the Armada. Not until 1591 did Grenville make his way to Roanoke, only to find that the settlers had disappeared without trace.

By the time Elizabeth died no English colony had been successfully established in the New World, but English sailors were to be seen in all quarters of the earth. As the Hanseatic League declined, the English Eastland Company took its place in trade with the Baltic, while the Muscovy Company built up a flourishing trade with Russia. In the Mediterranean, English commerce revived in the last decades of the sixteenth century and Leghorn became a great market for cloth. Further east the merchants of the Levant Company took over much of the trade of Venice, now in decline, and transmitted to the western world the spices and riches of the East. They were already trying to establish direct communication with India and the Spice Islands by sea, and in 1599 they took a leading part in the discussions that led to the decision 'to set forth a voyage this present year to the East Indies and other Islands and Countries thereabouts, and there to make trade'. On the last day of 1600 the Queen issued a royal charter to these adventurers and thereby began the official career of the East India Company.

England was not a major industrial producer at the beginning of the Tudor period, except for cloth, and even here production was concentrated on coarse white broadcloths which were shipped to Flanders and Italy to be dyed and finished. Nor was industrial activity self-contained and located in factories and urban areas as it is today. Wool, for instance, was collected from the sheep farmers by clothiers who distributed it, or 'put it out', to be spun, woven and carded in houses and cottages all over England and Wales. The major areas for manufacture were East Anglia, Yorkshire, Somerset, Gloucestershire and Wiltshire, and the people who made the cloth did so only as a part-time occupation. They also worked as farm labourers or scratched a living from the forests — for domestic industry was a valuable source of additional money in woodland and pasture regions where the population was increasing but openings for regular employment were scarce. Even heavy industry was located in rural areas, and although the total numbers employed in it were large, the actual units of production were small. If a firm consisted of as many as twenty men it was, in effect, big business.

Among the most important of the heavy industries was the manufacture of iron, especially after the 1540s, when a French engineer pioneered the casting of iron cannon in England, thereby giving this country a virtual monopoly of the process. English industry was very dependent upon the application of foreign inventions. Blast furnaces, for example, were in use on the Continent long before they were brought to England in the late fifteenth century. They were worked by water power and fuelled by charcoal, so had to be located in woodland regions where water was available. The Weald of Sussex and Kent proved to be well suited for this purpose, and of some seventy blast furnaces known to have been in existence by the 1570s — compared with only three before 1530 — more than fifty were located in the Weald.

Lead, tin and copper were the principal non-ferrous metals mined in England. The main deposits of lead were to be found in the north and south-west of the country, and once extracted the metal had to be transported long distances to the major outlets in the midlands, London and the Continent. Production was hit by the Dissolution of the Monasteries, because the lead stripped from the roofs of conventual buildings glutted the market, and by the development of new German mines in the second half of the sixteenth century. Tin came mainly from Cornwall, and was despatched to English and foreign destinations by sea. Copper also was to be found in Cornwall, but other centres of extraction were Wales and the Lake District. The biggest of all extractive operations took place, however, in the coal industry, located principally in the Durham region, from where the coal was sent for distribution to Newcastle. Some was shipped abroad, but the greater part was consumed in London, whose ever-growing population needed this cheap fuel to keep it warm in winter. 'Sea coals' from Newcastle were already a feature of the London scene during Elizabeth's reign, and so were the smogs which they produced.

Tudor governments were anxious to encourage industry, partly to find employment for an expanding population, but also to bring England abreast of continental techniques and free her from dependence upon foreign manufacturers. Sir Thomas Smith and William Cecil were active promoters of new projects, and one of the devices employed to protect these in their early stages was the grant of a patent of monopoly, giving the projector sole rights of manufacture for a given period. The first of these patents was issued for the glass industry in 1552, and they were also used to nurture the manufacture of refined cloths, or 'New Draperies', by refugees from France and the Netherlands who settled in England during Elizabeth's reign. Monopoly patents subsequently became a bone of contention between Elizabeth and her Parliaments, for they were increasingly used as a means of raising money for the crown rather than protecting new processes. Nevertheless they did serve to encourage infant industries. The stocking frame, invented by a Nottinghamshire parson in the 1590s, was protected by a patent and was soon being produced in considerable numbers and used, on a 'putting-out' basis, to establish a new industry of stocking-knitting. Elizabeth's reign also saw a big expansion in the manufacture of small but essential items such as pins and nails, and the growth of a consumer market meant that commodities which had earlier been the preserve of the rich were now becoming accessible to all but the very poor.

## Towns, and the Problem of Poverty

One of the most striking phenomena of the sixteenth century was the growth of London. At the beginning of the century it had a population of about 60,000, which made it far and away the biggest English town. By 1600, however, London and its suburbs contained some 225,000 inhabitants, and the number was steadily rising. This increase in population was entirely due to immigration into the capital, since the death rate exceeded that of live births. People flooded into London for a variety of reasons. Lawyers went there because the major law courts were located at Westminster. Government servants had to be resident there, for part of the year at least, and so did an increasing number of merchants, for during the Tudor period London became the commercial as well as the administrative capital of England.

As cloth exports came to be focused upon a single outlet at Antwerp, so London became the principal port from which they were despatched, and by the middle of the sixteenth century about 90 per cent of all cloth destined for overseas markets went through the capital. Not only that. London was also becoming a centre for luxury trades and was setting fashions that the rest of England had, willy nilly, to adopt. Its dominance was often resented in the provinces, and one writer complained at the way in which 'no gentleman can be content to have either cap, coat, doublet, hose or shirt made in his country [i.e. locality] but they must have their gear from London'. The 'outports', such as Bristol and Southampton, were badly hit by the shrinkage of their direct trade with the Continent, but their fortunes picked up in the second half of the sixteenth century, following the collapse of the Antwerp market.

The commercial predominance of London increased its appeal to all those who wanted to carve out a career for themselves in trade. Younger sons of gentry families who were barred from any major inheritance by the rule of primogeniture — which meant that the estates of a landed family passed to the first-born male heir — often bound themselves as apprentices to a London merchant and became inhabitants of the city, at least for a time. They had their professional counterparts in the trainee lawyers who took up residence in one of the Inns of Court that were sited on the north bank of the Thames, between the City proper and Whitehall. Apprentices, law students and the like were 'betterment migrants' who made their way to London in order to improve their career prospects. But their numbers were tiny compared with the thousands of 'subsistence migrants', poor people from all over England who made their way to the capital in the hope of scraping a living there. They flooded into the burgeoning suburbs, including those on the south bank, where they lived in conditions of acute squalor.

The slum tenements of the poor were in sharp contrast to the great mansions which the Tudor aristocracy had built on the riverside to the east of the royal palace of Whitehall. The land here had formerly belonged to the Church — as had Whitehall itself until Wolsey was persuaded to hand it over to Henry VIII — but the disappearance of the abbots and the diminishing wealth and importance of the bishops led to its secularisation. Mansions were to be found also within the City. In the 1560s Sir Thomas Gresham, who was a leading financier and raised loans on the Antwerp market for Edward VI, Mary and Elizabeth, built Gresham House in Bishopsgate Street as his principal London residence. Its arcaded ground floor, supported by marble pillars, was inspired by the buildings with which he was familiar in Antwerp, and his house in turn acted as a model for the Royal Exchange which he erected at his own expense in 1568 and gave to the City as a place where merchants could congregate and do business. Gresham was a member of the Mercers, and this and other livery companies, such as the Goldsmiths and Drapers, were the strongholds of the merchant oligarchs who dominated London life. It was from among their number that the Lord Mayor and aldermen, who actually governed the metropolis, were chosen, and although they were nominally inferior in rank to the aristocracy and often looked down upon by the gentry, their power and influence were considerable. Queen Elizabeth herself was descended from a Lord Mayor, and some of the leading figures of Stuart England like Oliver Cromwell, John Hampden and Sir Thomas Osborne (who became Earl of Danby and Duke of Leeds) were grandchildren of London aldermen. In this as in so many other ways the City made its mark on Tudor and Stuart history.

Outside London there were about half a dozen towns which were becoming, in effect, regional centres, of which the most important were Bristol, York, Norwich, Exeter and Newcastle. These had populations of around 10,000, small by London standards but significantly bigger than the 1,500–7,000 inhabitants of the hundred or so towns which were important centres only within their own counties. Apart from these there were some five hundred market towns with populations ranging from 600 to 1,000.

Generally speaking the first half of the sixteenth century was a difficult time for English towns. Industries, from which they had previously benefited, were moving into the countryside, where they were free of gild restrictions and also had easier access to water power and fuel. Overseas trade was dislocated by war and increasingly confined to London. High taxation, particularly in the 1520s and 1540s, fell heavily on the urban communities, and a further blow came with the Dissolution of the Monasteries, since the abbeys had been big purchasers and large-scale employers of labour. This difficult period reached its climax in the economic and social crisis of the mid-century, but after about 1560 conditions began to improve. The towns were helped to recover by the positive attitude of the Marian government and Parliaments, which passed an Act in 1554 giving corporate towns a virtual monopoly over retail trade in manufactured articles; another in the following year placing restrictions upon the rural textile industry; and one in 1557 which reinforced urban control over the processes of cloth manufacture. It was also during these middle years of the century that the merchant oligarchs who ruled most towns bought charters of incorporation from the crown. By 1547 there were some sixty corporate boroughs in England and Wales, and this figure was more than doubled by 1600. The royal government approved of oligarchic rule in the localities, since this was preferable either to magnate domination or to the involvement of the majority of the population, with all that this implied in the way of factiousness and undesirable influences. As for the oligarchs themselves, a royal charter gave them clearly defined powers and greatly strengthened their authority.

The members of the ruling elites in Tudor towns needed all the buttressing they could get, for they were a tiny minority of the urban population. Some two-thirds of the inhabitants of the bigger towns consisted of people living close to the poverty line, and their numbers were constantly swollen by the influx of subsistence migrants from rural areas. The growth of this urban proletariat represented a very real threat to the maintenance of the social order, and it was fear of unrest, as well as genuinely charitable inclinations, that drove municipal authorities to try to limit the inflow of destitute persons from outside their towns as well as provide a modicum of relief for the indigenous poor. Since the problems of poverty were common to all major cities it made sense for Parliament to provide common remedies, but in general legislation did little more than codify existing practices. It had long been customary, for instance, for urban authorities to arrest vagrants, punish them, and then return them to their homes. This was given statutory sanction by an Act of 1531 which laid down that a convicted vagrant was to be 'tied to the end of a cart naked and . . . beaten with whips . . . till his body be bloody'. After this benevolent treatment he was to be returned to his native parish, 'and there put himself to labour, like as a true man oweth to do'.

The 1531 Act assumed that the cause of poverty was idleness, the 'mother and root of all vices', but it followed late-medieval precedents in distinguishing between 'aged, poor and impotent persons', who were unable to work and were therefore to be licensed to beg, and 'persons being whole and mighty in body and able to labour'. This was still a valid distinction, but the implication that the able-bodied could find work if they wished was not. The circle of humanists surrounding Thomas Cromwell were aware of this and they drafted a scheme for employing the poor on public works, paid for by a graduated income tax and supervised by a specially created 'Council to avoid Vagabonds'. A Bill to this effect was introduced into the last session of the Reformation Parliament in 1536, and Cromwell persuaded Henry to appear in person and give it his backing. But members of Parliament, who represented the forces of order, found the measure unpalatable, and the Act, as it was finally passed, merely intensified the punitive measures against vagrants. In 1547, during the crisis years of the mid-century, Parliament was so alarmed by the prospect of more and more poor taking to the roads that it adopted the drastic remedy of ordering vagabonds to be enslaved, initially for two years, to ensure that they were put to work. However, the idea of turning Englishmen, even poor ones, into slaves was so unappealing that the Act remained a dead letter until its repeal in 1550.

One of the weaknesses of Tudor paternalism was that it had little statistical information upon which to base its policies. Cromwell attempted to remedy this in 1538 by requiring all parishes to record details of baptisms, marriages and deaths, but he fell from power before he could put his proposals into full effect. On a smaller scale, however, urban authorities were getting the information they needed: at Coventry, for example, in 1547 a census of the poor was conducted in an attempt to discover what caused poverty and how best it might be relieved. This initiative was seconded by Parliament in an Act of 1552 ordering the appointment in every parish of alms collectors who were to keep records of the numbers of the poor and of the amount of relief they paid out. In London a comprehensive scheme of poor relief had been created by the mid-sixteenth century. 'Idle rogues' were set to labour in a workhouse created out of the old royal palace of Bridewell, while former Church property was used to provide and maintain a number of hospitals to care for orphans, the sick and the aged. But there remained the task of providing relief for those who were temporarily out of work or otherwise ineligible for admission to a hospital, and the cost of this exceeded the sums given by way of voluntary contributions. In 1547, therefore, London instituted a compulsory poor rate, and other towns like York, Ipswich and Norwich adopted similar solutions. The state once again codified these local initiatives, and an Act of 1563 prescribed that anyone refusing to contribute to funds for poor relief was to be brought before the Justices of the Peace who could, if they saw fit, levy his contribution by distraint and send him to prison to meditate upon the evil of his unsocial ways.

The Tudor system of poor relief was finally extended and defined by an Act of 1598 which was confirmed, with only minor changes, in 1601. The distinction between able-bodied and 'impotent' poor was maintained, and vagabonds were still to be whipped and sent back to their native parishes or else set to compulsory work in specially erected Houses of Correction. As for the 'poor impotent people' they were to be provided by the parish with 'convenient Houses of Dwelling', and the money to build and maintain these was to be raised by a compulsory poor rate, collected by Overseers of the Poor, who were to be appointed by and responsible to the local Justices of the Peace. The Act also provided that if any parish was unable to raise sufficient money to meet its obligations, the Justices could require other parishes to assist it.

The Tudor poor law was designed as a framework within which national, local and individual initiatives could be combined. By itself it would have been insufficient, for it was only enforced sporadically, but the various systems of relief set up in the towns, where the problem of poverty was too self-evident to ignore, functioned regularly and were, on the whole, effective. Private charity also made a substantial contribution, particularly when individuals used their wealth to endow trusts which either relieved suffering through the payment of doles in money or kind, or stimulated self help by providing the deserving poor with the tools of a trade. It has been suggested that the volume of individual charity increased markedly after the Reformation, but this is an optical illusion caused by inflation. In real terms private charity was no greater than it had been earlier, and the recourse to compulsion in the collection of poor rates suggests that it may even have declined – though it is difficult to distinguish cause and effect in this particular instance. Nevertheless the charitable impulse was very much alive in Tudor and early Stuart England, and without private benefactions on a massive scale the poor would have been left in ever greater misery, and perhaps driven to violence on a scale that would have rocked the foundations of society.

Another example of Tudor paternalism was the great Statute of Artificers, or Apprentices, of 1563. This was an ambitious attempt to resolve the interrelated problems of poverty, vagabondage, unemployment and rising prices by conscripting the entire male population below the level of gentry. All craftsmen were to serve a seven-year apprenticeship, during which time they were to be under the control of their master. Non-craftsmen between the ages of twelve and sixty were to be set to work in agriculture. J.P.s were instructed to see that these provisions were put into effect, and were also authorised to regulate wage rates by annual assessments. But in practice the Act was only partially and sporadically enforced. The coercive mechanisms available to the Tudor state were far too limited to permit the regimentation of society on such a scale, and as economic conditions improved in the 1570s and '80s the Act lost much of its relevance.

## The Structure of Society

English society was a pyramid which broadened out from the crown at the top to the mass of the population in the lower layers. Immediately below the sovereign and royal family came the aristocracy. Half the noble families in existence when Henry VII came to the throne had become extinct in the male line by the time Henry VIII died, because of the natural failure of heirs, helped on by attainders. However, the aristocracy was reinforced by the grant of new titles, most of which went to men who had made their mark in the royal service. The older nobility was not excluded from the administration, but if individual members were employed it was because the King wished to employ them and not because of any prescriptive right on their part. When the Duke of Norfolk, for instance, dared to suggest that the borderlands in the north of England ought to be ruled by noblemen, the Council was quick to disillusion him. The King, said its reply, would choose whom he liked to serve him, and if he 'appoint the meanest man to rule there, is not his Grace's authority sufficient?' Norfolk's son, the Earl of Surrey, gave his answer to this question on the scaffold, for he died complaining that the King 'would deny the noble blood around him and employ none but mean creatures'.

The nobles were a small group, numbering just under fifty in 1547 and a little over in 1603. Elizabeth followed the example of her grandfather, Henry VII, when it came to granting peerages, and there were only two totally new creations during her reign. One of these was the barony of Burghley, granted to Sir William Cecil, but it says much about Elizabeth's attitude that the most long-serving, faithful and competent of her servants should have been advanced only to the lowest rung of the peerage ladder. At the top, the execution of Norfolk in 1572 removed the last surviving Duke, and no more were created, apart from members of the royal family, until 1623.

The peers were in general big landowners, and had suffered badly from the effects of inflation, for while they had to pay more for the goods and services they required, their income from rents remained static. By the late sixteenth century, however, leases were falling in, copyholds were running out, and noble landowners were able to bring rents and entry fines up to a more realistic level. As a consequence, their incomes began to rise at a rate which out-stripped inflation, and although there were big variations between one family and another, the economic crisis of the aristocracy was almost over by the time James I came to the throne. This did not mean that the nobles were out of debt. Far from it. But indebtedness was a reflection of their life style rather than of any fundamental financial weakness. They were addicted to conspicuous consumption: they built huge houses for themselves, they spent vast sums of money on entertaining, on extravagant clothes, on jewellery, plate, and innumerable law suits. The days of armed retainers had gone, but households were still large: the Earl of Derby, for example, had 150 men on his pay roll in 1590.

Below the aristocracy, and often connected with them by blood, came the gentry. They were already well rooted in the localities and in public life at the accession of Henry VII, but the redistribution of land which followed the Dissolution of the Monasteries gave them an even bigger stake in the country. Henry's lack of ready cash to pay for war was so crippling that part of the monastic prop-erty was sold off immediately while most of the rest was disposed of in the ensuing hundred years. In the 1540s the standard pur-chase price was fixed at twenty times the estimated annual profit, and at this rate there were plenty of bidders. A third of the land went to peers and courtiers; and those who happened to be in favour at the time, like the Dukes of Norfolk and Suffolk and the Earl of Hertford, added considerably to their estates. Some cour-tiers were lucky enough to get consolidated blocks of land which gave them territorial predominance in certain areas. John Russell,

who became the biggest landowner in the west country, was one
of these, and Thomas Wriothesley, who controlled Hampshire from
the great house he built out of Titchfield Abbey, was another.

Officials of the Court of Augmentations also did well for themselves, eventually acquiring about one-seventh of the land disposed
of, but there is no evidence of widespread speculation by groups
of London business men. When Londoners did buy up land they
were usually investing for themselves or acting as agents for country gentlemen who could not spare the time or energy to appear
personally before the Court of Augmentations. It was these country
gentlemen, medium-sized landowners whose families had often
been long established in their counties, who bought up the greater
part of the land that was available. Some merchants and lawyers
took the opportunity to acquire estates and turn themselves into
landed gentry, but it seems that the number of new families established on the basis of monastic property was relatively small.

Below the gentry came the yeomen. In theory these were the
possessors of freehold land worth a minimum of forty shillings a
year, but in practice a yeoman could hold by a variety of tenures,
and it was the size of his estate rather than its exact nature that
determined his status. A yeoman was a man who farmed fifty acres
or more, and substantial yeomen were virtually indistinguishable
from lesser gentry. If they had little or no rent to pay they were
well placed to take advantage of increased prices for their produce,
and many yeomen were flourishing during Elizabeth's reign, and
held their heads high. This did not necessarily meet with the approval of those who were nominally their social superiors. Thomas
Wilson, who wrote an account of *The State of England, 1600*, was one
of these, for as the younger son of a gentry family he had been left
to make his own way in the world. He commented bitterly on the
sons of well-to-do yeomen who were 'not contented with their states
of their fathers to be counted yeomen and called John or Robert'
but each must 'skip into his velvet breeches and silken doublet and,
getting to be admitted into some Inn of Court or Chancery, must
ever after think scorn to be called any other than gentleman'.

Not all yeomen were flourishing, of course, and at the other end
of the scale they merged into the upper sections of the husbandmen.
These were peasant cultivators who farmed anything from five to
fifty acres. Below them came the cottagers, who might have one or
two acres, and the landless labourers, who depended upon wages
for their livelihood.

The amount of land that a family held at any time gives an indication of its status, but Tudor society was far more fluid than
generalisations would imply, and although prevailing trends might
favour one group rather than another, much depended upon individual circumstances. Recusancy might cripple one family, ex-

travagance another, incompetence or sheer bad luck a third. In parts of the country — like Northamptonshire, for instance, which was ideal for sheep — agriculture alone was profitable enough for a landowner to flourish and extend his estates, while in other parts some extra source of income — the law, perhaps, or trade, or marriage to an heiress — was needed. Much depended, also, upon personal characteristics. One man might make a handsome profit out of holding public office while another would merely acquire extravagant habits that led him to live above his income: one man would run his estates with ruthless and profitable efficiency, while his neighbour would be held back by timidity, social conventions, tender-heartedness or simply lack of interest and ability.

## Education

Education was one of the principal means whereby a man could improve his status in Tudor society, and not only if he took holy orders, for a period of study at university, particularly if it was followed by a further period at one of the Inns of Court, became the standard opening to a career in the public service. At the time of Henry VII's accession, universities were still what they had been for several centuries, training centres for clerical administrators. But humanist influences were making themselves felt, and Erasmus struck a responsive chord when he declared that clergy should not simply be men who were expert in canon or civil law, but committed preachers engaged in active evangelisation. One of Erasmus's patrons was John Fisher, who became chancellor of Cambridge University in 1503. Fisher was also chaplain to Henry VII's mother, Lady Margaret Beaufort, and it was at his suggestion that she instituted the Lady Margaret chairs in Divinity at both universities and increased the educational provision for future preachers by founding first Christ's College and subsequently St John's, both at Cambridge. Her example was followed by Richard Fox, Bishop of Winchester and Lord Privy Seal, who founded Corpus Christi College at Oxford. He showed his humanist inclinations by laying down that all fellows of the college should be well versed in Latin, and he also put the study of Greek on a formal basis by endowing the first lectureship in this subject at either university.

The most magnificient of all the new foundations was, of course, Cardinal's College at Oxford. This survived Wolsey's fall, but was later suppressed by Henry VIII so that he could resurrect it as his own foundation of Christ Church. The new college was established in 1546, and in the same year Henry gathered a number of small Cambridge institutions into his palatial new foundation of Trinity College. Trinity was made responsible for the maintenance of regius professors in Divinity, Greek and Hebrew, and a similar responsibility was placed upon the new see of Oxford, which had as its cathedral the chapel of Christ Church. In this way Henry demonstrated his commitment to the new learning at minimum expense to himself.

The universities still regarded it as their main task to produce graduate clergy for the Church of England, and in Elizabeth's reign this function became increasingly important in view of widespread criticism of the ministry. But laymen from the upper sections of English society were also attending the universities in larger numbers than before, especially if they were thinking of a career in public life or administration, for the renaissance state needed educated men to serve it. In 1535, for instance, William Cecil went up to St John's College, Cambridge, where he stayed for six years and then moved on to Gray's Inn without taking a degree. Walter Mildmay, the future Chancellor of the Exchequer, did exactly the same, except that he chose Christ's as his college. Cecil, who was to become chancellor of Cambridge as well as Elizabeth's chief minister, always retained a deep affection for his university. Apart from anything else he had a family link with it, for he married the sister of John Cheke, the first regius professor of Greek at Cambridge. As for Sir Walter Mildmay, he showed his commitment by founding a new college, Emmanuel, and choosing as its first master Laurence Chaderton, another Christ's man. Chaderton was notorious for his puritan views, which was why Mildmay chose him, but the Queen was suspicious and asked her minister whether he intended to erect a puritan foundation. 'Far be it from me to countenance anything contrary to established laws', Mildmay replied, 'but I have set an acorn which, when it becomes an oak, God alone knows what will be the fruits thereof'.

There was no problem about finding students for the expanding universities, as demand for places was high, with the exception of the 1580s when it temporarily diminished. Most of the undergraduates were drawn from the upper sections of English society, and although this may have been good for the prestige of the universities it meant that they were unable, or indeed unwilling, to carry out their traditional function of educating the poor as well. As for the quality of teaching, this varied from college to college, and although the humanists had succeeded in modifying the medieval, scholastic curriculum, too much of its framework remained for some tastes: Francis Bacon, for example, who went up to Trinity at the age of twelve, was happy to leave it two years later, for he found Cambridge 'only strong for disputations and contentions, but barren of the production of works for the benefit of the life of man'.

While the Church maintained its tight hold upon the universities into the opening decades of the sixteenth century, it had already been forced to surrender its monopoly of education at secondary level. In 1411 a judgment in King's Bench had upheld the right of a layman to establish a school, and during the course of the fifteenth century more and more schools were founded not only by individuals but also by boroughs, livery companies and gilds. Yet whatever the nature of the foundation, the curriculum tended to be traditional, as did the ways in which subjects were taught. The first major change in this respect came with the establishment of Magdalen College School at Oxford in 1480, for the headmaster developed methods of teaching Latin grammar based on the enlightened Italian model. A number of his pupils stayed on to train as teachers, among them William Lily, who was chosen by John Colet to be the head of the new school which he set up at St Paul's in 1510. Colet wanted this to be a committedly humanist institution, where students would acquire not simply a basic knowledge of Latin but a real understanding of the works of both Christian and classical writers. There were no suitable textbooks available, so Lily wrote them himself, with the assistance of Erasmus.

Although St Paul's was intended as a model it was not widely imitated, for humanists were a small minority and teachers of the quality of Lily were thin on the ground. A major role in education was still played by the Church, including the monasteries which sometimes established schools of their own, as at Reading, and also acted as trustees for independent foundations. The Dissolution put an end to all this, of course, and although schemes were drawn up for re-establishing schools in the new dioceses that were created, they were not all put into effect. It was left to local and individual initiative to fill the gap. At Sherborne, for instance, the town bought the abbey church and set up a school of its own there, while in London the Mercers Company acquired a monastic institution and turned it into the Mercers School in 1542.

The dissolution of the chantries was an even greater threat to education than that of the monasteries. For one thing, chantry priests habitually supplemented their earnings by acting as schoolmasters; and, for another, many established schools had received bequests as part of a chantry foundation and now found their endowments at risk. The Edwardian government, which appreciated the value of secondary education in spreading protestant doctrines, instructed the Court of Augmentations to make appropriate provision, where necessary, and it also encouraged towns to set up schools of their own. The government's aim was to ensure that every county should have at least one school of real quality, soundly based under the direction of lay governors, and it used part of the funds raised by the dissolution of the chantries to endow, or re-endow, what were thenceforth to be known as King Edward VI's grammar schools.

Elizabeth's reign was a period of consolidation as far as secondary education was concerned. On the suppression of the religious community re-established by Mary at Westminster, the Queen authorised the transfer of part of its funds to what now became Westminster School, but this was virtually the end of her initiative. Once again the lead was taken by individuals, companies and corporations. London merchants were particularly active in setting up schools, and there were a number of instances of flourishing yeomen using their wealth for this purpose.

Although grammar schools could not be established without an adequate endowment, and were intended to be open to all and sundry, they were not totally free. Schoolmasters' stipends rarely kept pace with inflation, and in education, as in government administration, fees were used to supplement salaries. Those families at the lower end of the social scale were often unable to afford even nominal charges for the education of their children, who were thereby debarred from the grammar schools. But unless they were very poor they might be able to acquire rudimentary knowledge of reading, writing and arithmetic from the petty schools which many parishes maintained and where instruction was given either by the local curate or by a schoolmaster, who was usually an aspirant to holy orders.

One of the main reasons for the founding of schools in post-Reformation England was to promote the spread of literacy, so that people could read the Bible themselves and thereby strengthen their protestant faith. But literacy could not simply be imposed upon the population, and different sections of society varied in their enthusiasm for it. Landowners, professional men and tradespeople needed to be literate in order to carry out their work and duties, but this was not the case with wage-labourers and peasant cultivators. The most striking educational advance took place in the first three decades of Elizabeth's reign and by the 1590s the great majority of gentlemen were literate, as were some 60 per cent of yeomen and 45 per cent of those involved in commerce. Among husbandmen, however, the figure was much lower, a mere 13 per cent, and generally speaking the social distribution of literacy mirrored the hierarchical structure of Elizabethan England.

# 7

# Ireland and Scotland in the Sixteenth Century

## IRELAND

### Henry VII and Kildare

At the time of Henry VII's accession English rule in Ireland was confined to the Pale, a strip of coast stretching northwards from Dublin for fifty miles and extending some twenty miles inland. The rest of the country, the 'Irishry', was occupied by Gaelic-speaking clans, under their chieftains, but the most powerful families were the Anglo-Irish, descended from the Anglo-Norman adventurers of the twelfth century. Principal among these were the Butlers, Earls of Ormond, and the FitzGeralds (Geraldines), Earls of Kildare. The Lord-Deputy in 1485 was the eighth Earl of Kildare, who had held the same office under Edward IV and was a Yorkist sympathiser. Henry Tudor would no doubt have liked to remove him from office, but there was no obvious person to put in his place, and his control of Leinster, as well as his connexions with many of the leading Irish families, made him extremely powerful.

Kildare's loyalty was tested early on in the new reign when Lambert Simnel landed at Dublin in May 1487, claiming to be the Earl of Warwick, the Yorkist heir to the throne. Kildare and his associates were apparently taken in by the pretender, Simnel was crowned King as Edward VI in Dublin Cathedral, and an Irish contingent sailed with the Yorkist expedition to England. The revolt came to an end at the bloody battle of Stoke, and Henry had to decide how to deal with Ireland. Full-scale invasion would have been far too expensive an operation, since Ireland had little to offer an English King. Its chief importance was as a base from which the enemies of the Tudor dynasty could launch their attacks, and all that Henry required was an assurance from the Irish lords that they would remain loyal to him. Sir Richard Edgcumbe was sent to Ireland with five hundred men to administer an oath of loyalty. Kildare took this and remained in office as Lord-Deputy, but his acceptance did not spring from a change of heart and when the next pretender, Perkin Warbeck, appeared in 1491, Kildare accepted him as King.

Kildare's treachery prompted Henry to make a radical change of course in his policy towards Ireland. Instead of ruling via the established families he appointed his baby son, Prince Henry, as nominal Lieutenant of Ireland, and made Sir Edward Poynings his deputy. Poynings was given instructions to appoint Englishmen to the principal administrative positions in the Pale and to ensure that the institutions of Irish government should never again be taken over by Yorkist pretenders. The final step in this process of imposing direct English rule upon Ireland came when Poynings summoned the Irish Parliament in December 1496, for this passed the statute known as 'Poynings' Law' which stated that in future no Irish Parliament was to assemble or to pass any legislation without the prior approval of the English government.

Henry apparently hoped that Ireland, once it had been brought under effective English control, could be made to pay for itself, but it soon became apparent that the Irish revenues were insufficient to maintain an army of the size that would be necessary to guarantee the continuation of direct rule. Henry therefore decided to revert to indirect rule, but he left Poynings in Ireland for fear that Warbeck might make a reappearance. This in fact happened in 1495, when the pretender landed in Ireland and laid siege to Waterford, the second most important town in the country. But Waterford, with the aid of Poynings, held out, and Warbeck had to abandon the siege and sail away to Scotland. Poynings was now free to return to England, and Henry restored Kildare to the Deputyship. The Earl remained ruler of Ireland — or, rather, of the Pale and the FitzGerald sphere of influence outside it — until his death in 1513, when he was succeeded by his son, the ninth Earl.

## Henry VIII and the Kingdom of Ireland

The big advantage of indirect rule, from the crown's point of view, was its cheapness, but it left Ireland in an unsatisfactory, semi-detached state, subject to the whims of its magnate Deputies. The danger that Ireland might be used as a base by the King's enemies became acute in the 1530s, when Henry affronted catholic Europe by breaking with Rome, and Thomas Cromwell drew up plans for making it an integral part of the English monarchy. There was nothing revolutionary about his proposals — which included the appointment of an Englishman as Lord-Deputy, the strengthening of the Dublin administration, and the reduction of magnate power through the extension of royal authority into the Irishry — but he pushed them forward with a tenacity that was typical of him. He invited Kildare to England, probably in order to persuade him to co-operate in implementing the reform programme, but the Earl was reluctant to accept, for fear that he might be called to account for his actions. He eventually made the journey to London, in early 1534, but by this time he was a sick man, and before he could return to Ireland he died.

The ninth Earl had already warned his son, 'Silken Thomas', not to trust the English, and when the news of Kildare's death reached Ireland in the summer of 1534, 'Silken Thomas' called on the Geraldines to revolt and appealed to the Pope and the Emperor for support against the heretic King of England. It looked for a time as though English authority in Ireland would be swept away, but the Butlers remained loyal and Dublin held out against the rebels. Henry had no choice but to use force, and he raised an army of over two thousand men — the largest to be sent to Ireland since Richard II's reign — and gave command of it to Sir William Skeffington. In March 1535 Skeffington stormed 'Silken Thomas's' castle at Maynooth and slaughtered most of the garrison. 'Silken Thomas' kept up the struggle for a few months longer, but his followers deserted him and he eventually gave himself up. He was sent to England, with a promise of safety for his person, but in February 1537 he was hanged at Tyburn, along with five of his uncles. The Geraldine leadership had, in effect, been wiped out.

The collapse of the Geraldine rebellion opened the way to the imposition of direct rule, and Cromwell despatched a number of trusted officials to Dublin to take over the administration, under the aegis of Skeffington, who was appointed Lord-Deputy in May 1534. The money for these measures, and for the maintenance of Skeffington's army, was found by dissolving the Irish monasteries and confiscating the lands of the Geraldine leaders, who had been attainted of treason. But these windfalls were not sufficient to provide a permanent financial endowment for the maintenance of English rule, and by 1540 Ireland was costing Henry some £4,000 a year, which he could ill afford. With the fall of Cromwell in 1540 the advocates of direct rule lost their most powerful supporter, and Henry decided to revert to a policy of conciliation. In June 1541 the Irish Parliament formally recognised Henry as King of Ireland, and the chieftains of the Irishry were invited to surrender their lands to the crown and have them regranted as fiefs. They were also encouraged to adopt a more settled and 'civilised' way of life, including the use of the English language instead of Gaelic, and to recognise that their best chance of preserving their dominant role in the social hierarchy lay in co-operation with the crown. In 1542 a number of Irish chieftains made their appearance at court and were graciously received by Henry, who conferred titles of nobility upon them: the O'Neills, for instance, became Earls of Tyrone, and the O'Brians Earls of Thomond. In this way, it was hoped, Ireland would gradually divest itself of its separate identity and become an integral part of the Tudor state.

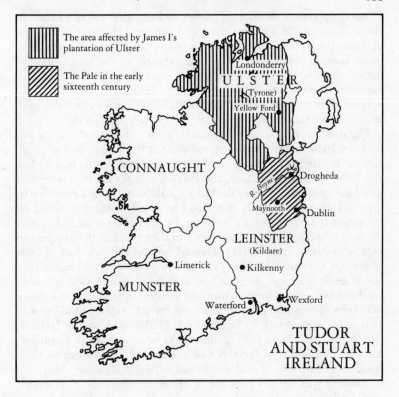

The area affected by James I's plantation of Ulster

The Pale in the early sixteenth century

ULSTER
(Tyrone)
Londonderry
Yellow Ford

CONNAUGHT

R. Boyne
Drogheda
Maynooth
Dublin

LEINSTER
(Kildare)

Limerick
Kilkenny

MUNSTER

Waterford
Wexford

TUDOR
AND STUART
IRELAND

## Elizabeth I and the Irish Rebellion

The process of 'surrender and regrant', which was designed to turn the Irish chieftains into English-style landlords, might well have been successful, given time. Religion was not, at first, a problem, for there was no great love for the Pope in Ireland, and most of the bishops as well as the nobles and chieftains had accepted the Act of Supremacy. When, in 1542, Jesuit missionaries arrived in Ulster they were given such a chilly reception that they sailed on to Scotland. The doctrinal changes of Edward VI's reign, however, were less acceptable to the Irish, and the attitude of the clergy was in general similar to that of the Archbishop of Armagh, who had supported royal supremacy but declared that 'he would never be a bishop where the holy mass was abolished'. The accession of catholic Mary as Queen was therefore welcomed, but Ireland remained only nominally under English control and the clash of family interests continued to dominate Irish affairs.

Mary appointed the Earl of Sussex as Lord-Deputy, and he made the security of the Pale his principal concern. He built a number of forts along its border and also encouraged English settlers to move into, or 'plant', the areas immediately to the west of it. He hoped thereby to create a buffer zone between the Pale and the turbulent Irishry and to accelerate the 'civilising' process, but his actions alarmed both the Anglo-Irish and the native chieftains and helped draw them together in defence of their territories.

Elizabeth at first continued Mary's policy of gradual infiltration into the Irishry, but the disordered state of this region was so great that it threatened the stability of the English administration within the Pale. In 1565, therefore, the Privy Council took into consideration the question 'whether the Queen's Majesty . . . be counselled to govern Ireland after the Irish manner as it hath been accustomed, or to reduce it as near as may be to the English government'. It opted for the second of these alternatives and thereby radically altered the course of Anglo-Irish history. Ireland beyond the Pale had its own language, customs and law, but these were now to be replaced by the English language, English law, and the system of local administration based upon counties that had evolved in England over many centuries. The assumption behind the Privy Council's thinking was that what worked well in England would also work well in Ireland, but this was to ignore the big differences between the two countries, for the inhabitants of Ireland had a stubborn attachment to their traditional institutions and would not willingly abandon them.

Trouble was already brewing in Munster, where the FitzGeralds and Butlers were, as usual, at loggerheads, and the Deputy's support of the Butlers drove James FitzMaurice FitzGerald into open rebellion in 1569. FitzMaurice appealed to the Pope and the King of Spain for help, but by the time their meagre supplies arrived the rebellion had collapsed. FitzMaurice fled to the Continent and returned to Ireland in 1579 with a mixed force of Spanish and Italian troops, financed by the Pope. For several years revolt smouldered in Munster, since Elizabeth could not afford a major expedition, and Spanish men and money kept the rebels going. Not until 1583 was Munster finally subdued, after a ruthless campaign which brought starvation to the Irish peasants, whom Spenser described 'creeping forth upon their hands, for their legs could not bear them. They looked like anatomies of death. They spake like ghosts crying out of their graves. They did eat the dead carrions, happy where they could find them'.

The suppression of the Munster rebellion meant that there was now no obstacle to the 'plantation' of that region. Burghley and Ralegh drew up a plan, based upon Ralegh's proposals for a settlement in the New World, by which four hundred thousand acres of Munster were confiscated and distributed to English immigrants.

Settlement was a slow business, as famine, disease and incompetence took their toll, but it was extended to Connaught and gradually undermined the traditional Irish way of life.

The English inhabitants of the Pale, and the Anglo-Irish, had a certain sympathy with and respect for the native Irish, based on long acquaintance. This was not the case with the English immigrants, who could not understand the Gaelic which they spoke and were shocked by their uncouth dress and primitive way of life. The attitude of these English settlers towards the Irish was very similar to that of the Spaniards towards the American Indians, and they saw their mission in much the same terms, as the imposition upon a backward people of a higher civilisation. The lack of harmony between the two elements was increased by the commitment of the Irish to Roman Catholicism, for protestantism had never taken root outside the Pale, and the influx of catholic missionaries from the Continent from the 1580s onwards had helped revive the old faith, particularly since it was now linked in the popular imagination with the defence of 'Irish' values against alien rule. Many of the English settlers were extreme protestants, who saw no difference between catholic ritual and pagan superstition, and this intensified their contempt for the native Irish. They regarded them in some ways as refractory children, in others as wild savages, and felt no compunction about treating them in a ruthless and often inhuman manner. Far from wishing to fuse the two cultures, which had been the aim of English policy in the 1540s, they saw it as their God-given duty to eradicate 'Irishness' in all its shapes and forms.

The Irish chieftains, who had earlier been encouraged to anglicise themselves, might have been able to bridge the gap between the natives and the immigrants. Hugh O'Neill, for instance, who was the second Earl of Tyrone, had spent several years at Penshurst as the guest of the Sidneys, and he and his sons spoke fluent English. But when men such as these were forced to choose between the English way of life and the Irish, blood ties and the sense of their own identity made it inevitable that they would opt for the latter. Tyrone, who had built up a powerful position for himself in Ulster, demanded that chieftain rule should be preserved and that the Irish should be allowed freedom of worship as Roman Catholics. When the Queen refused to guarantee these requests, he appealed for support to Philip of Spain. Philip sent money and also prepared an armada which sailed in 1596. The armada was turned back by storms before ever it reached Ireland, but the prospect of foreign aid ignited Irish nationalism and produced a major rebellion. English settlers were driven out of Munster in the south, while in the north an English army was crushingly defeated by Tyrone at the battle of the Yellow Ford. Only the Pale and some of the coastal towns remained loyal to the crown.

Elizabeth, who had already spent a million pounds on Ireland to little effect, was reluctant to pour more money away on a military campaign. But the threat of an independent Ireland under Spanish patronage was too real to ignore, and Essex, appointed Lord-Lieutenant in 1599, was despatched with about twenty thousand men — the largest army ever to be sent to Ireland in the Tudor period. Essex's campaign, however, was a failure. Instead of fighting Tyrone he negotiated a truce which left the Irish leader in control of Ulster, and promptly returned to England to put his case to the Queen.

Elizabeth refused to recognise the truce, and replaced her tarnished favourite by Charles Blount, Lord Mountjoy. He avoided pitched battles and waged a war of attrition instead, destroying the rebels' supplies and consolidating his gains by establishing powerful garrisons. By the autumn of 1601 Munster had been pacified and Mountjoy was ready to deal with Tyrone in Ulster, when news reached him that four thousand Spanish troops had landed at Kinsale. The success of Mountjoy's pacification was demonstrated by the marked lack of support given to these 'liberators', and when Tyrone marched south to link up with them he was heavily defeated. Early in 1602 the Spaniards surrendered and were allowed to return home. With them went the last hopes of the rebels, and in March 1603 Tyrone laid down his arms.

Tyrone's surrender completed the Tudor conquest of Ireland. He was treated generously and allowed to keep his lands, as were most of the other Irish lords, but they had to accept the suzerainty of the English crown. Their authority was slowly replaced by that of the English common law, supplemented by the conciliar Court of Castle Chamber in Dublin, but no change took place in religion. The stubborn Irish adherence to the old faith was to remain a perpetual challenge to English supremacy and a source of conflict in the future.

# SCOTLAND

## *James IV*

The principal difference between Scotland and Ireland in the sixteenth century was that Scotland had been for many years an independent country under the rule of its own kings. James IV, who came to the throne in 1488, was an ambitious ruler, determined that his country should play a more prominent role in European politics, and he seized on Perkin Warbeck as an instrument for this purpose. But if James hoped to make Warbeck a puppet king he was disappointed, and the failure of his attempted invasion of England encouraged him to come to terms with Henry VII. The truce of 1499 was extended into a 'perpetual peace' in 1502, and in the following year James married Henry's eldest daughter, Margaret.

Peace between the two kingdoms lasted for the rest of Henry's VII's reign, but the accession of the hot-blooded and ambitious Henry VIII in 1509 transformed the situation. Henry was contemptuous of the Scots and determined to take up again the struggle with France, to whom the Scots were bound by the 'auld alliance'. By 1512 England and France were at war, and Henry crossed the Channel to lead his armies in person, leaving the defence of England to the Earl of Surrey. In August 1513 James IV moved south, to attack the English in the rear, but Surrey had made good preparations. The two armies met at Flodden, southwest of Berwick, early in September, and in a battle that lasted well into the night the Scots were overwhelmed. James IV himself was killed, with the flower of the Scottish nobility and about ten thousand of his troops, and the northern kingdom was left in the hands of a boy king, James V.

## James V

Henry's sister, Queen Margaret, acted as regent for her young son, but in 1515 she was driven out of the country by the enemies of her second husband, the Earl of Angus. James's cousin, the Duke of Albany, who had recently arrived from France, was named as regent in her place. Henry VIII schemed for Albany's removal, since he did not want a francophil Scotland threatening him at a time when he was planning the renewal of his war against France. Throughout 1522 there was trouble along the border, and in the following year an English army carried out a number of punitive expeditions. Albany tried to rally the Scots lords and lead them against England, but fear of another Flodden paralysed effective action and in 1524 Albany returned, disgusted, to France. This left the way clear for Margaret and the anglophil group of lords who, in 1524, declared that James V was of age and therefore capable of ruling in his own right.

The Reformation did not have such a profound effect upon Anglo-Scottish relations as on those between England and Ireland, but it complicated the situation by making France the champion of Scottish catholics. Henry VIII had tried to persuade his Scottish nephew to join in the attack upon the Church, but James remained loyal to the old faith, particularly as he had been allowed to divert certain ecclesiastical revenues to secular purposes. In January 1537 he married a French princess, and after her untimely death he took as his second wife Mary, daughter of the Duke of Guise, the head of one of the greatest catholic houses in France. Henry VIII was faced with the unpleasant prospect of a francophil catholic kingdom on his northern frontier just at the moment when he was planning to invade France. Since persuasion had failed he had recourse to force, and in 1542 the Duke of Norfolk led a punitive expedition into Scotland. When the Scots counter-attacked in November 1542 they were heavily defeated at Solway Moss, and James, who was already ill, did not long survive the disgrace. In December he died, leaving as heir his baby daughter, Mary, only a week old, who now became Queen of Scots.

## English Intervention in Scotland

The death of James V brought to power the Earl of Arran, leader of the anglophil protestant party among the Scottish nobles. Henry saw an opportunity of extending Tudor sovereignty to Scotland, as he had already done to Wales and Ireland, and negotiations were set on foot for a marriage between Mary and Henry's heir, Prince Edward. These negotiations were successfully concluded in 1543, and the terms were formally set out in the Treaty of Greenwich. But this agreement, which implied the eventual subordination of Scotland to England, was deeply resented by the Scots, and Arran came under strong pressure to renounce it. Eventually he gave way, and admitted Cardinal Beaton, leader of the francophil, catholic party, to his council. Shortly afterwards the Treaty of Greenwich was denounced and the alliance with France reaffirmed.

Henry showed his fury at what he regarded as deception by sending Hertford with an army into Scotland, with orders to devastate the country. Hertford did his job well and left Edinburgh and Leith in flames behind him as he returned to England. The immediate effect of this vengeful policy was to close Scottish ranks against the aggressor, but the division between catholics and protestants was too deep to be permanently healed. John Knox was the leader of the protestants, whom he had imbued with his own particular brand of Calvinist fanaticism, and he looked to England for support. While an English fleet cruised off the Scottish coast the protestants could maintain themselves in power, but when, following Henry's death, the ships were withdrawn, the catholic party, supported by French arms, quickly triumphed. Knox himself was sent to the galleys and many of his followers were imprisoned.

Hertford, now Lord Protector Somerset, determined to retrieve the situation by a display of force. In September 1547 he invaded Scotland with an army of sixteen thousand men, supported by a powerful fleet, and routed the Scots at the battle of Pinkie. In order to solve the Scottish problem once and for all, he decided to station English garrisons in a number of key centres, so that they could serve as rallying-points for the protestant, anglophil elements among the population. At first this scheme worked well, but the cost of maintaining the garrisons was enormous: in two years Somerset spent £350,000 on military operations in Scotland, which was far more than the English Exchequer could afford. And the very success of his policy ensured its downfall by provoking French intervention. In July 1548 some 10,000 French troops landed in Scotland, occupied Edinburgh, and removed the young Queen Mary to France. The English garrisons came under increasing pressure, and eventually Somerset was compelled to withdraw them. For the next ten years Scotland remained under French control, particularly after 1554, when the queen mother, Mary of Guise, became regent. However, the appointment of Frenchmen to many of the highest positions in church and state created growing dissatisfaction, and many Scots came to detest the French so heartily that even the English seemed preferable.

The protestants were meanwhile increasing in numbers and strength, and they profited from their appeal to national pride, that 'the liberty of this our native country may remain free from the bondage and tyranny of strangers'. In 1557 the leading protestant nobles signed an agreement to set up 'The Congregation of Christ', to work for the establishment of the reformed religion in Scotland, and they were enormously strengthened when, in 1559, John Knox returned from exile.

By the time Knox came back a protestant sovereign was once again ruling in England. Elizabeth and her chief minister, William Cecil, might have ignored the appeal of their Scottish co-religionists had it not been that the political situation made English intervention imperative, for Mary, Queen of Scots, had been married to the Dauphin, who, in July 1559, ascended the throne as Francis II. It looked as though France and Scotland would now be united, and the danger to Elizabeth was increased by the fact that Mary was the catholic claimant to the English throne and had publicly asserted her rights.

In Scotland the queen-regent had decided to take action against the protestants who were a threat to her rule, but her military preparations drove the Lords of the Congregation to open rebellion. They occupied Edinburgh and appealed to England for help, while Mary of Guise remained in a strongly fortified position at Leith, waiting for French reinforcements to arrive. Urged on by Cecil, Elizabeth ordered an English fleet to cut the sea link between Scotland and France, and also issued instructions for assembling an army. By January 1560 the English fleet was anchored in the Forth, and a few months later an English army crossed the border. This English intervention was decisive, for it ensured the triumph of the protestants. By the terms of the Treaty of Edinburgh, signed in July 1560, both France and England agreed to withdraw their forces from Scotland and leave the religious question to be settled by the

Scottish Parliament. This body met in August and imposed the Reformation upon Scotland. The authority of the Pope was abolished, the celebration of mass was forbidden, and a protestant confession of faith was made the only authorised form of worship.

In December 1560 Francis II died, and in the following year his widow, Mary, returned to her Scottish kingdom. She found a very different situation from the one she had left twelve years before. Then the catholic Scots were fighting for their religion and their national independence against English invaders; now the French were regarded as the main threat to Scottish independence, and the government of the coutry was in the hands of the protestant, anglophil group. Mary, although a catholic, agreed to maintain the reformed religion, but the question of the queen's marriage was a major problem, as in England. The protestants were afraid that she would marry one of her own religion, and as Knox told the Scottish Parliament, 'whensoever the nobility of Scotland, professing the Lord Jesus, consents that an infidel — and all papists are infidels — shall be head to your sovereign, ye do so far as in ye lieth to banish Christ Jesus from this realm, ye bring God's vengeance upon the country, a plague upon yourself, and perchance ye shall do small comfort to your sovereign'.

Elizabeth was as anxious as Knox that Mary should marry a protestant, and put forward her own favourite, Robert Dudley, Earl of Leicester. Mary declared her willingness to marry Leicester if Elizabeth agreed to recognise her as heir to the English throne, but this was a condition that Elizabeth found totally unacceptable. The Queen of Scots therefore turned her attentions to Lord Darnley, who was, like herself, a great-grandchild of Henry VII. When the English Privy Council heard about this, it protested that a marriage between Mary and Darnley 'would be unmeet, unprofitable, and perilous to the amity between the queens and both realms', but once Mary was set on a course she never allowed political considerations to divert her. In July 1565, therefore, she married Darnley.

The protestant lords, led by the Earl of Moray and supported by Elizabeth, rose in rebellion against Mary, but the queen and her husband gathered their followers and chased the rebels across the border into England. The marriage, however, did not go well, for Darnley was insufferably arrogant and stupid, as Mary quickly discovered. She turned for comfort to her secretary, the Italian David Rizzio, who was rumoured to be her lover. Darnley, wounded in his pride, plotted with Mary's enemies, the protestant lords, who promised to accept him as king-consort if, in return, he would admit them to the council and get rid of Rizzio. The first part of the plan was put into operation in March 1566, when Darnley and his associates dragged Rizzio from the queen's presence and stabbed him to death. Shortly afterwards Moray and the exiles returned.

The queen never forgave Darnley, even though she dissembled her feelings. In June 1566 she gave birth to a son, Prince James; but there was no reconciliation between her and her husband. Instead, she drew closer to one of the protestant lords, the Earl of Bothwell, and it was at Bothwell's suggestion that Darnley, who had been ill, was sent to convalesce in a house called Kirk o'Field. In February 1567 the house was destroyed by a violent explosion, and Darnley was found, strangled, in the grounds. Public opinion assumed that Bothwell was responsible, but Mary showed her indifference by allowing the supposed murderer to abduct her. In May 1567 she and Bothwell (who had obtained a divorce from his wife) were married in a protestant ceremony at Edinburgh. By her actions Mary had forfeited public respect, and she was powerless in face of a rising of the protestant lords, led by Moray. In June 1567 she was captured and forced to abdicate in favour of her son, James. A year later she was a refugee in England, poised at the beginning of the long descent that was to bring her at last to Fotheringay and the scaffold.

## James VI

With Mary out of the way, Knox and the protestants consolidated their position. The structure of the Roman Catholic church was allowed to remain because the crown and aristocracy had succeeded in diverting part of its wealth into their own pockets. But all ministers were required, by 1573, to subscribe to a puritan confession of faith, and bishops, although still appointed by the crown, had to be approved by a panel of protestant ministers.

The mid-1570s saw the puritan movement enter a more intense phase in both England and Scotland. Knox died in 1572, but two years later Andrew Melville returned from Geneva and published his *Book of Discipline*. In this he went even further than the English puritans, by affirming that the Church was entirely independent of the state, responsible only to God, and bound to discipline the lay ruler if he transgressed. This was unacceptable to James, who held an exalted view of royal authority and certainly did not intend to be dictated to by puritan ministers.

James was inspired to take up the struggle against the puritan church — the Kirk — by Esmé Stuart, who arrived in Scotland in 1579 and quickly became the young king's favourite — the first of a long line. The influence of Stuart, whom James created Duke of Lennox, was resented not only by the Kirk but also by the protestant nobles who were afraid that James might be won over to catholicism. A plot was made, and successfully carried out, to kidnap James and hold him prisoner while Lennox was expelled. Not until June 1583 did James escape from captivity and re-establish his authority, by which time Lennox was dead.

The young king built up his position with great care and skill, and by 1584 he was ready to take the offensive. Melville and many puritan ministers fled to England to escape arrest on charges of treason, and a Parliament which met in that year passed the 'Black Acts', making the king head of the Church. The assemblies of the Kirk were not to meet without royal permission, nor were their decisions to be valid without royal approval. Government of the Church was to be in the hands of bishops appointed by the crown, and ministers were forbidden to discuss affairs of state from the pulpit.

James looked for support to Elizabeth, and in 1586 a treaty was concluded which gave the Scottish king a pension of £4,000 a year and bound the Queen to accept him as her successor, provided he did not, by some act of ingratitude, show himself to be unworthy of the English crown. James was certainly in need of the pension, for his own revenues were meagre, and at the time of his marriage to Anne of Denmark in 1589 one observer recorded that the king 'has neither plate nor stuff to furnish one of his little half-built houses, which are in great decay and ruin. His plate is not worth £100, he has only two or three rich jewels, his saddles are of plain cloth'. So anxious was James to preserve both the English pension and the right of succession that he made no protest when his mother, Mary, was executed. She had, in any case, played little part in his life since he was a baby, and the catholic claim to the throne, which she embodied, was just as much of a threat to James as to Elizabeth.

For the last ten years of his reign in Scotland James was occupied in consolidating his authority against the catholic earls, on the one hand, and the puritan Kirk, on the other. His aim was to exalt the royal dignity, as the Tudors had done in England, and make it the focus of national unity, but he met strong opposition from the leaders of the Kirk. The outspoken Andrew Melville, who had returned from exile in England, told the king that he was 'but God's silly vassal' and countered James's claim to supremacy with the assertion that 'there are two kings and two kingdoms in Scotland. There is Christ Jesus the king and His kingdom the Kirk, whose subject King James VI is, and of Whose kingdom not a king, nor a lord, nor a head, but a member'. Yet in spite of the determined opposition of puritan ministers James gradually extended his control over the Church. He encouraged the moderates by holding general assemblies away from extremist Edinburgh, and in 1600 he appointed a number of bishops, who were given seats in Parliament even though they had no clear role in ecclesiastical government.

As Elizabeth's life drew to a close, James waited impatiently for the news of his accession. He left Scotland without real regret, for, as he told the Hampton Court Conference, he was happy to be in 'the promised land, where religion was purely professed, where he sat among grave, learned and reverend men — not, as before, elsewhere, a king without state, without honour, without order, where beardless boys would brave him to his face'.

# 8

# Elizabeth I and the Church of England

## Elizabeth I

Elizabeth was an attractive young woman of twenty-five when she came to the throne. She was no classical beauty — her nose was too pronounced and her hair was reddish rather than golden — but she had character and intelligence as well as a commanding personality, and she knew how to charm men to her service. She was also well educated, for her tutors, John Cheke and Roger Ascham, had given her a good grounding in the classics and divinity as well as in several modern languages. And yet she was no pedant. The liveliness of her wit and the sharpness of her tongue were to become famous, and her speeches are models of their kind — involved and convoluted in the manner of the day, but full of salty comments and passages of magnificent rhetoric.

Elizabeth had inherited her father's exalted conception of the nature of kingship, and believed that God had made her head of the body politic so that she might guide her subjects into the right paths. Like her half-sister, Mary, she was proud and stubborn, but she had an ebullient self-assurance that the late Queen had never known, and the Spanish ambassador reported, two weeks after Elizabeth's accession, that 'she seems to me incomparably more feared than her sister was, and she gives her orders and has her way as absolutely as her father did'.

The Queen's advisers assumed that she would quickly marry, but this was not Elizabeth's intention. One reason for this was that all the time she remained single she could use the prospect of her marriage as a trump card in the game of diplomacy, to be brought out when hostile coalitions were threatening her. Another, and more powerful, reason was her reluctance to share power with a husband, for as the Scots ambassador told her, 'ye think that if ye were married ye would be but Queen of England, and now ye are King and Queen both. Ye may not suffer a commander'.

Elizabeth did, in fact, come near to marriage with Robert Dudley, son of the Duke of Northumberland and grandson of Henry VII's notorious minister. But Dudley was already married, and although this impediment was removed in September 1560 when Amy Robsart, his wife, was found dead in her house at Cumnor Place, the rumours of Dudley's complicity were too widespread for Elizabeth to ignore. She continued to love Dudley, and in October 1562, when she was lying desperately ill with smallpox and was not expected to recover, she recommended his nomination as Lord Protector of the Realm. But when she recovered she did not marry him.

Her illness brought the question of the succession into prominence. The Queen's early death would almost certainly have been followed by a disputed succession, for the obvious heir, Mary Stuart, had been married to the King of France, England's enemy, and was also a Roman Catholic. It was doubtful whether the leading English protestants would have accepted another catholic ruler after their experience of Mary Tudor's reign, but they wanted, above all, to put an end to uncertainty by persuading the Queen to nominate her successor. Elizabeth, however, would not do this. She had had experience of being a 'second person' herself in Mary's reign, and knew how intrigues sprang up around the heir to the throne. She also knew 'the inconstancy of the people of England, how they ever mislike the present government and have their eyes fixed upon that person that is next to succeed'. Her attitude was selfish, for she had to gamble on staying alive long enough for the succession problem to solve itself. The gamble paid off, but there was no reason why it should have done so. The early Parliaments of her reign had good reason, in fact, for their repeated requests that she should either marry or nominate a successor.

## The Religious Settlement

Elizabeth's inclinations in religion are suggested by the fact that she retained the silver crucifix and candles in her own chapel, and no doubt she would have liked cathedrals and parish churches throughout the land to follow her example. But there were two major restrictions upon her freedom of action. The first consisted of the group of Cambridge graduates, principal among them William Cecil, to whom she turned for advice, for they were committed protestants, who wanted to establish a truly reformed church in England, taking as their foundation stone the 1552 Prayer Book. The second was made up of the former exiles, who flooded back into England as soon as they heard the news of Mary's death. These covered a wide spectrum of religious opinions, within a protestant framework. Those who had settled at Geneva, and had come under the direct influence of Calvin, would have liked to see all remaining elements of popery swept away, including much of the ecclesiastical hierarchy as well as the vestments and ceremonies that the Edwardian Church had retained. Other exiles were more moderate in their approach. The Frankfurt group had looked for guidance to Richard Cox, who had assisted Cranmer in drawing up the Prayer Book and therefore had a personal commitment to it. Yet all the exiles, now that they had felt the impact of the continental Reformation at first hand, wished to go beyond the 1552 Book. Even the 'Coxians' at Frankfurt had modified their adherence to it in certain matters which they regarded as 'indifferent'. They abandoned the wearing of surplices, for instance, and they ignored saints' days. They also took communion seated, instead of kneeling, and they gave up the practice of signing with the cross in baptism. No matter what her own views were, Elizabeth could not possibly ignore those of the returned exiles, for these men were the cream of English protestants, whose knowledge, ability and, above all, passionate commitment, would be invaluable in creating a reformed church in England.

On the other hand Elizabeth also had to take into account the conservative attitude of the Marian bishops, who were entrenched in Convocation and the House of Lords. Furthermore, she was in a weak position diplomatically, for Mary had left her a legacy of an unsuccessful war with France and a depleted Exchequer. Elizabeth could not afford, at this stage, to antagonise the catholic powers, particularly Spain. Not until March 1559, when she heard that peace had been concluded at Câteau-Cambrésis, was she free to press ahead with her plans for restoring protestant worship.

In the event, the Elizabethan Church of England, as it was established by the Acts of Supremacy and Uniformity in 1559, was probably very close to what Elizabeth and her advisers had all along intended. The authorised form of worship, prescribed by the Act of Uniformity, was based on the 1552 Prayer Book, but included a number of changes designed to make it acceptable to moderates, and even, it was hoped, to catholics. The *Black Rubric*, for instance, was dropped, as was the petition to be delivered 'from the Bishop of Rome and all his detestable enormities', while in the communion service the wording of the first Prayer Book, which implied the real presence, was added to the commemorative phrases of the second Book. Perhaps most important of all, for its short-term consequences, was the clause in the Act of Uniformity which insisted that 'such ornaments of the Church and of the ministers thereof shall be retained and be in use as was in the Church of England by authority of Parliament in the second year of the reign of King Edward the Sixth'. This harmless-sounding provision — to which Elizabeth attached so much importance that, according to Archbishop Parker, without it she would not have accepted the amended Book — was a calculated blow at the Genevans. It meant that all clergy were now obliged to wear a surplice for ordinary church services, and — most galling of all to the extremists — 'a white alb plain, with a vestment or cope' for the administration of the holy communion.

The Act of Supremacy restored royal control over the Church, although Elizabeth was described as 'Supreme Governor of this realm ... as well in all spiritual or ecclesiastical things or causes as temporal' — a sop to those who believed that a woman could not be 'Supreme Head' of the Church. The change in wording was not the only difference between the Henrician and Elizabethan supremacies. Henry VIII's headship of the Church had merely been 'revealed' by Parliament, since it was deemed to be inherent in his position as King. But the Act of Supremacy of 1559, in restoring control over the Church to the crown, did so 'by the authority of this present Parliament', and the same authority was invoked in the Act of Uniformity, to prescribe the use of the new Prayer Book. All office-holders were required to take an oath accepting the supremacy, and the principle of compulsion was also applied in the Uniformity Act, where it was laid down that all the Queen's subjects should attend their parish church on Sundays and holy days, on pain of a shilling fine for every absence.

When the oath of supremacy was administered to the bishops, all but one refused to take it, even though they included men such as Bonner and Tunstall who had, in their younger days, accepted Henry's claim to headship over the Church. The bishops had to be replaced, but parish priests offered little resistance, and out of a total of about 8,000 only some 300 were deprived of their livings. This did not mean, of course, that all those who took the oath were genuinely committed to the new regime. Passive acceptance and outward conformity were all that the government insisted upon, and in 1566 the Dean of Durham complained that 'many people enjoy liberty and livings who have neither sworn obedience to the Queen nor yet do any part of their duty towards their miserable flocks'.

The returned émigrés, who had looked forward to building a new Jerusalem in their native land, found the Elizabethan compromise far from satisfactory, since it preserved many practices which they regarded with abhorrence. Yet Elizabeth needed the co-operation of these men, since only with their enthusiasm, purified and hardened by years of exile, could she build a really strong Church in England. They, similarly, felt the need to serve in the new Church, for fear that if they stayed out they would leave the door open for the catholic wolf to come in. Most of the émigrés eventually decided, as Grindal wrote several years later, 'not to desert our churches for the sake of a few ceremonies — and those not unlawful in themselves'. Grindal himself became Bishop of London, while other returned exiles were appointed to the sees of Ely, Worcester, Winchester and Durham. It was perhaps to counter this continen-

tal influence that Elizabeth chose as Archbishop Matthew Parker
who had spent Mary's reign in hiding in England. Parker, now over
fifty, was a link with the early days of the Reformation — he had
been a member of the 'Little Germany' group at Cambridge — and
he epitomised that continuity of the reformed tradition which was
lacking among the exiles.

## William Cecil

Cambridge provided the Queen not only with her Archbishop but
also with her chief secular adviser, for in one of the first actions of
her reign she appointed William Cecil, now thirty-eight years old,
as her principal Secretary. Cecil came from a family that had made
its way in the world by service to the crown. His grandfather, a
Welshman, had fought for Henry Tudor at Bosworth, and his
father held a minor position in the court of Henry VIII. The Cecils
were not numbered among the great families of medieval England:
they were new to power — as new as the Tudors — but they had
established themselves as country gentlemen at Stamford in Lincolnshire and were moving into the upper levels of society.

Cecil entered Parliament in 1543, when he was only twenty-one,
and was sufficiently well known by the time Henry VIII died to
be chosen by Somerset as his private secretary. At Somerset's fall
he was imprisoned for a time but he transferred his allegiance to
Northumberland, and received his reward in the shape of a knighthood, large grants of crown lands, and formal appointment as one
of the two Secretaries of State. He managed to survive Northumberland's fall, but gave up the Secretaryship after Mary's accession
and lived in semi-retirement, superintending the building of his
great house at Stamford. He kept in touch with Princess Elizabeth,
however, and when she came to the throne Cecil resumed his role
as Secretary. The Queen, when she appointed him to this key office,
told him: 'this judgment I have of you, that you will not be corrupted by any manner of gift, and that you will be faithful to the
state, and that without respect of my private will you will give me
the counsel which you think best'; and although in the early years
of the reign Cecil could not take Elizabeth's confidence in him for
granted, he soon established a close relationship with her that
lasted until his death.

Cecil might well have been appointed Lord Treasurer, had it not
been for the survival of the Marquis of Winchester, who had held
this office since 1550. Winchester had been involved in plans to
restore the currency, and he supervised the recoinage which was
carried out in 1561. This removed one of the elements contributing
to inflation, and it established Elizabethan public finances upon a
sound footing.

## Puritan Attempts to Modify the Religious Settlement

Although there were a number of features of the Elizabethan religious settlement which were unpalatable from the point of view
of the returned exiles — and, for that matter, of many people of similar persuasion who had remained in England during Mary's reign
— there was a widespread assumption that they were merely a
matter of form and would not, in practice, be insisted upon. When
Convocation met in 1563 a group of puritan ministers introduced
articles designed to eliminate these features. They called for the
abandonment of holy days, other than Sundays and the principal
feasts, and the removal of organs from churches. They argued that
ceremonies such as kneeling to receive communion and signing
with the cross in baptism should be left to the discretion of the
minister, and that compulsory vestments should be confined to the
surplice, which they regarded as relatively harmless. These articles,
however, were rejected by the lower house of Convocation —
though only by the narrow margin of fifty-nine votes to fifty-
eight — and at the same time the puritans came under increasing pressure to obey the rules of the Church to which they
belonged.

Elizabeth was determined to enforce conformity. 'We will have
no dissension or variety', she informed Archbishop Parker, 'for so
the sovereign authority which we have under Almighty God
would be made frustrate and we might be thought to bear the
sword in vain.' At her insistence Parker and four of his colleagues
drew up a list of minimum requirements, to which he demanded
the assent of his clergy. When the Queen refused to give these her
official sanction — for she always preferred to shift the blame for
unpopular measures on to someone else's shoulders — he issued
them on his own authority, in 1565, as a *Book of Advertisements*. In
this *Book* he did not insist on the use of eucharistic vestments, except in cathedral and collegiate churches, but he required all clergy
to wear a surplice for services and a long black gown and square
cap for everyday wear.

Parker probably assumed that these moderate requirements
would be generally acceptable, but he had reckoned without the
more extreme puritans. Thirty-four London ministers refused to
wear the prescribed vestments, and were subsequently deprived of
their livings. Some took refuge in more distant parts of England,
where they spread the infection of non-conformity, but the majority
joined the underground of unbeneficed, itinerant preachers who,
because they held no official position, were not amenable to episcopal discipline. In other words the *Book of Advertisements*, which
had been designed to unite the clergy under the firm leadership of
the bishops, had the contrary effect of creating a movement of rad-

ical dissent which was to develop into a major challenge to the ecclesiastical hierarchy.

The hostile reaction to the *Book of Advertisements* was not confined to the clergy. Congregations of churches whose minister had been deprived did not sit quietly back and accept a conforming replacement. Disturbances were reported in a number of London parishes, and even more alarming, from the point of view of the authorities, was the action of some hundred 'godly' citizens who separated from the Church altogether and held private meetings at which they used the Genevan Book. These people were not separatists on principle, but they were determined to withhold recognition from a Church which insisted on what they regarded as popish observances. As one of their spokesmen explained to Edmund Grindal, Bishop of London: 'When it came to this point, that all our preachers were displaced by your law, that would not subscribe to your apparel and your law, so that we could hear none of them in any church by the space of seven or eight weeks . . . and then were we troubled and commanded to your courts from day to day, for not coming to our parish churches: then we bethought us what were best to do; and we remembered that there was a congregation of us in this city in Queen Mary's days, and a congregation at Geneva'.

The effect of the Vestments Controversy was to change the attitude of the more extreme puritans towards episcopacy. Just as monarchical power, which the early reformers had elevated as a protection against papal claims, had come to be regarded as an impediment to further reform, so the authority of bishops was now challenged. 'What talk they', wrote one pamphleteer, 'of their being beyond the seas in Queen Mary's days because of the persecution, when they in Queen Elizabeth's days are come home to raise a persecution?' The reply to this was given by Pilkington, who had been a prominent member of the congregation of exiles at Frankfurt and was now Bishop of Durham. 'We are under authority', he said, 'and can innovate nothing without the Queen: nor can we alter the laws. The only thing left to our choice is whether we will bear these things or break the peace of the Church.'

Pilkington was himself a puritan, in the sense that he would have liked to strip the Church of its remaining popish traces. So was Grindal, another former exile, and so, in fact, were many, if not most, members of the ecclesiastical hierarchy. They differed from the radicals in their attitude towards the royal supremacy, for they were prepared to agree that vestments and other 'outward signs' were *adiaphora*, 'matters indifferent', to be regulated by the lay power. They also had a greater respect for the historical traditions of the English church and were not prepared to advocate innovation for its own sake. As Grindal told the members of the London separatist congregation: 'in this severing yourselves from the society of other Christians you condemn not only us but also the whole state of the Church reformed in King Edward's days . . . There be good men and good martyrs that did wear these things in King Edward's days. Do you condemn them?'

The more stiff-necked puritans defended their attitude on the grounds that if vestments and ceremonies were 'matters indifferent' their acceptance should be left to the individual conscience. Behind this difference of opinion was a more fundamental divergence of views about the nature of the Church: should it be self-governing, or should it be subject to the secular ruler? This issue was brought into the open by the lectures delivered at Cambridge in 1570 by Thomas Cartwright, the Lady Margaret Professor of Divinity.

Cartwright, who was only in his mid-thirties, represented a new generation of Elizabethan puritans, who took the achievements of their predecessors for granted and wished to push forward from the positions that they had established. Cartwright declared that the structure of the Church of England was contrary to that prescribed by Scripture, and that the correct model was that which Calvin had established at Geneva. Every congregation should elect its own ministers in the first instance, and control of the Church should be in the hands of a local presbytery, consisting of the minister and the elders of the congregation. The authority of archbishops and bishops had no foundation in the Bible, and was therefore unacceptable. Cartwright's definition lifted the puritan movement out of its obsession with details and threw down a challenge which the established Church could not possibly ignore. The counter-attack was led by John Whitgift, Master of Trinity College and Regius Professor of Divinity in the university. With the support of William Cecil, Cambridge's chancellor, Whitgift amended the constitution of the university in such a way that the heads of colleges, who were less given to radical views, became the effective rulers. They deprived Cartwright of his chair in December 1570, and the puritan spokesman left, appropriately enough, for Geneva.

Cartwright's expulsion did not mean an end to puritan pressure, for he had only put into clear terms what many people had long been thinking. As far as the London puritans were concerned, they looked for inspiration to the Calvinist churches set up in the capital by foreign congregations. The Huguenot church was particularly important in this respect, since it was frequented by John Field, an unbeneficed preacher who was to become a major figure in the puritan movement and act as a link between the puritan ministers and their supporters in Parliament. Puritan M.P.s had missed their opportunity to press for further changes in the religious settlement during the course of the 1566 session, because they were preoccupied with the question of the Queen's marriage and the succession, but by the time another Parliament met, in 1571, they were ready with their programme. Walter Strickland introduced a Bill designed to reform the Prayer Book by eliminating from it all those features which the puritans found unpalatable. This was a clear invasion of the Queen's prerogative, and the Councillors in the Commons advised the House to go no further. But they were up against men who would let nothing stand in the way of religious truth: such matters, said one member, were God's — 'the rest are all but terrene, yea trifles in comparison'. Strickland was summoned before the Privy Council and ordered to absent himself from the House, but members raised such an outcry against what they claimed was an infringement of their privilege of free speech that he was quickly restored to them.

Field and his clerical associates had no parliamentary privilege to protect them. They were summoned before the ecclesiastical commissioners whom Elizabeth had appointed to exercise the royal supremacy, and instructed to accept the Prayer Book in its entirety and to wear the prescribed vestments. Field refused, and was therefore forbidden to preach. He now had to earn his living as a schoolmaster, but this severe treatment goaded him to even greater efforts, and he set to work on an *Admonition to Parliament* which was designed as an appeal to the country at large and not simply to members of the Lords and Commons. In the *Admonition* Field openly attacked the system of government of the Church of England and set out the ground-plan of a presbyterian structure. As for the Elizabethan Prayer Book, this, he declared, was 'an unperfect Book, culled and picked out of that popish dunghill, the Mass Book, full of abominations'. Field was summoned before the Lord Mayor of London and sentenced to a year's imprisonment for his temerity, but this did not prevent the circulation of the *Admonition* and the widespread dissemination of Field's views.

The older generation of puritans was shocked by Field's intemperance. Anthony Gilby, for instance — a former exile who, as minister of Ashby-de-la-Zouch, had become one of the most celebrated puritan divines in England — gave it as his opinion that 'openly to publish such admonitions as are abroad I like not, for that in some points and terms they are too broad and overshoot themselves'. John Foxe, the martyrologist, would have nothing to do with the *Admonition*, and even Theodore Beza, Calvin's successor at Geneva, thought it 'indiscreet'. Many people who might otherwise have supported Field were afraid to do so after the Northern Rising of 1569 (see below, p. 177) and the publication of the papal bull of deposition in 1570, for any weakening of the Church of England at this stage seemed likely to play into the hands of the catholics. The views of Sir Thomas Norton M.P. are particularly interesting in this respect, for although he had translated Calvin's *Institutes* into English he had no wish to see a presbyterian church established in England. He believed that the existing Church should be revitalised, so that it could carry on the fight against the catholic enemy, and far from opposing the establishment, he preferred to work in collaboration with the Privy Council, most of whose members shared his moderate puritan attitudes. In other words, while Field spoke for the radical puritans, who were unwilling to accept the compromises involved in maintaining the Church of England as established by law, Norton and those who thought like him represented the broad range of moderate puritan opinion which, while recognising the defects of the established Church and wishing to remedy them, saw its task as that of strengthening, rather than undoing, the Elizabethan settlement. Field and his followers made the most noise, but in the long run it was the silent majority of conforming puritans who determined the future of the Church in England.

Thomas Cartwright, who returned to England in late 1572, went to see Field in prison and demonstrated his support for him by writing and publishing a pamphlet which he called *A Second Admonition*. This brought Whitgift back into the fray, and in the ensuing pamphlet war both Cartwright and Whitgift further defined their positions. Cartwright was not a separatist. He accepted the need for a state church and was prepared to tolerate the royal supremacy, but he believed that the English church had been wrongly constructed and needed radical alteration to bring it closer to the presbyterian model set out in the Scriptures. Whitgift's argument was that the Bible, while containing everything that was necessary for salvation, did not lay down any blueprint of Church government, and that Cartwright, whatever his stated intention, was undermining the Queen's authority. This was also the view of the ecclesiastical commissioners, who summoned Cartwright to appear before them in December 1573. Cartwright preferred discretion to valour, however, and avoided imprisonment by going into exile once again.

The initiation of proceedings against Cartwright was one of a number of indications in late 1573 that the secular and ecclesiastical authorities were mounting a counter-attack against the puritan extremists. At the time of the publication of the *Admonition* the bishops had felt depressed and isolated, and Edmund Sandys, the Archbishop of York, had declared that 'our estimation is little, our authority less, so that we are become contemptible in the eyes of the basest sort of people'. Elizabeth stood firm, however. She detested puritans, whom she described as 'greater enemies to her than the papists', and she was probably responsible for a proclamation issued in October which threatened imprisonment for anyone defaming the Prayer Book. In consequence there was a period of relative calm, which lasted for several years and provided an opportunity for the moderate, conforming puritans to reassert their leadership. Their moment of triumph came in December 1575 when, following the death of Parker, the Queen took Cecil's advice and appointed Edmund Grindal as Archbishop of Canterbury. Grindal had been a pupil of Bucer at Cambridge and had therefore, in Mary's reign, gone into exile at Strasburg. He was anxious to 'purify' the Church of England but not to remodel it, and he believed, like Bucer, that obnoxious features such as ceremonies and vestments would gradually disappear of their own accord and were not worth fighting over. He was, in short, a moderate, conforming puritan, but the opponent of radicals, presbyterians and separatists.

One of the major weaknesses of the Church was the low standard of education of many of its clergy, and Grindal's determination to remedy this led him to encourage the 'Prophesyings' which had sprung up in many parts of England. These consisted of meetings of ministers at which a learned preacher, acting as moderator, would lead the way in the analysis and exposition of a scriptural text. Prophesyings were highly popular with the laity, and the audiences would cover a wide cross-section of the local population. Where bishops took the lead in arranging prophesyings, and appointed the moderator, these meetings could serve to strengthen and revivify the Church; but many of the learned preachers were puritans, whose sympathies lay with Cartwright and Field rather than with the moderates. This alarmed Elizabeth, who believed, with some justification, that prophesyings could be the first step in the creation of a presbyterian system, and she therefore ordered Grindal to suppress them.

Grindal was understandably appalled by this directive, particularly when the Queen added her opinion that three or four preaching ministers were enough for any county. Prophesyings, he protested, were 'both profitable to increase knowledge among the ministers and tendeth to the edifying of the hearers', and he could not, therefore, 'with safe conscience and without the offence of the majesty of God give my assent to the suppressing of the said exercises'. Elizabeth responded to this act of defiance by sending direct instructions to the bishops in May 1577 that they were to put down these 'disputatious and new-devised opinions upon points of divinity far unmeet for vulgar people', and in the following month she took the unprecedented step of suspending the Archbishop from office. Since Grindal refused to resign, and the Queen was, with difficulty, dissuaded from dismissing him, he remained in limbo until his death six years later. It was a tragic conclusion to an archiepiscopate that had promised to unify the Church of England under moderate puritan leadership, and it seemed to prove the contention of the extremists that radical, structural change was essential.

Some people were already asking themselves why an individual should submit to the authority of either bishop or presbyter. Such an attitude was implicit in protestantism, which took its impetus from the revolt of individual conscience against an organised Church, and even in the early days of the Reformation there had been radical groups, like the Anabaptists, to whom the authoritarianism of Luther and Calvin was just as repellent as that of the Pope. There were Anabaptists in England, but they were few in number and of little influence. The handful of separatist congregations that did emerge, mainly in London, did so in revolt against the imposition of conformity, and found their inspiration in Lollard traditions and the memory of the 'privy churches' set up by protestants in Mary's reign. However, two Cambridge men, Robert Browne and Robert Harrison, came to believe that separate, 'gathered' congregations of the elect were the only true churches, and they put their ideas into practice in the diocese of Norwich. Repressive action by the bishop drove the two men and their followers into exile in Holland, and it was there, in 1582, that Browne wrote his *Treatise of Reformation without Tarrying for Any*. In this he proclaimed that every congregation was self-sufficient and did not need any form of central guidance or authority. The anglican church was, he declared, hopelessly corrupt, its ministers 'turned back after babbling prayers and toying worship . . . after popish attire and foolish disguising, after fastings, tithings, holy days and a thousand more abominations', and the presbyterians were just as bad. Browne's teaching, with its undertones of anarchy, was anathema to the government, and in 1583 two members of his sect were hanged for treason since they denied the royal supremacy. Browne himself was eventually reconciled to the anglican church, and spent the remaining forty years of his life as a country parson. But from his protest was to grow that tough and individualistic form of puritan 'Independency' that reached its apogee in the mid-seventeenth century.

By the early 1580s the anglican church had come of age and was no longer the temporary expedient it had seemed to be when Elizabeth ascended the throne. It had found able defenders, among them Bishop Jewel who, in his *Apology* — written at Cecil's suggestion, and published in 1562 — maintained that it was a true Church and not merely a compromise between two extremes. Even among the bishops there was far less inclination towards puritanism after the generation of Marian exiles died out. The new men, such as John Aylmer who became Bishop of London in 1577, were committed upholders of the royal supremacy and fully shared the Queen's determination to maintain the settlement of 1559. They were not necessarily hostile to Calvinism, but they did not regard Geneva as being any more infallible than Rome. As Whitgift said, later in the century, 'I reverence Mr Calvin as a singular man and worthy instrument in Christ's church, but I am not so wholly addicted unto him that I will condemn other men's judgments that in divers points agree not fully with him, especially in the interpretation of some places of the Scripture, when as, in my opinion, they come nearer to the true meaning and sense of it in those points than he doth'.

## Whitgift

On the death of Grindal in 1583, Whitgift was appointed Archbishop of Canterbury, and for the rest of Elizabeth's reign he devoted himself to defending the Church of England not simply against puritans and catholics but also against the laity, who had already stripped it of much of its wealth and hoped to grab more. At the parish level, priests were supposed to be maintained by tithes, paid either in kind or cash by their parishioners. During the course of the middle ages, however, the right of presentation to many livings had been given to monasteries, which appointed either one of their own number or a curate and appropriated the tithes for their own benefit. At the Dissolution these impropriate tithes were transferred to the new owners of monastic property, which meant that about a third of all the tithes paid throughout England now went to lay patrons who passed on only a small proportion to the actual incumbents. The anglican church, as Grindal told Elizabeth, had been 'spoiled of the livings which at the first were appointed to the offices of preaching and teaching . . . so as at this day, in my opinion, where one church is able to yield sufficient living for a learned preacher, there be at least seven churches unable to do the same'.

The Queen treated the bishops much as her wealthy subjects treated the lesser clergy, and although the plunder of the Church was carried out more discreetly than it had been under Northumberland, the result was the same. An Act passed in the first year of Elizabeth's reign gave the Queen the temporalities of vacant sees, as well as the right to exchange crown property for episcopal lands, and the temptation to hold up appointments so as to pocket the profits was too great to resist. The diocese of Oxford was without a bishop for over forty years, Ely for nineteen and Bristol for fourteen, and even when bishops were at last appointed they were often forced to exchange some of their more valuable lands for scattered royal manors or for impropriate tithes, which were difficult to collect and caused much hostility. The Queen and a small group of courtiers were the main beneficiaries: the Earl of Oxford, for instance, had £1,000 a year out of the bishopric of Oxford, while the coal-bearing lands of the bishopric of Durham were leased by the Queen and the Earl of Leicester to Thomas Sutton, who, in spite of the high rent he had to pay, made enough money to found the London Charterhouse.

Not surprisingly the value of bishoprics declined. Durham, which had been worth £2,800 in 1535, was valued at £1,800 forty years later, while Lincoln dropped from nearly £2,000 to under £900. The bishops, as individuals, often did well out of their depleted estates, which they treated as if they were personal property. Archbishop Parker, for instance, had a gross income of £3,000 a year — well above the average for lay peers — and was usually attended by seventy retainers when he went on progress. Yet at the bottom of the ecclesiastical hierarchy many parish priests and curates had to live on inadequate tithes or such sums as their patron made available. It was hardly to be wondered at that the quality of anglican clergy at the beginning of Elizabeth's reign was very poor, for ambitious young men, as one clergyman observed, 'when they look upon our contempt and beggary and vexation, turn to law, to physic, to trades, or anything rather than they will enter into this contemptible calling'.

Whitgift realised that reform was needed, but believed that it must be done gradually, so as not to shake the structure of the Church at a time when its opponents were waiting to dismantle it. The abuses, however undesirable, had something to be said for them. Impropriated tithes, for instance, swelled the revenues of bishops and university colleges, and pluralism did at least free the occupants of benefices from an obsession with getting their daily bread. A complete overhaul of ecclesiastical finances was needed, but only Parliament and the Queen were strong enough to carry this out, and these were the big property-owners, the very people who had a vested interest in maintaining the existing state of affairs. Whitgift therefore advised caution: 'the temporalty will not lose one jot of their commodity in any respect to better the livings of the Church. And therefore let us keep that we have. For better we shall not be. We may be worse, and that, I think, by many is intended.'

Whitgift chose Convocation as his instrument for reform from within the Church, and this body passed a number of decrees designed to improve the educational standard of the clergy and to limit the impact of pluralism. Bishops were instructed to conduct regular examinations of the clergy for whom they were responsible and to ensure that they had a good knowledge of the Scriptures. They were also required to subject candidates for ordination to careful scrutiny in order to keep out of the ministry those who were not fitted for it. As for non-residence, which was one of the worst consequences of pluralism, the 1589 Convocation decreed that all ministers holding one living should be resident in their parish, while those with two should split their time between them. If any minister had good reason to be absent, he should appoint a curate to carry out his duties.

The defence of the Church against lay assault required, in Whitgift's view, a united and conforming clergy. In 1583, therefore, he instructed all ministers formally to subscribe to the statement that the Prayer Book 'containeth nothing in it contrary to the word of God'. This aroused a storm of protest, and pressure from Cecil, among others, persuaded the reluctant Whitgift to allow ministers to subscribe that they accepted the Prayer Book in so far as it was compatible with the Scriptures. However, even this modified affirmation was too much for the more committed puritans. Some three or four hundred ministers refused to subscribe, but in the event only a handful of them were deprived of their livings. The fact that the vast majority of clergy made the affirmation shows that they put the unity of the Church above whatever scruples of conscience they may have had, and this same consideration persuaded Whitgift to treat the rebels leniently. Yet by taking such a firm stand on the Prayer Book issue Whitgift widened the gap between the episcopate on the one hand and the many hundreds of moderate puritan clergy on the other. In the long run the unity of the Church, which he was so anxious to maintain, might have been more effectively preserved by allowing a greater degree of divergence of opinion within the ministry.

From early in her reign the Queen had appointed ecclesiastical commissioners, including laymen as well as clerics, to exercise the royal governorship over the Church, and these had developed into autonomous Courts of High Commission, one for the province of Canterbury and another for that of York. Under Whitgift the southern High Commission, which was based in London, became the principal instrument for the enforcement of conformity, since it could deal with all matters affecting the Church — except where property rights were involved – and could impose fines and imprisonment as well as the spiritual penalties (mainly excommunication) to which Church courts were confined. However, the enforcement of conformity by the Court of High Commission aroused protests from puritan gentry and clergy in the southern, midland and eastern counties, and the Council summoned Whitgift to appear before it early in 1584 to answer charges made against him.

The Archbishop, aware of his dignity and of the need to resist lay control, declined to appear, but he modified his tactics in face of the opposition against him, and introduced the *ex officio* oath. . This gave any officer of the Church the right 'by virtue of his office' to question a man, on oath, about his beliefs. The common lawyers, who tended to be sympathetic to the puritans and in any case resented the High Commission as an upstart tribunal, challenged the validy of the *ex officio* oath on the grounds that a man should not be compelled to incriminate himself; but it was eventually decided, in Cawdrey's case in 1591, that the authority and procedures of the High Commission, deriving as they did from the royal supremacy, were legitimate. Whitgift meanwhile pressed ahead with his investigations, suspending as many as forty-five ministers in a single day in Suffolk.

The puritan sympathisers in the Privy Council kept up their criticism of Whitgift's policy. Sir Francis Knollys, for instance, who was the Queen's cousin and Treasurer of the Household, told William Cecil, now Lord Burghley, how much it grieved him 'to see the zealous preachers of the gospel, sound in doctrine (who are the most diligent barkers against the popish wolf to save the fold and flock of Christ) to be persecuted and put to silence'. Burghley was sufficiently impressed by this complaint to write to the Archbishop in similar terms, asserting the the *ex officio* oath was 'too much savouring of the Romish Inquisition'. Whitgift, however, refused to be deflected from his course, for he regarded opposition to him as proof not that he was acting harshly but that his predecessors had been too lenient and thereby weakened the Church. His suspicion of puritan activities was not without justification, for even before he was appointed Archbishop the presbyterian movement was making headway once again. In October 1582, for instance, a group of ministers from around the Essex village of Dedham decided to hold regular conferences to consider religious matters and to keep a record of their deliberations. These meetings, unlike the earlier prophesyings, were confined to clergy and held, with the minimum of publicity, in private houses. The Dedham group constituted, in presbyterian terms, a *classis*, and could be seen as the first step in setting up a presbyterian sub-structure within the English church.

Dedham's example was not widely or immediately followed, but in many parts of south-east and central England puritan ministers were establishing closer contact and co-ordinating their activities. This tendency to self-help on the part of the puritans was given additional impetus after the failure of the 1585 Parliament to secure further reform of the Church. Members of that Parliament had been hoping to goad the Queen into taking effective action, but Elizabeth had sent for the Speaker and ordered him to allow no debate on religious questions, since these fell within her sphere of authority as supreme governor. If members had any complaints, these were to be directed to the bishops or to her Councillors, or, in the last resort, to her herself, but 'she will receive no motion of innovation, nor alter or change any law whereby the religion or Church of England standeth established at this day'. The temper of the House was such that there were proposals to pass motions rejecting the Queen's command and censuring the Speaker for attending her without the

Commons' permission. These angry and extremist proposals came to nothing, but several Bills on Church matters did, in fact, pass through both Houses, and Whitgift had to appeal to the Queen to delay or veto them.

## The Classical Movement

By 1585 Cartwright was back in England, and he and Walter Travers — another Cambridge man, who had spent several years at Geneva, where he became a close friend of Beza — drew up a *Book of Discipline*, which was ready in time for a conference of puritan ministers that assembled in London at the time of the parliamentary session in 1586. This *Book* laid down the ground plan of a presbyterian organisation, or 'Discipline'. The smallest unit, the presbytery, consisted of a minister and a number of elected 'elders' or other officers. Next came the *classis*, consisting of representatives of several presbyteries. *Classes*, in turn, were to send delegates to provincial synods, from which would be chosen the members of the national synod, the governing body of the church. The big advantage of the 'Discipline' was that it was well thought out and provided a uniform pattern, instead of leaving each puritan congregation to make its own arrangements. In 1587 the 'Discipline' was set up in Northamptonshire, and two delegates from each of the three *classes* came together every six weeks or so to discuss matters of common concern. The *classes* themselves met every three weeks, and at the parish level congregations elected 'elders' to keep a watch over their moral lives and general behaviour.

The puritan leaders made elaborate preparations for the meeting of Parliament in 1586, and the increasing sophistication of their political techniques was shown by a letter which the head of the Dedham *classis* wrote to Field: 'I hope you have not let slip this notable opportunity of furthering the cause of religion by noting out all the places of government in the land for which burgesses for the Parliament are to be chosen, and using all the best means you can possibly for . . . procuring the best gentlemen of those places, by whose wisdom and zeal God's causes may be preferred.' Field also had ready a survey of the clergy in over two thousand five hundred parishes, covering London and the surrounding counties. This survey, which other evidence suggests is reasonably accurate, reported that in Essex, for example, over half the benefices were held by ignorant and unpreaching ministers. Many of the charges were based upon nothing more substantial than the fact that the minister in question did not live up to the puritan ideal — one was described as 'sometime a popish priest, a gross abuser of the scriptures' — but there was sufficient truth in the survey to make it a powerful indictment of the established church.

The 1587 Parliament contained a number of members who were committed to the establishment of a presbyterian system in England, and it was one of these, Anthony Cope, who acted as the spokesman of the radical puritans in the Commons. He introduced a Bill which would have abolished the Prayer Book, replaced it by the Genevan form of service, and swept away the entire ecclesiastical hierarchy. When the Speaker tried to hold up discussion of this highly provocative measure, another of the puritan radicals, Peter Wentworth, came to Cope's defence by putting to the Speaker a number of leading questions on the Commons' privilege of free speech, which he said should be immediately debated. The vigour of this puritan attack drove Elizabeth to stronger action than any she had hitherto taken. Cope, Wentworth and three other members were imprisoned, and the Speaker was commanded to prevent any consideration of religious matters. In fact the majority of the Commons were moderate rather than radical puritans, and they therefore gave a sympathetic hearing to Sir Christopher Hatton — one of the Privy Councillors in the House, and a man who was known to stand close to the Queen — when he led a counter-attack, pointing out that a presbyterian system would mean the establishment of a theocracy in which landowners' rights of patronage would be endangered. Yet there was a strong feeling in the Commons that continuing abuses within the Church should no longer be tolerated. A committee was set up to consider proposals for improving the educational standard of the clergy and for curbing the use of the *ex officio* oath. But Elizabeth again intervened and, insisting that the government of the Church was a matter for the royal prerogative alone, stopped any further discussion.

The puritans, blocked in Parliament, were forced back on self-help. As Field said, 'seeing we cannot compass these things by suit nor dispute, it is the multitude and people that must bring the "Discipline" to pass which we desire'. The *classes*, however, were divided. The radical puritans made a lot of noise, but they were thin on the ground. The Dedham *classis*, for example, had a total membership of only twenty ministers during the course of its seven-year existence, and in Northamptonshire under half of the known nonconforming clergy were active in the 'Discipline'. At this critical moment, while the puritans were divided between radicals and moderates, the tide of events and opinion receded and left them stranded. The defeat of the Armada in 1588 reduced the catholic threat which had made patriotism and puritanism virtually synonymous, and in the same year John Field, the organising genius of radical puritanism, and the Earl of Leicester, one of the most influential of the moderate puritans, both died. Moreover, the 1580s saw a recrudescence of the separatist, or Independent, movement under Browne's successors, Henry Barrow and John Greenwood. Many puritans now feared that if they resorted to *de facto* separation from the anglican church they would merely encourage the growth of Independency.

The radical puritans, who had scented victory in 1587, were bitter at the frustration of their hopes, and their feelings found vent in the *Marprelate Letters*, which began to appear in October 1588. These letters were masterpieces of invective, but their unremitting abuse acted like an inoculation and induced its own reaction. Bishops, for instance, were described as 'right poisoned, persecuting and terrible priests . . . petty anti-Christs, petty popes, proud prelates, intolerable withstanders of reformation, enemies of the Gospel', while the clergy in general were dismissed as 'so many swine, dumb dogs, non-residents . . . so many lewd livers, as thieves, murderers, adulterers, drunkards, cormorants, rascals, so many ignorant and atheistical dolts'. Cartwright was appalled by the tone of these letters, and assured Burghley that he had 'continually upon any occasion testified both my mislike and sorrow for such kind of disorderly proceeding'. The search for the author of the letters led to the house of a prominent Northamptonshire puritan, Sir Richard Knightley, where the printing press had been concealed. Knightley was arrested, along with many of his associates, and this led to the uncovering of the underground presbyterian organisation in the midland region. Whitgift took action against the puritan ringleaders in Star Chamber, where he argued that their attempt to substitute the 'Discipline' for the Prayer Book amounted to sedition. His case was weak in law, and Star Chamber refused to convict the ministers, but they remained in prison until 1594, when they acknowledged the unwisdom of their actions and promised never to behave in like manner again.

The *Marprelate Letters* and the increasing evidence of subversive presbyterian activities within the Church of England angered and alarmed Elizabeth. When John Penry, a puritan minister who was suspected of being the anonymous Marprelate, took refuge in Scotland, the Queen wrote to James to warn him that 'there is risen both in your realm and mine a sect of perilous consequence such as would have no kings but a presbytery, and take our place while they enjoy our privilege'. In 1593 Penry, who had returned to England, was brought before Queen's Bench on a charge of fomenting insurrection. He was found guilty, sentenced to death, and executed in May of that year. The previous month had also witnessed the hanging, at Tyburn, of Barrow and Greenwood, the leaders of the Independents. If further confirmation was needed that public opinion was turning against non-conforming puritanism it came in this year, 1593, when Parliament passed the Conventicle Act. This laid down that any person refusing to attend his parish church or forming part of a puritan conventicle should go into exile. If he returned to England he would be guilty of felony, the punishment for which was death by hanging.

These harsh measures effectively crushed the presbyterian and separatist movements, which remained in a state of limbo for the rest of Elizabeth's reign. The last recorded provincial conference of Midland and East Anglian puritans took place at Cambridge in September 1589. As for the Dedham *classis*, it held its eightieth, and final, session in June of that year, when it wrote its own epitaph: 'thus long continued through God's mercy this blessed meeting, and now it ended by the malice of Satan'.

It would be quite wrong, however, to assume that Elizabeth had succeeded in suppressing puritanism or driving it out of the established church. At the parish level many puritan ministers were firmly entrenched, and neither the ecclesiastical nor the secular authorities could take consistent and effective action against them if they had the support of the local gentry. Many of the gentry were themselves puritans, and their dominance of local administration meant that they could block royal initiatives of which they disapproved. Although the Queen insisted that no-one but herself was responsible for the government of the Church, she actually increased the influence of the landowners over it by selling off more than two thousand impropriate tithes which usually carried with them the advowson, or right of presentation. This meant that the purchasers, who included many gentry, could appoint as ministers men who shared their own attitudes in religion. In other words, while the Queen was fighting for control over the Church at the centre, she was conceding it at the grass roots.

Puritanism was well rooted in many urban as well as rural areas. In Leeds, for instance, which was contained within a single parish, the inhabitants raised the considerable sum of £130 to purchase the advowson, and promptly appointed a puritan to the living. Similarly, in 1561, the corporation of Hull invited a well-known puritan to be their vicar. He refused to wear the prescribed vestments, but this did not prevent him from retaining his post until his death thirty years later. In 1573 the corporation decided to appoint a lecturer, or unbeneficed preacher, at a stipend of £40 per annum, and did so with the enthusiastic support of Archbishop Grindal. The first lecturer was a Cambridge man, who on a number of occasions was summoned before High Commission for non-conformity , but he remained a respected and popular figure in the locality until the time of his death in 1598. Northampton was another town where puritanism had taken a firm hold, and when, shortly after the death of Elizabeth, an attempt was made to enforce the Prayer Book, the corporation complained that this would mean adopting ceremonies that had not been in use for forty years. In other words, puritan practices were the norm at Northampton: it was the advocates of conformity who appeared to be the innovators.

In 1573 the Queen had ordered the suppression of prophesyings in the southern province, but these frequently continued under the form of Exercises, in which local clergy came together to be instructed by a preacher, often of puritan persuasion. Public fasts were another means of bringing the 'godly' into contact with each other and strengthening their sense of purpose. And in the closing decade of Elizabeth's reign puritan energies found another outlet in Sabbatarianism — the insistence that Sunday should be regarded as the Jewish sabbath, a day set apart for prayer and meditation.

During the first half of Elizabeth's reign puritan ministers were, in general, better educated than the ordinary run of parish clergy, but the disparity lessened in the 1580s and 1590s as more graduates entered the Church. In London, for example, only 40 per cent of the clergy were graduates in 1560, but by 1595 the proportion was over 70 per cent. Bishops usually made no difficulty about issuing a preaching licence to graduates, so the Church under Whitgift was gradually moving towards attainment of the aim which both the episcopate and the puritans shared, of creating an educated, preaching ministry. But better-educated clergy were not necessarily closer to their flocks, for learning could be a barrier where simple men and women were concerned. Graduate ministers, whether or not they were puritans, could sometimes display such 'puritan' characteristics as intellectual arrogance, contempt for 'popular culture', and a sense of commitment to their own order which was a form of clericalism.

## The Reaction against Puritanism

Changing attitudes were also to be seen in the upper levels of the ecclesiastical hierarchy, for in reaction to the criticisms voiced by presbyterians and the claim that episcopacy had no biblical foundation, some bishops — though as yet a small minority — were swinging to the opposite pole and claiming that their authority was *jure divino*. Richard Bancroft, who was appointed chaplain to Archbishop Whitgift in 1592, was firmly committed to this view, and publicly asserted in 1593 that government of the church by bishops had been ordained by God and was therefore not only acceptable but essential.

The anti-Calvinist reaction made itself felt in theological studies. At Cambridge in the 1580s the Huguenot refugee Peter Baro, who had been appointed Lady Margaret Professor of Divinity, gave a series of lectures in which he submitted fundamental Calvinist doctrines to critical and often hostile scrutiny. At the same time Lancelot Andrewes, the future Bishop of Winchester, was expounding the belief — which Calvinists regarded as heretical — that divine grace and human nature, far from being in opposition, worked in harmony. The expression of such views provoked a lively controversy, and Whitgift was called upon to define where exactly the Church of England stood. He gave qualified support to the Calvinists, and the *Lambeth Articles*, which he helped draw up in 1595, affirmed that God had from eternity predestined some persons to eternal salvation and reprobated others to everlasting damnation. The *Lambeth Articles*, if they had been given official sanction, would have put the Calvinist nature of the Church of England beyond dispute, but Elizabeth was determined that no such sanction should be given them. She stood by the *Thirty-Nine Articles* adopted by Convocation in 1563 and confirmed by statute in 1571, and she therefore instructed Robert Cecil to tell Whitgift 'that she mislikes much that any allowance hath been given by your grace of any points to be disputed of predestination (being a matter tender and dangerous to weak, ignorant minds) and thereupon requireth your grace to suspend them [i.e. the *Lambeth Articles*]'.

Elizabeth has been criticised for taking too narrow a view of the Church of England and failing to realise that minor modifications, designed to make it more acceptable to the puritans, would in the long run have strengthened it. This may be true, but it can also be argued that without Elizabeth's resolve to maintain the settlement established in 1559 the anglican church would never have struck roots and established its hold upon the English people. The Queen's attitude was not dictated solely by stubborn conservatism. While critics of the Elizabethan settlement regarded it as simply a stage in the process of creating a truly reformed Church in England, Elizabeth believed that it was as near to an ideal solution as could be hoped or expected. As she told the members of Parliament assembled in 1589, she was 'most fully and firmly settled in her conscience, by the word of God, that the estate and government of this Church of England, as now it standeth in this reformation, may justly be compared to any church which hath been established in any Christian kingdom since the Apostles' times: that both in form and doctrine it is agreeable with the scriptures, with the most ancient general councils, with the practice of the primitive church, and with the judgments of all the old and learned fathers'.

# 9

# Elizabeth I. Roman Catholics and Foreign Policy

## The English Catholics

England did not suddenly become protestant in 1558. The degree of genuine commitment to Roman Catholicism in Mary's reign had varied from one region to another — though generally speaking it was greater in the north than in the south — but all areas had their catholic elements; in west Sussex, for example, there were twice as many Roman Catholics as there were protestants among the gentry families in the 1560s. In parts of the north such as Lancashire those priests who accepted the Elizabethan settlement did so in a half-hearted fashion and continued to hold what were in effect catholic services. Meanwhile their brethren who had preferred to leave the Church rather than take the oath of supremacy, kept up an unofficial ministry, relying for maintenance on voluntary contributions.

Although the Elizabethan government was committed in principle to the eradication of catholicism, in practice it was dependent upon the co-operation of local gentlemen and clergy, and this was not always forthcoming. Catholicism therefore survived, but during the 1560s many catholics would attend their parish churches out of a sense of social obligation. The church was, after all, the focal point of the life of the community and if gentlemen absented themselves from it they were, in a sense, failing to live up to the responsibilities of their position. 'Church-papists', as these conforming catholics were called, remained committed to the old faith, but they did not believe that this commitment entailed an ostentatious rejection of the state Church — of which, like all the Queen's subjects, they were deemed to be members. In any case the Prayer Book services were derived from catholic models and, as the puritans pointed out with increasing bitterness, contained many 'popish' features. The administration of the sacrament was likely to cause difficulties, but in practice communion services were held very rarely — at the most four times a year — and those with scruples of conscience could usually think up a good reason for staying away.

The loyalty of the English catholics to Elizabeth was demonstrated most strikingly by their refusal to support the Northern Rebellion in 1569 (see below, p. 177). In fact, catholic passivity was causing alarm at Rome, where it was feared that the old faith would die out completely unless its English adherents were pushed into a more active commitment. Pope Pius V therefore issued the Bull *Regnans in Excelsis*, in which he declared Elizabeth excommunicate and 'deprived of her pretended title to the kingdom . . . And we do command and charge all and every the noblemen, subjects, people and others aforesaid that they presume not to obey her or her orders, mandates and laws'.

This Bull, which was published in February 1570, was not intended as a direct challenge to Elizabeth. It was meant to give guidance to English catholics so that when a moment of crisis came — such as the Northern Rebellion — they would know how to act. In theory Roman Catholics now had to choose between their religious faith and their secular loyalties, but in practice the majority managed to avoid doing any such thing. The government, however, could not afford to take a relaxed attitude, particularly in view of the foreign situation. By giving the impression that every Roman Catholic was a potential traitor the Bull put an end to a decade of relative tolerance and confirmed Philip II's prediction that 'this sudden and unexpected step will make matters worse and drive the Queen and her friends the more to oppress and persecute the few good catholics remaining in England'.

Elizabeth was far less alarmed than many of her advisers by the catholic menace. Parliament was informed in 1570 that as long as the catholics observed her laws and did not 'wilfully and manifestly break them by their open acts, her Majesty's meaning is not to have any of them molested by an inquisition or examination of their consciences in causes of religion', and she vetoed a Bill which would have made attendance at the communion service compulsory. Yet she could not turn back the tide of anti-catholicism which was now rapidly rising, and she felt it politic to accept a Bill making it treasonable to procure a papal Bull for the specific purpose of reconciling her subjects to Rome. This was the first of a series of Acts which placed the catholic community in England under increasing pressure, at a time when the arrival of the missionary priests was forcing it to re-examine the implications of its religious commitment.

During the first decade of Elizabeth's reign more than a hundred Oxford graduates went into exile rather than acknowledge the newly-established protestant Church. Among them was William Allen who, in 1568, when he was in residence at the university town of Douai in the Spanish Netherlands, decided (in his own words) 'to establish a college in which our countrymen, who were scattered

abroad in different places, might live and study together more prof-
itably than apart. Our next intention was to secure for the college
an unbroken and enduring existence by means of a constant succession of students coming and leaving; for we feared that if the
schism should last much longer, owing to the death of the few who,
at its beginning, had been cast out of the English universities for
the faith, no seed would be left hereafter for the restoration of religion, and that heresy would thus obtain a perpetual and peaceful
possession of the realm'.

Allen assumed that in due course the catholic faith would be restored to England, but the young men who flocked to Douai were
not prepared simply to sit and wait for this moment to arrive. They
believed it was their duty, after they had been adequately prepared,
to return to England and, as Allen put it, 'train catholics to be
plainly and openly catholics, to be men who will always refuse
every kind of spiritual commerce with heretics'. This changed the
whole nature of the college and turned it into a seminary for missionary priests. The first of the missionaries landed in England in
1574, and by the time Allen left Douai in 1585 it had produced
nearly three hundred priests. Their impact was immediate, for the
Bishop of London told Secretary Walsingham in 1577 that 'the
papists marvellously increase both in numbers and in obstinate
withdrawal of themselves from the Church and services of God'.

Among the offshoots of Douai was the English College established at Rome in 1576. This was originally intended, like Douai,
to be a haven and a study centre for English catholics in exile, but
after a few years the Pope gave control of it to the Society of Jesus
— one of the new orders to which the catholic reformation of the
mid-century had given birth. The Jesuits were committed to missionary endeavour, and at Allen's suggestion they agreed to send
some of their recruits from the English College to join the seminary
priests on the mission to England.

The men chosen to inaugurate the Jesuit campaign were Robert
Parsons and Edmund Campion, who arrived in England in the
summer of 1580. More Jesuits followed them, and as the number
of priests — both seminarists and Jesuits — increased, it became
essential to organise them more effectively. The Jesuits, whose
membership of a regular order gave them a sense of corporate identity that was lacking among the secular, seminary priests, brought
a greater professionalism to the English mission. They arranged for
the reception and shelter of newly-arrived priests and in due course
despatched them to the area in which they were to work. The mission was based on London — inevitably so, since it was not only
the capital but also easily accessible from the south-east coast,
which was the main point of entry for the priests — but gradually
established a regional organisation.

The big problem facing the missionaries was that of moving around the country, for the government's repressive measures were beginning to bite, and even people with catholic sympathies were often afraid to give shelter to priests. There were some areas, in Lancashire for instance, where catholics were so thick on the ground that the priests could move around openly, without the need of disguise, but these were the exception. Elsewhere they were dependent upon the hospitality of catholic gentry whose houses were big enough to conceal them. As the mission developed, networks of 'safe' houses were established, and priests were passed on from one to another as they went about their dangerous business of bringing spiritual guidance and comfort to the English catholics. Without such networks the mission might never have got off the ground, but there was a price to be paid for this, and it consisted in the fact that the missionary priests became increasingly identified with the gentry and shared their attitudes and assumptions. There were parts of England, particularly in the north, where catholicism had survived as a genuinely popular movement, but the lack of resident gentry in these regions meant that they were not easily accessible to the priests. The basing of the mission in London was also detrimental in this respect, for it focused activity on the south and east, in which catholicism was weak, at the expense of the north and west, where it had been strongly entrenched at the end of Mary's reign.

The Jesuits had acquired a reputation as the shock troops of the Counter-Reformation, and they were deeply involved in the political as well as the religious life of catholic Europe. It was realised that their participation in the English mission might alarm Elizabeth's government and strengthen the hard-line protestants. They were therefore instructed to confine their activities to those who were already catholic, to take no part in English politics and to profess no views on political matters. The Jesuits observed these instructions carefully, but they were operating in a country in which Church and state were so closely integrated as to be inseparable. Nothing in Elizabethan England could be 'purely religious' any more than it could be 'purely secular', and although the Jesuits were genuine in their protestations of political non-involvement, they were the sworn servants of the papacy at a time when it was committed to the overthrow of Elizabeth and had given aid to FitzMaurice in his rebellion against the Queen's rule in Ireland.

It was therefore hardly surprising that the English government intensified its repressive measures. An Act of 1581 stated that anyone attempting to subvert the loyalty of the Queen's subjects, or to convert them as a means to this particular end, was to suffer death as a traitor, while catholic 'recusants' — so-called because they refused to attend anglican services — were to be fined the crippling sum of £20 a month instead of a shilling, as earlier. Missionary priests were hunted down, imprisoned, tortured and frequently executed, and in 1585 an Act was passed declaring that any catholic priest who remained in England was committing treason by doing so and was therefore liable to death by hanging, drawing and quartering.

During the course of Elizabeth's reign about half the English mission were captured, and well over a hundred were executed. Among them was Campion, who went to the scaffold in 1581. He maintained until the last moment that he had been condemned unjustly, because his mission was only a spiritual one, and that the catholics were 'as true subjects as ever the Queen had'. The Privy Council took a different view, however, and required catholic prisoners to answer the notorious 'Bloody Question': 'if the Pope or any other by his appointment do invade this realm, which part would you take, and which part ought a good subject to take?' One answer to this was given by Robert Parsons when he wrote a virulent tract against Elizabeth, to be distributed by Spanish troops after they had landed from what he assumed would be the victorious Armada.

Lay catholics, who were caught up in the struggle between the government and the missionary priests, inevitably suffered. The government insisted upon outward conformity in religion, but the priests encouraged catholics to assert their faith by becoming recusants. The success of the priests was shown by the marked decline in the number of 'Church-papists' as recusancy became more general and widespread. In the eyes of the missionaries recusants were the only true catholics, and they preferred a smaller group of committed adherents to the larger, more amorphous and less zealous catholic community that had survived from Mary's reign. It has been estimated that by the end of the sixteenth century there were only about 35–40,000 catholics in England; however, this leaves out all those who were forced into conformity by social or economic pressures, but remained catholic at heart.

These pressures could be extreme, especially after 1587, when it was provided by statute that if recusants failed to pay the monthly fine for non-attendance at church, two-thirds of their land could be seized by the Exchequer. Since a month was calculated at 28 days, recusants were liable, in theory, to a fine of £260 a year. In fact, not more than sixteen people paid this enormous amount in Elizabeth's reign, but poorer recusants were often made to pay the shilling fine, and the need to preserve their property drove an increasing number of heads of households into occasional conformity from the 1590s onwards. The seizure of lands was not quite the harsh measure it seems, since property valuations were always low, and a nominal two-thirds was in practice far less. The confiscated lands were leased out by the Exchequer in order to recover the amount due, but the purchasers of the leases frequently sold them back to the recusant owner or to trustees acting on his behalf. In these ways the impact of confiscation was lessened, but it remained an expensive and frightening penalty.

The tension between secular and religious loyalties affected even the missionary priests. The Jesuits were firmly committed to the ideals of the Counter-Reformation, and regarded England as only one of many mission fields in a church whose range was world-wide. The seminarists, on the other hand — or some of them, at any rate — thought in more specifically English terms, and believed that by accepting a subordinate role for catholicism and emphasising their allegiance to the Queen they could persuade the government to relax its persecution. They wanted to return to normality by re-establishing the traditional hierarchy. This would have the further advantage of placing control of the catholic church in England firmly in the hands of the bishops and secular clergy, and reducing the role of the Jesuits, whom they distrusted. The seculars were deeply affronted when, in 1598, the Pope, far from acceding to their requests, appointed an Archpriest to take charge of the mission and went out of his way to praise the Jesuits for their work. Those seculars who felt particularly deeply on this issue made repeated appeals to Rome for a change of attitude, and in 1602 the Pope responded by instructing the Archpriest to take three of the Appellants as his assistants and to report direct to Rome instead of consulting with the Jesuits, as he had earlier been required to do. In the following year thirteen Appellants made a public assertion of their loyalty to Elizabeth, and it seemed for a time as though the 'Archpriest Controversy' would fatally divide the mission. This did not happen, however, for the Appellants were never more than a small minority among the three hundred or more priests now in England. Tension between the various elements among the missionaries remained, but the mission itself continued to flourish and expand well into the next century.

## Foreign Policy

At the outset of Elizabeth's reign France, with her ally Scotland, was the main enemy, but in 1562 the political situation in Europe was transformed by the outbreak of the French wars of religion. For the next twenty years French influence fluctuated violently as aristocratic families, at the head of religious factions, struggled for supremacy. In the peaceful interludes between bouts of fighting the French monarchy attempted to resume its European role, and this, as well as ingrained habits of thought, blinded many English people to the fact that a dramatic shift in the balance of power had taken place.

With the decline of France, Philip II of Spain emerged not only as the greatest catholic prince in Europe but also as the chief threat to English independence, and as if to demonstrate this he moved an army, under the Duke of Alva, into the Spanish Netherlands in August 1567 to crush the revolt that was smouldering there. Elizabeth could hardly ignore such a move, for a powerful army in the Netherlands was always a potential threat to England.

The situation in the Netherlands was complicated by internal divisions between the greater and the lesser nobles, the aristocracy and the urban bourgeoisie, the Calvinists and the catholics. In the northern provinces the most prominent figures among the rebels were the Calvinists from the ports of Zeeland and Holland, who had taken up privateering against Spanish shipping and called themselves the Sea Beggars. They used the ports of south-east England as a base for their operations, but in 1572, in response to Spanish pressure, Elizabeth ordered them to leave. The unexpected effect of her action was to transform the whole nature of the Netherlands' revolt, for the Sea Beggars did not simply return peaceably to Holland; they attacked a number of ports, drove out the Spanish garrisons, and shifted the focus of the rebellion from the southern to the northern provinces.

William of Orange, the Burgundian noble who had emerged as the champion of Netherlands' autonomy against the Spanish attempt to reimpose direct rule, realised that if the rebellion was to stand any chance of success it must be as broad-based as possible. He therefore gave his patronage to the Sea Beggars, and in 1573 took the politically significant step of joining the Calvinist church, even though this made him less acceptable to the catholic, conservative nobles of the south. He also appealed for help from abroad, and called on Elizabeth to support the rebels with men and money. Elizabeth had no love for rebels, however, and was not interested in independence for the Netherlands. She wanted a return to the autonomy they had enjoyed before Philip II, and feared that by aiding the rebels she would be rendering a negotiated settlement less likely. She therefore rejected William's appeal. But at the same time she urged Philip to concede home rule to the Netherlands and warned him that failure to do so would make English intervention in the long run inevitable.

In 1577, Don John of Austria, who had been sent by Philip, his half-brother, to govern the Netherlands, granted them autonomy, but this was merely a tactical gesture, and before the year was out he had resorted to the earlier policy of trying to impose Spanish rule by force of arms. This abrupt change of course so angered Elizabeth that she now offered the Dutch 6,000 troops, under the command of her favourite, the Earl of Leicester — who was also the leader of the group of committed puritans in the Privy Council which wanted England to give support to the protestant cause wherever it was threatened. But Elizabeth had not lost her native caution, and in June 1578 she sent her Secretary of State, Sir Francis Walsingham, to the Netherlands, in the hope that he might be able to bring about a peaceful settlement. Walsingham was in despair at what he regarded as dangerous vacillation on the part of the Queen. 'The only remedy left to us,' he declared, 'is prayer. Where the advice of counsellors cannot prevail with a prince of her judgment, it is a sign that God hath closed up her heart from seeing and executing what may be for her safety'.

Since Elizabeth had failed him, William turned to the Duke of Anjou, the brother of Henri III of France. Anjou had hopes of creating a powerful anti-Habsburg bloc, under French protection, and was willing to consider accepting sovereignty over the Netherlands as the first step towards this. But he did not wish to commit himself until he had tested the feasibility of the second step, which consisted in bringing England into the coalition by means of a marriage with Elizabeth. Negotiations opened in 1578, and in August of that year Anjou was invited to be the Queen's guest at Greenwich. Elizabeth apparently took Anjou's courtship seriously. The marriage had much to be said for it on diplomatic grounds, and a number of Privy Councillors, including Lord Burghley, were in favour of it. The majority, however, were opposed, and as the prospect came closer to realisation Elizabeth herself turned against it. Anjou therefore returned to France, leaving the question of his future unresolved.

The next two years saw the balance of power in Europe swing ever more strongly in favour of the Habsburgs. In 1579 the provinces of the southern Netherlands gave up their struggle for autonomy and accepted Spanish rule, while in the Iberian peninsula the death of the King of Portugal in 1580 allowed Philip to take over that country and bring its colonial empire, as well as its powerful navy, under his control. The only hope of saving at least part of the Netherlands from ultimate subjection to Spain now seemed to rest in Anjou, and Elizabeth therefore reopened the marriage negotiations, using them this time as a lever to push Anjou into accepting the offer of sovereignty over the provinces. Walsingham was again sent on mission, to France, to urge Henri III to give his support to the proposed marriage and also to join in the formation of a defensive league against the Habsburgs. Yet on this occasion, as earlier, Elizabeth could not bring herself to give an unequivocal undertaking to marry. Whatever her feelings about Anjou, she clung to her independence and was understandably reluctant to play the last diplomatic trump card that was left in her hand.

Walsingham was left to make what sense he could out of conflicting instructions, and confessed to Burghley that he was completely baffled. 'I wish to God her Highness would resolve one way or the other touching the matter of her marriage ... When her Majesty is pressed to marry, thus she seemeth to affect a league; and when a league is proposed, then she liketh better of a marriage!'

One thing that did become plain to Walsingham was that under the irresolute Henri III France could not be counted on to play a major role in Europe: if Elizabeth was to achieve anything, she would have to act on her own initiative. Events were in any case pushing her in this direction. Anjou had accepted sovereignty over the Netherlands, but he was caught up in the factional strife that bedevilled the provinces and finally abandoned them to their fate. He died in June 1584, and the following month saw the assassination of William of Orange. Now, at last, Elizabeth acted. Leicester was sent across with an expeditionary force, but not until the Dutch agreed to hand over Flushing and Brill as security for the repayment of Elizabeth's expenses. Leicester, who arrived in Holland in December 1585, had instructions to put an end to squabbles among the rebels but to keep out of any firm commitments on Elizabeth's behalf. It took Leicester only a short time to discover that without some clearly defined position of authority he could not possibly overcome Dutch factiousness. He therefore accepted the office of Governor and Captain-General, but this brought Elizabeth's wrath down upon him and he returned to England in November 1586. In the following year he was back in the Netherlands with more men and money, but he found, as Anjou had done, that the factions were too strong for him. In 1588 he left the Netherlands for good, having accomplished little of significance; only the nobility of Sir Philip Sidney, dying on the battlefield at Zutphen, redeemed his campaign from total oblivion. However, Elizabeth left the English troops to carry on the fight, under Dutch control, and she continued payment of a subsidy which amounted to some £125,000 a year — about a third of her ordinary annual revenue.

## Mary, Queen of Scots

It has been argued, both at the time and since, that Elizabeth was over-cautious in her approach to the Netherlands problem, and intervened only when it was too late. There is obviously some truth in this, but Elizabeth was aware of the enormous disparity between English and Spanish power. She also had to deal with the difficult situation that confronted her at home after May 1568, when Mary, Queen of Scots, took refuge in England. Elizabeth did not want the catholic claimant to the English throne so near at hand, but she could hardly use English arms to reimpose Mary's rule on the protestant Scots; nor could she allow Mary to take refuge in the courts of France or Spain, where she would undoubtedly be used as a valuable pawn in the power game against England. There was no alternative, in the short run, to keeping the Queen of Scots in honourable captivity in England, and in 1569 she was therefore sent to Tutbury castle, in Staffordshire, under the guardianship of the Earl of Shrewsbury.

No sooner had Mary reached Tutbury than she became the focus of intrigues. Some English nobles of ancient lineage, prominent among them the Duke of Norfolk, resented the rule of Cecil and other 'new men' and drew up a plan by which Elizabeth should recognise Mary as her heir and give permission for Norfolk to marry her — thereby ensuring the rule of the 'old' nobility after Elizabeth's death. There was nothing treasonable about this proposal, which in fact had the support of a number of Privy Councillors — including Leicester, who saw this as a possible way of getting rid of Cecil, his rival for power. But Norfolk was also linked, through his brother-in-law, the Earl of Westmorland, with a group of northern peers who felt increasingly out of sympathy with the government in London. They shared Norfolk's hatred of 'new men', particularly the members of the Council of the North who were eroding the independence that the Percies, the Nevilles, the Dacres and other long-established families had taken for granted as theirs by hereditary right.

Henry Neville, Earl of Westmorland, was in touch with Thomas Percy, Earl of Northumberland, and the two men, who were both catholics, were already considering rebellion as the only way in which to make their grievances known. There were tenuous links between them and Norfolk, and when the Duke left court, in dudgeon, in September 1569, they took this as a signal for their revolt to go ahead. In fact they were mistaken, for Norfolk returned to court the following month and thew himself on Elizabeth's mercy. The Queen, who had heard reports about the disturbed situation in the north, summoned the two earls to London, but rather than risk their lives by obeying, they took the plunge into open rebellion. They quickly assembled an army, made up largely of their retainers, and moved south, announcing that their intention was to put an end to the 'new-found religion and heresy' that was infecting the Queen's dominions. In mid-November they occupied Durham, and the banner of the Five Wounds was once again carried into the cathedral as mass was celebrated there. From Durham the rebel host advanced to Tadcaster, where they were within striking distance of Tutbury. But the Yorkshire gentry, whom the earls had expected to rally to the catholic cause, held aloof, and there was no defection among the Queen's officers in the north. While the earls hesitated, uncertain what to do next, the rebellion lost its impetus and their followers melted away. Before 1569 came to an end the rebellion was over. Westmorland fled abroad and spent the rest of his life in exile; Northumberland evaded capture until 1572, when he was executed at York. The rank and file were not spared. Elizabeth ordered·that at least one man should be hanged from every town and village that had contributed recruits to the rebel host, and although this bloodthirsty directive was not carried out to the letter, some 450 of the poorer sort of rebels were put to death.

The Spanish ambassador in England had apparently been in touch with Norfolk and also with the leaders of the Northern Rebellion through a Florentine banker named Ridolfi. Anglo-Spanish relations had taken a sharp turn for the worse in December 1568 when Elizabeth ordered the seizure of a substantial quantity of bullion on board a Spanish fleet that had put into English ports on its way to the Netherlands. The Queen justified her action on the grounds that the bullion was the property of Italian bankers, who had merely loaned it to Philip II so that he could pay Alva's army. In fact she may have been prompted to take this action by the news, which had just reached her, of the Spanish attack on the ships of John Hawkins in the Mexican port of San Juan de Ulloa (see above, p. 117). Even if this played no part in her decision — which could also have been made on the spur of the moment, with no clear justification other than the immediate financial gain — the growing challenge by English seamen to the Spanish monopoly of American trade was undoubtedly contributing to the souring of relations between the two countries.

Further evidence of Spanish ill will was provided in March 1571, with the uncovering of a plot which involved the King of Spain and the Pope, along with the Queen of Scots and the Duke of Norfolk. The arch-conspirator who was trying to knit these disparate elements together was Ridolfi, and his idea was that Norfolk should call on the English catholics to rise in rebellion, seize Elizabeth and free Mary from captivity, at the same time as a Spanish expeditionary force landed on the east coast. It is most unlikely that the plot would ever have succeeded, but Cecil discovered what was afoot and grasped the opportunity to remove Norfolk, once and forever, from the political scene. The Duke was arrested, put on trial for high treason, and found guilty. Six months later, after the Queen's doubts and hesitations had been overcome, he was executed on Tower Hill.

Relations between England and Spain were apparently moving towards breaking point, but neither side wanted a rupture, and Elizabeth took the initiative in opening negotiations with Alva — who had reacted to her seizure of the bullion intended for his army by imposing an embargo on English trade with the Netherlands. These negotiations were successful, and by 1575 normal commercial relations had been restored. But there could be no long-term agreement between England and Spain while Philip persisted in his attempt to reimpose Spanish rule on the Low Countries, for Elizabeth was bound to oppose this. Her open intervention in 1585, when she sent Leicester with an English army to the aid of the rebels, made a clash with Spain inevitable, and matters were not improved by Drake's privateering expedition to the West Indies, which set out in the same year. By the time he returned to England in 1586, Drake had burnt and plundered Spanish ships and cities and extorted vast sums by way of ransom. He had also demonstrated that Spain, despite her wealth and power, was not invulnerable, and that England's naval strength was potentially formidable.

Philip II's policies would have stood a better chance of succeeding if Elizabeth could have been removed from the English throne. Throckmorton's plot, in 1583, was designed to achieve just this, and the Spanish ambassador therefore gave it his blessing. But the plot was uncovered before it could come to anything, and the ambassador had to pack his bags and leave. Mary, Queen of Scots, had also been party to the conspiracy, and the Privy Council, which regarded her as a major threat to Elizabeth, drew up the *Bond of Association*, pledging all its signatories, in the event of a successful attempt on Elizabeth's life, to hunt down and destroy the person on whose behalf the assassination had been carried out. Mary was not explicitly named, but she was clearly uppermost in the minds of those who flocked to sign the *Bond*, and in Parliament and the Council the prevailing opinion was that the Queen of Scots should be put to death.

Elizabeth, who knew that the stability of her own throne depended, in the last resort, upon a general reverence for monarchy, was unwilling to execute a fellow-sovereign, and she refused to be convinced of Mary's complicity in the plots against her. It was left to Sir Francis Walsingham to provide irrefutable evidence. In 1586 he discovered a new plot to murder Elizabeth and release the Queen of Scots with the help of a Spanish army, in which the go-between was a young English catholic named Anthony Babington. Walsingham tapped Babington's correspondence with Mary, and through his agents he prompted the sending of a letter asking for Mary's explicit approval of all the details of the plot, including Elizabeth's assassination. In July 1586 came Mary's reply, giving her full assent. Even Elizabeth could not ignore this evidence, and she ordered Mary to be put on trial.

The result of the trial was a formal condemnation of the Scottish queen, and Parliament petitioned for Mary's execution. But Elizabeth still could not steel herself to this action, which would outrage public opinion in France and Spain and complete the isolation of England. As always she hoped to shift the responsibility for action on to other shoulders, and hinted that Mary's murder would not be displeasing to her. The hint was not taken, but in the end the Council acted on its own initiative and despatched the death warrant to Fotheringay Castle in Northamptonshire, where Mary was held prisoner. On 8 February 1587 she was led out to a scaffold specially constructed in the castle hall and there executed.

Elizabeth was furious when she heard the news, refused to admit Burghley to her presence, and sent William Davison, the Secretary of State who had been entrusted with the warrant, to the Tower. Her anger was genuine, for her ministers, even though they acted in good faith, had disobeyed her trust. But she was too much of a realist not to appreciate the advantages of Mary's removal from the scene. Among these was the fact that the new catholic claimant to the English throne was the daughter of Philip of Spain. English catholics, who might have risen in Mary's cause, were unlikely to feel much enthusiasm for a Spanish pretender.

## Spanish Armadas

The removal of the Queen of Scots from the political scene made Philip's way plain, for while she was alive he had always been aware that by placing her on the English throne he would risk putting England into the orbit of France. Yet even before the news of Mary's execution reached him, Philip had decided to invade England. His plan was for a great fleet to sweep the English Channel and leave it clear for the Duke of Parma and his Spanish infantry to cross over from the Netherlands. Throughout 1586 ships were being built and assembled along the Channel coast, and in England the Council ordered the setting up of beacons at prominent places so that news of a Spanish invasion could be quickly transmitted. The Armada was almost ready in 1587 and might have sailed then, had not Drake swooped on Cadiz and destroyed the ships and stores assembled there. In fact it did not leave until May 1588, and even then it was short of provisions and ammunition, and lacking sufficient guns.

Lord Howard of Effingham, the English commander, and Drake, the Vice-Admiral, wanted to attack the Armada off the Portuguese coast, but bad weather, lack of supplies, and the Queen's own wishes, kept them in home waters. By July 1588 the Armada was in the Channel, where William Camden, the antiquary, saw it 'built high like towers and castles, rallied into the form of a crescent whose horns were at least seven miles distant'. The Spanish admiral, the Duke of Medina Sidonia, had about 130 ships, carrying more than 20,000 soldiers and sailors, and he kept them in tight formation which the English could not break up. Howard had

about the same number of ships, but they were far more man-
oeuvrable than the cumbrous Spanish ones — 'so fast and nimble',
wrote Medina Sidonia, 'they can do anything they like with them'.
The English ships were also much better armed, and their long-
range iron guns inflicted heavy damage on the Spaniards when they
came to close quarters.

Medina Sidonia's orders were to keep his fleet intact until the
rendezvous with Parma, and in fact he held his ships together until
the night of 28 July 1588, when they anchored off Calais to await
news from the army. This was the opportunity Howard had been
waiting for. He sent fire-ships sailing downwind towards the anchored ships, and in the resulting confusion the Spaniards cut their
cables and stood out to sea. By the time daylight came the great
fleet was scattered over the waters, and the English ships darted
in among it, doing great damage. They could have done more had
they not run out of ammunition.

The battle was, in fact, over, for the Spanish ships were short
of ammunition, food and water, and had been so badly damaged
by English fire that they would fight no more. Since Howard
blocked the return passage south, the Duke had no option but to
order his leaking ships to sail north, round the coast of Scotland
and Ireland, where rough winds and high seas took a heavy toll.
Only half of the great fleet that had set out to humble the protestant English ever returned to harbour, and the enemies of the
catholic church all over Europe hailed this defeat as a sign of God's
blessing on their cause. Elizabeth, too, saw the manifestation of
divine judgment in the success of her arms, for the commemorative
medal which she ordered to be struck recorded not the skill of her
sailors but the favour of an almighty providence. *Afflavit Deus et
dissipati sunt*, it declared, with laconic directness: 'God blew and
they were scattered.'

The defeat of the Armada did not mean the end of the war. The
problem for the English was how to make the most of their victory,
and opinions were divided. Hawkins wanted to bankrupt Spain by
blockading her coast and cutting her lifeline with the New World,
while Drake proposed detaching Portugal from Spain by attacking
Lisbon and sparking off a rebellion. Drake's plan was adopted, and
in April 1589 a fleet carrying 20,000 men set sail for Portugal.
However, the expedition was a total failure. Land and sea operations were not co-ordinated, and more damage was done to the
English forces by drink, incompetence and disease than by the
Spanish defenders. Vigo was sacked, but apart from that nothing
was accomplished. American bullion continued to flow into Spain,
Portugal remained part of the Spanish empire, and the half
of the Armada which had returned to port was left to refit in
safety.

In 1595 another expedition was sent out, under the command of Drake and Hawkins. It was intended to revive the glories of former years by attacking the Spanish Main, but the Spaniards had by now built up their defences in the New World and they beat off an English assault on Puerto Rico. The ships therefore had to return ingloriously home, bringing with them the sad and depressing news that both Hawkins and Drake had died during the voyage.

English privateering continued, of course, but was now left largely to individuals and small groups. The only other major expedition that was mounted in Elizabeth's reign was that to Cadiz, which set sail in 1596 under the command of Howard of Effingham and the young Earl of Essex — Leicester's stepson and his successor as the Queen's favourite. This expedition marked the adoption of Hawkins's policy of maintaining a permanent blockade of the Spanish coast, and was at first brilliantly successful, for Cadiz was captured. But the English did not have the will or the resources to hold it indefinitely, and after sacking the town the victors returned home. While they had wounded Spanish pride, they had not established English supremacy at sea. This was shown by the fact that before the year was out Philip despatched a second armada towards England. Fortunately it was turned back by strong winds and high seas, and the same fate befell it when it made another attempt in the following year.

Part of the blame for the limited success of English naval activities after 1588 must be attributed to the peculiar nature of the expeditions, for they were financed by a number of shareholders, of whom the Queen was only one, and their main objective was to make money. The Queen could not possibly have met the entire cost of these ventures, for her finances were under heavy and increasing strain. Following the assassination of Henri III in July 1589 the protestant Henri of Navarre became titular King of France. He was opposed by the Catholic League, however, and therefore called on Elizabeth to support him. She responded by sending money and 4,000 men, but this merely provoked the League to appeal to Philip II. Spanish troops now moved into France and threatened to occupy the Breton coast, where they would be well placed to launch an invasion of England. Elizabeth therefore sent over more troops in 1594, and she kept up her assistance until the conclusion of peace between France and Spain in 1598. Her commitment to Henri IV involved a total of some 20,000 English soldiers, of whom about half were killed, as well as many thousands of pounds in money. At the same time Elizabeth was maintaining a force of 4,000 men in Dutch service, and a large army in Ireland. Little wonder, then, that she could not afford to finance naval operations on an adequate scale.

# 10

# Elizabeth I. Parliament and the Royal Finances

## *Elizabethan Parliaments*

Elizabeth summoned ten Parliaments in the course of a reign that lasted forty-four years. There were thirteen sessions in all, and the average length of each session was less than ten weeks. There were many years in which no meeting of Parliament took place, and the interval between sessions was approximately three years. Yet although Parliament was an intermittent assembly, its prestige was high and there was intensive competition for seats in the Commons. The Queen was pressed to create additional parliamentary boroughs, and in the first thirty years of her reign she added sixty-two members to the House by so doing. The majority of these new members were not, however, townsmen, for more and more boroughs were choosing neighbouring gentlemen rather than residents to represent them. By 1600 gentry outnumbered townsmen in the Commons by four to one, and the proportion of merchants in the House declined from 17 per cent at the beginning of the reign to 13 per cent at the end.

The landowners and other members of the political nation valued Parliament not simply because it provided them with an opportunity to go to London and express their opinions on issues of major importance in politics and religion. It was also extremely useful to them as a way of resolving problems affecting their local community by way of legislation. While the government's main concern was with public statutes, they were at least as interested in the private Acts which secured their particular ends. Under Henry VIII the number of private Bills per session had averaged a little more than eight; the corresponding figure for Elizabeth was well over thirteen.

The big advantage of Parliament from the government's point of view was that it provided a microcosm of the whole nation and symbolised the unity between the Queen and her people. It thereby facilitated the making of law, and, above all, the granting of supply with which to replenish the royal Exchequer. In eleven out of the thirteen sessions the government asked for supply; in six it proposed major legislation. Yet Parliament was not merely a money-voting and law-making machine. Because it embodied the political nation it made possible the reconciling of differences of attitude and opinion in a peaceful manner and the harmonisation of conflicting interests in order to channel them into positive action.

The House of Commons, which had 462 members by 1601, was very much bigger than the House of Lords, which numbered about 60. Procedure in the Commons was crystallising, and by the end of the reign Bills were usually read three times, with a committee stage after the second reading. The full House met in the morning from 8 till 11, and divisions were common: the afternoon was reserved for committees. The proliferation of committees was a consequence of the increasing amount of business that Parliament had to deal with — as well as the Queen's desire, widely shared by members, to keep sessions short. By discussing Bills informally in committees, when members were allowed to speak more than once on the same topic — which was not the case in debates in the whole House — the Commons' procedure was speeded up. Committees were not an anti-government device. They were usually chaired by Privy Councillors or their nominees, and other Councillors were invariably to be found among the most frequent speakers.

## The Commons' Privilege of Free Speech

The Commons had a number of privileges, of which the most highly valued was freedom of speech, but this was not at all clearly defined. Elizabeth was faced, in her early years, with a difficult situation abroad which needed tactful handling, and she was also involved in domestic disputes about the succession and the ecclesiastical settlement. She claimed that these matters, since they affected her so closely, were not for discussion by the House, but many members were of the opinion that it was their duty as well as their right to discuss them. In opening the first Parliament of her reign the Queen granted freedom of speech without defining it, but when the Commons later petitioned her to marry she sharply reminded them that it was a 'very great presumption, being unfitting and altogether unmeet for you to require them that may command'. The Commons, undaunted, revived their petition in 1566, and were not silenced by a message assuring them that the Queen was minded to marry. Elizabeth thereupon commanded the House, via her Councillors, to discontinue the debate, but this brought Paul Wentworth to his feet to ask whether such a commandment 'be a breach of the liberty of the free speech of the House?'. This appeal to self-interest rallied the Commons, who drew up a petition in which they described their privilege as 'an ancient laudable custom, always from the beginning necessarily annexed to our assembly'.

The petition was never presented, for the Queen withdrew her prohibition, but in her closing speech she told members that while she had no intention of infringing their lawful privileges, neither did she wish their liberty to make her bondage.

Perhaps as a result of this tussle, the Queen gave a more precise definition of freedom of speech when Parliament again assembled in 1571. The Lord Keeper, speaking in her name, told the Commons they would 'do well to meddle with no matters of state but such as should be propounded unto them, and to occupy themselves in other matters concerning the commonwealth'. 'Matters of state' were not defined, but the practice of Elizabeth's reign showed that she included in this category anything that directly affected herself or her prerogative — the succession, for instance, and her own marriage, the royal supremacy over the Church, the conduct of foreign policy, and the regulation of trade. These were all topics on which the Queen needed room to manoeuvre, and Acts of Parliament — which were the natural conclusions of parliamentary debate — tied her far too rigidly. She could hold up a Bill, or, in the last resort, veto it, but this type of clear-cut decision was always disagreeable to Elizabeth. She wanted the Commons to use the much more flexible procedure of petitioning, since this brought grievances to her attention while leaving her free to decide on the best way of dealing with them. Unfortunately for her, the very rigidity of procedure by Bill appealed to those members who wanted to tie her hands, in the conviction that they knew best what was for her own good and that of the Church and state over which she ruled.

The limitations of freedom of speech, as indicated by the Queen at the outset of the 1571 session, did not inhibit the Commons from debating religious matters, for it was in this session that Strickland introduced his Bill for reforming the Prayer Book (see above, p. 154). He was summoned before the Council and told to stay away from the House, but this only led to further, and more heated, discussion. One of Strickland's supporters shifted the issue on to the question of the Commons' privileges, asserting that 'all matter not treason, or too much to the derogation of the imperial crown, was tolerable there [in the Commons]'. He went on to say that it was proper for princes to have their prerogatives, but that these were 'to be straitened within reasonable limits'. At moments like this Elizabeth's cause would have been lost without her Councillors. It was they who, on this occasion as on many others, 'whispered together. And thereupon the Speaker made this motion, that the House should stay of any further consultation hereupon.' Next morning Strickland was back in his place. The Queen had given way on this particular issue, while still maintaining the principle.

The 1571 session saw the maiden speech of Peter Wentworth,

brother of Paul, who was to become the champion of freedom of speech in the Commons. His great moment came, however, in the 1576 Parliament, when he delivered a speech he had been brooding on for several years. His theme was freedom of expression, and when he considered the forces which endangered this liberty, he put 'rumours and messages' first. The House, he said, was full of rumours such as 'take heed what you do. The Queen's Majesty liketh not of such a matter. Whosoever preferreth it, she will be much offended with him', and occasionally there were messages 'either of commanding or inhibiting, very injurious unto the freedom of speech and consultation. I would to God, Mr Speaker, that these two [rumours and messages] were buried in hell.' Developing his argument he went on to claim that the Queen was bound to maintain the law and that 'free speech and conscience in this place was granted by a special law, as that without which the prince and state cannot be preserved or maintained'.

Wentworth was in no way a typical member of the Commons, and the House was so shocked by his outspokenness that it sent him to the Tower. There he stayed for a month until the Queen ordered his release, and one of the Councillors used the occasion of this generous gesture to remind the House that liberty did not mean licence. 'Though freedom of speech', he said, 'hath always been used in this great council of the Parliament, and is a thing most necessary to be preserved among us, yet the same was never, nor ought to be, extended so far as though a man in this House may speak what and of whom he list.'

Elizabeth could never afford to relax in her struggle to keep her wealthy, independent-minded Commons under control, and from 1571 onwards her reply to the Speaker's petition for freedom of speech emphasised that this privilege did not extend to matters of state. She never entered the House of Commons, let alone listened to a debate, but from her palaces at Whitehall, Richmond, Nonsuch or Greenwich, she kept a constant watch on parliamentary affairs and inspired those 'rumours and messages' of which Wentworth complained. She was fortunate in having Councillors who were not only loyal to her but men of considerable stature in their own right. After Cecil left for the Lords in 1571, leadership of the Commons passed to Sir Christopher Hatton, who was ably supported by three of his colleagues, Knollys, Walsingham and Mildmay — all of them widely respected in the House.

Elizabeth's attitude was never, in any case, merely negative. In the 1589 session, for instance, financial grievances came to the fore and two Bills were introduced to check abuses concerning the Exchequer and the practice of purveyance. The Queen informed the Commons that since these matters affected her closely she would take action herself, and she asked that four members of Parliament should be chosen to confer with a group of Privy Councillors and household officials about the best ways in which to remedy the grievances. In this way she preserved her prerogative while at the same time satisfying the Commons' desire for the redress of grievances.

In 1593, when Parliament met again, Hatton, Mildmay and Walsingham were all dead and a new generation had emerged which did not unquestioningly accept traditional restraints. Perhaps for this reason the Lord Keeper's reply to the petition for freedom of speech defined the privilege most carefully. 'For liberty of speech', he said, 'her Majesty commandeth me to tell you that to say "Yea" or "No" to Bills, God forbid that any man should be restrained or afraid to answer according to his best liking, with some short declaration of his reason therein, and therein to have a free voice — which is the very true liberty of the House: not, as some suppose, to speak there of all causes as him listeth, and to frame a form of religion or a state of government, as to their idle brains shall seem meetest. She saith no King fit for his state will suffer such absurdities.'

Elizabeth was far less tolerant of breaches of her instructions in this session. She sent Peter Wentworth to prison for publishing a tract on the succession, excluded from the House two members who dared to attack the High Commission, and reminded the Speaker that she had the right not only to summon and dissolve Parliament, but also to tell members what they were and were not to discuss. She was, by 1593, sixty years old, and had been ruling England before some of the members of the Commons had even been born. She regarded them as young hotheads, who needed to be disciplined, and she particularly resented 'such irreverence [as] was showed towards Privy Councillors'. Yet even young hotheads had their way to make in the world and were aware that a speech in opposition to the Queen's policy could end their chances of promotion. When the Earl of Essex tried to obtain an office for a friend in the Commons he failed because, as he wrote, the Queen 'startles at your name, chargeth you with popularity, and hath every particular of your speeches in Parliament . . . She stands much upon the bitter speech against Sir Robert Cecil.'

## Monópolies

Monopolies replaced the established church as the main target for parliamentary criticism in the last years of the reign. Monopolies were patents granted by the Queen to a favoured courtier, or sold to a business man, and they gave the holder the sole right to manufacture or trade in a certain commodity. This system, justified as a means of protecting new inventions, was applied to everyday articles simply as a means of raising revenue, and the Commons resented it as a form of indirect taxation. Since monopolies were created by the Queen they fell within the category of 'matters of state', not to be discussed without prior permission. But the Queen, no doubt informed about the temper of the House, chose to defend her prerogative by taking action herself. In 1597 she ordered her Councillors to examine all monopolies to see if there were any against the public interest, and the grateful Commons turned their petition of complaint into a thanksgiving address. The Queen, in reply, reminded her 'dutiful and loving subjects' that they must not entrench on her prerogative, which was 'the chiefest flower in her garland and the principal and head pearl in her crown and diadem'.

Although the Queen cancelled some of the more objectionable monopolies, her desperate need for money to meet the costs of war and of the Irish rebellion led her to grant at least thirty new patents on items that included currants, iron, bottles, vinegar, brushes, pots, salt, lead and oil. In these circumstances it was hardly surprising that the 1601 Parliament, the last of the reign, took up the issue again. One member called monopolists 'bloodsuckers of the commonwealth', and told how they brought 'the general profit into a private hand'. 'The end of all', he declared, 'is beggary and bondage to the subject.' Bacon tried to persuade the House not to take direct action itself but to petition the Queen to do so. 'The use hath ever been', he said, 'by petition to humble ourselves unto her Majesty and by petition desire to have our grievances redressed, especially when the remedy toucheth so nigh in point of prerogative.' But members were in an angry mood, disillusioned by the Queen's failure to take effective action after their earlier petition. When the Speaker tried to switch the debate on to discussion of the subsidy he was shouted down, and several members were unable to make themselves heard in the general confusion. Robert Cecil, who had been, as he reminded the Commons, a member of six or seven Parliaments, said that he had never seen the House in so great a confusion: 'This is more fit for a grammar school than a court of Parliament.'

The Queen realised that her prerogative would be endangered if she clung to monopolies, for they were a real grievance and opposition to them was widespread — Cecil, for instance, reported that while he was in his coach he had heard someone say, 'God prosper those that further the overthrow of these monopolies! God send the prerogative touch not our liberty!' Proclamations were therefore issued cancelling the principal monopolies complained of, and authorising anyone with a grievance to seek for redress in the courts of common law.

## '*Opposition*'?

Although Elizabeth had her difficulties with the Commons, it would be mistaken to assume that members regarded themselves as an 'opposition' — indeed, the very concept of a 'loyal opposition' was alien to the Tudor period. The House, like any large assembly, needed tactful and informed handling, but on the whole the Councillors provided this and thereby preserved harmony. The occasional outbursts of criticism or anger on the part of individual members created a disproportionate stir simply because they were untypical. Accounts of the 1576 Parliament, for instance, often suggest that the affair of Peter Wentworth dominated business; yet in fact, out of the thirty-five days for which the session lasted, only three were spent on Wentworth.

When disputes did arise they did not necessarily result from a clash between the Queen and her Council on one side and the Commons on the other. The Privy Council was itself divided on major issues, such as foreign policy and the reform of the Church, and policy divisions were accentuated by personal rivalries, such as that between Leicester and William Cecil at the beginning of the reign, or Essex and Robert Cecil at the end. One group within the Council was not above stirring up parliamentary opinion in order to discountenance its opponents, and when members of the Commons criticised certain aspects of royal policy they might be speaking for elements within the government as well as for themselves. The links between the Council and the House were not only close but complex, and an 'official' opinion could well be expressed by someone who held no official position. Sir Thomas Norton, for example, was not a Councillor and appeared at times to be among the foremost critics of the government in the Commons. Yet, as he made clear after the 1581 session, 'all that I have done I did by commandment of the House, and specially of the Queen's Council there, and my chiefest care was in all things to be directed by the Council'.

There were occasions, of course, when the Council was united against the Queen, as over the execution of Mary, Queen of Scots, and made use of Parliament to bring pressure to bear upon her. But such occasions were exceptional. In general the Councillors were concerned to ensure that the Queen's business was carried through Parliament with the greatest possible expedition, and they could count on the support of the vast majority of members of both Houses, who were not simply loyal to the Queen but regarded co-operation with the royal government as being in their own best interest. Conflict was the exception, not the rule, and the really important work of Commons and Lords consisted in the often tedious and certainly unglamorous task of carefully considering the Bills that were submitted to their scrutiny and passing them through the various stages that were necessary before they could receive the royal assent and reach the statute book.

While the Queen relied on her Councillors, and on the Lord Chancellor and Speaker, to ensure the smooth running of her Parliaments, they in turn were dependent upon her for support. Elizabeth's success as politician came from a remarkable blend of rigidity and flexibility. She knew when and how to give way gracefully, but she was no trimmer: she maintained the Church of England unaltered against opposition that would have overwhelmed an ordinary person, and she refused to abate one jot of her royal prerogative. Although the Commons were allowed a measure of free speech, they did not enjoy it even to the extent that Sir Thomas More had claimed in 1523. And if any member crossed the invisible line that divided 'liberty' from 'licence' the Queen had no qualms about barring him from the House or sending him to prison. Her authoritarian attitude would have provoked considerable resentment had it not been for the fact that she was identified with achievements that most English men and women valued dearly — above all the defence of the protestant cause against catholic Spain. She became the great 'Gloriana', a legend in her own lifetime, and even the quirks of her personality, including a stubborn aversion to change, had to be accepted as political realities.

The secret of Elizabeth's success was her identification with her people. From the beginning of her reign she cultivated her public image and went on progresses that took her all over the southern and central regions of England. These came to a virtual halt in the crisis years of the 1580s, but she revived them in the last decade of her reign, for she knew that by showing herself to her people she was deepening those bonds of affection which strengthened her throne. She was a majestic figure, and her subjects went in awe of her. Yet she knew how to descend from majesty and express herself in vivid, racy language. It was her gift for words that enabled her time and again to defuse an explosive situation and turn her critics into admirers. She used it to great effect in 1601, when she addressed the last Parliament of her reign in what came to be known as her 'Golden Speech'. 'There will never Queen sit in my seat', she told the members, 'with more zeal to my country, care for my subjects, and that will sooner with willingness venture her life for your good and safety, than myself. For it is my desire to live nor reign no longer than my life and reign shall be for your good. And though you have had and may have many princes more mighty and wise sitting in this seat, yet you never had, nor shall have, any that will be more careful and loving.'

## The Royal Finances

When Elizabeth ascended the throne the ordinary revenue amounted to some £200,000 a year, to which parliamentary subsidies added £50,000. By the 1590s the ordinary revenue had increased to £300,000, and parliamentary subsidies were now worth £135,000, giving Elizabeth a total annual income of about £450,000. Yet her expenditure had gone up far more than her income, particularly after her involvement in open war in the 1580s, and although she sold off lands to close the gap between the two she thereby reduced the yield of what remained.

Burghley, who became Lord Treasurer in 1572, pursued a policy of retrenchment at home and restraint abroad. He was a conservative in financial matters and believed in making the best of the existing system rather than reforming it. As a consequence royal revenue did not keep pace with inflation. Customs, for instance, which had brought in about £90,000 per annum in the early years of the reign, dipped to £60,000 in the 1570s and only regained their earlier level in the 1590s. In other words, Elizabeth was receiving the same amount in money from Customs in 1600 that she had done in 1560, yet during that time prices had risen by at least 75 per cent. Burghley would have been well advised to issue a new Book of Rates, but this might have provoked opposition in Parliament and elsewhere. He therefore preferred to stick with the increasingly outdated one that had been drawn up in Mary's reign.

Burghley's conservatism was also to be seen in the Court of Wards, of which he was appointed Master in 1561, for the revenue from wardship declined from £24,000 a year to £13,000 during Elizabeth's reign. When Robert Cecil took over from his father in 1598 he quickly doubled the yield, but this still meant that in real terms the Queen was receiving less from wardship at the end of her reign than at the beginning. The same lack of expansion was apparent in the land revenues. Crown estates were not exploited to anything like the extent that private estates were — partly because they were used as much for patronage as for revenue — and although the nominal yield increased during Elizabeth's reign from under £80,000 a year to about £100,000, this concealed a diminishing return in real terms, when inflation is taken into account.

Elizabeth could not have avoided bankruptcy had it not been for the subsidies voted by Parliament. Until 1589 it had been customary for Parliament to vote one subsidy by way of supply, but in that post-Armada year two were granted. The continuing demands of war on the royal finances made further recourse to Parliament inevitable, and in 1593 the Lords persuaded a reluctant Commons to increase their supply to three subsidies. The next Parliament, in 1597, saw another grant of three subsidies, and in 1601 the last Parliament of the reign took the unprecedented step of voting four. Members expressed doubts about whether the country could actually bear so heavy a burden of taxation, and the fact that they supported the crown in this apparently generous manner is a sign that the policies which Elizabeth was pursuing were widely supported.

Yet there was an element of hypocrisy in the Commons' attitude, for although they were voting more subsidies, the yield of each subsidy was steadily diminishing. This was because the commissioners who drew up the assessment in every county were local gentry, and they were concerned to reduce the rate at which they and their fellow gentry were taxed. A Cambridgeshire peer told Burghley in 1589 that 'there is no man assessed before me but is known to be worth at least in goods ten times as much as he is set at, and six times more in land', and the truth of this observation was confirmed by Sir Walter Ralegh when he reminded the Commons in 1601 that 'our estates [which] are £30 or £40 in the Queen's books [are] not the hundredth part of our wealth'.

The desperate need for money drove the royal government into imposing forced loans and demanding benevolences. In 1596, in order to set out the Cadiz expedition, it also instructed the maritime counties to provide ships at their own expense, while the inland counties were ordered to give money in lieu. Such measures provoked opposition in the localities, particularly as they came on top of heavy and continuous taxation and at a time of acute economic distress (see above, p 115). Public opinion was further alienated by devices such as monopolies; and landowners, in particular, were unhappy about the activities of the common informers who were encouraged by the government to pry into property titles and see if they included 'concealed' monastic lands. A great deal of land had in fact passed, unacknowledged, into new ownership when the property market was thrown into turmoil by the Dissolution, but the landowners by now regarded it as rightfully theirs and resented any suggestion that they should compound for their offence (or that of their forefathers) and purchase a valid and legal title.

## *Patronage*

Resentment against the crown was intensified by the fact that many of the patentees and projectors who battened and grew fat on Tudor society were the clients of courtiers and royal servants. The English monarchy had traditionally depended for administration on ecclesiastics who could be rewarded by advancement in the Church, but the anti-clericalism released by the Reformation changed this. Bishops remained men of substance, but the decline

of their political importance is reflected in the fact that no bishop
sat in Elizabeth's Council until Whitgift was appointed to it in
1586. Government, which had formerly been the preserve of the
Church, had been taken over by laymen. These secular administrators could not be rewarded by advancement in the Church, yet
no Tudor monarch could possibly afford to pay them a realistic
salary. Expenditure on the royal household had risen to a peak in
the early years of Mary's reign, as the government accepted its
obligation to increase stipends in line with inflation, but thereafter
economy had become the order of the day. Elizabeth, by the end
of her reign, was actually spending less on her household than
Henry VIII had done sixty years earlier. Since office-holders could
not live on their official salaries they had to supplement them with
fees and gratuities from those men and women who were
unfortunate enough to have need of their services. They were
also engaged in a perpetual struggle to obtain some grant from
the crown which would bring in money either directly or indirectly.

Royal patronage fell into three main categories. First of all there
was the grant of titles of honour, but Elizabeth cut down on these,
and at her death the peerage was smaller than it had been at her
accession. The same is true of the knightage. In 1560 there had
been some 600 knights, but by 1580 the figure was down to 300,
and although it rose to about 550 by 1603 this was largely the work
of military commanders, who had the right to confer knighthoods
on the battlefield. Essex alone created some 150 knights, showing
a recklessness that was typical of him but certainly not of his royal
patron.

The second category of patronage included appointment to offices in the crown's gift. There were about two hundred positions
in the royal household, traditionally reserved for the leading families, and other offices were available in the central administration
— the Treasury, the Secretariat and the Court of Wards. The Judiciary also provided many opportunities of profit — though appointment was limited to men trained in the law — and so did the
armed forces, whose commanders disposed of temptingly large
sums of money. The Queen appointed to many lucrative offices in
the Church as well, and she alone could confirm a man's local
standing by making him Lord-Lieutenant or Justice of the Peace,
or by conferring on him some nominal office — such as stewardship
of a royal park or manor — which carried great prestige. Tudor
England was a hierarchical society, and a man's place in it at any
given moment depended upon the titles, offices and perquisites with
which he was endowed. Unfortunately, there were only about a
thousand such offices to be distributed among over double that
number of claimants.

The third category of patronage included more obvious marks of royal favour, such as gifts and pensions, leases of crown lands, and monopolies. Direct grants from the Queen were generally confined to a handful of favourites, but they could be a valuable prize — Leicester, for example, had an annual pension of £1,000 and Christopher Hatton was given £400 a year in 1576. Leases of royal estates could be almost as valuable, since crown lands were usually under-exploited and might be made to yield a big profit to a hard-headed lessee: a typical example was that of the Earl of Essex, who paid £23 a year to the crown for the lease of Uttoxeter Moors which he sublet for £167. The Queen could also be occasionally persuaded to exchange some of the scattered manors of the crown for a more consolidated block belonging to a subject. The new owner could make a handsome profit by selling enough of the manors to cover his purchase price and increasing the rents on those he kept. Monopolies were another valuable (though double-edged) gift in the Queen's possession, and she gave the valuable patent of sweet wines successively to her two favourites, Leicester and Essex.

The demand for patronage was insatiable and the Queen could not deal with it all herself, but looked for advice to those around her. The well-placed persons who were able to channel the flow of royal favour became some of the most influential figures in Elizabethan society, and constellations of suppliants clustered round them. Burghley received between sixty and a hundred letters a day from clients and would-be clients, begging for favours, and much the same was true of Leicester, for as one contemporary remarked 'advancement in all worlds be obtained by mediation and remembrance of noble friends'.

One of the key posts where patronage was concerned was the Mastership of the Wards. In theory the Master's task was the straightforward one of selling the guardianship of tenants-in-chief who were under age, but in practice he acted as the nerve centre of a complex system of money deals, often of dubious morality, in which the upper levels of English society were all involved. To take only one example: Sir Edward Coke bought a valuable wardship from the Court, for which he paid £300. This was a substantial sum, but it was little compared with the £1,000 which he gave to the Master as a sign of his gratitude. Nor did he lose on the transaction, for no sooner had he been granted the wardship than he sold it for £4,000. The Queen was lucky if she received as much as a fifth of the profits of wardship during Burghley's period as Master from 1561 to 1598, but after Robert Cecil took over he increased the official price of wardships and brought the Queen's share up to about a third.

## Essex and Cecil

Although Burghley guided the Queen in her patronage policy, other courtiers — Ralegh, Hatton and Walsingham among them — could usually make their voices heard, and Elizabeth would often please herself. Burghley realised that the success of the Elizabethan system of patronage was in proportion to the number of important families it embraced, and he was not so much concerned to build up a private empire as to cement the bonds between the Queen and the political nation. In the closing years of his life, however, when he was anxious to ensure that his political influence would pass to his second son, Robert, he became aware that the Queen's young favourite, the Earl of Essex, was determined to acquire a monopoly of power and was setting about it in a ruthless fashion. In 1594, for instance, when Essex was trying to obtain the post of Attorney-General for his client Francis Bacon, he announced that 'the Attorneyship for Francis is that I must have, and in that I will spend all my power, might, authority and amity, and with tooth and nail defend and procure the same for him against whomsoever'.

This sounds like a declaration of war, which indeed it was, and Burghley reacted by fighting Essex with his own weapons and building up a patronage empire which acquired the nickname of 'Cecil's Commonwealth'. The balance which Elizabeth and Burghley had earlier established was destroyed by this conflict, for it came at the very moment when poverty was forcing the Queen to cut down, and there was less patronage available to meet an ever-growing demand. The struggle between Essex and Cecil was a bitter one because the stakes were so high. Burghley frequently complained about the meagre rewards of royal service. In 1585, for example, he declared that 'my fees of my Treasurership do not answer to my charge of my stable — I mean not my table!' In one sense he may have been speaking the truth, for his official stipend as Lord Treasurer was only £400. But this did not take into account the patronage which this office gave him and which yielded at least £1,000 a year. If Burghley really was impoverishing himself by serving the Queen, how was it that he became one of the richest landowners in England, built two enormous palaces at Stamford and Theobalds, left plate worth £15,000 behind him, and established his family so securely in the upper echelons of English society that it remains there to this day? Burghley, in fact, was a classic example of a man who rose to great wealth as well as great power in the royal administration, and Essex was determined to follow the same lucrative path.

Essex, who was not yet thirty when he sailed with the Cadiz expedition in 1596, fought brilliantly and became the idol of the soldiers. He hoped for his reward in the shape of the Mastership of the Wards, but Elizabeth, although she had a great affection for the Earl, distrusted his popularity and also resented the imperious manner in which he claimed advancement. She left the Mastership vacant, and Essex therefore accepted command of the army which was being despatched to Ireland. No doubt he was reckoning on the fact that a string of victories there would confirm the reputation he had established at Cadiz and make him so popular that even his enemies would have to come to terms with him. But he knew that his Irish venture was a gamble, for as he wrote to a friend, 'I am not ignorant what are the disadvantages of absence — the opportunities of practising enemies when they are neither encountered nor overlooked; the construction of princes, under whom *magna fama* is more dangerous than *mala*, and *successus minus quam nullus* . . . All these things which I am like to see, I do foresee.'

Essex's forebodings were justified. The Council, either by accident or design, was slow to send supplies, and he saw himself committed to a long campaign which would keep him far from the Queen. His rivals had already taken advantage of his absence — Robert Cecil, for instance, had secured the coveted Mastership of the Wards — and the longer he stayed away the weaker his influence became. In defiance of the Queen's explicit orders he therefore threw up his command in Ireland, even though the rebellion was still alive, returned to England in September 1599, and rode posthaste to Elizabeth at Nonsuch.

The Queen was at first glad to see him, but as she reflected on his disregard of her wishes her anger mounted. 'By God's son', she burst out to one of her gentlemen, 'I am no Queen! That man is above me. Who gave him commandment to come here so soon?' Essex's valuable monopoly of sweet wines was taken away from him and he was kept prisoner until June 1600 when a special tribunal stripped him of his offices.

Out of his anger against those who, he was convinced, had ousted him from Elizabeth's favour, Essex hatched a plot for an armed rising, to take over the government and force the Queen to accept new advisers. It looked as though faction struggles were once again going to lead to civil war, and Essex House became a centre where groups of discontented nobles and gentry, including Shakespeare's patron, the Earl of Southampton, discussed their plans. The Council was alarmed, particularly when Shakespeare's company staged *Richard II* at the Globe — the story of an English monarch who had been deposed because he listened to evil counsellors — and Essex was summoned to appear before it. This challenge sparked off the rising, and on 8 February 1600 the Earl rode into the City at the head of two hundred armed men, crying out, 'For the Queen! For the Queen!' Nobody joined him, but troops were drawn up to block his way. The rebellion was over before it had even begun.

The Essex rising showed how close factional strife had come to destroying Elizabethan harmony. Not for nothing did Edward Coke, who led the prosecution against Essex, hark back to the Wars of the Roses when he prayed that 'this Robert might be the last of his name, Earl of Essex, who affected to be Robert the first of that name, King of England'. Essex was executed, but his removal did not solve the problem of an ageing Queen and an empty treasury, even though by confirming Robert Cecil in power it restored at least a semblance of the order that Burghley had established.

Cecil's supremacy apparently depended on the Queen's life, for James had no love for the Cecils, whom he held responsible for Elizabeth's refusal to nominate him as her successor. In the last years of the Queen's reign Robert Cecil spent £25,000 on land, to cushion his possible fall from power, but at the same time he was working hard to make sure that such a fall would not take place. In 1601 he opened secret negotiations with James and prepared arrangements for the peaceful accession of the King of Scots. James's suspicion changed overnight to warm friendship, and when Cecil sent him the draft proclamation announcing his succession, he made no corrections: this music, he said 'sounded so sweetly in his ears that he could alter no note in so agreeable an harmony'.

By March 1603 the Queen was obviously dying and sat for long periods saying nothing. When, however, Cecil and the other officers of state asked her to name her successor, she was said to have given a sign that she acknowledged James. After that she prayed with Whitgift until she fell into a stupor. Early on the morning of 24 March 1603 she died, and a few hours later, while a messenger rode north as fast as relays of horses could carry him, James was proclaimed King of England.

# I I

# James I

## James I

James left Edinburgh in April 1603, and so many Englishmen flocked north to see their new monarch that his journey turned into a triumphal progress. As James himself was to recall, 'the people of all sorts rid and ran, nay rather flew to meet me, their eyes flaming nothing but sparkles of affection their mouths and tongues uttering nothing but sounds of joy'. The King showed his pleasure by creating over three hundred knights on his way south, and he revelled in the entertainments provided for him at the great country houses where he stayed. It was May before he eventually entered London and took up residence at Whitehall.

James was only thirty-six at Elizabeth's death, and the fact that he had two sons seemed a guarantee of a long period of stability. As King of Scotland he had been a success, and his writings — especially the *Basilicon Doron*, a philosophical tract on kingship addressed to his eldest son, Prince Henry — had been well received in England. There was some apprehension that a king who had not been raised in the common-law tradition, with its emphasis on the subjects' rights, might act in too high-handed a manner, but wariness was outweighed by relief at the fact that the throne was safely occupied, and by someone who was, in his own words, 'an old and experienced king'.

There was, in short, a great fund of goodwill towards James, which reflected in part the discontent that had been mounting in the closing decade of Elizabeth's reign. Her noted prudence in financial matters had become, in the eyes of many of her more important subjects, tight-fistedness, and her failure to provide adequate rewards for those who served her had led to widespread corruption. As the members of James's first Parliament were to record, 'in regard of her sex and age, which we had great cause to tender, and much more upon care to avoid all trouble which by wicked practice might have been drawn to impeach the quiet of your Majesty's right in the succession, those actions were then passed over'. But they added that they hoped, 'in succeeding times of freer access to your Highness of renowned grace and justice', that these abuses would be remedied. Their expectations, unfortunately, were not to be fulfilled, for corruption remained endemic in public life, and James's good intentions were nullified by the intractable financial problems which confronted him, and which he made worse by his own extravagance.

## *James and the Royal Finances*

Elizabeth bequeathed James a debt of £400,000, but this was not as bad as it seemed, for the subsidies voted by her last Parliament had not yet been collected in full, and by the time they were all paid in to the Exchequer the net debt was a mere £100,000. Elizabeth had reigned during a period of acute inflation, whose effects were exacerbated by war, and it is a tribute to her determination and skill in managing her finances that she left James a smaller debt than she herself had inherited. Yet in some ways her success was self-defeating, for she thereby encouraged her subjects to believe that the royal finances were fundamentally sound — which was far from the case — and she also misled James into assuming that he could give up all attempts to curb his natural generosity now that he had left his poverty-stricken Scottish kingdom and entered a land flowing with milk and honey.

Even if James had been as thrifty as Elizabeth he would have found it hard to make ends meet, for unlike his unmarried predecessor he had three households to support — his own, the Queen's and Prince Henry's. He was also expected to maintain the dignity of the crown in an age when expenditure on courts throughout Europe was rising dramatically; to reward his loyal servants, both Scottish and English; and to signal an end to the stringency of Elizabeth's closing years. There was no possibility of doing all this without massive support from Parliament, yet one of James's first actions was to put an end to the long war with Spain, and this removed a major incentive for Parliament to grant supply. It so happened that when James called on Parliament for assistance in 1606, after the last of the Elizabethan subsidies had been collected, he met with a generous response. Parliament voted him three subsidies and six fifteenths, worth nearly £400,000, but this may have given James the mistaken impression that whenever his financial circumstances became desperate he could always rely on Parliament to bail him out.

While James's subjects were looking forward to the end of Elizabethan stringency they can hardly have anticipated such a violent swing of the pendulum, from miserliness to extravagance. When Robert Cecil, Earl of Salisbury, took over the Treasury in 1608 he discovered that the King was well over half a million pounds in debt and running an annual deficit approaching £100,000. Salisbury took all the obvious steps, such as chasing up outstanding debts and ordering a survey of all the royal lands, with a view to raising rents. He even resorted to the collection of a feudal aid for the knighting of Prince Henry, though this produced such a small amount that it was hardly worth the trouble. He was reluctant to revert to the practice of selling off crown lands, since the short-term capital gain was offset by the long-term loss of income, yet the situation was so desperate that he had no choice, and he therefore disposed of properties worth more than £400,000. He also extended the number and range of Impositions — duties on selected imports and exports which were levied by virtue of the royal prerogative and without any parliamentary sanction. As a result of his herculean efforts the debt was substantially reduced, but he could not eliminate it altogether. He now became convinced that tinkering with the financial system would never produce the desired results. What was needed was a fundamental reorganisation which would repair the damage done by a century of inflation and effectively re-endow the crown. In 1610, therefore, he invited the House of Commons to co-operate with him in drawing up the 'Great Contract'.

What Salisbury proposed was that Parliament should vote the King a 'supply' of £600,000, so that the debt could be eliminated and a reserve fund established. It should also provide for an annual 'support' of £200,000, in return for the surrender by the crown of a number of its feudal prerogatives, the abolition of purveyance (the crown's right to buy goods for the royal household at lower than market prices), and the reform of the Court of Wards. These proposals, if carried through, would have transformed the crown's financial situation and set English history on a different course. But the sums involved were enormous, and the Commons never, in fact, gave more than cursory consideration to the demand for 'supply'. Instead they concentrated on 'support' but made it plain that they were not interested in the relatively minor concessions which Salisbury had proposed. Abolition of purveyance was welcome to them, but what they wanted more than anything else was the total abolition of wardship. James was persuaded to agree to this, in principle, and Salisbury and the Commons then spent several months haggling over the amount of compensation. Eventually, in the summer of 1610, the Commons gave a formal commitment to provide £200,000 a year for the crown in perpetuity.

Salisbury's triumph, however, was short-lived, for when the House re-assembled after the summer recess it quickly became clear that opinion had swung against the Contract. This was no doubt because members had consulted their constituents and found that there was widespread opposition to the idea of accepting a tax burden equivalent to nearly three subsidies every year. There was also justifiable scepticism about the King's ability to restrain his extravagance so as to keep within the limits of his expanded income. Even if the principle of 'support' had been conceded, there was no agreement on 'supply'; nor, for that matter, was there any agreement on how the 'support' would be raised. The King insisted that it should be by a land tax, since this was certain and invariable, but there was a body of opinion in the Commons which wanted a tax on trade. This was because the House as a whole had never accepted the legality of Impositions, despite the judgment in their favour in 1606 (see below p. 212), and now the negotiations over the Great Contract opened the possibility of eliminating them at minimum cost. James was by no means inflexible on this issue. He offered to accept a bill outlawing Impositions for the future. He even offered to abandon existing Impositions provided the Commons would make up the shortfall in his income. But what he could not afford to do was give up Impositions without compensation. If he were to surrender purveyance, wardship and Impositions in return for an annual grant of £200,000 he would actually be worse off than he was already. Impositions, therefore, although they never constituted a formal part of the Great Contract, cast their shadow over it and helped create the atmosphere of mutual suspicion and ill will in which it foundered. James, who felt that he had compromised his dignity by allowing public haggling over the details of the royal income, blamed Salisbury for the debacle. 'Your greatest error', he told him, 'hath been that ye ever expected to draw honey out of gall, being a little blinded with the self-love of your own counsel in holding together of this Parliament, whereof all men were despaired, as I have oft told you, but yourself alone'.

Although Salisbury was out of favour he retained the Lord Treasurership until his death in 1612. James did not immediately appoint another Lord Treasurer, but he turned for advice to members of the Howard family, and in particular to Henry Howard, Earl of Northampton. By this time the crown's debt had again reached half a million pounds, and was increasing at the rate of £50–100,000 a year. Numerous projects were considered for improving the royal finances, and Northampton performed a major service for the crown by calling on the services of a self-made City merchant and financier, Lionel Cranfield. It was some years, however, before Cranfield began to make his presence felt, and meanwhile the financial problem was becoming more and more acute. So serious was it by 1614 that James decided on another appeal to Parliament, but no sooner had members assembled, in April of that year, than they renewed their assault on Impositions. After two months of stormy and sterile debates James lost patience and dissolved this 'Addled Parliament'.

Soon after the dissolution, Northampton died, but James confirmed the supremacy of the Howards by appointing Northampton's nephew, Thomas Howard, Earl of Suffolk, as Lord Treasurer. Unfortunately both for himself and the King, Suffolk was singularly lacking in Northampton's qualities of determination, ruthlessness and commitment to reform. He was a much pleasanter man but an inefficient administrator — except when it came to enriching himself, for his profits from office enabled him to build a vast palace at Audley End in Essex. There was no obvious threat to his position, however, particularly since Robert Carr, Earl of Somerset, who had married into the Howard family and therefore had a vested interest in its continuing predominance, was the King's favourite. But Carr's hold on the King's affections was threatened by the emergence of a rival favourite, George Villiers, the future Duke of Buckingham, and as early as 1615 Villiers had established friendly relations with Cranfield, whose continuing investigation into the royal administration was daily revealing more evidence of Suffolk's laxness. In 1617 one observer reported that 'the King is now preparing an exact examination and censure of the abuses in the Exchequer, which in all men's opinions are likely to prove very foul', and as the corruption in the revenue departments was exposed it became clear that Suffolk's days were numbered. In July 1618 he was dismissed from office and subsequently brought to trial in the Star Chamber on charges of malversation.

Just as he had done after Salisbury's death, the King left the office of Lord Treasurer vacant and relied on commissioners to carry out its functions. Cranfield was appointed to the Treasury commission in 1619 and under his guidance expenditure was further reduced, especially in the Navy and Ordnance departments, while the yield from Customs and Impositions was increased. By 1620 the commission had come within sight of eliminating the annual deficit, but it could do nothing about the debt, which now stood at about £900,000. Meanwhile the foreign situation was causing alarm, for the Thirty Years War had broken out, and there was an obvious need for money to be spent on diplomacy and defence preparations. These considerations were behind the decision to summon the Parliament which met in January 1621. This voted two subsidies, but the £160,000 which these brought in did not even cover James's extra expenditure: they made no contribution towards solving the basic financial problem, which was that of under-endowment.

Before the second session of Parliament opened in November 1621, James appointed Cranfield as Lord Treasurer and soon after elevated him to the Earldom of Middlesex. This signalled a continuation of the same unglamorous policies of restraint and retrenchment with which Cranfield had become identified. Perhaps the Treasurer's greatest success consisted in persuading James to curb his extravagance, for expenditure on the royal household, which had been rising inexorably in the first decade of the reign, was down to Elizabethan levels by 1624. Yet even had James been as parsimonious as his predecessor the royal revenue would still have been insufficient. Inflation had sent prices up fivefold during the sixteenth century, and James would have needed close on £600,000 a year if his income was to match, in real terms, that of Henry VII. This was far more than he was getting even at the end of his reign.

War, allied with inflation, had wrecked the royal finances, and Middlesex was appalled at the prospect of a renewal of war against Spain in the 1620s. His hopes rose when, in 1623, Prince Charles made a secret and hasty journey to Madrid, accompanied by Buckingham, in the hope of finally concluding the marriage negotiations, which had been dragging on for years, and bringing back a Spanish Infanta as his bride. Had he been successful the royal Exchequer would have benefited from a dowry of half a million pounds — enough to eliminate the debt — and war preparations, with all the expense that they entailed, would have been unnecessary. But Charles returned from Spain without the Infanta, and it soon became clear to Middlesex that Buckingham was determined to force James into war. He did everything he could to prevent this, even going so far as to promote an alternative favourite, but all he achieved was his own downfall. No sooner had Buckingham returned from Spain, in late 1623, then he set about Middlesex's destruction. James, who still valued his gritty and rough-spoken Lord Treasurer, did his best to shield him, but when the last Parliament of James's reign assembled in 1624 the leaders of the Commons were only too happy to second Buckingham's efforts. The Lord Treasurer was impeached on charges of 'bribery, oppression, wrong and deceit', found guilty, and sentenced by the Lords to be dismissed from office, imprisoned and heavily fined. It was a poor recompense for all the good work that he had done, but James made the most perceptive, if cynical, comment on his fate when he told the Lords 'he cannot, you know, but have many enemies, for a Treasurer must have hatred if he love his master's profits'.

## James I and the Church of England

The accession of a new sovereign had been, for the last three reigns, the occasion for a redefinition of religious policy, and in 1603 the puritans were hoping that James, whose background in religious matters was presbyterian, would show sympathy with their demands for modification of the Elizabethan settlement. They struck early, by presenting him with the Millenary Petition while he was on his way south from Scotland. This was the work of a number of puritan ministers who described themselves as neither 'fractious men affecting a popular parity in the Church', nor 'schismatics aiming at the dissolution of the state ecclesiastical' but 'faithful servants of Christ, and loyal subjects to your Majesty'. What they wanted was what their Elizabethan predecessors had tried, in vain. to get from the Queen — namely, an end to pluralism and non-residency, the establishment of a preaching ministry, and the abolition of such 'popish' ceremonies as signing with the cross in baptism, using the ring in marriage, and wearing the cap and surplice.

James sympathised with the basic aim of eliminating pluralism and improving the quality of clergy, and in July 1603 he had given an earnest of his intentions by writing to the Vice-Chancellors of Oxford and Cambridge informing them that he intended to devote the proceeds of all impropriations in royal hands to increasing the value of poorer livings, so that they would be able to attract and maintain learned ministers. He also invited representatives of the puritans to meet him and the bishops at Hampton Court, early in 1604, to consider what further reforms needed to be carried out. The puritans were delighted by this response and in a number of counties, of which Northamptonshire was perhaps the most committed, began drawing up reform petitions and organising public opinion. They seem to have envisaged a repetition of the 1586–7 campaign, including a survey of the clergy and the sending of delegates to London to act as informal advisers to their representatives at Hampton Court.

This flurry of puritan activity alarmed the bishops, who feared that the new sovereign might not be so stout in defence of the established church as his predecessor. Yet in fact they had little to fear. James did not regard the Church of England as perfect, but he had no wish to see it swept away and replaced by a presbyterian system, for his experience in Scotland had taught him the dangers of this. It is not clear who actually chose the four ministers who eventually argued the puritan case at Hampton Court, but they were all moderates, having more in common with the mainstream of the episcopate than with their radical presbyterian brethren. When they argued the case for a learned, preaching ministry they were pushing at an open door, for this was everybody's aim: the disagreement was on the best way in which to achieve it. However, when they urged that the disciplinary powers of bishops should be modified by the inclusion, as assessors, of representatives of the lesser clergy, they awoke James's fears of Scots'-style presbyterianism and stung him into a characteristically forceful outburst: 'I will think of this matter seven years before I resolve to admit of a presbytery, and by that time happily I may wax fat, and if then

I think it behoveful for me to have any to stir me up and awaken me, I will then have a presbytery by me'.

After the final meeting of the Hampton Court conference, on 18 January 1604, a declaration was issued summarising its conclusions. There were to be minor changes in the descriptions of certain services in the Prayer Book, an expansion of the articles of religion, and a slight reduction in the powers of the Court of High Commission. The conference also committed itself to the objectives of providing a learned ministry, encouraging preaching, and limiting pluralism. The amendments to the Prayer Book were authorised by a royal proclamation issued in March, but the tone of this indicated James's basic conservatism in ecclesiastical matters, for he announced that he had found 'no cause why any change should have been made at all in that which was most impugned, the Book of Common Prayer . . . neither in the doctrines, which appeared to be sincere, nor in the rites and form, which were justified out of the practice of the primitive church'. Not surprisingly, the radical puritans, particularly those who had gone to London to act as a pressure group, blamed the moderation of the puritan representatives at the conference, as well as the intransigence of the bishops, for what they regarded as its failure. Indeed, the only major and positive outcome of the conference was a new translation of the Bible, the Authorised Version, which was published in 1611.

A month after the ending of the conference, John Whitgift died. Although, as Archbishop of Canterbury, he had been responsible for the government of the Church under the King, old age and increasing ill health had led him to hand over many of his duties to his former chaplain, Richard Bancroft, who was now Bishop of London. This meant that even before Bancroft succeeded Whitgift as Archbishop he was the most influential figure on the episcopal bench. He had been one of the principal spokesmen at Hampton Court, and he was also responsible for guiding Convocation in its task of codifying Church law — something that had not been done since Henry VIII's reign. The results of his work were seen in the *Canons*, published by royal authority in September 1604. These defined, in considerable detail, the doctrines and structure of the Church of England, and Bancroft clearly intended them to put an end to nonconformity, once and for all, by laying down regulations which every minister and ordinand must accept. Bancroft was very much in the mould of Whitgift, though perhaps even more determined in his insistence on uniformity, and the *Canons* included a requirement that every candidate for holy orders should subscribe to three articles modelled on those drawn up by Whitgift in 1583. The most contentious of these was that 'the Book of Common Prayer . . . containeth in it nothing contrary to the Word of God . . . and that he himself will use the form in the said Book prescribed in public prayer and administration of the sacraments, and none other'.

Bancroft, with James's support and encouragement, set about enforcing conformity, and as a consequence some ninety ministers were deprived of their livings. Although they constituted a mere one per cent of all clergy they were often men of considerable talent as well as integrity, and the action taken against them led to protests in Parliament and to a revival of the petitioning campaign. The climax of this came with the presentation to James of a petition from the gentlemen of Northamptonshire calling on him to prevent the deprivation of 'many faithful preachers who . . . out of the tenderness of their consciences and fear to offend the King of Heaven . . . make scruple to use the ceremonies and yield to the subscription enjoined'. James was furious, and ordered the framers of the petition to be deprived of their official positions in the county administration, yet his essential moderation quickly re-asserted itself and there was a marked slackening in the campaign against puritan nonconformists. No doubt James was encouraged by the fact that the vast majority of ministers had accepted the *Canons*, and that the minority of obdurate protesters presented no real threat either to the Church or to the royal supremacy.

As far as theology was concerned, James had no quarrel with the puritans, nor had most of his bishops. There was general agreement on the doctrine of predestination and the commemorative nature of the communion service: indeed, in many parish churches the communion table had long since been removed from the chancel — where it looked too much like an altar — and placed in the nave, where it was treated with scant respect. There was a 'high church' wing in the episcopate, whose members — later referred to as Arminians — believed that Calvinist influences in the anglican church had become too strong, but they were few in number and of limited influence while James was alive.

James, like Elizabeth, took his stand on the *Thirty-Nine Articles* and believed that they should be left unchanged even when they were open to differing interpretations, as was the case with the article on predestination. His objection to the Dutch Arminians was not based so much on theological differences as on the fact that they had challenged the prevailing orthodoxy and thereby created disunity — at a time, moreover, when the Dutch were faced with the prospect of a renewal of their war of independence against Spain. When, in 1619, he sent representatives to the conference called at Dordrecht (Dort) to settle the dispute between the Arminians and their opponents, he instructed them to act as peacemakers and try to restore harmony. He saw no need for public debate on abstruse theological matters, for as he told one of his bishops 'it appeared to him a very bold attempt for men to dispute . . . about such ques-

tions of God's predestination, and so peremptorily to decide matters as if they had been in heaven and had assisted at the divine
council-board'.

James showed by his appointments to the episcopal bench that
he was determined to make the Church of England representative
of a broad spectrum of protestant belief. Lancelot Andrewes, the
most distinguished of the 'high' churchmen, was given the bishopric of Chichester in 1605 and subsequently translated to Winchester. John Overall, who had strongly criticised the Lambeth
Articles, held the sees, successively, of Coventry and Norwich,
while Richard Neile, a determined opponent of the hard-line Calvinists, was appointed to Lincoln in 1614 and later promoted to
Durham. Neile picked as his chaplain William Laud, who represented the younger generation of high churchmen, and it was
partly as a result of Neile's advocacy that Laud became Bishop of
St David's in 1621. But the key positions in the Jacobean church
went to committed Calvinists. In 1607 James chose as Archbishop
of York Toby Matthew, who established a reputation for himself
as an assiduous preacher and took a tolerant line towards the puritans, preferring to focus his attack upon the catholics. As for the
province of Canterbury, it was widely assumed that Bancroft would
be succeeded by Andrewes, but when the Archbishop died in 1610
James elevated the Bishop of London, George Abbot, a former lecturer who was a conforming puritan.

Under the leadership of Abbot and Matthew the Jacobean
church retained the adherence of the great majority of puritans, but
there were some who found conformity too high a price to pay, and
the early decades of the seventeenth century saw a proliferation of
congregations which either cut themselves off altogether from the
established Church or else adopted a semi-separatist position by
remaining within it but forming what were in effect separate cells.
Sometimes congregations would include both separatists and semi-
separatists. This was the case with the group which gathered round
Henry Jacob, a former Brownist, at Southwark in 1616.

Formal separation from the established church was a crime, and
conventicles, where they were discovered, were broken up. But in
practice the Church of England permitted a degree of diversity that
satisfied the consciences of most of its members. If the minister in
one parish was a non-preaching 'dumb dog', the more zealous
among his parishioners could always take themselves off to a neighbouring church, or go to their market town to hear the lectures
which the diocesan authorities provided by drawing on the services
of a panel of local clergy. And as the seventeenth century went on,
so the quality of new entrants to the Church improved. By the time
James died, the aim of providing a learned, preaching ministry for
the Church seemed to be drawing ever closer to fulfilment.

## Roman Catholics

The puritans were not the only people who hoped that a new reign would open a new, and better, chapter in their history. The same was true of the Roman Catholics, and they had good reason to be hopeful, for James was not an intolerant man by nature, and shortly before his accession he had been in correspondence with one of their leading figures, Henry Howard, later Earl of Northampton, and had promised him that 'as for the catholics, I will neither persecute any that will be quiet and give but an outward obedience to the law, neither will I spare to advance any of them that will by good service worthily deserve it'. The King was as good as his word, and catholics enjoyed a degree of tolerance that they had not known for a long time. They took comfort from the knowledge that James's wife, Anne of Denmark, was an adherent of the old faith (though a discreet one) and even catholics who had hitherto kept their beliefs to themselves now came out into the open. One contemporary commented: 'it is hardly credible in what jollity they now live. They make no question to obtain at least a toleration, if not an alteration of religion, in hope whereof many who before did dutifully frequent the Church are of late become recusants.'

The ninety-nine per cent of Englishmen who were not catholics were appalled and alarmed by the evidence of catholic vitality and began to suspect that James himself might not be as sound in religion as they had assumed. When James realised this he not only made it plain that he was a committed protestant, determined to uphold the Church as it existed in England, but also ordered that the penal laws should again be put into effect. The catholics — like the puritans after the Hampton Court conference — felt bitter at the collapse of all their hopes, particularly since the signing of peace with Spain in 1604 meant that they could no longer look to that country for support. They were faced with the realisation that they were an isolated minority in a hostile community, and that time was running against them. This produced a mood of desperation that drove a number of young catholic gentlemen to devise a plan to blow up the Houses of Parliament at the very moment when James was formally opening the session.

Fortunately for James the Gunpowder Plot was discovered before it could be put into effect, and Guy Fawkes and his fellow conspirators were arrested, tried and subsequently executed. Among those who suffered was Henry Garnett, head of the Jesuit mission in England. The evidence against him was largely circumstantial, but the government was determined to tar all the missionary priests with the brush of sedition in the hope of thereby depriving them of the support of the lay catholic community. A further step in this direction came in 1606, with the drawing up of an oath of allegiance

which all catholics were required to take. The aim of the oath was
to distinguish between loyal and disloyal catholics, but while all
except a few fanatics were prepared to swear that they would 'bear
faith and true allegiance to his Majesty, his heirs and successors,
and him and them will defend to the uttermost of my power against
all conspiracies and attempts whatsoever', many of them had reservations about that section of the oath which required everyone
taking it to declare that 'I do from my heart abhor, detest and ab-
jure, as impious and heretical, this damnable doctrine and position,
that princes which be excommunicated or deprived by the Pope
may be deposed'. In other words, while perfectly happy to accept
James as King, even in the event of his being excommunicated,
English catholics would have preferred not to become involved in
controversies about the exact nature and limits of papal power. In
the event, most catholics, clerical as well as lay, took the oath, but
instead of serving, as James had hoped, as a means to reconcile the
English catholics with the protestant community in which they
lived, it became yet one more obstacle in the way.

Garnett's arrest and execution did not mean the end of the English mission. As far as the Jesuits were concerned, their numbers
grew rapidly, from under twenty at the end of Elizabeth's reign to
over a hundred by the end of James's. In 1623 their increasing
strength was recognised by the decision to elevate England into a
province of the Order of Jesus, and the following years saw the
establishment of twelve districts, each under the leadership of a
superior, who was required to keep in close touch with the provincial of the Order at his headquarters in the London region. The
Benedictine mission was also increasing in size, and eventually
numbered about half that of the Jesuits, but the largest group still
remained the seculars, headed by the Archpriest. Many of the seculars had a degree of commitment at least equal to that of the regulars, but their organisation was poor, and since there were far too
few of them to operate in every parish, they were distributed ir-
regularly throughout England.

The seculars were envious of the regulars and particularly of the
Jesuits, who were increasingly taking up residence in gentry households and acting as confessors to the family. After Garnett the Jesuits had accepted the fact that England was going to remain (as
they saw it) a heretical country for the foreseeable future. They
were therefore prepared to co-operate with the gentry in preserving
and nourishing the tender plant of English catholicism without concerning themselves overmuch with the relationship between the
English catholic community and the Roman church as a whole.
The seculars, on the other hand, hoped, even if they did not believe,
that England would be restored fully to the Roman obedience and
that the organisation of the Church in their country should ap-

proximate to that laid down by the Council of Trent. In particular they wanted the episcopal hierarchy to be restored, for if a bishop was appointed he would automatically take charge of all the mission priests in England, regular as well as secular, and cut the Jesuits down to size. He would also be well placed to insist that financial contributions from English catholics should go to him and be used for the general good of the mission. This, once again, would benefit the seculars, since at present a considerable proportion of the funds that were made available by the catholic gentry went either to the Jesuits or to limited and specific purposes. The papacy was reluctant to restore the hierarchy in its traditional shape and form for fear of offending James, but in 1623 William Bishop was appointed Bishop of Chalcedon, with jurisdiction over all English and Scottish catholics. He died early the following year, but was succeeded as bishop by Richard Smith. The seculars were delighted by the way in which Smith asserted his authority over the catholic laity, but catholic gentlemen, who shared the anti-clerical prejudices of their protestant neighbours, were deeply offended by it. The seculars' triumph was achieved only at the cost of alienating the very people upon whose support they were ultimately dependent, and of cementing the alliance between the gentry and the regulars which they had hoped to weaken or even destroy.

Royal policy towards the catholics fluctuated according to the pressures that James was subjected to. There is little doubt that if he had been free to act as he wished he would have adopted a relaxed and tolerant attitude. But when Parliament was in session he had to take account of the violently anti-papist sentiments which members expressed; and in view of his precarious financial situation he could not afford to deprive himself of the revenue from recusancy fines, which by 1614 amounted to some £8,000 a year. On the other hand, James's principal aim in foreign policy was to bridge the gap between protestant and catholic Europe and part of his strategy consisted in the arranging of a marriage between Prince Charles and a Spanish Infanta. The Spaniards insisted that one of the elements in any marriage treaty should be a promise of better treatment for the English catholics, and whenever negotiations reached a certain level of intensity James would relax the enforcement of the penal laws. The climax came in 1623, when Charles and Buckingham were in Spain for what it was assumed would be the closing stage of the negotiations. James now gave a solemn assurance to the Spanish ambassadors in England that he would suspend the penal laws and do all in his power to persuade Parliament to repeal them.

When news of this leaked out it was not well received by James's subjects. Archbishop Abbot, in particular, had grave reservations about the wisdom of James's policy, and a letter appeared under his name warning the King of the danger 'lest by this toleration and discountenancing of the true profession of the gospel, where-with God hath blessed us, and this kingdom hath so long flour-ished under it, your Majesty do not draw upon the kingdom in general, and yourself in particular, God's heavy wrath and indig-nation'. Abbot denied that he had written any such letter, and no doubt he was speaking the truth. But there is equally no doubt that it accurately reflected his feelings and those of the vast majority of his fellow countrymen.

## James I and the Common Law

James was a stranger to common law, for in Scotland the civil law, which was generally assumed to be more concerned with the rights of the ruler than the liberties of the subject, had gained a consider-able measure of acceptance during the course of the sixteenth cen-tury. This might not have given cause for alarm south of the border had it not been for the fact that in his published writings James put so much emphasis upon the royal authority. In the *Trew Law of Free Monarchies*, for instance, he asserted that 'the King is above the law, as both the author and giver of strength thereto'. A good king, he added, would 'frame all his actions to be according to the law, yet is he not bound thereto but of his good will and for good example-giving to his subjects'.

In one way James was saying nothing new. English kings had always been above the law to the extent that there was no pre-scribed, legal way in which they could be called to account for their actions. The judges were appointed by the King, writs ran in his name, and although the creation of new law was a function of Par-liament the statutes which it made had no validity until the King had signified his assent to them. What worried many Englishmen, particularly that cross-section of the political nation which had re-ceived at least part of its education at one or other of the Inns of Court, was the fear that James might make law independently of Parliament. The King already had the right to issue proclamations which had the force of law, and James made frequent use of these in the early years of his reign. This created problems of overlap-ping, and the decision was therefore taken to publish all extant proclamations in book form, so that their exact text would be avail-able for careful study and interpretation. The book was published in 1609, and when Parliament reassembled in the following year it immediately took up the matter. The Commons drew up a pet-ition complaining that the printing of proclamations 'in such form as Acts of Parliament formerly have been and still are used to be . . . seemeth to imply a purpose to give them more reputation and more establishment than heretofore they have had'. Furthermore, the Commons argued, the extensive use of proclamations had spread a general apprehension that they would 'by degrees grow up and increase to the strength and nature of laws [and] in process of time bring a new form of arbitrary government upon the realm'.

James gave a conciliatory reply, in which he made it plain that he regarded proclamations as inferior to common and statute law, but defended their use as temporary measures when a statutory remedy was not available. James also consulted the judges about the limitations upon his authority where proclamations were concerned, and Sir Edward Coke later recorded how he gave his opinion 'that the King by his proclamation cannot create any offence which was not an offence before'. This bald statement failed to reflect the careful phrasing of the judges' response, for in .fact they agreed that in cases of necessity the King could create an offence and provide for its punishment in the prerogative court of Star Chamber. But although James continued to issue proclamations far more frequently than Elizabeth had done, he never gave any indication that he wanted to extend them into an instrument of arbitrary government. James may have been inclined to absolutism in theory, but in practice he remained a strictly constitutional sovereign. As he told Salisbury in 1610, although he was King by hereditary right, and not dependent in any way on public approval, yet 'the law did set the crown upon his head, and he is a king by the common law of the land'. It was dangerous, James added, to try and define the authority of a king, but 'he did acknowledge that he had no power to make laws of himself, or to exact any subsidies *de jure* without the consent of his three Estates [i.e. Parliament]'.

James's explicit denial that he had any right to tax at will arose out of the problems associated with Impositions, and in particular the judgment given in Bate's case in 1606. Impositions had been levied first of all by Mary and subsequently by Elizabeth, but had never received parliamentary sanction. It was on these grounds that John Bate, a merchant and member of the Levant Company, refused to pay them. Since this was a matter affecting the royal prerogative James could have refused to allow it to be tried at common law, but since he had no wish to rule in an arbitrary fashion he let it go before the judges, or barons, of the Court of Exchequer, which specialised in financial matters. The judges decided in favour of the crown, and Chief Baron Fleming, when he passed judgment, distinguished between two aspects of the royal prerogative. There was the ordinary prerogative, which was defined and limited by the common law and could not be enlarged or otherwise altered except through Parliament. But there was, in addition, an absolute prerogative, which was not 'guided by the rules which direct only at the common law, and is most properly named policy and government'. He included in this category 'all commerce and affairs with foreigners, all wars and peace, all acceptance and admitting for current foreign coin . . . No exportation or importation can be but at the King's ports. They are the gates of the King, and he hath absolute power by them to include or exclude whom he shall please.'

Fleming's analysis of the prerogative was in accordance with current legal opinion, but members of Parliament were alarmed by the implication that the King could levy taxes at will, for if this were the case he would have no need of Parliaments in the future. In the debate on Impositions which took place in the 1610 session, several speakers came within striking distance of the concept of sovereignty — of a power within the state which is superior to all other powers. James Whitelocke, for instance, argued that the King's power was twofold; he could act alone and he could act through Parliament. 'And if, of these two powers in the King, one is greater than the other and can direct and control the other, that is *suprema potestas*, the sovereign power, and the other is *subordinata*. It will then be easily proved that the power of the King in Parliament is greater than his power out of Parliament, and doth rule and control it.'

To modern ears this sounds like an unqualified assertion of parliamentary sovereignty, but in 1610 very few people were thinking in such terms. The current assumption was that England was a 'mixed monarchy', or, to use the term coined by the distinguished fifteenth-century jurist Sir John Fortescue, a *dominium politicum et regale*, in which the monarch was not absolute but limited by law. As a system of government it was no doubt lacking in clarity, but it had the big advantage that it worked — or at least it had worked satisfactorily in the past. James and his subjects were in agreement that it was unwise to subject this pragmatical system to too close or too critical an analysis, for as Sir Thomas Wentworth was later to say 'he . . . which ravels forth into questions the right of a king and of a people shall never be able to wrap them up again into the comeliness and order [in which] he found them'.

As it happened, Dr John Cowell, a distinguished civil lawyer, had recently been involved in just such a 'ravelling forth'. He believed that the civil law and the common law had a lot to learn from each other, but that mutual ignorance barred the way to fruitful interchange. As part of his attack on ignorance he published, in 1607, a legal dictionary called *The Interpreter*. This contained, amidst a mass of uncontroversial definitions, a number of statements about the nature of royal power which caused a furore in Parliament when they were brought to the attention of the Commons in 1610. Under the heading *King*, Cowell had written that 'though at his coronation he take an oath not to alter the laws of the land, yet this oath notwithstanding, he may alter or suspend any particular law that seemeth hurtful to the public estate'. As for *Pre-rogative*, this was the 'especial power, pre-eminence or privilege that the King hath in any kind, over and above other persons and above the ordinary course of the common law'. *Parliament*, according to Cowell, was the highest of all courts, but it was subordinate to the King, and although he would be well advised to use it for the making of laws, such laws could not possibly bind him.

In order to defuse the explosive situation created by the debate on Cowell's book, James intervened directly and suppressed the *Interpreter* by proclamation. He also went down to Parliament to assure members of his commitment to the common law, and in the speech which followed he drew a distinction between primitive states, in which the ruler's will was law, and states 'settled in civility and policy', where the king ruled according to law. 'Therefore all kings that are not tyrants or perjured will be glad to bound themselves within the limits of their laws, and . . . as for my part, I thank God I have ever given good proof that I never had intention to the contrary; and I am sure to go to my grave with that reputation and comfort, that never king was in all his time more careful to have his laws duly observed, and himself to govern thereafter, than I.'

James regarded it as an essential part of his kingly function to watch over the administration of law in his dominions and resolve disputes where they arose. But this brought him into conflict with one of the most formidable common lawyers of his day, Sir Edward Coke. During the sixteenth century the appearance of new courts, such as the Councils of Wales and the North, as well as the expanding jurisdiction of courts of equity like Chancery and Requests, had led to overlapping and confusion. Matters were made worse by the fact that cases concerning the Church were handled by its own courts or by the prerogative courts of High Commission. Unscrupulous litigants could inflict damage upon innocent defendants by constantly switching courts, and there was an obvious need for clear lines of demarcation to be drawn between them, so that one should not trespass on the territory of another. During the closing decade of Elizabeth's reign the central courts at Westminster had been making increasing use of 'Prohibitions' to prevent inferior courts adjudicating on matters which were outside their sphere of competence, but the number and range of prohibitions increased dramatically after the appointment of Coke as Chief Justice of Common Pleas in 1606. The Church courts, in particular, found their proceedings inhibited, particularly in tithe cases, which straddled the hazy boundary line between religion and property. Archbishop Bancroft regarded Coke's use of prohibitions as part of a general assault upon episcopal authority and appealed to James for support. James felt, not unreasonably, that as head of the state and supreme governor of the Church it was his responsibility to sort out this clash of jurisdictions, but Coke would not agree. For him, the common law was a craft or 'mystery', knowledge of which could only be acquired by arduous study over many years. It was true that the King was gifted with 'excellent science and great endowments of nature', but he was not learned in the law. He should therefore leave all legal matters to the judges, who were experts, since only by so doing would he enable the law to act as 'the golden metwand and measure' which held in due balance the rights of the subject and the authority of the ruler.

Coke's vision of the law as an impartial arbiter between government and the governed was a noble one, but not entirely in accordance with the facts either of history or of the age in which he lived. James's approach made better sense, and he had the support of lawyers like Francis Bacon, the Attorney-General, and Ellesmere, the Lord Chancellor, who were just as learned as Coke and no less distinguished. Yet James — despite, or perhaps because of, the suspicion that he was only a lukewarm upholder of the common law — did not choose to assert his authority by forbidding or regulating the use of prohibitions. These were, after all, well-established and useful means by which disputes about jurisdiction could be resolved, and he could only hope that the judges would ensure that they were employed in a responsible manner.

Coke remained to some extent the odd man out in the judiciary, immensely learned but cantankerous and wilful. In 1616 he launched an assault upon the right of Chancery to redress unfair judgments given in common-law courts, and created a great deal of bad blood before he was eventually forced to concede defeat. He then adopted an even more extreme stance by asserting that the King had no right to ask the judges to hold up consideration of a case in which the royal prerogative was involved until they had been fully informed of the facts. This was the final straw, as far as James was concerned. He did not want his judges to be mere yes-men, but neither did he think it right for them to be wilfully obstructionist. In 1616, therefore, he broke with precedent by dismissing Coke from the judicial bench. Coke's place was taken by Sir Henry Montagu, who signalled a change of course to a more conventional direction by announcing that he would not be 'a heady judge ... busy in stirring questions, especially of jurisdictions'.

## James and Parliament

As King of Scotland, James had come into conflict with the more extreme presbyterians, who maintained that the Church was entirely separate from the state and that the secular ruler had no authority over it. And, from the other end of the religious spectrum, he had been reminded by Roman Catholics that all earthly sovereigns were subordinate to God and therefore to God's deputy on earth, the Pope. James countered these implicit threats to his independence by asserting the divine origin of kingly authority and in his writings as in his speeches he consciously and deliberately exalted monarchical power. In 1610, for instance, he informed members of Parliament that 'kings are justly called gods, for that they exercise a manner or resemblance of divine power upon earth . . . They make and unmake their subjects; they have power of raising and casting down, of life and of death, judges over all their subjects and yet accountable to none but God only'.

There was nothing new in James's belief that kings were appointed by God and ruled in His name. The 'godly prince' had been the Reformation's substitute for papal authority, and Elizabeth, no less than James, had taken it for granted that her office was of divine origin. There was widespread acceptance of this assumption, even among those who were later to be prominent critics of the crown: Pym, for instance, told James in 1621 that 'the image of God's power is expressed in your royal dignity'. But James's insistence on his divine right to rule seemed to imply that the liberties of his subjects only existed upon sufferance, and this was something which the political nation, the propertied section of English society, would never accept. Apprehension on this score helps to explain the ambivalent attitude of the Commons in James's first Parliament, which lasted, on and off, from 1604 to 1610. Their protestations of loyalty and affection for their new monarch were genuine and sincere, but they were determined to preserve both their privileges as a House and the common-law rights which protected their property against any extension of the royal prerogative. So suspicious were they that they sometimes saw danger where no danger existed.

When James opened Parliament he reminded members that he was the descendant of the royal houses of both York and Lancaster. 'But the union of these two princely houses is nothing comparable to the union of two ancient and famous kingdoms, which is the other inward peace annexed to my person.' James had been brought up to believe that he would accomplish a total union between England and Scotland. Not only did he hope to see one law, one Parliament and one Church for the united kingdom; he also wanted the separate names and identities of England and Scotland to be submerged in the new, all-embracing one of Britain. This was in many ways a noble aim, but his attempt to achieve it brought James up against the House of Commons, for members feared that any change would lead to a diminution of those rights which Englishmen had won by their own endeavours over the course of their history. The common law, they were persuaded, was superior to Scots' law; the English church, with all its imperfections, was preferable to Scots-style presbyterianism; and as for the Scots themselves, they were a backward and barbarous race, only waiting for the opportunity to flood south over the border and take the bread out of English mouths. One member of the Commons, Sir Christopher Pigott, expressed these sentiments in a particularly blunt manner. The Scots, he told the House, were beggars, rebels and traitors, who had murdered all their kings. It was as reasonable to unite England and Scotland as it would be to place a judge on an equal footing with a prisoner at the bar. James was highly indignant when Pigott's remarks were reported to him, and insisted that the Commons should take appropriate action. The House duly expelled Pigott and sent him to the Tower, but it is significant that they did so only after pressure had been exerted upon them. There is little doubt that many members, probably the great majority of the House, shared Pigott's sentiments, even though they would not have expressed themselves so forthrightly.

Pigott was speaking in the second session, in 1607. During the first session, James took Cecil's advice to move cautiously, and merely asked for parliamentary sanction for him to assume the style of King of Great Britain, and for the appointment of commissioners to negotiate the details of union with the Scots. The Commons reluctantly accepted the second proposal, but refused to abandon the name of England. James, losing patience, issued a proclamation announcing his new royal style, and thereby confirmed the fears of the Commons about the extension of the prerogative. In subsequent debates the Commons refused to accept the view of the commissioners that all Scots born after James's accession to the English throne (the *post-nati*) were automatically English. James therefore turned to the common law, and, in a test case, won the approval of the judges for the commissioners' view. This was not only a further rebuff to the Commons; it was a reminder that the common law, which they venerated, might not be as effective in guarding English liberties as they had hitherto assumed. In this respect, the *post-nati* ruling confirmed the unfavourable impression given by the judgment in Bate's case (see above, p. 212).

In the early years of his reign James relied a great deal on Robert Cecil, whom he created Earl of Salisbury, but Cecil's elevation to the Lords meant that he was unable to keep a close personal watch on affairs in the Lower House. This would not have mattered so much if James had appointed good men to take his place, but during the first session of the 1604 Parliament there were only two Privy Councillors in the Commons, neither of them men of great ability, and as late as 1610 there were still only three. Salisbury should bear at least part of the blame for this, since he had been a member of the Commons since 1584 and knew from personal experience just how important a role was played by Councillors in moulding opinion there. In fact it was the Councillors who, in the last decade of Elizabeth's reign, had prompted the Commons to set up large committees to discuss important and controversial issues, since this would free them from the rules of debate which forbade members of the House to speak more than once on the same topic. Some of these committees were so large that they included any member of the House who chose to attend, and 'Committees of the Whole', as they were called, became quite common during the early Stuart period. But their usefulness to the crown depended upon the presence of well-briefed and able Councillors. In the absence of these, the committees, like the House itself, would tend to fall under the sway of forceful speakers whose views might be at variance with those of the government.

James has often been criticised for his inept handling of Parliament, yet in fact he went out of his way to try to establish a harmonious relationship with the Commons. At the very beginning of the 1604 session a dispute arose over which of two contestants had been lawfully returned for the county of Buckinghamshire, and this resurrected the issue — which had been raised, but never settled, in Elizabeth's reign — of whether matters affecting the membership of the Commons should be settled by the House or, as hitherto, by the crown. The dispute held up discussions on other topics, particularly the Anglo-Scottish union, and there appeared to be no way of resolving it until James intervened and called a conference at which the judges and Privy Councillors were present, as well as the Commons. At James's suggestion it was decided to annul the Buckinghamshire election and hold another — a solution which preserved the Commons' dignity, especially since James acknowledged that the House was a court of record and had a valid, though not an exclusive, jurisdiction in electoral matters. The Commons showed their pleasure by appointing a committee to wait on the King and express their thanks.

James had been made aware on his way south from Edinburgh that two particular aspects of the royal prerogative, wardship and purveyance, were deeply resented, and his willingness to have them discussed is indicated by the fact that one of Salisbury's associates in the House of Commons introduced a motion to this effect in 1604. But if James hoped that the subsequent debate would lead to a re-structuring of the royal finances he was disappointed, for discussion on wardship never really began, while that on purveyance got nowhere. One of the reasons for this was a split in opinion in the Commons. Since royal progresses were normally confined to the southern half of the country, it was this region that had to bear the burden of purveyance. Members who sat for southern consti-

tuencies were, therefore, prepared to consider buying out purveyance, but northern members did not see why they should consent
to taxation from which their constituents would derive no obvious
benefit.

James, who was used to Scottish Parliaments which were very
effective in carrying through business, lost patience with the way
in which proposals became bogged down in the English one. He
was already angry with the Commons for dragging their feet in the
matter of the Union, and relations were not improved when members took up the cause of clergy who had been deprived of their
livings as a consequence of the 1604 *Canons*. James's sense of frustration as he saw his reform initiatives come to nothing vented itself
in outspoken criticism of the Commons. This provoked the House
into drawing up *The Form of Apology and Satisfaction*, in which they
defended their proceedings and claimed that if time had been
wasted it was because their privileges had been attacked. The *Apology* was never officially adopted by the House — an indication that
members did not wish to push matters to extremes — nor was it
formally presented to James. But the King was aware of its con-
tents, which included the assertion that 'the prerogatives of princes
may easily and do daily grow; the privileges of the subject are for
the most part at an everlasting stand'. James no doubt felt the injustice of such an accusation, since he regarded himself as bound
to defend his subjects' liberties as much as his own, but the statement reflects the fear of the Commons that the accession of a foreign monarch — and one, moreover, who was determined to unite
his two kingdoms — had opened the way to all sorts of undesirable
innovations and weakened the foundations upon which the traditional liberties of the English political nation were built.

James kept up his attempts to achieve the Union. In 1607 he told
Parliament that when he first proposed it 'I thought there could
have been no more question of it than of your declaration and acknowledgment of my right unto this crown, and that as two twins
they would have grown up together'. But he hastened to assure
members that he blamed himself and not them for the lack of progress. 'The error was my mistaking. I knew mine own end, but not
others' fears.' He tried to remove these fears by emphasising 'the
truth and sincerity of my meaning, which in seeking union is only
to advance the greatness of your empire seated here in England',
but the Commons were not easily swayed. Their stubbornness
came in part from prejudice, but they were also aware that the
political liberties of Englishmen were an inheritance which they
were responsible for defending, and that freedom, once lost, is not
easily regained. They did not doubt James's sincerity but they believed he had not fully appreciated the risks involved. As Sir Edwin
Sandys told the first session of Parliament 'the King cannot pre-

serve the fundamental laws by uniting, no more than a goldsmith two crowns ... We shall alter all laws, customs, privileges, by uniting.'

The failure to bring about the Union soured the atmosphere of James's first Parliament, and when to this was added criticism of the King's generosity to his Scots' favourites, opposition to his ecclesiastical policy, the attack on Impositions and the ultimate refusal to implement the Great Contract, it is hardly surprising that by the time Parliament was dissolved, in 1610, James had had his fill of it. Four years later, however, shortage of money drove him to summon another. Before he did so he was offered conflicting advice on how to ensure that it was successful. One former member suggested — no doubt with an eye to his own advancement — that James should give office to men who were well thought of by the Commons and would therefore be in a position to 'undertake' the handling of the crown's business. Francis Bacon, on the other hand — who was at this time Attorney-General – urged James to 'manage' the House by co-operating with the 'courtiers and the King's servants' who were members of it and trying to intimidate or win over potential critics.

In the event James did nothing until the last moment and then tried a mixture of 'undertaking' and 'management' that had little effect except to create an atmosphere of alarm and suspicion. James could no longer rely on Salisbury, who had died in 1612, but he may well have thought that in view of the failure of his first Parliament he could do without Salisbury's advice. Indeed, when he opened the 1614 Parliament he expressed the hope that it would end more amicably than the last, and implied that Salisbury had been responsible for the earlier failure. Yet the new Parliament was even less co-operative than the old one, for the Commons quickly succumbed to the influence of 'fiery spirits' who led it in a bitter attack on both Impositions and the Scots. James could have done with more and better-briefed Councillors in the House, for his chief representative was Sir Ralph Winwood, who had only been appointed Secretary shortly before the opening of the session, and had no parliamentary experience. Winwood urged the Commons to ensure the King's goodwill by voting supply, but the House preferred to take up the matter of grievances, and when it became clear that nothing constructive would be accomplished, James dissolved this 'Addled Parliament' after it had sat for little more than two months.

James showed his anger with the Commons by sending four of its members to the Tower. They included Thomas Wentworth — who was following in the footsteps of his father, Peter — and John Hoskyns. Wentworth had outraged James by declaring that the levying of Impositions by the French kings had led them to die 'like calves upon the butcher's knife'. Hoskyns' offence consisted in a bitter attack upon Scottish favourites and a reference to the Sicilian Vespers — a notorious massacre — which implied that the same might happen in England. The intemperance of such language went well beyond the bounds of what was permissible, so far as James was concerned, and his opinion was widely shared. But James was also critical of the inefficiency of Parliament, particularly the Commons, for the volume and intensity of debate seemed to be an impediment to business rather than a means of getting things done. The Lower House, he told the Spanish ambassador, 'is a body without a head. The members give their opinions in a disorderly manner. At their meetings nothing is heard but cries, shouts and confusion.' He added that he would never have allowed such an ineffective institution to come into existence, but since he could not get rid of it he was obliged to put up with it.

The Addled Parliament had done nothing to solve James's financial problems, and the only way in which to deal with these seemed to be a renewed programme of retrenchment and reform. Among the Councillors who urged this most strongly were the Lord Chancellor, Ellesmere; the Lord Chamberlain, the Earl of Pembroke; Archbishop Abbot, and Sir Ralph Winwood. These men were sometimes referred to as 'the protestant interest' because they were strongly opposed to Roman Catholicism, particularly insofar as it was linked with the political ambitions of Spain. They knew that James, desperate to find a way out of his financial difficulties and egged on by the Howards, was hoping to marry his surviving son, Prince Charles, to a Spanish princess, who would bring with her a dowry of at least half a million pounds. They also knew that their alternative policy of retrenchment would take time to make its effects felt, and that James might well lose patience. Rather than allow the Howards to increase their hold on James, they took the dangerous step of promoting an alternative, non-Howard, favourite. James had already met George Villiers, the handsome twenty-two-year-old son of a Leicestershire knight, and fallen under his spell. Abbot now pressed the King to ignore the objections of the Earl of Somerset, the current favourite, and choose Villiers as one of the Gentlemen of his Bedchamber. James agreed, and in 1616 Villiers was appointed to this position, which placed him in close attendance upon the King. He was also knighted, made Master of the Horse, and awarded a pension. Later that same year he became Viscount Villiers, and James presented him with a landed estate to maintain his newly-acquired dignity. In 1617 he was created Earl of Buckingham, in the following year he became a Marquis, and by 1623 he was Duke of Buckingham and the most important subject in the kingdom.

Buckingham's rise, even though it led to the fall of the Howards, did not alter the course of English foreign policy, because this was determined by James himself. He wanted the Spanish match, not simply because it would fill his depleted coffers but also because it would link him with the premier catholic ruler in Europe. He had already brought about, in 1613, the marriage of his daughter, Elizabeth, with the Elector Frederick of the Palatinate, who was head of the Union of protestant German princes. With a leading protestant and a leading catholic as his relatives James would be well placed to rein back religious passions and preserve the peace of Christendom — or so he hoped. But in fact Elizabeth's marriage contributed, indirectly, to the outbreak of the war which James was trying to avert, for in 1618 the protestant nobles of Bohemia renounced the allegiance they had sworn to the Archduke Ferdinand, heir to the Holy Roman Emperor, and offered the throne instead to Frederick. They reckoned that with James and the whole of protestant Europe behind him, Frederick would be able to hold Bohemia against any attempt by the Habsburgs to wrest it back. Frederick asked James's advice before accepting, but did not wait for the answer. James was against the whole idea, since he saw its dangers, but by the time his message reached Frederick, the Elector was on his way to Prague. He took with him the hopes of protestant England, for James's subjects thought in black-and-white terms when it came to foreign policy, and believed that the best way to cope with the threat from international catholicism was by fighting it.

James had no wish to fight, but public opinion was flowing strongly in favour of war. He was even under pressure from members of his own household, for Charles and Buckingham were urging him to take the sword in his hand. War fever mounted when Frederick was defeated at the battle of the White Mountain in November 1620 and driven out of the kingdom of Bohemia in which he had spent only one brief winter. From now on the 'Winter King' and his English wife, the 'Winter Queen', were refugees. They could not even return to their hereditary palatinate on the Rhine, since this had been overrun by imperial troops and also by an army sent from Spain. In such circumstances it obviously made sense for James to look to his defences, but he could not possibly do so without the assistance of Parliament. In any case it was always advisable in moments of crisis for the King to summon the representatives of his people to Westminster, to demonstrate the unity of purpose between him and them and to open a dialogue which, ideally, would remove all the elements of friction. Yet in many ways the circumstances were unpropitious. England was in the throes of an economic depression, and even if members of Parliament had been willing to vote sums of money on a realistic scale they would have had to take account of feeling among their constitutents, whose financial problems were quite bad enough without adding the burden of taxation to them.

With money in short supply and prices rising, the seven-year in-termission in Parliaments meant that pressure had built up for an attack upon abuses. Principal among these were the hated mono-polies, which were seen as worsening the depression even if they did not cause it. Much of this resentment was focused upon Buck-ingham, for the King had showered money, lands and honours upon the new favourite, as well as his relations, friends and clients, at the very moment when he was claiming that the royal Exchequer was empty and calling on Parliament to fill it. Buckingham was no more scrupulous than Somerset where money was concerned, and the line between legitimate perquisites and bribery, which had never been easy to determine, virtually disappeared during the years of his ascendancy. Anything was for sale — crown lands, offices in the King's gift, even titles of honour. James had already cheapened the prestige of knighthood by the lavish grants he made in the opening years of his reign, and it was common knowledge that the dignity was for sale. Ben Jonson was imprisoned for mak-ing a character in one of his plays say (in a broad Scottish accent — perhaps not unlike the King's?) 'I ken the man weel. He's one of my £30 knights', and another dramatist wrote

> But now, alas, it's grown ridiculous,
> Since bought with money, sold for basest prize,
> That some refuse it, which are counted wise.

As the prestige of knighthood declined the need arose for a more respectable title, and the dignity of baronet was created in 1611, open to anyone who would pay £1,000 to maintain thirty soldiers in Ireland. But by 1622 baronetcies were being sold for £250 apiece, and the prestige declined with the price. The same was true of peer-ages. In the last thirty years of her reign Elizabeth had created only one new peerage, and the pent-up demand caused by social change led to pressure on James to be more generous. At first James was comparatively restrained in his grants, but after Buckingham's rise to power peerages were sold for cash, and the number of peers in-creased from just over eighty in 1615 to almost one hundred and thirty by 1628.

James summoned the 1621 Parliament mainly in order to get supply, and the members duly voted him two subsidies: they did not add the customary fifteenths, the surviving relic of the medieval system of taxation, since these were held to press too heavily upon the poor. The two subsidies eventually brought in £145,000, but this sum bore no relation to the amounts James would need if he was really to engage in hostilities. He had set up a Council of War to advise him on what measures he should take, and this recommended the creation of a force of 30,000 men to help defend what was left of Frederick's possessions in the Palatinate. It estimated that the raising of such a force would cost a quarter of a million pounds, while just under a million pounds a year would be needed to maintain it. Clearly a grant of two subsidies, however generous it seemed in the eyes of members of Parliament, would go nowhere near meeting commitments of this sort, and it may be that James was secretly relieved, and his pacific inclinations strengthened, by this latest evidence that his subjects' bellicosity would not be expressed in realistic cash terms. He obviously could not afford to go to war. He could not even create an army, however small. He therefore resorted to the more congenial tactic of negotiation and despatched envoys to the major European capitals.

From James's point of view Parliament had served its purpose by voting supply. For members, on the other hand, the main purpose of Parliament was to remedy the abuses of which their constituents complained. This meant striking at the monopolists, and they began with one of their own members, Sir Giles Mompesson, who was also a kinsman of Buckingham. Mompesson was involved, along with Buckingham's half-brother, in the monopoly patent for the manufacture of gold-and-silver thread, which had aroused the opposition of a number of London artificers and led to a clash between the patentees and the City authorities. He also held a patent for licensing inns, which many members of the Commons found offensive not simply because of the corrupt way in which he used it to make money but also because it undermined the authority of Justices of the Peace which they were determined to uphold. Feelings in the House were running high, but it was not clear whether the Commons had any jurisdiction in such matters. It was decided to search for precedents, and as a result of this the Commons resolved to act in consort with the Lords, who constituted the High Court of Parliament.

James made no objection to this revival of parliamentary judicature. He was no lover of monopolies, as he had shown at the very beginning of his reign by issuing a proclamation against them. Moreover, he recognised the right of the Commons to take action over undoubted grievances: in his own words 'the Commons best know the state of the country and are to inform the King of the disorders so that he may show himself a just King'. No doubt James also relished the prospect that with the Commons in pursuit of monopolists he would be freed from the constant pressure of suitors demanding grants. He was also aware that the Commons were being guided by Councillors such as Cranfield and Sir Edward Coke, who saw Parliament as a means of strengthening the King's will and freeing him from those constraints which inhibited the carrying-out of their reform programme. James showed his sympathy for the Commons by cancelling the patents of inns and gold-and-silver thread which Mompesson had brought into discredit, and during the parliamentary recess he issued a proclamation annulling virtually all those patents of which the Commons had complained.

Among the reformist Councillors was Francis Bacon, who was now Viscount St Alban and Lord Chancellor. In money matters, however, Bacon was far from scrupulous, and during the course of their investigations the Commons came across evidence that he had been taking bribes. They presented this evidence to the Lords, who carried out their own investigations and prepared to bring Bacon to trial. Not since the fifteenth century had a great officer of the crown been overthrown in Parliament, and Bacon no doubt assumed that he could count on James's protection. But James told the Lords that while they should proceed with all due care they should not scruple to pass judgment where they found good cause. Bacon could recognise defeat when he saw it, and instead of defending himself acknowledged his guilt. The Lords thereupon sentenced him to be fined and imprisoned and never again to hold public office. By refusing to shield his Chancellor James had identified himself with the parliamentary attack upon abuses and had thereby retained the initiative. When the Commons, flushed with success, turned their fire on the Lord Treasurer, Viscount Mandeville, James told Cranfield to inform the Lower House that he 'wished that we should not be so careful for his honour as to destroy his service'.

In June 1621 James prorogued Parliament, but before the Commons went into recess they returned briefly to the subject of foreign affairs and passed a motion declaring that if the King's efforts to achieve a peaceful resolution of the problem of the Palatinate should meet with no success they would be 'ready, to the utmost of their powers, both with their lives and fortunes, to assist him'. As the international situation grew ever more alarming, James summoned the Houses to reassemble in November to hear a report from Lord Digby, who had just returned from an embassy to the imperial court at Vienna. Digby called for firm action by England, but although the Commons agreed with this in principle they were uncertain how to proceed in practice. Foreign policy was, after all, a prerogative matter, and they were reluctant to discuss it without guidance. Such guidance came, or at least appeared to come, from Sir George Goring, one of their members who was known to be in Buckingham's confidence. Goring told the House about a letter which James had written to the King of Spain, calling on him to bring about the restoration of the Palatinate to Frederick, and suggested that they should petition James to make it clear that unless he received a satisfactory reply he would be prepared to declare war. The Commons thereupon drew up a petition along these lines, but they went considerably beyond the limits which Goring had laid down. In particular, the petition included a request that 'our most noble Prince may be timely and happily married to one of our own religion'. This offended Charles as well as James, and by striking at the Spanish match it threatened to eliminate the diplomatic option which the King was most anxious to keep open.

James showed his anger by ordering the House not to 'presume henceforth to meddle with anything concerning our government or deep matters of state, and namely not to deal with our dearest son's match with the daughter of Spain'. The Commons, convinced that they had only followed the path which James, via Goring, had indicated, were shocked by this message. Although, in their reply, they protested that they never meant 'to encroach or intrude upon the sacred bounds of your royal authority, to whom and to whom only we acknowledge it doth belong to resolve of peace and war and of the marriage of the most noble Prince your son', they added that they had an 'ancient and undoubted right' to freedom of speech.

James responded to this by pointing out that the privileges of the Commons 'were derived from the grace and permission of our ancestors and us', though he gave his word that he would maintain them 'as long as you contain yourselves within the limits of your duty'. Such an assertion awakened all the Commons' latent fears about the expansion of prerogative power and the contraction of their own and the subjects' liberties. They therefore drew up a *Protestation* which was formally entered into their Journal. In this they deliberately echoed the writ of summons to Parliament by declaring that 'arduous and urgent affairs concerning the King, state, and defence of the realm and of the Church of England, and the maintenance and making of laws, and redress of mischiefs and grievances which daily happen within this realm, are proper subjects and matter of counsel and debate in Parliament; and that in the handling and proceeding of those businesses every member of the House of Parliament hath, and of right ought to have, freedom of speech, to propound, treat, reason and bring to conclusion the same'. It was a high-sounding declaration, but James showed what he thought of it by sending for the Commons' Journal and tearing out the *Protestation*. Subsequently he dissolved Parliament.

The two subsidies voted in 1621 were not enough to enable James to pursue a warlike policy, even if he had wished to do so. He now placed all his hopes on the Spanish marriage, especially since Digby, who was now Earl of Bristol and James's principal ambassador at Madrid, reported favourably on his negotiations. It was well known, however, that the Spaniards were adept at spinning matters out, and no-one could be sure that they were negotiating in good faith. It was probably in order to test their sincerity that in February 1623 Prince Charles and Buckingham slipped away from the English court, crossed the Channel into France, and then rode hard until they reached the Spanish capital. Had their journey been announced beforehand the Spaniards would almost certainly have blocked it. As it was, the first they knew about it was when the Prince and his companion arrived, weary and travel-stained, at Bristol's house.

Charles and Buckingham had assumed that within a few weeks they would be sailing back to England with the Infanta. In fact they had to spend many months in the Spanish capital, and during the course of their negotiations Buckingham became convinced that the Spaniards were not acting in good faith but were mainly concerned to keep England out of the war until the military situation had swung irreversibly in their favour. He now became aware of the scope of Spanish ambitions, of the danger that the Habsburgs might re-establish a preponderance in Europe not seen since the days of Charles V. When Buckingham and the Prince eventually left Spain, in September 1623, the marriage articles had been signed and it had been agreed that the Infanta would be sent over to England in the spring. But the Duke, at any rate, was determined that no marriage would take place. He was persuaded that the anti-Habsburg powers must join together for their own safety, and had already made contact with the French court, with a view to bringing about both a French match and a military alliance.

Although James was delighted to have his son and his favourite restored safely to him, he had no intention of suddenly abandoning his pacific foreign policy. And although a significant proportion of the Privy Council was in favour of war with Spain, many members found it hard to accept that Buckingham, who had hitherto been the King's mouthpiece, had genuinely changed course. Buckingham, with the invaluable assistance of the Prince, now concentrated on persuading the King to summon Parliament, hoping that he would be able to win the support of that body and persuade it to vote the necessary supply. James eventually agreed, and in February 1624 the two Houses assembled at Westminster.

Buckingham had prepared the ground well and was now the hero of the hour. Yet there was a fundamental divergence between his aims and those of most of the members of Parliament. They wanted a war of religion against the catholic enemy, a revival of what they conceived (mistakenly in many ways) to have been the Elizabethan strategy of fighting Spain at sea and leaving the Continent to look after itself. Such a strategy had the further advantage that it would cost far less than military intervention. As Sir John Eliot put it: 'Spain is rich. Let her be our Indies, our storehouse of treasure'. Buckingham, on the other hand, knew that James would never willingly become involved in a war of religion. He also believed that such a war would not be in the best interests of England, since both the immediate aim of recovering the Palatinate and the long-term one of checking the expansion of Habsburg power, demanded a secular alliance which should include France, a major catholic state, as well as protestant countries like the United Provinces, Denmark and Sweden.

The King had asked Parliament for six subsidies and twelve fifteenths — about £800,000 — for the proposed war. This was, if anything, an underestimate, but the Commons, who were only too well aware that in the continuing economic recession their constituents would resent any taxation, were appalled by such a demand. In the words of Sir Edward Coke, 'all England hath not so much'. In the end they voted three subsidies, accompanied by fifteenths, which they smugly declared to be 'the greatest aid which ever was granted in Parliament, to be levied in so short a time'. Even this concession was obtained only after James, at Buckingham's insistence, had agreed that the subsidies should be appropriated to the war and paid into the hands of treasurers appointed by Parliament. The King also promised the assembled members that he would not 'treat nor accept of a peace without first acquainting you with it and hearing your advice, and therein go the proper way of Parliament in conferring and consulting with you in such great and weighty affairs'.

While Parliament was in session, negotiations were taking place for a French marriage and military alliance. As far as the marriage was concerned, difficulties arose over the religious provisions, for the French were determined to demonstrate to the outside world that their involvement with a protestant power did not imply any weakening of their commitment to Roman Catholicism. They therefore demanded concessions to English catholics similar to those which the Spaniards had insisted on. Buckingham, who numbered catholics among his relatives and close friends and did not share the anti-popish prejudices of his fellow-countrymen, was prepared to make such concessions. So was James, though he insisted that they should not constitute a formal part of the marriage treaty. But members of Parliament, and of the Commons in particular, would never have agreed to relaxation of the penal laws. Indeed they believed that at this moment, when war against the popish enemy was about to be declared, the persecution of English papists should be intensified. It was to reassure the two Houses and open the way to the vote of subsidies that Charles made a formal promise that 'whensoever it should please God to bestow upon him any lady that were popish, she should have no further liberty but for her own family [i.e. household] and no advantage to the recusants at home'. In other words, Parliament had been told one thing, the French another. Buckingham presumably hoped that the ambiguities inherent in such contradictory assurances would be obscured by swift victories on the battlefield.

By the end of 1624 the two sets of negotiations, for a French marriage and a military alliance, had both been concluded. The first fruits of the alliance were to consist of an expedition under an experienced German mercenary captain, Count von Mansfeld, which should attempt to recapture the Palatinate. Mansfeld's force was to be made up of twelve thousand English infantry who were to be shipped to France, where they would be joined by three thousand French cavalry. But difficulties arose before the troops left Dover, for James — who was still King and was fighting a skilful delaying action against the bellicose designs of his son and favourite — insisted that Mansfeld's force should not pass through any of the possessions belonging to Spain or her allies. Since it was virtually impossible to get from France to the Palatinate without infringing such a condition, Louis XIII declared that he would not allow the English force to land in his country. At the last moment, therefore, and in the depths of winter, the English soldiers — recruited from the dregs of the population, ill equipped and barely trained — had to be shipped to Holland, where nothing had been prepared for them. What disease and desertion failed to accomplish was completed by starvation, and Mansfeld's force melted away before it had accomplished anything. Instead of the swift victory Buckingham had hoped for, he had been given an ignominious failure. It was an inauspicious opening for the as-yet-undeclared war and cast a pall over the Anglo-French alliance at its very outset.

# 12

# Charles I

## Charles I

James I died in March 1625 and was succeeded by his only surviving son, who now, at the age of twenty-four, became King
Charles I. For the first twelve years of his life Charles had lived
in the shadow cast by his self-assured and immensely popular elder
brother, and even after Prince Henry's death in 1612 he remained
introverted and reserved. He had an impediment in his speech that
made him a man of few words, and he told his first Parliament how
grateful he was that the business in hand required so little explanation, 'for I am neither able to do it, nor doth it stand with my
nature to spend much time in words'. This brevity was not, at first,
unwelcome to his subjects, and Sir John Eliot reported that 'both
the sense and shortness of this expression were well liked, as meeting with the inclination of the time, which wearied with the long
orations of King James that did but inherit the wind'.

There was a marked change of tone at court, for as the puritan
Mrs Hutchinson was later to recall 'King Charles was temperate,
chaste and serious, so that the fools and bawds, mimics and cata-
mites of the former court [i.e. James's] grew out of fashion, and the
nobility and courtiers who did not quite abandon their debauch-
eries yet so reverenced the King as to retire into corners to practise
them. Men of learning and ingenuity in all arts were in esteem and
received encouragement from the King, who was a most excellent
judge and a great lover of painting, carvings, gravings, and many
other ingenuities less offensive than the bawdry and profane abus-
ive wit which was the only exercise of the other court.'

## Charles I and Parliament, 1625–9

Charles's high seriousness and depth of religious commitment were
qualities which appealed to his subjects. He therefore had good
reason to hope for a friendly relationship with Parliament, especially since he had been an active member of the Lords since
1621 and had co-operated with the leaders of both Houses in persuading his reluctant father to break off the negotiations with

Spain in 1624. As he told the assembled members in June 1625, 'it is true that I came into this business willingly, freely, like a young man . . . but it was by your entreaties, your engagements . . . I pray you remember that this being my first action and begun by your advice and entreaty, what a great dishonour it were, both to you and me, if this action, so begun, should fail for that assistance you are able to give me.'

It looks as though Charles and Buckingham were relying upon goodwill and shared objectives to carry the Houses along with them, for they made no attempt to brief Councillors or to guide business. This was a major error, for the Commons, after voting a mere two subsidies for the impending war, were left to their own devices and promptly took up the question of religion. They had been shocked by the arrival of the new Queen, Henrietta Maria, since she brought with her a train of catholic priests who wandered round London in their outlandish garb, to the amazement and horror of the citizens. Charles's accession coincided with one of the worst outbreaks of plague England had so far experienced, and there were many people who took this as a sign of God's displeasure. Another sign was the failure of Mansfeld's expedition. Surely the remedy lay in strict enforcement of the penal laws? Yet such action would run counter to the spirit, if not the letter, of the marriage treaty and alienate the French at a time when their military assistance was essential.

At the beginning of a new reign it had long been the practice for Parliament to vote the sovereign the Customs duties — Tonnage and Poundage — for life. These duties formed a substantial part of the royal revenue, and would be more important than ever now that war was looming. But Tonnage and Poundage were not the only levies on trade. There were also Impositions, which the Commons continued to regard as illegal despite the judgment in Bate's case. If they simply voted Charles Tonnage and Poundage without raising the question of Impositions, it might seem as though they were tacitly sanctioning these arbitrary levies. And since Charles was such a young man, a lifetime grant of the Customs would leave the issue of Impositions unresolved for so long that the crown would eventually establish a prescriptive right to them. Tonnage and Poundage, in short, were much too valuable as bargaining counters to be lightly thrown away.

Moreover, there were some members of the Commons, principal among them John Pym, who believed that the dispute over Impositions could not be resolved without taking into account the whole question of the inadequacy of the royal revenue. The crown needed re-endowing, so that it could meet the normal costs of government without always having to call on Parliament and the people for assistance. Re-endowment, however, would be a complex business requiring a great deal of time, yet members were anxious to make the session as brief as possible, so that they could escape from London before the plague struck them down. The Commons therefore decided to grant Tonnage and Poundage for one year only, in the first instance. Their intention was that the crown should enjoy its customary revenue, while Parliament would be given the opportunity to reconsider the problem of the royal finances at a subsequent meeting, when it would not be under such pressure.

The Commons' action might have been acceptable had the Upper House taken the same view, but the Lords were affronted by the breach of precedent implied in a one-year grant, and threw out the Tonnage and Poundage bill. As a consequence, Charles was deprived of a vital part of his revenue just as he was about to spend great sums of money on a war into which — or so he believed — Parliament had encouraged him to enter. In fact he continued to collect Tonnage and Poundage on grounds of necessity, but this put the Customs duties in the same category as Impositions and re-awakened the Commons' old fears that by resorting to prerogative taxation the crown would remove the need for Parliament's existence.

These fears were based, consciously or unconsciously, upon the realisation that Parliament had less and less to offer. The gentry, in their local capacity as subsidy commissioners, had failed to keep assessments in line with inflation. The subsidy was already bringing in less at the beginning of Elizabeth's reign than it had done during that of her father, when it was a new tax based on realistic assessments of wealth. One subsidy in 1559 yielded £137,400, yet the three subsidies voted to James in 1624 averaged £67,000 apiece: in other words the parliamentary subsidy was diminishing even in face value, at a time of galloping inflation. This explains why the Stuart kings were so reluctant to surrender Impositions. If Parliament had offered a regular annual subsidy by way of compensation, this would have produced a sum varying from £70,00 at the beginning of James's reign to about £55,000 at the end of Charles I's. But Impositions were already yielding £70,000 by 1610, and thirty years later they were bringing in nearly a quarter of a million pounds annually to the royal Exchequer.

Charles regarded the vote of two subsidies by his first Parliament as little more than a token, and called the Houses into a second session at Oxford. This time they were well briefed, first of all by Sir Edward Conway, Secretary of State, and subsequently by Sir John Coke, who was known to be Buckingham's right-hand man at the Admiralty. The Privy Councillors spoke up in favour of a generous grant of supply, but the Commons refused to follow their lead. They declared that the country could not afford more taxes at a time of plague and economic recession: as Sir Thomas Wentworth said, 'we fear the granting thereof will be esteemed by his subjects no fair acquittal of our duties towards them or return of their trusts reposed in us'. They were also swayed by increasing doubts about Buckingham's suitability as the King's chief adviser. If the crown was poor, was this not because so much of its wealth had been diverted into his hands? And if more money was provided what guarantee was there that it would not be used in expeditions as futile as Mansfeld's? Despite a long speech from Buckingham to both Houses, in which he defended his policies, assured them of his commitment to the war, including a naval assault upon Spain, and gave them details of the King's financial obligations, they refused to vote additional supply. The King therefore dissolved Parliament.

The Commons had clamoured for a sea war against Spain, and Buckingham provided just this in the shape of an expedition to Cadiz. Money was raised by holding back the payment of wages, by pledging the credit of the crown, and by consuming the £120,000 paid by France for Henrietta Maria's dowry. The counties were ordered to raise troops at their own expense and to provide equipment, and ten thousand men — mostly gaolbirds and vagabonds — were somehow assembled for the expedition. The lack of organisation, of adequate supplies, and of any clear strategy, did not promise much hope of success, yet Buckingham cannot be entirely blamed for this. Combined expeditions were notoriously difficult to arrange, as the Elizabethans had found to their cost and as Cromwell was to discover thirty years later. England had neither a professional army nor a professional navy, and the marvel is that the troops were actually embarked and eventually landed on the Spanish coast. There they captured a fort and marched on Cadiz, but before ever they reached the town the heat, the lack of food and the abundance of local wine had turned the army into an undisciplined rabble. Any attack was now out of the question. The troops — or as many of them as were in a fit state — were re-embarked, and the ships sailed back to England with their cargo of sick, starving and dying men. Sir John Eliot saw some of the remnants landed at Plymouth and never forgot the shame of it. Until this time he had been a client of Buckingham, but now he turned against his patron.

The need for money forced the King to summon his second Parliament in 1626, but it met under the cloud of the Cadiz fiasco, and Eliot launched a bitter attack on those he held responsible for the failure. 'Our honour is ruined', he thundered, 'our ships are sunk, our men perished, not by the sword, not by an enemy, not by chance, but . . . by those we trust.' Eliot himself had no doubt where the responsibility lay. The King's revenues, he declared, were 'consumed as well as the treasures and faculties of the subject

... But the harvest and great gathering comes to one who must protect the rest, and for his countenance draws all others to him as his tributaries.' At Eliot's suggestion the House refused to consider the King's request for subsidies until their grievances, including the greatest grievance of all, were remedied.

Charles had few friends, but he was unswervingly loyal to those he had. He knew that Buckingham had spent much of his own money, as well as energy, in preparing the expedition, and he regarded the Commons' criticism not only as grossly unfair but as an attack upon himself, the King, who had entrusted Buckingham with the direction of affairs. He told the Commons in reply to their address: 'certain it is that I did command him to do what he hath done therein. I would not have the House to question my servants, much less one that is so near me', and two weeks later he summoned both Houses to Whitehall where he warned them that liberty must not be confused with licence. He assured them that 'never any King was more loving to his people nor better affectioned to the right use of Parliaments', but he reminded the Commons that since they had encouraged him to go to war they were morally bound to support him in it. 'Now that you have all things according to your wishes and that I am so far engaged that you think there is no retreat, now you begin to set the dice and make your own game. But I pray you be not deceived. It is not a parliamentary way, nor is it a way to deal with a King.' If Parliament acted responsibly, by voting supplies and enabling the war to be continued, Charles would be prepared to redress their grievances. If not, he warned them to 'remember that Parliaments are altogether in my power for their calling, sitting and dissolution. Therefore as I find the fruits of them good or evil they are to continue or not to be.'

The Commons would not accept Charles's interpretation of their actions. What he regarded as sterile and destructive criticism, they believed was the expression of their main function — to expose grievances and petition the King to remedy them. In the remonstrance which they drew up at Eliot's suggestion they affirmed 'that it hath been the ancient, constant and undoubted right and usage of Parliaments to question and complain of all persons, of what degree soever, found grievous to the commonwealth in abusing the power and trust committed to them by their sovereign', and to demonstrate their right they went ahead with a formal impeachment of the Duke of Buckingham.

Throughout these proceedings Eliot protested his loyalty to the King. 'In nothing,' he said, 'we intend to reflect the least ill odour on his Majesty or his most blessed father of happy memory.' The aim of the Commons was, he declared, to protect the honour of the King by removing all those who threatened to eclipse his royal glory, and of these Buckingham was the worst. 'His profuse expenses, his superfluous feasts, his magnificent buildings, his riots, his excesses — what are they but . . . a chronicle of the immensity of his waste of the revenues of the crown? No wonder, then, our King is now in want, this man abounding so. And as long as he abounds, the King must still be wanting.' Eliot, carried away by his feelings, went on to compare the hated favourite with Sejanus, the adviser of the tyrannical emperor Tiberius. 'If the Duke is Sejanus', said Charles, when he was told of Eliot's comment, 'I must be Tiberius', and he decided to dissolve Parliament rather than let the attack on Buckingham continue.

Since Parliament had never voted the four subsidies requested by the King, he was unable to meet his commitments to his allies. Charles therefore ordered the raising of an equivalent amount of money by way of a loan. When the Lord Chief Justice questioned the legality of this, Charles dismissed him. He also ordered the imprisonment of all those who refused to pay, including John Hampden, Sir John Eliot and Sir Thomas Wentworth.

The loan brought in nearly a quarter of a million pounds, but aroused widespread resentment. So did the demand that coastal towns should provide ships at their own charge for the royal service, and that the counties should provide free billeting for troops raised for another expedition which Buckingham was planning. This time it was to France, for relations between the two countries had deteriorated as the result of an uprising by the French protestants, the Huguenots. Cardinal Richelieu was by now Louis XIII's chief minister, and it was fear of his intransigent catholicism that had prompted the Huguenots to rebel. Richelieu held it as axiomatic that France could not engage in foreign ventures while torn by internal dissent; he therefore moved away from cooperation with England and mended his bridges with Spain. Such action confirmed all Buckingham's latent suspicions, and he decided to intervene on behalf of the Huguenots in the hope that he could either topple Richelieu from power or force him to change course. In any case Buckingham had little choice, for public opinion in England was so strongly in favour of the Huguenots that he dared not ignore it.

La Rochelle was the main centre of Huguenot resistance, and Buckingham planned to assist it by seizing the nearby island of Ré. Since the failure of the Cadiz expedition had been blamed on him, though he had not been present, he planned to lead the attack on Ré in person, and took charge of the preparations. Shortage of money was, as always, the main problem, but by the end of June 1627 the expeditionary force — consisting of some seven thousand men and close on a hundred ships — was at sea, and two weeks later the troops landed on Ré. A counter-attack by the French was beaten off, but the defenders subsequently took refuge in the citadel of St. Martin, from which it proved impossible to dislodge them. In November, after a gallant but futile attempt to storm the citadel, Buckingham had to retreat to his ships, losing many men in the process. When the news of this latest defeat reached England it created bitterness and anger. Sir Thomas Wentworth declared that 'since England was England it received not so dishonourable a blow', and balladmongers pinned responsibility for the disaster on Buckingham's 'treachery, neglect and cowardice'. Only Charles, who blamed himself for the failure to supply the Duke with the promised and much-needed supplies and reinforcements, struck a different note. 'With whatsoever success ye shall come to me,' he told him, 'ye shall be ever welcome.'

The plight of La Rochelle was now desperate, for Richelieu had invested it from both land and sea, and was determined to starve the inhabitants into surrender. Only England could prevent the collapse of Huguenot resistance, but if another expedition was to be mounted money would somehow have to be raised. Buckingham therefore persuaded the King to summon Parliament, but before this met the seventy or so gentlemen who had been imprisoned for refusing to pay the forced loan were freed. They included five knights who had tried to obtain release by bringing an action for *habeas corpus* before the King's Bench. They hoped this would raise the fundamental question of whether forced loans were legal, but the crown circumvented the issue by certifying that the knights had been imprisoned 'by special command of the King'. Since English rulers had always exercised a right to arrest suspects — in treason cases, for instance — and hold them incommunicado, the judges had little choice but to decide that the knights could not be bailed. But they were clearly unhappy about sanctioning such arbitrary action in a case which did not involve the security of the state, and declined to give any formal and specific approval to the crown's arguments. However, the Attorney-General, as the chief law officer of the crown, subsequently attempted to tamper with the record in order to imply that judgment in the King's favour had been given. Meanwhile Parliament had assembled, in March 1628, and it was not long before one of the lawyer members of the Commons revealed what had happened. The House was shocked and alarmed. Bate's case had shown that the common law could not be relied on to defend Englishmen from arbitrary taxation. Now the Five Knights' case had demonstrated its inability to secure them from arbitrary arrest. If English liberties were to be preserved, Parliament would have to clarify and strengthen the law.

Sir Thomas Wentworth put the blame for this unhappy state of affairs on evil counsellors, who had 'extended the prerogative of the King beyond the just symmetry which maketh the sweet harmony of the whole'. He proposed that the House should concentrate upon four specific issues, of which the two most important were freedom from arbitrary imprisonment and from arbitrary taxation. Sir Edward Coke supported him. 'Let a Bill be drawn [up] to supply defects of the law,' he urged. 'The prerogative is like a river without which men cannot live, but if it swell too high it may lose its own channel.' A committee was therefore appointed to draw up a Bill of liberties, a seventeenth-century *Magna Carta* as it were, but the King made it known that while he was willing to confirm existing statutes which defended the subjects' freedom he was not prepared to accept any new ones. It was at this point that Sir Edward Coke took up an earlier suggestion and proposed that the House should proceed by a petition of right.

Coke's proposal was quickly adopted, and after numerous conferences with the Lords — who felt that the petition should be made more acceptable to the King by including a specific acknowledgement of his prerogative, but dropped their demand when the Commons insisted that it would vitiate all the other provisions — the *Petition of Right* was formally presented to the King. In this the two Houses requested that unparliamentary taxation, imprisonment without good cause, the billeting of troops and the imposition of martial law should be declared illegal. Charles, in his reply, declared his willingness to see 'that right be done according to the laws and customs of the realm and that the statutes be put in due execution', but this did not satisfy the Commons. They wanted the traditional response to petitions of right, for only this, they were persuaded, would give it the full force of law. The King was obviously reluctant to make this commitment, but he needed the five subsidies the Commons had agreed to vote and he was anxious to re-establish harmony between himself and the representatives of the political nation. He therefore summoned the Houses to his presence a second time, and instructed the clerk to pronounce the customary words of approval: *soit droit fait comme est désiré* (let right be done as is desired). The assembled members cheered and threw their hats in the air, and as the news spread there were similar rejoicings in towns and villages throughout the land.

The parliamentary session was not over, however, and when the Commons resumed their discussions it was not in any spirit of compromise. Distrust of Buckingham was still acute. So was resentment at the continued collection of Tonnage and Poundage despite the fact that Parliament had not granted these duties. Sir John Eliot suggested that remonstrances on these two subjects should be drawn up and presented to the King. Charles, who had hoped that his acceptance of the *Petition of Right* would lead to co-operation instead of confrontation, at last lost patience. On 26 June he sent for the two Houses and announced his decision to prorogue them. The main reason, as he informed them, was their intention 'to take away my profit of Tonnage and Poundage (one of the chief maintenances of the crown) . . . This is so prejudicial unto me that I am forced to end this session some few hours before I meant it, being not willing to receive any more remonstrances to which I must give a harsh answer'. He also reminded his audience that the *Petition of Right* had only confirmed existing liberties and not created any new ones.

A month later the King was at Portsmouth, waiting to send off Buckingham, who had organised another expedition for the relief of La Rochelle. It was while he was at prayers that the news was brought him that the Duke had been assassinated. The murderer was John Felton, an army officer who had fought in the Ré campaign and held a grudge against Buckingham for failing to promote him. But Felton, when he was questioned, made it plain that he had been prompted to do the deed through 'reading the remonstrance of the House of Parliament' against Buckingham, for this persuaded him that by 'killing the Duke he should do his country great service'. Charles concealed his emotions at the loss of his closest friend, but there is little doubt that he regarded the leaders of the Commons as accessories to Buckingham's murder.

Although the assassination of the Duke was a personal blow to Charles it ought to have opened the way to happier relations between him and Parliament. But when the two Houses re-assembled, in January 1629, it soon became clear that confrontation would continue. One of the reasons for this was the absence of moderate leaders. Sir Edward Coke, now approaching eighty, stayed at home, while Sir Thomas Wentworth had at last achieved his ambition of holding office under the crown — as President of the Council of the North — and was now a viscount and member of the House of Lords. This left the Commons under the influence of hotter-headed men such as Sir John Eliot, Denzil Holles and Benjamin Valentine. They took up the question of grievances, and focussed the attention of the Commons not only upon Tonnage and Poundage, but also upon the growth of Arminianism. This matter had first been brought to the Commons' notice in 1624, when complaint had been made of Richard Montagu, an anglican controversialist who, in defending the established church against Jesuit attacks had asserted that, far from being Calvinist, it was the only true catholic church. Such an assertion raised many hackles in the Commons, where members were inclined to see high churchmen as papists in disguise, and before the opening of the 1626 session a conference had been held at York House, Buckingham's London residence, at which the whole issue of 'Arminianism' had been discussed. No formal decisions were announced as a result of the York House Conference, but the so-called Arminians had not been publicly disavowed and Charles made his own preferences plain by choosing Montagu as his chaplain and, in July 1628, appointing him Bishop of Chichester.

The Commons regarded this as an affront, and in the 1629 session religion became, for the first time, a major bone of contention. High churchmen, aware of the hostility towards them in Parliament, looked to the King for protection and consciously exalted the prerogative. Roger Manwaring, for instance, in a sermon preached before the King in July 1627, declared that resistance to the royal authority was sinful, and that kings had the right to take their subjects' property if they needed it for 'the supply of their further necessities'. At Pym's suggestion, the Commons impeached Manwaring in 1628, and the Lords sentenced him to fine and imprisonment. But Charles directed a pardon to be drawn up for Manwaring and appointed him to the living recently vacated by Montagu.

In an attempt to put an end to religious controversy the King issued a declaration in December 1628, affirming that the *Thirty-Nine Articles* were the foundation of the Church's doctrines, and forbidding any further public discussion of controverted issues. This declaration, far from lowering the temperature, caused alarm among the committed Calvinists within the Church, for it had become apparent as early as the 1590s that the *Thirty-Nine Articles* did not unequivocally endorse their hard-line view on such matters as predestination. Speaking in the opening debates of the 1629 Parliament, Sir John Eliot attacked the declaration and the toleration shown to high churchmen. 'In all other particulars of our fears concerning popery or Arminianism,' he told the members, 'we are endangered by degrees . . . But in this, like an inundation, they break on us with such impetuous violence that . . . they threaten to overwhelm us by plain force.'

Although Eliot was criticising the actions of the crown he was careful to exclude Charles personally from any blame. This was not simply a matter of form. Eliot was a convinced monarchist and a deeply loyal subject, who saw the King as the victim of a popish-Arminian conspiracy rather than the agent. Similarly with Tonnage and Poundage, he blamed this on evil advisers, particularly the new Lord Treasurer, Richard Weston. What is true of Eliot is not necessarily true of other members, for the House of Commons was a collection of individuals, many of whom had strongly developed personalities and made up their own minds. But the loyalty of the House and the commitment of its members to Charles as King and to established ways of government was undoubted. What they feared more than anything else was innovation, for any change could only be away from liberty towards absolutism, as was being currently demonstrated in states such as France and Spain. They knew that under the stresses of inflation, population explosion,

financial stringency, and above all war, the power of princes was
daily growing, and they were acutely aware that, as Sir Robert Phe-
lips told the 1625 Parliament, 'we are the last monarchy in Christendom that retain our original rights and constitutions'. It was their
determination to defend these rights, not against the King but
against those sinister forces which seemed to be driving him in the
wrong direction, that led them to act in the way they did.

Whatever the motives of the Commons' leaders, however, their
actions persuaded Charles that he had little to gain from prolonging the session. If Parliament would not vote him Tonnage and
Poundage and created dissension by criticising his religious policy,
what point was there in keeping it sitting? Far from being a source
of harmony between himself and his people it was turning into a
public demonstration of disunity. In March 1629, therefore, he decided on an adjournment, as a prelude to dissolution. The House
of Lords immediately obeyed his command, but the reaction in the
Commons was unexpected and violent. When the Speaker arose to
close proceedings, Holles and Valentine forced him back into the
chair and held him there while Eliot delivered a passionate attack
upon popish influences at court and called on the House to pass
three resolutions. These affirmed that anyone advising the King to
collect Tonnage and Poundage, or paying this levy before it had
been granted by Parliament, or propounding innovations in religion, should be reputed 'a betrayer of the liberties of England and
an enemy to the same'. With Black Rod knocking at the door and
the House in indescribable confusion the Commons at last ad-
journed themselves.

Charles never recalled this Parliament. As for the men who had
led the Commons in such unprecedented action, Eliot, Valentine
and Holles were tried before King's Bench and sentenced to imprisonment until such time as they acknowledged their fault. Valentine remained in prison until January 1640; Eliot stayed there
until his death in 1632; Holles alone managed to escape abroad.
For the next eleven years Charles ruled England without Parliament. There is no reason to suppose that he never intended to
summon it again, but he wanted time to show how beneficial
royal government could be when it was given a chance to operate
freely.

### The Personal Rule. I: Laud and the Church of England

The Elizabethan religious settlement had created a Church which,
while it owed a great deal to Lutheranism, Calvinism, Zwinglian-
ism and other varieties of protestant belief, was not totally committed to any of them. During the course of Elizabeth's reign,

however, the Calvinist elements within it became more pronounced — a development that was to some extent masked by the vociferous puritan campaign for faster and more radical change. This prompted a reaction among some of the higher clergy, inspired by Lancelot Andrewes, who deplored the way in which the Calvinist insistence on the primacy of preaching — the religion of the Word — had pushed into the background the older and more traditional concept of the Church as the body of God on earth, preserving in its liturgy and sacraments a visible link with spiritual realities. This reaction was not confined to England; in Holland, for instance, a similar revolt had taken place against the aridity and novelty of puritan attitudes. The Dutch theologian Arminius had played a leading part in this movement towards traditionalism, and the followers of Andrewes were given the name 'Arminians' by their puritan opponents.

One of the leading figures among the 'Arminians' by the 1620s was Neile's protégé, William Laud. He had already made a name for himself as a formidable controversialist, and this prompted the King to call on his services in 1622. The Countess of Buckingham, mother of the favourite, had fallen under the spell of a Jesuit priest — one of a number who circulated, under cover, in court circles — and was on the verge of becoming a catholic. James chose Laud to engage in debate with the Jesuit in the Countess's presence, and so well did he argue his case that the Countess retained her faith — for the time being, at any rate. Buckingham was impressed with Laud's performance and extended his patronage to him, but while James was alive Laud never rose higher in the Church than the bishopric of St David's. James acknowledged Laud's skill in debate but feared, with reason, that he might emulate the Dutch Arminians by stirring up controversy and undermining the unity of the Church. 'He hath a restless spirit', James observed, 'and cannot see when matters are well, but loves to toss and change and bring things to a pitch of reformation floating in his own brain.' Charles I, however, was not so concerned to maintain harmony in the Church. What he wanted was someone who would take it in hand after the lax rule of Archbishop Abbot and impose discipline and uniformity in the way that Whitgift and Bancroft had done. From his point of view Laud was the ideal man. In 1627 he appointed him to the Privy Council; in 1628 he made him Bishop of London; and in 1633, following the death of Abbot, he elevated him to the Archbishopric of Canterbury. No one was more closely identified with the period of Charles's personal rule than Laud, and when that rule collapsed Laud went with it.

Laud concentrated first on the bishops, ordering them not to part with their lands on long leases, nor to make a quick profit by ruthless exploitation of natural resources. When sees fell vacant he secured the appointment of men who shared his own high ideals and, if possible, some of his own intolerance, and he urged bishops to impose uniformity in their dioceses. He was also concerned with the need to improve the quality of the ministry as a whole, and he showed his appreciation of the role of education in this process by making generous gifts to Oxford University, of which he was chancellor. He insisted that candidates for ordination should be men of learning if at all possible, and his efforts, coming on top of those made by Whitgift, Bancroft and others, did have a marked effect in raising standards. In the diocese of Worcester, for example, the proportion of graduates among the clergy rose from under 20 per cent in 1560 to more than 80 per cent by 1640, and much the same was true of other dioceses.

Laud encouraged the clergy to hold their heads high, for like his fellow bishop Matthew Wren, he 'hoped to live to see the day when a minister should be as good a man as any Jack Gentleman in England'. By securing the appointment of parish clergy as J.P.s, and upholding ministers in their frequent disputes with local gentry, he did much to improve their morale. Many gentlemen, of course, resented this threat to their status, particularly since the 'Arminian' bishops were often of non-gentry stock: Matthew Wren, for instance, was a mercer's son, Neile's father was a tallow-chandler, while Laud's was a Reading clothier. Puritan militants, such as the lawyer and pamphleteer William Prynne, took great delight in pointing out the bishops' lowly origins and condemning them as 'tyrannising lordly prelates raised from the dunghill'. One of the reasons why Laud was so sensitive to these attacks and punished them severely was that they struck at his whole concept of the clergy as a spiritual elite.

Laud's aims ran counter to the ingrained anti-clericalism which had such deep roots in England, and they implied a threat not only to the social supremacy of the landowners but to their property as well. Church reform was held up by shortage of money, yet a big share of the Church's wealth was diverted into the hands of lay impropriators, who used it either to enrich themselves or to undermine episcopal authority by appointing puritan ministers or lecturers. Laud believed that these lay impropriators had a moral obligation to provide an adequate stipend for the vicars they appointed, and he encouraged clergy to sue for their rights. Church courts were the most convenient instruments for this purpose, but prohibitions from common-law courts, forbidding them to take cognisance of property matters, limited their effectiveness — even though Charles ordered in 1638 that such prohibitions should not be issued without the Archbishop's consent. Laud therefore turned to the Privy Council for support, and many a recalcitrant impropriator found himself summoned before this august assembly and browbeaten for his refusal to part with his tithes. Such actions did not increase the popularity of the Council or the prerogative courts, and Clarendon described how 'persons of honour and great quality', who regarded courts of law as guarantors of the existing social order, never forgot 'the shame which they called an insolent triumph upon their degree and quality and levelling them with the common people'.

Laud was not only concerned to recover impropriated tithes: he also wanted to make sure that they were used for the right purpose, and for this reason he suppressed the 'Feoffees for Impropriation' — a puritan body which raised over £6,000 to buy up impropriations and use the income to improve the stipend of 'godly' ministers and lecturers. It was these ministers and lecturers — particularly strong in urban areas where tithes were difficult to collect and clergy depended largely on voluntary contributions — who were the main obstacles to Laud's plan to restore ceremony and a uniform liturgy — the 'beauty of holiness' — to the Church. He checked them by extending episcopal control and by insisting that certain minimum requirements be observed. Among these was the regulation that the communion table should be moved to the east end of the church and there protected by rails 'one yard in height and so thick with pillars that dogs may not get in'. This deeply offended puritans, who were so anxious to avoid any suggestion of venerating the sacraments that they frequently placed the holy table in the body of the church, where it served as a hatstand: Laud was not exaggerating when he complained that 'tis superstition nowadays for any man to come with more reverence into a church than a tinker and his bitch come into an ale house'. He also insisted on the wearing of the surplice, and on bowing at the name of Jesus.

Laud has been painted, with justice, as a narrow fanatic, but he believed he was restoring the Church of England to its rightful and historical role as a *via media* between Rome and Geneva. In the early days of the Reformation Starkey had declared that ceremonies and traditions were *adiaphora*, 'matters indifferent', which the state might regulate to suit its own convenience. Laud took his stand on the same ground, accepting the authority of the Bible in questions of faith but insisting on his duty, as well as his right, to regulate matters on which the scriptures were silent. 'Unity cannot long continue in the Church,' he said, 'when uniformity is shut out at the church door. No external action in the world can be uniform without some ceremonies . . . Ceremonies are the hedge that fences the substance of religion from all the indignities which profaneness and sacrilege too commonly put upon it.'

Many clergy welcomed Laud's reforms, since the effect of these was to strengthen their authority within their parishes and to give them a prestige which they felt was justified by their educational and other attainments. They approved of greater care being taken

over the fabric of churches, even though the cost of this had to be
borne by their parishioners, who often resented it. There were, of
course, puritan clergy, just as there were high-church and non-
committed clergy, and what pleased one minister might well be unacceptable to another. The same was true of the laity who made
up their congregations. In one sense Laud was shifting the Church
of England into a new position, breaking away from the Calvinist
consensus, returning to clericalism. But in another sense he was
building on the foundations laid by Whitgift and Bancroft: it was,
after all, the *Canons* of 1604 which laid down that 'when in time of
divine service the Lord Jesus shall be mentioned, due and lowly
reverence shall be done by all persons present'; that ministers,
when they were taking services, should wear surplices and, if graduates, hoods; and that holy communion should be administered at
least three times a year. Part of the reason for Laud's unpopularity
consists not in the novelty of what he did but in the way in which
he did it. As John Selden, the distinguished lawyer and member
of Parliament, later observed, 'the bishops were too hasty; else,
with a discreet slowness, they might have had what they aimed at'.

Both Laud and his 'godly' opponents — whom he categorised
as 'puritans', though they were, and had always regarded themselves as, members of the Church of England — shared the belief
that society needed disciplining. But as Archbishop, responsible to
a royal governor, Laud took it for granted that the lead should
come from the crown and the hierarchy. This meant the bishops
taking an active part in government: 'You must not measure
preaching,' he said, 'by a formal going-up into the pulpit. For a
bishop may preach the gospel more publicly, and to far greater
edification, in a court of judicature or at a council table, where
great men are met together to draw things to an issue, than many
preachers in their several charges can.' Laud set an example himself by regularly sitting in Star Chamber and the Court of High
Commission. Star Chamber had hitherto been a respected institution, but as it became increasingly identified with the defence of
the Laudian church it lost much of its popularity. Elizabeth had
been careful to allow only one bishop at a time to sit in Star Chamber, but after 1630 there were three, and they were some of the
most active members of the Court. As criticism of the bishops became more outspoken, Laud used Star Chamber to punish the offenders, and in so doing he gave it the unjustified reputation for
savage sentences that still endures. In fact, in most cases that came
before the Court, fines were inflicted — not usually crushing, and
rarely collected in full. Corporal punishment was reserved for those
who, by slandering great men, had brought the Church or royal
government into disrepute. This explains the harsh treatment of
Prynne, Burton and Bastwick in 1637. They had published libels

against the bishops and were sentenced to stand in the pillory, have their ears cropped and spend the rest of their lives in prison. Such harshness had the opposite effect from what Laud intended. The three men were treated as heroes, and property-holders were more impressed by Prynne's words than by his fate. 'You see,' he declared from the pillory, 'they spare none of what society or calling soever. None are exempted that cross their own ends. Gentlemen, look to yourselves. You know not whose turn may be next.'

Critics of Laudian 'innovations', who looked on themselves as the true custodians of the Church of England as it had been established under Elizabeth I, were particularly incensed at the contrast between the way in which they were persecuted while papists, the real enemy of the Church, were treated with relative mildness. Yet in some ways the appearance of mildness was misleading, for it was largely confined to court, where the influence of Henrietta Maria made catholicism fashionable and led to a number of conversions. Among the King's ministers, Richard Weston, the Lord Treasurer, had a catholic wife, and was known to favour the idea of reunion between the Roman and anglican churches. Secretary Windebank shared these sentiments, and so did Francis Cottington, the Chancellor of the Exchequer, who was generally suspected of being a covert catholic. But the greatest advocate of reunion was Charles himself, and he held long and frequent discussions on this subject with a papal agent, George Con, who was officially in attendance upon the Queen but became, in effect, the Pope's representative in the royal court. Laud's enemies often accused him of being a catholic at heart, and the Pope went so far as to offer him a cardinal's hat if he changed his religious allegiance. But Laud was totally committed to the Church of England: indeed, one of the reasons for his advocacy of greater ceremonial in anglican services may have been his desire to counter the attraction of catholicism and check the flow of conversions to Rome. Laud was no friend of the Queen and her circle. It was at his insistence that Charles, in 1637, issued a number of proclamations forbidding proselytising by catholics, whether priests or laymen, and threatening severe punishment for all those who attended the Queen's chapel, which was theoretically reserved for Henrietta Maria and members of her household. These measures had little or no effect, but they demonstrated Laud's awareness of the dangers of court catholicism and his determination to curb it, if he possibly could.

Outside the circle of the court there was no weakening in the official attitude towards recusants, especially since the fines which they paid were an important part of the royal revenue. In 1625, under pressure from his first Parliament and in contravention of the assurances given to the French, Charles ordered the penal laws to be enforced, and a special department was set up within the Exchequer to handle the revenue from recusancy. Yet in one respect catholics were better off than before, since Charles encouraged them to compound for their recusancy by agreeing to pay a regular annual fine. In return they were freed from the harassment of informers, and largely left to their own devices.

The alliance between the catholic gentry and the religious orders, especially the Jesuits, was cemented in Charles's reign. Richard Smith made himself so unpopular by trying to assert his episcopal authority that he sparked off an anti-clerical reaction among the catholic laity — similar to that which Laud provoked among their protestant counterparts. In late 1628 Smith was denounced to the Privy Council, which ordered his arrest. He took refuge in the French embassy, hoping that the Pope would intervene in his behalf. But the papacy came to the conclusion that the restoration of the hierarchy had been a mistake, and it encouraged Smith to return to France, where he spent the rest of his life.

The secular priests, who had looked to the hierarchy to establish their supremacy over the regulars, were now without a head, and in effect there were two missions, only loosely connected. The seculars' numbers continued to increase, and by 1640 there were well over four hundred of them, twice as many as at the beginning of the century. But the regulars had achieved a fourfold expansion. In 1640 there were close on two hundred Jesuits on the mission, and a hundred Benedictines. This was a scale of provision for the catholic community not matched again until the nineteenth century, but the concentration on the gentry, particularly by the regulars, confirmed the pattern already emerging in Elizabeth's reign. The south and midlands had more than their fair share of priests, while the catholic areas in the north and west were poorly provided for. The mission certainly kept English catholicism alive, but only at the cost of narrowing its geographical range and accepting its sectarian, minority status.

### The Personal Rule. II: Administration and Finance

No minister, after 1628, ever monopolised the royal authority in the way that Buckingham had done. Power was distributed rather than concentrated, but among the most important members of Charles's government was the Lord Treasurer, Richard Weston, whom he created Earl of Portland in 1633. Portland was not an original or creative thinker. He worked within the existing system, much as Burghley had done, and his enemies nicknamed him 'Lady Mora [Delay]' because of the time he took to get things done. But in his own unspectacular way Portland was an efficient Treasurer, pursuing the inevitable policies of pruning the expenses of the royal household and the administrative departments at the same time as he exploited all means of increasing the royal revenue. Weston, like Cranfield before him, was an advocate of peace, since Charles could clearly not afford to engage in war, and he wholeheartedly approved of the treaties which brought to an end the state of hostilities first with France (1629) and then with Spain (1630).

As far as enlarging the King's revenue was concerned, there could be no question of levying new taxes. The English were notoriously resistant to taxation at the best of times, and in the absence of Parliament Charles had to make sure that he kept within the bounds of the law. That is why his advisers sought to resurrect old measures, which had at least a colouring of legality, rather than adopt new ones. There was no logic behind this, other than the need for money. The financial system was already ramshackle, and the devices adopted during the Personal Rule made it more so.

The first device was Distraint of Knighthood. In theory all men with land worth £40 a year were required to take up knighthood, but rapid inflation during the Tudor period pushed many into the £40 p.a. bracket who were below the social level of knights and had no relish for an honour which might well oblige them to perform functions in the local communities for which they had neither the leisure, the qualifications, nor the necessary status. The summons to take up knighthood was confined, by the sixteenth century, to occasions such as coronations. Elizabeth made no use of it, but the summons was issued at the time of James I's coronation, though never apparently enforced. Because of the uncertainty surrounding the whole procedure, Charles I declined to use it, but following the dissolution of Parliament in 1629 the need for money persuaded him to agree to the appointment of commissioners to collect fines from more than nine thousand people who, while being in the strict legal sense 'qualified' for knighthood, had failed to take it up. This was in effect a land tax, and while the average fine was in the £10–25 range, wealthier gentlemen found themselves paying more than twice as much. In financial terms Distraint of Knighthood was very successful, bringing in a total of £175,000, but as Clarendon later observed, 'though it had a foundation in right, yet in the circumstances of proceeding [it] was very grievous and no less unjust'.

The revival of Distraint of Knighthood had been prompted by Sir Julius Caesar, a civil lawyer and Master of the Rolls. The revival of the forest laws was initiated by a common lawyer, William Noy, who was Charles I's Attorney-General. Forests were, in effect, huge game reserves, subject to a special law, but over the centuries their boundaries had shrunk and in many places it was not clear whether land was or was not technically 'forest'. Since the crown wished to exploit its rights over the royal forests it needed to establish their exact limits, and Noy revived the medieval practice of holding forest 'eyres' which the local inhabitants were required to attend, so that they could be questioned on the nature of their tenure. There was nothing wrong with Noy's scheme, but he died in 1634 and his work was continued by another common lawyer, Sir John Finch — who had been Speaker in Charles's third Parliament and had suffered the indignity of being held in his chair while trying to adjourn the House. On the basis of old records which he professed to have discovered, Finch began to widen the boundaries of the forests until the area subject to forest law became almost as extensive as it had been in the Middle Ages. Many people were prosecuted for breaches of the forest law who were unaware that they had committed any offence. After fining them, the crown would then offer to sell them the legal right to opt out of the 'forest'. This made the crown a profit, but only at the cost of losing the goodwill of many landowners, on whose co-operation it was ultimately dependent.

The most notorious of all the financial devices of the personal Rule was Ship Money. It had long been accepted that, in times of emergency, the ports and coastal regions should provide ships for the defence of the kingdom — or, if they had no ships available, money in lieu. Shortly before Elizabeth's death the Privy Council had been planning to call for contributions from the whole country, and early in 1628 Charles I had announced his intention of charging all counties a share of the cost of setting forth a royal fleet. He did not, as it happened, put this scheme into effect, but in 1634 he sent out Ship Money writs to the seaports, and in the following year he extended the levy to inland counties as well, on the grounds that 'that charge of defence which concerneth all men ought to be supported by all'. This proved so lucrative that Ship Money was thereafter demanded every year. While remaining strictly within the letter of the law, the King had circumvented the convention that taxation should only be levied with parliamentary consent.

Strictly speaking, Ship Money was not a tax but a rate, and it was no doubt in order to emphasise this crucial distinction that the Privy Council devised a new way of administering it. Instead of leaving the assessment to local gentlemen, as was the case with subsidies, it fixed the total sum it intended to raise from the whole kingdom and then apportioned this among the counties. Furthermore, it made the sheriff of each county its local agent, not the Justices of the Peace. In financial terms Ship Money was very successful. The crown aimed to raise about £200,000 a year from it — the equivalent of four subsidies — and until the outbreak of the Scottish revolt, which undermined royal authority, this target was very nearly met. Only in and after 1638 did refusals to pay make a major impact. It should be added that the crown was not being totally cynical when it demanded Ship Money. The seas were infested by privateers from Dunkirk and the dreaded Barbary corsairs from the coast of North Africa, who in 1631 sacked Baltimore. The money raised was paid direct to the Treasurer of the Navy, and was used solely for the construction of a fleet. But this did not alter the basic objection to Ship Money, that it was a non-parliamentary tax, and while the majority of people complained but paid up, there were one or two who determined to take a stand on principle.

These included the leading members of a company which had been set up to establish a colony on Providence Island in the Spanish West Indies, from which the English settlers — no doubt recruited from the 'godly' — would be able to prey on Spanish shipping, like latter-day Drakes. Among the shareholders were some of the men who were to mastermind the opposition to Charles I. They included Lord Saye, well known for his puritan views, and John Hampden, a Buckinghamshire gentleman of considerable wealth. Saye refused to pay Ship Money, and sued the constable who distrained his goods. The crown was careful not to take up this challenge, and merely called for a formal opinion from the judges, who decided that Ship Money was legal. It was left to Hampden to provoke the crown into action, for by stubbornly refusing to pay he achieved what he had been aiming at, namely a formal trial in which he hoped to raise the basic issue of whether a regular tax could be levied without the consent of Parliament. The case aroused widespread interest, and the speech made by Hampden's counsel, Oliver St John — who was also solicitor to the Providence Island Company — centred on the argument that if the King could force his subjects to contribute taxes at his pleasure, their property would be at his mercy.

However, the judges, as in previous cases, were not well placed to consider the broader implications of the crown's actions. The King had stated that an emergency existed and that by virtue of his absolute prerogative he was empowered to levy contributions from his subjects without waiting for their formal consent. Sir Robert Berkeley, Chief Justice of the King's Bench, upheld this, and declared 'that it is a dangerous tenet, a kind of judaizing opinion, to hold that the weal public must be exposed to peril of utter ruin and subversion rather than such a charge as this, which may secure the commonwealth, may be imposed by the King upon the subject, without common consent in Parliament'. Berkeley was careful to add that the King's absolute prerogative applied only in cases of emergency, and that in the normal course of affairs he would raise money solely through Parliament. But who was to decide when an emergency existed? The common law could give no guidance on such a subject, and Berkeley could only affirm that the King could be relied on not to abuse his trust. Not all his colleagues were so confident of the King's intentions, however, and the degree of resistance which Charles's policies had aroused is indicated by the fact that out of twelve judges, five gave their verdict in Hampden's favour. Charles had hoped that a unanimous decision in his support would stifle opposition to Ship Money, but in point of fact the views of the dissenting judges carried more weight with public opinion than those of the majority. As the sheriff of Cheshire told the Council in 1638, he had been unable to collect the full quota for the county because 'the general bruit of the late arguments of those judges who concluded against Ship Money is so plausibly received by those who were too refractory, and countenanced by some of rank, that I have found more difficulty than in all the rest'.

In terms of their effect upon popular opinion, the financial expedients of the Personal Rule were disastrous, but they did at least succeed in expanding the crown's revenue. Every source of income was exploited. The Court of Wards, for instance, which had produced just over £20,000 a year when Robert Cecil was Master, provided more than £70,000 under Cottington in the late 1630s, but only because gentry purchasers of wardships now had to pay up to £1,000 instead of the £100 which was the average under Elizabeth. Impositions, as already mentioned, brought in nearly a quarter of a million pounds, while the great farm of the Customs, which had been set at £112,00 in 1604, was raised to more than £170,000 in 1638. Much the same was true of smaller sources of income, such as recusancy fines, which increased from £5,000 a year at the beginning of Charles's reign to £30,000 under Bishop Juxon, who succeeded Portland as Lord Treasurer in 1635. It was financial motives which prompted the government to take legal action against the City of London for failing to fulfil its obligations to establish a plantation in Londonderry and for mismanaging the sale of royal estates conveyed to it in 1628 as satisfaction for outstanding loans which the crown was unable to repay.

The effect of all these measures was to bring the total royal revenue to close on a million pounds by the end of the 1630s. This figure is misleading in that it does not take account of the considerable proportion of the revenue which had been pledged in advance to debt repayment, yet the fact remains that during the period of Personal Rule the crown's income came to equal, and eventually exceed, its annual expenditure. This was a striking demonstration of the inherent financial strength of the monarchy — and, by implication, of the financial irrelevance of Parliament — but what the crown gained in money it lost in goodwill. Much the same was true of governments throughout Europe, but whereas Louis XIII — whose income was five times as great as Charles I's — had a standing army which he could employ, if necessary, against his over-taxed and rebellious subjects, Charles did not. He was dependent for the running of his government in the localities upon the active co-operation of the political nation and the passive acquiescence of the underprivileged majority. By exploiting — or at least seeming to exploit — his subjects, Charles strained their loyalty, in some cases to breaking point.

Yet throughout the greater part of the Personal Rule the property-owners did co-operate, if only for the reason that they stood to gain, as well as the crown, from the preservation of order. The period following the dissolution of the 1629 Parliament coincided with bad harvests that caused severe distress and rioting in several parts of England. In January 1631, therefore, the Council issued the *Book of Orders*, laying down in great detail the duties of J.P.s. They were told to take particular care over the enforcement of the poor law and vagrancy regulations, in order to stop distress getting out of hand. They were also required to hold monthly meetings and to report to the sheriff about the conditions prevailing in their area. The sheriff was charged with drawing up a composite statement on the whole county, to be presented to the assize judges on their bi-annual visitations and passed on by them to the Privy Council.

A copy of the *Book of Orders* was sent to every county and corporate town, and this evidence of governmental vitality has often been taken as indicative of the efficiency of the Personal Rule, in contrast to the laxness of earlier periods. In fact, however, the government was following the path laid down by its predecessors. It had long been established practice, in times of emergency such as plague and famine, for the Council to issue precise directions to J.P.s and to supervise their work. Elizabeth's reign had seen the first appearance of a printed book of dearth orders, codifying the measures to be taken to preserve grain stocks, as well as a book of plague orders. The 1631 *Book* had no precise precedent, but it did not go beyond established practices. Indeed it was the brainchild of the Earl of Manchester, who had first sketched it out at an earlier period of social distress in the middle years of James I's reign, basing it upon his knowledge of what was being done in his native county of Northamptonshire. J.P.s in general complied with the *Book of Orders*, since it was in their own best interests, but they resented the demand that they should make regular reports, and rarely did so after 1632, when the immediate crisis had passed. Nor did the Council continue to press for these, since it was turning its attention increasingly to revenue-raising devices, which entailed much more consistent and greater pressure upon the localities.

Although many Englishmen came to resent the Personal Rule, at least in some of its aspects, and would have welcomed the summoning of Parliament, there are no indications that they were prepared to contemplate rebellion. The habit of obedience was too ingrained, the costs of disturbing the social order were too high, and in any case Charles's concern to keep his actions within the formal boundaries of the common law drew the sting from the potential opposition. He had not bound himself never to summon another Parliament, but he had no need to do so as long as he remained at peace. There were members of his entourage, however, who wanted a more active commitment to the protestant cause and a revival of Buckingham's policy of alliance with France against Spain and the Habsburgs. They included Buckingham's close friend and protégé, the Earl of Holland, who was the first governor of the Providence Island Company and the brother of a noted puritan peer, the Earl of Warwick. Surprisingly enough this 'puritan' group won the support of the Queen, who approved of their pro-French attitude and hoped that in return for her assistance she could persuade them to take a more moderate line towards the English catholics. By late 1636 the 'war party' seemed to be in the ascendant, and the Elector Palatine, Charles Louis (who had succeeded his father, Frederick, in 1632) came over to England to make a personal appeal to his royal uncle. At the same time Warwick assured Charles that if he did decide to go to war with Spain, Parliament could be relied on to vote him supply.

The King was hesitant, however, for he knew from bitter experience that war would place him at the mercy of Parliament, and that assurances of supply were unlikely to be translated into grants. He was doing well out of peace, for in 1630 he had made an agreement to mint Spanish silver in England in return for a commission, and send it in English ships to Antwerp, where it was used to pay the Spanish armies fighting the Dutch. While the Continent was convulsed by war, England, in the words of the Flemish painter, Rubens, was 'rich and happy in the arts of peace'. Rubens arrived in England in 1629 and began work on the magnificent painting with which he decorated the ceiling of Inigo Jones's Banqueting House in Whitehall. He was followed, a few years later, by his pupil, Van Dyck, who produced a series of portraits of Charles, Henrietta Maria and members of the royal court which constitutes one of the most resplendent legacies of the Personal Rule. Charles was a connoisseur of painting and the collection which he built up at Whitehall was the finest ever assembled by an English monarch. Nothing was allowed to stand in the way of this passion for pictures. Even in 1627, when money was desperately short and Buckingham, marooned in the Ile de Ré, was crying out for supplies, the King diverted £15,000 from his almost empty coffers in order to purchase the magnificent collection of the Duke of Mantua, and he kept up his spending on works of art throughout the period of the Personal Rule. But Charles's achievements as a collector, while they have dazzled posterity, did little to win his subjects' respect. They tended to regard the Italian masterpieces which he loved as dangerously popish in taste, and they were alarmed by the fact that the artists whom he patronised were Roman Catholic, and that these included not only foreigners like Rubens and Van Dyck but also Englishmen such as Inigo Jones. In its culture, as in so many other aspects, the court was becoming increasingly isolated from the country.

## The Destruction of Prerogative Monarchy

In October 1636 the King ordered a new service-book, modelled on the English Prayer Book, to be brought into general use in Scottish churches. His aim was to extend to Scotland the uniformity of worship which Laud was already imposing in England, and perhaps to continue that process of integrating the two kingdoms which his father had begun. But when, in July of the following year, the book was used for the first time in St Giles's Cathedral, Edinburgh, it provoked a riot. 'The mass is entered among us!' shouted one woman, another flung her stool at the preacher, and soon the whole cathedral was in an uproar. The revolt spread quickly, and found support and leadership among the Scottish nobles who feared that the King's next step would be the confiscation of such of their lands as had formerly belonged to the Church. Puritanism, in its presbyterian form, was much stronger in Scotland than in England, and thousands of people, encouraged by their ministers, flocked to sign the *National Covenant*, in which they pledged themselves to defend their system of worship.

Charles gave himself a breathing-space by suspending the new service-book, but at the same time he prepared to use force and ordered the trained bands of the northern counties to be called to arms. Years of peace, however, had left the country unprepared for war, and one observer reported that 'the King's magazines are totally unfurnished of arms and all sorts of ammunition, and commanders we have none either for advice or execution: the people through all England are generally so discontented . . . I think there is reason to fear that a great part of them will be readier to join with the Scots than to draw their swords in the King's service.'

By the end of 1638 Charles was ready for action. He hoped that patriotic sentiment would cause his English subjects to rally behind him and seemed to be unaware that many of them in fact approved of the Scottish stand against Laudianism. Nor did he realise just how much alarm had been caused in England by the growth of popery at court: had he done so he would hardly have appointed the Earl of Arundel to command his army, for Arundel was reputed to be a catholic at heart. But Charles went further than this by appealing to Spain to supply troops for the suppression of the Scottish rebellion and welcoming a suggestion that English catholics should raise a voluntary contribution to aid the royal war effort. All these panic measures were in vain, however, for when Charles joined his army at York, in March 1639, he had to acknowledge that the ragged collection of conscripts arrayed under his banner was no match for the Scots, who were led by men who had made their name and fortune as professional soldiers in foreign armies. In June 1639, therefore, he agreed to the Pacification of Berwick, whereby both armies were to be disbanded while a Scottish Parliament and Assembly of the Kirk were to advise on what action should be taken to restore peace.

Charles now realised that he needed a strong man at his side, and he sent for Wentworth. 'Come when you will,' he wrote, 'ye shall be welcome to your assured friend Charles R.' Wentworth, created a viscount in 1628, had been appointed Lord President of the Council of the North, but Charles never really trusted him. Wentworth was a self-confident, somewhat overbearing man, who longed to employ his talents to their maximum advantage. He had established a close friendship with Laud, and in their correspondence the two men coined the term 'Thorough' to describe the sort of policies they believed Charles should follow during the 1630s. 'Thorough' meant cutting through red tape and administrative delay — which they identified with Lord Treasurer Portland, 'Lady Mora' — and making sure that the Kings's rights were fully enforced. In 1632 Wentworth had been sent to Ireland, as Lord-Deputy, and it was widely assumed that his rule there was a try-out for 'Thorough'. He took the initiative in recovering for the crown and the Church lands which had been alienated during the previous half-century of disturbance. When he was opposed by the common lawyers, Wentworth secured letters patent from Charles giving the prerogative court of Castle Chamber final authority in such matters. Royal power was, of course, less restrained in Ireland than in England, since there was no strongly-entrenched gentry group to oppose it, but English property owners were afraid that in due course they also would be called on to give up former Church and crown lands in their possession, and that the common law would show itself yet again powerless to protect them. They feared and hated Wentworth because he had the capacity, or so they thought, to turn Charles's personal rule into absolutism.

Wentworth now advised the King to summon Parliaments in England and Ireland as well as Scotland, arguing that the traditional enmity between England and Scotland would rouse members in defence of their native land. In the Scottish Parliament and Assembly members voted, as was to be expected, for the abolition of episcopacy, but the Irish Parliament, well managed by Wentworth, set a better example by voting over £150,000 for the King's needs. Yet if Wentworth thought that the English Parliament, which met in April 1640, would be as amenable as the Irish one, he was swiftly disillusioned.

The King depended for the presentation of his case to the Commons on the recently appointed Secretary, Sir Henry Vane, who had little skill in parliamentary tactics and was envious of Wentworth. His fumbling gave an opportunity to John Pym. This bull-necked west-countryman had been born four years before the Armada and grew up hating catholicism and longing to restore the total commitment to protestantism which he believed had been the hallmark of Elizabeth's reign. Charles proposed that subsidies should be voted in the first session of Parliament and that grievances should be left until the second, but Pym, who feared that once subsidies had been granted there would be no second session, insisted that grievances should be redressed first. His attitude alarmed Charles, especially in view of rumours that he and other prominent critics of the government were in touch with the Scots and intended to draw up a protestation against the war. Wentworth, who was now Earl of Strafford, was in favour of keeping Parliament in session, but the majority of the Privy Councillors were against him, and in May 1640 the King dissolved this Short Parliament only three weeks after it had met. By this hasty action Charles lost a good chance of coming to some sort of agreement with the parliamentary leaders, for the Commons and Lords, while they insisted on the need for reform, were not so intransigent as they were later to become.

Although Parliament had been dissolved, the King ordered Convocation to continue sitting. This clerical assembly voted £20,000 a year for the cause of the King and Church, and it also passed a number of canons defining the doctrines of the anglican church in what appeared to be an uncompromisingly authoritarian manner. Particular offence was given by the requirement that all clergymen, teachers and doctors should take an oath to maintain the government of the Church by 'archbishops, bishops, deans and archdeacons, etc.', for no-one could be certain what was included in that final, ambiguous abbreviation. The 'Etcetera Oath', far from putting an end to controversy, inflamed it.

Strafford now urged the King to renew military operations against Scotland, but this second 'Bishops' War' was even less successful than the first. The Scots poured south across the border and occupied the northern counties without meeting any effective resistance, and Strafford, who assumed that the King's benevolent rule had made his government popular, was forced to recognise that the converse was true. 'Pity me,' he wrote to a friend, 'for never came any man to so mightily lost a business. The army altogether unexercised and unprovided of all necessaries. That part which I bring now with me from Durham the worst I ever saw. Our horse all cowardly, the country from Berwick to York in the power of the Scots; an universal affright in all men; a general disaffection to the King's service; none sensible of his dishonour. In one word, here alone to fight with all these evils, without anyone to help.'

The King, in desperation, decided to summon a great council of peers to meet him at York, but when this assembled all it could propose was the conclusion of a truce with the Scots, to last until such time as another Parliament could settle the affairs of the kingdom. Writs were accordingly sent out, and on 3 November 1640 members of both Houses assembled in London for what was to be the last Parliament of Charles's reign. The King could not, this time, risk an early dissolution, for the terms of the truce negotiated with the Scots were that their army should remain in possession of Northumberland and Durham and receive £850 a day until a final settlement was agreed upon. Not until Parliament had guaranteed repayment of any monies advanced were the City authorities prepared to raise a loan to pay the Scots.

Pym was again the effective leader of the Commons and was more convinced than ever that the troubles of the King and kingdom had been caused by the machinations of papists and neopapists: as he told the House in his first major speech of the session, 'there is a design to alter law and religion. The party that affects this are papists, who are obliged by a maxim in their doctrine that they are not only to maintain their religion, but also to extirpate others'. Strafford was a long way from being a papist, but as far as Pym was concerned he was part of the conspiracy, for he was known to be a close friend of the 'Arminian' Laud; he had raised a catholic army in Ireland for use against the Scots; and, at the King's orders, he had been engaged in negotiations for a substantial loan from Spain, the greatest and most feared of all catholic powers.

Strafford missed the opening of Parliament, for the King had appointed him to command the royal army in the north, and he could not get away until the details of the truce with the Scots had been settled. During his absence Pym whipped up fears of a popish plot, centring on the powerful minister, and by the time Strafford reached London the Commons were ready to impeach him. Strafford had few friends in either House, and when the Lords heard the Commons formally accuse the minister of high treason they ordered that he should be sequestered from their House and held in custody until he was brought to trial. Two weeks later the Commons presented to the Lords a list of articles against Strafford. These included the assertion that he had 'traitorously abused the power and authority of his government, to the increasing, countenancing and encouraging of papists, so that he might settle a mutual dependence and confidence betwixt himself and that party, and by their help prosecute and accomplish his malicious and tyrannical designs'.

The writing was clearly on the wall for those members of Charles's government who were identified with 'Arminianism' or suspected of being papists. Archbishop Laud was impeached and sent to the Tower (where he remained until his execution in January 1645). Secretary Windebank only avoided a similar fate by fleeing to France. The Commons also attacked those ministers who had been linked with the extension of prerogative rule. Lord Keeper Finch, accused of bringing pressure to bear upon the judges in the Ship Money case, was a leading candidate for impeachment, but after making a robust defence of his actions before the House of Commons he followed Windebank's example and escaped overseas. Meanwhile the release had been ordered of all those who had suffered at the hands of the bishops, and in November 1640 Prynne and Burton made a triumphal entry into London: they were followed a week later by Bastwick.

Strafford's trial before the Lords opened in Westminster Hall on 22 March 1641. He was charged with nine general and twenty-eight specific offences which, so the Commons claimed, were treasonable. The major problem facing the Commons was that treason was defined, under the terms of the Act of 1352, as an offence against the King, but Strafford had been the King's officer, acting with the sovereign's authority. Pym, therefore, in his address to the Lords, argued that while Strafford's individual actions might not, of themselves, be treasonable, they amounted in total to an attempt to change the basis of English government which, if it had succeeded, would have made the King odious to his people. What could be more treasonable than this? As Pym said, 'other treasons are against the rule of the law: this is against the being of the law. It is the law that unites the King and his people, and the author of this treason hath endeavoured to dissolve that union, even to break the mutual, irreversible, indissoluble band of protection and allegiance whereby they are, and I hope ever will be, bound together.'

Strafford, who defended himself with great skill and courage, denied that he had extended the prerogative beyond its proper range or aimed at tyranny. 'I did ever inculcate this,' he declared, '[that] the happiness of a kingdom consists in the just poise of the King's prerogative and the subject's liberty, and that things should never be well till these went hand in hand together.' As for Pym's argument in favour of constructive treason, 'how can that be treason in the whole which is not in any of the parts?' If the Lords accepted such a novel doctrine they would be undermining the rule of law and opening the way to their own destruction: 'These gentlemen [i.e. his accusers] tell me they speak in defence of the com-

monweal against my arbitrary laws; give me leave to say that
I speak in defence of the commonweal against their arbitrary
treason'.

The Lords were impressed by Strafford's defence, and it became
clear that the impeachment might well fail. Pym still wanted to
press ahead with it, but his leadership of the Commons was not
unchallenged, and the more fiery spirits insisted that the judicial
proceedings against Strafford should be abandoned and that he
should be dealt with instead by Act of attainder. This simply recited the offences of which Strafford was accused and declared that
he should 'be adjudged and attainted of high treason, and shall
suffer . . . pains of death and incur the forfeiture of his goods and
chattels, lands, tenements and hereditaments'. The Bill passed the
Commons by a majority of 204 votes to 59, but these figures show
that only about half the members were present. Many of those who
absented themselves presumably did so because, while they wanted
to get rid of Strafford, they also wanted to confine their actions
within the boundaries of the law. To bring a man to trial and then,
when it looked as though he would be found not guilty, condemn
him by legislative enactment, was too much for their consciences.
Even at this early stage, then, the House of Commons was beginning to split between those who believed that the law must guide,
and if necessary curb, their actions, and those who believed that
if the law obstructed their political aims it must be bent or altered.

While Pym's immediate concern was to secure Strafford's destruction, as part of a general assault upon prerogative rule and
popery, he wished to preserve the royal government by strengthening it and making it more popular. The House had already been
persuaded to vote subsidies, and St John, who was Pym's ally, also
won support for a proposal that it should consider the crown's finances, with a view to putting them on a sounder basis. Charles
welcomed this initiative, but was more guarded in his response to
suggestions that he should bridge the gap between his government
and the political nation by appointing to high office some of his
leading critics. The main advocate of this policy was Pym's patron,
the Earl of Bedford, who had Charles's respect, and an early sign
of success came with the appointment of St John as Solicitor-
General in January 1641. Rumour had it that more substantial
changes would shortly take place, bringing Bedford into the administration as Lord Treasurer, accompanied by Pym as Chancellor of
the Exchequer. In February Bedford was made a Privy Councillor,
as were Essex and Saye, who were known to be deeply critical of
Charles's attitude towards both religion and the prerogative, but
the anticipated major appointments never took place. It may be
that Charles was waiting for proof that the Commons really would
solve his financial problems — which, in fact, they showed little

intention of doing. He was also probably alarmed by the massive demonstrations against Strafford that took place outside the House of Lords and were clearly intended to intimidate those members who might be tempted to take a moderate line: could he really trust men like Pym if they were committed to mob rule?

The true test of Pym's intentions, as far as the King was concerned, was his attitude towards Strafford. Charles accepted that Strafford's days as a minister were over, but he was determined, if at all possible, to save his life. Bedford and Pym might have been prepared for compromise on this issue, but by insisting on it they would almost certainly have forfeited their positions of unofficial leadership, for opinion in both Houses, as in the country at large, was intensely hostile towards Strafford. Bedford tried to persuade the Earl of Essex that Strafford's life should be saved, but Essex's response was a blunt negative: 'stone dead hath no fellow'. As for Pym, he could not possibly have carried the Commons with him if he had proposed sparing Strafford's life. He would have been accused of selling out to the King, and the members' fears of betrayal would have become even more acute if Pym had subsequently accepted high office. In short, the plan for bridge appointments never had much chance of success, and the last faint hope disappeared in May 1641 when Bedford was struck down by smallpox and died. There had been some measure of trust between Bedford and the King, but none between Charles and Pym. Charles seems to have believed from quite early on that Pym was aiming at his overthrow. Pym, on the other hand, suspected Charles of being lukewarm in his defence of protestantism and dangerously inclined towards absolutism. He was particularly alarmed by Charles's refusal to disband the army which Strafford had raised in Ireland, since he suspected it might be brought over to England for use against the King's critics.

There was now no hope for Strafford, and in early May the Lords passed the attainder Bill by 26 votes to 19. Charles had promised Strafford that if he came to London he would not be harmed. But now, from the Tower, Strafford wrote to the King releasing him from his promise: 'to set your Majesty's conscience at liberty, I do must humbly beseech your Majesty (for prevention of evils which may happen by your refusal) to pass this Bill'. Charles had to weigh the life of his minister against the danger to himself and his crown, and it was only after long and agonising deliberation that he gave his assent. 'My lord of Strafford's condition', he said, 'is happier than mine.' Strafford went to his execution on 11 May, looking up at Laud's window as he passed, to receive the Archbishop's benediction. A huge crowd had gathered to witness the end of 'Black Tom' and one of them described how 'many that came up to town on purpose to see the execution rode in triumph back, waving their hats and with all expressions of joy through every town they went crying "His head is off! His head is off!"' Laud was one of the few people who mourned Strafford's death, and he permitted himself a rare criticism of the King who had brought this about: Strafford, he wrote, 'served a mild and gracious prince, who knew not how to be, or be made, great'.

The destruction of Strafford opened the way to the destruction of the prerogative. Bills were passed abolishing the Courts of Star Chamber and High Commission, declaring Ship Money illegal, forbidding Distraint of Knighthood, and limiting the royal forests. Another Bill made a temporary grant of Tonnage and Poundage and Impositions to the King, but declared that the earlier collection of these taxes had been illegal. Even before the opening of Strafford's trial the King had accepted a Triennial Bill, providing that Parliament should meet at least once every three years, but he was subsequently presented with one prescribing that the existing Parliament should not be dissolved without its own consent. This Bill was presented to Charles at the same time as that for Strafford's attainder, and such was the distressed state of his mind that he eventually accepted it. For the first time in English history the sovereign was saddled with a Parliament which he could not legally get rid of.

Without Strafford, Laud, and other of his former Councillors to advise him, Charles was open to persuasion from those who urged him to take a firm stand against his enemies. In May he had given his blessing to a scheme whereby the garrison in the Tower — where Strafford was imprisoned — would be replaced by men who were known to be loyal to him, and as rumours of a military coup, or 'Army Plot', became current they created an atmosphere of alarm and suspicion. Pym took advantage of this to introduce a Bill proposing that Parliament, and not the King, should nominate the Lord Lieutenants who commanded the county militias. He also prompted the Commons to draw up a *Protestation*, to be taken on a nationwide basis, binding all those who subscribed to it to defend 'the true reformed protestant religion expressed in the doctrine of the Church of England against all popery and popish innovation'. But in Pym's eyes some of the major agents of popery were the 'Arminian' bishops, and it was therefore essential to remove them from their positions of influence in the House of Lords. The Commons passed the Bishops' Exclusion Bill in May 1641, but the Lords, who resented this interference with the composition of their own House, threw it out.

The Lords' action strengthened the position of the more radical members of the Commons who wanted not simply the exclusion of bishops from the Upper House but the total abolition of episcopacy. Not long after Parliament assembled in November 1640 a petition from the City of London had been presented calling for the destruction of episcopacy and 'all its dependencies, roots and branches'. Supporting petitions flowed in from other counties which had felt the impact of Laudianism, but it was not until after the Lords' rejection of bishops' exclusion that a Root-and-Branch Bill was introduced to the Commons. Debates on this showed a marked division of opinion, for there were many members of the Commons who, while detesting Laudian bishops, had no wish to destroy episcopacy, which they regarded as a traditional and essential feature of the Church of England. While one section of Parliament — and, indeed, of the political nation — was being driven by fear of popish and army plots into advocacy of unprecedented actions such as the abolition of episcopacy and the removal of the King's right of appointment to Lord Lieutenancies, another section was taking its stand upon defence of the *status quo* and the traditional constitution. It was too early as yet to talk of opposing sides, but the unity of the House of Commons could not be taken for granted. Pym was aware of this, and used devices such as petitions and the *Protestation* to rally opinion, both inside and outside Parliament, behind his policies. In June he persuaded both Houses to accept the *Ten Propositions*, which called, among other things, for the King 'to remove such evil counsellors against whom there shall be just exceptions' and to commit 'his own business and the affairs of the kingdom to such counsellors and officers as the Parliament may have cause to confide in'. Here, by implication, was a further restriction on royal authority.

The immediate purpose of the *Ten Propositions* was to persuade Charles to abandon a plan he had formed to leave London and go north to Scotland. Charles was adamant, however. London was no place in which to pass the summer months, particularly when the mobs were in the streets. Although he had a handful of guards, they could not be relied on to protect him and his family against an explosion of popular violence, and he no doubt recalled how similar circumstances had earlier led to the assassination of his favourite, Buckingham. But there could well be positive advantages to be gained by a Scottish visit. By timely concessions to the Scots he might be able to restore them to obedience and break the links between them and his enemies — for so he was coming to regard his critics — at Westminster. He would also be able to make personal contact with the officers of the English army still stationed in the north, and test the degree of their loyalty. He needed to move quickly, for Parliament had passed a poll tax Bill designed to raise money for disbanding the army, and suspicions of Charles's intentions had been increased by the revelation in June 1641 of a second Army Plot. Brushing aside all objections, therefore, Charles set out for his northern kingdom in August 1641.

## *The* Grand Remonstrance *and the Five Members*

It was while Charles was away from London that the news arrived
that the catholics in Ireland had risen in revolt against the English
settlers and were massacring them. Pym could have asked for no
more graphic proof of his belief in the existence of a popish conspiracy, for as one member of the Commons declared, 'all these
plots in Ireland are but one plot against England, for it is England
that is the fine sweet bit which they so long for and their cruel teeth
so much water at'. What was even more alarming, from Pym's
point of view, was the rebels' assertion that they were acting with
the King's authority and under a royal commission. It now seemed
to him to be a matter literally of life and death that the King's freedom to appoint Councillors and Lord Lieutenants should be restricted and that control of the army that would have to be raised
to put down the rebellion should be vested in men in whom Parliament had confidence. He had already been at work on a remonstrance, listing Parliament's achievements, which was designed
to appeal to the localities and swing opinion beyond Westminster
in his favour. Now he turned this into the *Grand Remonstrance* — a
long list of all the grievances under which the country had groaned
during the years of prerogative rule, and a call for determined action to make sure that they should never recur. Pym was careful
to focus blame not upon the King but on those who had misled
him. These included 'the Jesuited papists, who hate the laws as the
obstacles of that change and subversion of religion which they so
much long for; the bishops and the corrupt part of the clergy, who
cherish formality and superstition as the natural effects and more
probable supports of their own ecclesiastical tyranny and jurisdiction; [and] such Councillors and courtiers as for private ends have
engaged themselves to further the interests of some foreign princes'.
The aim of all these evil advisers had been, so the *Remonstrance* declared, to subvert 'the fundamental laws and principles of government upon which the religion and justice of this kingdom are firmly
established'. In order to frustrate their 'malignant and pernicious
design' it was necessary for the King not only to remove such men
from the circle of his advisers but also to 'vouchsafe to employ such
persons in your great and public affairs, and to take such to be near
you in places of trust, as your Parliament may have cause to confide
in'. Charles was also asked to agree that bishops should be deprived
of their votes in the Upper House; that tender consciences in religion should be salved 'by removing some oppressive and unnecessary ceremonies'; and that there should be 'a general synod of the
most grave, pious, learned and judicious divines . . . who may consider of all things necessary for the peace and good government of
the Church'.

Pym must have known that the *Grand Remonstrance* would split the Commons, for the conservatives were already organising themselves under the leadership of a Wiltshire country gentleman and common lawyer, Edward Hyde. But the outbreak of the Irish Rebellion had convinced him that time was running short and that if the godly did not take steps to defend themselves they would be overwhelmed. The final debate on the *Grand Remonstrance* opened at noon on 22 November 1641 and went on until past midnight. The House eventually divided, and the vote was taken by candlelight: 159 members voted in favour of the *Remonstrance*, 148 against — a majority of eleven. The conservatives immediately claimed the right to enter a protest, and members sprang to their feet reaching for their swords. 'I thought we had all sat in the valley of the shadow of death,' wrote one of them, 'for we, like Joab's and Abner's young men, had catched at each other's locks and sheathed our swords in each other's bowels, had not the sagacity and great calmness of Mr Hampden, by a short speech, prevented it.'

The *Grand Remonstrance* was regarded, at the time and later, as a turning point. The member for Cambridge, Oliver Cromwell, told Falkland that if it had not been passed 'he would have sold all he had the next morning and never seen England more, and he knew there were many other honest men of the same resolution'. Hyde now despaired of winning the Commons over to moderation, and offered his services to the King, hoping to prevent Charles from making mistakes which would widen the gulf between him and Parliament.

While the House of Commons was debating the *Grand Remonstrance* Charles was in the closing stages of his return journey to London. His visit to Scotland had been successful in the sense that he had come to terms with Argyll, the leading figure north of the border, whom he created a marquis. He was also encouraged by the evidence of the continuing popularity of the monarchy in the villages and towns through which he passed on his way to and from Scotland, for crowds of people flocked into the streets to cheer him. Even London gave him a warm reception when he made his state entry on 25 November, and Charles showed his pleasure by knighting the Lord Mayor. But appearances were in some ways deceptive, for although the City elite, made up principally of the directors of the East India and Levant Companies, looked to the crown as the guarantor of their privileged position, the many merchants and businessmen who were outside the charmed circle pinned their hopes on Pym and Parliament. In the elections for the Common Council which took place in December 1641 the radicals won control, and from then on the City was to be numbered among the King's most committed opponents.

Charles, at Hyde's suggestion, now set out to win over the mod-

erate members of Parliament by making the sort of bridge appointments that Bedford had earlier advocated. He even went so far as
to offer Pym the Chancellorship of the Exchequer, and when Pym
declined he gave it instead to Sir John Culpepper, one of Hyde's
associates. Another of the moderates, Viscount Falkland, renowned
for his integrity and love of peace, was persuaded by Hyde, who
was his close friend, to accept office as Secretary of State

However, at the same time as Charles was making these gestures
of conciliation he was preparing to take much firmer action against
the militants, for he shared Pym's belief in the existence of a conspiracy, though he was convinced that the principal conspirators
were to be found in the House of Commons, not the Privy Council,
and that they aimed at the destruction of his monarchy. Charles
saw no inherent contradiction between winning over the moderates
and attacking the hardliners: on the contrary, he believed that the
moderates would only rally round him when they saw that he was
determined to take a stand against the extremists. On 3 January
1642, therefore, the Attorney-General, acting on the King's direct
instructions, appeared before the House of Lords, where he impeached one peer and five members of the Commons on a charge
of treason. Lord Mandeville, John Pym, John Hampden, Arthur
Haselrig, Denzil Holles and William Strode were identified as the
ringleaders of the opposition, and they were accused of subverting
the fundamental laws by attempting to deprive the King of his
rightful prerogatives, alienating the affections of his subjects from
him, and conspiring with the Scottish rebels.

Charles was no doubt hoping that the Lords would order the
arrest of the impeached members as they had done with Strafford,
but he had miscalculated. The Lords were deeply unhappy about
Charles's initiative, which they thought was ill-timed as well as ill-
conceived, and refused to take any immediate action. On the next
day, therefore, Charles made his way to Westminster, accompanied
by a bodyguard, and entered the Commons. 'By your leave, Mr
Speaker,' he said, 'I must borrow your chair a little', and stepping
on to the dais he scanned the rows of faces to see if the Five Members were among them. When he realised that they had fled, he
turned to the Speaker and demanded to know where they had gone.
But William Lenthall, in an uncharacteristic moment of greatness,
fell on his knees and answered: 'may it please your Majesty, I have
neither eyes to see nor tongue to speak in this place but as the
House is pleased to direct me, whose servant I am here'. Charles
knew then that his coup had failed. 'Well,' he said, 'since I see all
the birds are flown, I do expect from you that you shall send them
unto me as soon as they return hither', and he made his way out
of the House amid a clamour of voices and shouts of 'Privilege!
Privilege!'

The Five Members, who had been warned that Charles was contemplating the use of force, were in fact in the City, where the puritan radicals of the parish of St Stephen's, Coleman Street, had given them refuge. Charles drove to the City and called on the Common Council to hand over the fugitives so that they might stand trial, but the City would not abandon its heroes, and angry crowds surged round the King's carriage as he drove, empty-handed, back to Whitehall. London was becoming too dangerous a place for Charles to stay in, and on 10 January he left for Hampton Court. Next day the Five Members returned in triumph to Westminster.

## The Drift towards War

By abandoning London the King had given a trump card to his opponents, for the capital was traditionally the seat of government. As reports reached the two Houses of armed men gathering in various parts of the country they ordered that the counties should 'put themselves in a posture of defence', which meant calling out the trained bands and preparing to suppress disorders. Technically speaking such commands were invalid, since only the King had the right to issue them, but the very name of Parliament carried authority and the governors of the localities were not well placed to decide whether or not particular orders were from Parliament alone or from King-in-Parliament. In any case the *Grand Remonstrance* had done its work, for petitions from all over England demonstrated a common belief in the existence of a popish plot in which all the enemies of the commonwealth — evil counsellors, Arminian bishops, monopolists and projectors — were involved. No overt blame was attached to the King, for he was regarded as the potential victim of the conspirators and not as their protector. Yet it was Parliament to which the petitions were addressed, and this in itself was a sign that Pym's identification of Parliament with opposition to popery had made it a focus of popular loyalty in a way that would earlier have been inconceivable.

The general fear of catholic conspiracy made it essential that the trained bands, the county militia, should be in the hands of men who were committed both to protestantism and parliamentary rule. Charles, who was still making gestures towards compromise, agreed, in principle, that Parliament should nominate the Lord Lieutenants, as long as their commission ran in his name and could be revoked when he saw fit. He also accepted the Bishops' Exclusion Bill which the Lords, in the panic atmosphere following the attempt upon the Five Members, had at last passed. But Pym and a majority of the Commons were determined not to compromise on the vital question of control of the militia, and the two Houses therefore issued the Militia Bill as an 'ordinance' to which they required obedience on the grounds that the King's 'public will' was expressed only by and through Parliament.

The exact legal position of the militia had been unclear ever since the repeal of the Marian statutes defining military obligations at the beginning of James I's reign. It could therefore be argued that the Militia Ordinance was not taking away the King's authority in such matters, since by law he had never had any. But the appointment of Lord Lieutenants had always been a royal prerogative, and, whatever its case in law, Parliament now seemed to have stepped over the line which divided constitutional action from innovation. In other words it had been driven by fears for its own safety and that of the kingdom into taking 'emergency powers' in just the same way as the King had done in the period of Personal Rule. Charles could now claim that it was Parliament which was destroying the constitution by breaking the fundamental laws, while he, under Hyde's guidance, was emerging as its champion. By June the royal propaganda campaign was in full flood, and in the following month Charles published an open letter to the judges who were about to set out on their assizes. In this he asserted his determination to maintain the protestant Church of England and to rule according to law. In many places his words fell on receptive ears.

Whether or not Charles was genuine in his protestations that he was now a constitutional monarch is open to question, for the circumstances were such that he could not rely on a slow swing of public opinion in his favour. He was convinced that his enemies would stop at nothing to destroy him, and in February 1642 he had sent his wife over to Holland, carrying with her the crown jewels, which she was to pawn in order to raise money for the purchase of arms and ammunition. He was obviously determined to fight rather than make further concessions. 'What would you have?' he asked a parliamentary delegation waiting on him at Newmarket in March. 'Have I violated your laws? Have I denied to pass one Bill for the ease and security of my subjects? I do not ask you what you have done for me. God so deal with me and mine as all my thoughts and intentions are upright for the maintenance of the true protestant profession and for the observation and preservation of the laws of this land.' The Earl of Pembroke, who was one of the delegation, urged him to give up his right of appointing Lord Lieutenants, even if only for a time, but Charles would have none of it. 'By God, not for an hour!' he told him. 'You have asked that of me in this was never asked of a king.'

Charles may have been thinking in terms of armed resistance to Parliament but if so he can only have been discouraged by the lukewarm reception he was given as he made his way north to York.

There was no lack of respect or loyalty, but it was clear that what his subjects wanted more than anything else was a peaceful resolution of the differences between him and the two Houses. He had already called on Parliament to state its terms for a peaceful settlement, and it eventually did so in the *Nineteen Propositions* which were sent to Charles at York in June 1642. These contained demands that Parliament should control appointments to the principal military and civil offices, that 'no public act ... may be esteemed of any validity, as proceeding from royal authority, unless it be done by the advice and consent of the major part of your Council, attested under their hands', and that 'such a reformation be made of the Church government and liturgy as both Houses of Parliament shall advise'. Acceptance of such terms would have meant total capitulation for the King, but the parliamentary leaders felt certain he would have to accept them in the end because he had no alternative. Charles and Hyde were now in agreement that the only chance of a negotiated settlement rested in strengthening the King's position. Since Parliament had taken over control of the Lieutenancy system through the Militia Ordinance, Charles now reverted to the pre-Lieutenancy device of issuing Commissions of Array. These were directed to named individuals in every county and major city, and instructed them to raise forces on the King's behalf. The commissions were sent out in June 1642; in July the King's recruiting campaign got under way; and on 22 August Charles raised his royal standard at Nottingham. It was a call to arms, for civil war was now inevitable.

# I3
# The Civil War and Interregnum

## *Roundheads and Cavaliers*

In June 1642 the Commons felt certain that the King would have
to accept their demands because he would find no one to fight for
him; yet four months later Charles was advancing on London with
an army of 13,000 men. From that time to the present day the problem of who fought for whom, and why, has intrigued historians and
defied any clear-cut explanation. As far as the ordinary soldier was
concerned, pay and the chance of plunder, as well as traditional
loyalties, seem at first to have been the main incentives, and when
captured he was usually quite willing to change sides. But the political nation, which had been united against the King in 1640, split
for a variety of reasons, and none of the general explanations is
entirely satisfactory.

For S. R. Gardiner, the great nineteenth-century historian of the
Stuart period, the dispute was primarily one of ideas, with the
champions of religious liberty fighting side by side with defenders
of constitutional government in opposition to the crown. Some
twentieth-century historians, however, writing under the stimulus
of Marx, found the explanation of the civil war solely in religious
and constitutional terms insufficient, because it took no account of
the economic realities which underlay and, so they believed, served
to mould the attitudes of the property-owners who led the struggle.
For fully-fledged Marxists the civil war was the revolt of the up-
and-coming capitalist gentry against the feudal aristocracy who
were clinging to power and could only be dislodged by violence. As
for the victory of the gentry, this was an essential part of the process whereby England was transformed from a feudal-agricultural
society into a capitalist-commercial one. This interpretation
was strengthened by the study which R. H. Tawney — not himself
a Marxist — made of the gentry, showing how they had been increasing in wealth and influence as a result of their acquisition of
monastic lands, and it seemed to explain why the economically
advanced south and east, led by London, supported Parliament,
while the backward north and west were predominantly royalist.

The weakness of the Marxist hypothesis is that the gentry were not capitalist nor were the aristocracy feudal. There were capitalists in England, but they were to be found among the richer City merchants, who did not play a major role in the revolution and, in the early stages at any rate, supported the crown. There were also a few aristocrats who might be legitimately described as 'feudal', because they could call up armies of retainers to fight for them. The Earl of Derby was one of these, and he, it is true, supported Charles I; but the Earl of Northumberland, head of the great house of Percy and one of the most powerful magnates in England, was to be found on the side of Parliament. Such men were, in any case, exceptions, for the long period of Tudor rule had seen the decline and disappearance of feudalism (except as a money-raising device). It had also seen the disappearance of the feudal aristocracy: the majority of English nobles in 1640 came from gentry families that had been elevated to the peerage only during the preceding hundred years. There was no great gulf fixed between the gentry and the aristocracy in birth, wealth or attitude. John Hampden, for instance, was a mere gentleman, but he was richer than most of the nobles, and after the attempt on the Five Members a thousand of the tenants from his Buckinghamshire estates marched to Westminster to offer their services to Parliament. Hampden also had at least eight relatives in the Long Parliament, but they did not form a united group and they included not only Oliver Cromwell but the King himself!

Professor Trevor-Roper put forward quite a different interpretation, though one that was also based on property. According to him the revolt was led by the declining or 'mere' gentry — those who had no access to office, the law or trade, and were determined to break the power of the 'court' gentry, who supplemented their landed wealth from these other sources. Oliver Cromwell comes to mind immediately as an example of a 'mere' gentleman who managed not simply to force his way into the gilded circle but to make himself the centre of it. It is also the case that as the war progressed the leadership of the county committees, which organised the supply of men and money for the parliamentary armies, fell increasingly into the hands of men whose families had not formerly been numbered among the elite of their county. Yet this interpretation, attractive as it is, does not accord with some of the most important evidence. The court gentry were not a homogeneous group: when war came some supported one side, some the other, and the choice seems to have been dictated by personal convictions. The Roman Catholics were declining gentry, if only because of the heavy recusancy fines they had to pay, but they were to be found mainly in the King's armies. The parliamentary leaders included some of the most prosperous landowners in England, while on the other hand the 'mere' gentry of the north and west placed their money and lives at the King's disposal.

So far, no all-embracing and watertight explanation has been found of why some people chose one side and some another. This is hardly surprising, since human beings are complex creatures who do not fit easily into general categories. But Gardiner was right when he put the emphasis upon religious attitudes, for religion was something about which most men and women felt strongly, and it was so intimately connected with politics that frequently the two fused into one.

In many, if not most counties, the immediate reaction to the outbreak of fighting was one of shock and of determination to keep it away. Where the county community was divided in its opinions, 'neutralism' was a positive, not simply a negative, response. It reflected the desire to restore and maintain harmony, for the gentry were well aware that divisions between them would endanger the social order. Yet commitment to the county community might well run counter to commitment to the religious community, whether of the 'godly', the anglicans (though this term was not in use at the time), or the papists. In Herefordshire, for example, where the gentry were overwhelmingly royalist, the puritan Sir Robert Harley and his wife, despite their ties of blood and friendship with their neighbours, felt compelled to side with Parliament.

Elsewhere the converse was true, for although the godly professed their desire to maintain the social order it seemed to many of their compatriots that they were unleashing forces which threatened it far more than the King had ever done. Moderates were appalled by reports from many parts of the country that common men, and even women, were mounting into pulpits and preaching what they believed to be the word of God. Sir Edward Dering, a Kentish gentleman who, in a rash moment, had been persuaded to introduce the Root-and-Branch Bill into the Commons, quickly repented of his action. He told the House in November 1641 how shocked he had been when a 'bold mechanic [i.e. artisan] had said to him, "I hope your worship is too wise to believe that which you call your Creed"'. Dering's comment that 'one absurdity leads in a thousand, and when you are down the hill of error there is no bottom but in hell' must have struck home. It was echoed in an outburst by a former Lord Mayor of London about the general lack of respect for rank and dignity. 'Before God!' he exclaimed, 'I have no more authority in the City than a porter . . . If to be governed by people whose authority we know not, and by rules which nobody ever heard of or can know, be a sign of arbitrary power, we have as much of it as heart can wish.'

The King knew that one of his major strengths came from his identification with order. When Culpepper drew up the royal reply to the *Nineteen Propositions* he warned that by breaking with precedent and committing itself to innovations, Parliament was striking at the foundations of society. Parliament claimed authority as representative of the people, but what if the people were to 'set up for themselves, call parity and independence liberty ... destroy all rights and proprieties, all distinctions of families and merit'. By such means, he declared, 'this splendid and excellently distinguished form of government' would collapse in chaos and confusion, 'and the long line of our many noble ancestors in a Jack Cade or a Wat Tyler'. It was this same linking of religious and political dissent that inspired Charles when he told his troops in September 1642 that they would 'meet with no enemies but traitors, most of them Brownists, Anabaptists and atheists, such who desire to destroy both Church and state'.

Not everybody was convinced by the King's arguments, however. His opponents numbered many gentry and 'middling sort' who were concerned to see the social order preserved, along with a truly protestant church, but believed that only Parliament could be trusted to ensure this. The long opening section of the *Grand Remonstrance* covering the years from Charles's accession down to the assembling of the Long Parliament was designed to show how far the King had strayed from the path of religious and constitutional probity. Even if his intentions had been good, he had been too weak to carry them out, and had, instead, come under the sway of evil counsellors who aimed at the subversion of the existing order in both Church and state. But for Parliament — or so it was argued — their wicked designs would have been carried through, and the King's unwillingness or inability to reach a peaceful settlement with his Parliament now that civil war was impending was a further sign of his unreliability. Parliament, admittedly, had been forced into innovation, but as the two Houses declared in a remonstrance of May 1642, 'if we have done more than ever our ancestors have done, we have suffered more than they have ever suffered'. It was true that Parliament had had to establish new precedents, but 'we have made them for posterity, upon the same or better grounds of reason and law than those were upon which our predecessors first made any for us'. In other words it was the King who, by his arbitrary actions, had driven Parliament into innovation. The aim of the two Houses remained what it had always been, the restoration and preservation of the traditional order in Church and state.

The very fact that both the King and Parliament claimed to be fighting for the same causes made it difficult for people at all levels of society to choose between them. Many took the line of least resistance by making no choice, and either followed the lead of their social superiors or clung to the hope that by adopting a neutralist stance they could opt out of the conflict altogether. This gave the edge to the minorities which were committed, and the adherence of a county to one side or the other was often determined by the balance of power between these minorities. This is why it is misleading to assume that certain regions were wholeheartedly parliamentarian while others were wholeheartedly royalist. Almost the only area of which this was true was Wales, which never wavered in its commitment to the King. Elsewhere the pattern was a complex one of varied and shifting allegiances. Essex, for instance, was noted for its puritanism. It was one of the first counties to put the Militia Ordinance into effect, and took the lead in providing troops for the parliamentary armies; yet there was a significant body of opinion within the county which wanted a compromise with the King. The problem for the moderates, and not only in Essex, was that their very moderation made them ill suited to give a lead, and they were therefore outflanked and outwitted by those who were committed.

In the last resort the allegiance of the local communities was determined by the presence of the field armies of either side. Neutralism was no longer a viable option when armed men were in control of a county or town, and where a royalist or parliamentarian group had seized power it could be toppled by outside intervention: this was the case with Hertfordshire, where the activities of the King's supporters were crushed by a parliamentary troop of horse, and much the same happened in Kent. The sad truth was that whether the people of England wanted war or not — and the overwhelming majority of them did not want it — they had no choice once armies were called into existence and began their manoeuvrings. The future of all regions — royalist, parliamentarian or neutralist — would now be decided on the battlefield.

## The Civil War

By the autumn of 1642 the King had an army of some 6,000 foot and 3,500 horse, and was ready to strike at London, the nerve-centre of his enemies. In mid-October he left Shrewsbury and moved south-east towards the capital, taking with him his twenty-three-year-old nephew Rupert, younger son of the Winter Queen, who had come over to fight for him. The Earl of Essex, who had been appointed by the two Houses to command the parliamentary field army, marched out to meet the King, and the two armies clashed at Edgehill. In this first big engagement of the war the pattern was set for many of the later encounters. Rupert's cavalry, on one wing, charged right through their opponents and disappeared into the distance. But the roundhead cavalry, on the other wing, broke the royalist line and captured the King's standard. It was left to the infantry to decide the outcome, but by the time night fell neither side had won a decisive advantage. The King was ready to give battle again next morning, but Essex drew off his men and left the road to London open.

Rupert was all for a swift advance on the capital, but the King, shocked by the slaughter he had witnessed and realising for the first time what war entailed, moved only slowly south-east, and let Essex march round him and enter London first. There the Earl mobilised the citizens for their defence and marched them out to Turnham Green — then a small village surrounded by market gardens whose hedges provided good cover against attack. By early November the King's army had reached Brentford, which Rupert captured and fired, but there his advance stopped. Winter was drawing in, and the approaches to London were so heavily defended that savage fighting would have been needed to break through. Rupert, thinking in military terms, might have been prepared for this, but the King did not wish to make himself master of a ruined city. His aim was to demonstrate his strength and force his opponents to negotiate with him as an equal, and the Edgehill campaign had achieved just this. He therefore drew back his troops and established his headquarters at Oxford.

In London discontent was spreading. The King controlled Newcastle and had cut the supply of coal to the capital, where a little over half the Commons and about a fifth of the Lords exercised power in the name of King and Parliament. Theatres were closed, food was dear and fuel prohibitively expensive, and the failure to obtain the swift victory which Pym had predicted revived the peace party in Parliament. Early in 1643 parliamentary commissioners arrived at Oxford to try to negotiate a settlement, but on the fundamental questions of Church reform and accountability of royal ministers the gap between the two sides was too great to be bridged. There was not even agreement on a temporary cessation of hostilities. Charles was elated by the news that his forces in the west had been victorious at Braddock Down. He was coming to realise, as Parliament was later to do, that armies raised to strengthen one's position and force the enemy to negotiate, opened the way to total victory, after which no concessions would be necessary.

The failure of the attempt to produce a negotiated settlement strengthened Pym's authority in the Commons. He was by no means the unchallenged master of this assembly. Holles — who, as one of the Five Members, had no reason to love Charles — was in favour of peace at almost any price, while at the other extreme there were men like Henry Marten who was prepared to fight until the King was destroyed. Between these two wings came the mass of members, and Pym had to move skilfully to avoid antagonising them and to secure the passing of the measures which he believed were necessary for financing the war. He persuaded the House to order the confiscation of all property belonging to royalists in areas controlled by Parliament, and to impose a regular weekly assessment throughout the kingdom for the maintenance of the parliamentary armies. Pym could count on the support of London, where his ally Isaac Pennington had been elected Lord Mayor in 1642, but City opinion was as divided as that in the House of Commons. The richer merchants were in favour of peace and gave a sympathetic ear to royalist propaganda, but there was also a radical group which set up its own committee and took as its hero Sir William Waller, the parliamentary commander in the west, rather than Essex, whom it accused of not wanting to win the war.

Both sides used the winter of 1642–3 to improve their organisation. The King ordered the sequestration of the estates of parliamentary sympathisers, and also imposed a regular assessment on the counties under his control. He was not desperately short of money. His richer supporters made generous gifts to the royal coffers as well as raising men at their own expense, and Oxford and Cambridge colleges sent the King much of their plate. But the defection of the fleet — which, under the Earl of Warwick, had declared for Parliament — was a serious blow, since it meant that the King could not collect Customs from the ships entering London and other big ports. For arms he depended on the capture of local arsenals and on supplies from abroad. Hull would have been a valuable acquisition, not only as a port but as a well-stocked magazine, but it stood firm for Parliament. However, there were many smaller places from which royalists could operate: they included Bridlington, on the Yorkshire coast, where the Queen landed in February 1643, bringing with her a cargo of munitions from Holland. And in the autumn of that year the capture of a number of south coast ports by the cavaliers ensured that the King's supply routes to the Continent would be kept open.

Charles had established his headquarters at Oxford, which, despite the fact that it was surrounded by hostile territory, was well placed to serve as a rendezvous for the forces being raised in the west and midlands. He intended to concentrate his main fighting units at Oxford in the spring of 1643 and then distribute them in such a way as to bring maximum pressure to bear on London. He hoped to inflame discontent among the citizens and thereby force the parliamentary leadership to reopen negotiations. At first all went well with these plans. The Earl of Newcastle, commander of the northern army, brought Sir Thomas Fairfax to battle at Adwalton Moor in June and heavily defeated him. Yorkshire was now effectively under royalist control, and siege was laid to Hull. In the following month the parliamentary forces under Sir William Waller were virtually wiped out at the battle of Roundway Down, outside Devizes, and by September Sir Ralph Hopton, who commanded the King's troops in the west, had pushed as far east as Arundel. But the most resounding victory was won by Rupert, who had been sent to besiege Bristol, the second largest port in the kingdom and far too powerful and dangerous to be left in the rear of the advancing cavalier armies. In July 1643 Rupert took the city by storm, and the news sent royalist spirits soaring.

These defeats intensified the jockeying for power in Parliament. Three main groups had emerged, though each could count on only thirty or so adherents, and their total numbers amounted to less than half of the active membership of the Commons. The peace party wanted a settlement at almost any price. As long as the King agreed to maintain the constitutional, non-prerogative monarchy re-established by the legislation of 1641 — to which he had given his assent — they were prepared to trust him. The war party, on the other hand, wanted outright victory leading to a dictated settlement which would go well beyond that of 1641. They were determined on a major puritan reconstruction of the Church of England and on a limitation of the King's power in secular government which would make it impossible for him to go back on his concessions even if he wished to do so. Between these two extremes tacked a middle group, of which Pym was the most prominent member. Its adherents agreed with the peace party in being prepared to accept the 1641 settlement as a basis, but they also wanted ecclesiastical reform and shared the war party's distrust of Charles.

Following the defeat of the parliamentary forces in the summer of 1643 the peace party put forward its proposals, which were only narrowly rejected. Now the initiative passed to the war party, which, with the support of its radical allies in the City, campaigned for the vigorous prosecution of the war and the appointment of a more committed commander-in-chief in place of Essex. Pym may have had reservations about Essex's military ability, but he could not afford to desert the Earl. Essex, Pym and Hampden had stood for a negotiated peace, even though they were unwilling to negotiate until they were in a position of strength, but Hampden was killed early in 1643 in a skirmish outside Oxford, and as far as Pym could see only Essex stood between him and domination by the war party. He persuaded the Commons to give Essex command of an army, to be raised largely from the London trained bands, which should march north-west to block the King's advance. He also persuaded them that new forces must be brought in to redress the balance in Parliament's favour. The Scots, who had earlier come to the help of the English Parliament, were alarmed by the King's successes and were ready to march south if only terms could be agreed on. At Pym's suggestion parliamentary commissioners, of whom the most influential was Sir Henry Vane the younger, son of Charles's former Secretary, were sent to Edinburgh to arrange a treaty with the Scots.

This was almost Pym's last service to the parliamentary cause, for he was a dying man, but he managed to complete his reorganisation of the financial system by getting the Commons to agree that an excise should be levied on wine, sugar and other articles. Pym never fought in the armies, but no man did more to make sure of Parliament's victory in the civil war. He provided the money, without which no army could have been raised, and he called in the Scots when they were most needed. But more important even than these was the way in which he steered Parliament between the two extremes and kept alive in 1642 and '43 the principles which had guided it in 1640. Pym's death in December 1643 removed from the scene the one man who might have made sure that those principles found expression in the peace that followed victory.

Pym lived long enough to know that his faith in Essex had been justified. Charles had decided not to advance on London until Gloucester had been captured, and Essex marched to the city's relief. The King called off the siege, but moved rapidly round Essex's army and took up his position at Newbury, between the Earl and London. The battle of Newbury, which took place in September, might have been decisive, for a royalist victory would not simply have opened the way to London but would also have increased the dissensions within Parliament. Essex, however, handled his men well, and although the King was not defeated he drew off his forces during the night, leaving the parliamentary army to return home in triumph.

By the end of 1643 stalemate had been reached, and both sides were looking for ways out of it. The King was hoping for reinforcements from Ireland, where his commander, the Earl of Ormond, had signed a truce with the rebels in September 1643. Charles was also, on Hyde's advice, preparing to appeal to all moderate men by summoning a Parliament to Oxford. This body, which assembled early in 1644, consisted of about thirty peers and over a hundred members of the Commons, and Hyde hoped that it would serve as a reminder and a guarantee that the King had abandoned all thought of ruling by virtue of his absolute prerogative.

The Westminster Parliament had also extended its appeal by setting up an Assembly of Divines to discuss religious differences and make recommendations about a settlement of the Church. There was no question of continuing episcopal government, for the Scots demanded as the price of their military intervention that the Church should be reformed on a puritan pattern. Parliament committed itself to this by taking the *Solemn League and Covenant*, by which members swore to 'endeavour the extirpation of popery, prelacy ... and whatsoever shall be found to be contrary to sound doctrine and the power of godliness', and to reform religion 'according to the word of God and the example of the best reformed churches'. The Scots assumed that by subscribing to the *Solemn*

*League and Covenant* the English had subscribed also to a presbyterian settlement on the Scottish model. But not all puritans were presbyterians. Vane, for instance, who had carried through the negotiations with the Scots, was deeply opposed to presbytery, and when the Committee of Both Kingdoms was set up in January 1644, as a co-ordinating body for the direction of the war, only six of the twenty-one members were staunch presbyterians.

In 1644 the tide of war began to turn against the King. The Scots crossed the border in January with an army of twenty thousand men and drove the Marquis of Newcastle back towards York. In the same month Fairfax, in a sudden swoop from Yorkshire across to the west, fell on the troops who had just landed from Ireland and captured most of them at Nantwich. A further setback for the King came in March, when Waller defeated his western army at Cheriton in Hampshire. It was now a matter of urgency to save the northern army, which was bottled up in York. Charles therefore instructed Rupert that 'all new enterprises laid aside, you immediately march. . .with all your force to the relief of York'.

Rupert had about fifteen thousand men and was outnumbered by his opponents, for the Scots had been joined by the army of the Eastern Association under the Earl of Manchester, and the northern army under Fairfax. As the Prince advanced, the investing forces drew off and marched to intercept him, but in a brilliant manoeuvre Rupert swung round them and entered the city that Newcastle had so gallantly defended. Newcastle wanted to rest his tired men, but Rupert, conscious of the King's command, insisted on an immediate engagement.

The two armies drew up on Marston Moor outside York, on 2 July 1644. Cromwell and the cavalry of the Eastern Association were on one wing of the parliamentary army, Fairfax and the northern cavalry on the other, while the Scottish infantry were concentrated in the centre. In the royalist army, Rupert commanded the cavalry opposite Cromwell, Lord Goring was in charge of the other wing, while the centre was composed of Newcastle and his infantry. The day was drawing to a close and Rupert, deciding there would be no fighting until the morning, allowed his troops to break ranks. Cromwell saw his opportunity, charged, and drove Rupert's cavalry from the field. As he did so, Goring's horse advanced to the attack, and broke right through Fairfax's cavalry. Everything now depended on the speed with which either side could exploit its victory, and here the advantage went to Cromwell, who had trained his men not to scatter in pursuit but to rein in their horses and wait for further orders. Newcastle's infantry were gradually overcoming their Scottish opponents when Cromwell brought his cavalry back on to the battlefield, swept away the remnants of Goring's horse, and attacked Newcastle's men from the flank.

The Yorkshire infantry refused to give way and were cut down
where they stood. With them died the King's hopes of holding the
north. York, which Charles regarded as one of the brightest jewels
in his crown, surrendered to Fairfax, the Earl of Newcastle fled to
the Continent, and Cromwell wrote to the Speaker to tell him that
'truly England and the church of God hath had a great favour from
the Lord in this great victory given to us, such as the like never was
since this war began . . . God made them as stubble to our swords'.

Parliament could have won the war after Marston Moor if its
armies had been united and had been commanded by men determined on victory. But Essex was entangled with the King's forces
down in Cornwall, while Manchester was playing for time. He had
been an opponent of the King from the early days, and had been
named (as Lord Mandeville) along with the Five Members as an
enemy to the crown. But like Pym, Manchester had fought only to
make a negotiated peace possible, and he feared that victory would
play into the hands of the radicals in the war party. He was also
shocked by the bitter disputes that had broken out in his Eastern
Association army between the presbyterians and Independents,
and was convinced that only a negotiated settlement could rein in
sectarian passions and prevent a collapse into religious anarchy.

The two Houses at Westminster were far from united on the religious issue. In the Commons the majority of members probably
wanted to preserve a national Church. Some members were in
favour of episcopacy on the 'primitive' or Elizabethan model, but
since the alliance with the Scots ruled out bishops they were prepared to go along with a watered-down version of presbyterianism
— what one disgusted Scottish commissioner subsequently described as a 'lame, erastian presbytery'. There were, however, committed presbyterians in the House, who longed for the
establishment of an autonomous Scots-style Church in England.
And at the other extreme there was a small but influential minority
of Independents, who believed that every congregation should be
self-sufficient. Some of them were prepared to accept a loose association of congregations on a national basis as a bulwark against
anarchy, but not the rigidly centralised structure of provincial and
national synods advocated by the presbyterians.

The situation at Westminster was made even more complex by
the fact that religious and political attitudes did not always coin-
cide. It might be thought that Independents, who wanted to go well
beyond the 1641 settlement in religion, would be found only in
the war party: in practice they were to be found in the middle
group as well, though not in the peace party. As for presbyterians,
they covered the whole of the political spectrum, and had adherents
in all three of the major groupings. The peace party included the
majority of episcopalians and for that reason had been opposed to

the alliance with the Scots. Yet they soon came to realise that the
Scots were as afraid of the Independents as they were, and as
anxious to obtain a negotiated settlement with the King. The peace
party and the Scots were therefore allies in persuading Parliament
to agree to negotiations. These opened at Uxbridge early in 1645,
but they got nowhere. The parliamentary commissioners insisted
that Charles should commit himself to the abolition of episcopacy,
the setting up of a presbyterian church, and parliamentary control
of the militia. Charles offered compromises — which may or may
not have been genuine — on all these issues, but the lack of trust
in him that had done so much to precipitate the war now blocked
the path to peace.

Meanwhile the war party, with strong support from the Independents, had been pressing ahead with its plan to reshape the
parliamentary armies as a prelude to a military solution. They
needed to get rid of the aristocratic commanders who, they
believed, were holding up the war effort, but to do so without
antagonising the House of Lords. They therefore promoted a
Self-Denying Ordinance, by which all members of Parliament were
required to lay down their military commands. The Lords held this
up while they awaited the outcome of the Uxbridge negotiations,
but by mid-February 1645, when it became plain that these would
not succeed, they passed not only the Self-Denying Ordinance but
also one creating a New Model army. Sir Thomas Fairfax was appointed to command this force, and he gave charge of the cavalry
to Oliver Cromwell, who was temporarily exempted from the provisions of the Ordinance.

The New Model was a national army, as distinct from the various county associations which had hitherto fought the war, but its
military significance should not be over-estimated. It had been in
existence only a few months when the King was finally defeated at
Naseby, and in that battle it was the steadiness of Cromwell's cavalry — mostly drawn from the eastern counties, and renowned for
their discipline long before the New Model was first thought of —
which won the day. Naseby lies north of Oxford, and it was there
that on 14 June 1645 Fairfax brought Rupert and the King to battle. Rupert again succeeded in driving his opponents from the field,
but Cromwell, on the other flank, broke the royalist cavalry and
then turned to attack the infantry. When Rupert returned with his
exhausted horsemen he could only look on helplessly as the King's
last army was destroyed.

Charles knew after Naseby that it was merely a matter of time before he would have to surrender. Rupert urged him to win over the
Scots by agreeing to the establishment of presbyterianism, but
Charles was not prepared to compromise on what he regarded as
essentials: 'speaking as a mere soldier or statesman', he declared,

'I must say there is no probability but of my ruin. Yet as a Christian I must tell you that God will not suffer rebels and traitors to prosper, nor this cause to be overthrown ... A composition with them at this time is nothing else but a submission, which, by the grace of God, I am resolved against, whatever it cost me.' He still hoped that more troops might arrive from Ireland, or that Montrose's astonishing successes in Scotland might eventually save him, but by the spring of 1646 he could fight no more, and in May he rode in to the Scottish camp outside Newark and gave himself up to the Scots.

## The Problems of the Post-War Settlement

Now that the war was over — except for mopping-up operations against royalist garrisons — the problems of peace came to the fore, and among these the most intractable was that of the religious settlement. In July 1643 a parliamentary ordinance set up the Westminster Assembly of Divines, with instructions to consider how 'such a government shall be settled in the Church as may be most agreeable to God's holy word'; but the Assembly, which included both presbyterians and Independents, was as divided as Parliament itself and could not reach agreement. Meanwhile Parliament was driven by the demands of war into alliance with the Scots and acceptance of the *Solemn League and Covenant*, but not until the war was over did it implement its promise to establish presbyterianism. By the beginning of 1645 the Westminster Assembly had drawn up a *Directory of Worship* to replace the Prayer Book, and in the summer of that year it submitted to Parliament its proposals for setting up a presbyterian church. Members of Parliament, however, were unwilling to see the last word on religious matters, namely the authority to excommunicate, left in the hands of ministers, however godly, for they had not destroyed Laudian clericalism merely to submit themselves to a presbyterian version of it. Their insistence that Parliament should be the final court of appeal in ecclesiastical matters was resisted by the Assembly, but eventually it gave way, and in March 1646 Parliament ordered a presbyterian organisation to be set up in every county.

By this time, however, it was too late to preserve religious uniformity. With the breakdown of ecclesiastical discipline in and after 1642 many congregations had come into existence which acknowledged no external authority, and they were not prepared to abandon their right to worship as they wished simply in response to a parliamentary edict. If Parliament had been all-powerful it might have been able to impose its will, but it had to take account of feeling in the army, which was strongly sympathetic not only to Independents but also to the newly emerging sects, such as the

Baptists. Cromwell was the spokesman of the army in his determined opposition to the imposition of an intolerant presbyterian system. He believed that the army's success in the civil war had been a sign of God's approval of the way in which religious differences had been subordinated to the common aim. 'Presbyterians, Independents, all have here [i.e. in the army] the same spirit of faith and prayer', he told Parliament in September 1645. 'They agree here, have no names of difference: pity it is it should be otherwise anywhere ... For brethren in things of the mind we look for no compulsion but that of light and reason'.

The ending of the war did not put an end to divisions within Parliament. The adherents of the former war party were now known as the Independents, since they drew their main strength from the congregationalists in the two Houses and their sympathisers among the army officers. The peace party, by contrast, became known as the Presbyterians, though not all of its members were of that religious persuasion. The middle group survived under its own name and continued its advocacy of Pym's policy of a settlement based on the legislation of 1641 but with additional safeguards in the shape of parliamentary control over the militia and appointments to high office.

Not all members of Parliament, by any means, belonged to one or other of these parties, and the committed minorities were engaged in a constant struggle to win over the uncommitted majority. The most influential of the groups was the Presbyterians, under the leadership of Denzil Holles, but the middle group — of which Oliver St John and Lord Saye were the most prominent members — feared that the Presbyterians' overriding aim of returning the country to normality as soon as possible might lead to a sell-out to the King. In order to prevent this they allied with the Independents, and thereby kept a restraining hand on Holles and his adherents. One consequence of this was that the propositions presented to the King at Newcastle in the summer of 1646 were so hard-line as to be unacceptable to him. Not only was Charles to take the *Covenant* and agree to the permanent establishment of presbyterianism; he was also to give up royal control of the armed forces for a minimum of twenty years. As Hyde commented, 'whoever understands them [the propositions] cannot imagine that, being once consented unto, there are any seeds left for monarchy to spring out of'.

The King's rejection of the *Newcastle Propositions* left the Scots in an awkward position. They could not stay in England indefinitely, but they had no intention of taking the King with them to Scotland, where he might become a focus for dissension. All that kept them south of the border was shortage of money, for their occupation costs had not been fully paid. In September 1646, however, Parliament took steps to raise the required amount by formally abolishing episcopacy and putting the bishops' lands up for sale. By the end of January 1647 the first instalment of money had been paid to the Scots, who were now ready to leave. Before doing so they handed the King over to parliamentary commissioners, who in February escorted him to honourable captivity at Holdenby House in Northamptonshire.

Holles and his allies hoped that with the King in their custody they would be better placed to arrive at an agreement with him. But they were not prepared to await the outcome of negotiations before pressing ahead with the disbandment of the army, which they regarded as a hotbed of religious and political radicalism. Military rule was unpopular in the localities, for although the county committees which had organised the parliamentary war effort had been remarkably efficient, they were all too frequently dominated by relative newcomers to local government, lacking the social prestige that made the elite of upper gentry the natural rulers of the shires. The domination of these upstarts was resented, and their efficiency made them less, rather than more, popular: 'Thorough' government was no more acceptable when it came from Parliament than when it was imposed by ministers of the crown. In any case military rule and the maintenance of the army were appallingly expensive: Kent, for instance, was paying more by way of the assessment every month than Ship Money had cost it for an entire year. Holles and the moderate leaders of the Commons knew that if they could make a substantial reduction in the size of the army and return the country to civilian rule by the traditional elites, they would confirm their hold on power.

One section of the army was to be sent to restore order in Ireland, but if the remainder was to be peacefully disbanded its arrears of pay would have to be met. Parliament had shown itself during the war to be highly effective at raising money, but it never had enough to cover its huge expenditure. When the New Model was created it was promised regular pay, and at first this was forthcoming. By the middle of 1647, however, the wages of the infantry, who constituted the greater part of the army, were four months in arrears, while the cavalry had remained without pay for the best part of a year. If these arrears had been met the regiments due for disbanding would probably have gone quietly, but Parliament had committed all its available resources to paying off the Scots and it dared not raise additional funds by taxation for fear of provoking uprisings in the localities which were crying out for relief.

Holles and the Presbyterians, who were in effective control of the Commons, went some way towards meeting the soldiers' demands. In May 1647 funds were voted for the payment of part of their arrears, and a comprehensive Indemnity Ordinance was approved. This was very important from the soldiers' point of view, for many of the actions which the exigencies of war had driven them to commit — commandeering horses, for instance — had created widespread resentment among the civilian population, and if they returned home without legal indemnity they were likely to face prosecution. But the goodwill created by these gestures was offset by Parliament's failure to recognise the army's sense of its own identity and the *esprit de corps* that it had acquired. Parliament insisted that the soldiers' primary function was to obey, and it therefore refused to accept a petition setting out their case for better treatment. This provoked mutinies in several regiments and the election of 'agitators' to act as the spokesmen of the rank and file. It seems likely that these agitators were behind the scheme to remove Charles from Parliament's control, for it was a very junior officer, William Joyce, a Cornet of Horse, who appeared at Holdenby House with a troop of horse in early June and ordered the King to go with him to Hampton Court.

Charles was now the prisoner of the army, and while he was on his way south the regiments were holding a rendezvous at Newmarket, at which it was decided to set up an Army Council in which both the officers and the men should be represented. The assembled soldiers also took the 'Engagement', by which they swore not to disband until their grievances had been remedied. Later that month the Council drew up a declaration which proudly asserted that 'we are not a mere mercenary army, hired to serve any arbitrary power of a state, but called forth . . . by . . . Parliament to the defence of their own and the people's just rights and liberties'.

Holles and his Presbyterian supporters, now thoroughly alarmed, were attempting to build up a counter-force to the army from among the London militia and the many ex-soldiers looking for employment. It was this threat that drove the army, for the first time, to take direct action against the Parliament which had created it and to which it was, in theory, still subordinate. Moving towards London, it established itself at St. Albans and called for the impeachment of Holles and ten of his associates in the Commons. When Parliament ignored its call, it moved closer in, to Uxbridge, whereupon the eleven accused members — following the example of the five impeached by Charles in 1642 — withdrew to the safety of the City. The agitators on the Army Council wanted the advance on London to continue, so that the Independent minority within Parliament would be given the chance to seize the initiative and work out a settlement for Church and state more in line with the Army's aims. They were restrained by Cromwell, who — as both an army officer and a member of Parliament — wished to preserve an element of co-operation between the two institutions rather than impose the army's will. However, his hand was forced by the action of the City apprentices and other supporters of the Presbyterians who invaded the House of Commons in late July and held down the Speaker while they called for the upholding of the *Covenant* and the return of the Eleven Members. Faced with the threat of continuing violence, the Speaker and some sixty members — including middle-group adherents as well as Independents — sought refuge with the army. Fairfax was now ready to take the final step, and in early August his soldiers moved into London and occupied the city.

The future pattern of English government now depended on the army, and it presented the King with the *Heads of the Proposals*, which summarised its demands. These were in many respects more moderate than the *Newcastle Propositions*. As far as the Church was concerned the way was left open for the restoration of episcopacy, on condition that the bishops should have no coercive powers and that no set form of liturgy should be made compulsory. In secular matters, Parliament was to have control over the militia and appointment to major offices for at least ten years. But the most remarkable provision was that which called for biennial Parliaments, elected in such a way as truly to reflect the distribution of property and wealth throughout the kingdom. This embodied the army's view that parliamentary tyranny was no more acceptable than royal despotism, and that the Commons must respond to the will of the people rather than impose their own.

At this stage another group entered the debate by publishing its demands. The Levellers had emerged as a movement in post-war London, where they found supporters among the small traders, craftsmen and shopkeepers who had been brought to an exceptional degree of political awareness during the hothouse years of the 1640s and were not prepared meekly to return to the *status quo*. They declared their preference for biennial Parliaments, and wanted them elected by a much broader section of the population than had hitherto been the case. They called on the Army Council for a public discussion of the various schemes for religious and political reconstruction, and in October 1647 a remarkable series of debates took place in Putney church. The principal spokesman for the officers was Henry Ireton, who was not simply the formulator of the *Heads of the Proposals* but also Cromwell's son-in-law, and he made plain his opposition to Leveller pleas for radical change. 'I think we ought to keep to that constitution that we have', he argued, 'because it is the most fundamental we have, and because there is so much reason, justice and prudence in it.' He was supported by Cromwell, who reminded the Levellers that if they insisted on a new form of government there was nothing to stop other innovators insisting on theirs: 'while we are disputing these things, another company of men shall gather together and put out a paper as plausible perhaps as this . . .'. Such a plethora of proposals would lead, he assured them, only to anarchy.

The Putney debates broke up without agreement. Cromwell and Ireton were now aware of the widespread sympathy for Leveller ideals within the army and therefore alive to the danger of taking too conservative an approach, for fear that this might spark off rebellion and shake the foundations of society at the very moment when they were trying to underpin them. Outside the army, however, conservative opinion was appalled by the Leveller demands and feared that any concessions would open the way to the destruction of the social order. Reports reaching the King at Hampton Court painted the radical threat in its most lurid colours, and Charles, who feared that an attempt would be made on his life, escaped from his mild captivity in November 1647 and fled to Carisbrooke Castle, in the Isle of Wight. From there he proposed negotiations with Parliament and the Scots, hoping that with the help of a Scottish army and the acquiescence of the Presbyterian party in the two Houses, he would be enabled to reverse the verdict of the civil war.

Except for a tiny handful of anti-monarchists, both Lords and Commons were agreed that there could be no permanent settlement without the King. The only disagreement came over the terms that should be offered to him. The Independents and their middle-group allies were insistent that the King should accept certain conditions, such as parliamentary control of the militia, before discussions could take place. But Charles was pinning his hopes on the Scots, and therefore rejected Parliament's preconditions. This confirmed many of the Independents in their distrust of the King, and Oliver Cromwell spoke for them when he told the Commons that Charles was 'so great a dissembler and so false a man that he was not to be trusted'.

The two Houses responded to the King's rejection of their preconditions by passing a vote of No Addresses in January 1648, which put an end to all negotiations. The middle group played a major part in this, yet the ground was slipping under its feet, for it was still committed to Pym's aim of a negotiated settlement. Members of Parliament were not, of course, operating in a vacuum. They had to take note of the opinions of their constituents, who were crying out for a settlement with the King and a return to something like normality. Even while the war was still on, revulsion against it had provoked neutralist movements known as the 'Clubmen' revolts, and the Sussex Clubmen had drawn up a declaration which could serve as an accurate statement of opinion in the localities in the immediate post-war period. It referred to 'the insufferable, insolent, arbitrary power that hath been used amongst us, contrary to all our ancient known laws . . . by imprisoning our persons, imposing of sums of money . . . and exacting of loans by some particular persons stepped into authority who have delegated their power to men of sordid condition whose wills have been laws and commands over our persons and estates, by which they have overthrown all our English liberties'. These sentiments were echoed in the petitions which were sent to Parliament early in 1648, urging the disbandment of the army, the reduction of taxation, and a return to the rule of law. These petitions came particularly from counties in the south and east which had been parliamentary strongholds during the civil war, and they show the extent to which the local communities had become alienated. This revolt of the localities was an integral element in the uprisings which broke out in the spring of 1648 and are usually known as the second civil war. In south-east England and in Wales royalist risings took place, and petitions were sent in to Parliament from Kent and Surrey demanding the restoration of the King. If the Scots had been ready to move, the risings might have challenged the parliamentary regime, but Fairfax had time to subdue Kent, while Cromwell put down the Welsh rising before going north to deal with the Scots.

The pressure of public opinion, and the need to restore order, forced Parliament to reconsider its ban on negotiations with the King. The Independents were adamant in their opposition to any discussions with a man whom they regarded as totally untrustworthy, but they could no longer carry the middle group with them. St John, Saye and those who thought like them were committed to the principle of a negotiated settlement and were prepared to switch their support to the Presbyterians if that was the only chance of obtaining one. They hoped that by doing so they would be able to persuade Charles to accept the preconditions which he had earlier rejected. In May 1648, therefore, Parliament rescinded its vote of No Addresses and in the following September commissioners were despatched to Newport in the Isle of Wight to open discussions with the King. The new pattern of alliances was symbolised by the fact that the commissioners included not only Holles, the leader of the Presbyterians, but also Saye and a substantial middle-group contingent.

By the time the commissioners reached Newport events were moving strongly in favour of the army and their Independent allies. During the early part of 1648, when Parliament was holding aloof from the King, Charles had reached a settlement with the Scots by agreeing to the temporary establishment of presbyterianism in return for the restoration to him of all the royal prerogatives, including control of the militia. In May, while members of Parliament were agonising over whether or not to rescind their vote of No Addresses, the Scots were arming, and in early July they moved south across the border once again. This second invasion, however,

met with a very different response from the first, for the English
army was by now highly trained and commanded by experienced
officers. As the Scots pushed down through Lancashire, Cromwell
caught up with them at Preston in August and, in a hard-fought
battle, drove them from the field.

In reporting his victory to Parliament, Cromwell called on it to
recognise that 'this is nothing but the hand of God' and to 'take
courage to do the work of the Lord in fulfilling the end of your
magistracy in seeking the peace and welfare of this land'. Such sentiments might seem unexceptional, but Cromwell's views on the
nature of a just settlement and those of the Presbyterian-middle
group supporters in Parliament were by now poles apart. Cromwell
had been with his brother officers at Windsor in the spring of 1648
when the second civil war broke out, and had taken part in the
prayer-meeting at which they were led 'to a very clear and joint
resolution. . . that it was our duty . . . to call Charles Stuart, that
man of blood, to an account for the blood he had shed and mischief
he had done . . . against the Lord's cause and people in these poor
nations'. In other words, the settlement to which the army was now
committed had no place in it for the King.

## Pride's Purge and the Trial of Charles I

As the army put down rebellion in England and drove the Scots
back across the border, it became clear to members of Parliament
that time was running against them, for if they did not swiftly reach
a settlement with the King, the army would impose its own.
Charles had already agreed to give up control of the militia for
twenty years, but he would only consent to the establishment of
presbyterianism for a three-year period. These concessions fell short
of what the Presbyterians and their middle-group associates had
been hoping for, but the circumstances were such that they
felt compelled to accept them. On 5 December 1648, therefore,
Parliament resolved that the King's answer was 'a ground for
the course to proceed upon for the settlement of the peace of the
kingdom'.

Events were no longer under Parliament's control, however. Following the break-up of the alliance between the Independents and
the middle group, the more radical Independents had reached the
conclusion that the only hope of achieving their aims lay in the
army. The officers were of the same opinion. Ireton was in favour
of a forcible dissolution of Parliament, but the radical Independents
persuaded him to transfer power to them by a purge. On 6 December, therefore, as members arrived to take their seats, they
found their way blocked by Colonel Pride, holding a list of names
in his hand. Some forty members were arrested, others were turned

away, and only a rump of a hundred or so was allowed in to the Commons' House.

Pride's Purge, then, was a coup carried out by the radical wing of the Independents against moderates of all persuasions. This explains why the Rump included a number of hard-line Presbyterians while moderate Independents were among those excluded. Yet the radicalism of the men who conceived and carried through Pride's Purge was more apparent in the religious than the political sphere. They had no love for established churches, whether anglican or presbyterian, but they cherished the established order of society — indeed, they had been driven to act as they did from fear that the reactionary nature of the settlement reached between the King and the Presbyterian-middle group alliance would create an explosion which might well destroy the social fabric.

Now that the radical Independents had seized power their immediate aim was to reduce the political temperature below boiling point, but they realised that in order to do this they would have to make at least a gesture towards popular radicalism. The most obvious gesture, and the one to which both the Rump and the army were committed, was the bringing to trial of the King. A special high court was created for the occasion, under the presidency of an obscure lawyer named John Bradshaw, and it opened its sessions in Westminster Hall on 20 January 1649. Charles had been brought back to London as a prisoner of the army, and was now summoned before the high court to answer the charge that 'being admitted King of England, and therein trusted with a limited power to govern by and according to the laws of the land, and not otherwise', he had wickedly designed to erect 'an unlimited and tyrannical power to rule according to his will, and to overthrow the rights and liberties of the people'.

Charles never showed to better advantage than at this, the supreme moment of his life. Throughout the proceedings he conducted himself with a calm dignity that impressed even his opponents, and he steadfastly refused to acknowledge the jurisdiction of the court. He took his stand on the known laws. If, he said, the army could set up a court and impose its will by force, 'I do not know what subject . . . can be sure of his life or anything that he calls his own . . . I do plead for the liberties of the people of England'.

As the King refused to acknowledge the court, Bradshaw proceeded to pronounce judgment 'that he, the said Charles Stuart, as a tyrant, traitor, murderer and public enemy to the good people of this nation, shall be put to death by severing of his head from his body'. Fifty-nine judges were persuaded to sign the death warrant, and by their authority a scaffold was constructed outside the Banqueting House that Inigo Jones had built in Whitehall. An enormous crowd gathered there on the afternoon of 30 January 1649, when the King was led out to execution, but only those near the scaffold heard Charles declare that he died in the cause of law and the Church. 'For the people', he said, 'truly I desire their liberty and freedom as much as anybody whomsoever, but I must tell you that their liberty and freedom consist in having of government — those laws by which their life and their goods may be most their own. It is not for having share in government, Sirs; that is nothing pertaining to them. A subject and a sovereign are clean different things.' As for the Church, 'I declare before you all that I die a Christian according to the profession of the Church of England as I found it left me by my father.'

There was no jubilation as at Strafford's execution. The vast crowd was silent until they saw the axe swing in the air, 'at the instant whereof', according to one eye-witness, 'there was such a groan by the thousands then present as I never heard before and desire I may never hear again'. By the manner of his death Charles went far towards wiping out the memory of his eleven years' prerogative rule. For the anglicans he was a saint, for the royalists a martyr who had sacrificed his life to protect the old constitution from the abuse of arbitrary power. Cromwell may have been right in believing that the execution of the King was a political necessity, but he created a spectre that was to haunt his own regime and frustrate his efforts to build a new and more godly society out of the ruins of Charles I's England.

## The Rule of the Rump

The Rump, having got rid of the King, went on to abolish the monarchy, on the grounds that it was 'unnecessary, burdensome and dangerous to the liberty, safety and public interest of the people'. Experience had also shown 'that the House of Lords is useless and dangerous to the people of England', so this institution was abolished as well. England was now declared to be a 'Commonwealth and Free State' under the rule of a unicameral Parliament, and the government was entrusted to a Council of State, under the provisional chairmanship of Cromwell.

Radicals of all sorts welcomed these moves, for they seemed to presage even more fundamental changes. Yet the revolution, if such it may be called, was in effect over, for the Rump, despite its public commitment to early elections, showed no signs of dissolving itself and clearly intended that political reform should not open the way to reconstruction of society. The Levellers were bitterly disappointed. In January 1649 they had persuaded the Army Council to adopt their programme as set forth in the *Agreement of the People*. This called for biennial Parliaments, to be elected on a basis of manhood suffrage (though the right to vote should not extend to servants or persons in receipt of poor relief). Parliament was to have 'the supreme trust' but was to be limited in its authority: it was not to have the right, for instance, to conscript men for service outside their own county, and it was to uphold equality before the law as well as 'the foundations of common right, liberty and safety'. As for religion, there should be no established church or doctrine, but the widest possible measure of toleration.

There was nothing extreme about these proposals, but the Rump was not prepared to consider them, nor was Cromwell. He was alarmed by the revival of Leveller agitation in the army, which caused sporadic revolts, and by the proliferation of sects like the Baptists and the Fifth Monarchists (who believed in the destruction of existing institutions as the work of sin). In the *Agreement of the People* the Levellers had committed themselves not to 'level men's estates, destroy property, or make all things common', but this was not the case with the 'True Levellers', or Diggers, who believed in agrarian communism and set up a community at St George's Hill near Weybridge in Surrey. Cromwell was of the opinion that a period of firm government was needed to allow the country to re-cuperate and that 'there is more cause of danger from disunion amongst ourselves than by anything from our enemies'. He put down the revolts in the army by force, executing the leaders, and summoned John Lilburne, the Leveller spokesman, before the Council of State, where that irrepressible champion of popular liber-ties heard him thumping his fist 'upon the council table until it rang again, and saying, "I tell you, Sir, you have no other way to deal with these men but to break them in pieces . . . If you do not break them, they will break you"'.

From August 1649 until the spring of the following year Crom-well was in Ireland, restoring order to that unfortunate country and forcing it to accept the authority of the new rulers of England. He returned just in time to deal with the Scots, who had been angered by the high-handed way in which the English Parliament had dealt with Charles I — who was, after all, King of Scotland as well as of England — despite having promised in the *Solemn League and Covenant* 'to preserve and defend the King's Majesty's person and authority'. In February 1649, therefore, following the execution of Charles, they proclaimed his eldest son King of Scotland, on con-dition that he accepted the *Covenant*, and began raising an army to restore him to the English throne.

Cromwell went north to check the Scots before they should have a chance of crossing the border. In September 1650 he routed them at Dunbar, by December he had occupied Edinburgh, and his ad-vance was halted only by illness, which brought him close to death and kept him off the battlefield until the following summer. The

Scots used this pause to re-form their army, and in August 1651 Charles II, with Scottish troops, struck south across the border and occupied Worcester. There Cromwell caught him on 3 September and in a hard-fought battle put an end to royalist hopes. For Cromwell it was, in his own words, 'a crowning mercy'. The young King had to make his way, disguised, to the south coast, where he took ship for France. He left behind him a country which, however unsettled, could offer no effective opposition to Cromwell and the Rump.

While Cromwell and his fellow officers were away fighting, the Rump ruled England. Despite the fact that it was widely regarded as a temporary expedient it was in power for over four years, yet during that time it accomplished remarkably little. This was partly because of its composition. Socially speaking the Rump was a conservative body, and the genuinely radical elements within it were singularly lacking in influence. After the immediate shock of the King's execution had passed, members of Parliament who had been excluded by Pride's Purge were encouraged to make their peace with the new regime and take their seats once again. Many of them did so, but this served to swell the ranks of the moderates and leave the radicals even more isolated.

The religious divisions in the Rump were as marked as those in the Long Parliament. Presbyterians, Independents and sectaries were strong enough to block moves of which they disapproved but not to impose their own orthodoxies. The result was deadlock. Tithes were retained, since there was no agreement on what, if anything, should replace them, and the supervision of ministers was left, in practice, to county committees. Presbyterians and even some Independents were appointed to parishes, and the Elizabethan ideal of uniformity gave way to diversity — though Prayer-Book services and Roman Catholic ones were still officially proscribed. Local congregations were left with a great deal of autonomy, particularly since the Rump repealed the statutes requiring all parishioners to attend Sunday services at their parish church. The inhabitants of the localities were now free to worship as and where they pleased and were no longer subject to the rival temptations of Sunday games, since these were firmly put down.

The lack of positive policies also characterised the Rump's attitude towards law reform. The Levellers had called for the creation of county courts and the end of imprisonment for debt, and the Rump duly appointed a committee to consider these matters. In 1652 it also set up an extra-parliamentary commission under Sir Matthew Hale, a distinguished judge, to give its advice and make proposals for reform. The Hale commission adopted many of the Levellers' suggestions, though with modifications to make them more acceptable, but in the event the Rump took no action on its

recommendations. One of the reasons for this was the large number
of lawyers in the House. They constituted nearly a third of its active
membership and appointed themselves as guardians of the existing
system. They were not necessarily opposed to the principle of reform, but their ideas of what constituted significant change were
a long way removed from those of the Levellers.

Another influential pressure group consisted of members with
trading interests, who regarded the United Provinces as a dangerous commercial rival. In May 1641, as the storm clouds were
gathering around him, Charles I had demonstrated his protestant
commitment by marrying his daughter, Mary, to William, Prince
of Orange. The Dutch had therefore been favourably disposed towards the King, and were shocked by the news of his execution
— particularly as they believed it to have been carried out by Independents, whom they regarded as enemies of their own presbyterian faith. When the Rump sent envoys to Holland to propose a
union between the two republics, they were deliberately insulted,
and this was the opportunity for the commercial interests in the
Rump to win support for a trade war. The Rump passed a Navigation Act in 1651, designed to cripple Dutch trade, and war soon
followed. The English navy, led by Robert Blake — the son of a
Bristol merchant, and the greatest English sailor since Drake —
now came into its own. In a number of hard-fought engagements
the Dutch fleet was defeated and the coast of Holland blockaded.
When the Dutch admiral, van Tromp, tried to break out in July
1653, his ships were routed and he himself was killed.

If English trade expanded into areas formerly filled by the
Dutch, as the commercial interests hoped, the yield from Customs
revenues would increase substantially and the Rump's financial
problems would be solved. But in the short run the war made the
problems even more acute, for the fleet cost some £300,000 a year
to keep in service. The Rump had also despatched an army to Ireland, while another was needed first to defeat the Scots and then
to hold them in check. The expenditure which these measures involved put an end to all hope of tax reductions, and the monthly
assessment was actually increased. In these circumstances it is
hardly surprising that the Rump, and the Commonwealth which
it had brought into being, became increasingly unpopular,
especially in the localities, where the 'Commonwealthsmen' were a
feared and often hated minority. Lilburne, now a prisoner in the
Tower, was expressive of general opinion when he told one of his
visitors: 'I had rather choose to live seven years under old King
Charles's government (notwithstanding their beheading him as a
tyrant for it) when it was at the worst, before this Parliament, than
live one year under their present government that now rule. Nay,
let me tell you, if they go on with that tyranny they are in they will

make Prince Charles have friends enough not only to cry him up but also really to fight for him, to bring him into his father's throne.'

Although the Rump was unpopular it was efficient, and the administrative reforms which it initiated provided a ground plan for the sweeping changes of the later Stuart period. Its pragmatic approach to problems was widely condemned at the time, but given the lack of consensus on major issues there was much to be said for it. This was later recognised by Cromwell, when he took over the procedures developed under the Rump for supervising parochial clergy. Yet the Rump's determination to maintain social stability, however understandable, made it unresponsive to the idealistic aspirations of many English men and women, and particularly of religious enthusiasts who were longing for a campaign of active evangelisation to be set on foot. The Rump made a gesture in this direction, by passing an Act for the Propagation of the Gospel in Wales, but members were increasingly alarmed by the growth of religious radicalism and by the proliferation of sects such as the Ranters and Quakers. In April 1652, therefore, when the Act was due for renewal, no action was taken, and the evangelising campaign, such as it was, came to an end.

By distancing itself from the radicals the Rump hoped to make itself respectable in the eyes of the property-owners and gradually win their support. But its efforts in this direction were frustrated by its obviously unrepresentative character. The Rump had a nominal membership of over 200, but only 60–70 members took a regular part in debates. This small group of more or less full-time politicians included 34 who were also members of the Council of State, which was responsible for day-to-day administration. In other words, the government of the Commonwealth was in the hands of a self-appointed oligarchy which, however well intentioned, had no popular mandate. Yet the Rumpers were clearly enjoying power and showed no haste to dissolve Parliament and order new elections. They were not motivated solely by selfishness. The reaction against military rule throughout the country had been so marked that if free elections had been held an anti-army majority, and even conceivably a royalist one, would have been produced. Such a result would have been unacceptable both to the army and the Commonwealthsmen, for what was the point of fighting a bloody civil war merely to restore the old regime? Yet if elections were ruled out, what other solution was there to the problem of legitimacy? The Rump had no answer to this question. It was playing for time, hoping that simply by staying in power it would become a guarantor of stability and eventually win over the political nation.

The army officers, however, were not prepared to wait indefinitely. If the Rump had committed itself to a programme of godly reformation they might have been prepared to maintain it in authority, but they found the combination of timid pragmatism and immobilism unacceptable. Once they had suppressed the rebellions at home and brought Ireland and Scotland to heel they were free to turn their attention to political matters, and called on the Rump to dissolve itself. In February 1652 the Rump as last decided to terminate its existence, but not until November of the following year. It was to be replaced by a single chamber of 400 members, elected from among persons of 'known integrity, fearing God, and not scandalous in their conversation'. Since these qualities, however desirable, were not easily assessable, the Rump reserved to itself the right to scrutinise the list of those elected to the new assembly and weed out any of whom it did not approve.

Given the prevailing climate of opinion in the country, this provision had much to recommend it. But to the army officers it was one more example of the Rump's delaying tactics, designed to perpetuate its hold on power. Cromwell, who was not noted for his patience, decided on personal intervention, and strode off to the House, calling on his guards to follow him. Once inside he listened to the debate for a while, his anger mounting until he could sit still no longer. Rising to his feet he shouted at the assembled members: 'Come, come! I will put an end to your prating. You are no Parliament. I say you are no Parliament. I will put an end to your sitting.' As the members continued to sit in their places, stupefied, Cromwell called his troops into the House and told them to clear it. Speaker Lenthall was hustled from his chair so quickly that he left the mace — the symbol of civil authority — behind him. When Cromwell caught sight of it he told one of his soldiers to 'take away this bauble', but as Bradshaw proudly informed him, 'you are mistaken to think that the Parliament is dissolved, for no power under heaven can dissolve them but themselves. Therefore take you notice of that'.

### Oliver Cromwell and the Parliament of Saints

Oliver Cromwell was descended from Henry VIII's minister, Thomas Cromwell, through a nephew who had done well out of the dissolution of the Monasteries and had taken his uncle's name as a sign of gratitude. Oliver was born in 1599 to a branch of the family that had settled in Huntingdon, and his early links were all with East Anglia. This was an area where puritan attitudes were widespread, and Cromwell fully shared them. In particular he looked back nostalgically to the great days of Queen Elizabeth, and longed for England once again to give a lead to protestant Europe and humble the might of Spain.

Cromwell was first elected to the Commons in 1628, but he only emerged from obscurity during the Long Parliament. In that assembly he sat as the representative for Cambridge, and a fellow member of the House described him as 'very ordinarily apparelled, for it was a plain cloth suit which seemed to have been made by an ill country tailor. His linen was plain and not very clean, and I remember a speck or two of blood upon his little band, which was not much larger than his collar. His hat was without a hat-band. His stature was of a good size, his sword stuck close to his side, his countenance swollen and reddish, his voice sharp and untunable, and his eloquence full of fervour.'

The war showed Cromwell to be a natural leader of men, and it also brought out the radical streak in him. He was a conservative, in that he wanted to preserve as much of the old order as possible, but he also recognised that merit took no account of wealth or breeding. At times he could use Leveller language, as on the occasion when he told the Earl of Manchester that he hoped to live to see the day when there was not a nobleman left in England. But he also had an awareness of the need for government and of the precariousness of the foundations on which English society rested.

Cromwell had got rid of the Rump because of its unwillingness to risk an immediate election, but once he was confronted with the realities of power he was forced to acknowledge that the Rump's caution had been justified. What the country needed before any election could be held was a period of truly godly rule, the benefits of which would become so apparent that the English people would eventually be happy to vote for its continuance. But where were godly rulers to be found? Major-General Harrison, who had recently become a Fifth Monarchist, was convinced that he knew the answer, and he persuaded Cromwell to look to the puritan 'saints' who had set up their Independent and sectarian churches all over England and Wales. These 'gathered congregations' were not formally invited to propose members for a new assembly — although some of them did so uninvited — but when the Council of Officers met to nominate the representative institution which they had decided to create, they included a substantial number of 'saints'. For this reason the 'Nominated Assembly' soon became known as the 'Parliament of Saints'. It was also called the 'Barebones Parliament', after one of its most prominent members, Praise-God Barbon, a London leather-seller and Independent minister.

Not all the 140 members of the Nominated Assembly were 'saints'. The majority were property-owners, men of substance in the traditional mould, and the Speaker was Francis Rous, Pym's half-brother. Cromwell probably intended the Assembly to sit for little more than a year and then to hand over power to an elected body, but Harrison and the hard core of 'saints' were determined to seize this opportunity to carry through all those reforms which the Rump had failed to enact. Their vision of godly rule embraced a substantial part of the secular Leveller programme, and since they had no respect for existing institutions, which they regarded as the work of sinful man, they had no hesitation about remodelling or replacing them.

The Assembly followed in the steps of the Rump by appointing a committee to consider law reform, but there the resemblance stopped, because this committee had no lawyers on it. Perhaps for that reason it made far-reaching recommendations, which included the abolition of the Court of Chancery (already notorious for its interminable delays) and the simplification and codification of the law, especially where it related to debt. These measures alarmed the conservative majority in the Assembly, which regarded the law as one of the last surviving bulwarks of property, but they were outwitted and outmanoeuvred by the committed minority of some forty radicals, of whom at least a quarter were Fifth Monarchists.

The Assembly managed to maintain some semblance of harmony until it turned to the question of reform of the Church. Most members wanted to retain tithes as a means of paying ministers. Advocates of a state church, whether they were enthusiastic presbyterians or covert anglicans, believed that tithes, which were collected and paid automatically, gave ministers a necessary degree of security. Independents were in favour of retaining them on the grounds that the state ought to contribute to the maintenance of the Church and ensure that a reasonable provision was made for all parishes. And property-owners of whatever religious persuasion were also aware that a change in the existing system would deprive many of them of their income from impropriated tithes, which was often substantial. The sectarians, however, believed that every congregation should accept responsibility for maintaining its minister and that the state, as an ungodly institution, should not be involved. When the question was debated in December 1653 it was their views which prevailed, by a narrow majority, and the way now seemed open for a radical reconstruction of the Church, which would shake the foundations of property.

Cromwell was not prepared to stand by and watch the social order undermined. The effect of the Assembly's measures, he declared, was to 'fly at liberty and property . . . Who could have said that anything was their own if they had gone on?' It was no doubt with his tacit encouragement that on 12 December the moderates came to the House very early, made speeches accusing the radical minority of threatening the Church, the army, property and the law, and then marched to Whitehall where they formally resigned their authority into the hands of Cromwell. When the radicals eventually arrived at the House and discovered what had happened, they de-

cided on a sit-in. Cromwell sent troops to remove them, and when
the colonel in charge asked the members what they were doing,
they replied, 'We are seeking the Lord'. 'Then you may go elsewhere,' replied the colonel, 'for to my certain knowledge He has
not been here these twelve years!'.

## The Protectorate

The failure of the Nominated Assembly was, in a sense, a post-
humous triumph for the Rump, since it confirmed what Rumpers
had instinctively known, that godly rule, at least as it was conceived
by the sects, was incompatible with the existing framework of society. Cromwell's brief honeymoon with the sects was now over,
and he accepted the suggestion put forward by another of his generals, John Lambert, that there should be a written constitution
embodying elements of the traditional one as well as provisions
designed to safeguard the gains of the 1640s. Lambert had already
been working on this *Instrument of Government*, which was based on
the earlier *Heads of the Proposals* and the *Agreement of the People* accepted by the Army Council in January 1649. The Rump and the
Nominated Assembly had inadvertently demonstrated the need for
a powerful executive authority to hold the legislature in check. The
*Instrument* therefore declared that 'the supreme legislative authority
. . . shall be and reside in one person and the people assembled in
Parliament, the style of which person shall be the Lord Protector
of the Commonwealth of England, Scotland and Ireland'.

The Lord Protector, with the assistance of a Council of State, was
to be responsible for administration and foreign affairs, but although he was provided with a permanent revenue to maintain his
household and the armed forces, he was dependent upon Parliament for any extra supply. Parliament, under the terms of the *Instrument*, was to be summoned at least once every three years and
was not to be dissolved without its own consent until it had sat for
a minimum of five months. The Protector could hold up Bills for
twenty days, but after that they were to become law with or without
his consent, unless they were clearly contrary to the provisions of
the *Instrument*.

The inauguration of the Protectorate signalled the end of a decade of innovation and a turning back to the traditional pattern of
English government. In many respects Cromwell was a monarch.
After his formal installation as Lord Protector he and his family
took up residence in Whitehall Palace, where they lived in great
state, and he also had the use of Hampton Court. The *Instrument*
contained a number of safeguards against arbitrary rule on the
Protector's part, but otherwise it was a moderate and even conservative document. The unicameral Parliament was to consist of

400 members for England and Wales, with thirty each for Scotland and Ireland. Some places not previously represented, such as Manchester and Durham, were now given seats, while many rotten boroughs were abolished. The franchise was restricted to those who held property or goods worth £200, and the number of county members was increased at the expense of the boroughs. It was hoped by this means to produce a Parliament of independent country gentlemen of the sort Cromwell admired.

Only in the religious sphere did the *Instrument* break with tradition, for Cromwell and the army officers shared the Independents' conviction that while the state should give its formal approval and support to the Church it should not impose uniformity. Cromwell believed that religious liberty had been the greatest gain from the civil war. 'Religion was not the thing at first contended for,' he said, 'but God brought it to that issue at last, and . . . it proved that which was most dear to us. And wherein consisted this, more than in obtaining that liberty from the tyranny of the bishops to all species of protestants to worship according to their own light and consciences?' It was in accordance with this belief that the *Instrument* laid down 'that such as profess faith in God by Jesus Christ (though differing in judgment from the doctrine, worship or discipline publicly held forth) shall not be restrained from, but shall be protected in, the profession of the faith and exercise of their religion'.

This liberty was not, in theory, extended to anglicans or Roman Catholics, but in practice they were allowed a great deal of latitude. In London and many country areas anglicans were able to attend services at which the Prayer Book was used, and as for catholics, the abrogation of the penal laws and the abolition of High Commission and the Church courts meant that they were probably freer than at any time since the Reformation. Nor was the principle of religious liberty applied only to Christians, for in 1656 Cromwell persuaded the Council of State to agree to the readmission of the Jews to England. As far as the parochial organisation of the Church was concerned, Cromwell built on the foundations laid by the Rump. Livings were in the gift of patrons still, but in 1654 'Triers' were appointed to examine candidates for the ministry and make sure that they met minimum standards of learning and godliness. These Triers, like the ministry itself, were drawn from a wide range of protestant belief: the majority of them were Independents, but they also included presbyterians and Baptists. And in order to prevent the re-emergence of clericalism, a third of the Triers were laymen. The Triers were complemented, at county level, by lay Ejectors (with clerical advisers) who were authorised to expel ministers and schoolmasters found guilty of 'scandalous living'.

The first Protectorate Parliament did not meet until September 1654, and in the interim Cromwell and the Council of State ruled

alone, issuing ordinances which, under the *Instrument,* had the force
of law. These dealt mainly with security and legal matters. In the
first category came the ban on race meetings, cock-fights, and similar public assemblies which could provide a cover for seditious activities, while the second category included an ordinance
regulating, but not abolishing, the Court of Chancery. The ordinances were essentially pragmatic and did not add up to a coherent
reform programme. In this they reflected Cromwell's own attitude.
He was a practical man, not a theoretician, and was content to
leave long-term planning to Parliament.

The Parliaments of the Protectorate were in theory new institutions, depending for their authority solely upon the *Instrument of
Government.* Yet the elected members soon made it clear that they
regarded themselves as inheritors of the parliamentary tradition.
They chose William Lenthall, who had presided over the Commons
in the Long Parliament, as their Speaker, and they ordered the
mace — which Cromwell had scorned when he expelled the Rump
— to be brought in by the Long Parliament's Sergeant-at-Arms.
More than a hundred former members of the Long Parliament were
elected to the first Proctectorate Parliament: they included a number of republicans, who regarded Cromwell as the betrayer of 'the
good old cause' and were determined to cripple his autocracy if
they could not put an end to it.

The Lord Protector had supporters in the House — Councillors
of State, for instance, household officials and members of his own
family — but he made no attempt to organise and direct them, as
Elizabeth would have done. Failing a lead from the government,
the republicans seized the initiative and immediately challenged the
validity of the *Instrument.* Cromwell's reply was to surround the
House with soldiers and call on members to recognise the fundamental principle of government by a single person and Parliament.
The republicans withdrew from the House rather than acknowledge
the Protectorate, but the members who remained included many
critics of Cromwell's policies, and in particular his religious tolerance. They were alarmed by the growth of sects such as the Baptists and Quakers, whose members openly displayed their contempt
for established social hierarchies, and they therefore proposed that
the Protector's veto should no longer apply to Bills against blasphemy and heresy or for enforcing attendance at church. This drove
Cromwell into dissolving Parliament in January 1655. 'Is there not
yet upon the spirits of men a strange itch?' he angrily demanded.
'Nothing will satisfy them unless they can put their finger upon their
brethren's consciences, to pinch them there ... What greater
hypocrisy than for those who were oppressed by the bishops to become the greatest oppressors themselves so soon as their yoke was
removed!'

Opposition to the Protectorate was not confined to Parliament. Major-General Harrison had been cashiered for refusing to recognise the new regime, but this did not prevent the circulation of an army petition in the autumn of 1654 which called for the end of military rule. The three colonels who promoted this petition were forced to resign their commissions, and Cromwell persuaded the Council of Officers to make a public declaration that they were 'resolved to live and die with his Highness and the present government'. But the open expression of military support for the Protectorate did not make the regime any more acceptable to the population at large. As far as they were concerned the standing army was the cause of continuing high taxation which they deeply resented and longed to be freed from.

Even if Cromwell had wished to dispense with the army altogether he could not have done so, because of the threat from unreconciled royalists at home and abroad. In March 1655 a royalist rising broke out in Wiltshire under John Penruddock. It was easily suppressed, but the mere fact of its occurrence seemed to suggest that the J.P.s and other local officials were not carrying out their duties properly. Cromwell therefore took the drastic step of imposing direct military rule in the localities. He divided the whole country up into eleven districts, and appointed major-generals to govern them. Their responsibilities covered security, public morals, poor relief, regulation of the economy, and the enforcement of godliness, and to aid them in their task — and also to relieve the army of its policing functions — Cromwell ordered the raising of a new militia, to be paid for by a 10 per cent decimation tax on royalist estates.

The Major-Generals varied in effectiveness. In Lincolnshire Edward Whalley made himself thoroughly unpopular by hounding the J.P.s to put down alehouses and suppress many of the entertainments to which the gentry were devoted. Elsewhere the new rulers of the localities were given grudging acceptance and a measure of co-operation: indeed, without the assistance of local office-holders they would have been unable to carry out their prescribed duties. Yet however well-intentioned and efficient the Major-Generals were, their presence was an affront to the local elites, who were beginning to return to public life now that the Commonwealth had been replaced by the Protectorate. Even Cromwell was forced to realise that if he wished to base his regime on consent he would have to recall his satraps: as he told the army officers, 'it is time to come to a settlement and lay aside arbitrary proceedings, so unacceptable to the nation'.

The outbreak of war with Spain in 1656 made another Parliament necessary, since Cromwell's administration was already in debt and there was no money to spare. Cromwell, like the Stuarts before him, had already been driven into punishing those who challenged his right to tax. In November 1654 George Cony, a silk merchant, refused to pay charges on Spanish wine on the grounds that they had been imposed by ordinance of the Protector and not by Parliament. In fact the Protector's right to issue ordinances was clearly set out in the *Instrument of Government*, so Cony's challenge was directed at the legal basis of the protectoral regime. Cromwell was not prepared to have the validity of the *Instrument* tested, since in law it had none: it had been imposed on the nation by command of the army. He therefore ordered that Cony and his lawyers should be imprisoned until they dropped the case. Two judges had earlier been dismissed for questioning the authority of the *Instrument*: now one of the Chief Justices resigned rather than be party to the high-handed treatment of Cony which savoured too much of prerogative rule.

The second Protectorate Parliament assembled in September 1656. The Council of State excluded nearly a hundred members whom it regarded as troublemakers, whereupon another sixty refused to take any further part in the proceedings. The two hundred or so members who remained voted £400,000 for the Spanish war, but they showed their disapproval of sectarians — and, by implication, of Cromwell's policy of religious toleration — by inflicting a savage punishment on James Nayler, a Quaker who had been accused of blasphemy. Parliament claimed the right to act as a court by virtue of its descent from earlier Parliaments, and although Cromwell challenged this assumption he did not intervene to save Nayler. Perhaps he gave priority to the need for harmony now that war had broken out, but the episode clearly rankled, particularly as it had shown up the weaknesses of the existing constitution. Members of Parliament, he told the officers, 'by their judicial authority . . . fall upon life and limb, and doth the *Instrument* in being enable me to control it? . . . The case of James Nayler might happen to be your own case'.

## *The* Humble Petition *and the Overthrow of the Protectorate*

Cromwell was already considering the need for a new constitution, in which the arrogance of the Commons should be checked by countervailing institutions. His view was shared by the moderates in Parliament, who wanted Cromwell to detach himself from the army and become a truly civilian ruler. If he were to assume the crown, he would immediately acquire the considerable powers that had formerly belonged to that high office: he would also be able to perpetuate the Protectorate in the shape of his own descendants. The moderates managed to carry the House with them, and in March 1657 they presented Cromwell with the *Humble Petition and Advice*, which called on him to assume the office and title of King.

Cromwell took time to consider this offer. He was not blind to the considerable advantages of becoming King, but he had to take account of opinion in the army, and this was strongly opposed to such a change. Some of the generals, such as John Lambert, had ambitions of their own, and did not want to be ruled out of the succession in favour of Cromwell's family, while among the junior officers and soldiers there were many who felt that the war had been fought to overthrow monarchy and that any return to kingship would be a betrayal. What weighed most with Cromwell, however, was the realisation that many honest men, 'men that will not be beaten down with a carnal or worldly spirit', would not welcome the advent of King Oliver. In a confused speech, which showed his genuine uncertainty, Cromwell therefore declined the crown and asked 'that there may be no hard thing put upon me — things, I mean, hard to them [men of goodwill] that they cannot swallow'.

Although Cromwell refused the crown he accepted the rest of the *Humble Petition and Advice*, which now became law. It was the first of the constitutional experiments of the Interregnum to have some measure of public support, for it originated from Parliament and not from the army. It was also a carefully constructed attempt to remedy the deficiencies of the *Instrument* and to deal with the problems that had emerged during Cromwell's period of power. The future of the Protectorate was assured, so far as could be, by the granting of authority to Cromwell 'to appoint and declare the person who shall, immediately after your death, succeed you in the government of these nations'. As for the arrogance of the single House of Parliament, this was to be restrained by the revival of a second chamber.

The *Humble Petition* recognised the financial weakness of the protectoral regime, and made provision for 'a yearly revenue of £1,300,000, whereof £1,000,000 for the navy and army, and £300,000 for the support of the government'. But the framers of this new constitution were not prepared to give Cromwell everything he wanted: the Lord Protector, as well as Parliament, would have to compromise. The *Humble Petition* therefore laid down that 'those persons who are legally chosen by a free election of the people to serve in Parliament may not be excluded from sitting in Parliament to do their duties but by judgment and consent of that House whereof they are members'. No doubt Cromwell was prompted to accept this on the assumption that the harmony produced by the new constitution would obviate the need for conciliar control of the membership of Parliament. But he cannot have been so happy about the religious clauses of the *Humble Petition*. These followed the principles laid down in the *Instrument* when they asserted that 'the true protestant Christian religion, as it is contained in the Holy Scriptures of the Old and New Testament, and no other, be held forth and asserted for the public profession of these nations', but they went further, and into a more dangerous region, by providing for 'a Confession of Faith, to be agreed by your Highness and the Parliament', which should be 'recommended to the people of these nations'. The idea that the government should commit itself to a statement of doctrine was unwelcome to Independents and sectarians, for although the *Humble Petition* added the rider that no one should be compelled to accept the official formula, the religious minorities feared that at some future stage they would be faced with the reimposition of uniformity.

If Cromwell hoped that by accepting the *Humble Petition* he would inaugurate a period of harmonious relations between himself, as Lord Protector, and the representatives of the people, he was quickly disillusioned. The last of his Parliaments assembled in January 1658, but the Commons contained, as usual, a hard core of republicans, while the government was weakened by the elevation of some thirty of its supporters to the second chamber. No sooner had Parliament opened than members of the Commons began to question the authority of the 'other House' and to pour scorn on the newly-created titles of nobility. As the political temperature rose, a petition was circulated in the City, calling for the abolition of the Protectorate and the restoration of a sovereign unicameral Parliament. Cromwell was alarmed by the threat to order that this implied, and embittered by the negative attitude of the Commons. Impatience overcame him, and although Parliament had been sitting for little over two weeks he dissolved it. When members protested against this abrupt conclusion to their meetings, Cromwell appealed, like Charles I before him, to divine sanction. 'Let God judge between you and me', he said; to which some of the republican members replied 'Amen!'.

Cromwell's failure to establish a firm constitutional basis for his rule was in sharp contrast to his success in establishing his reputation abroad. He began by putting an end to the war with Holland which the Rump had begun, and tried to negotiate a union between the two protestant states. He subsequently concluded treaties with Denmark, which reopened the Baltic to English shipping, and with Portugal, thereby gaining access for English merchants to the Portuguese colonies. He also decided on war with Spain, to revive the glories of Elizabeth's reign and wipe out the humiliation of the 1625 Cadiz expedition. In December 1654 an expedition was sent to the West Indies, where it failed, much to Cromwell's chagrin, to capture Hispaniola, but made amends by taking possession of Jamaica.

Cromwell recognised the importance of sea power to Britain, and turned the navy into a full-time regular service with a ladder of promotion and standard rates of pay. He left Robert Blake in charge of the fleet, which carried out an arduous but successful blockade of the Spanish coast all through the winter of 1657 and, in April of the following year, destroyed a Spanish treasure fleet in the bay of Santa Cruz. Blake died on the journey back to Plymouth, but his skill had given England command of the sea.

Cromwell's aims in foreign policy were a not untypical mixture of old and new. In his use of sea power and his enthusiastic promotion of English trade he foreshadowed the Elder Pitt and the 'blue water' school of strategists of the eighteenth century. Yet his desire for a union of protestant states and his encouragement of buccaneering expeditions against Spain were increasingly anachronistic in contemporary Europe, in which power politics were replacing religion as the basis for relationships between states, and in which France was rising towards dominance as Spain declined. However, Cromwell's determination to wipe out the Spanish privateering base at Dunkirk had much to be said for it, since the 'Dunkirkers' had long been a menace to English trade. In order to achieve this he allied with France, and English troops fought alongside the French in the Battle of the Dunes in June 1658. The consequence of this victorious campaign was that Dunkirk was not merely captured but handed over to England: the Lord Protector had turned the clock back to the sixteenth century, and for the first time since Mary's reign England held a beachhead on the continent of Europe. As an achievement it was full of ambiguity.

## The Restoration

In 1658 George Fox, the Quaker, went to visit the Lord Protector at Hampton Court, and described how 'I saw and felt a waft of death go forth against him, and when I came to him he looked like a dead man'. Cromwell died on 3 September 1658, the anniversary of the battle of Worcester, having named his eldest son, Richard, as his successor. The fact that Richard's accession was peaceful demonstrated the innate strength of the Protectorate, but Richard suffered from the handicap that he had never been a member of the army and did not have the confidence of the officers or the rank and file. Oliver had achieved the impossible by maintaining a balance between the conflicting interests of Parliament and the army, between the presbyterians and erastians on one side, and the Independents and sectarians on the other. This had been essentially a personal achievement, and Richard could not emulate it. He hoped to build up a civilian basis for his rule, but the army feared that this would be at their expense and would mean, among other things, an end to religious toleration. Rather than risk such an outcome, Fleetwood and Lambert forced Richard Cromwell to abdicate and brought the Protectorate to an abrupt end.

The generals now recalled the Rump, hoping that a common

commitment to republicanism would enable the army and Parliament to work together. When the Rump reassembled, however, members showed that they had lost none of their old spirit, and they determined to demonstrate the superiority of duly-constituted civil authority by disbanding the army. Such a proposal met with no support from the generals, whose position depended solely on the number of soldiers they could command, and in October 1659 Lambert once more used troops to drive out the Rump.

North of the border, however, General Monck had one of the finest armies in Britain, and he was ready to use this to prevent anarchy. Monck was in touch with Fairfax — who had retired from public life soon after the execution of the King, in which he played no part — and Fairfax agreed to use his prestige to win over malcontents from Lambert's army and hold Yorkshire for Monck. The plan worked well. Monck and his army crossed the border unopposed and made a triumphal progress to London, where the Rump had already reassembled. In February 1660 Monck ordered that the members whom Pride had excluded should be invited to return to their places in the Commons, and when the augmented House met it voted that the Long Parliament, after twenty years of existence, should at last be legitimately dissolved.

The tide of royalism was now flowing strongly, for the experience of military dictatorship, particularly under generals as incompetent as Fleetwood and Lambert, had created a strong desire for a return to traditional forms of government. Cromwell had virtually brought back the old constitution: all that was missing was the old reigning family. When elections for a Convention were held in March, the republicans were routed, and the last obstacle to a restoration was removed when Charles II, at Monck's suggestion and with the help of his Chancellor, Edward Hyde, published a declaration from Breda promising a general pardon, liberty of conscience, and the determination of all disputed matters 'in a free Parliament, by which, upon the word of a King, we will be advised'.

Fairfax, who had done more than any man alive to defeat Charles I, headed the commission which the Convention sent to The Hague to greet Charles II and invite him to return to his kingdom. In May 1660 the King arrived in London, where that staunch anglican John Evelyn described how 'the ways were strewed with flowers, the bells ringing, the streets hung with tapestry, fountains running with wine'. 'I stood in the Strand', he added, 'and beheld it and blessed God. And all this was done without one drop of blood shed, and by that very army which rebelled against him.' The irony of it all was not lost upon the new King, for he was heard to observe that since his subjects were obviously so delighted to see him back it was doubtless his own fault that he had been away so long.

# 14
# Early Stuart England

## The Government of the Realm

Government was the responsibility of the crown and its ministers, but the four million or so inhabitants of early Stuart England were not simply puppets who jerked to the string pulled by their royal master. This was particularly the case with the propertied minority, which cherished its privileged position and was determined to maintain it against threats from above as well as below. But even the obedience of humbler subjects could not be taken for granted, for if they were pushed beyond a certain point they might be driven into riot or rebellion. This was something that governments wanted to avoid at all costs, for they had no standing armies or police force at their disposal and their powers of coercion were extremely limited. But coercion was only necessary where persuasion had failed, and this was not often the case, for governments were aware of the need to carry public opinion with them by acting in customary and accepted ways. Only in the last resort, and usually in response to outside pressures, did they take the risk of innovating.

Under the early Stuarts, as under the Tudors, the administration of every county was in the hands of a comparatively small group of families who owed their position to birth and land. These aristocrats and gentry were mostly of recent origin, even though they invented pedigrees which took them back to the Conqueror. There were few families in England that could claim more than a hundred and fifty years of local predominance: the majority had climbed to power after the Reformation by taking over land that had formerly belonged to the Church. Yet however recent their establishment, the local rulers firmly controlled county life, and their families were interlinked by ties of marriage. Many of them had followed the same pattern of education, at the universities or Inns of Court, and the more important ones had sat as county or borough members at Westminster. But although every county was linked, administratively, with London, its society was largely self-contained, and very few families maintained a permanent town house. Sir Henry Hyde, Clarendon's father, never went to London after he attended

Queen Elizabeth's funeral, even though he had thirty more years of life ahead of him, and his wife never went there at all. They were, perhaps, untypical, for many, if not most, gentlemen had to pay the occasional visit, particularly if they were involved in litigation (a not infrequent occurrence), or were members of Parliament, or needed the advice or assistance of a minister, courtier or administrator. They often went alone, but they had to face increasing pressure from their wives and families, who were less averse to travelling now that they could go in a coach instead of on horseback and who welcomed the prospect of a break from routine existence and a chance to catch up with the latest fashions. Very few gentlemen, with or without their families, were resident in London for more than part of the year. Most of their time was spent at home, indulging in the pleasures of the chase and of reciprocal hospitality.

Their presence in the country was highly desirable from the crown's point of view, for they played a vital part in local government. The upper gentry usually provided the Deputy-Lieutenants, who were chosen mostly from among the Justices of the Peace and were the effective rulers of the counties. Below them came a large group of middling gentry, from whom the other J.P.s were drawn. Below these again were the lesser or parochial gentry, who served, if at all, in the lower ranks of the administration — as coroners or escheators, perhaps, or as high constables.

The J.P.s, who were appointed (and usually re-appointed) annually by the Commission of the Peace, were the lynch-pins of local government. In their judicial capacity they dealt with the entire gamut of crime, passing serious cases on to the judges of assize but punishing lesser offenders themselves, either at Quarter Sessions or in the more frequent smaller meetings that were eventually to be formalised as Petty Sessions. In addition to being judges the J.P.s were also administrators, having had, in the words of one contemporary, 'not loads but stacks of statutes . . . laid upon them'. They were responsible for supervising poor relief, keeping roads and bridges in repair, licensing and controlling alehouses, regulating wages according to the Statute of Artificers, and deciding who should be responsible for looking after illegitimate children. In their legal work they were advised and assisted by the Clerk of the Peace, a full-time official, usually a professional lawyer, who was responsible for keeping the records of Quarter Sessions and had a small clerical staff under him. In their administrative duties they were dependent upon the unpaid services of local constables, churchwardens and Overseers of the Poor.

The sixteenth century saw a growth in the number of gentry, partly as a consequence of the land redistribution that followed the Dissolution of the Monasteries, and this was reflected in an enlarged Commission of the Peace at county level. In the early Tudor period there were about ten J.P.s per county, but by the end of Elizabeth's reign the average was closer to fifty. Not all J.P.s were active members of the Commission. Some were impeded by age or illness, others were content to enjoy the prestige of the office without performing its duties. There were frequent complaints in the Privy Council that J.P.s were failing to carry out their principal task of law enforcement, especially in the 'penal' sphere of social and economic regulations — so-called because the statutes laid down that a financial penalty should be imposed for infringement of them. In 1576 the Lord Keeper gave a warning that if such negligence persisted the Queen would be driven 'to appoint and assign private men for profit and gain's sake to see her penal laws to be executed'. In fact this was already being done, for the majority of prosecutions for breaches of penal statutes were initiated by private informers. If they were successful they were rewarded with a share of the penalty, but many cases never came to trial because the victim preferred to buy off his accuser.

Common informers, not surprisingly, were generally loathed, but the crown was reluctant to dispense with their activities, particularly since it made a profit from them. Under James there was increasing recourse to the practice of transferring functions, such as the licensing of alehouses, from J.P.s to groups of individuals who were authorised to act by a royal patent. All too often, however, the patentees were men of the stamp of Sir Giles Mompesson, more concerned with private profit than the impartial and effective execution of the law, and their activities, like those of the common informers, were counter-productive in that they turned public opinion against the crown and tainted it with corruption. The government was being driven beyond the bounds of the acceptable, and as a Norfolk man complained in 1593, 'the good subjects, specially of the meaner sort, are preyed upon as kites prey upon carrion, and not to her Majesty's use, nor for defence of the realm, but by others (commonly the worst of all others) by patents, penal laws and many other practices to make themselves rich and all the realm poor'.

The great outcry against patentees came in the 1621 Parliament, but tension between the crown and the localities had been mounting since the 1590s, under the twin pressures of war and inflation. A statute of Mary's reign required every county to organise its adult male population into a militia for defence purposes, and to see that at least the core of this part-time army was given regular training and provided with modern arms and equipment. By the 1580s the cost of maintaining these trained bands was about £400 per county, but since they were confined to home duties other troops had to be raised for service abroad. The latter, usually drawn from the dregs of the people, had first to be clothed and then conducted, under escort, to the place of rendezvous. Although 'coat-and-conduct money' was in theory refunded by the central government it was in practice a further drain on limited county resources: Northamptonshire had to find £1,000 for coat-and-conduct money in 1588, the year of the Armada, and Norfolk spent four times that amount on defence preparations. When expenditure on this scale is taken into account, it becomes less surprising that local gentlemen were unwilling to increase the rate of assessment for parliamentary subsidies — though the ultimate effect of their attitude was to make the crown poorer and therefore increase its pressure upon the localities.

J.P.s were not well suited to organise the militia, for there were too many of them and they were too amenable to pressure from their neighbours. The Council therefore placed increasing reliance on the men it appointed as Lord Lieutenants. This office had been created under Henry VIII, to maintain order at a time when it was threatened by disputes over religion, and had been revived from time to time in subsequent reigns during periods of emergency. With the threat of Spanish invasion in the 1580s, Elizabeth's government nominated Lord Lieutenants and made them responsible for co-ordinating defence preparations, but since these officers were usually peers and Privy Councillors and often had more than one county under their jurisdiction, selected members of the upper gentry were appointed as Deputy-Lieutenants. This meant, in effect, that the government was by-passing the Commission of the Peace and enforcing its will in the localities via an elite of some ten to twelve persons. This made for greater efficiency, but it tended to polarise the county community into those — the minority — who were in the government's confidence, and those — the majority — who were not.

Although both the Queen and the war against Spain were popular, the demands made by the government were a cause of mounting friction. When, in 1596, the ports were called on to provide ships for the Cadiz expedition and the counties were instructed to give them financial assistance, there was an outcry. Resentment at this breach of precedent was focused on the Deputy-Lieutenants, and many J.P.s in Norfolk and Suffolk refused to obey what they regarded as unconstitutional orders. Matters were far worse in the 1620s, because Buckingham's wars against Spain and France were widely regarded as misconceived and unnecessary. In 1626, when invasion was threatened once again, the Privy Council followed Elizabethan precedent, and instructed the maritime counties to aid the hard-pressed ports in supplying ships. Again there was opposition, and the Dorset J.P.s protested that they could not 'find any precedent for being charged in a service of this nature': to which the infuriated Council made the terse, but ominous, reply 'that state occasions and the defence of a kingdom in times of extraordinary danger do not guide themselves by ordinary precedents'.

Recollection of the J.P.s' opposition to Ship Money may have been one of the reasons why Charles I, when he levied it during the Personal Rule, made the sheriff his agent. The sheriff had originally been the principal officer of the crown in the shires, but his powers had been gradually eroded since the fourteenth century and his functions were now confined to arranging parliamentary elections for his county, serving writs, empanelling juries and carrying out sentences imposed by the courts. Sheriffs served for a year only and were not allowed to leave the county during their term of office — as Charles I remembered in 1625 when he 'pricked' a number of his critics as sheriffs in order to keep them out of the next Parliament. The office of sheriff was not popular, for it cost the holder more than he made through fees, and it entailed a great deal of work. This was particularly the case after 1635, since the sheriff was charged with the responsibility of apportioning and collecting Ship Money, and held personally responsible for any sums outstanding.

The government was not entirely dependent upon local residents for local administration. Twice a year the judges of the common law courts set out on circuits that took them through the whole of England. The principal object of their assizes was to try offenders accused of serious crimes, but from the 1590s onwards they were addressed by the Lord Chancellor or Keeper shortly before their departure and given a 'charge' which they were to pass on to the J.P.s. This 'charge' was, in effect, a brief statement of the problems which the government thought needed particular attention, and the judges were required not simply to do justice but to enquire into the whole working of county administration. Their duties were summarised by James I, when he told them, in 1616, to 'remember that when you go your circuits you go not only to pursue and prevent offences but you are to take care for the good government in general of the parts where you travel . . . You have charges to give to Justices of Peace, that they do their duties when you are absent as well as present. Take an account of them and report their service to me at your return.' The involvement of the judges in county administration reached its peak in the 1630s, when they were made responsible for supervising the enforcement of the *Book of Orders* (see above, p. 251) and collecting the regular reports which the J.P.s were supposed to submit.

The common law, of which the judges were the guardians and interpreters, was the ancient and customary law of England. It had never been fully written down or codified, but had been defined and made coherent by judicial decisions over the course of several centuries. Criminal proceedings at common law, in assize courts as in Quarter Sessions, were usually initiated by the J.P.s, who submitted

a bill of indictment to a grand jury consisting of the more substantial inhabitants of their locality. Only if the grand jury found
that the bill was 'true' — in other words, that the accusation was
well founded — did the case go to trial. If an individual wished to
begin an action before King's (or Queen's) Bench or Common
Pleas, the two main courts of common law, he had first to purchase
a writ. These were theoretically limited in scope, and it was partly
for this reason that the two courts had been losing business during
the early sixteenth century. Plaintiffs preferred to take their complaints to Star Chamber (a prerogative court) or to Chancery (a
court of equity), especially when Wolsey was in power, for they
could hope for a swift decision and the minimum of technicalities.
However, the common-law courts responded to this challenge by
developing more flexible procedures and enlarging their
competence: for instance, they began dealing with questions of
copyhold, which had previously been left to Chancery. As a
consequence, they were doing six times as much business at the end
of Elizabeth's reign as they had done at the accession of Henry VII.
Yet the struggle for survival had left its mark, for King's Bench and
Common Pleas were competing for business both among themselves
and with the many other courts that were functioning in Tudor and
early Stuart England. When the common-law judges issued
prohibitions to Church courts, forbidding them to proceed in certain
cases, they were acting in defence of their own jurisdiction rather
than, as James and the bishops assumed, challenging the royal
supremacy.

In some respects, such as the continued use of Norman-French
for formal proceedings, the common law was wilfully archaic, but
the increasing recourse to the courts showed that it was successfully
adapting to the needs of a changing society. The law had its critics,
of course, not least among lawyers, and there were suggestions that
it could be improved by adopting certain features of other systems
of jurisprudence. Yet the common law was not as self-contained as
it appeared to be; even Sir Edward Coke, its most outspoken champion, had the major works of Roman, or civil, law in his library.
Civil law was still studied in England, its practitioners were active
in the Court of Admiralty and the ecclesiastical courts, and they
were often on close terms with their common-law brethren. In
short, while the common law might appear to be rigid and insular,
it was in practice remarkably flexible and responsive.

Lawyers could be tenacious in their defence of individual or corporate rights, and were frequently to be found among the principal
critics of royal policy in the House of Commons. James I did not
disguise his feelings towards 'wrangling lawyers' and was eventually goaded into dismissing Coke from his post as Lord Chief Justice. But the common law provided ministers for the crown as well

as critics. The offices of Solicitor-General and Attorney-General were invariably filled by lawyers, and in the post-Reformation period the Lord Chancellor or Keeper was almost always a member of the legal profession. Too often the common lawyers are seen through the eyes of Coke; it should also be remembered that Francis Bacon, who was no whit inferior to him in knowledge or understanding of the law, served James I as Lord Chancellor and described the judges as 'lions under the throne'.

While the law was available to all citizens, there was considerable reluctance on the part of neighbours to use it against each other. One reason for this was that it made future good relations difficult. There was also the consideration that many offences — particularly theft, which was the most common of crimes — carried the death penalty, and even the angriest of plaintiffs would think twice before exposing a man to this. Most communities, whether they were medium-sized towns or small villages, exercised a degree of toleration of petty crime as long as it did not seriously threaten the general well-being, and local officials were more concerned with settling disagreements between neighbours than with imposing a rigid discipline.

This tolerance was severely weakened, however, under the pressure of social and economic change. As Elizabeth's reign drew to a close the gap between rich and poor was widening, and in both urban and rural areas there was an increasing number of poor people for whom the community had no obvious place. This alarmed the 'middling sort' of yeomen farmers, substantial tradesmen and minor gentry who formed an elite in many parishes — particularly in the nucleated villages of the lowland zone — for the poor rate which they paid was an ever-growing burden. They were also afraid that the social order might break down, for they were coming to regard the poorer members of their communities as feckless, irresponsible and immoral. Not surprisingly, the middling sort were often puritan in their religious outlook, for the assumption that they had a right, as an elite minority, to direct the unregenerate mass could be justified if it was set in the Calvinist context of the rule of the 'elect' (whom God had fore-ordained to salvation). Where the local minister was himself of puritan inclination, the middling sort could prove an irresistible combination, and would impose upon the community a discipline that was simultaneously secular and religious. Immoral behaviour, for example, was punished not simply because it was ungodly but because it might also lead to the birth of illegitimate children who would have to be maintained at the parish's expense. Alehouses were suppressed because they encouraged drunkenness and debauchery but also because they provided a counter-attraction to Church services.

The emergence of parish elites, at or below the level at which political participation in Stuart England usually stopped, should have made the government's task of maintaining order easier. But the early Stuarts and their advisers were opposed to the rule of Calvinist minorities which they saw as a challenge to their authority rather than a reinforcement of it. They also rejected the narrowness and divisiveness of the Calvinist attitude, for as kings they accepted a responsibility for the well-being of all their subjects, not simply the godly. They saw their task in the conventional terms of maintaining minimum standards of conformity in the Church and obedience in the state, rather than actively rooting out idleness and sin. James I made clear his response to puritan demands for stricter enforcement of the sabbath by issuing a *Declaration of Sports* in 1617. This was reissued by Charles I in 1633, and laid down that the King's 'good people', after they had attended church on Sundays, were not to be 'disturbed, letted or discouraged from any lawful recreation, such as dancing, either men or women, archery for men, leaping, vaulting, or any other such harmless recreation, nor from having of May-games, Whitsun-ales and Morris-dances, and the setting up of Maypoles — so as the same be had in due and convenient time, without impediment or neglect of divine service'.

The *Declaration of Sports* struck at the foundations of puritan discipline, for the godly minority who were the upholders of strong government in the localities, provided that they exercised it themselves, now found that they were disowned by the royal administration. Indeed, the Laudians whom Charles favoured were so determined to demonstrate their rejection of puritan claims that they frequently ignored or belittled the elites of middling men which had established themselves in parishes, villages and towns throughout the kingdom. In these circumstances it was hardly surprising that the middling sort, like their social superiors among the godly gentry and aristocracy, found it increasingly difficult to reconcile their loyalty to the King with their commitment to God's cause. There was no obvious way out of this dilemma while Charles I remained in power, but with the overthrow of the monarchy and the destruction of the Laudian church their turn came at last. It was during the Interregnum that the godly campaign to impose discipline upon the entire nation — this time with the blessing of the central government — reached its peak. By an irony of history it thereby created a reaction that not only blocked its chances of success but opened the way to the restoration of the old order that it had been so determined to transform.

## Trade and Finance

English cloth exports took some time to recover from the slump of the mid-sixteenth century, but by the time James I ascended the throne they were in a flourishing condition. The end of this boom period was brought about by Alderman Cockayne's project in 1614. Cockayne, who was a member of the Eastland Company, pointed out that the Merchant Adventurers, who controlled the English trade in shortcloths, exported mainly 'white', or unfinished, cloth, which was dressed and dyed in Germany and the Low Countries. If, argued Cockayne, this work were done at home, unemployment would be checked and English profits would rise. The scheme met with royal approval, in 1614 the privileges of the Merchant Adventurers were suspended, and a new company — the 'King's Merchant Adventurers' — was set up to handle the trade in finished cloth to the Continent.

The government was hoping to encourage English exports, thereby increasing the Customs revenue, but Cockayne's motives were more doubtful. He had made no preparations for marketing the finished cloth, and it soon became apparent that he and his associates were far more interested in breaking the monopoly of the Merchant Adventurers and transferring it to themselves than in changing the pattern of the English cloth industry. The whole project was based upon the assumption that England had a monopoly of the continental market, but this was not the case. Foreign countries reacted by forbidding the import of dressed cloth from England, and the only result of the scheme was to disrupt the English cloth industry and give its continental rivals an advantage which they never lost. The King cancelled Cockayne's concession in December 1616 and restored the Merchant Adventurers to their former privileged position, but by that time the damage was done.

For many years after 1614 the cloth industry, and with it English commerce as a whole, was in a slump. Exports to Germany and the Low Countries fell, and by 1622 the amount of cloth shipped from English ports was only 40 per cent of what it had been in 1614. Riots were reported from the west country and from East Anglia, and in 1624 Parliament debated the sad state of English trade and tried to find a cure for its ills. One answer it gave was the Statute of Monopolies of 1624, which placed all monopolies under the control of the common-law courts, except for those grants designed to protect the inventors of new processes against imitation. The statute was aimed mainly at the patents granted by James I to his courtiers, but there was also a free trade lobby in the Commons which was opposed to the restrictive activities of the trading companies — particularly the Merchant Adventurers — and believed that if trade was thrown open to all comers it would flourish. The triumph of the free traders was seen in the decision that the monopoly of the Merchant Adventurers should in future be limited to the export of white cloth.

The causes of the 1620s slump are not easy to diagnose. One of the most important seems to have been currency depreciation in Germany and eastern European countries following the outbreak of the Thirty Years' War. English merchants could not afford to accept at their face value coins which in England and western Europe would have been worth far less, and they therefore put up their prices. This gave local manufacturers an enormous advantage, and for several years, until recoinage became effective, English cloth priced itself out of the German market.

Although the trade in shortcloths steadily declined, there was a big expansion in the production and export of the so-called 'New Draperies'. These were lighter cloths — bays, says and perpetuances — more suitable for warmer climates, and they found a ready sale in Mediterranean countries. Spain was an important market for the New Draperies, particularly after the signing of peace in 1604. Italy was another, especially the free port of Leghorn, and the New Draperies also found a ready sale in the Levant. Piracy in the Mediterranean was a major problem, and although an English fleet under Sir Robert Mansell attacked the Barbary Corsairs in 1620, it was not until Blake's Mediterranean expedition of 1654 that piracy was really brought under control.

Piracy was not confined to the Mediterranean. In the Channel and North Sea the 'Dunkirkers' preyed on shipping, and the Eastland merchants had to organise convoys for their ships. The wars against Spain and France, which lasted from 1625 to 1630, seriously disrupted trade in the New Draperies and brought unemployment to East Anglia, which was one of the main centres of production. It may be that too much cloth was being produced, for even after the restoration of peace the East Anglian industry remained depressed, and discontent was increased by the poor harvests of 1630 and 1631, with the subsequent increase in grain prices. Depression continued through the 1630s, and unemployment and poverty combined with puritanism to spread disaffection in the eastern counties. The emigrants who left Essex and Suffolk for Holland and the New World were frequently inspired by hatred of Laudianism, but years of slump also played their part in making men decide to break with their native land.

By the time civil war came in 1642 the export of New Draperies equalled, in value, the export of shortcloths, and this reflected an important extension of the range of English trade. Shortcloths were associated with the European market, but the New Draperies were sent to America, the Levant, Africa, India – in short, all over the world. This expansion was not confined to England. In the new markets as in the old, English merchants found that they were up against competition from the Dutch who, because they had few natural resources of their own, specialised in carrying the goods of other nations. In the struggle for trade, diplomacy often came to the aid of the merchants. In 1648, for instance, the Dutch persuaded the King of Denmark to sell them the right for their ships to pass through the Sound without paying toll, and six years later the Sound was closed to English shipping. Dutch and English merchants were rivals also in the East Indies, where they were struggling for control of the empire which Portugal was too weak to hold. In 1623 seven English merchants were tortured and executed at Amboyna, and when the news of this 'massacre' reached England it caused a public outcry and created a desire for revenge that was not satisfied until the first Dutch War.

The Dutch were generally held to blame for the slow expansion of English overseas trade. James and Charles both made belligerent gestures towards them, but nothing effective was done until the passing of the Navigation Act in 1651. This measure was designed to cut the Dutch out of the carrying trade with England, and it ordered that all goods coming into the British Isles should be carried in British or colonial ships or in ships belonging to the country in which the goods originated. The Act could not be rigidly enforced because there was not enough English shipping available, and it was only a contributory cause of the war with Holland which broke out in the following year, but it demonstrates more clearly than any other measure the way in which the Commonwealth government was prepared to use political means to obtain commercial advantages.

There was nothing new about close links between the mercantile interest and the government: under James I, for instance, a leading City merchant and financier, Lionel Cranfield, had been ennobled and appointed to the important office of Lord Treasurer. But the merchants were not a solid bloc. The interlopers, who resented the power of the chartered companies and were determined to break into the American and West Indian trade, wanted war against Spain and attacks upon Spanish settlements in the New World. But the directors of the East India, Levant and other major companies were generally in favour of peace and shared Wentworth's belief that war tended 'to the decay of trade and losing entrance to the enlargement thereof that hath of many years been open to us'.

These merchant magnates were also linked to the crown by mutual need. They wanted the privileges, including monopoly rights, that only the King could give them, while the King needed the loans that only they could raise. James and Charles borrowed large sums of money both from individuals and from privileged groups, which included the Livery Companies and the City Corporation. Repayment was a slow business that dragged on for many years — long after the dates originally fixed. In 1628 the crown was so deeply in debt to the City that it handed over £350,000 worth of land on condition that a further cash advance of £100,000 was made. De-

lays in repayment did the crown's credit much harm, and both
bribery and threats were used to persuade potential lenders to part
with their money. Sir Baptist Hicks, for instance, who was made
a viscount in 1628, paid little or nothing for his title because he had
already lent so much to the crown; but companies which declined
to meet the King's request for financial aid might find their charters
confiscated and their privileges transferred to rival organisations,
while individuals would find themselves subjected to the sort of
treatment that one courtier advocated: they were like nuts, he said,
that 'must be cracked before one can have any good of them, and
then too at first they appear dry and choky, but bring them to the
press, they yield a great deal of fat oil'.

One of the most lucrative privileges in the gift of the crown was
the grant of the Customs farm. Early in James's reign it was decided that Customs should no longer be collected by royal officials
but by a private company which paid a fixed rent for its rights. The
advantage of this was that the crown got a regular revenue while
the Customs farmers made a substantial profit over and above the
rent. As trade expanded and profits increased, the government
could, of course, increase the rent, but even so the Customs farmers
did well out of the bargain — so well, in fact, that they became one
of the main sources of loans for the crown. In the crisis year of
1640 they advanced more than £100,000 to the King, and they
were to be found, not unnaturally, among the supporters of the
crown as the dispute between King and Parliament developed.

# 15
# Charles II

## Charles II

Charles II — 'a long, dark man, above two yards high', as the roundheads had described him when they were searching for him after Worcester — arrived in London on his thirtieth birthday, having spent his adult life in exile. The experience of poverty, humiliation and danger had taught him to take a cynical view of human behaviour and to value every man only for what he could get out of him. Where Charles I had been stiff and reserved, Charles II was easy and friendly and charmed all who spoke to him, until they discovered, in Burnet's words, 'how little they could depend on good looks, kind words and fair promises, in which he was liberal to excess because he intended nothing by them but to get rid of importunities and to silence all farther pressing upon him'. Charles had not known security since he was a young child, and now that providence had restored him to his throne he was determined, as he told his brother James, not to set out on his travels again. To this end he was prepared to sacrifice almost anything — advisers, friends, principles, even religion. His political morality, in short, was one of survival, and this gave him a degree of flexibility that enabled him to ride out storms and anchor the monarchy deep in his people's affections.

## The Restoration Settlement. I: The Constitution

The King's chief adviser was his Lord Chancellor, Edward Hyde, created Earl of Clarendon in 1661. Hyde was a common lawyer who came from a gentry family and had made his name by leading the moderates in the Long Parliament. After the defeat of the cavaliers he joined the young King in exile, and he, more than anyone else, had schooled Charles II in the art of government and kept him faithful to the Church of England. Charles had no first-hand experience of kingship; he relied upon Hyde, and for the first years of his reign was content to leave government largely in the Chancellor's hands.

Clarendon was a conservative. He believed that the traditional constitution, the 'mixed monarchy', had happily combined freedom with authority and that all that was needed was to restore it to working order. The experiments of the previous thirty years had produced chaos and disaster, but now, as he told the Convention, 'our own good old stars govern us again'. It was in this spirit that he called on members to restore 'the whole nation to its primitive temper and integrity, to its old good manners, its old good humour, and its old good nature'. For Clarendon the Personal Rule of the 1630s had been as much of an aberration as the republican government that followed it, and for this reason there was no restoration of the prerogative monarchy. Those Acts to which Charles I had given his assent in the opening months of the Long Parliament remained in force, and Star Chamber, High Commission and the Council of the North were consigned permanently to oblivion.

It is often assumed that Parliament, by restoring the monarch, had thereby asserted its supremacy over the crown, but this was far from the case. The previous decade had seen Parliament, as well as the monarchy, in eclipse, and the failure of Cromwell's constitutional experiments had shown how mutually dependent were the two institutions. The tide of public opinion in 1660 was flowing strongly in favour of monarchy, and without Clarendon to guide him Charles might have been tempted to opt for a more despotic settlement. Clarendon, however, restored as much as he could of the traditional constitution. The 'mixed monarchy', the mystical and indivisible union of the kingly and representative elements, had been torn apart by the war and could not be put together again. Instead, there was an attempt to establish an equilibrium between the authority of the crown and the rights of the subjects as represented in Parliament. The two institutions, or so it was hoped and assumed, would operate separately but harmoniously within their respective spheres, thereby preserving those traditional liberties which Englishmen, and in particular members of the political nation, valued so highly. Under the terms of the Triennial Act of 1641 Parliament was required to assemble once every three years even if the King neglected to summon it. Such an infringement of royal authority was unacceptable in the climate of Restoration England, and in 1664 a new Triennial Act swept away the provisions for automatic assembly, describing them as being 'in derogation of his Majesty's just rights and prerogative'. Instead, it was enacted 'that hereafter the sitting and holding of Parliaments shall not be intermitted or discontinued above three years at the most'. What if the King chose to ignore this provision and rule without Parliament? The Act was silent on that point, for it was based upon the assumption that the executive and the legislature would not only see the need to work together but would wish to do so.

## The Restoration Settlement. II: Finance

One of the basic assumptions of the traditional constitution was
that the King should 'live of his own', but although crown lands
which had been alienated during the Interregnum were restored to
Charles II they brought in a mere £100,000 a year — a stark reminder of the extent to which inflation and war had reduced the
King's 'own' during the century that had elapsed since the Dissolution. A committee of the Commons was set up to decide just
what the crown needed and how this should be provided. The committee fixed on the sum of £1,200,000 a year, which was somewhat
more than Charles I had been receiving at the end of his reign, but
less than Cromwell had enjoyed, since it was assumed that the restoration of the monarchy would be accompanied by the disbandment of the standing army which had been a major item in
Cromwell's expenditure. Customs would, it was thought, bring in
£400,000; the rest was to be provided by an excise on liquor, which
it was hoped would produce £400,000 a year, and a number of
minor duties. Half the excise was voted to the crown in perpetuity,
in return for the abolition of the hated feudal dues. The Court of
Wards had not been abolished until 1646 and in theory could have
been revived by the restored monarch, but Charles and Clarendon,
who knew how much bitterness had been created by feudal tenures,
were content to abandon them in return for a permanent grant,
thereby fulfilling, fifty years too late, the contract which Salisbury
had proposed in 1610.

The Convention had originally intended to compensate the King
for the abolition of feudal dues by a tax on land, but land taxes,
or subsidies, had traditionally been reserved for extraordinary supply, and it was typical of the conservative attitude that prevailed
in these early years of the Restoration that Parliament preferred to
work on old assumptions rather than formulate new ones. Yet by
so doing it defeated its constitutional aims, for it unwittingly deprived the crown of the regular and certain income that it needed
if it was to carry out its executive functions. Since land is a fixed
quantity the amount of tax levied on it can be estimated with considerable precision, but the same is not true of indirect taxes such
as Customs and the excise, which vary with the volume of trade.
In the opening years of Charles II's reign the excise yielded less
than half the estimated £400,000, and although Parliament showed
its good intentions by voting an additional Hearth Tax to the crown
in 1662 this was not enough to overcome the shortfall in the royal
finances. During the 1660s ministers had to make frequent appeals
to Parliament for additional supply, and although this was
usually forthcoming it limited the independence of the crown
and ran counter to the constitutional principle that the King's

own income should be sufficient for the ordinary needs of government.

While members of Parliament genuinely wanted to put this principle into effect they could not see how to do so. This was partly because accounting techniques were primitive and the science of statistics was in its infancy. The Treasury was inefficient, and Charles made matters worse by appointing the aged Earl of Southampton as Lord Treasurer. Southampton was a man of integrity and good intentions, and the Treasurership was a reward for the faithful service he had given Charles I, but he could not provide either the King or Parliament with an accurate picture of the financial situation. As the first flush of enthusiasm for the restored monarchy faded it was only too easy for members of Parliament to slip into the old assumption that extravagance was the cause of the King's difficulties. They were not entirely wrong, since Charles was indeed extravagant, especially when it came to making gifts to his mistresses, but royal extravagance merely made a bad situation worse: it was not the root cause of the problem.

It was not long before members of Parliament realised the advantages that this unintended imbalance in the constitution brought them, for as one of their number commented in 1677, ''tis money that makes a Parliament considerable, and nothing else'. There was, however, another side to this picture, for awareness of his dependence upon Parliament made the King increasingly disenchanted with the Restoration settlement and with those persons, especially Clarendon, who had been responsible for it. As long as he was short of money he could do little to redress the situation, but by the late 1670s, as trade expanded and the yield from Customs and the excise constantly increased, he became aware of new possibilities, which included reducing or even eliminating the role of Parliament.

The Commons might have been more concerned to provide an adequate endowment for the crown had they not been obsessed with the need to raise large sums of money to disband the army. Members knew from their own experience that a standing army was inimical to constitutional rule, and they were also aware that soldiers would disband peacefully only if they were fully paid. In the event, the large sums were raised and the army was disbanded. However, the King retained Monck's regiment for his own service, and this — the Coldstream Guards — became the nucleus of a regular force. Charles II was the first monarch since the Middle Ages to have a standing army at his disposal, and although the numbers involved were small its very existence — in the teeth of parliamentary complaints — gave him a degree of security that his father had never enjoyed.

## The Restoration Settlement. III: Land

Parliament restored to the crown and Church all the lands that had been taken from them during the Interregnum. As for private individuals, they were left to fend for themselves. So much land had changed hands in the previous two decades that Parliament despaired of unravelling the legal intricacies and arriving at a just solution. It resolved that land which had been confiscated should be restored to the original owner, but passed no general Act to enforce this. Returning cavaliers had to try to come to an arrangement with the occupier of their estates, failing which they could sue for possession. Law suits, however, were expensive, and the aggrieved cavalier could not always be sure that judgment would be given in his favour. Noblemen were in a stronger position, since they could more easily obtain private Acts of Parliament and they had the powerful backing of the House of Lords which issued direct orders to sheriffs, commanding them to see that confiscated lands were returned to their noble owners.

This settlement was not as unfair as it seems to be at first glance. Many cavaliers who had been forced to sell their lands or had allowed them to be confiscated and sold by the state had managed to buy them back again before the Restoration took place, while others found that the new owners were content to become rent-paying tenants in 1660 rather than risk expropriation. Most royalists got their land back, before or after the Restoration, though the cost of recovery sometimes led to collapse in subsequent decades. For families which had been in financial difficulties prior to 1640 the civil war was in many instances the final blow, but they would probably have succumbed sooner or later in any case. Generally speaking, the permanent changes in the pattern of landholding which took place as a consequence of the civil war and Interregnum were no greater than would have been the case in any twenty-year period.

Royalists who had suffered from plundering, or had sold land to pay composition fines, had no grounds for redress at law. Few of them were actually ruined, but they felt bitter at the contrast between their continuing impoverishment and the relative affluence of the fortunate majority who had regained their estates. It became an accepted maxim among this group that the Act of Indemnity and Oblivion passed by the Convention meant indemnity for the King's enemies and oblivion for his friends. Yet in fact this was far from the case. Most of those men who had been closely associated with the Commonwealth or Protectorate suffered as a consequence. Of the twenty-six regicides, nine who remained in England were executed, along with four other men who had been involved in Charles I's execution even though they had not signed the death warrant. Other prominent republicans had to choose between exile or imprisonment, and even those who escaped punishment altogether were sooner or later forced out of public life. In general, only those figures who had come to terms with Charles II before the Restoration took place survived the change of regime unscathed.

## The Restoration Settlement. IV: The Church

The restoration of the monarchy was bound to entail the restoration of the Church of England. During the Interregnum about half of the existing incumbents had retained their livings by agreeing not to use the Prayer Book and not to preach against the new political and religious order. More important, so far as the restoration was concerned, were those ministers who refused to conform and took refuge in the houses of cavalier families, where they kept the traditions and ceremonies of the anglican church alive in readiness for happier days. They included men like Gilbert Sheldon who had been educated in Laud's own university of Oxford, and their devotion to the ideals for which Charles I and his Archbishop had died assured Laudianism of survival. Other clergy went into exile rather than abandon the Church of England. A century earlier the Marian exiles — creators of a Church that had barely established itself — had fallen under the influence of continental religious practices and had brought radical ideals back with them to England. But the Caroline exiles were confident in their anglican faith and unimpressed by the varieties of religious practice, Roman Catholic or protestant, which they encountered on the Continent. For them the years of exile meant a confirmation of all they had earlier taken for granted, and they returned to England more strongly anglican than when they had left.

The anglicans in exile derived great comfort from the unswerving support of Edward Hyde, the King's right-hand man. Hyde had earlier been a critic of episcopacy, and he never shared Laud's belief that the Church should take a prominent role in the state. Laudianism in this sense, however, died with the Archbishop, and Hyde found himself strongly in sympathy with the principles of royal supremacy, hierarchical government and uniformity of religious practice which characterised latter-day Laudians. He was prepared to make concessions to the puritans if this was the price that had to be paid for the restoration of the Church and monarchy, but, as he told John Cosin, he saw such concessions simply as a means of ensuring that 'the Church will be preserved in a tolerable condition, and by degrees recover what cannot be had at once'.

Hyde's attitude was not shared by the King. Charles wanted to re-establish the Church of England on the broadest possible basis and was determined to avoid his father's mistake of allowing control of it to pass into the hands of an intolerant minority. Of his new appointments to the episcopal bench, only three had been closely connected with Laud. They included Cosin, who went to Durham, and the aged William Juxon, who was elevated to Canterbury. Matthew Wren, however, was passed over, as were a number of other prominent Laudians, and in his use of patronage at a lower level Charles showed the same commitment to a broad-based settlement.

As the Restoration turned from a dream into reality in the early months of 1660, Hyde was working towards an accommodation with the puritans, who appeared to be still in the majority in England. It was to quieten their fears that Charles issued, in April, the *Declaration of Breda*, in which he promised 'a liberty to tender consciences, and that no man shall be disquieted or called in question for differences of opinion in matter of religion which do not disturb the peace of the kingdom'. At the same time informal discussions were taking place between anglican and presbyterian representatives, which achieved a large measure of agreement. The presbyterians acknowledged the right of expelled ministers to regain their livings. The anglicans, in return, accepted that puritan incumbents who had never been ordained by a bishop should not be required to undergo ordination.

Puritan distrust of bishops was of long standing, but Charles took a significant step towards reconciliation by publishing the *Worcester House Declaration* in October 1660 in which he ordered that every bishop should be assisted in ordination and excommunication by the 'most learned and pious presbyters of the diocese' and that no one should be persecuted for refusing to use the Prayer Book. The presbyterians were delighted by this evidence of royal goodwill, and their representatives in the Convention, led by the irrepressible Prynne, urged that the *Declaration* should be given statutory confirmation. But they came up against opposition not only from the minority of committed anglicans but also from many Independents, who feared that agreement between the King and the presbyterians would restrict religious freedom and open the way to an intolerant settlement. It was this alliance between anglicans and Independents which ensured, by a narrow majority, the rejection of the presbyterians' proposal, and from that moment their cause was lost. Hyde did not bother to conceal his pleasure at this outcome. In his closing speech to the Convention he described the Church of England as 'the best and the best reformed in the Christian world' and declared his belief that 'God would not so miraculously have snatched this Church as a brand from the fire, would not have raised it from the grave after He had suffered it to be buried so many years . . . to expose it again to the same rapine, reproach and impiety'.

Although Hyde welcomed the triumph of anglicanism he still

assumed that concessions would have to be made to the presbyterians, at least in the short run. He held out an olive branch to
them by offering bishoprics to three of their leaders, Richard
Baxter, Edmund Calamy and Edward Reynolds. Only Reynolds
accepted, however. Baxter was far less prepared for compromise, and
his intransigent attitude largely accounted for the failure of the
Savoy Conference, which opened in April 1661. He was working
on the assumption that the presbyterians held the trump cards and
could afford to play for time. What he did not appreciate was that
all over the country anglican ministers were resuming possession
of their livings and that the re-establishment of the Church of England was a *fait accompli.* Moreover the elections that took place in
the spring of 1661 were a triumph for the anglicans and cavaliers.
Charles and, to a lesser extent, Hyde might be willing to negotiate
a compromise settlement, based on toleration, but the Cavalier
Parliament which assembled in May 1661 was determined to re-
establish uncompromising and intolerant anglicanism.

While negotiations between anglican and presbyterian representatives were taking place, the bishops were producing a revised
version of the Prayer Book. They made a number of alterations
designed to meet puritan criticisms, but Baxter declared that the
new Book was even less acceptable than the old. His condemnation
carried no weight with Parliament, however, and it was this body
which now determined the nature of the religious settlement. The
new Prayer Book was incorporated into the Act of Uniformity of
1662, and all ministers were required not only to use the Book before the following St Bartholomew's Day but to make public declaration of their 'unfeigned assent and consent to all and every
thing contained and prescribed in and by the Book'. They were also
ordered to acknowledge 'that it is not lawful, upon any pretence
whatsoever, to take arms against the King', and to renounce the
*Solemn League and Covenant* as 'an unlawful oath ... imposed upon
the subjects of this realm against the known laws and liberties of
this kingdom'. St Bartholomew's Day was awaited with some trepi-
dation, but it came and went quietly enough, and Pepys recorded
in his diary that the presbyterian clergy had 'gone out very peaceably, and the people not so much concerned therein as was
expected'.

Just under a thousand ministers were deprived of their livings,
for refusing to make the prescribed declarations. This showed a far
greater degree of resistance to the reimposition of anglicanism than
the bishops had anticipated, and they were hard put to it to find
suitable replacements. Nor was it the case that all those ministers
who remained within the Church were wholeheartedly committed
to the new settlement. Anglicanism had been imposed from above,
by the Cavalier Parliament, and it took many years to filter down

to parish level. Until this happened the bishops had to turn a blind eye to non-conformity. In the Essex village of East Colne the minister, Ralph Josselin, managed to avoid wearing a surplice until 1680, and even by the time Charles II died, five years later, many parishes were without a surplice for the minister, a chalice for the administration of holy communion, or, in some cases, a Prayer Book.

Parliament confirmed the victory of intolerant anglicanism by passing a series of Acts known collectively as the Clarendon Code — although Clarendon was not responsible for them. The Corporation Act of 1661 empowered commissions of local gentlemen to administer oaths of loyalty to the governing bodies of corporate towns and remove aldermen and councillors who refused to take them. It also prescribed that in future nobody should be eligible for appointment to a corporation unless he took the sacrament 'according to the rites of the Church of England'. The Conventicle Act made it an offence for any person to attend a service other than that set forth in the Prayer Book, and gave J.P.s authority to break into private houses if they thought that illegal conventicles were being held there. In spite of this legislation puritan assemblies continued and were often presided over by former ministers, ejected from their livings. The Five Mile Act was aimed at these men, and tried to limit their influence by forbidding them to go within five miles of any corporate town.

Not everybody shared the Cavalier Parliament's intolerant attitude. In December 1662 the King issued what is sometimes referred to as the first *Declaration of Indulgence*, reminding members of Parliament of the promise of toleration he had made in the *Declaration of Breda* and requesting them to 'concur with us in the making some such Act . . . as may enable us to exercise with a more universal satisfaction that power of dispensing which we conceive to be inherent in us'. This plea fell on deaf ears, yet after a brief flurry of persecution following the passing of the Conventicle Act the local authorities in both town and countryside adopted an attitude of benign neglect. As the memory of the puritan excesses of the Interregnum faded and it became apparent that the restored Church and monarchy were built upon secure foundations, persecution was in general confined to those such as Quakers who went out of their way to challenge the social order.

The Clarendon Code, by its explicit acknowledgment of the existence of dissent, marks the *de facto* abandonment of the ideal of comprehension, of a single Church to which all English men and women must belong. The ideal was not formally renounced until the Toleration Act of 1689, and attempts at reconciliation continued on and off until that date, but the Church could never again assert its right to speak for all the people. It became increasingly the Church of the gentry and lost touch with labouring men and their families. It also lost its dominant position in politics, and after 1664, when Gilbert Sheldon — who succeeded Juxon as Archbishop of Canterbury — accepted Clarendon's proposition that the clergy should no longer tax themselves but should contribute to national taxation at the same rate as the laity, Convocation did not meet for a quarter of a century. The bishops remained important as individuals in the House of Lords, and they set a high standard of learning and piety. Many ministers also gave faithful and devoted service to their parishioners. But the Church had lost its independence. Church courts continued to function, but they were confined to spiritual penalties, which were of limited effectiveness. High Commission was never restored, and the exercise of ecclesiastical discipline was in practice left to country gentlemen, acting as J.P.s, and to Parliament. In its commitment to ritual, ceremony and hierarchy the Restoration church was Laudian, but it had gained acceptance by the political nation only through abandoning those claims to primacy in the secular sphere which Laud himself had championed.

## Clarendon

Clarendon's administration consisted of old cavaliers, like himself, Ormond and Southampton, and former Commonwealth men like the Earl of Manchester, now Lord Chamberlain; Monck, created Duke of Albemarle and appointed Captain-General for life; and Ashley Cooper, who became Chancellor of the Exchequer in 1661. Clarendon, the Lord Chancellor, was no mere figurehead. Because he had the ear of the King he was the chief minister and dominated the Privy Council, to which decisions on a whole host of matters, major and petty, were referred.

Clarendon's conservatism was particularly dangerous where Parliament was concerned. He recognised the need for the Council to give a lead in the Commons, and at the beginning of the reign he 'had every day conference with some select persons of the House of Commons' to consult together 'in what method to proceed in disposing the House'. Yet although he was prepared, like Elizabeth, to watch over debates and to intervene where necessary, Clarendon had no intention of building up a 'King's party' in the Commons, nor did he believe that Parliament should take more than an occasional part in the government of the country. He had been away from England during the years when the Long Parliament, out of necessity, had been forced to master the arts of administration, and he could not accept that the divided society revealed in 1642 was to be a permanent feature of English political life. In 1660 there was a superficial appearance of unity, but the fissures between anglicans and dissenters, supporters of divine right and opponents of absolutism, ran too deep to be healed. National unity could no longer be taken for granted, and if the King's government was to be carried on efficiently the 'King's men' in the House of Commons would have to be organised. Clarendon was not prepared to do this dirty work, but other politicians were less scrupulous.

The Cavalier Parliament had not been long in session before an opposition group began to form in the Commons. The Chancellor was not popular. Ardent cavaliers blamed him because he had made the constitutional settlement too moderate, while dissenters accused him of making the religious settlement too extreme. Many people were jealous of his wealth and of his exalted position. Clarendon's daughter Anne had married James, the heir to the throne, and courtiers commented with acid tongues on the means through which a man who was by birth an obscure country lawyer had wormed his way into the royal family. The Chancellor was also blamed for allowing France to purchase Dunkirk, which Cromwell had captured, even though it cost far more to keep up than it brought in to the Exchequer. The hostility of public opinion was shown when the mob rioted outside the great house which Clarendon was building for himself in Piccadilly and broke its windows.

Clarendon was a far finer character than any of his critics, but they were more in tune than he was with the amoral, cynical and witty tone of Restoration England. Even the King, although he valued Clarendon's loyalty and wisdom, had no love for him and preferred the company of younger, more amusing men and women — particularly women. He was prepared to keep Clarendon in office as long as the administration functioned smoothly, but when the second Dutch War revealed appalling corruption and inefficiency, he hastily got rid of him.

War was forced on Clarendon by the younger men, like Thomas Clifford and Henry Bennett, who had the Commons behind them. The Dutch were hated as commercial rivals whose trading empire and control of the European carrying trade threatened to block the expansion of the English economy. War against Holland offered the prospect of rich prizes, and young cavaliers hoped to show that the restored monarchy could acquit itself just as honourably as the Commonwealth when it came to fighting. The self-confidence engendered by the Restoration had developed into aggressiveness, and the widespread desire for war was reflected in the results of by-elections which increased the number of members who despised the pacific Chancellor and longed for his overthrow. They now had Clarendon in a cleft stick, for if the war went well, they, as its instigators, would take the credit. If it went badly they would put all the blame on the Chancellor. Charles forced Clarendon to include some of the younger men in his administration by appointing Clifford to the Privy Council and by giving seats on the Treasury Commission to him and Ashley. Everything now depended on the outcome of the war.

Fighting between the Dutch and the English in America and Africa created the situation that led to a formal declaration of war in March 1665. At first English arms were triumphant. James, the Lord High Admiral, routed the Dutch fleet in the battle of Lowestoft in June 1665, and killed the enemy admiral, Opdam. But this victory was not followed up, and the Dutch made such a good recovery that a year later they pounced on a squadron commanded by Prince Rupert, and in the Four Days' Battle sank about twenty ships and would have done even more damage had not Albemarle arrived with the rest of the fleet in time to save his fellow admiral from destruction.

While the navies grappled in the Channel and the North Sea, two natural disasters fell upon England. In May 1665 the first signs were observed of bubonic plague, which spread with frightening rapidity in the narrow, smelly streets and rat-infested slums of London. In the heat of the summer thousands of people died every month, and all who could afford to do so fled from the polluted city. Houses where the plague had struck were closed up, with a red cross painted on their door and the inscription *Lord have mercy on us*, while at night carts rumbled through the deserted streets, gathering up the dead and tumbling them into pits for common burial.

In September 1665 the plague claimed over thirty thousand victims, but after that it began slowly to decline as the survivors developed immunity. Hardly had life in the City returned to normal, however, than the Great Fire broke out. It started in September 1666 in a baker's shop in Pudding Lane, not far from the place where the Monument now stands, and for three days and nights it burned its way westward, fanned by a strong breeze. Pepys, who watched it all, describes the 'poor people staying in their houses as long as till the very fire touched them, and then running into boats or clambering from one pair of stairs by the waterside to another', and as darkness fell he saw the fire spread 'in corners and upon steeples and between churches and houses, as far as we could see up the hill of the City, in a most horrid, malicious, bloody flame . . . The churches, houses and all on fire and flaming at once, and a horrid noise the flames made, and the cracking of houses at their ruin.'

Charles went down to the City and supervised the blowing up of houses to make a fire break. Little could be done, however, until the wind dropped and the fire burned itself out. By that time the old City of London had been destroyed, and St Paul's, which Laud had struggled to restore, was a hollow shell. Over thirteen thousand homes and nearly ninety churches had been ruined by the fire, and the homeless citizens camped out in the fields that stretched towards the villages of Highgate and Hampstead. After the first shock was over, various plans were drawn up and submitted to the King for the rebuilding of the City in a more rational, and more grandiose, manner. The most famous of these came from the hand of Sir Christopher Wren, who was commissioned to rebuild St Paul's and many parish churches, but in the end little was done to alter the ground plan of the medieval City. Minor changes of some significance were, however, made. The height of houses was regulated and a minimum width was laid down for principal streets. Charles also ordered that the new City should be built of brick and stone and not of inflammable wood.

Those who believed that plague and fire had been sent by God to punish a wicked and blasphemous people, sought for a scapegoat. The honeymoon years which followed Charles's restoration were now over and in the country as well as in Parliament there was increasing criticism of the profligate court and of Clarendon's administration. If the war with Holland had ended in triumph, public opinion might have swung round once again in the court's favour, but there was no hope of this since the King could not afford to equip the fleet for the campaign of 1667. In the early part of that year peace negotiations were opened with the Dutch at Breda, while the greater part of the English fleet was laid up in the Medway. It was there that the Dutch found it in June 1667 when, with magnificent effrontery, they sailed up the river, burnt three English ships and towed away two others, including the *Royal Charles*, the flagship of the fleet. The *Royal Charles*, originally the *Naseby*, had been rechristened by Charles when it brought him back from his long exile. Its humiliating capture pointed the contrast between the efficiency and warlike strength of republican England and the maladministration and weakness that seemed to be the hallmark of the Stuarts.

Charles realised that he would have to provide a scapegoat, for the tide of criticism was washing round the throne itself; Pepys, for instance, recorded a rumour that 'the night the Dutch burned our ships the King did sup with my Lady Castlemaine [one of his mistresses] and there were all mad in hunting of a poor moth'. Clarendon was the obvious victim. Not only was he the head of the administration which had been responsible for failure in war; he was also blamed for marrying Charles to a Portuguese princess, Catherine of Braganza, who had failed to produce an heir. She had brought with her as dowry Bombay and Tangier, which were so expensive to maintain that Clarendon was considering selling them. Pepys describes how, when the news of the Medway humiliation reached London, a crowd of 'rude people' demonstrated outside the Lord Chancellor's new house and painted a gibbet on his gate, with 'these words writ: "Three sights to be seen — Dunkirk, Tangier and a barren Queen"'.

Charles could hardly dismiss Clarendon before peace was concluded with Holland, but this was accomplished in July 1667 when, by the Treaty of Breda, the *status quo* was restored — except in America, where the Dutch colony of New Netherland was transferred to England. Clarendon's dismissal followed shortly afterwards. The King was tired of the ageing statesman who reproached him for his mistresses, rebuked him when he did not take the advice of the Privy Council, opposed his scheme for toleration, and had deliberately (or so it was suggested) limited the revenue that Parliament voted him so that he should not be able to undermine either the constitutional monarchy or the established church.

Clarendon's dismissal did not satisfy the young men in the Commons who wanted to make sure that the fallen Chancellor would never again be able to threaten them. They decided on impeachment, and rallied their forces in the Commons. They could count on presbyterian sympathisers, who hated the intolerant anglicanism with which Clarendon was associated, and on the independent country gentlemen who saw in the Chancellor the embodiment of court corruption and intrigue. They could also count upon the eighty or so holders of office at court, who had entered the House in one or other of the numerous by-elections and were tied to Charles by bonds of patronage that Clarendon had regarded as unworthy of his consideration. Clarendon was prepared to face his accusers, confident in the knowledge that he had done nothing illegal, but when it became clear to him that the King had united with his enemies in the Commons, he realised the futility of opposition and fled to France. The King allowed him to keep his titles and the profits of his estates, but Parliament passed an Act of perpetual banishment against him. The man who, more than any other person, had brought about the Restoration spent the rest of his life in exile, reflecting on the vanished virtues of an earlier age and recording them for posterity in the *History of the Rebellion and Civil Wars in England*, which remains to this day one of the finest pieces of historical writing in the English language.

## The Cabal

The politics of the next few years are associated with the Cabal — Sir Thomas Clifford, appointed Treasurer of the Household; Anthony Ashley Cooper, Baron Ashley, who kept his post as Chancellor of the Exchequer; the Duke of Buckingham, son of Charles I's favourite; Henry Bennet, Lord Arlington, one of the Secretaries of State: and John Maitland, Earl of Lauderdale, who ruled Scotland for the King. In this ill-assorted group Arlington and Lauderdale were the oldest members, but the other three were in their late thirties or forties, some twenty years younger than Clarendon, and representatives of a new political generation. In spite of its name the Cabal was never a tight-knit body and members had little more than their initials in common. They were united only in their ambition and in their opposition to Clarendon and all that he stood for. They disliked the cumbersome Privy Council, preferring less formal and more intimate consultations. They also had little affection for the Church of England. Clifford and Arlington were Roman Catholic sympathisers; Lauderdale was a former presbyterian; Ashley had close links with the dissenters; and Buckingham had married the daughter of Sir Thomas Fairfax, the puritan commander of the parliamentary army in the civil war.

There was no question of the Cabal meeting regularly to advise the King on policy. Charles listened now to one minister, now to another, and played on personal rivalries in such a way that he was free to pursue his own desires. His experience with Clarendon had taught him never again to become the pawn of a statesman, but although he kept a careful watch on government, and attended meetings of councils and committees, he was not suited by temperament to the working out of general policies. He preferred an empirical approach, and the Cabal served as a screen behind which he could plot his constantly shifting course.

The European political scene was dominated by Louis XIV of France, the 'Sun King'. One of Louis' main aims was to take over the Spanish Netherlands, thereby putting at risk the continued independence of the Dutch republic. Had Charles been a free agent he would probably have allied with Louis, for he was half French by birth, and his years of exile in France had given him considerable affection for that country. Unfortunately for Charles he was not free to act as he pleased, for shortage of money made it necessary for him to take parliamentary opinion into account. Many members of the Commons disliked the Dutch as commercial rivals, but informed opinion was becoming increasingly hostile to France, which was now replacing Spain as the symbol of monarchical absolutism and uncompromising catholicism. Charles therefore, while he kept in secret touch with Louis, authorised Arlington to go ahead with plans for a league against France. These reached fruition in January 1668 when the Triple Alliance was signed between England, Holland and Sweden. The popularity of this 'Protestant League' in England gave Charles a breathing space; it also increased his value in the eyes of Louis XIV who, Charles hoped, might be tempted to buy him off at a handsome price.

Early in 1669 James, Duke of York and heir to the throne, disclosed to Charles, Clifford and Arlington that he had become a convert to the Roman Catholic faith. Charles took this opportunity of declaring that he also would like to promote catholicism in England, and asked for advice on how best to do so. As a result of the discussions that followed, new negotiations were opened with France, which led to the signing of the secret Treaty of Dover in May 1670. Charles agreed to assist Louis in war against Holland in return for a French subsidy. Payment of this, however, was to be dependent upon Charles's conversion to catholicism, and in the second clause of the treaty it was recorded that 'the King of England, being convinced of the truth of the Roman Catholic religion, is resolved to declare it and to reconcile himself with the Church of Rome as soon as the state of his country's affairs will permit. He . . . will avail himself of the assistance of the King of France who . . . promises to pay to the King of England the sum of two million *livres tournois*, the first half payable three months after ratification of the present treaty, the other half three months later. In addition, the King of France undertakes to provide, at his own expense, six thousand troops for the execution of this design, if they should be required. The time for the declaration of catholicism is left entirely to the discretion of the King of England.'

The significance of the secret treaty of Dover has remained a matter for controversy ever since it was signed. Charles was inclined towards catholicism and died in the Roman Catholic faith, but his lack of any fervent religious convictions makes it difficult to believe that spiritual factors alone prompted his action; financial considerations must also have played a major part. The costs of the second Dutch war, which amounted to more than five million pounds, had been covered by parliamentary grants, but the dislocation caused by war, plague and fire had seriously reduced the King's ordinary income. Even prior to 1665 he had only been receiving about £800,000 a year, a mere two-thirds of what Parliament had thought appropriate in 1660, but in the second half of the decade this figure slumped to less than £650,000. Louis, under the provisions of the Treaty of Dover, had agreed to pay Charles £225,000 a year as an inducement for him to join in the war against the Dutch, and a lump sum of £150,000 in return for Charles's announcement of his conversion. Although Charles never made his conversion public Louis gave him the £150,000, and in 1672 and 1673 Charles also received the promised £225,000. In other words, French subsidies during this brief period increased the King's ordinary revenue by nearly 50 per cent. From Charles's point of view it was a good bargain.

Buckingham and the 'protestant' members of the Cabal were not aware of the secret clauses. They were shown only the 'open' Treaty of Dover, concluded in December 1670, which contained the provisions relating to joint action against Holland and nothing else. Parliament was not informed about either treaty, since foreign af-

fairs came within the scope of the royal prerogative. When the two
Houses reassembled in October 1670 they assumed that the protestant league created by the Triple Alliance was still the corner-
stone of Charles's policy and showed their approval of it by voting
subsidies estimated to bring in £800,000 as well as an additional
excise. The success of the government was partly due to the skilful
way in which Clifford, working on Arlington's behalf, had organised the 'King's men' in the Commons. The lesson was not lost on
one of Buckingham's protégés, Sir Thomas Osborne, nor on the
King himself who, some time later, reported that in this session the
majority of the Commons 'were tied to his interests either by offices
or by pensions'.

From April 1671 until February 1673 Parliament was in prorogation while the King made his preparations to put the Treaty of
Dover into effect. The parliamentary grant enabled him to set out
the fleet but did nothing to reduce the backlog of accumulated debt
with which he was burdened. Much of his annual revenue was
mortgaged in advance to his creditors, but with the approach of
war the King needed all the money he could lay his hands on. In
January 1672, therefore, by the Stop of the Exchequer, he put an
end to repayment of loans and took all the revenue into his own
hands. He offered his creditors interest on sums outstanding but
no longer acknowledged his obligation to repay the principal. Not
surprisingly he thereby lost the confidence of merchants and businessmen and found it even more difficult to raise fresh loans.

The Stop of the Exchequer was followed, in March 1672, by the
issuing of a second *Declaration of Indulgence*, suspending the penal
laws against Roman Catholics and dissenters. Roman Catholics
were now free to worship in private; dissenters could worship publicly as long as they obtained an official licence. It may be that
Charles planned the *Declaration* as a way of preparing public opinion for the announcement of his conversion, but it seems more likely
that it was intended to keep the dissenters quiet during the forthcoming war against the Dutch. Dissenters had been holding meetings for worship despite the provisions of the Conventicle Act, and
the *Declaration* was stating little more than the truth when it said
that 'the sad experience of twelve years' had shown 'that there is
very little fruit of all those forcible courses'.

Public opinion — the opinion, that is to say, of the politically
articulate — had been gradually moving towards the acceptance
of toleration in practice, but there was widespread opposition to
Charles's *Declaration*. For one thing it implied that the King had
a right to suspend the operation of statute law, which was calculated to alarm property-owners. And, for another, it was issued at
a time when rumours about the King's private leanings were encouraging the suspicion that his secret purpose was not to relieve

the sufferings of protestant dissenters but to prepare the way for the re-establishment of Roman Catholicism. The long period of relatively harmonious relations between King and Parliament was now approaching its end, for more and more members were coming to see in Charles not the guardian of the traditional order in Church and state but a potential threat to it. This was to bring about a marked rise in the political temperature.

The future pattern of English politics depended, to a considerable extent, upon the outcome of the third Dutch War, which opened in March 1672, when Louis XIV's preparations were complete. Charles did his best to win support for his plans. Lauderdale was made a duke, Arlington an earl, and Clifford a baron, while Ashley was given the Earldom of Shaftesbury. It was at this date also that Sir Thomas Osborne, who had shown his financial ability as Treasurer of the Navy, was appointed to the Privy Council. Arlington, who opposed the war, dropped into the background. The leading members of the administration were Clifford and Shaftesbury, who had a deep interest in commercial matters, regarded the Dutch as dangerous rivals, and valued the policy of toleration. In November 1672 Shaftesbury was made Lord Chancellor, while Clifford was given the white staff of the Lord Treasurer.

The joint strategy worked out by England and France for the war was that French troops, with a small English contingent, would be responsible for land operations, while the English fleet, aided by a French squadron, would attack the Dutch at sea. The opportunity to win a decisive victory, which would have opened the coast of Holland to invasion, came in May 1672 when the Earl of Sandwich, commanding the English fleet, joined battle with De Ruyter in Solebay (Southwold Bay) off Suffolk. Both sides fought stubbornly, but Sandwich was killed after his flagship blew up and the Dutch fleet was able to withdraw, battered but intact. Meanwhile, on land, the French invasion of Holland had met with rapid success and had driven the Dutch to sue for peace. The terms dictated by Louis were, however, so humiliating that the Dutch preferred to continue fighting. The republican leaders, whom the Dutch blamed for their desperate plight, were assassinated and the Prince of Orange was recalled to power. He ordered the dykes to be cut, and the French advance slowed to a halt in a slough of mud.

Charles could not fight the war without parliamentary grants, and the two Houses assembled in February 1673. Shaftesbury made his famous *Delenda est Carthago* speech, declaring that 'the States of Holland are England's eternal enemy both by interest and inclination', and the Commons proposed to vote generous supply, but only on condition that the King abandoned his 'right' to suspend the laws. In an address to Charles they asserted that 'penal statutes, in matters ecclesiastical, cannot be suspended but by Act of

Parliament', and when the King assured them in his reply that he did not 'pretend to the right of suspending any laws wherein the properties, rights or liberties of any of his subjects are concerned', they told him that his answer was 'not sufficient to clear the apprehensions that may justly remain in the minds of your people'.

Buckingham and Clifford advised Charles to protect his prerogative by refusing to withdraw the *Declaration*, and Lauderdale even suggested the use of Scottish troops to enforce the royal will, but Arlington urged the King to abandon not only the *Declaration* but the whole pro-French, anti-Dutch policy of which it was a part. In order to win Shaftesbury over to his view, Arlington revealed to him the details of the secret Treaty of Dover, and from this moment onwards the Lord Chancellor, angry at the way in which he had been deceived, began to move away from the court and appeal to the 'Country' — all those who distrusted the papist tendencies at Whitehall and wanted to see the re-establishment of what they thought to be traditional English virtues.

Charles cancelled the *Declaration of Indulgence* in March 1673, and Parliament responded by voting just under £1,200,000 for the war. But at the same time it passed the Test Act, banning from office all who refused to take the sacrament according to the rites of the Church of England and to make a public declaration against transubstantiation. The aim of the Act was to put an end to rumours of papists in high places and to make it clear that the Commons were voting money only for a 'protestant' war. When it became law, however, the rumours were given unexpected confirmation, for James resigned his office as Lord High Admiral, while Clifford gave up the Treasury.

## Danby

Charles's major problem at this stage was shortage of money, but he was also aware of the need to restore public confidence in his administration. Rumours about secret commitments to France were circulating widely, and William of Orange had been so alarmed by the pro-French drift of Charles's policy that he had sent an agent to England. It was this agent who, in March 1673, published *England's Appeal from the Private Cabal at Whitehall to the Great Council of the Nation*, in which he developed the persuasive argument that the alliance with France was the key element in a policy aimed at overthrowing the protestant religion in England and destroying English liberties. Charles made an effective reply to this challenge by choosing as Clifford's replacement Sir Thomas Osborne, who was a committed supporter of the Church of England and an advocate of an anti-French foreign policy, as well as a staunch upholder of the monarchy.

Osborne's long-term aim was to win the co-operation of the Commons by persuading Charles to follow policies of which they approved, and thereby open the way to a parliamentary solution of the King's financial problems. Meanwhile, he cut down on pensions and salaries and made honesty and economy his watchwords. He had already demonstrated his financial acumen as Treasurer of the Navy, and after he was appointed Lord Treasurer in July 1673 he extended his grasp over the administration and became, in effect, the King's chief minister. By this time the Cabal had disintegrated. Clifford committed suicide, Shaftesbury adopted an ostentatiously 'Country' position, Arlington wavered, and as for Buckingham, he was, in the words of Dryden:

> A man so various that he seemed to be
> Not one, but all mankind's epitome:
> Stiff in opinions, always in the wrong,
> Was everything by starts and nothing long;
> But in the course of one revolving moon
> Was chemist, fiddler, statesman and buffoon.

Shaftesbury was dismissed from the Lord Chancellorship in November 1673 — 'It is only laying down my gown and putting on my sword', he commented — and Heneage Finch, a lawyer and ally of Osborne, became Lord Keeper in his place. Arlington stayed in office long enough to negotiate the Treaty of Westminster, which brought about a separate peace between England and Holland in February 1674, but resigned his Secretaryship later in the year. Osborne was gradually attaining a primacy in the King's counsels unparalleled since the fall of Clarendon, and in June 1674 he was created Earl of Danby.

Danby was inclined at first to rely upon the attractiveness of his policy to win the favour of the House of Commons, but in this he reckoned without Louis XIV. The emergence of England as an active protestant champion threatened to check French expansion, and Louis was ready to use French money to bribe members of Parliament and encourage them to an open breach with the executive. It is unlikely that the money paid by Louis or by anyone else created changes of opinion in the Commons: its effect was to persuade those who were already critical of government policies to organise themselves.

The opposition in Parliament had good enough reasons for its attitude without French gold. The King's brother, James, Duke of York, who was also heir to the throne, had recently taken a Roman Catholic princess, Mary of Modena, as his second wife, following the death of Anne Hyde. This intensified rumours and fears about popery at court, and although Charles tried to stifle these by ordering that the penal laws should be enforced, he could not dispel

the cloud of mistrust that was gathering around him. Suspicion of
Charles spread over on to Danby, for how could members of Parliament be sure that the King and his chief minister were not plotting to deceive them once again by demanding supply for a
protestant war that would, in fact, be used for the creation in England of a French-style, catholic absolutism?

If Charles had stood firmly behind Danby, harmony between
King and Parliament might eventually have been achieved. Mutual
confidence was all that was lacking, and time could have created
this. There is no reason to suppose that Charles was deliberately
working against such a reconciliation. Those who picture the King
as a Machiavellian intriguer, juggling men to suit his long-prepared
designs, surely do him a disservice. Charles's main aim was to keep
his throne and live comfortably, and he was prepared to embrace
a protestant policy if this would achieve the required result; Louis
XIV, at any rate, was sufficiently convinced of Charles's change
of heart to spend thousands of pounds on frustrating Danby's
plans. But Charles II did not want to be caught in the same trap
as his father, who had committed himself to war at the Commons'
request, only to find, as he told them bitterly, that '[now] I am so
far engaged that you think there is no retreat . . . you begin to set
the dice and make your own game'. The King therefore kept up
the secret link with Louis as an insurance in case Danby should
not succeed. Unfortunately, by doing so he created an atmosphere
of suspicion that ensured Danby's failure.

Throughout 1675 Danby tried to reach agreement with Parliament, and began organising the King's men in the Commons as
Clifford had done before him. Pensions and offices were carefully
distributed, and the nucleus of a royalist 'party' was created. This
produced a natural reaction. By emphasising that certain members
were *in* the golden circle of court patronage it encouraged the *outs*
to organise themselves. The hard core of the Commons remained,
as always, the independent, uncommitted country gentlemen, but
on either wing there were organised groups, neither of them
strong enough to command a majority, but each working constantly
to win over a sufficient number of the uncommitted to give it
victory.

Danby effectively blocked many of the opposition's moves, but
they were equally effective in blocking his own. Parliament, in the
autumn session of 1675, had voted supply, but only on a small scale
and for strictly defined purposes. The main concern of members
of the Commons was to secure the recall of the British troops fighting alongside the French. They disapproved of such open support
of Louis XIV; they also feared that a standing army used to promote absolutist policies abroad might subsequently be employed
for the same purpose at home. Their apprehensions were given

forceful expression in the *Letter from a Person of Quality to his Friend in the Country*, which appeared in November 1675. This pamphlet, which may well have been the work of Shaftesbury and John Locke, argued that ever since the Restoration there had been plans afoot to create an absolute monarchy in England and that these were now coming to fruition. Parliament's functions would be restricted to the granting of money and any opposition would be put down by the army. These assertions were, of course, exaggerated, but there was sufficient truth in them to carry conviction, and even Danby had to accept that in such a hot-house atmosphere his hopes of achieving harmonious co-operation between King and Parliament could not be fulfilled. What was needed was a long period of political inactivity in which passions could die down and rational attitudes assert themselves. The King therefore decided on a fifteen-month prorogation, and in November 1675 Parliament went into recess. Louis XIV, who had feared that parliamentary pressures might force Charles into war against him, showed his relief by paying the King a 'reward' of £100,000. This was little, compared with the sort of sums that a co-operative Parliament might provide. But Parliament was not co-operative, and in any case the King's financial position was improving. English withdrawal from the war, at a time when the French and Dutch were still locked in bitter conflict, had led to a marked expansion in British trade and a big increase in the yield of Customs and Excise. For the first time the King's ordinary revenue was approaching the 'target' figure of £1,200,000.

When the Cavalier Parliament met for its fifteenth session in February 1677 Danby and the court party were well organised, and the Commons voted £600,000 for the Navy as well as renewing the additional excise originally granted in 1670. The voting of supply on this scale was a major victory for Danby and might have led to closer co-operation between King and Parliament had it not coincided with news of a big French offensive against the Dutch. The Commons petitioned Charles to make a firm alliance against France and promised him further supply once he had declared war. Charles wanted the grant before he committed himself irrevocably, but the Commons would not agree to this: their attitude was expressed by the member who recalled 'that example of Harry the Seventh, who got aids for the war and presently struck up a peace'. This was the testing moment for Danby's policy, and he came within an ace of success. But the King would not take the decisive step until he was sure of supply, and consequently the session petered out in acrimonious exchanges, the King reminding the Commons that 'should I suffer this fundamental power of making peace and war to be so far invaded (though but once) as to have the manner and circumstances of leagues prescribed to me by Parliament, it is plain that no prince or state would any longer believe that the sovereignty of England rests in the crown'.

Political deadlock, and the frustration which it engendered, sent the temperature rising once again, and old fears were given new expression by Andrew Marvell, whose pamphlet on *The Growth of Popery and Arbitrary Government in England* appeared in late 1677. In this he developed the theme that 'there had now for divers years a design been carried on to change the lawful government of England into downright popery'. Parliament alone had the strength to block this design, but Marvell asserted that the majority of the Commons were on the government's patronage list and cared nothing about principles so long as they were in receipt of their pensions.

If Marvell had been correct, then Charles would have had little to worry about. The reality was very different, for the King was losing hope of reaching any agreement with Parliament, which he regarded as intransigent, and was willing to accept French offers of financial assistance in return for a further prorogation. Danby, however, encouraged the King to pitch his demands high. Perhaps he hoped that Louis, in disgust, would withdraw his offer: at the very least there would have to be lengthy negotiations, and these would give Danby time, which he badly needed. For the Treasurer had by no means given up hope of building bridges between the court and the Commons. On the contrary, he persuaded Charles to bid for the support of Parliament by agreeing to a marriage between William of Orange, the protestant champion, and James's daughter, Mary. The marriage took place in November 1677, and in the following January England and Holland bound themselves by treaty to impose peace terms on Louis, if necessary by force.

When Parliament reassembled, early in 1678, Charles called on it to vote supply, so that he could raise an army of 30,000 men and set out the fleet in conformity with his obligations under the Dutch treaty. The Commons, however, were unwilling to commit themselves to so potentially dangerous a move, and Danby therefore went ahead without them. When it became apparent that the government really was carrying out its promises, Parliament voted a poll tax, which eventually brought in £300,000. This was less than half what Danby had already spent, however, and a long way short of the £2.5 million which full-scale war would cost. Danby's belief that he could solve Charles's financial problems through cooperation with Parliament seemed increasingly chimerical. The Commons were still suspicious of the King's intentions and rejected Danby's proposal that they should at last fulfil the intention behind the Restoration settlement by bringing the ordinary revenue up to £1,200,000 a year. Their attitude was epitomised by one member who said, 'I am for keeping the revenue from being too big, for then you'll need Parliaments'.

Louis was so alarmed by the direction in which Danby was moving that he authorised his ambassador to spend on a massive scale in order to encourage opposition to him. Most of Danby's critics in Parliament, including the well-known republican, Algernon Sidney, were on the French pensions list, for they believed that Louis was less of a threat than Charles and that the army being raised to fight France would in fact be used to suppress English liberties. Their fears increased when it became known that Louis and the Dutch were on the point of agreement, for although peace was concluded at Nymegen in August 1678 Charles declined to disband his forces. The international situation was still volatile, and there were good reasons for keeping the army in being, but to the opposition this seemed proof that the King's aims — or at least those of his chief minister — were sinister. The Commons insisted that the army should be disbanded, and made it clear that there was no possibility of further supply. Even Danby seems to have despaired, at this stage, of winning them over, and at the King's command he therefore wrote to Ralph Montagu, the ambassador in Paris, ordering him to speed up negotiations for a French subsidy. It was at this point, in September 1678, that Titus Oates — a turncoat Jesuit and a liar of the first quality — and his associate, Israel Tonge, made their astonishing revelations about a Popish Plot.

## The Popish Plot and Exclusion Crisis

The catholic community in England had lived quietly and unobtrusively in the years following the Restoration. Its numbers were stable or declining, and much the same applied to the English mission: in the 1670s there were some 230 seculars at work — a fall of 40 per cent since the 1630s — while the regulars amounted to about 260, of whom just under half were Jesuits. But *de facto* acceptance of catholics as individuals and at a local level was only one side of the coin. The other was made up of acute suspicion of 'popery', by which was meant the operations of international catholicism with the aim of destroying English protestantism. This explains why it was that when Oates revealed that the Pope had ordered the Jesuits to overthrow the English government, kill the King, and place his catholic brother on the throne, he was instantly believed. When he added that French troops were to be used to carry out this design and that it was to be accompanied by a general massacre of protestants, whatever lingering doubts there might have been about his veracity were immediately dispelled. Consciously or unconsciously he had used the type of apocalyptic language that was exactly tuned to English anti-catholic paranoia. He had also timed his revelations well, for Charles, by his simultaneous pursuit of mutually incompatible policies, had created such uncertainty about his real motives that anything seemed possible. By the time Parliament assembled in October 1678, therefore, the Plot was a major topic of discussion. Among the people whom Oates had accused of being implicated was Edward Coleman, a Roman Catholic in the service of the Duke and Duchess of York. When Coleman's papers were seized, it was discovered that he had been engaged in extravagant schemes for the re-conversion of England and had told his foreign correspondents of the 'mighty work' which lay ahead and involved the subduing of 'a pestilent heresy which has domineered over part of this northern world a long time'.

Before the end of 1678 Shaftesbury had taken up Oates and made himself the champion of the Plot. Shaftesbury was a Dorset landowner with commercial connexions, especially with the American colonies. He was a ruthless politician but not unprincipled; among his close friends he counted the philosopher John Locke, who was already at work on the *Two Treatises of Government*, which provided a theoretical basis for Shaftesbury's assumption that government depended on an implied contract between the property-owners and the ruler — a contract which was automatically invalidated if the ruler attempted to renege on his obligations by turning himself into an absolute monarch.

Shaftesbury was not a republican, like Algernon Sidney. He was in favour of limited monarchy on the traditional pattern, and twenty years earlier he had been prominent among those who urged Cromwell to take the crown. He saw in James a threat to everything he believed in, for, in the words of a fellow member of Parliament, 'the protestant religion is so intermixed with the civil liberties of the nation that it is not possible to preserve them if a popish successor comes'. Shaftesbury's aim was to use the anti-catholic paranoia inflamed by Oates to force Charles to accept a Bill excluding James from the succession. In order to achieve this he built up a powerful party in Parliament, linked with the Green Ribbon Club in London and with similar organisations throughout the country. Pamphlets were published, processions organised, and public opinion marshalled in such a manner that the opposition in Parliament became for a few years a party in the modern sense, with a political programme and national organisation. And at the centre, working tirelessly to achieve the single end of exclusion, was Shaftesbury, small in stature, great in his ambitions. Dryden, in *Absalom and Achitophel*, has left an unforgettable picture of him:

> For close designs and crooked counsels fit.
> Sagacious, bold, and turbulent of wit,
> Restless, unfixed in principles and place,
> In power unpleased, impatient of disgrace;

A daring pilot in extremity,
Pleased with the danger when the waves went high,
He sought the storms; but, for a calm unfit,
Would steer too nigh the sands, to boast his wit.

The opposition won their first victory when Montagu, now a member of the Commons, was persuaded to reveal to a shocked House the details of Danby's negotiations for a French subsidy. This seemed to confirm that Danby, while pretending to be a supporter of the protestant interest, had all the time been working to destroy it, and the Commons voted his impeachment. Rather than risk further disclosures the King prorogued Parliament, and in January 1679 he at last dissolved it. The Cavalier Parliament had been in existence for nearly eighteen years, during which time the crown had built up its influence in such a way that long parliaments seemed to be almost as much of a danger to the liberty of the subject as no parliaments. The opposition had been clamouring for dissolution and now they were rewarded.

The election was, as always, fought over local rather than national issues, but when the new Commons assembled in March 1679 it became clear that the majority of members were strongly exclusionist. Parliament immediately revived Danby's impeachment, and the fact that the King had given him a pardon under the great seal only added to the members' indignation. The Treasurer was clearly of no more use to the King. In March he resigned his office, and in the following month the House of Lords committed him to the Tower to await trial.

Charles was doing his utmost to defuse the situation. In the closing months of 1678 he had ordered the rigorous enforcement of the laws against popish recusants and Jesuits, and he also accepted a second Test Act excluding catholics from both Houses of Parliament. James was not directly affected by this measure since it was explicitly stated that 'nothing in this Act contained shall extend to his royal Highness the Duke of York'. But his continued presence at court was clearly an embarrassment to Charles, and in February 1679 the King persuaded him to go into voluntary exile at The Hague. Charles now made a bid for broader support by enlarging the Privy Council and restoring it to the position it had earlier held. The period after the Restoration had seen the emergence of a smaller body, sometimes called the Cabinet Council, which was more fitted, as Charles explained, for the 'secrecy and dispatch that are necessary in many great affairs'. Now, however, he made Shaftesbury Lord President of a Council that included not only courtiers and officials, like the Earl of Sunderland, but also such opposition leaders as the Earl of Essex and William, Lord Russell. By doing this Charles hoped to divide the opposition leaders from their followers and avoid the mistake that his father had made in a similar situation in 1641.

When the Commons turned to business they began with the old question of the standing army, and voted £200,000 for its disbandment. Next came a Bill, introduced by John Hampden's grandson, excluding James from the throne and providing that the crown should revert to the next in succession, as though James had been dead. Shaftesbury was busy whipping up anger against James, whom he described as a man 'heady, violent and bloody, who easily believes the rashest and worst of counsels to be most sincere and hearty . . . His interest and designs are to introduce a military and arbitrary government'. Charles, however, was firmly opposed to exclusion. He offered instead to accept statutory limitations on his brother's authority, which would have left Parliament with control over all appointments to high offices in Church and state. But how could members be sure that the King would not later use his dispensing power to evade the provisions of the statute? And what certainty could there be that James, once he came to the throne, would observe its limitations? Exclusion seemed, on the face of it, to be more clear-cut, more incontrovertible, and the Commons therefore passed the Bill. Charles riposted by proroguing Parliament at the end of May 1679 and in the following July he dissolved it, with nothing accomplished except the Habeas Corpus Act, which gave statutory backing to the common-law right of freedom from arbitrary arrest and imprisonment.

Elections for a new Parliament were to be held in August and September, and Shaftesbury kept passions alive by indicting James before the grand jury of Middlesex on the grounds that he was a popish recusant. Only the judge's intervention prevented the jury from returning a true bill and thereby opening the way to James's prosecution. This was technically a defeat for Shaftesbury, but he had probably anticipated such a result and had planned his action mainly for its propaganda value. The exclusionists — or Whigs, as they were coming to be called — were very active in the elections, and when Charles resorted to repeated prorogations to postpone the moment when he would have to confront Parliament they organised a campaign of mass petitions calling for its immediate assembly.

Shaftesbury had assumed that Charles would give way under pressure, for the King had never been renowned for his adhesion to principle. But over the issue of exclusion Charles stood firm. He recognised his brother's faults, but he had a genuine affection for him and was, in any case, determined to maintain the fundamental law of hereditary succession without which he himself might not have come to the throne. In his attitude to the law Charles was consistent, for he let it take its course even though this led to injustice. During the period 1678–81 the English catholics underwent their last period of intense persecution. The missionary priests suffered worst of all, for about a hundred were arrested, of whom seventeen were executed and another twenty or so died in prison. The Jesuits were particularly hard hit, for nearly half their number were imprisoned, and the provincial of the Order was among those executed. Roman Catholic peers were not exempt from persecution. Many went into exile and waited for the storm to blow over, but eleven who remained behind were arrested on treason charges, one was executed and one died in the Tower. Catholic gentry fared better, though some four hundred of them were imprisoned, but catholic tradesmen came under strong attack in London, where some twenty of them were executed or died in custody.

In October 1680 Charles at last allowed the new Parliament to assemble, and in a mere nine days a second Exclusion Bill was rushed through the Commons. It was careful not to name the alternative successor to James, however, for the opposition was divided on this issue. Some members wanted Mary, James's daughter and the wife of William of Orange; others, including Shaftesbury, hoped to win over Charles by promoting the claims of his illegitimate son, the Duke of Monmouth. The decisive debate came in the Lords which, unlike the Commons, was never solidly Whig. Charles attended the debates in person, standing with his back to the fireplace, noting the points put forward by successive speakers, and now and again making an effective intervention. He was aided by the Earl of Halifax, who argued that limitations, of the sort proposed by Charles, were a better bet than exclusion. During the course of the heated debate Halifax rose to speak sixteen times, and his pleading, combined with Charles's presence, was effective. The Lords rejected the Bill by sixty-three votes to thirty.

In January 1681 Charles dissolved this second Exclusion Parliament and summoned a third to meet at Oxford. No doubt he remembered the way in which the Long Parliament had drawn strength from the City of London when it confronted his father, and was determined not to let the same thing happen again. In the elections the Whigs showed themselves to be masterly tacticians. They kept up their pamphlet campaign, they maintained the focus on national rather than local issues, and they drew up draft instructions to candidates which were presented to them, upon election, and committed them to the support of exclusion in the name of the electorate. The Tories — as the defenders of the monarchy were now called — also organised themselves, adopting many of the devices pioneered by the Whigs, and this in itself was an indication that the tide was ceasing to flow so strongly in the Whigs' favour. So was the fact that in the new House of Commons their strength was slightly reduced. Nevertheless they could be sure of a big majority for exclusion. Their only problem was what to do if the Lords — or, failing them, the King — rejected it. There was talk of using force, but this was little more than rhetoric, for nobody wanted another civil war. Shaftesbury was counting on the King's need for parliamentary subsidies to secure the acceptance of exclusion. He did not know that as trade continued to expand the King's ordinary income was, for the first time, up to or even above the figure of £1,200,000, or that Louis had promised Charles £125,000 a year in return for a dissolution.

In his opening speech to the Oxford Parliament Charles emphasised that he had taken his stand on law, and that if the rules governing succession were changed no man's property would be safe. He offered to accept any limitations on James that Parliament proposed, but made it clear that he would never accept exclusion. Whether he was genuine in his offer of limitations was never put to the test, for Shaftesbury clung to exclusion, convinced that if sufficient pressure was put on the King he would eventually give way. 'If you are restrained only by law and justice,' he said to Charles in the Lords, 'rely on us and leave us to act. We will make laws which will give legality to a measure so necessary for the quiet of the nation.' 'Let there be no delusion,' replied the King. 'I will not yield, nor will I be bullied. Men usually become timid as they become older. It is the opposite with me, and for what may remain of my life I am determined that nothing will tarnish my reputation. I have law and reason and all right-thinking men on my side. I have the Church' — here he pointed to the bishops — 'and nothing will ever separate us.'

The Commons insisted on going ahead with exclusion. On 28 March, therefore, Charles went to the Lords as usual but then sprang a surprise by appearing robed and crowned and commanding members of both Houses to attend him. The Whigs were still confident of victory, but when Charles spoke it was only to announce his decision to dissolve Parliament. Had his enemies been warned they might have organised, and had they been in London they might have seized the initiative. Charles, however, had made his preparations with great care. Six hundred infantry were present to guard him at Oxford, while a strong force of cavalry kept open the road back to London, which was itself garrisoned by several thousand men. Charles, in short, was ready to fight if need be. His enemies were not. Some of the Whigs talked violence, but in the end they dispersed peacefully while the King rode back at full speed to the capital. The Exclusion Crisis was over.

## The Royalist Reaction

Charles exploited his victory by issuing a declaration explaining why he had dissolved Parliament. This document, which he ordered to be read from pulpits throughout the land, portrayed the King as the saviour of his country, the man who had prevented a second civil war, and this theme was developed by the journalist Roger L'Estrange in his newspaper, the *Observator*. The high point of the royalist propaganda campaign came in November 1681 with the publication of Dryden's brilliant satire, *Absalom and Achitophel*, in which Shaftesbury and his adherents are portrayed as unscrupulous adventurers while Charles is compared to King David, the guardian of his people.

Shaftesbury himself was arrested on a charge of high treason, sent to the Tower, and subsequently indicted before the London grand jury. But the Whig sheriffs, elected when exclusion sentiment was still strong, ensured that the jurors were of their persuasion, and the indictment was not upheld. Shaftesbury was a free man once again, but this was only a temporary reprieve, for London was not immune from the royalist fervour that was now sweeping through England, and in July 1682 two Tory sheriffs were elected. Shaftesbury immediately went into hiding and subsequently escaped to Holland, where he died the following year. In June 1683 the other Whig leaders were accused, justly or unjustly, of planning to assassinate Charles at the Rye House, near Hoddesdon in Hertfordshire, on his way back from the races at Newmarket. The Earl of Essex committed suicide after his arrest: William, Lord Russell, and Algernon Sidney were tried, condemned and executed.

Charles remodelled the judicial bench, to make sure that it would not oppose his will. For the first eight years of his reign he had appointed judges *Quamdiu se bene gesserint* (during good behaviour), which gave them virtual security of tenure, but thereafter he changed this to *Durante beneplacito* (during good pleasure), which meant he could dismiss them as and when he thought fit. Charles I had been accused of eroding the impartiality of the bench by dismissing one judge and suspending another in a reign of twenty-four years, but Charles II went far beyond this. By the end of 1683 he had removed eleven judges in eight years, and he appointed as Chief Justice the notorious timeserver George Jeffreys. With the judges firmly behind him Charles could act as autocratically as his father had done through the prerogative courts, and he turned his attention to the municipal corporations.

At the Restoration the Corporation Act had authorised the King to appoint commissioners to remodel the governing bodies of corporate towns, but this had been only a temporary measure. During

the Exclusion Crisis the corporations had become Whig strongholds, but now the Tories were winning places, and they looked to
the crown to ensure their victory. They pressed for borough charters to be confiscated and new ones issued which would confirm
them in control. Charles therefore instructed his judges to undertake
*Quo Warranto* enquiries, to determine 'by what warrant' the corporations exercised their functions. In many, though not all, cases
borough privileges were derived from royal charters, but over the
course of years the governing bodies had assumed powers for which
there was no specific authorisation. Now they were called to account, and often made a voluntary surrender of their charters
rather than face the costs of a judicial enquiry. Those which held
out were subject to the full force of the law. Even London, the
greatest corporation of all, was punished for its initial refusal to
indict Shaftesbury by being called upon to defend its claims in
King's Bench. Judgement was given against it and an order was
made 'that the franchise and liberty of London be taken into the
King's hands'.

Charles was pleased to restore all the traditional rights of his
capital city, but only on condition that no official should be elected
in future without his approval. The same condition was imposed
on fifty or so other municipalities. This gave the King virtual control over a significant number of borough seats in the House of
Commons and opened up the pleasing, and unusual, prospect of
a co-operative, if not subservient, Parliament when he next pleased
to summon one.

The closing years of Charles II's reign were the Indian summer
of the Stuarts. Tories replaced Whigs in county administration as
well as the boroughs, and from every pulpit the sinfulness of resistance to the will of a divinely-appointed monarch was
preached. So secure was the King that when, under the terms of
the Triennial Act of 1664, another Parliament became due in 1684,
he flouted the law by failing to summon it. Halifax protested, but
there was was no general outcry. Halifax was increasingly out of
favour, and the King now looked for advice to Robert Spencer,
second Earl of Sunderland, who became Secretary of State in 1683,
and Sidney Godolphin, who was appointed to the commission which
ran the Treasury after Danby's fall. The principal commissioner was
Godolphin's associate Laurence Hyde, Clarendon's second son, who
was created Earl of Rochester in 1682. Rochester was a skilled eco-
nomist and a highly competent administrator. He followed the example of Danby, who had abandoned the farming of the Customs in
1671 with beneficial results, and instituted direct collection of the
excise and the hearth tax. The result was a substantial increase in the
yield of both taxes, but Rochester went further than Danby had ever
been able to do by persuading Charles to restrain his natural extrava-

gance and live within, or even below, his income. This was not all that much of a hardship, for by the end of Charles's reign the ordinary revenue was not far short of £1,400,000 a year, and French subsidies brought it well above that figure. The Restoration financial settlement, which had been designed to restore a balanced constitution in which King and Parliament should co-operate, had opened the way to a second Stuart despotism, and Charles, much to his delight and amazement, was able, like Henry VII before him, to enjoy 'the felicity of full coffers'.

In 1684 Danby was released from the Tower, but he was not recalled to office. The anglican-parliamentary policy for which he had stood was dead, so far as Charles was concerned, and the King came to lean more and more upon his brother James. It was James who, in February 1685, when the King had a stroke and was obviously dying, sent for a Roman Catholic priest to administer the last rites. At this late stage, therefore, Charles carried out the promise he had made fifteen years before in the secret Treaty of Dover, and declared himself a catholic.

Charles had kept his throne and preserved his prerogative intact by a combination of good luck and good judgment. By showing up the weaknesses of the Restoration settlement he prepared the way for the constitutional changes of 1689, but these might never have come about had Charles been succeeded by a ruler as flexible as himself. The irony of Charles's reign lies in the fact that his greatest success carried the seeds of failure in it: by safeguarding the succession of his brother James he ensured the destruction of the monarchy and dynasty he had so skilfully preserved.

# 16

# The Glorious Revolution

## James II

'If it had not been for his popery he would have been, if not a great, yet a good prince.' In these words Bishop Burnet pithily and accurately summed up James II. The new King had much to be said in his favour. He was honest and hard-working, and he wanted to see his country become once again a major power in Europe – not for him the dependence on France that had come to characterise Charles II. He had, it is true, an exalted view of kingship which would sooner or later have brought him into conflict with Parliament, but he shared so many of the attitudes of the Tory squires who dominated the Commons that he could probably have arrived at a *modus vivendi* with them. Yet he threw away all his advantages because of his determination to secure toleration for his fellow catholics. Such was the prevailing suspicion of popery that any move towards relaxing the penal laws was interpreted by James's subjects as the first stage in the re-establishment of catholicism in England. Suspicion of James's intentions was reinforced by knowledge of his character. Lauderdale observed that he 'loves, as he saith, to be served in his own way, and he is as very a papist as the Pope himself, which will be his ruin . . . If he had the empire of the whole world he would venture the loss of it, for his ambition is to shine in a red letter after he is dead'.

## James and the Anglicans

James did not regard himself as an intolerant man. In his view it was his subjects who were intolerant, for they denied catholic Englishmen the civil liberties which they themselves enjoyed. James told the Spanish ambassador that 'he would force no man's conscience, but only aimed at the Roman Catholics being no worse treated than the rest, instead of being deprived of their liberties like traitors'. He was convinced, against all the evidence, that many, if not most, Englishmen were catholic at heart and were only held back by the penal laws from openly acknowledging their faith. Once these inhibiting factors were removed James confidently anticipated a flood of conversions and a rapid, though voluntary, return of England to the catholic fold.

James hoped to secure the repeal of the penal laws through cooperation with the anglican Tories, and in order to dispel any doubts about his motives he assured the Privy Council that he would 'preserve this government both in Church and state as it is now by law established. I know the principles of the Church of England are for monarchy, and the members of it have showed themselves good and loyal subjects. Therefore I shall always take care to defend and support it.' The composition of James's first ministry showed that he meant what he said, for Rochester was appointed Lord Treasurer while Henry Hyde, second Earl of Clarendon, became Lord Privy Seal. These two brothers, James's relations by marriage, were pillars of the anglican church, and so were Godolphin, now Chamberlain to the Queen, and Halifax, who retained his post as Lord President of the Council. Only Sunderland, who managed to keep his Secretaryship, was lacking in any real enthusiasm for the Church of England.

Sunderland prepared for the election of Parliament with considerable thoroughness, sending letters to Lord Lieutenants and influential noblemen asking them to make sure that only the 'well-affected' were returned. He was helped by the fact that the remodelling of the municipal corporations had brought them under much closer royal control, and when Parliament met it turned out to be the most loyal that any Stuart ever had the pleasure to encounter. Even James reckoned there were only about forty members of whose devotion he could not be certain.

James did not wait for Parliament to settle his revenue before he began collecting the Customs and excise duties, and the Commons therefore had little alternative but to make the same financial provision for him that they had earlier made for Charles II. However, James also asked for extraordinary supply, to help him pay off Charles II's debts and restore the strength of the navy. The Commons met his wishes by voting extra duties for an eight-year period. The expansion of trade had brought the ordinary revenue to about £1,600,000 a year, and with the temporary grant James was in receipt of well over £2 million annually. Even though he used the extra duties for the purposes for which they had been granted, he still had enough money to cover his expenditure, including the maintenance of an enlarged standing army.

In June 1685, a month after Parliament had assembled, the Duke of Monmouth landed in the west country and called on its inhabitants to join him in a protestant rebellion. But his appeal evoked no response among the men of property. His supporters were drawn, in the main, from those of little substance who had nothing to hope for from the existing system and may also genuinely have believed that their religion was in danger. Monmouth led these men against the royal forces encamped on Sedgemoor, but his amateur soldiers were easily crushed by John Churchill, the King's commander, and he himself was captured, tried and executed.

The rebellion had been put down with ease, but James was shocked by the fact that it had taken place at all, and scented treachery all around him. His anger was shown in his instructions to Judge Jeffreys, who was sent to the west country to do justice on the defeated rebels. Some 300 men were sentenced to death, and another 800 were transported as serfs to the West Indies. By this savage repression James made sure that Devon and Somerset would not rise again in support of a rebel.

Members of Parliament, which reassembled in November 1685 for the winter session, were shocked by the violence of James's revenge and by the contempt with which Jeffreys had swept aside legal safeguards. They were also alarmed by the flood of protestant refugees pouring in from France in the days preceding Louis XIV's revocation of the Edict of Nantes in October 1685. In that month also Halifax was dismissed from office and from the Privy Council, and the hated Jeffreys was appointed Lord Keeper. The Commons were not, therefore, in so loyal a frame of mind when James demanded a large supply in order to increase the size of the standing army to protect him from possible future rebellions. They particularly resented the announcement that he intended to keep the Roman Catholic officers he had recruited, in defiance of the Test Act, since they were the only persons on whose loyalty he could rely. Even so £700,000 was voted for the army, but James regarded this as an inadequate sum and told the Commons that 'I had reason to hope that the reputation God has blessed me with would have created and confirmed a greater confidence in me'.

The Commons refused to increase the proposed grant. One member went so far as to say 'we are all Englishmen, and not to be frightened out of our duty by a few high words'. There could have been no clearer indication of the extent to which James had dissipated the goodwill that greeted his accession, and had turned the loyalty of Parliament into suspicion. Rather than face a prolonged struggle he gave up the hope of a grant and prorogued Parliament. It never met again.

James was not yet ready for an open break with the Tories. Rochester stayed on as Lord Treasurer, but Clarendon was sent into honourable exile as Lord-Lieutenant of Ireland, and his place as Lord Privy Seal was taken by Sunderland, who retained his Secretaryship. Sunderland was by now the King's chief minister, and the 'cabinets' which met at his house were more important in policy-making than the Privy Council. These cabinets had no formal standing and no fixed membership. They could therefore include catholics, and Father Petre, James's Jesuit confessor, was a frequent attender.

Until such time as James could obtain parliamentary sanction for the repeal of the penal laws, he used his prerogative powers to relieve his catholic subjects from the disabilities imposed upon them. There was some doubt, however, whether the King had the legal right to dispense with statutes. The matter was brought to a head through a test case, Godden *v.* Hales, in which Edward Hales, a Roman Catholic whom James had appointed as an army officer despite his refusal to take the oaths prescribed by the Test Act, defended himself on the grounds that he had a royal dispensation. James had earlier called on the judges to acknowledge his dispensing power, and dismissed two who refused to do so. In April 1686, shortly before the opening of Hales's trial, he dismissed four more. This pressure may have contributed to the favourable verdict given in Godden *v.* Hales, for eleven of the twelve judges maintained that the dispensation was valid. Chief Justice Herbert went so far as to say 'that the Kings of England are sovereign princes; that the laws of England are the King's laws; that therefore 'tis an inseparable prerogative in the Kings of England to dispense with penal laws in particular cases and upon particular necessary reasons . . . [and] that this is not a trust invested in or granted to the King by the people, but the ancient remains of the sovereign power and the prerogative of the Kings of England, which never yet was taken from them, nor can be'.

This momentous judgment, with its insistence on the inalienable prerogative, meant that there was now no legal barrier preventing James from carrying out his policy of infiltrating catholics into public life. However, this brought him up against opposition from the Church. The bishops, and in particular William Sancroft, Sheldon's successor as Archbishop of Canterbury, had welcomed the Tory reaction after 1681, since this had led to increased attendances at Church services and a renewal of the persecution of dissenters. They hoped to maintain the alliance between Church and crown into James's reign, and were therefore prepared to turn a blind eye to the non-enforcement of the penal laws against the catholics. But James's determination to secure the repeal of these laws alarmed them, since this would destroy the anglican monopoly over public life to which they attached so much value. In an effort to persuade James to change his mind they began making critical and outspoken sermons, but this merely goaded James into setting up an Ecclesiastical Commission in July 1686, with instructions to bring the clergy under tighter royal control. The Ecclesiastical Commission was not a court, neither did it have jurisdiction over laymen, but it bore a sufficiently close resemblance to the hated

Court of High Commission — abolished by the Long Parliament
— to encourage the belief that James intended to use the same repressive tactics and weapons as his father had done. Among the
first persons to be disciplined by the Commissioners was Henry
Compton, Bishop of London, who had refused to take the required
action against one of his clergy for preaching an anti-catholic sermon. For this offence Compton was suspended from his functions
— a clear warning to any other bishop who was considering
resistance.

### *James and the Dissenters*

The dismissal of Clarendon and Rochester in January 1687 marked
the end of James's attempt to achieve his aims through co-
operation with the Tories. The alliance between crown and Church,
which had been cemented after the dissolution of the Oxford Parliament in 1681, had served the monarchy well, but James was now
preparing to come to terms with his former enemies, the Whigs,
and their supporters among the dissenters. He began by making
overtures to William Penn, the leader of the Quakers, and Penn
joined him in drafting the *Declaration of Indulgence*, which was pro-
mulgated in April 1687. This condemned the principle of compulsion in religion, on the grounds that 'it has ever been directly
contrary to . . . the interest of government, which it destroys by
spoiling trade, depopulating countries and discouraging strangers'
and that 'it never obtained the end for which it was employed'. The
*Declaration* affirmed the King's intention to protect the Church of
England and its ministers, but went on to announce his 'royal will
and pleasure that from henceforth the execution of all and all manner of penal laws in matters ecclesiastical . . . be immediately suspended'. Generally speaking the Quakers and the Baptists
welcomed the *Declaration* and took it as evidence of the genuineness
of the King's commitment to the principle of religious toleration.
The presbyterians were more cautious, and paid heed to Halifax's
warning, in his *Letter to a Dissenter*, that 'you are therefore to be
hugged now, only that you may be the better squeezed at another
time'.

In the *Declaration* James had made it clear that 'we cannot but
heartily wish, as it will easily be believed, that all the people of our
dominions were members of the catholic church', and he was convinced that now that the penalties on catholics had been removed
there would be a flood of conversions. As he told the French ambassador, 'the possibility of holding offices and employments will
make more catholics than permission to say mass publicly'. James
had already appointed a number of Roman Catholics to the Privy
Council, and he now extended this to the Commission of the Peace:

of 455 new J.P.s chosen in early 1687, more than 60 per cent were catholics.

One of the biggest problems facing James was the shortage of Roman Catholics of sufficient ability and experience to fill key positions. The anglicans had long monopolised the universities, which existed to train young men for these places, and in the spring of 1687, therefore, James began putting pressure on Oxford and Cambridge to admit papists. When Cambridge refused to give a degree to a Benedictine monk, the Ecclesiastical Commission deprived the vice-chancellor of his office; and when the fellows of Magdalen College, Oxford, refused to elect a Roman Catholic head, James eventually turned out all twenty-five of them and appointed catholics in their place. It seemed as though Magdalen was now all set to become a seminary for training the future rulers of catholic England.

James had not abandoned hope of securing the repeal of the penal laws. Although he intended that his suspension of these statutes should remain in force until such time as Parliament formally annulled them, he was aware, as were his catholic subjects, that earlier Declarations of Indulgence had proved abortive. Only Parliament could sweep away, once and for all, the disabilities which crippled catholics and leave them free to practise their faith openly without fear of unpleasant consequences. James wanted to increase the number of avowed catholics for political as well as religious reasons. Since he had no male heir he would be succeeded by his eldest daughter, Mary, and her husband, William of Orange, who were both committed protestants. In 1687 James was fifty-four and could not be sure of having many more years before him. It became a matter of increasing urgency, therefore, that catholics should establish themselves so firmly in positions of influence in central and local government that a protestant successor would have to come to terms with them. It was also essential, from James's point of view, that the penal laws should be swiftly repealed, for the use of the prerogative to suspend them would clearly not outlast his own lifetime. In July 1687, therefore, James announced the dissolution of the Parliament which he had prorogued in November 1685, and ordered Sunderland to begin preparations for an election.

There would be no point in holding an election if the only result of it was the return of a House of Commons dominated by the anglican Tories. James therefore exerted the maximum pressure upon the constituencies, in order to ensure victory for the Whigs and dissenters — as well as to give his fellow catholics a secure foothold in local administration. The climax of his campaign came in October 1687, when Lord Lieutenants were ordered to put three questions to the J.P.s in their counties. Would they live in friendship with their neighbours of all religious persuasions? If elected

to Parliament, would they vote in favour of repealing penal legislation? Or, if they were not candidates themselves, would they support the election of those who were so committed? About a quarter
of all J.P.s came out in support of the King's policy, but these, of
course, included many of the catholics whom James had recently
appointed. Only 16 per cent of protestant magistrates were prepared to give an affirmative answer. Twice as many were opposed,
while most of those J.P.s who gave conditional acceptances or no
reply at all may be counted as hostile.

The Three Questions were followed by a massive purge of local
governors. By the following year, 1688, Roman Catholics, despite
being a tiny minority of the population, held fifteen Lord
Lieutenancies. Among the Deputy-Lieutenants, over 30 per cent
were catholic, as were nearly 20 per cent of the remaining J.P.s.
Since catholics were relatively thin on the ground and, for obvious
reasons, inexperienced in local government, James had to cast his
net wide. This antagonised the old established gentry families, and
one Yorkshire squire, who had served Charles II and James II loyally, wrote of his astonishment at the quality of the new Justices of the
Peace for his county. 'The first', he said, 'can neither write nor read;
the second is a bailiff ... and neither of them have one foot of
freehold land in England.'

The appointment of catholics to offices in central and local administration coincided with the active encouragement of catholic
evangelisation. For this purpose the country was divided into four
districts, each under the direction of a Vicar-Apostolic, who was
in effect a bishop. James had given a lead by opening a catholic
Chapel Royal in Whitehall, and a number of other catholic chapels
sprang up in London and provincial towns. There were also a few
catholic schools, including two run by the Jesuits in London. Despite the greater freedom with which missionaries could operate,
there was no mass·movement of conversion. But among those who
went over to Rome were prominent figures like the poet laureate,
John Dryden, and Secretary Sunderland, and it is hardly surprising
that the anglican political nation felt the ground slipping under its
feet.

While the selection of catholics as J.P.s aroused most comment,
more significant from the point of view of the forthcoming election
was the appointment of a much larger number of dissenters, for
they could be relied on to work for a Whig victory. The same process was to be seen in the urban corporations. Charles II had
shown the way, by remodelling some fifty boroughs in order to entrench the Tories in power. James went further, by granting or re-
granting charters to more than 120 boroughs, but he used this
device as a means of ejecting the Tories and replacing them by a
Whig-dissenter combination. James hoped that he would thereby

secure a Whig majority in the House of Commons, which could then be relied upon to repeal the penal laws.

The anglicans were so alarmed by what was happening that their leaders made contact with the agents whom William of Orange had sent over to sound out opinion. The Prince had been careful not to offend James, and at the time of the Monmouth rebellion had returned the English troops in his service so that they might be used against the rebels. But as James continued on his headstrong course, William came to fear that the King would be driven into increasing dependence upon France, to save him from the anger of his own subjects. William had devoted his life to fighting France and checking the ambitions of Louis XIV. He was not prepared to stand by while England became, once again, a French satellite, and in April 1688 he let it be known that if he was invited by 'some men of the best interest . . . to come and rescue the nation and the religion' he would be ready to do so.

April also saw James make a further bid for the support of the dissenters in the imminent election by issuing his second *Declaration of Indulgence*. He planned to obtain the maximum publicity for this by instructing all anglican clergy to read it from their pulpits. Archbishop Sancroft and six of his fellow bishops, who feared that unless they gave a lead the Church might crumble before the King's assault, sent a petition to James, asking him to cancel his instruction. They were not, they emphasised, lacking in obedience to the royal will, nor were they opposed to some measure of toleration for the dissenters, but they called in question the validity of 'such a dispensing power as hath been often declared illegal in Parliament', especially in 'a matter of so great moment and consequence to the whole nation'. James met this challenge to his prerogative by ordering the arrest of the Seven Bishops on the charge of publishing a seditious libel. Excitement was mounting in London, and the bishops became, perhaps for the first time, popular heroes. But before the trial began, a major blow was struck at protestant hopes. In June 1688 James's wife, Mary of Modena, whose earlier hopes of providing an heir had been frustrated by miscarriages, at last gave birth to a son.

## The Glorious Revolution

The birth of a Prince of Wales meant that James would be followed not by the protestant Mary but by another catholic King. The anglican leaders showed their bitterness by refusing to accept that James Edward was in truth the King's son. While James hailed the birth of his child as a signal mark of divine favour, his opponents spread the rumour that the baby had been smuggled into Mary's bed in a warming-pan and had no drop of royal blood in him.

Whether or not they really believed their story is of little importance. Its significance is that it gave them an excuse to disregard
the principles of non-resistance which they professed, and to take
action against James in order to preserve the 'legitimate' succession
of his daughter Mary. On 30 June the Seven Bishops were acquit-
ted by a London jury, and while bonfires were being lit in the
streets Admiral Herbert slipped quietly away on the first stage of
his journey to Holland. He took with him an invitation to William
of Orange to invade England and defend those who, they feared,
would be 'every day in a worse condition than we already are, and
less able to defend ourselves'.

The seven signatories of the invitation were rebels only in a narrow sense. They included two former Roman Catholics, the Earl
of Shrewsbury and Lord Lumley; two staunch anglicans, Danby
and Henry Compton, Bishop of London; and three Whigs, the Earl
of Devonshire, Edward Russell and Henry Sidney — the last two
being respectively the cousin and the brother of their namesakes
who had been executed in 1683 for their involvement in the Rye
House Plot. All these men were from the upper stratum of English
society and knew that rebellion might lead to the destruction of the
social order upon which their property and their liberties depended.
But the establishment of an autocratic catholic monarchy, to which
James now seemed to be committed, was in their eyes an even
greater threat and one they felt impelled, out of self-interest, to
oppose. There was little chance of success for a rebellion without
assistance from outside, for James had substantially expanded his
standing army and distributed it, for the most part, throughout the
country in such a way that it could be used to suppress disturbances. The army was officered by country gentlemen, whose sympathies were likely to be Tory, but their sense of *esprit de corps* was
strong and they might well put their loyalty to James first. In any
case there were reports that the King intended to increase the number of Roman Catholic officers, on whose total commitment he
could rely. A revolt against the King's rule could only succeed if
a countervailing force was introduced. Hence the appeal to the
Prince of Orange.

This was, in effect, the second invitation that William had received to intervene in English affairs, for at the time of the Exclusion Crisis he had been urged to throw his weight into the scales
against James. On that occasion he had opted for neutrality, but
the subsequent course of events convinced him that he had mis-
judged the situation. He was determined not to make the same
mistake again. All he now demanded was an assurance that his
intervention would be well received, but this was contained in the
invitation, which stated that 'there are nineteen parts of twenty of
the people throughout the kingdom who are desirous of a change

and who, we believe, would willingly contribute to it if they had such a protection to countenance their rising as would secure them from being destroyed'.

James was aware that naval and military preparations were being made in Dutch ports, but he was not inclined to take the rumours seriously. He had lavished money on the navy, which was one of the finest in Europe, and he had an army of some 40,000 men at his disposal. If William was foolhardy enough to attempt invasion, he would, James felt confident, be crushed. James also doubted whether William would in fact risk leaving Holland denuded of troops at a time when Louis XIV was poised to strike against it. He therefore decided to let events take their course, and in August issued writs for the general election. By October, however, James had become convinced that the danger was greater than he had realised. He now decided to postpone the election while he made a bid to win over public opinion. He dissolved the Ecclesiastical Commission and restored charters to those boroughs which had forfeited them. He also appointed new, protestant Lord Lieutenants and replaced J.P.s who had been dismissed for giving unsatisfactory replies to the Three Questions. But these measures were interpreted as panic signals by James's opponents, and the credit for them was given to William.

There was no widespread movement of revolt against James. Danby planned to raise rebellion in Yorkshire as soon as he heard of William's landing — which he assumed would take place on the north-east coast — and other conspirators had made similar preparations. The prevailing mood was one of hesitancy, however, and it looked as though success would depend upon the speed with which William arrived. After one false start, the Prince eventually set sail on 1 November and was blown down the Channel by the 'protestant wind' which stopped the English fleet from coming out. On 5 November, the anniversary of an earlier English deliverance from a catholic threat, he landed in Torbay.

The west country had learnt its lesson after Monmouth's rebellion, and there was no general rising in William's favour. However, he had some fifteen thousand men with him, and could afford to wait for James to make the next move. James left London in mid-November to join his soldiers, but while he was on his way he was given news of a rising in Cheshire, and during the week that he spent in Salisbury the Earl of Devonshire seized Nottingham, while Danby took control of Yorkshire. If James had given a firm lead, the army would probably have followed him, but he seemed overcome by doubts, and decided to return to London. The officers, many of whom were wavering in their allegiance, took James's hesitation as a sign of weakness and deserted to William in increasing numbers. Among the first to go was John Churchill, the King's friend and commander of the royal army. His wife had stayed in London, where she organised the flight of James's daughter, Princess Anne, to the rebels at Nottingham.

On the last day of November James issued a proclamation in which he announced a general pardon, gave assurances of security for the Church of England, and summoned Parliament to meet in the following January. On the face of it, William had achieved all his objectives, and indeed there were some leading figures among the English nobility who suggested that he should now return to Holland. But William had no intention of going home until the concessions announced by James had been put into effect. He therefore advanced slowly on London, and James, obsessed by the recollection of Charles I's fate, fled from the city. After an unsuccessful first attempt he managed to find a boat which took him across the Channel, and on Christmas Day 1688 he landed in France.

## The Revolution Settlement

James had ordered his army to disband, but without requiring it first of all to be disarmed. He had also thrown the Great Seal into the Thames. No doubt he hoped that the ensuing chaos would lead to a demand for his recall, but although there were popular disturbances — particularly in London, where catholic chapels were sacked — it was William who gained from them, since only he could guarantee the restoration of order. An *ad hoc* assembly of peers, former MPs and representatives of the City of London, which William convened in late December, requested him to take over the administration and arrange for the elections to go ahead. Since William was not King, the body which he summoned could not be a Parliament, but a precedent had been established in 1660 for the election of a Convention, and this was now followed. It was the Convention, therefore, which assembled in London on 22 January 1689.

In the Convention the Whigs were in a majority, but this was relatively small and they therefore had to take account of Tory opinion. While the Whigs welcomed James's flight, since by 'excluding' himself he had enabled them to attain the objective for which they had struggled unavailingly in 1679–81, the Tories were hesitant and divided. Their commitment to the principle of hereditary succession was such that they would have liked to maintain James's nominal right to the throne by appointing William and Mary as regents only. However, they failed to carry the Convention with them; nor were the Lords, in which the Tories were strongly entrenched, able to persuade the Commons to accept their alternative proposal that Mary alone should be recognised as sovereign.

Even had they done so it would have made little difference, for Mary rejected the suggestion and told Danby that 'she would take it extreme unkindly if any, under a pretence of their care of her, would set up a divided interest between her and the Prince'. As for William, he let it be known that he would never consent to be his 'wife's gentleman-usher': either he must be offered the throne or he would shake the dust of England off his feet and leave its un-grateful inhabitants to defend themselves as best they could.

The Commons had already resolved 'that King James II, having endeavoured to subvert the constitution of the kingdom by breaking the original contract between King and people, and by the advice of Jesuits and other wicked persons having violated the fundamen-tal laws, and having withdrawn himself out of his kingdom, has abdicated the government, and that the throne is thereby vacant'. The Tory lords objected to the statement that the throne was va-cant, particularly since this implied that the Convention had a duty to fill it, but William's ultimatum left them no further time for struggling with their consciences. The Upper House therefore agreed with the Lower that the crown should be offered jointly to William and Mary, and on 13 February, in a ceremony at the Ban-queting House — from which Charles I had stepped to the scaffold forty years earlier — the Prince of Orange and his wife were for-mally proclaimed King and Queen of England.

In 1660 Charles II had been restored without conditions, and the failure to balance the constitution had ultimately opened the way, once again, to autocratic government. The leaders of Parliament were determined that this mistake should not be repeated, and the formal offer of the crown to William and Mary was therefore preceded by the presentation to them of a *Declaration of Rights*. This was subsequently embodied in statutory law as the Bill of Rights, and formed the constitutional basis of the Revolution settlement.

The Commons' committee responsible for drafting the *Declaration of Rights* had divided its recommendations into those which merely restated existing liberties and those which contained novel elements and would therefore require legislation. In the event, however, the *Declaration* was confined to the first category, for insistence on the second was likely to prolong debate, particularly in the Lords, and was certain to be unacceptable to William. This gave the Bill of Rights a conservative appearance, yet some of its provisions went well beyond the statement of the accepted and traditional. For ex-ample, despite the fact that the Militia Act of 1661 had declared that 'the sole supreme government, command and disposition of the militia and of all forces by sea and land . . . is and by the laws of England ever was the undoubted right of his Majesty and his royal predecessors, Kings and Queens of England, and that both or either of the Houses of Parliament cannot nor ought to pretend to

the same', the Bill of Rights asserted parliamentary control by forbidding 'the raising or keeping a standing army within the kingdom
in time of peace, unless it be with consent of Parliament'. As far
as the succession was concerned, the Bill broke fresh ground by
providing 'that all and every person and persons that is, are, or
shall be reconciled to, or shall hold communion with, the see or
church of Rome, or shall profess the popish religion, or shall marry
a papist, shall be excluded and be for ever incapable to inherit,
possess, or enjoy the crown and government of this realm'. It also
swept aside the principle of strict hereditary succession by ignoring
James II's heir and providing that if William and Mary remained
childless the throne should pass to Mary's sister, Anne, and her
heirs.

Even when it came to the restatement of existing liberties, the
Bill of Rights did so in a way that shifted the balance of the constitution significantly in favour of Parliament. The suspending
power was declared illegal, while the dispensing power was to operate only in those cases where statutory provision was made for
it. The Ecclesiastical Commission 'and all other commissions and
courts of like nature' were declared illegal and pernicious'. The levying of money, except by parliamentary grant, was condemned,
and the right of subjects to petition the King was upheld. As for
Parliament, the 'election of members', it was stated, 'ought to be
free'; while a century of dispute, much of it violent, was concluded
in the declaration 'that the freedom of speech and debates or proceedings in Parliament ought not to be impeached or questioned
in any court or place out of Parliament'.

Two other statutes completed the constitutional settlement. The
Mutiny Act, passed for a year at a time in order to preserve parliamentary control, gave the King authority to impose military discipline on the armed forces which were to be raised 'during this
time of danger . . . for the safety of the kingdom [and] the common
defence of the protestant religion'. The Triennial Act — which was
not passed until 1694, because of William's resistance to the invasion of his prerogative — dealt with the twin perils of no parliaments and perpetual ones by providing that in future a new
Parliament should meet not more than three years after the dissolution of its predecessor, and that 'no Parliament whatsoever,
that shall at any time hereafter be called, assembled or held, shall
have any continuance longer than for three years only at the
farthest'.

The Restoration constitutional settlement had been undermined
by the financial arrangements which Parliament made. Members
were determined not to repeat the same mistake, for as one of them
wryly observed, 'if you give the crown too little, you may add at any
time. If once you give too much, you will never have it back again'.

William expected to obtain a financial settlement no less generous than that which James II had enjoyed, but in 1689 the Commons proposed voting him a revenue of only £1,200,000 a year, of which half should be spent on the civil administration. William rejected this limitation on his right to do as he pleased with his own income, but the idea of a 'civil list' remained. The 1690 Parliament voted him the excise for life but the Customs duties for only four years — another major break with tradition. The war with France, which occupied the greater part of William's reign, reduced the yield from Customs, and William had also surrendered the unpopular hearth tax. As a consequence his ordinary revenue rarely rose above £1,000,000 a year. Moreover the war blurred the distinction between 'ordinary' and 'extraordinary' revenues, for it went on so long that it became, in effect, the norm. By the time it came to a temporary halt, in 1697, William was ready to accept the principle of a civil list, since only by doing so did he have any chance of escaping from his increasing indebtedness. Parliament voted him taxes designed to bring in £700,000 a year, to cover the costs of the civil administration; all other costs were to be met by direct parliamentary grant. William, then, unlike his predecessors, no longer had control over the entire expenditure of the state. Even his freedom to spend the much smaller sum at his disposal was limited by the fact that Parliament broke it into sections, each with a maximum limit. There was no question of the King ruling without Parliament, even if he had wished to do so. The Revolution financial settlement, therefore, showed a greater realism than the Restoration one. Not only did it reinforce the constitutional provisions; it intensified their effect and substantially reduced the power of the crown.

In the religious sphere the Revolution marked the reluctant acceptance by the political nation of the principle of toleration. The dissenters and the anglicans had been driven closer together by their joint opposition to James II, and dissenter leaders demonstrated their friendly feelings by visiting the Seven Bishops during their imprisonment in the Tower. Following William's accession it was generally assumed that some measure would be passed for relieving protestant nonconformists from the penalties imposed upon them, but a group of high churchmen, led by the Earl of Nottingham, hoped to promote the alternative principle of comprehension. This involved modifying the doctrines of the Church of England so that puritans could once again be comprehended within it. Nottingham introduced two Bills into the Lords, one designed to facilitate comprehension, the other to provide a very limited measure of toleration for the stiff-necked puritan minority which rejected it. But there was little enthusiasm for comprehension either among the anglicans or the dissenters, and suspicion of William's intentions

— he was, after all, a Calvinist, and therefore closer in his religious attitudes to the puritans than to the anglican establishment — made members of Parliament reluctant to free the dissenters altogether from restraint. Nottingham's second measure, therefore, which had been intended only for a recalcitrant minority, was turned into the Toleration Act of 1689. This freed nonconformists from the operation of the penal laws as long as they took the oath of loyalty and made a declaration against transubstantiation; but the penal laws themselves were not repealed, and the dissenters, like the Roman Catholics, were still barred from public life. However, they were now permitted to worship freely, as long as they obtained a licence from the civil or ecclesiastical authorities. In the first year of operation of the Toleration Act more than 900 meeting houses were licensed, and by the end of Anne's reign the figure was well above 2,500. The anglican monopoly of the religious life of the nation had been finally abandoned, and parish priests now had to fight to maintain their congregations in the face of competition from dissenting ministers.

In its broad outlines the Revolution settlement was conservative. It did not establish parliamentary government. The King was left free to choose and dismiss his ministers as well as his judges, and he could summon, dissolve, prorogue and adjourn Parliament as he thought fit, provided he did not transgress the provisions of the Triennial Act. Nothing was said about placemen in the Commons, nor was the King's prerogative in foreign affairs brought into question. Generally speaking the framers of the settlement wanted a return to the principles of the ancient constitution. They wanted, in other words, to carry through to completion the work that had been botched in 1660 by establishing a durable balance of power between the executive and the legislature. But experience had taught them that however carefully constitutional arrangements were worked out, kings usually managed to alter them to their own advantage. It therefore seemed only prudent to build in an imbalance at the outset, to weight the scales in favour of Parliament in order, eventually, to achieve and maintain equilibrium. This was a realist attitude — though where some M.P.s were concerned a more appropriate term would be cynical. There was little desire on the part of the majority of the political nation to abandon the ancient constitution, for it had given them liberties which were the envy of their contemporaries in less favoured countries — or so, at least, they believed. Indeed, the 'glory' of the Revolution came from the fact that it was designed to preserve the constitution against an innovating and autocratic monarch. However, by choosing to exercise the power which control of the purse strings gave it, Parliament had ensured that in any future conflict of wills its own was likely to prevail.

This shift in power was not necessarily irreversible, but a combination of factors made it so. William was by temperament, as well as by birth, a true Stuart, and just as much inclined to autocracy as Charles or James, but he could not draw on those deep wells of loyalty which were available to hereditary monarchs. His wife, Mary, was loved and respected, and might have recovered a good deal of ground for the crown if she had been so inclined. So might Anne, in the twelve years of her reign, but neither of the two Queens had the degree of political understanding and commitment required for such a task. In any case the period from William's accession to the death of Anne was dominated by war, which entailed expenditure on a scale that only Parliament could even contemplate, let alone authorise. Whatever chance the crown might have had of restoring a true balance in the constitution was lost on the battlefields of the Netherlands.

## Political Parties and the War

William III was a man who inspired affection in few people. His constant struggle against ill-health left him short-tempered, and he concealed his feelings beneath a cold mask of indifference. The controlling passion of his life was the destruction of French power, and to this he devoted all his energy. Because England was essential to the fulfilment of his plan he had taken the English throne, but he had no love for the country he ruled and usually spent half of every year out of it. In his high views of the prerogative he came close to the Tories, but they could never forgive him the fact that he had driven out the legitimist King, and they could not focus on him the devotion they had given to the divinely-appointed Stuarts.

The Whigs, on the other hand, although they were no great lovers of monarchy, felt that William ought to rely on them because they were whole-heartedly committed to the Revolution and its consequences. Their attitude was expressed by the Earl of Shrewsbury when he told William 'that your Majesty and the government are much more safe depending upon the Whigs ... than [on] the Tories who, many of them, questionless would bring in King James, and the very best of them I doubt have a regency still in their heads. For although I agree them to be the properest instruments to carry the prerogative high, yet I fear they have so unreasonable a veneration for monarchy as not altogether to approve the foundation yours is built upon.'

The Tories only tolerated William because they had no alternative to him. Mary, with her charm and vivacity, was far more popular than her husband (to whom she was devoted) and provided some of the warmth in which he was so conspicuously lacking. The Tories comforted themselves with the thought that she was a

Stuart, and would be succeeded by the devoutly anglican Anne. Meanwhile, they concentrated on defending anglicanism against the dangerous combination of a Calvinist King and low church-dissenter Whigs. The anglican clergy had accepted the change of dynasty with surprisingly little fuss, in spite of the fact that they had been more fervent than anybody else in preaching the evils of resisting monarchical authority. Only four hundred non-jurors, including five of the famous Seven Bishops, gave up their livings rather than take the oath of allegiance to the new sovereigns.

William had no wish to be either a Whig or a Tory King, and his first administration was balanced between the two groupings. Halifax, who was not really a party man, held office as Lord Privy Seal, while the Tory Danby was appointed Lord President of the Council. One Secretary of State was the second Earl of Nottingham, a devout anglican, but his Tory fervour was offset by the Whiggish leanings of the other Secretary, Shrewsbury. These ministers did not form a united 'Cabinet' with a common policy. Their job was to serve the King and to advise him when necessary. Policy-making was William's prerogative, and one that he exercised to the full. He was his own chief minister, and used his Dutch favourite, William Bentinck, Earl of Portland, as the link between him and his administration.

In May 1689 William declared war on France, in the expectation that the country would unite behind him. But there was little enthusiasm for war at this stage, and the Whigs, who were in any case incensed by William's lukewarm response to their advances, spent their energies on divisive campaigns against their Tory opponents. They pushed through a Bill annulling the sentences passed against Russell and Sidney at the time of the Rye House plot and were pressing ahead with a proposal to confine borough government to men of their own persuasion when William, disgusted by such partisan behaviour, dissolved Parliament in January 1690. Halifax resigned in the following month and Danby now became the dominant figure in an administration that was increasingly Tory.

Danby used all his old arts of parliamentary management, noting of one member 'not willing to lose his place', and of another 'I think hath a pension', and his seven 'managers' in the House of Commons kept in touch with the 'King's men' and ensured a reasonably smooth passage for finance Bills and other important government measures. Yet Danby never had the full support of the Tory country gentlemen, who found the heavy land tax, levied for the war, a crippling burden. From their stronghold in the Commons they attacked the government for fighting expensive land campaigns instead of winning prizes at sea, for permitting corruption to divert national wealth into private pockets, and for failing to bring the war to a close.

Danby suffered from this resentment and could offer little in the way of victory. William was bogged down in siege warfare in the Netherlands and was unable to break the French stranglehold. In July 1692 he had to abandon Namur to the enemy, and a year later he was heavily defeated at Landen. At sea the French won command of the Channel in the summer of 1690, after the Battle of Beachy Head, and although they were heavily defeated two years later at the battle of La Hogue — which put an end to James's hopes of invasion — the credit for this went to the Whig Admiral Russell and not to the Tory ministry. Russell was so unco-operative that he was replaced by a trinity of Tory admirals, but these only succeeded in bringing the administration into even greater discredit by permitting the French to wipe out the Levant Company's convoy in May 1693 and inflict losses estimated at £1 million.

What William required of his ministers was that they should maintain good relations with Parliament so that the supply of money which kept his armies and navies in action should not dry up. Danby was at first successful in meeting this requirement, but by 1693 he was finding it increasingly difficult. One of the reasons for this was that the men he relied on to manage the Commons were not as efficient at the job as he himself had been. But Danby's failure was not simply one of management. The 'court party' in the Commons was always a small group, and flourished when the political temperature was low. When, on the contrary, members were stirred by great causes, they were less susceptible to bribery, family connexions and all the other influences that tugged at them. The country gentlemen wanted an end to heavy taxation, and the only hope of this lay in an end to the war. They blamed Danby for military and naval reverses which destroyed hopes of an early peace, and they bitterly attacked the placemen in the House who, they were convinced, were the sole reason why an inefficient, unsuccessful and corrupt administration remained in power.

Danby suffered from the effects of the Glorious Revolution, which had made Parliament more powerful but left the King in charge of policy. As the King's representative in Parliament he had to take the blame for William's actions; yet as Parliament's representative to the King he had to bear the brunt of royal anger against parliamentary criticism. While the King chose his ministers regardless of their following in the Commons, this situation was bound to recur. The ultimate solution was for the King to accept as ministers the representatives of the predominant parties or groupings in the Commons, but this implied a tacit surrender of prerogative powers which William was unwilling to concede.

The King's defence of his prerogative added to the resentment felt in Parliament. In 1692, for instance, he vetoed a Bill making the judges' tenure *Quamdiu se bene gesserint* instead of *Durante bene-*

*placito* (though he had no objection to this in practice); in March 1693 he vetoed a Triennial Bill, and in January of the following year he refused to accept a Bill to exclude placemen from the House of Commons. Altogether William used his veto five times, where Charles II had used it twice and James II not at all. This shows that liaison between crown and Parliament was not as good as it ought to have been, for skilful management of both Houses might have diverted discontent into relatively harmless channels before it reached the stage where the veto had to be used.

The decline of the Privy Council was partly responsible for the unsatisfactory state of the linking mechanism between King and Parliament. Under Elizabeth, members knew that Councillors were, in fact as well as in name, the sovereign's advisers and were familiar with her policies. Under William they could not be sure of this. The King was out of the country for half the year, and even when he was in it allowed few men into his confidence. During his absences a small committee, called the Cabinet Council, handled government business and tendered advice to Mary, but from about 1695 onwards this 'Cabinet' continued meeting even when the King was in England. William himself was frequently present, and it was at these small, informal assemblies that the decisions were taken which transformed his policy into action.

Members of Parliament knew, of course, that such meetings went on, but resented the fact that because of the uncertain membership of these 'Cabinets' they could never be sure who to blame for measures of which they disapproved. The advantage of the Privy Council was that its membership was formal and defined, but this was not the case with the Cabinet Council — and there were other meetings which did not have even the limited degree of formality towards which the Cabinet Council was moving. The confusion to which this situation could give rise was shown in 1694 when Lord Normanby claimed a right to membership of *all* councils on the grounds that William had promised him this privilege. The King, however, replied that 'it is true that I did promise my lord Normanby that when there was a Cabinet Council he should assist at it, but surely this does not engage either the Queen or myself to summon him to all meetings which we may order on particular occasions ...?'

## William and the Whigs

The Place Bill which William vetoed in 1694 was the work of the Tory country gentlemen in the Commons, and a constitutional crisis was only prevented by William's conciliatory reply to their protest, in which he assured them that 'no prince ever had a higher esteem for the constitution of the English government than myself, and ... I shall ever have a great regard to the advice of Parliaments'. This quarrel persuaded William that in spite of his high views of monarchy he could no longer depend on the Tories. The Whigs might be, as he suspected, neo-republicans, but they were at least in favour of the war, and it was this consideration which prompted the King to broaden the basis of his administration by including more Whigs — a process that over the course of the next few months turned a predominantly Tory ministry into one that was mainly Whig.

Although William was forced to abandon the Tories he did not wish to become the prisoner of the Whigs. What he needed, as always, was a non-party man who would put the interests of the crown above everything else. He therefore turned to Sunderland, who had served many causes but committed himself to none, and whose attitude to party was summed up by the observation — delivered in the languid drawl for which he was famous — 'What matter who saarves his Majesty so long as his Majesty is saarved?' Sunderland took over from Danby the task of 'managing' the placemen in the Commons, and it was at his insistence that the King eventually agreed, in November 1693, to part with Nottingham. Danby, created Duke of Leeds, was kept in office to preserve a semblance of continuity and to avoid antagonising the Tories, but he was no more than a figurehead.

The important members of the reformed administration were Edward Russell, appointed First Lord of the Admiralty in May 1694; Charles Montagu, who became Chancellor of the Exchequer; and Shrewsbury, who accepted office once again as Secretary of State. Russell and Montagu were members of the 'Junto', the group of influential Whig leaders who were wholeheartedly in favour of the war and who commanded a big following in the Commons. Other members of this group were John Somers, John Trenchard and Thomas Wharton, and they were the spiritual descendants of Shaftesbury's Whigs. For William, alliance with such men was at best a marriage of convenience, but as Sunderland pointed out 'it was very true that Tories were better friends to monarchy than the Whigs were, but then his Majesty was to consider that he was not their monarch'.

The reformed administration suffered from the disadvantage of all mixed ministries. Because it contained a number of Tories, the Whigs were dissatisfied and clamoured for complete control. At the same time the Tories were horrified that the King's government should be largely in the hands of enemies to monarchy and the anglican church. If party allegiances had been clear-cut, disputes could have been settled by a mere counting of heads, but party feeling was only one of several influences that played on the Commons and made it so difficult to control. Personal feelings about the war and about the Church were of great significance in determining a man's attitude; but so were his family relationships, his involvement in one or other of the aristocratic 'connexions', and his hopes of gaining office or a commission in the armed forces.

Ever since their emergence as a political entity at the time of the Exclusion Crisis the Whigs had drawn strength from the fact that they were an opposition party and could therefore appeal to 'Country' sentiment. In 1694, however, they changed their nature by going over to the 'Court' and becoming a party of government. This left a vacuum that was only filled by the emergence of the Harley-Foley grouping, which later became known as the New Country party. Paul Foley and Robert Harley were both Whigs, but as the Whig Junto moved into government, they moved into opposition. They became the spokesmen for 'Country' suspicion of the court, and their attacks on placemen and corruption won them the support of many Tories. The New Country party thrived on resentment at the way in which men who had formerly served the cause of Stuart absolutism were now serving William III and using the same dubious methods to preserve their hold on power. In April 1695 this new opposition mounted an attack on Danby, now Duke of Leeds, who was the embodiment of everything they feared and despised in politics, and William had to prorogue Parliament in order to prevent his minister facing impeachment for the second time.

Fortunately for the King the war in the Netherlands had taken a turn for the better, and in August 1695 William achieved his greatest success when he recaptured the fortress of Namur. The favourable climate of opinion produced by this victory persuaded him to dissolve Parliament, in hopes that a less fractious assembly would be elected. The new Parliament was not, in fact, any more friendly towards William than the old one had been, particularly as the death of Mary in December 1694 left the King as sole ruler. But in February 1696 a Jacobite plot to assassinate William was discovered, and in the reaction against this William acquired, for the first time, some semblance of popularity. An association was formed, on the model of the one that had been set up to protect Elizabeth, and an Act of 1696 declared that William was 'rightful and lawful King' — terms which the Tories, with their scruples about hereditary succession, had kept out of the legislation which followed the Revolution. Throughout the summer of 1696 fears of a Jacobite invasion stifled the critics of the war, and the Junto became increasingly powerful. In 1697 Somers was made Lord Chancellor, Russell was created Earl of Orford, and Montagu became First Lord of the Treasury.

Harley and the opposition did not abandon their attacks on the administration, but they had to concentrate on matters other than the war. One obvious target was the lavish grants of land made by the King to his Dutch favourites out of confiscated Jacobite estates in Ireland. The opposition demanded that these grants should be revoked, and denounced them as examples of the way in which the wealth of the country was being squandered while the landowners, under the burden of heavy taxation, were bleeding to death. The country gentry in the House of Commons were also prepared to join with Harley and the dissident Whigs of the New Country party in attacks on the Bank of England. This had been created in 1694, and much of its capital was subscribed by City merchants and financiers who were Whig in sympathy. These men were doing well out of the war, making big profits on the supply of weapons, ammunition and clothing to the armed forces, and the smaller landowners bitterly resented the fact that the proceeds of the Land Tax, which they paid at so great a cost in suffering, should pass through the Bank of England into the pockets of the Whigs. They supported Harley's scheme for a Land Bank, to function in the same way as the Bank of England but with its capital provided mainly by landowners. The Bill setting up the Land Bank received the royal assent in April 1696, but the scheme was stillborn. The City magnates and big landowners who had invested in the Bank of England had no intention of supporting a rival institution, and the gentry alone were too poor to raise more than a few thousand pounds. The failure of the Land Bank became just one more item in the balance sheet of resentment.

The Whig Junto remained in power as long as the war lasted, but in May 1697 peace negotiations opened and in the following September the Treaty of Ryswick brought the war to a close. Both sides agreed to return their conquests, and Louis XIV announced his acceptance of William as King of England, and his abandonment of the Jacobite cause.

Harley and the New Country party welcomed the end of the war and proposed that the army should be immediately reduced to 7,000 men. William, who realised that the Peace of Ryswick was only a truce and that Louis XIV had not abandoned his ambitions, struggled to preserve at least four times that number, but he could not win over the gentry in the Commons who, when they chose to unite — and they were united on this issue — could be sure of a majority. Sunderland, afraid of a revengeful Tory attack on him, insisted on leaving the King's service in December 1698, and this deprived William of a useful link between himself and the Junto ministers. The Whig leaders knew that their predominance was threatened, and demanded guarantees from William in the shape of a Secretaryship for Wharton. But William never liked being dictated to, particularly by Whigs. He was drawing close to John Churchill, Earl of Marlborough and a favourite of Princess Anne, and felt that he could dispense, if need be, with the services of the Junto.

## Succession Problems

Under the terms of the Triennial Act, Parliament was dissolved in July 1698. In the new Commons which met in December of that year the Tories and New Country party had a majority and immediately demanded a reduction in the army. William was so disgusted at their parochial attitude that he drafted a speech of abdication, in which he proposed to tell them that since they had 'so little regard to my advice that you take no manner or care of your own security, and expose yourselves to evident ruin by divesting yourselves of the only means for your defence, it would not be just or reasonable that I should be witness of your ruin'.

William never delivered the speech, for England was more than ever essential to the fulfilment of his plans. The problem of the Spanish Succession still dominated European politics, and in 1698 William had concluded a secret Partition Treaty with France and Holland. It was agreed that Louis' grandson, Philip, should have the southern Italian possessions of Spain, while the Archduke Charles, younger son of the Emperor, was to have north Italy. The great bulk of the Spanish Empire — Spain itself, the Netherlands and America — was to go to the Emperor's grandson, the Electoral Prince of Bavaria. In this way the Spanish Empire would be prevented from passing into the hands of Louis. In January 1699, however, while William was engaged in bitter dispute with Parliament, the Electoral Prince died, and the question of the Spanish Succession was once again wide open. It was for this reason that William decided to hold on to his crown and try to arrive at some *modus vivendi* with his turbulent Parliament.

Since Parliament was strongly Tory in sentiment a Tory ministry offered the best chance of harmony, but the King had first to disembarrass himself of the Junto without giving them such offence that they would decline to serve again, if he needed them. The Junto ministers were therefore turned out of office one by one. Orford resigned from the Admiralty in May 1699, Montagu left the Treasury commission in the following November, but Somers held on to his office as Lord Chancellor until April 1700. His dismissal cleared the way for a Tory ministry, and only just in time, for the Commons were getting out of control. In April 1700 they passed a Bill revoking all the grants William had made of Irish estates, and threatened to attaint the King's Dutch favourites. Rumours of dissolution were in the air, mobs gathered outside Parliament, and at Harley's suggestion the Commons carried on their debate behind locked doors. The King, angry and embittered, decided to accept the Bill without resisting, but he prorogued Parliament rather than agree to a formal request that he should employ no foreign advisers except Prince George of Denmark, husband of Princess Anne.

This Parliament did not meet again, for William dissolved it in December. Before summoning another he made approaches to the Tories and the New Country party, hoping that a ministry based on these two interests would be able to lead the Commons into a constructive solution of the urgent problems that had to be dealt with. In March 1700 William had secretly concluded a second Partition Treaty, giving Spain, America and the Netherlands to the Archduke Charles, while Philip was to have the Spanish possessions in Italy. Six months later, however, in October 1700, the King of Spain at last died, and left a will bequeathing all his great empire to Philip on condition that the crowns of France and Spain were never united. Louis decided to accept the will on behalf of his grandson, and there were no obvious grounds for objecting to this decision since it fulfilled the main aim of the partition treaties — namely, the separation of the French and Spanish empires. William, however, was convinced that Louis would ignore the provision about keeping the two crowns apart and would try to present Europe with a *fait accompli*. He could not risk struggles with Parliament while such a threat hovered on the horizon.

William also had to deal with a succession problem nearer home, and one that could be solved only by statute. In July 1700 the Duke of Gloucester, Princess Anne's only surviving child, died, and since it was certain that Anne would have no more children steps had to be taken to assure the succession. Only William, a sick man, and Anne, a sick woman, stood between England and the prospect of a Jacobite restoration.

By the time a new Parliament met in January 1701 the administration had again been reformed. Rochester was now Lord-Lieutenant of Ireland, while Godolphin was First Lord of the Treasury. In other words, William, in these closing years of his reign, had come to rely on the two men who had served Charles II in a similar capacity after the Exclusion Crisis. The Tories were, of course, delighted, but the Whigs could be excused for wondering why the Glorious Revolution had ever taken place.

The Rochester-Godolphin ministry was successful in pushing the Act of Settlement through Parliament, thereby ensuring — as far as statute alone could do — an undisputed succession after Anne's death. But the high Tories insisted on adding provisions to the Act which were deliberately critical of William and the practices that had grown up during his reign. As far as the succession was concerned, the Act of Settlement provided that the crown should pass, on Anne's death, to the Electress Sophia of Hanover, daughter of Elizabeth of Bohemia, 'the Winter Queen', and grand-daughter of

James I. The heirs of Sophia were to inherit the throne after her death, Roman Catholic claimants were specifically excluded, and it was ordered that in future every monarch should be a communicant member of the Church of England.

This last provision was an implied criticism of William; so were the clauses requiring that 'this nation be not obliged to engage in any war for the defence of any dominions or territories which do not belong to the crown of England, without the consent of Parliament', and that no future sovereign should leave the country without first obtaining parliamentary permission. To prevent Dutchmen, Germans or any other foreigners from playing, in future, the key role that they had filled under William, it was ordered that no person born outside the British Isles should be capable of enjoying 'any office or place of trust, either civil or military, or to have any grants of lands'.

As for the true-born Englishmen who were held to have betrayed their honour by serving as the King's retainers in the Commons, the triumphant Tories decreed 'that no person who has an office or place of profit under the King, or receives a pension from the crown, shall be capable of serving as a member of the House of Commons'. Government by 'Cabinets' was forbidden by the provision that 'all matters . . . which are properly cognizable in the Privy Council by the laws and customs of this realm, shall be transacted there', and to prevent the King from interfering with the course of justice it was ordained that judges should in future be appointed *Quamdiu se bene gesserint*, and that 'no pardon under the Great Seal of England be pleadable to an impeachment by the Commons in Parliament'.

The passing of the Act of Settlement did not produce the harmony between crown and Parliament for which William had hoped. News of the Partition Treaties had leaked out, and the Tory gentry, furious at the way in which they had been committed behind their backs, showed their anger by proposing to impeach the leading members of the Junto. But while the Commons were working themselves into a fury over the defence of their constitutional liberties, a much more substantial and dangerous threat was growing in Europe. Louis XIV had sent his troops into the Spanish Netherlands, officially to aid his grandson but in fact to annex them to France. Even a peace-lover like Harley was beginning to talk of a 'necessary war', and the feeling of the country was indicated by a petition presented to the Commons in April 1701 by representatives of the gentlemen of Kent. In this petition the Commons were asked to vote supplies to the King so that he could form his alliances before it was too late. The indignant members, outraged at this criticism of their public spirit, committed the delegates to prison, but they could not so easily stifle public opinion. Robert

Walpole was a member of this Parliament, and one of his Norfolk correspondents, writing to him in May, assured him that 'our people . . . seem pleased with the sentiments of the Grand Jury of Kent [and] think this time ought not to be neglected to make haste to secure ourselves and allies'.

The Lords refused to accept the Commons' articles of impeachment against the Junto leaders, and a violent dispute between the two Houses was only averted by William's dissolution of Parliament in November 1701. In September of that year he and Marlborough had been in Holland, building up a coalition against France, and their work came to fruition in September with the signing of the Grand Alliance. By the terms of this agreement, England, Holland and the Empire bound themselves to force Louis to accept partition of the Spanish Empire. Philip was to be left in possession of Spain and America, but the Archduke Charles was to have the Italian territories and the Spanish Netherlands. France was not to be allowed to monopolise trade with the New World, nor were the crowns of France and Spain to be united.

English opinion, which was already turning in favour of war, swung solidly behind William when, on the death of James II in September 1701, Louis recognised his son, the Old Pretender, as King of England. This was a direct violation of the Treaty of Ryswick. It was also an insult to the English people and Parliament, since it implied that they had no right to decide the succession to the English throne. It was in the heated atmosphere created by this challenge that the general election of December 1701 took place.

When William's last Parliament met, the Commons were almost evenly balanced between the Tories and the New Country party on one wing and the adherents of the Whig Junto on the other. The Tories still felt bitter over what they regarded as William's betrayal of them, but all groups, Tory and Whig, recognised the necessity for war. The King, in his opening speech, reminded them that 'the eyes of all Europe are upon this Parliament. All matters are at a stand till your resolutions are known . . . If you do in good earnest desire to see England hold the balance of Europe and to be indeed at the head of the protestant interest, it will appear by your right improving the present opportunity.' Parliament responded to this appeal, and assured William that 'all true Englishmen, since the decay of the Spanish monarchy, have taken it for granted that the security of their religion, liberty and property, that their honour, their wealth and their trade depend chiefly on the measures to be taken from time to time against the growing power of France'.

William, by treating foreign policy as an exclusively prerogative matter and keeping it secret from Parliament, had contributed to the insularity and xenophobia of the political nation. Perhaps it was because he now recognised the need to educate his subjects in the realities of power that he made known the details of the Grand Alliance to both Houses. At the very least this would prevent members from complaining, as they had done over the Partition Treaties, that they were being committed without their approval. There was general agreement among members that the terms of the Alliance were in the interests of Britain, since they offered the prospect not only of a check to French expansion but also of security for British trade in the Mediterranean and West Indies. The Commons showed their approval by voting that an army of forty thousand soldiers should be raised, and they passed an Act of attainder against the Pretender. There was no room, at this moment, for Jacobite scruples about legitimacy.

William had already appointed Marlborough to command the troops being assembled in Holland and was looking forward to joining them there, but as he was riding from Kensington Palace to Hampton Court in February 1702 his horse stumbled on a molehill and threw him. He died the following month, aged fifty-one — much to the delight of the followers of 'James III', who raised their glasses to toast the Jacobite mole, 'the little gentleman in black velvet'. But the mole had done his work too late. William died only after he had committed England to war, and the reign of his successor witnessed the triumph of all he had fought for.

# 17

# Queen Anne

## Queen Anne

Anne was the last Stuart to wear the crown of England, and she had all the pride and stubbornness that typified her family. She was only thirty-seven when she came to the throne, but youth had long ago deserted her. Anne was crippled by gout and dropsy, which made public appearances agony, yet she believed that God had given her the throne and she was determined not to evade the responsibilities that went with this high trust. She had disliked William, referring to him in her private correspondence as 'Mr Caliban', and proudly assured her first Parliament that 'I know my heart to be entirely English'. Yet she shared William's exalted view of the prerogative, and struggled throughout her reign to prevent the crown from becoming the pawn of any political group or party. One of her ministers wrote, 'she will be Queen of all her subjects and would have all the parties and distinctions of former reigns ended and buried in hers', and Anne herself described her aim as that of having 'my liberty in encouraging and employing all those that concur faithfully in my service, whether they are called Whigs or Tories'.

The fact that Anne was a Stuart was not simply a matter of interest: it was a political factor of the first importance. Since 1688 the Tories had been longing for a monarch on whom they could focus their loyalty, and who would preserve those twin pillars of society — the royal prerogative and the anglican church. Anne seemed to fit these requirements exactly. In spite of her size and limited intelligence she had a natural dignity, and she emphasised her hereditary right to the throne by once again exercising those sacred functions which her predecessor had though it prudent to let lapse. She revived, for instance, the practice of 'touching' for the Queen's evil — a type of scrofula supposed to be curable by contact with a royal body — to the benefit, it is to be hoped, of many of her subjects, including the young child who was to become famous as Dr Johnson. She also took her duties as supreme governor of the Church with great seriousness, for as she told Parliament 'my own

principles must always keep me entirely firm to the interests and
religion of the Church of England, and will incline me to countenance those who have the truest zeal to support it'.

## ·Marlborough, Godolphin and the Tories

The Marlboroughs came to power with Anne, for Sarah Churchill,
the Earl's wife, was the Queen's intimate friend and adviser. Marlborough himself was the son of Sir Winston Churchill, a royalist
squire who had been impoverished by the civil war, and he had
risen to power by service at court, where at an early age he had
become page to James II. Marlborough played a major part in the
suppression of Monmouth's rebellion, but in 1688 he led the de-
serters into William's camp. William, although he rewarded Marlborough with an earldom, was not disposed to take him into his
confidence. He may have been jealous of Marlborough's military
ability and he certainly resented the fact that the Earl was held in
such high esteem by Anne. The nadir of their relationship came in
1692 when Marlborough spent several months as a prisoner in the
Tower of London, on suspicion of treasonable correspondence with
James, but some years before William died the two men were reconciled, and in 1702 Marlborough was ready to take over the task
that William had left unfinished. His ally in the political world was
Sidney Godolphin — whose son had married Marlborough's
daughter — and while the Earl was engaged in fighting the Queen's
enemies on the Continent, Godolphin looked after affairs at home
and persuaded Parliament to vote the vast sums of money needed
to finance war on a scale greater than anything England had yet
known.

The Tories believed that with the accession of Anne they had
come into the promised land, and the first administration of the
reign seemed to confirm all their hopes. Rochester and Nottingham,
both staunch anglicans, were appointed respectively Lord-
Lieutenant of Ireland and Secretary of State, while Somers, Halifax
and Orford, the representatives of the Junto, were dismissed from
the Privy Council.

The administration was, however, only superficially Tory, for the
key figures in the government were Marlborough and Godolphin,
who were neither of them party men. Their main concern was the
prosecution of the war, and while they assumed that co-operation
with the Tories would be the best means of achieving victory, they
were prepared to work with the Whigs if necessary. They were a
long way removed, in sympathy, from Rochester and Nottingham,
who were convinced that the anglican religious settlement was in
danger and made the preservation of it their major concern. Such
fears may seem unjustified in view of the accession of so commit-

tedly anglican a Queen, but the high Tories were alarmed at the way in which nonconformists were qualifying for public office by occasionally attending anglican services and receiving the sacrament, in order to evade the penalties prescribed by the Test Act. This practice of Occasional Conformity had enabled the dissenters to retain their influence in the municipal corporations. In 1697, for example, the Lord Mayor of London had openly attended a dissenting service, dressed in full regalia, and by the time Anne came to the throne there were signs that the alliance between the Whigs and the dissenters, which James had promoted, was beginning to bear fruit at a local level. The prospect that James's strategy for creating a Whig majority in Parliament might achieve success in the reign of his daughter was more than the high Tories could bear to contemplate, particularly in view of their quite unjustified assumption that all Whigs were dissenters at heart. Hence their concern to put an end to Occasional Conformity.

The high Tories were also in favour of fighting a naval rather than a military war. Nottingham told Marlborough that he was 'biast by an opinion that we shall never have any decisive success nor be able to hold out a war against France but by making it a sea war', and such a view commanded the support of the Tory gentry, who believed that the costs of a naval campaign could be offset in part by the capture of prizes and that they were, in any case, well below those entailed in the maintenance of large armies. Marlborough did not reject the idea of fighting the French at sea, but insisted that this did not rule out the need for a major commitment on land. He was certain in his own mind that the French could only be finally checked by the defeat of their forces in the field. He also believed that he was the man who could lead the allied armies to victory.

In May 1702 Anne dissolved the Parliament which she had inherited from William, and issued writs for a general election. The campaign that followed was not fought on party lines: about half the total number of seats were uncontested, and in those constituencies where an electoral battle took place, local interests and family influence were at least as important as national issues. In the new House of Commons the combination of the Marlborough-Godolphin connexion with the high Tories and Harley's New Country party gave the ministry a majority, but not one on which it could rely, since the coalition was based on personal attitudes which were constantly shifting.

War against France was formally declared by England and Holland in May 1702, and Marlborough took charge of operations in the Netherlands. He was hampered by the Dutch political representatives on his staff, who were terrified of losing the war and preferred inaction to the taking of risks, but in spite of this he man-

aged to capture a number of important strongholds and to push the
French out of the valleys of the Lower Rhine. His success, in striking contrast with William's early failures, made Marlborough a
public hero, the Commons voted that he had 'retrieved the ancient
honour and glory of the English nation', and the Queen made him
a duke.

The high Tories were suspicious of Marlborough's success since
it confirmed their fears that England was going to expend the
wealth of her landowners in a continental war. They had favoured
an attack upon Spain, and although an expedition against Cadiz
had been a miserable failure, their self-confidence was revived when
they heard that the returning fleet had come across some Spanish
treasure-ships in Vigo Bay and sent them to the bottom. Rochester
was already on bad terms with Godolphin, whom he suspected of
being lukewarm in his opposition to Occasional Conformity, and
an open break came in February 1703 when Godolphin persuaded
the Queen to dismiss her uncle.

Nottingham remained a thorn in the Lord Treasurer's flesh,
however, since he and Sir Edward Seymour — the leader of the high
Tories in the Commons — were threatening to divide Parliament
and the country by their passionate advocacy of a Bill to prevent
Occasional Conformity. Marlborough confessed to Sarah that
though he felt 'bound not to wish for anybody's death . . . should
Sir Edward Seymour die it would be no great loss to the Queen
nor the nation'. But Seymour remained obstinately alive, and in
December 1703 the Commons passed the Occasional Conformity
Bill by a big majority. Marlborough and Godolphin felt obliged
to vote for the Bill in the Lords, since they knew the Queen was
in favour of it, but they were relieved when the House threw it out.

Nottingham continued as a member of the administration until
April 1704, when his demand that Whig members of the Privy
Council should be expelled brought matters to a head. Anne was
anxious to keep this pillar of the established church but not at the
cost of giving in to blackmail. When Nottingham realised that he
could not count on the Queen's support he resigned, and Seymour
went with him. The brief reign of the high Tories had come to an
end, and the moderate Tories who supported Harley were brought
in to fill the vacuum. Harley himself took Nottingham's place as
Secretary of State, while his protégé, Henry St John, was appointed
Secretary-at-War.

The war aims of the allies had been significantly changed by the
Methuen treaty, signed with Portugal in May 1703. Portugal
agreed to join in war against France, and also made Lisbon available as a British naval base, but demanded that the Archduke
Charles should be sent to the Peninsula, with a force of allied
troops, to try to establish himself on the throne of Spain. When

William had signed the Grand Alliance he had not envisaged giving Spain to the imperial claimant, since this would have opened the way to the reunification of the Habsburg empire — a prospect almost as alarming as the union of the Spanish and French crowns. But by the Methuen treaty England became committed to a campaign in the Peninsula that was to keep the war dragging on long after it should have been over. The Tories at first welcomed this Peninsular commitment, but when they realised that it meant a longer, not a shorter, war, they came to oppose it.

Hopes of a speedy end to the war rose in 1704 when Marlborough won the first of the magnificent victories which destroyed the legend of French invincibility and marked the re-emergence of Britain as a major military power. Marlborough hoped to avoid siege warfare of the type that had hamstrung William by an advance down the Moselle, and had persuaded his reluctant Dutch allies to agree to this. But in the heart of Europe French armies were threatening Vienna, and the Emperor sent urgent appeals for help. Marlborough knew that if Vienna fell and the Empire was knocked out of the war the chances of allied success would be slender; but he also knew that the Dutch would never consent to sending their troops hundreds of miles away from their homeland. The Duke therefore had resort to deception and allowed it to be assumed that he was preparing an attack down the Moselle while in fact he was in secret communication with the imperial commander, Prince Eugene, planning a surprise campaign on the Danube.

Marlborough left Holland at the beginning of May with an army of over fifty thousand men, about half of whom were paid for by Britain, although only nine thousand were actually British. For three months he marched south-east, following the Rhine, then suddenly and secretly switched course towards the Danube. On 13 August 1704 he came up against the French, who were occupying a defensive position by the little village of Blenheim, not far from Augsburg. In a battle which lasted until late into the afternoon the French were utterly routed. Marlborough laconically summarised his achievement in the note which he hastily scribbled to his wife. 'I have not time to say more', he wrote, 'but beg you will give my duty to the Queen and let her know her army has had a glorious victory. Monsr Tallard [the French commander] and two other generals are in my coach, and I am following the rest . . .'

Marlborough had saved Vienna and had thereby saved the Grand Alliance. He had also made British arms more feared on the Continent than they had been since the days of Henry V. Even before he left England he had been a popular hero, but on his return he was idolised. The Emperor made him a prince of the Empire, while Anne presented him with the royal manor of Woodstock, just outside Oxford, and commissioned

Sir John Vanbrugh to build a palace for him there at her own expense.

The Godolphin-Harley ministry was enormously strengthened by Marlborough's victory, which temporarily stifled criticism and discontent. The high Tories, led by Rochester and Nottingham, looked around for another hero, who could be used to dim Marlborough's glory and that of the ministry to which he belonged. They found such a man in Admiral Rooke, who had been responsible for the capture of Gibraltar ten days before Blenheim was fought. Marlborough himself welcomed this achievement. He was aware, like William before him, of the importance of naval operations in the Mediterranean, and appreciated that British supremacy there would not only afford protection to commerce but would also influence the outcome of the Peninsular campaign. The high Tories, however, managed to give the impression that the Duke was interested only in military operations in the Netherlands, and that every victory won at sea was a blow to his reputation. Daniel Defoe. who was employed by Harley as a government propagandist and sounder of public opinion, reported from Bury St Edmunds that Rooke was 'exalted above the Duke of Marlborough; and what can the reason of this be, but that they conceive some hopes from this that their high church party will revive under his patronage?'

In the winter session of 1704 the high Tories revived the Occasional Conformity Bill, and proposed that it should be 'tacked' to the Supply Bill in order to ensure its passing the Lords. The supporters of the ministry defeated this proposal, but the untacked Bill passed the Commons and was sent up to the House of Lords, who followed the lead given by Marlborough and Godolphin and rejected it. The Commons were furious, but could hardly claim that the Lords had acted unconstitutionally. They vented their anger by taking up the cause of William White, mayor of Aylesbury. White was a Tory, and had struck off many Whig voters from the electoral roll, confident that when the case came before the Commons — who claimed the sole right to decide disputed elections — the Tory majority in the House would uphold him. However, one of the deprived electors, Matthew Ashby, was encouraged by the Whig leaders to bring an action against White, and this eventually came, by way of appeal, to the Upper House. The Lords decided in Ashby's favour, on the grounds that while the Commons undoubtedly had authority to decide disputed elections they had no right to deprive a man of his vote, which was a piece of property. The Commons had already decided in favour of White, and when a number of other Aylesbury men followed Ashby's example the House ordered them to be arrested for breach of privilege. The situation was made even more explosive when the prisoners appealed to the House of Lords to uphold a writ of *habeas corpus* and order their release. The Commons had long resented the increasing power of the Lords, and now it seemed as if the Upper House was going to sit in judgment on them. Tempers rose to such a pitch that government business came to a halt, and Anne had to put an end to this unedifying conflict by dissolving Parliament in April 1705.

## The Drift towards the Whigs

The factionalism of the high Tories drove Marlborough and Godolphin towards the Whigs, but they were not yet willing to bring the Junto lords into the administration. They allied instead with the Duke of Newcastle, a moderate Whig with vast estates and therefore considerable electoral influence, who was appointed Lord Privy Seal in April 1705. The Queen hoped to arrest the drift of her government towards the Whigs, and to keep herself free, as far as possible, from party ties. She wrote to Godolphin urging him to find a moderate Tory for the post of Lord Chancellor: 'I must own to you,' she continued, 'I dread the falling into the hands of either party, and the Whigs have had so many favours showed them of late that I fear a very few more will put me insensibly into their power, which is what I'm sure you would not have happen to me, no more than I . . . I do put an entire confidence in you, not doubting but you will do all you can to keep me out of the power of the merciless men of both parties.'

Godolphin, however, although he shared the Queen's ideals, had to look to his majority in the Commons, and for this the support of the moderate Whigs was essential. The Queen had to contain her fear and indignation and agree to the appointment of a Whig as Lord Keeper. But incidents such as these gradually undermined the confidence between the Queen and her chief minister, and inclined her to look for support to other men — Harley, for instance, who wrote in 1706: 'I have no obligation to any party . . . I know no difference between a mad Whig and a mad Tory . . . . It will be very hard ever to bring the nation to submit to any other government but the Queen's. In her they will all centre.'

When Parliament met for the winter session of 1705 the high Tories temporarily abandoned Occasional Conformity and instead tried to embarrass the government by a proposal that the Electress Sophia should be invited to take up residence in England. They knew that Anne would resent any such suggestion since, like Elizabeth before her, she did not wish to be constantly reminded of her own mortality. They calculated that the government would have to choose between the unwelcome alternatives of offending the present Queen, by supporting the proposal, or alienating her successor by opposing it. Godolphin and Harley, however, aided by the

Whig Junto, neatly turned the flank of this attack by rejecting the proposal but at the same time passing the Regency Act to ensure the smooth succession of the Electress Sophia or her heir. The Act provided that, on the death of Anne, the Privy Council should immediately assemble and 'with all convenient speed cause the next protestant successor entitled to the crown . . . to be openly and solemnly proclaimed'. The opportunity was also taken to modify some of the constitutional provisions of the Act of Settlement. The clause requiring all government business to be dealt with by the Privy Council was repealed, while that which barred placemen from the Commons was modified by allowing members who accepted offices — with the exception of newly-created ones and certain named posts — to be re-elected.

Military operations had made a little progress in 1705. In the Mediterranean area Gibraltar had survived a six-month siege, and in October 1705 'King Charles', with the assistance of allied troops, had captured Barcelona. In tentative peace negotiations that took place between Holland and France during the summer the allies had formally committed themselves to the support of Charles's claims, and Marlborough wrote to the Dutch to remind them that 'England can like no peace but such as puts King Charles in the possession of the monarchy of Spain'.

In the Netherlands and central Europe Marlborough had been unable to exploit the victory of Blenheim. He always had difficulty in persuading his allies to sink their individual fears and differences and to leave him free to determine strategy. When the military situation was unfavourable they turned to the Duke for support and gave him all the authority he required, but after a victory they became over-confident and stubborn. This accounts for the two-year cycle of success followed by stagnation that prevented a speedy end to the war.

By the spring of 1706, however, a major French offensive on all fronts had united the allies behind Marlborough, and in May of that year the Duke won his second great victory at Ramillies in the Spanish Netherlands. 'The consequence of this battle', he wrote to Godolphin, 'is likely to be of greater advantage than that of Blenheim, for we have now the whole summer before us, and with the blessing of God I will make the best use of it.' As the allied forces swept south, capturing 'so many towns . . . that it really looks more like a dream than truth', Marlborough began to hope for an early peace, and told Sarah to hurry on the building of Blenheim Palace so that they could move into it as soon as the war was over. Antwerp, Ostend and Brussels were all captured, and by the time the campaigning season came to an end the allied armies were poised for an advance into France itself.

1706 had also been a year of success for the allies in Italy, where

Prince Eugene had expelled the French and proclaimed Charles as king. In the Peninsula, Barcelona held out against French attempts to recapture it, and an allied force from Portugal struck into the heart of Spain and actually captured Madrid. This gave an opportunity for 'King Charles' to turn his claim to the Spanish throne from pretence into reality, but Charles had none of the personal magnetism that might have persuaded the Spanish people to rally round him. The allied aim to place Charles on the throne of Spain came increasingly up against the difficulty that the Spaniards had accepted Philip as their sovereign, and were not prepared to tolerate anyone else. Spain was ideal country for guerrilla warfare, in which the native inhabitants excelled, and the military balance moved even further against the allies when the Duke of Berwick returned to Spain to take command of the French and Spanish forces there.

The parliamentary session which opened in the winter of 1706 saw the Godolphin-Harley administration pushed further towards the Whigs. The Regency Act had settled the succession as far as England was concerned, but relations with Scotland were so bad that a full union seemed the only way of averting a disputed succession and possible war between the two kingdoms. The Whigs were in favour of such a union, but the Tories dreaded the prospect of Scottish presbyterians arriving to sit as members of the Commons, and were opposed to giving formal recognition to the puritan Church of Scotland. Once again the opposition of the high Tories drove Godolphin, against his will, into the arms of the Whigs. The Whig leaders, however, demanded concrete rewards for their support, and insisted that one of their number, Charles Spencer, third Earl of Sunderland, should be appointed Secretary of State. The Queen was opposed to Sunderland in person and in principle. 'All I desire' she declared, 'is my liberty in encouraging and employing all those that concur faithfully in my service, whether they are called Whigs or Tories; not to be tied to one nor the other.'

Such sentiments as these were to be expected from Clarendon's grand-daughter, but the Queen was no longer entirely free to choose her servants as she wished. The demands of the war made parliamentary co-operation essential, and this could only be achieved by the support of the Whigs. Sarah, Duchess of Marlborough, who was a close friend of Godolphin, put pressure on Anne to accept Sunderland. She knew that no compromise was possible, for Sunderland (who was her son-in-law) had told her that he and the Junto had 'come to our last resolution in it, that this, and what other things have been promised, must be done, or we and the Lord Treasurer must have nothing more to do together about business'. Anne reluctantly gave way and in December 1706 appointed Sunderland as Secretary of State. But although she had bowed to the inevitable she resented the pressure put upon her, and her feelings were not mollified by Sarah's tactless observation that 'it looks like infatuation that one who has sense in all other things should be so blinded by the word Tory'.

Robert Harley did not approve of the drift towards the Whigs, and he was already establishing direct links with the Queen behind Godolphin's back. The intermediary in these was unwittingly provided by the Duchess of Marlborough, who introduced into the Queen's presence Abigail Hill, Mrs Masham. The ambitious Abigail swiftly replaced Sarah in the Queen's confidence, and by the winter of 1707 the embittered Duchess was describing to one correspondent how she never had 'the honour to speak of anything but what concerns my own offices, and in that I can't prevail — all which is compassed by the black ingratitude of Mrs Masham, a woman that I took out of a garret and saved from starving!' Mrs Masham was the friend of Harley, and through her a relationship was established that gradually began to undermine Godolphin's authority.

Godolphin sensed that his position was becoming less secure, especially when, in the summer of 1707, he learned that the Queen had nominated two Tories for election as bishops without consulting him. The Junto lords were furious, because two extra Tory votes in the House of Lords could make a big difference, and Godolphin was appalled at the thought that the Queen, by her action, might alienate the Whigs and thereby impede the voting of supplies when Parliament assembled in the winter. 'The liberties of all Europe and the glory of your reign', he reminded the Queen, 'depend upon the next session of Parliament. This being truly the case, what colour of reason can incline your Majesty to discourage and dissatisfy those whose principles and interest lead them on with so much warmth and zeal to carry you through the difficulties of the war?'

The Queen eventually agreed to make some Whig bishops, in order to cancel out the Tory advantage — thereby demonstrating the extent to which Church appointments, even under a devout monarch, had become a matter of political wrangling. The Whigs were not satisfied, however, and kept up the pressure on Godolphin, while the high Tories pursued their own vendetta against the chief minister. At the Battle of Almanza in April 1707 the allied forces in Spain were heavily defeated by the Duke of Berwick, while in the Netherlands a combination of Dutch caution and allied bickering prevented Marlborough from exploiting the favourable situation created by Ramillies. The high Tories blamed defeat in Spain upon the inadequate supply of troops, and in December 1707 Rochester and Nottingham formally proposed that several thousand men should be transferred from the Netherlands to the Peninsula. Their allies in the Commons followed up this proposal by demanding to know why less than nine thousand English troops had actually been present at Almanza when Parliament had appropriated supply for thirty thousand.

By January 1708 Godolphin and Marlborough had decided to throw in their lot with the Whig Junto. They were beginning to suspect Harley's treachery, they were exhausted by the perpetual struggle against the high Tories, and they realised that Whig co-operation was essential, especially as the Union with Scotland, brought about in 1707, had added to Whig strength in the Commons. The Junto had always been in favour of Marlborough's conduct of the war and had now openly committed themselves to the principle of 'No peace without Spain'. There seemed little reason for keeping them out of the administration except Anne's dislike of party rule — by which she seemed to mean, more often than not, Whig party rule. Anne was prepared to get rid of Godolphin rather than accept the Whigs, and tried to persuade Marlborough to serve under Harley, but the Duke refused to do so after 'the treacherous proceedings of Mr Secretary Harley to Lord Treasurer and myself'. Since Anne could not possibly, at that stage, dispense with the services of Marlborough, she had to let Harley go instead. Harley resigned in 1708, St John went with him, and Robert Walpole, a moderate Whig who was on good terms with the Junto, became the new Secretary-at-War.

In May 1708, after the administration had been reformed, a general election was held. War fervour had been revived by the repulse of a French invasion attempt two months earlier, and this helped the Whigs — both the moderates and the Junto. Many Tories, including St John, lost their seats, and Walpole, in a letter to Marlborough, reported that 'the Whigs have had the advantage very much. I believe by the most modest computation there are near thirty more Whigs chosen in the room of Tories than Tories in the room of Whigs, which makes them in Parliament stronger by double that number.'

In July 1708 Marlborough defeated the French for the third time, at Oudenarde, but was persuaded by Eugene not to advance on Paris until the great fortress of Lille had been taken. The siege lasted until December, when Lille at last capitulated, and Marlborough extended the campaigning season long beyond its normal course by capturing Ghent and Bruges in January of the following year. These victories were welcomed in England, particularly by the Whigs, but the Tory gentry were longing for peace and could not understand why, after three major triumphs, Marlborough had still not been able to bring the war to a close. They suspected him of wanting to be another Cromwell, rising to supreme power through a standing army, and they came to believe that he was deliberately prolonging the war for his own personal advantage. In the Mediterranean theatre Port Mahon, in Minorca, had been captured in September 1708, and provided an invaluable naval base, but the war in the Peninsula was going badly and there seemed little prospect of Charles ever establishing himself securely on the Spanish throne.

The Tories, who had originally urged the claims of the Peninsular campaign in preference to those of the Netherlands, had now swung into opposition to it. St John gave expression to their feelings when he angrily told Harley that the ministers' plan to raise yet more regiments 'is to my apprehension downright infatuation, and what I am glad of. They hasten things to a decision, and our slavery and their empire are put upon that issue. For God's sake let us be once out of Spain!'

As the Tories became more clamorous in their desire for peace, the Junto demanded a bigger share in the government, and insisted that Somers should be given a post. Anne held out against this demand, but in October 1708 the death of her husband prostrated her with grief and broke her resistance. Lord Somers was appointed President of the Council and the Earl of Wharton was made Lord-Lieutenant of Ireland. Godolphin and Marlborough were now to all intents and purposes the heads of a Whig administration, but public opinion was turning in favour of the Tories and against the war, and discontent was increased by the severe winter of 1708–9, when the Thames froze and prices soared.

The strain of war was felt in France as well as England, and in the spring of 1709 Louis sued for peace. He offered to accept the transfer of the whole Spanish Empire to Charles of Austria, except for those places that should be claimed by England or Holland, as long as Philip was compensated for the loss of his Spanish crown by being given territories somewhere else — preferably in Italy. These terms represented total defeat for France and would certainly have been acceptable to William III. But the allies insisted that Louis should join them in driving his grandson out of Spain if the young man refused to leave of his own free will. Even Marlborough was shocked at such terms, commenting that 'if I were in the place of the King of France, I should venture the loss of my country much sooner than be obliged to join my troops for the forcing of my grandson', yet he did nothing to moderate them. Marlborough's enemies had some grounds for their argument that he was deliberately prolonging the war, for he was prepared to go on fighting until the French surrendered unconditionally, and his victories only confirmed him in the belief that such a solution was possible. He was not an opponent of peace, but he was in fact an obstacle to a negotiated settlement.

By the summer of 1709 the allies had at last forced their way

across the French border, and in September Marlborough captured
Tournai. The same month saw the last of the great battles of the
war, and Marlborough's last triumph, at Malplaquet. But this was
a pyrrhic victory, for the allies lost more than the French, and the
flower of the Dutch infantry was wiped out. If the French defended
every inch of their soil with the determination they had shown at
Malplaquet the war would turn into a holocaust, and the Tories
were already talking about the 'butcher's bill'. Marlborough knew
that his position was being undermined, but was also convinced,
with good reason, that if he were dismissed there would be no more
allied victories. The planning of strategy and negotiations with allies were long-term projects that demanded a greater measure of
security than Marlborough could be certain of. He was therefore
toying with the idea of asking to be made Captain-General for life,
although he knew that his enemies would see in this proof of his
ambitions to be a military dictator. In the autumn of 1709 he at
last formally demanded the life tenure of this high office, but Anne
refused to comply. She, like the Tories, was tired of the war and
disillusioned with the man who seemed able to win everything except peace.

By this mid-way stage in Anne's reign English society was more
deeply and openly divided than at any time since the Exclusion
Crisis. In London there were Whig coffee houses and Tory coffee
houses; and when the Tories took over the theatre in Drury Lane
the Whigs clubbed together and built a rival to it in the Haymar-
ket. After the lapsing of the Licensing Act in 1695 Tory and Whig
news-sheets became increasingly common, and by 1709 there were
some twenty papers circulating in London alone. The most influential Tory weekly was the *Examiner*, and so successful was it that
Marlborough and Godolphin gave government patronage to Daniel
Defoe, whose *Review* now became a forum for the expression of pro-
war, and therefore pro-Whig, views. For some time the *Review* had
the edge over its rival, but Defoe lost confidence after the Whig
defeat in 1710 and left the field open for Jonathan Swift, who took
over the *Examiner* and placed his brilliant talents at the disposal of
Robert Harley.

The Tories were often referred to as the 'landed interest' and
thought of themselves as such. In fact, not all landowners were
Tory; a number of the biggest ones were Whig. But the smaller
landowners, who were dependent upon rents for their livelihood,
were almost exclusively Tory and they viewed with the utmost suspicion the growth of what they regarded as an alien 'monied interest'. The citadel of the monied interest was the Bank of England,
whose major stockholders included men of French, Dutch and Jewish extraction whom the Tories regarded as un-English and sinister.
Even the smaller stock-holders were merchants, office-holders and

professional men, mainly from London and the home counties: there were very few genuine landowners among them. The Tory gentry were paying for the war through a punitive Land Tax, and they were incensed at the way in which the proceeds were passed on to the financiers, to businessmen who were doing well out of army and navy contracts, and to the increasing number of regular officers. Henry St John gave voice to their sense of outrage when he referred, in 1709, to 'a new interest . . . a sort of property . . . not known twenty years ago . . . now increased to be almost equal to the *terra firma* of our island'.

As the gap between pro-war Whigs and anti-war Tories widened, so both sides took up more and more extreme positions. The Tories prided themselves on their devotion to monarchy, in contrast to the 'republican' Whigs, and they chose to ignore the role played by Tories in the Glorious Revolution and to blame the sorry state of the country upon the failure to live up to their avowed principles of passive obedience and non-resistance. They also identified themselves with the Church of England, despite the fact that the majority of Whigs were anglican. Religious toleration was the dividing line here, for while the Whigs were committed to it on principle the Tories were in general opposed. They particularly resented the degree of toleration allowed to dissenters, for this, in their view, weakened the foundations of English society at a time when it was already under threat from the dissenters' allies, the Whigs and the monied interest. They were also horrified at the way in which the removal of restrictions on the press had led to the appearance of a number of works highly critical not only of the established Church but of religion in general.

The deep-felt emotions and prejudices of the Tory gentry found open and powerful expression when, on Gunpowder Day 1709, Henry Sacheverell preached a sermon in St Paul's Cathedral. Sacheverell was a noted high Tory, and took as his text, 'In peril among false brethren'. The Church of England, he said, had had 'her pure doctrines corrupted and defiled; her primitive worship and discipline profaned and abused; her sacred orders denied and vilified; her priests and professors (like St Paul) calumniated, misrepresented and ridiculed; her altars and sacraments prostituted to hypocrites, deists, socinians and atheists', and he implied that this tragic decline was due to the resistance that had been offered to the Stuart monarchy in 1688. The only hope, he was convinced, lay in 'an absolute and unconditional obedience to the supreme power in all things lawful', and he insisted on 'the utter illegality of resistance upon any pretence whatsoever'.

The Whigs, who had almost convinced themselves that they alone had carried out the Revolution, took up the challenge thrown down by Sacheverell, and all the pent-up party strife was concentrated on this single issue. The Whig majority in the Commons decided to impeach Sacheverell, and Walpole was one of the managers of the trial which took place in Westminster Hall, where Charles I had defended the same twin causes of monarchy and the Church sixty years earlier. Sacheverell was accused of maintaining 'that the necessary means used to bring about the said happy Revolution were odious and unjustifiable', and Walpole, speaking for the prosecution, denounced the doctrine of non-resistance. He agreed that violent opposition to government should never be declared legal, but countered this by the assertion that 'the doctrine of unlimited, unconditional, passive obedience was first invented to support arbitrary and despotic power'.

The trial excited enormous popular interest. Sir Christopher Wren was commissioned to build galleries for the fashionable world and a box for the Queen, who was in daily attendance. Outside the Hall, the Tory mob, in what was probably an orchestrated campaign of violence designed to frighten the government, gave itself up to the congenial task of burning down dissenters' meeting-houses. It even threatened to attack the Bank of England, the visible embodiment of Whiggery and the monied interest, and the Horse Guards had to be called out to preserve the nation's credit.

Sacheverell was condemned, but the punishment inflicted upon him — he was forbidden to preach for three years, and his sermon was ordered to be burnt by the common hangman — was so light that it amounted to a victory. The trial had shown just how strong Tory sentiment was, and this helped persuade Anne to remodel her ministry. The leading Whig ministers were gradually removed, and the Queen turned for support to that middle group of moderate Whigs and moderate Tories of which Harley was a leading member. In April 1710 the last meeting between Anne and the Duchess of Marlborough took place, and the beginning of a new era, in which the Marlboroughs should no longer be dominant, was signalled by the appointment of the moderate Shrewsbury as Lord Chamberlain.

Godolphin complained to Anne about the way in which she had 'taken a resolution of so much consequence to all your affairs both at home and abroad, without acquainting the Duke of Marlborough and me with it till after you had taken it', but the Queen did not listen to him. Her policy was guided now by Robert Harley and his intermediary, Mrs Masham, and Harley appealed, as always, to those who put service to the crown and state before consideration of party. 'As soon as the Queen has shown strength and ability to give the law to both sides,' he declared, 'then will moderation be truly shown in the exercise of power without regard to parties only'. In June 1710 Sunderland, who was the link between Marlborough and the Whig Junto, was dismissed from office. Finally, on 8 Aug-

ust, the Queen sent a curt message to Godolphin, ordering him
to break the white staff that had given him authority not only as
Lord Treasurer but also as the chief minister of the crown. In September Rochester was appointed Lord President in place of Somers,
and St John was given office as Secretary of State.

## Harley, the Tories and Peace

Only after she had demonstrated her attitude by dismissing the
Whigs did Anne dissolve Parliament and order a general election.
The result was a Tory landslide, which shocked Harley as much
as it surprised him. He had hoped to build a ministry of moderates,
free from the extremists of both wings, but now he was dependent
for his majority upon a House of Commons in which the high Tories were extremely powerful. Marlborough made the perceptive
comment that if Harley could, by allying with the Whigs, form 'a
party stronger than that of the Tories, he would do it tomorrow'.
But the Duke was not entirely correct in deducing that, because the
'Octobrists' were so numerous in the Lower House, Harley, 'who
will always sacrifice everything to his ambition and private interests, will be obliged, if he is to keep his place, to devote himself to
them and to embrace all their schemes'.

The 'Octobrists' were the 160 or so high Tories who formed
themselves into the October Club and demanded the dismissal of
all Whigs from office, the impeachment of former Whig ministers,
and the condemnation of Occasional Conformity. They were also
the voice of the 'Country', calling for an end to bribery in elections
and corruption in government. They wanted a limitation on the
number of placemen allowed to sit in the Commons, and insisted
that public expenditure should be brought under the scrutiny of the
House. Harley skilfully placated this right wing by supporting a
number of measures of which it approved, but opposing those
which he regarded as unnecessarily divisive. The Place Bill fell into
the latter category, and Harley persuaded the Commons to reject
it. But he gave his support to an Act making a minimum land quali-
fication essential for election to Parliament. The high Tories hoped
that this measure would, in the words of one member, 'prevent the
monied and military men becoming lords of us who have the land',
but the Act was stillborn, for temporary conveyances of property
in the period preceding an election enabled unqualified candidates
to evade its restrictive intentions.

The euphoria created among Tories by the outcome of the Sacheverell affair had revived the hopes of all those who longed to restore the Church of England to what they regarded as its rightful
position in the life of the nation. There were suggestions that the

Church courts should be re-invigorated and that all schools should be brought under the control of the diocesan authorities. But Harley deplored these attempts to put the clock back and effectively blocked them. By way of compensation, however, he sponsored a Bill in January 1711 which authorised the government to provide funds for the construction of fifty new churches in London. He also agreed to the setting up of a committee to investigate the public accounts.

The main aim of the Tories was, of course, to put an end to the debilitating war against France, and they were quite prepared to go behind the backs of their allies in order to achieve this. The Tories had come to loathe the Dutch in particular, and believed that the war would not have gone on as long as it had if only English interests had been given primacy. Many of the smaller landowners were facing bankruptcy as a result of heavy war taxation and did not see why they should be ruined for the benefit of foreign nations. The Whigs were, in general, more outward-looking and regarded the Dutch alliance as the key to stability and security in Europe, but they were aware that it could be bought at too high a cost: even Marlborough expressed his fears that 'besides the draining our nation both of men and money almost to the last extremity, our allies do by degrees so shift the burthen of the war upon us that, at the rate they go on, the whole charge must at last fall on England'.

The Tories had only reluctantly accepted the Whig view that any peace settlement must include the expulsion of Louis XIV's grandson, Philip V, from the Spanish throne, and the defeat of an allied army at Madrid in December 1710 merely provided them with a valid reason for abandoning this principle. In the secret negotiations already opened with France Harley had anticipated this change of attitude by instructing his agent to let it be known that 'we will no longer insist on the entire restoration of the monarchy of Spain to the House of Austria, or, if we do, it will be weakly and *pro forma*, and we shall be content provided France and Spain will give us good securities for our commerce; and as soon as we have got what we need and have made our bargain with the two crowns, we will tell our allies'.

In April 1711 Henry St John was made responsible for negotiating a settlement with France, and by September of that year provisional terms had been drawn up. Louis XIV was now willing to withdraw recognition from the Old Pretender, agree to the cession to England of Gibraltar, Port Mahon and Newfoundland, and concede English merchants a monopoly of the valuable slave trade with Spanish South America. The Netherlands, like the Italian possessions of Spain, were to go to the Emperor, except for a barrier of fortress towns to protect the Dutch against further French aggression, and it was also formally agreed that the crowns of France and Spain should never be united.

These terms were very satisfactory from England's point of view. Port Mahon and Gibraltar would give the English navy control of the Mediterranean and encourage the expansion of English commerce in Italy and the Levant; Newfoundland would give English fishermen a privileged position in the valuable fishing banks; while the slave trade monopoly, though nominally limited to thirty-three years, might well be extended indefinitely. Harley — who, in April 1711, had been created Earl of Oxford and appointed Lord Treasurer — saw in this last provision an opportunity to free himself from dependence upon the Whig Bank of England and also to strengthen Tory ties with the City and financial interests. He therefore set up the South Sea Company and gave it a monopoly of trade with South America on condition that it took over part of the national debt.

English pleasure at the proposed peace terms was not shared by the Emperor and the Dutch, who felt they had been betrayed; nor were the German princes pleased at the settlement which left France as a potential menace to their security. Marlborough made himself the spokesman of the allies and it was to counter this powerful criticism that Oxford called on Swift to write the pamphlet which appeared in November 1711 under the title of *The Conduct of the Allies*. In this brilliant and savage piece of propaganda Swift built up a distorted, but convincing, interpretation of the war. It had been started, he said, by a united nation in order to ensure the partition of the Spanish Empire. But Marlborough and the Whigs had become infatuated with military glory and with the prospect of their own continual enrichment, and had turned a deaf ear to French offers conceding all their original demands. They had deliberately kept the war going, not only in the Netherlands but in Spain, where they had undertaken commitments which they had no intention of meeting. The only gainers from these long years of exhaustion were the Whig profiteers and the foreign allies who had bled the English squirearchy to death while they waxed fat.

*The Conduct of the Allies* sold over eleven thousand copies within a month of its appearance and provoked a pamphlet war more violent than anything seen since the days of the Exclusion Crisis. The Whigs were so determined to prevent acceptance of the proposed peace terms that they made an unholy alliance with Nottingham and the high Tories. They committed themselves, at last, to accepting the outlawing of Occasional Conformity on condition that the high Tories joined them in insisting that there should be 'No Peace without Spain'. In December 1711 the Occasional Conformity Bill, which imposed penalties on any office-holder found attending a dissenting service, became law, and the House of Lords passed a resolution against peace without Spain. But Oxford and the moderate Tories in the Commons closed ranks in face of this danger and were ready, with the Queen's support, to counter-attack. On the last day of 1711 Anne dismissed Marlborough from all his employments by a note which was so curt that the Duke tossed it into the fire. In January of the following year Robert Walpole, the leader of the Whigs in the Lower House, was im-peached on a charge that he had been guilty of corrupt practices during his time as Secretary-at-War; and to ensure the acceptance of the proposed peace terms by the House of Lords Anne created twelve new peers.

A formal peace conference opened at Utrecht in January 1712. The principal English representative was Henry St John, who was a high Tory by inclination but remained outwardly loyal to Oxford in the hope of eventually taking his place. Anne, however, disliked and distrusted St John, and in July 1712 she refused his request for an earldom and created him Viscount Bolingbroke instead. Bol-ingbroke resented this slight — 'I remain clothed with as little of the Queen's favour as she could contrive to bestow,' he commented bitterly — but it only intensified his ambition and his determi-nation to win power. 'I am afraid,' he wrote many years later, 'that the principal spring of our actions was to have the government of the state in our hands; that our principal views were the conser-vation of this power, great employments to ourselves and great op-portunities of rewarding those who had helped to raise us, and of hurting those who stood in opposition to us ... I believe few or none of us had any very settled resolution.'

Bolingbroke, who echoed Swift's criticism of the conduct of Eng-land's allies, felt no obligation towards them. He was afraid that military success would encourage the Dutch to raise their terms, and for this reason he sent a message to Marlborough's successor in command of the British army, giving him 'the Queen's positive command to ... avoid engaging in any siege, or hazarding a battle, till you have further orders from her Majesty. I am at the same time directed to let your grace know that the Queen would have you disguise the receipt of this order; and her Majesty thinks that you cannot want pretences for conducting yourself so as to answer her ends without owning that which might, at present, have an ill effect if it was publicly known.' He added as an afterthought: 'I had almost forgotten to tell your grace that communication is given of this order to the court of France ...'

Bolingbroke was, in short, treating the French as allies and the allies as enemies. In July 1712 English troops were withdrawn from active service, leaving Eugene to be heavily defeated, and in the following October Bolingbroke notified the French of Eugene's plan of attack so that they could take the necessary counter-measures.

This sort of treatment, combined with her own exhaustion, drove
Holland to accept the terms drawn up by England and France, and
in April 1713 the war was formally concluded by the signing of the
Treaties of Utrecht. Only the Emperor held out for another year,
until he too was obliged to come to terms.

## Bolingbroke and the Succession

A general election held in the summer of 1713 confirmed the Tories
in possession of power. Now that the war was over the succession
was the major political issue. In law there was no succession problem, since the heir to the throne was the Electress Sophia of Hanover. But Sophia was an ageing woman, not expected to live long,
and it seemed certain that the crown of Great Britain would therefore pass to her son, Prince George. The disadvantage of this arrangement from the Tory point of view was that George was one
of the German princes who had taken a prominent part in the war
against France, and he regarded the 'English Peace' as a betrayal
of all he had fought for. George was in touch with Marlborough
and the Whigs, and the general assumption was that his accession
would be followed by Whig rule.

Such a prospect did not appeal to the Tories, and about a
hundred of them, including Bolingbroke, were flirting with the idea
of bringing back the Stuart line in the person of the Old Pretender,
James Edward, the 'warming-pan baby'. The biggest obstacle to
this was James's Roman Catholic religion, especially since the young
man, in spite of considerable pressure put upon him, refused to
renounce his faith. James would return to England as a catholic
King, or he would not return at all.

Bolingbroke was not so besotted with the Stuarts that he believed
their restoration was possible without a change of religion. He knew
that the country would not accept another catholic King, yet he
also knew that the accession of George of Hanover would mean the
end of his political career. He therefore struggled for power, hoping,
as he later said, 'to break the body of the Whigs, to render their
supports useless to them, to fill the employments of the kingdom
down to the meanest with Tories. We imagined that such measures,
joined to the advantages of our numbers and property, would secure us against all attempts during [the Queen's] reign, and that
we should soon become too considerable not to make our terms in
all events which might happen afterwards.'

For the fulfilment of his plan Bolingbroke needed control of royal
patronage, but this was vested in Lord Treasurer Oxford. Bolingbroke had therefore to drive Oxford from power, and to do it speed-
ily, so that he could push Tories into all the key posts before Anne
died. Oxford, who led the somewhat smaller wing of the Tory party

which was committed to the Hanoverian succession, was not easily moveable, however. Indeed he was determined to hold on to office in order to frustrate Bolingbroke's plans.

In June 1714 Bolingbroke made a bid for the support of the high Tories by leading a campaign to put down dissenting academies and forbid anyone to teach who was not in possession of an episcopal licence. The Schism Act was introduced into the Commons to give effect to these proposals, and Bolingbroke hoped that Oxford, who had good reason to think well of nonconformist teachers, would oppose it and thereby discredit himself with the Queen and the Tories. But Oxford, although he proposed amendments to the Bill when it reached the Lords, did not vote against it, and he counter-attacked by persuading the Queen to issue a proclamation denouncing James Stuart and offering a reward of £5,000 to anyone who captured him, should he attempt to land in Britain.

Anne was slowly turning against her Treasurer, but Oxford was still in power when Parliament was prorogued in July 1714. Swift described the Tory ministry as 'a ship's crew quarrelling in a storm, or while their enemies are within gunshot', and it was true that by mid-July the situation had become critical, for Anne fell ill and was not likely to recover. Bolingbroke was frantic in his efforts to oust Oxford, and bitter quarrels took place between the two men in the presence of the dying Queen. Eventually, on 27 July, Anne dismissed her Lord Treasurer, but she did not immediately offer the white staff to Bolingbroke.

Before the Queen could make up her mind her illness took a turn for the worse. The Cabinet, reinforced by two Whig members who had not attended since the making of the Peace of Utrecht, decided against Bolingbroke, and recommended to the Queen that the Duke of Shrewsbury, a moderate Whig, should be appointed Treasurer. Bolingbroke, hoping to make the best of a situation that was rapidly slipping out of his control, headed the procession of Councillors which made its way to the dying Queen to obtain her consent to this appointment. Shrewsbury became Lord Treasurer on 30 July, and early on the morning of 1 August 1714 Anne died at Kensington Palace. She had lived long enough to deprive Bolingbroke of any chance of success and to ensure the smooth accession of George I. 'The Earl of Oxford was removed on Tuesday,' Bolingbroke recorded in his diary, 'the Queen died on Sunday. What a world is this, and how does fortune banter us.'

# 18

# Ireland, Scotland, and Overseas Possessions in the Seventeenth Century

## IRELAND

### *The Plantation of Ulster*

The Tudors had imposed English rule on Ireland by force. The problem facing James I was how to establish his authority on something more durable and less expensive. One method, which had already been tried with some success, was to dispossess the Irish landlords and replace them by English settlers, but this had caused rebellion in the closing years of Elizabeth's reign. Hugh O'Neill, Earl of Tyrone, who had led the rebellion, had been pardoned, but he and his fellow chieftain, the Earl of Tyrconnel, both felt apprehensive about the fate that might be reserved for them by the protestant English government, and in 1607 they fled to France.

The 'Flight of the Earls' left Ulster open to plantation, and the crown took over the six northern counties, confiscating most of the land and offering it, in small parcels, to English and Scots 'undertakers', who had to agree, as one of the terms of their tenure, to accept only British settlers as tenants. Like so many Stuart enterprises, the plantation of Ulster was only a partial success. Ireland was in such a disturbed state, and land titles were so uncertain, that settlers were not forthcoming in any considerable numbers. By 1628 there were only some two thousand British families in Ulster, and many of the 'undertakers' had allowed the original Irish tenants to stay on. The two most successful features of the scheme were associated with Scotland and London. Scottish emigrants, suffering from a shortage of land in their own country, were prepared to try their fortunes in Ireland, and as their numbers slowly increased they turned Ulster into a Presbyterian enclave and gave it a flavour, quite different from the rest of Ireland, which has endured to this day. The contribution of London came through the City corporation, which decided to invest money in establishing a major port in Ulster, and achieved a remarkable success by creating Londonderry.

The dispossessed Irish landowners, the great majority of them Roman Catholic, found themselves paupers and outlaws in their own country. They were, as one of their bishops described them, 'excluded from all hopes of restitution or compensation, and are so constituted that they would rather starve upon husks at home than fare sumptuously elsewhere. They will fight for their altars and hearths, and rather seek a bloody death near the sepulchres of their fathers than be buried as exiles in unknown earth and inhospitable sand.' The Anglo-Irish, or 'Old English' landowners were not affected by the plantation of Ulster. These men, descendants of settlers who had come to Ireland in the Middle Ages, shared the Roman Catholic faith of the native Irish but were not prepared to make common cause with them at this stage against the 'New English', the government officials, soldiers and 'adventurers', who, with the blessing of the royal administration, were taking over Irish estates.

The Old English began to suffer as James gradually extended his plantation policy. They were also angered by the creation of a Court of Wards for Ireland in 1622, which represented a threat not only to their property but also to their religion, since it was part of the policy of the court to bring up all wards as protestants. By the time Charles I came to the throne the loyalty of the Old English had been strained almost beyond endurance, but the outbreak of war with Spain made it essential for the King to secure his position in Ireland. Negotiations took place between Lord-Deputy Falkland (father of Clarendon's friend) and representatives of the Anglo-Irish landowners, and agreement was reached in 1628. The landowners offered to pay the King £120,000 on condition that the enforcement of the oath of supremacy was relaxed and that security of land titles was guaranteed to anyone who had held his estates for sixty years.

The King accepted these terms, and made his concessions as an act of grace. It was intended that these 'Graces' should be given statutory confirmation by the Irish Parliament, but this had not been done by the time Falkland left Ireland in 1629. Falkland had hoped to establish the King's authority in Ireland by an alliance with the Old English, but he was frustrated by the New English who were strongly entrenched in the Irish administration. These men, of whom the most influential was Richard Boyle, Earl of Cork, regarded Falkland's dismissal as a triumph and looked forward to a period of co-operation and profit-sharing with the new Deputy. Unfortunately for them the new Deputy was Thomas Wentworth.

## Lord-Deputy Wentworth

Wentworth had nothing but contempt for Cork and his associates, whom he regarded as 'a company of men most intent upon their own ends that ever I met with'. He believed that Charles's rule in

Ireland should be based not upon any group or faction but upon the goodwill of the people as a whole, assuming that the firm, impartial, uncorrupt administration which he intended to establish would command obedience by its own obvious virtues and would bring under its sway not only the Irish and Old English but the New English as well.

The authoritarian attitude of the new Deputy was clearly shown when the Irish Parliament assembled in 1634. The Old English wanted statutory confirmation of the Graces, but Wentworth would not condescend to bargain. 'It is far below my great master', he told them, 'to come every year's end with his hat in his hand, to entreat you that you would be pleased to preserve yourselves', and he insisted that the first session should be devoted to the needs of the crown. Only in the second session, after Parliament had shown its goodwill, would he be prepared to consider grievances.

The Old and New English were united in their desire to gain security for their title-deeds and hoped to make certain of this by a generous vote of supply. They accordingly granted the King six subsidies, and then waited hopefully for the announcement of the promised reforms. But Wentworth would not agree that sixty years' tenure should give security. He had good reason to believe that the crown and the anglican church had both been deprived of a great deal of land during the previous hundred years, and he did not wish any investigation into the legality of title-deeds to be held up by statutory barriers. He was thinking mainly of the New English, whose methods in land-grabbing had often been very doubtful, but by his refusal to confirm the Graces he alienated the Old English as well.

Wentworth realised that the common-law courts would defend property rights in Ireland as in England. He therefore secured from the crown letters patent giving the Court of Castle Chamber authority to make final decisions in matters affecting the Church. With this weapon he prepared to restore to the crown and Church many estates of which they had been cheated. The biggest offender in this respect was the Earl of Cork, and Wentworth had a list of all Cork's property drawn up so that the title-deeds could be examined and if necessary disproved. Some of these deeds went back to the reign of Elizabeth, when Cork had first arrived in Ireland, and the Earl fought a bitter battle, with no quarter given, to preserve his property. He was forced to disgorge part of his possessions and his fate served as a warning to the other New English landowners.

Wentworth was not deterred by opposition. He was convinced that his policy in Ireland was the right one and that it would ultimately redound to the credit of the King. He also took pride in the fact that, as a result of his strong government, Irish trade was flourishing. Piracy round the coasts was put down, communications were improved, and the linen industry was encouraged. Wentworth had a direct interest in the success of such measures, since he had taken over the farm of the Irish Customs and was doing well out of it. He condemned the abuse of office by other men, but he was not free from it himself — although he could claim that he only enriched himself by enriching the King his master. By the time he left Ireland in 1640 Wentworth had no doubts about the success of his rule there, for he declared that the Irish were 'as fully satisfied and as well affected to his Majesty's person and service as can possibly be wished for'.

The events of the next few years were to show how wrong the great Deputy had been in the estimate of his achievement. Wentworth had done nothing to solve the basic problems of Ireland. He had hoped to smother all discontents in the blanket of royal authority, but such a solution — assuming that it could ever have worked — would have needed a much longer time than Wentworth had at his disposal. As it was, he had succeeded only in angering all the various groups. The Irish and Anglo-Irish hated him because he had refused to give them security of tenure and had extended the system of plantations; the New English loathed him because he had shown up their corruption and attacked their hold on office; while the presbyterians in the north detested him because he had tried to impose Laudian anglicanism and had ordered them to take the 'black oath' to obey royal commands unconditionally.

## The Irish Rebellion

The discontent which Strafford had held in check boiled to the surface after his departure when, in October 1641, the native Irish rose in rebellion against the new settlers in Ulster and massacred them. The Old English were torn between their faith and their loyalty, but in the end their faith proved stronger and they threw in their lot with the rebels. Successive English governments had done nothing to keep their allegiance, and they saw in the growing strength of the puritans in England a menace to their own position.

Londonderry and a few other towns held out in Ulster, while in the Pale loyalist forces were commanded by the Earl of Ormond — head of the Butlers, one of the oldest and greatest of the Old English families, but a protestant as a result of his upbringing as a royal ward. Ormond appealed to England for reinforcements, but King and Parliament were in deadlock and there were few troops to be spared. Parliament proposed that ten million acres of Irish land should be confiscated and used to repay those who would advance money to the state for the suppression of the rebellion. The King accepted this proposal, but by the summer of 1642 both sides were preparing for civil war and Ireland was left to fend for itself.

The Irish rebels were guided by the Roman Catholic bishops, who set up the Confederation of Kilkenny, with a supreme council of two members from each province, pledged to carry on the war until Roman Catholicism was accepted as the official religion of Ireland. The Confederation controlled most of the country, except for pockets of resistance in Ulster and the Pale. Ormond was still the nominal commander of all the protestant forces, but his primary loyalty was to the King, and Charles was constantly urging him to come to terms with the rebels so that his forces could be transferred to England.

In September 1643 Ormond agreed to a cease-fire — the 'Cessation' — but little came of this. The Scots army in the north ignored the Cessation and subscribed to the *Solemn League and Covenant*, while the Munster protestants called on Parliament for support. Ormond was betrayed even by the King, for Charles was in secret negotiation with the rebels, and gave the impression that if only they would come to his assistance he would accept all their demands.

The Old English leaders in the Confederation were anxious for agreement with the King, partly out of loyalty and partly because they saw in a royal victory the best chance of toleration for their catholic religion. The Old English were in a strong position on the supreme council, and early in 1646 came to terms with Ormond. But in June of that year the Confederate forces in Ulster, under the leadership of Sir Phelim O'Neill, heavily defeated the Scots. O'Neill was now the chief man in the Confederation, and dissolved the supreme council. He distrusted Charles, and insisted that the demands of the Roman Catholic church must be met in full before any pact was made with the King. Not until January 1649, by which time the royal cause was lost, did Ormond and the confederates accept the Treaty of Kilkenny, guaranteeing religious toleration and an independent Parliament for Ireland.

## Cromwell and Ireland

Just over six months after the signing of the abortive Treaty of Kilkenny, Cromwell landed in Ireland with twelve thousand men. He had been shocked, like all his contemporaries, by the reports of massacres and atrocities committed in Ulster, and was determined to exact vengeance. In September he assaulted Drogheda, after the garrison had refused to yield, and took the town by storm. 'Being thus entered,' he proudly recorded, 'we refused them quarter, having the day before summoned the town. I believe we put to the sword the whole number of the defendants. I do not think thirty of the whole number escaped with their lives. Those that did are in safe custody for Barbados.' He had no reason to anticipate criticism of his actions from the English Parliament, but he made his position clear. 'I am persuaded', he wrote, 'that this is a righteous judgment of God upon those barbarous wretches, who have imbrued their hands in so much innocent blood.'

Cromwell left Ireland after nine months, leaving Ireton and Ludlow to complete the conquest. Ormond fled into exile, O'Neill died, and by May 1652 Ireland lay prostrate before the English invaders. The conquerors' terms were set out in the Act for Settlement of Ireland, which provided that every Irish landowner, protestant or catholic, should lose his estates unless he could prove that he had shown 'constant good affection to the interests of the Commonwealth of England'. There was nothing new about this policy. It marked the extension to the whole of Ireland of the system of plantation that had previously been applied only to parts, and it resulted in a gigantic change of landownership. Protestant landowners might, with luck, hold on to their estates, or at least part of them, but the majority of the eight thousand catholic landlords were expelled from their property. They were replaced by English soldiers, who accepted land in compensation for arrears of pay, and by the 'adventurers' who had loaned money to the government in order to make the reconquest of Ireland possible. In 1641 catholics had owned some 60 per cent of Irish land, but by the time Charles II was restored to the throne in 1660 their share had slumped to 20 per cent.

From 1655 Ireland was under the governance of Cromwell's younger son, Henry, who was given the title of Lord-Deputy in 1657. He worked in close co-operation with the New English — or, as they now came to be known, the Old Protestants — much to the chagrin of the new immigrants, who believed that all the established landowners, protestant as well as catholic, had been involved in the Rebellion and should therefore suffer expropriation. Henry Cromwell's aim was to restore as wide a measure of harmony as possible to the troubled island and to reconcile former enemies in support of the Protectorate which his father had established. It was no coincidence that Lord Broghill — who was a close associate of Henry and, as the son of the Earl of Cork, a very prominent Old Protestant — supported the Cromwellian regime in Parliament and was one of the promoters of the *Humble Petition and Advice*, which urged the Protector to make a complete return to civilian rule by taking the crown.

As far as Henry Cromwell's administration was concerned, it was not noticeably more effective than that of his predecessors. Ireland remained a drain on the English Exchequer, especially since an army of 35,000 men had to be kept there, and although the Protectorate Parliaments contained thirty Irish representatives the majority of members had little understanding of Irish affairs and worked on the principle that what was best for England would ultimately be best for Ireland.

## The Restoration Settlement

Charles II was faced with a land problem in Ireland even more intractable than that with which he had to deal in England. He promised to confirm the titles of existing owners and at the same time to restore to their estates all those who had been evicted for fighting on the royalist side, but as Ormond wryly commented, 'there must be new discoveries of a new Ireland, for the old will not serve to satisfy these engagements!' An Irish Parliament, summoned in 1661, passed the Act of Settlement, which left existing owners secure in the possession of their estates, promised restitution for evicted protestants, and made grudging provision for Roman Catholics who could be shown to have suffered for the King's cause. As Ormond had foretold, however, there was not enough land to meet this settlement, and four years later an Act of Explanation was passed, requiring the Cromwellian settlers to part with a third of their property in order to compensate land-hungry claimants, and ordering that in all disputes between catholics and protestants, the latter were to have the benefit of the doubt.

This solution to the land problem satisfied the protestants since it confirmed their ascendancy, but the catholics felt, with reason, that they had been robbed, and they continually agitated for the repeal of the Act of Settlement. As far as religion was concerned, however, they had much to be thankful for. Ormond returned to Ireland as Lord-Lieutenant, and although he was a devout anglican he was prepared to obey Charles II's orders and turn a blind eye to catholic practices. Roman Catholic clergy were allowed to move freely about the country, schools and monasteries were set up, and the mass was openly celebrated. There was less tolerance of dissenters, however, and in Ulster the bishops began evicting presbyterian ministers. Persecution continued, on and off, until the *Declaration of Indulgence* of 1672, which opened a new era for the nonconformists in Ireland as in England.

Prosperity helped to keep discontent at a safe level. Cattle-raising turned out to be a profitable enterprise and became the basis of Irish wealth. English commercial jealousy resulted in the exclusion of Irish cattle from England, but continental markets remained open and a flourishing trade was built up with them. Ormond also continued Wentworth's policy of fostering the linen industry which, since it did not obviously compete with English manufactures, was relatively free from restrictive tariffs.

It is possible that Charles II intended to try out in Ireland the re-establishment of the Roman Catholic church which he had in mind for England. But whatever his long-term plans, he never attempted anything more than toleration. James went much further, by appointing the catholic Earl of Tyrconnel as Lord-Lieutenant in January 1687 and instructing him to weed out protestant officers from the Irish army, appoint Roman Catholic judges, and generally repeat in Ireland the policy that was being pursued in England. Tyrconnel was so successful that when the Glorious Revolution took place in England, Ireland remained loyal — except for the Ulster protestants, who proclaimed William as King and were driven by Tyrconnel to take refuge in Londonderry.

## The Penal Laws

James landed in Ireland in March 1689, and two months later he met the 'Patriot Parliament', which was dominated by Roman Catholics. This Parliament proceeded to establish liberty of conscience, and to repeal the hated Act of Settlement. In theory the land question was once again wide open, but in fact little could be done until James had achieved control over the whole country. In April 1689 he laid siege to Londonderry, but the city stubbornly held out until relieved by an English fleet. William authorised the despatch of an expedition to Ireland in August 1689, but it was not until June of the following year that he himself took charge of it. The decisive encounter between the two kings came in July 1690, at the Battle of the Boyne, and it resulted in the total defeat of James, who gave up the struggle and retired to France. William and the protestant cause had triumphed, and in October 1691 Limerick, the last catholic stronghold, surrendered.

By the terms of the Treaty of Limerick, which put an end to the fighting, Irish soldiers were to be free to take service in the armies of France, while Roman Catholics were to enjoy 'such privileges as are consistent with the laws of Ireland, or as they did enjoy in the reign of King Charles II'. The military articles of the Treaty of Limerick were duly observed, and English ships were provided for 'the flight of the wild geese' — the departure into voluntary exile of thousands of Irish catholic soldiers. The Irish Parliament, however, once again under the control of the protestant landlords, refused to ratify the civil articles. The protestants were determined to monopolise power, and they could not do this if catholics were allowed to take part freely in public life. They were prepared to tolerate the open exercise of the catholic religion, but only on condition that catholics accepted a position of permanent social and political inferiority.

During the reigns of William and Anne Irish Parliaments passed the penal laws which confirmed the protestant ascendancy. Roman Catholics were excluded from Parliament, the civil service, the armed forces, local government and the law. They were not allowed to educate their children at universities, nor were they free to acquire land. The estates of a Roman Catholic landowner were to be divided, after his death, among all his children, unless the eldest became a protestant, in which case he was to have the entire property. These and other restrictive measures could not be rigidly enforced, but they did succeed in crippling the catholic Irish and keeping them out of public life throughout the eighteenth century. The transformation that the Tudors had started and Cromwell had accelerated was completed by the penal laws, and a legacy of hatred and violence was handed down to future generations.

# SCOTLAND

## *James VI*

James VI of Scotland, who in 1603 became James I of England, hoped that the union of crowns would shortly be followed by a statutory union of the two states. He persuaded both the English and the Scottish Parliaments to set up commissions to consider this question, but in the end the mutual distrust and dislike between the two peoples, and England's fears that her commercial supremacy might be weakened by Scottish competition, frustrated all James's hopes. The only crumb of comfort came with the judgment given in 1606, in Calvin's case, that persons born in either of the two kingdoms after the date of James's accession to the English throne should have dual nationality.

When James left his native land he was full of expressions of regret and of his longing to return, but in fact he went back only once, and for the greater part of his reign Scotland had to be content with an absentee king. James boasted that he ruled Scotland with his pen, and it is true that government was carried out by the Scottish Privy Council, acting on orders from the King. The Scottish Parliament was of little account. It met only occasionally and its agenda was prepared by the Lords of the Articles, who were, in effect, royal nominees.

From London, James continued the fight to check the power of the presbyterian Kirk in Scotland. In 1606 Andrew Melville, one of the most determined of the puritan leaders, was sent into exile, and in the same year the Scottish bishops were strengthened by a statute restoring to them revenues that had earlier been transferred to the crown. Four years later a Court of High Commission, on the English pattern, was set up to impose royal authority on the Church, and the position of the Scottish bishops was confirmed when they were formally consecrated by their English brethren. James presumably hoped to persuade his Scottish subjects to accept the same form of ecclesiastical government that buttressed his authority in England, but he moved carefully and took his time. In 1618, by the *Five Articles of Perth*, the King ordered the observance of certain practices in the Scottish church, including kneeling to receive the sacrament. This last provision caused uproar among the puritan Scots, who regarded it as synonymous with popery, and although James did not cancel the *Articles* he did not insist on their rigid enforcement. The same was true of the Prayer Book which was drawn up, at his command, in 1619. It was left to Charles I and his Archbishop to carry the battle against the Kirk into its next phase.

## Charles I and Scotland

One of the reasons for James's success in Scotland was that he kept the nobles and the Kirk apart by playing on the jealousies between them. Charles, however, pushed the two groups together at the very outset of his reign by the Act of Revocation, which asserted the right of the crown and Church to resume any lands which had been taken from them since the Reformation. Charles had no intention of immediately dispossessing all the nobles — most of whom, like their English counterparts, held Church lands — but it was his ultimate aim, as Wentworth was showing in Ireland, to counterattack the forces of secularism and greed which had undermined royal and spiritual authority. The ministers of the Kirk were not impressed by the prospect of having lands restored to them; they were far more concerned about the threat which Arminianism represented, and they began to look upon the nobles as possible allies.

Open revolt came when Charles went ahead with his father's plan to impose a new Prayer Book on the Scottish church. The Scots' bishops had been consulted about drawing up the Book, but it was never submitted to the Scottish Parliament or to the General Assembly of the Kirk. The uproar in St Giles's Cathedral that greeted the introduction of the Book sparked off a general rising, and all classes united in signing the *Covenant*, by which they swore to uphold the honour of the King, but to resist all popish innovations.

The Covenanters were organised by John Leslie, Earl of Rothes, whose family held many estates which had previously belonged to the Church, and he was assisted by the Earls of Argyll and Montrose. Charles's chief adviser in Scotland was the Marquis of Hamilton, and the King ordered him to play for time while he mustered an army. 'I expect not anything can reduce that people, but only force', he wrote. 'I give you leave to flatter them with what hopes you please . . . till I be ready to suppress them.' Suppression was out of the question, however, for Charles had no effective army, and he therefore instructed Hamilton to suspend the Prayer Book (a mere formality, since it was not being used) and to summon a General Assembly of the Kirk.

The Assembly opened in November 1638, but no bishops were present. The Covenanters had spread the rumour that the bishops were to be tried for 'crimes' they had committed, and this had the desired effect of keeping them away from the Assembly. Hamilton realised that he could do nothing with this collection of ministers and lay elders, and decided on a swift dissolution. The Assembly, however, refused to dissolve. Members allowed Hamilton to depart, but they stayed in session themselves, annulled the *Articles of Perth* and the Prayer Book, and declared the abolition of episcopacy.

Both sides were now preparing to fight, and the Scots chose Alexander Leslie, a veteran of the Thirty Years' War, to command their forces. Charles's raw levies could not stand up to such troops, and in June 1639 the King accepted the Pacification of Berwick, by which he agreed to leave all matters in dispute to the decision of the Scottish General Assembly and Parliament. But when these bodies assembled, in August, they proved to be as intransigent as their predecessors. The General Assembly confirmed the abolition of episcopacy and ordered all Scots to take the *Covenant*, while the Parliament, in which the Covenanters were strongly represented, broke with its servile past and insisted on its right to appoint the Lords of the Articles. Charles might have been prepared to accept a temporary abandonment of episcopacy, but he would not consent to its total abolition. Negotiations between the two sides came to nothing, and the Scots had recourse to arms again. In August 1640 the Covenanting army crossed the border into England and by the end of the month had occupied Newcastle.

The Scots remained in possession of the northern English counties until the Long Parliament met and drew up terms of peace. The King agreed to withdraw his condemnation of the *Covenant* and Covenanters, to remove his garrisons from Scotland and to hand over Edinburgh Castle, and in return the Scots agreed to recall their troops from England. Charles was now hoping to gain a party for himself in Scotland, and on his visit there in 1641 he tried to win over his former opponents by distributing honours among them. Argyll, for example, was made a marquis, while Alexander Leslie, the Scottish commander, was created Earl of Leven. This policy of conciliation did not, however, pay off. The Covenanters were very powerful and not disposed to put their trust in Charles's apparent change of heart. Montrose, it is true, was anxious for a reconciliation with the King, but he was outmanoeuvred by Argyll who, in spite of his marquisate, was using all his influence to cement the coalition against Charles.

The Covenanters were far more likely to support Parliament than the King, but after sparking off the civil war they held aloof until the closing months of 1643. Their aim was to establish presbyterianism in England, thereby giving themselves the sort of religious security that Charles had tried to obtain by imposing episcopacy on Scotland, but the Long Parliament, having just thrown off one ecclesiastical despotism, was unwilling to subject itself to another. English puritans had never wholeheartedly accepted the political implications of Calvinism, and preferred an erastian settlement to any form of theocracy. They were only persuaded to make an agreement with the Scots after Charles had come within an ace of winning the civil war. The Scots were confidently awaiting the plea for help that Pym made shortly before his death, convinced that God had used the weapon of defeat to bring the English to their senses. For them the *Solemn League and Covenant* was the first step in the creation of a presbyterian England, but for Vane and many other members of the Long Parliament it was mainly a military alliance, with doctrinal undertones that were best left undiscussed.

A Scottish Covenanting army, under the Earl of Leven, invaded England early in 1644 and played a major part in the campaign that eventually brought Charles I to defeat. But while the Covenanters were marching south, Montrose, now completely disillusioned with his fellow-rebels, raised a rebellion in the highlands and won a series of astonishing victories. If Charles could ever have reached him or could have sent troops to him from Ireland, defeat would have been staved off, but the war in England was going too badly for any men to be spared, and Montrose had to fight alone. His luck and his skill enabled him to survive until September 1645, but in that month he was heavily defeated at Philiphaugh and had to flee to the Continent.

## Cromwell and Scotland

The Scots failed to come to terms with Charles I, after he surrendered himself to them in 1646, and eventually handed him over to Parliament. But they had sworn, in the *Covenant*, to protect the honour and person of the King, and became increasingly alarmed by the news which reached them from England. When Charles escaped from the army and fled to Carisbrooke they were ready to open negotiations with him again, and the King eventually agreed to accept presbyterianism for three years in return for Scots' support. This 'Engagement', as it was called, led at last to Scottish intervention on the King's side, but the Covenanters still distrusted Charles and were unwilling to give him their full assistance unless and until he took the *Covenant*. The 'Engagers', unable to depend upon the Covenanting army, had to raise their own troops, and it was their force, badly trained and badly led, which Cromwell swept away at the battle of Preston in August 1648.

A year later, however, Covenanters and Engagers had united against England. They were shocked by the execution of Charles I and by the failure of the republican government to establish presbyterianism in England, and when Charles II agreed to accept the *Covenant* they proclaimed him King. It was an unhappy alliance. Charles had to abandon Montrose to the revengeful fury of the Covenanters, who executed him, and he was plagued by Scottish divines anxious to probe into the secrets of his soul and assure themselves that his 'conversion' was genuine. In fact it was far from genuine, but Charles preferred a Covenanting crown to no crown at all, and the Scots were quite confident that, with the Lord on their side, they would humble the proud Parliament and at last impose 'the godly religion' on England.

Their certainty, their self-confidence and their hopes were shattered at Dunbar. They had appealed to the Lord and the Lord had spoken! The defeat at Worcester, which came a year later in September 1651, merely confirmed the verdict. Scotland was now, like Ireland, prostrate before the English invader, and the conquest that Cromwell had started was completed by General Monck.

During the Interregnum, Scotland remained under military rule, and although it was formally integrated into the united republic which Cromwell established, the thirty Scottish representatives who sat at Westminster were in fact the nominees of the army. Cromwell left the presbyterians undisturbed in their worship, but insisted that toleration should be shown towards the sects. The ministers of the Kirk did not thank him for his lack of fanaticism, and opposition to the Protectorate was increased by the heavy taxation needed to maintain the army. Monck observed in 1657 that 'the Scots are now as malignant as ever they were', and the Restoration was welcomed in Edinburgh as in London.

## The Restoration Settlement

The short-lived union of England and Scotland was ended in 1661, as was freedom of trade between the two countries, and presbyterians were once again subjected to persecution. The bishops returned, conventicles were forbidden, and illegal assemblies were put down by force. The Scottish Parliament could offer no resistance to these measures because it was once again under the control of crown-appointed Lords of the Articles, and after formally annulling all the legislation of the Interregnum and voting the King a considerable annual revenue, it was dissolved. Scotland was henceforward ruled by the Privy Council, under the direction of the King's commissioner in Edinburgh.

The policy of repressing the puritans lasted until 1666, when it provoked the Pentland Rising. This minor rebellion was easily put down, but it persuaded Charles to abandon persecution and to accept Lauderdale's proposals for increasing toleration. Lauderdale, who was Secretary for Scotland throughout the greater part of Charles's reign, was a former presbyterian, and he wanted to put an end to religious and factional strife by elevating royal authority, as Wentworth had done in Ireland forty years earlier. The *Letter of Indulgence* of 1669 allowed ejected ministers to return to their livings, as long as they agreed to accept episcopacy, and the number of conventicles increased. But Lauderdale, who had hoped to quieten passions by a policy of toleration, was alarmed to find that he had opened the way to a revival of the power of the Kirk. Rather than risk a renewed challenge to royal authority he began repression once again. In 1670 a new Act against conventicles was passed, and in the years that followed troops were once more employed to suppress illegal assemblies. The Covenanters, despairing of any improvement in their condition, rose in rebellion in 1678 and murdered James Sharp, the oppressive Archbishop of St Andrews. But they had no clear plan, their hastily raised army was no match for the trained English troops, and they were crushed by Monmouth at the Battle of Bothwell Bridge in May 1679.

Monmouth persuaded his father to get rid of Lauderdale and to be lenient in his treatment of the rebels, but Lauderdale was succeeded by James, Duke of York, who immediately brought the machinery of government under close control. All officials were required to renounce the *Covenant* and to take an oath of non-resistance. The opponents of James's policy had to choose between suffering in silence or emigrating, except in the south-west of the country, where perpetual guerrilla warfare was waged between English troops and dissident Cameronians.

The success of James's rule in Scotland was shown by the fact that when he became King in 1685 an attempted revolt against him, led by Argyll (the son of the first marquis, who had been executed after the Restoration), was easily put down. Even James's policy of toleration for Roman Catholics aroused little protest, since the dissenters also profited by it. Scotland took no part in the Glorious Revolution, and not until February 1689 did a Convention of Estates, meeting at William's invitation, recognise the new English sovereigns as rulers of Scotland.

## Scotland and the Glorious Revolution

Although the Scots had not joined in expelling James, they took advantage of the Revolution to secure their religious and constitutional liberties. The *Claim of Right* went further than the English Bill of Rights by asserting that Parliament was justified in deposing any ruler who violated the law, and when the Convention was formally declared a Parliament it forced William to agree that the Lords of the Articles should be abolished. As for the Church, episcopacy was abandoned, ministers who had been ejected by the Stuarts were restored, and a General Assembly of the Kirk was summoned for the first time since 1653. The contrast between the treatment of Scotland and of Ireland could not have been greater. In Scotland the Revolution marked the triumph of all the Scots had struggled for, whereas in Ireland it meant defeat and humiliation for the Roman Catholic population. The key to the differences lies in the fact that Scottish puritanism had never affronted English susceptibilities in the same way as Irish catholicism, and there had been no attempt to establish plantations in Scotland. While Ireland had been divided by Tudor and Stuart rule, Scotland had remained united.

Although the accession of William and Mary had been accepted by the greater part of Scotland, the Jacobites found many supporters among the highlanders, and in July 1689 they defeated William's troops at Killiecrankie. But the rebels could not hold together for a long campaign and by 1690 the pacification of the highlands was well under way, with Fort William being constructed as a base from which to complete operations. Highland chiefs were offered a free pardon if they made their submission to William, but some of the King's advisers felt that an example should be made of one of the more recalcitrant clans, to overawe the others. The Macdonalds of Glencoe were chosen as victims and in February 1692 troops from Fort William, who had been billeted on the Macdonalds, suddenly turned on their hosts and murdered them. Many of the intended victims escaped, but the chief and thirty of his followers were slaughtered. It is doubtful whether William himself had any knowledge of what was intended, but the Massacre of Glencoe poisoned relations between him and his Scottish subjects.

Bad feeling was also stirred up by the Navigation Acts, which treated the Scots as foreigners where trade was concerned. Scotland was not rich in natural resources, but in the face of English jealousy Scottish merchants looked to their own salvation. In 1695 a Bank of Scotland was successfully created, and in the same year the Scottish Parliament authorised the establishment of a company to trade with Africa and the Indies. It was hoped that this company would be a joint venture between England and Scotland, for many English merchants who were excluded from trade with the orient by the monopoly of the East India Company hoped to find an outlet for their capital and enterprise in the Scottish venture. The English Parliament took up the question, however, inspired not so much by love of the East India Company as by fear of Scottish competition, and threats of impeachment persuaded English merchants to pull out of the scheme.

The Scots, smarting under a sense of betrayal, decided to go ahead on their own. About £200,000 was raised by a national effort, and it was decided to send an expedition to establish a settlement at Darien, on the Isthmus of Panama. This plan was foolhardy, in face of the terrible climate and of the fact that Darien was claimed by the Spaniards. William was engaged in complicated diplomacy over the Spanish succession, and the last thing he wanted was an overt act of hostility against Spain. He therefore instructed neighbouring English colonies to give no assistance to the Scottish venture, and by April 1700, after three expeditions had been decimated by disease and Spanish opposition, the Scots gave up. The money which had been subscribed, and which had meant a heavy sacrifice for a poor country like Scotland, had been dissipated without result, and the Scots put the blame for their failure firmly on England.

## The Union

The Darien fiasco had shown up the weakness of William's position. As King of England he was opposed to the project, while as King of Scotland he might have been expected to support it. The only way in which to prevent the re-emergence of this split personality was to unite the legislatures of the two countries, but William died before he could accomplish this. Anne continued his work and immediately appointed commissioners to treat for union, but little progress was made, for the English were determined to keep the Scots out of their commercial empire, and negotiations were eventually broken off. The Scottish Parliament showed its anger against this unfriendly treatment by emphasising the isolation thrust upon Scotland. By the Act anent Peace and War, passed in 1703, it declared that Scotland should not be automatically committed to war or peace by English policies, but should arrive at her own decisions. In the following year the Act of Security laid down that Scotland would not accept the Hanoverian Succession unless her constitutional, economic and religious liberties were guaranteed.

The English Parliament riposted with the Aliens Act, ordering that all Scots were to be treated as foreigners and that trade between the two countries was to come to an end. But the prospect of a Hanoverian successor arriving in England at the same time as the Old Pretender landed, with a French army, in Scotland, was more than English ministers could bear. The Aliens Act had already opened the way to a solution by providing that its terms should not come into effect if the Scottish Parliament appointed commissioners to treat for union. This invitation was taken up, terms were swiftly agreed, and in 1707 England and Scotland were formally combined into Great Britain.

The Union confirmed the Hanoverian succession. It also opened the trade of England to all British subjects, which meant that Scottish landowners and merchants now had access to the largest free-trade area in Europe for their corn, cattle, linen, coal and salt. Further concessions to the Scots included the right to keep their own established presbyterian church, their own law, and, for a time, their own Privy Council. They lost their separate Parliament, but were compensated for this by being allotted forty-five newly-created seats in the Lower House of the United Kingdom Parliament as well as sixteen in the Upper. The Scots agreed to share the burden of the national debt, but in return they received a lump sum of £400,000, to be used to compensate those who had suffered from the Darien disaster — thereby removing, it was hoped, at least one source of Anglo-Scottish hostility.

The English government was generous in its offers of places and pensions to the Scottish nobles, and opponents of the Union north of the border claimed that it had only been made possible by massive bribery. Yet the terms of the Union took generous account of Scottish desires and sensibilities, which hardly suggests that the English negotiators believed they were dealing with servile pensioners whose views could be discounted. The Union did not, of course, put an immediate end to friction between the two countries and peoples. The period of Tory rule at the end of Anne's reign placed severe strains on the new relationship, since the government insisted on restoring the rights of lay patrons in Scotland and permitting episcopal worship there. Bitterness reached such a peak that in 1713 a motion to dissolve the Union was only narrowly defeated in the House of Lords, but the following year saw the triumph of the Whigs, who had framed the original agreement and were determined to maintain the Union. It has survived to the present day, bringing incalculable advantages to both sides and showing that the politicians of Anne's reign could act with far-sighted generosity when self-interest and protestantism combined.

# OVERSEAS POSSESSIONS
## *Virginia*

Elizabethan attempts to found a colonial empire failed because they
were given only a low priority. The resources which might have
enabled infant settlemens to survive were consumed in privateering
expeditions and other activities which, it was assumed, would yield
a swifter and more profitable return, However, the accession of
James I to the throne was followed by the conclusion of peace with
Spain and a ban on privateering. This released resources for renewed attempts to establish plantations overseas. These were commercial ventures, inspired in part by economic nationalism, for it
was hoped that the colonies might make England self-sufficient by
producing the naval stores and 'Mediterranean' goods which she
could not produce herself. Settlers were not easy to come by at first,
but the economic depression which set in about 1620 created unemployment and acted as a spur to emigration; so also did the persecution of the puritans, which became more severe after Laud's
rise to power.

The first big attempt at colonisation in the Stuart period was
directed towards Virginia, where Ralegh had pointed the way.
Ralegh sold his patent for colonising Virginia to a group of London
business men who included Sir Thomas Smythe, son of a Customs
farmer and himself a prominent member of the Merchant Adventurers, the Levant Company and the Muscovy Company. Smythe
was the moving spirit behind the formation of the Virginia Company in 1606, and it was as a result of his efforts that in December
of that year three ships, the *Susan Constant, Godspeed* and *Discovery*,
set sail from London, carrying almost a hundred and fifty settlers.
They arrived in Chesapeake Bay in May 1607, sailed up the river
which they named after King James, and established a settlement
at the site which was eventually to become Jamestown.

For many years the future of the colony hung in the balance. The
swampy site and hostile Indians accounted for many deaths, and
the settlers were dependent on the supplies which reached them
from England. A royal Council of Virginia had been set up in England during the first flush of enthusiasm, but as it became clear that
no easy fortunes were going to be made the King lost interest, and
in 1609 he issued a new charter making the Virginia Company the
proprietors of the colony.

Money for the venture came from 'adventurers' who bought
shares in the company; the cost of transportation was paid either
by the settlers themselves, who were then free to start up their own
farms as soon as they arrived, or by the company, in which case
the assisted person had to agree to work for the community for a
number of years. By 1617 the colony was firmly established, and

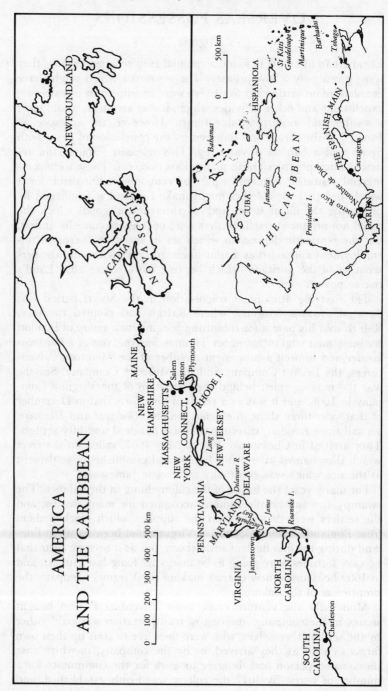

had made tobacco its staple crop. Unfortunately for the company the habit of smoking developed only slowly and met with the disapproval of the King. Profits were never sufficient to repay adventurers the money they had invested, and new capital was consequently hard to attract. Smythe was unpopular with many of the shareholders, who blamed him for the lack of profits, and he was also opposed by some of the leaders of parliamentary opinion, who saw in Virginia a chance to put their own principles into practice. By 1619 Smythe had been pushed out of office and Sir Edwin Sandys, that doughty champion of the privileges of the House of Commons, became Treasurer in his place.

Sandys' rule lasted only a few years, but it led to the summoning of the first representative body ever to meet on American soil. The general assembly of Virginia, elected by the settlers themselves, met in July 1619 and again the following year, and this movement towards self-government, which Sandys had encouraged, survived his fall. In 1624, after complaints that the administration of the Virginia Company was more concerned with politics than commerce, the crown confiscated the company's charter and assumed direct control itself. A royal governor was despatched, but he had orders to continue summoning the representative assembly, and it was also made clear that settlers, being under the authority of the English crown, were to enjoy the law and liberties that belonged to Englishmen at home.

## New England

Just over a year after the little fleet had sailed from London for Virginia, a group of Nottinghamshire puritans, who could not find it in their consciences to give outward conformity to the practices of the Church of England, emigrated to Holland and there established a spiritual community. But in spite of the tolerance that Holland offered, they missed their native land and hoped that they might one day be able to live, if not in England, at least among Englishmen. The Virginia Company, prompted by Sandys, gave them a licence to settle in the New World, a joint-stock company was set up, and in September 1620 the Pilgrim Fathers set sail from Plymouth in the *Mayflower*. Out of more than a hundred passengers only thirty-five were members of the original separatist congregation: the rest of the emigrants had come direct from England and did not all share the puritan attitudes of their colleagues. No provision had been made for the separate government of this community, since it was assumed that it would come under the jurisdiction of the authorities in Virginia, but just in case the emigrants should land in an unknown region their leaders drew up the *Mayflower Compact*, providing for the making of laws and the estab-

lishment of a civil administration. It was as well they did so, for
the Pilgrim Fathers landed well to the north of Virginia and had
to establish an isolated settlement at Plymouth. They managed to
survive, though conditions were hard, and by sending corn, timber
and furs to England they made sufficient profits to buy out the
home-based shareholders. By this means they created the first self-
contained, self-governing English community in America.

The Pilgrim Fathers had begun the colonisation of New England
and in 1629 they were followed by another puritan congregation,
which had obtained a separate charter for itself as the 'Company
of the Massachusetts Bay'. These new settlers founded Salem, and
they shortly copied the example of the Plymouth settlers by deciding
that 'the whole government, together with the patent for the said
plantation, be ... legally transferred and established to remain
with us and others which shall inhabit upon the said plantation'.
In 1630 John Winthrop, elected governor of the company and colony, set sail for Salem, taking with him not only the charter itself
but a thousand new emigrants. These men were nearly all religious
refugees, and they paid their own passage. Poor men had to go to
the southern colonies and sell their labour to pay off their debt, but
the New England colonists were, from the beginning, men of substance and of independent spirit.

During the reign of Charles I some 60,000 emigrants left the
shores of England, and of these about a third went to New England.
The ideal of the puritan settlement in New England was not religious toleration but a different form of intolerance from that which
obtained in England itself. In Massachusetts, government was confined to elders of the Church, who constituted only about one-fifth
of the adult males, and anyone who objected to the rule of this theo-
cratic oligarchy was expelled.

The intolerance of Massachusetts led to the foundation of a number of other colonies. One group of dissident settlers hived off and
established themselves in Connecticut. Another group followed the
irrepressible Roger Williams, champion of religious liberty, who
was driven out of Massachusetts for declaring that the civil government had no authority in religious matters. In 1636 Williams
took refuge among the Indians, and he insisted on treating them
as equals and on buying from them land on which he might establish a new, and free, settlement. The community which he set
up developed eventually into the self-governing colony of Rhode
Island.

By the time civil war broke out in England, the colonies of North
America were firmly established and already valued their virtual
independence of the mother country. Further south, across the gap
formed by the Dutch colony of New Netherland, Virginia had been
joined by Maryland, created in 1632 by the Roman Catholic Lord

Baltimore, and named in honour of Charles I's Queen. The northern colonies made their living out of agriculture and the trade in fish, furs and naval stores, but in Virginia and Maryland tobacco and cotton were the main crops. These were ideally suited for cultivation on big plantations, and because immigrant labour was not readily available for such work negroes were imported from West Africa. The New England settlements had built up a flourishing trade by supplying the plantation colonies with food, and they worked in close co-operation with the Dutch merchants and shipowners of New Netherland.

## The West Indies

Of the islands off the American Coast, Bermuda was the first to be settled by the English. Sir George Somers, sailing out to Virginia with fresh emigrants in 1609, was wrecked on the 'Somers Islands', but he found life there very agreeable and sent back reports which not only inspired Shakespeare to write *The Tempest* but also encouraged the formation of the Somers Islands Company. Further south, in the Caribbean, the first English settlement was on St Kitts, discovered in 1624, but in the following year an English ship returning home came across the uninhabited island of Barbados, and annexed it to the English crown. Sir William Courteen, partner in an Anglo-Dutch trading concern, provided the funds for the settlement of the island and began a profitable trade in tobacco, but his rights were challenged by one of James I's Scottish favourites, the Earl of Carlisle, who had been given a patent creating him proprietor of the 'Caribee Islands'. Carlisle was not personally interested in colonisation, but he hoped that profits from the West Indian plantations would help pay off his debts, and he fought a prolonged legal battle which eventually confirmed his ownership. For some years Barbados and other West Indian islands concentrated on the production of tobacco and cotton, but by the time the civil war broke out they had begun the cultivation of sugar cane on a large scale.

## Cromwell and the Colonies

The colonies took no direct part in the civil war, and although the sympathies of the New England settlements were clearly with Parliament their main objective was the preservation of their freedom of action. The puritan triumph in England caused a second big wave of emigration — this time of royalists, most of whom went to the southern colonies. Others settled in Barbados and Antigua, and royalist predominance in the southern colonies explains why, after the execution of Charles I, the governments of these settlements recognised Charles II as King.

The English Parliament was not prepared meekly to relinquish control over the West Indian and southern mainland colonies, which were so valuable for English trade. In 1651 Sir George Ayscue was sent with a fleet to restore them to obedience, and this he did without any difficulty — a striking demonstration of the effectiveness of sea power. Cromwell hoped to use the Commonwealth navy not simply to enforce obedience but to extend the area of English sovereignty in the West Indies. He realised that this would be to his country's economic advantage, and the idea of uprooting Spanish power in that area appealed to the Elizabethan in him. He had already been involved with the company that attempted to establish a puritan settlement on Providence Island, but this was far too near the mainland coast, and the settlers had been driven out by the Spaniards in 1641. Cromwell's expedition, despatched in 1654, failed in its main objective of capturing Hispaniola, but it added Jamaica to England's colonial empire.

The governments of the Interregnum took the first big steps towards breaking the Dutch monopoly of trade in the American region, and of knitting together the commerce of England and her colonies. Early Stuart governments had not been entirely neglectful of colonial needs: the first committee of the Privy Council for Foreign Plantations, for instance, had been set up in 1634, and as early as 1621 James had ordered that colonial tobacco should be sent only to England and that, in return, the growing of tobacco in England should be forbidden. In 1651 these *ad hoc* measures were gathered together in the Navigation Act, which laid down that 'no goods or commodities whatsoever of the growth, production or manufacture of Asia, Africa or America, or of any part thereof . . . shall be imported or brought into this Commonwealth of England' except in such ships 'as do truly and without fraud belong only to the people of this Commonwealth, or the plantations thereof . . . and whereof the master and mariners are also for the most part of them of the people of this Commonwealth'. The intentions behind this Act were clear. The growth of English shipping was to be stimulated, and the Dutch were to be forced out of the dominant position which they had won for themselves in international commerce.

## The Restoration of Royal Authority

The government of the restored Charles II continued the policies of its Interregnum predecessors, as was shown by the passing of another Navigation Act in 1660 and the Staple Act three years later (see below, p. 430). It also completed the process of driving out the Dutch by taking over the colony of New Netherland in 1664 and renaming it New York. Expansion continued to the south and north of Virginia, though the settlers for these new colonies were drawn from Europe and the existing settlements rather than from England, where the growth of trade and industry was creating a demand for labour. In 1663 a group of courtiers, including Clarendon, Albemarle and Ashley, was given proprietorship over the area which they named Carolina. They intended to produce Mediterranean goods there — wine, oil and fruit — but the project was not a great success; smuggling flourished more than viticulture, and by 1700 there were only two small settlements which eventually developed into the separate colonies of North and South Carolina.

To the north of Virginia, Pennsylvania was colonised after William Penn had been given proprietary rights in 1681. Penn was the Quaker son of one of the admirals who had commanded Cromwell's Hispaniola expedition, and Charles II granted him territory in the New World to cancel out a debt owed by the crown to the admiral. The colony was at first settled by Quakers, glad to escape from religious persecution in England, and Penn's high ideals were reflected in the framing of an elaborate constitution and in the careful design of the city of brotherhood, Philadelphia, which he built by the Delaware river. Soon, however, the Quakers were outnumbered by other immigrants, who refused to accept Penn's direction and gradually took over control of the colony themselves.

The distance between England and America, and the conditions of life in the New World, promoted the growth of popular assemblies and self-government. The Navigation Acts, however, made some sort of central control imperative, in order to see that the regulations were not evaded, and under Charles II and James II an attempt was made to bring the colonies more directly under royal authority. The weapon of *Quo Warranto*, which had been used with such effect against the English corporations, was employed to bring the American settlements to heel. In 1684 the charter of Massachusetts was declared forfeit; two years later similar action was taken against Connecticut; and in 1687 Rhode Island was turned into a crown colony. James consolidated the northern settlements into a single Dominion of New England, and appointed a governor for the whole area, with orders to suppress popular assemblies and to rule through a nominated council.

## America and the Glorious Revolution

Autocracy, in New England as well as old, was ended by the Glorious Revolution. Most of the colonies had their charters restored, although in the case of Massachusetts the rule of the Church elders was brought to an end. The attempt at central control was abandoned, but further steps were taken to ensure that the Acts regulating trade were observed. In 1697 Customs officials were given the same rights of search as their English counterparts, and governors of colonies were required to take an oath to enforce the Navigation Acts on pain of £1,000 fine for negligence. The following year saw the setting up of Vice-Admiralty courts, which worked without juries and were therefore specially suitable for dealing with smuggling cases.

The long war with France, which dominated the reigns of William and Anne, resulted in a number of changes in the pattern of ownership of colonies in the New World. The Treaty of Utrecht, among many other provisions, transferred to England the French settlements in Newfoundland and the Hudson Bay region and set the stage for the last act of the colonial conflict, that was to take place in the eighteenth century. By the time the treaty was signed, the British possessions stretched unbroken along the east coast of America, and included many of the more important West Indian islands. The total population of this whole area, white and black, was about 350,000 — less than the number of people living in London and only about one-fifteenth of the total population of England. Yet these figures signified an astonishing achievement on the part of a small country, and although the English colonies were usually a disappointment to the early speculators who hoped for swift rewards, they brought enormous wealth to the Britain over which Anne ruled, and confirmed Hakluyt's prediction that 'this western voyage will yield unto us all the commodities of Europe, Africa, and Asia, as far as we were wont to travel, and supply the wants of all our decayed trades'.

## Africa and India

The settlement of the New World led to the development of commerce with Africa, and the years that followed the Restoration saw the establishment of a number of British trading stations on the west coast. In 1664 Fort James was founded on an island in the river Gambia, and the Treaty of Breda of 1667 transferred to England the Dutch settlement at Cape Coast Castle. These posts, and others like them, served as warehouses for human cattle, where black slaves were held before being shipped, in appalling conditions, across the Atlantic.

Further east, English traders had made settlements in India. When Charles II came back to his throne England did not actually own any Indian territory; the various trading stations, or 'factories', were held on lease from native rulers. This situation was changed by Charles's marriage to a Portuguese princess and by the breakdown of imperial government in India. Catherine of Braganza brought with her, as dowry, the port of Bombay, and this possession of the King of Portugal passed into outright English ownership. Charles II found it too expensive to maintain and in 1668 handed it over to the East India Company, who later made it their headquarters.

The company was concentrating on the development of its Indian links, leaving the East Indies to Holland, but it looked for protection to the Mogul emperors. This protection declined as the emperors lost effective control of the great empire which they ruled, and long before Aurungzeb died in 1707 the company had taken measures for its own defence. Royal charters from Charles II and James II had already given it authority to form alliances, declare war, make peace, issue coins, and carry out many other functions which were normally the preserve of sovereign powers. The trading company was, in fact, being slowly transformed into a sovereign state in India, and in 1687 the directors ordered the governor of Surat to 'establish such a polity of civil and military power, and create and secure such a large revenue . . . as may be the foundation of a large, well-grounded, sure English dominion in India for all time to come'. When this declaration was made it was little more than a statement of intention, and the years that followed saw bitter disputes between members of the old and the new East India Companies (see below, p. 429). Not until a united company was once again established, in 1708, could trade and diplomacy take advantage of the disintegration of central authority in India to establish British influence on foundations that were to endure for nearly two and a half centuries.

# 19

# Late Stuart England

## Population, Agriculture, and the Structure of Society

The Tudor and early Stuart period had seen the population increasing at an unprecedented rate. In 1541 there were some 2.8 million people in England, but the comparable figure for 1601 was more than 4 million and by 1656 it was well over 5 million. There followed a thirty-year period of decline until a slow growth set in again in the mid-1680s, which brought numbers up to 5.25 million by the time Queen Anne died. English agriculture had responded to this massive increase and, with the exception of brief periods when the harvest failed for several years in succession, had succeeded in meeting the demand for more food. The late Stuart period was one of consolidation, but also of experimentation in new crops and new and improved techniques. In Suffolk, for example, the cultivation of turnips was being practised on a large scale by the time Charles II was restored to the throne. Turnips were planted in late summer, after the harvest had been gathered, and were used mainly as cattle feed. This made it possible to keep animals in reasonable condition throughout the winter, and the advantages of this were so apparent that the practice gradually spread to neighbouring counties. Some of these had also pioneered improvements of their own. In Norfolk the use of lime, marl and manure to enrich sandy soils was already widespread, as was the growing of clover and other grasses.

Agricultural labourers, even though they were not destitute, normally lived near the poverty line. Their wages were low, their living conditions primitive, and they depended on communal grazing rights and the collection of brushwood to keep themselves going. Urban workers were no better off, and could not count even on the occasional benevolence which the country squire bestowed on his tenants. Justices of the Peace were still theoretically responsible for fixing wages, and occasionally did so, but they were usually more concerned with holding wages down than with enforcing a minimum. Strikes and combinations were illegal under common law, and in 1706 the Leeds Quarter Sessions heavily fined some cloth workers who had agreed among themselves to demand a penny-halfpenny an hour for their work, when the current official rate was only one penny. Nevertheless, the poorer sections of society, like the richer, benefited from the fact that prices in the non-agricultural sector were falling with the expansion of trade; and as more and more men were swept up into the armed services a scarcity of labour developed in certain areas, which gave the workers greater bargaining power. These factors contributed to the relative quiescence of the lower levels of English society, in marked contrast to the radicalism of the mid-seventeenth century. Had it not been for this, the Glorious Revolution and the intense party conflict of Anne's reign might have sparked off explosions.

Life was, as always, harsh for those who had no work and were dependent upon the charity of their neighbours. Tudor governments had been obsessed with the problem of the migrant poor, who were travelling in search of jobs, and the vagrants, who had lost their roots altogether and were perpetually on the move, since these were a threat to social stability. The same hostility was reflected in the Act of Settlement of 1662. This made the familiar assertion that 'the necessity, number, and continual increase of the poor . . . is very great and exceeding burthensome', and reiterated the long-established principle that paupers should be the responsibility of their native parishes. If any dared to leave home, they were to be arrested and sent back there — or, failing this, returned to the last place where they had been settled for any length of time. Otherwise it was feared they would become a burden on the more prosperous centres to which they were attracted. J.P.s were strict in enforcing the terms of this Act. By 1700 the cost of returning migrant poor to their home parishes had become a regular charge on the county rates, and in some places salaried contractors were appointed for the purpose.

The pressures which led to migrancy were reduced by the more effective administration of relief at the parish level. The able-bodied poor were set to labour in specially-built institutions, and from the 1690s onwards Corporations of the Poor were set up to cut down on outdoor doles and institute a strict regime in these workhouses, so that they should be regarded as places of last resort. The aged and enfeebled were usually looked after by Overseers of the Poor and were maintained out of the proceeds of a compulsory poor rate. The J.P.s, meeting in Quarter Sessions, would supervise the work of the Overseers and supplement it if need be. They would sometimes order rented accommodation to be provided for the deserving poor, or even the erection of cottages for them at the public expense. Such measures were expensive, but the cost of poor relief to local communities would have been even greater had it not been for the charitable foundations set up under the Tudors and early

Stuarts and for the endowment of almshouses by private patrons, which became increasingly common during the reigns of William and Anne. There was nothing enviable about the position of the poor, but at least the richer members of society acknowledged, and to some extent fulfilled, an obligation to provide for them.

These richer members were not, of course, without troubles of their own, particularly if they were middle or smaller gentry dependent upon rents for their livelihood. Poor harvests in the 1690s often left tenants with insufficient money to pay their rents, yet there was little point in evicting them, since they could not be easily replaced. The gentry could meet the shortfall in their incomes by borrowing, and could use the same method to finance improvements in their estates which would pay off in the long run. But lenders were reluctant to invest in land, which offered a return of only 3 per cent, when they could get around 8 per cent from the East India Company and 7–16 per cent from the Bank of England. Big landowners, on the other hand, were not so dependent upon the money market. They often had access to non-landed sources of wealth, and in any case could use the profits from one part of their estates to offset losses in another.

The outlook for the gentry was not all black. For one thing the expansion of trade and the increase in the size of the armed forces meant that there were more openings available to the sons of landed families. The law offered good prospects, not simply in London, and so did the Church, now that the social status of ministers was rising. Medicine was another career which was becoming socially acceptable, as was government service, particularly in the expanding revenue departments. Yet it remained the case that the best positions tended to go to those with most influence, which meant, in effect, to the children of the greater landowners, wealthy financiers and leading merchants. The lesser landowners lost out even in the marriage market, for their daughters had to be well endowed if they were to find a suitable husband, and the cost of this could be crippling. Marriage portions, like money for improvement of estates, could be raised by borrowing, but with the government taking such a large share of the national wealth for war purposes the interest rate was high. Officially it stood at around 5 per cent, but in practice borrowers might have to pay twice or three times as much.

It is hardly surprising that in these circumstances the lesser landowners, most of whom were Tory, developed a vehement and at times neurotic hatred of the Whigs, with whom they associated what they called the 'monied interest', or that they adopted an intransigently 'Country' stance and denounced the corruption of ministers and courtiers of whatever political persuasion.

The clergy, who from the economic point of view counted as

smaller landowners, shared these Tory and 'Country' prejudices. Now that the Church had moved into alliance with the political nation there was no shortage of recruits for the ministry, and most of them were men who had received a university education. The value of livings remained low, however, and pluralism was common. Poorly paid curates were all too frequently left in charge of parishes, while the holder of the living acted the part of a country gentleman or served as chaplain to some great household. Queen Anne showed her affection for the Church, and her appreciation of its needs, by surrendering the First Fruits and Tenths which Henry VIII had originally annexed to the crown. The income from this source was used, as 'Queen Anne's Bounty', to supplement the income of poorer clergy, but there was still an enormous gap between the average incumbent earning about £50 a year and some of the wealthier bishops who lived like princes on £5,000.

The greater bishops, the greater merchants, the greater landowners — these were the people who ultimately profited from the social and political changes of the sixteenth and seventeenth centuries. The Stuart attempt to give the central government control over local affairs had brought such discredit on this practice that it was not repeated. The landowners were left free, like the late medieval barons, to rule the areas over which their influence extended, and their mansions became the administrative centres from which the localities were run. They could usually depend on sources other than land to swell their incomes, offset the demands of taxation, and provide capital for expansion. The profits of trade, for instance, enabled Sir Josiah Child, a prosperous East India merchant, to build his great house at Wanstead; the profits of office — amounting in this case to £40,000 — provided the Earl of Nottingham, after six years as Secretary of State, with the capital he required to build his mansion at Burley-on-the-Hill; even war could be turned to profitable account, as the Duke of Marlborough discovered when a grateful Queen and country presented him with Blenheim Palace and an extensive estate as a thank-offering for his services on the battlefield.

The vacuum left by the contraction of royal authority was everywhere filled by the great landowners, and their influence extended even into that gentry stronghold, the House of Commons. Parliament met annually after 1689, and ambitious men were now prepared to devote not only much of their time but also much of their money to securing a seat. After the passing of the Triennial Act in 1694 it was illegal for a Parliament to remain in existence longer than three years, and frequent elections became the rule. In the counties the right to vote was confined to forty-shilling freeholders, but because of inflation this category now included not simply most of the 'middling sort' but even some of their social inferiors. In boroughs there was far greater variety, for during the early Stuart period the House of Commons had used disputed elections as a means of widening the franchise in urban constituencies, and this process had continued up to the Restoration. There were, of course, rotten boroughs, with only one or two voters, but there were also open boroughs, where the franchise extended to the majority of ratepayers. Overall it seems as though a quarter of the adult male population of England had the right to vote in Queen Anne's reign — a higher proportion than at any subsequent time until the late nineteenth century — and even the inhabitants of towns such as Birmingham, Manchester, Sheffield and Leeds, which had no seats in the House of Commons, made their views known by taking part in county elections.

Such was the intensity of political passions in late Stuart England that borough as well as county seats became prizes to be fought for, and the electorate had to be taken into account. Candidates did not rely simply on propagating their views to win support. They also resorted to various forms of 'influence', which could range from outright bribery to offers of patronage or support, or even to threats and occasional violence. The cost of influencing a county electorate could be enormous, but even in boroughs the price of votes was rising to the point where only very rich men could afford to compete. Peers could not be members of the Commons, but by using their money and their prestige they could bring considerable pressure to bear upon the electors who chose those members. By an ironic twist of fate, the gentry House of Commons, which had successfully led the struggle against monarchical absolutism, was now in danger of losing its independence to the newly emerging oligarchs.

## Trade and Industry

The years following the restoration of Charles II saw a rapid increase in the rate at which English commerce expanded. In the Tudor and early Stuart period English trade had been based upon the export of wool and woollen cloth to Europe, and by the time civil war broke out more distant markets had been opened for the New Draperies in India, the Levant and America. Until the Restoration, then, English industry and English trade were wool; everything else was incidental. After this date, the pattern of English commerce was transformed by the exploitation of oceanic trading routes and overseas possessions.

By 1700 nearly a third of all English imports came from outside Europe, and about half of these were re-exported — at a profit, of course. This was partly due to the opening up of new sources of supply, but it would have been impossible without the lowering of prices and the growth of a mass market. Tobacco, for instance, which in the early years of the century had been a luxury, costing at least twenty shillings a pound, became the indulgence of all classes as the price dropped to under a shilling. There was consequently an enormous increase in the amount imported. Virginia and Maryland, which had despatched a mere 20,000 pounds in weight to England in 1619, sent 21 million in the last year of the century, and colonial production was being constantly expanded to meet an apparently insatiable demand.

The same pattern was followed in the sugar trade, though here the expansion was not so dramatic. The Portuguese colonies in South America held a virtual monopoly of sugar exports until the 1640s, and it was not until James II's reign that sugar from the British West Indies began pouring into London and thence to all the major European centres. The third important item in this flourishing re-export trade was calicoes, which the East Indian Company began importing in considerable quantity. These fine cotton cloths, well suited to the style of living of an elegant age, were particularly valued by the fashionable ladies of late Stuart and early Georgian England, and their taste was shared by their contemporaries throughout Europe.

The government was alarmed by the threat which foreign textiles offered to the native woollen industry and did its best to protect the home product. The export of wool was forbidden, so that English clothmakers should have first call on the raw material available, and in 1678 the dead as well as the living were called on to maintain England's greatest manufacture by an Act ordering that all shrouds should be made of wool. These and other measures no doubt helped to check the decline of the cloth industry, but the salvation of the cloth merchants came in the end from their own efforts. They could not hope for a big expansion of their trade with hot regions like India, China and the Levant, but they exploited colder markets and sent increasing quantities of woollen goods to northern Europe and the American colonies. Although cloth no longer accounted for 90 per cent of English exports it was still more important than any other single item.

The spice trade lost its significance as tastes changed and more fresh meat became available in the winter, but tea and coffee both made their appearance in post-Restoration England, and quickly became popular. The East India Company flourished, as a consequence, but its monopoly was threatened by interlopers and resented by City merchants who did not belong to it. This jealousy found expression in the decision taken by Parliament in 1698 to create a new company, but the representatives of the old one fought a stubborn battle to preserve their privileges and in 1709 the two bodies were amalgamated once again into a single East India Company.

Although Parliament had been, in the early seventeenth century, an opponent of monopoly companies, its increasing power did not lead to free trade. In fact the post-Restoration period saw the creation of a number of new chartered companies — among them the Royal African Company, which bought slaves in West Africa and shipped them to the West Indies where they were exchanged for sugar; and the Hudson's Bay Company, which was formed to exploit the fur trade of North America. The general assumption, in an age when first the Dutch and then the French offered such a threat to the expansion of English trade, was that only organised groups of merchants could hope to raise the capital and provide the services necessary to ensure this expansion.

As far as trade to and from the American colonies was concerned, a monopoly was granted not to any specific company but to English merchants as a whole. The Staple Act of 1663 required the colonies to send 'enumerated' goods — of which the most important were sugar, tobacco and cotton — only to England, and forbade them to buy European goods until these had first been imported into England. This legislation was designed to protect English merchants against the Dutch, who were strongly entrenched in the carrying-trade both between one colony and another and between the colonies and Europe. Nothing effective could be done, however, while the Dutch held colonies on the North American mainland, and while the number of English ships was insufficient to cope with the demands made on them. Shortage of ships and sailors prompted the Navigation Act of 1660 which closed several loopholes in the 1651 Act by requiring that foreign-built ships in English ownership should be registered, and that English ships should have predominantly English crews. These measures presumably contributed to the great expansion of English shipping after 1660 and prevented the diversion of men and capital to less protected occupations. So did the freeing of trade from official restrictions. Corn exports, for instance, which the Tudors and early Stuarts had restrained in the cause of self-sufficiency, were stimulated by a government subsidy from 1673. Export duties on woollen goods were abolished in 1699, and ten years later the duty on coal was removed. These changes had a direct effect upon British shipping, for it was bulk cargoes like corn and coal that offered the chance of big profits, as the Dutch had earlier discovered.

The freeing of trade was accompanied by the freeing of industry, though this was the result of natural changes rather than of official action. In theory, industries were under the control of companies, which derived their authority from government charters, and they were also shackled by the Elizabethan laws regulating apprenticeship. In practice, however, the authority of the companies was declining, and the apprenticeship laws were moribund, except as an administrative convenience where paupers were concerned. The Livery Companies survived in London, but their members were recruited by patrimony rather than by occupation, and they were more concerned with social functions and City government than with the close supervision of particular occupations. The apprenticeship laws had attempted to impose a strait-jacket on English industry, and were the product of an age when men were plentiful and jobs were scarce. This was no longer true in the late seventeenth century. The rise in population was slowing down, while the demands of a wealthy community were encouraging industry to expand. The use of machines such as the stocking-frame and the gig-mill, which had earlier been opposed on the grounds that they put weavers out of work, was now encouraged, and experiments were taking place to harness steam power to the needs of industry. In 1712 the first steam pump, invented by Thomas Savery and Thomas Newcomen, was installed in a coal mine, and by the time George I came to the throne several more were at work. The exploitation of deeper seams was made necessary by the demand for coal. London alone burnt a quarter of a million tons a year, and the shortage of wood encouraged manufacturers to use coal instead. The iron and steel industry remained dependent upon charcoal, because the sulphur contained in coal made the metal brittle, but even here future developments were anticipated, for some time during Anne's reign a Quaker ironmaster, Abraham Darby, turned coal into coke, which he used to feed his blast furnaces.

Late Stuart England was, generally speaking, a country in which the way was being prepared for the agrarian and industrial changes that were to transform English society in the following century. New techniques were being tried out. Old restrictions were being swept away. Most important of all, the growth of great estates and the expansion of foreign trade were making possible the accumulation of capital on such a scale that it could eventually finance revolutionary changes.

## *Financial Institutions and Public Administration*

The expansion of English commerce made London one of the focal points of world trade, and brought not only wealth but elegance to the capital city. The London of Pepys and Defoe was a long way removed from the London that Shakespeare had known. After the Restoration it extended westwards into the area around Piccadilly and Jermyn Street, while in the early eighteenth century Edward Harley, son of Anne's Lord Treasurer, perpetuated his family's name and fortune by building Harley Street, Oxford Street and other fashionable thoroughfares on the open spaces that surrounded Tyburn. The streets of London were broader and cleaner after the Great Fire; hackney coaches and sedan chairs made travelling much more comfortable; theatres were crowded by the fashionable world, anxious to see the latest productions of Dryden, Congreve, Wycherley and Farquhar; and coffee-houses provided meeting places not only for the ladies and gentlemen of London 'society' in the narrower sense, but also for businessmen. One of these coffee-houses — that started by Edward Lloyd — was a favourite haunt of ship-owners, and gradually developed into the headquarters of marine insurance in England, while other coffee-houses were associated with particular political groups or with men of letters.

Lloyds was one example of the way in which the merchants of London were coming to provide the financial mechanisms demanded by a great trading community. The merchants were also responsible for persuading the government to establish a national bank. Ever since Charles II had declared, in 1672, his inability to repay his debts unless special parliamentary provision was made, but had offered the regular payment of interest, a national debt had existed, but public opinion was reluctant to accept such an innovation, especially when it was involved with the shaky financial system of the Stuart monarchs. The long war against France, however, made government borrowing on a big scale inevitable, and in 1694 a Bill was passed authorising the establishment of a national bank. Subscribers guaranteed to raise £1,500,000 and advance the entire sum to the government, in return for the regular payment of interest. The money was quickly raised, the Bank was an immediate success, and the key role played by the City is indicated by the fact that among the first directors were no fewer than seven future Lord Mayors. The Bank was given permission to issue its own notes as long as the total of these did not exceed the sum originally advanced to the government, and three years later, after the failure of the Land Bank, Parliament confirmed the Bank of England in its privileged position, and made the forging of its notes a felony. To ensure that the resources of the Bank were never used to finance monarchical despotism it was laid down that no advances were to be made to the government without the express approval of Parliament, and the combination of parliamentary security with assurance against royal intervention persuaded the wealthier sections of English society to contribute to the needs of the state on a scale that would have been impossible while Charles II or his brother was on the throne.

The Bank of England did not take over the existing national debt, although from time to time government bonds were transferred to it, but it made the idea of a national debt acceptable — even though it was hoped and assumed that the government would

eventually return to solvency. The government in fact made a remarkable effort to meet its financial obligations through taxation
rather than by borrowing, but the costs of the long war against
France were so enormous that taxation could go only part of the
way towards meeting them. It was hardly surprising, then, that by
the time Anne died the national debt stood at more than
£36,000,000 and that interest charges on it consumed three-fifths
of the annual revenue.

The main source of government income was the Land Tax,
which, in the post-Restoration period, gradually superseded the
older subsidy. It was based on the assessments collected during the
civil war — which themselves owed much to Ship Money — and
every county was required to provide a stated share of the total sum
fixed upon by the Treasury. When the Land Tax stood at four shillings in the pound, as it did throughout the greater part of Anne's
reign, it became a major, and at times intolerable, burden. In particular it struck at the shaky financial position of the lesser landowners, proving the last straw which forced many of them to sell
up and leave the land altogether.

The government imposed indirect as well as direct taxes, the
most important of which were the excise and the Customs. The
excise was a major source of revenue and was extended from beer
and cider to many other commodities and articles in daily use. By
1715 it was bringing in £2,300,000 a year, while the Customs were
contributing a further £1,700,000. The close connexion between
trade and revenue prompted post-Restoration governments to take
an interest in commercial matters. In 1660 a Council for Trade was
set up to advise the Privy Council on such matters and to work in
co-operation with the Council for Foreign Plantations, which handled colonial business. These two bodies survived until 1665, when
they were replaced by standing committees of the Privy Council, but
the triumph of the Cabal brought to power men who were much
more interested in commerce than Clarendon had been, and in 1668
a new Council for Trade was set up, which, by 1673, had also become responsible for plantations. Shaftesbury was active on this
body, of which John Locke was secretary, and it began the important process of collecting and interpreting statistical information.
This Council lasted only two years, when it was replaced by committees of the Privy Council, and not until 1696 was a permanent
Board of Trade set up, to keep in touch with the merchants and to
advise the government on commercial policy.

The expansion of government finance meant that the Treasury
became increasingly important, and during the late Stuart period
it not only developed more efficient book-keeping and budgeting
techniques but also extended its control over other departments.
These included two or three which had been of little importance

hitherto but developed rapidly under the impact of war. The industrious Samuel Pepys, now famous for his diary, served as a highly efficient Secretary of the Admiralty under Charles II and James II, and created what was virtually a new department. William Blathwayt did much the same during his long tenure of office as Secretary-at-War. Men such as these were professional administrators, and their emergence was one indication of changing attitudes towards government office — although much of the work continued to be done by deputies, and old habits died hard. Another indication was the shift, which set in during Charles II's reign, from life tenures, reversionary grants, and dependence upon fees, towards reversible appointments and realistic salaries.

All departments were grossly understaffed by modern standards. The two Secretaries of State had only about a dozen clerks to serve them, and had to write most of their letters themselves, while the permanent staff of the Treasury was seldom much more than twenty. Nevertheless, the years between 1660 and 1714 witnessed the development of an administrative machine far more complex than anything envisaged by, for instance, Thomas Cromwell, and one that, because of its complexity, was no longer under the immediate control of the King. No single minister controlled it either, for the Lord Treasurer (or, when the office was in commission, the First Lord of the Treasury) had not yet obtained the position of primacy which Walpole was to secure. But the collection and expenditure of public moneys were the most important governmental functions, as the Commons recognised when, in 1713, they passed a standing order giving the government sole right to initiate financial business in Parliament. While Anne was alive the emergence of a Prime Minister was hardly possible, but the half-century which followed her death showed that the minister who controlled the financial policy of the government could, in certain circumstances, become more important even than the sovereign.

## Political and Scientific Thought

Politics and religion were the cause of such intense controversy in the late Stuart period that a casual observer might well have assumed that fanaticism and intolerance were still integral features of English public life. This was true, but it was not the whole truth, for while the disputes between Whigs and Tories and dissenters and anglicans were genuine they concealed a considerable measure of agreement over fundamentals. The Tories were admittedly uneasy about their role in the Glorious Revolution, and an increasing number of them were in favour of the accession of the Old Pretender, following Anne's death. But a substantial section of the Tory party remained firm in its commitment to the Hanoverian succession and was prepared to work with the Whigs to bring this about. Even if the Jacobite line had been restored it would have been upon conditions that would have made permanent the positive gains of the Revolution settlement, for there was no disagreement between the various groups about the dangers of absolutism and the essential role of Parliament in the government of the country. The Tories professed their devotion to the cause of monarchy, but they did so within the context of the traditional constitution, which enshrined the liberties of the subject as well as the prerogatives of the ruler.

Similarly in religion, there was widespread acceptance of toleration for protestant nonconformists, in practice if not in principle. Some Tories, no doubt, would have liked to return to the days of Laud, but this was clearly out of the question. Anglican enthusiasts devoted their energies instead to such worthy causes as establishing Church schools and promoting the activities of the Society for the Reformation of Manners — founded in 1691 to combat the immorality which, they believed, was the inevitable accompaniment of the spread of heterodox and 'atheistical' doctrines. There was also a greater awareness on the part of Christians of all denominations of the need to evangelise the world outside Europe, and societies like those for Promoting Christian Knowledge (1698) and the Propagation of the Gospel (1701) were established to provide missionaries for the conversion of the heathen.

One of the reasons for the grudging acceptance of toleration was the realisation that persecution was ineffective, and that men's consciences could not, in the long run, be coerced. This case was argued most convincingly by John Locke, who, in his *Letters on Toleration,* emphasised that true religion consisted in 'the inward and full persuasion of the mind'. 'I cannot be saved', he added, 'by a religion that I distrust and by a worship that I abhor.' Locke's rational and dispassionate approach was also demonstrated in his political writings, which provided a philosophical basis for many Whig beliefs.

Locke's immediate predecessors in the field of political philosophy had been mainly concerned with justifying absolutism, reflecting in this — as did Locke in his own time — the age in which they lived. Thomas Hobbes, for instance, put forward in his *Leviathan* the doctrine that self-preservation is the basis of society. 'The condition of man', he wrote, 'is a condition of war of everyone against everyone', and in the state of nature which preceded the establishment of civil society there were 'no arts, no letters, [only] continual fear and danger of violent death; and the life of man, solitary, poor, nasty, brutish and short.' To free themselves from this terrible condition, human beings had (so Hobbes maintained) abdicated all their rights to the ruler — whether one man or a group — and the sovereign was justified in commanding absolute obedience, since any criticism of his authority would threaten to throw society back into the condition of primitive anarchy from which it had so laboriously raised itself.

Hobbes's view shocked his contemporaries, who had not grasped the nettle of sovereignty as firmly as he had. Royalists distrusted him because he seemed to justify power, no matter how that power had been acquired; while Parliamentarians disapproved of his theories because they could be taken as a defence of royal absolutism. Even Locke, who was critical of Hobbes's theories, declined to attack the *Leviathan* directly, for fear that he should become involved in the unsavoury reputation of its author. Instead he took as his target the doctrine of divine right, as expounded by Sir Robert Filmer in his *Patriarcha*, written during the Interregnum but not published until 1680.

Locke took a far more optimistic view of human nature than Hobbes or Filmer. He believed that men were born with certain rights which belonged to them as individuals. They had a right to life and to liberty, and because they had added their labour to the raw material that nature provided, they had a right to the property so created. Locke agreed with Hobbes that the basis of society was contractual, but where Hobbes had imagined primitive men contracting to abandon all their freedom of action to a sovereign power, Locke conceived of them making a bargain. They would agree to obey the sovereign because by so doing they could better preserve their natural rights. But if the sovereign himself became a threat to those rights, then the contract was automatically dissolved and the obligation of obedience annulled. 'A government', he wrote, 'is not free to do as it pleases . . . The law of nature stands as an eternal rule to all men, legislators as well as others.'

Locke was no republican. Like his friend and patron, Shaftesbury, he thought that limited monarchy represented the happy mean between tyranny and anarchy, but he was concerned above all that the community should be the ultimate arbiter. Government had been created by and for the people, and the people should decide what form of government they wanted at any given time.

The even tone of Locke's writings, the absence of passion and the appeal to common sense, were, like latitudinarian attitudes in religion, the heralds of the age of reason. Nothing contributed more to the triumph of reason than the progress of science, for by calling established truths into question and subjecting them to critical examination, the scientists increased the prestige and the self-confidence of man as a rational being.

The scientific revolution which began in the sixteenth century was a European phenomenon to which Englishmen made a number of important contributions. They were not among the first to challenge accepted explanations of the structure of the universe, but the Scotsman John Napier produced in 1614 the first tables of logarithms, which were used by Kepler in his work on ellipses, and Queen Elizabeth's physician, William Gilbert, published a book *On the Magnet and Magnetic Bodies and that Great Magnet the Earth* which so impressed Galileo that he gave a detailed account of it in his *Dialogues*.

The first major English figure in the scientific revolution was not, however, a practising scientist. Francis Bacon, a distinguished lawyer who became James I's Lord Chancellor, made himself the propagandist of the scientific method and constantly urged the need for experiment and research. The high position that he held and the fame of his name formed a shelter behind which enquiring men could pursue their researches, and the freedom given to scientific speculation in England may account for the fact that by the late seventeenth century London had become the capital of the scientific as well as the commercial world. It was Bacon's hope that academies would be formed where scientists could exchange information, for he recognised the paramount importance of communications to the spread of knowledge. No such academy was founded during his lifetime, but the Royal Society acknowledged him as its spiritual founder, and his picture appears next to the bust of Charles II in its official history.

In spite of Bacon and of the isolated achievements of such men as William Harvey, the discoverer of the circulation of the blood, English scientists did not come into their own until after the Restoration. Charles II was interested in mathematics and experimental science, and gave his patronage to the Royal Society which was formed in 1660. Among the early members of this distinguished body were Robert Boyle — son of Strafford's old enemy, the Earl of Cork — who was the first person to make a quantitative test of the elasticity of air, and Robert Hooke, who gave the first detailed description of a microscope and of the observations he had obtained by using one.

Most famous of all members of the Royal Society was Sir Isaac Newton, who fitted the isolated segments of scientific knowledge into a coherent pattern. Copernicus had shifted the earth from the centre of the universe, where Ptolemy had placed it; Galileo had confirmed, by his own observations, that heavenly bodies did not revolve around one fixed centre; while Kepler had discovered that the planets moved in ellipses and not circles. These men between them had destroyed the old picture of the universe, but had not succeeded in putting anything in its place. As John Donne, the Jacobean poet, complained:

The sun is lost, and th' earth, and no man's wit
Can well direct him where to look for it.
'Tis all in pieces, all coherence gone;
All just supply, and all relation.

It was left to Newton to restore coherence to the universe. Born in 1642, the year of Galileo's death, he studied at Cambridge under the mathematician Isaac Barrow, and eventually succeeded to Barrow's chair. During the Great Plague, Newton left Cambridge, like most of his contemporaries, and returned home to Lincolnshire. It was during this enforced vacation that he worked out the principles which were to form the basis of his system. He combined Kepler's laws and the observations of Galileo into a single theory of gravitation, and showed that the same force which makes an apple fall to the ground sends the heavenly bodies swinging on their courses.

The extension of scientific knowledge transformed older and traditional attitudes in much the same way, and at the same time, as protestantism and the expansion of trade broke up the fabric of medieval Christendom. The destruction of the old order with nothing to replace it would almost certainly have led to reaction, but the success of the scientists in creating a new synthesis had the opposite effect — it encouraged criticism and experiment, and it produced a veneration for the faculty of human reason that ushered in the Enlightenment.

# Suggestions for Further Reading

This bibliography does not include works published before 1970.

## THE TUDOR PERIOD

ALSOP, J. D. 'The Theory and Practice of Tudor Taxation', 97 *English Historical Review*, 1982.

CHALLIS, C. E. *The Tudor Coinage*, Manchester University Press, 1978.

CROSS, CLAIRE. *Church and People 1450–1660*, Fontana, 1976.

DAVIES, C. S. L. *Peace, Print and Protestantism 1450–1558* (Paladin History of England), Granada, 1976.

ELTON, G. R. *Reform and Reformation: England 1509–58* (The New History of England Vol. 2), Edward Arnold, 1977.

ELTON, G. R. *Studies in Tudor and Stuart Politics and Government*, Cambridge University Press, Vols I & II 1974, Vol. III 1983.

ELTON, G. R. *The Tudor Constitution*, Cambridge University Press, 2nd edition 1982.

FLETCHER, ANTHONY. *Tudor Rebellions* (Seminar Studies in History), Longman, 3rd edition 1983.

HAIGH, CHRISTOPHER. *Reformation and Resistance in Tudor Lancashire*, Cambridge University Press, 1975.

HEINZE, R. W. *The Proclamations of the Tudor Kings*, Cambridge University Press, 1976.

IVES, E. W. *Faction in Tudor England* (Appreciations in History No. 6), Historical Association, 1979.

LOADES, D. M. *Politics and the Nation 1450–1660: Obedience, Resistance and Public Order*, Harvester/Fontana, 1974.

RUSSELL, CONRAD. *The Crisis of Parliaments: English History 1509–1600* (The Short Oxford History of the Modern World), Oxford University Press, 1971.

SMITH, ALAN G. R. *The Emergence of a Nation State: The Commonwealth of England 1529–1660* (The Foundations of Modern Britain), Longman, 1984.

WILLIAMS, PENRY. *The Tudor Regime*, Clarendon Press, 1979.

YOUNGS, JOYCE. *Sixteenth-Century England* (The Pelican Social History of Britain), Penguin, 1984.

YOUINGS, FREDERIC A. *The Proclamations of the Tudor Queens* Cambridge University Press, 1976.

# THE NEW MONARCHY

CAMERON, A. 'The Giving of Livery and Retaining in Henry VII's Reign', 18 *Renaissance and Modern Studies*, 1974.

CHRIMES, S. B. *Henry VII*, Eyre Methuen, 1972

CHRIMES, S. B. 'The Reign of Henry VII: Some Recent Contributions', 10 *Welsh History Review*, 1981.

CHRIMES, S. B., ROSS, C. D. & GRIFFITHS, R. A. (Eds), *Fifteenth-Century England 1399–1509*, Manchester University Press, 1972.

COOK, DAVID. *Lancastrians and Yorkists: The Wars of the Roses* (Seminar Studies in History), Longman, 1984.

GUY, J. A. 'A Conciliar Court of Audit at Work in the Last Months of the Reign of Henry VII', 49 *Bulletin of the Institute of Historical Research*, 1976.

HICKS, M. A. 'Dynastic Change and Northern Society: the Career of the 4th Earl of Northumberland 1470–89', 14 *Northern History*, 1978.

HOROWITZ, MARK R. 'Richard Empson, Minister of Henry VII', 55 *Bulletin of the Institute of Historical Research*, 1982.

KIPLING, GORDON. 'Henry VII and the Origins of Tudor Patronage' in LYTLE, G. F. & ORGEL, S. *Patronage in the Renaissance*, Princeton University Press, 1981.

LANDER, J. R. *Crown and Nobility 1450–1509*, Edward Arnold, 1976.

LANDER, J. R. *Government and Community: England 1450–1509* (The New History of England Vol. 1), Edward Arnold, 1980.

LOCKYER, ROGER. *Henry VII* (Seminar Studies in History), Longman, 2nd edition 1983.

MYERS, A. R. 'Parliament 1422–1509' in DAVIES, R. G. & DENTON, J. H. *The English Parliament in the Middle Ages: A Tribute to J. S. Roskell*, Manchester University Press, 1981.

PRONAY, NICHOLAS. 'The Chancellor, the Chancery and the Council at the End of the Fifteenth Century' in HEARDER, H. & LOYN, H. R. *British Government and Administration*, University of Wales Press, 1974.

ROSS, CHARLES. *Edward IV*, Eyre Methuen, 1974.

WOLFFE, B. P. *The Crown Lands 1461 to 1536. An Aspect of Yorkist and Early Tudor Government* (Historical Problems. Studies and Documents), Allen & Unwin, 1970.

WOLFFE, B. P. *The Royal Demesne in English History. The Crown Estate in the Governance of the Realm from the Conquest to 1509*, Allen & Unwin, 1971.

# WOLSEY AND THE PRE-REFORMATION CHURCH

DERRETT, J. DUNCAN M. 'The Affairs of Richard Hunne and Friar Standish' in TRAPP, J. B. (Ed.). *The Complete Works of St. Thomas More*, Vol. 9 Appendix B, Yale University Press, 1979.

GORING, J. A. 'The General Proscription of 1522', 86 *English Historical Review*, 1971.

GUY, J. A. 'Wolsey, the Council and the Council Courts', 91 *English Historical Review*, 1976.

GUY, J. A. *The Cardinal's Court: the Impact of Thomas Wolsey in Star Chamber*, Harvester Press, 1977.

GUY, J. A. *The Public Career of Sir Thomas More*, Harvester Press, 1980.

GWYN, PETER. 'Wolsey's Foreign Policy: The Conferences at Calais and Bruges', 23 *Historical Journal*, 1980.

HARPER-BILL, CHRISTOPHER. 'Archbishop John Morton and the Province of Canterbury 1486–1500', 29 *Journal of Ecclesiastical History*, 1978.

SCARISBRICK, J. J. 'Cardinal Wolsey and the Common Weal' in IVES, E. W., KNECHT, R. J. & SCARISBRICK, J. J. (Eds). *Wealth and Power in Tudor England. Essays presented to S. T. Bindoff*, Athlone Press, 1978.

WILKIE, WILLIAM E. *The Cardinal Protectors of England. Rome and the Tudors before the Reformation*, Cambridge University Press, 1974.

# HENRY VIII

BOWKER, MARGARET. 'Lincolnshire 1536: Heresy, Schism or Religious Discontent?' in BAKER, DEREK (Ed.). *Schism, Heresy and Religious Protest* (Studies in Church History Vol. 9), Cambridge University Press, 1972.

BOWKER, MARGARET. 'The Henrician Reformation and the Parish Clergy', 50 *Bulletin of the Institute of Historical Research*, 1977.

BOWKER, MARGARET. *The Henrician Reformation: The Diocese of Lincoln under John Longland 1521–47*, Cambridge University Press, 1981.

BRIGDEN, SUSAN. 'Popular Disturbance and the Fall of Thomas Cromwell and the Reformers 1539–40', 24 *Historical Journal*, 1981.

ELTON, G. R. *Policy and Police: The Enforcement of the Reformation in the Age of Thomas Cromwell*, Cambridge University Press, 1972.

ELTON, G. R. *Reform and Renewal: Thomas Cromwell and the Common Weal*, Cambridge University Press, 1973

GUY, J. A. 'Henry VIII and the Praemunire Manoeuvres of 1530–31', 97 *English Historical Review*, 1982.

HARRISS, G. L. 'Thomas Cromwell's "New Principle" of Taxation', 93 *English Historical Review*, 1978.

IVES, E. W. 'Faction at the Court of Henry VIII: The Fall of Anne Boleyn', 57 *History*, 1972.

JAMES, M. E. 'Obedience and Dissent in Henrician England: the Lincolnshire Rebellion 1536', 48 *Past & Present*, 1970.

LEHMBERG, S. E. *The Reformation Parliament 1529–36*, Cambridge University Press, 1970.

LEHMBERG, S. E. *The Later Parliaments of Henry VIII 1536–47*, Cambridge University Press, 1977.

PALMER, M. D. *Henry VIII* (Seminar Studies in History), Longman, 2nd edition 1984.

SCARISBRICK, J. J. *The Reformation and the English People*, Blackwell, 1984.

YOUINGS, JOYCE. *The Dissolution of the Monasteries* (Historical Problems. Studies and Documents), Allen & Unwin, 1971.

# EDWARD VI AND MARY I

BARTLETT, KENNETH R. 'The English Exile Community in Italy and the Political Opposition to Mary I', 13 *Albion*, 1981.

BEER, BARRETT L. *Northumberland: the Political Career of John Dudley, Earl of Warwick and Duke of Northumberland*, Kent State University Press, 1974.

BEER, BARRETT L. *Rebellion and Riot. Popular Disorder in England during the Reign of Edward VI*, Kent State University Press, 1982.

BUSH, M. L. 'Protector Somerset and Requests', 17 *Historical Journal*, 1974.

BUSH, M. L. *The Government Policy of Protector Somerset*, Edward Arnold, 1975.

CORNWALL, JULIAN. *Revolt of the Peasantry 1549*, Routledge & Kegan Paul, 1977.

ELTON, G. R. 'Reform and the "Commonwealth Men' of Edward VI's Reign' in CLARK, PETER, SMITH, ALAN G. R. & TYACKE, NICHOLAS (Eds). *The English Commonwealth 1547–1640. Essays in Politics and Society presented to Joel Hurstfield*, Leicester University Press, 1979.

HOAK, D.E. *The King's Council in the Reign of Edward VI*, Cambridge University Press, 1976.

JONES, WHITNEY R. D. *The Mid-Tudor Crisis 1539–63*, Macmillan, 1974.

LOACH, JENNIFER & TITTLER, ROBERT (Eds). *The Mid-Tudor Polity c. 1540–1560* (Problems in Focus), Macmillan, 1980.

LOADES, D. M. *The Reign of Mary Tudor: Politics, Government and Religion in England 1553–58*, Ernest Benn, 1979.

MACCULLOCH, DIARMID. 'Kett's Rebellion in Context', 84 *Past & Present*, 1979.

PALLISER, D. M. 'Popular Reactions to the Reformation during the Years of Uncertainty 1530–70' in HEAL, FELICITY & O'DAY, ROSEMARY (Eds). *Church and Society in England Henry VIII to James I* (Problems in Focus), Macmillan, 1977.

POGSON, R. H. 'Revival and Reform in Mary Tudor's Church: a Question of Money', 25 *Journal of Ecclesiastical History*, 1974.

POGSON, R. H. 'Reginald Pole and the Priorities of Government in Mary Tudor's Reign', 18 *Historical Journal*, 1975.

THORPE, MALCOLM. 'Religion and the Wyatt Rebellion of 1554', 47 *Church History*, 1978.

TITTLER, ROBERT. *The Reign of Mary I* (Seminar Studies in History), Longman, 1983.

# TUDOR ENGLAND

## Agriculture and Enclosures

BLANCHARD, IAN. 'Population Change, Enclosure and the early Tudor Economy', 23 *Economic History Review*, 1970.

BRIDBURY, A. R. 'Sixteenth-century Farming', 27 *Economic History Review*, 1974.

DYER, CHRISTOPHER. 'Deserted Medieval Villages in the West Midlands', 35 *Economic History Review*, 1982.

WORDIE, J. J. 'The Chronology of English Enclosure 1500–1914', 36 *Economic History Review*, 1983.

## Economy and Society

CHARTRES, JOHN. *Internal Trade in England in the Sixteenth and Seventeenth Centuries* (Studies in Economic and Social History), Macmillan, 1977.

CLARKSON, L. A. *The Pre-Industrial Economy in England 1500–1750*, Batsford, 1971.

COLEMAN, D. C. *Industry in Tudor and Stuart England* (Studies in Economic and Social History), Macmillan, 1975.

COLEMAN, D. C. *The Economy of England 1450–1750*, Oxford University Press, 1977.

COLEMAN, D. C. & JOHN, A. H. (Eds). *Trade, Government and the Economy in Pre-Industrial England: Essays presented to F. J. Fisher*, Weidenfeld & Nicolson, 1976.

DAVIS, RALPH. *English Overseas Trade 1500–1700* (Studies in Economic History), Macmillan, 1973.

HOSKINS, W. G. *The Age of Plunder: The England of Henry VIII 1500–47* (Social and Economic History of England), Longman, 1976.

JAMES, M. E. *Family, Lineage and Civil Society: a Study of Society, Poli-*

*tics and Mentality in the Durham Region 1500–1640*, Oxford University Press, 1974.

PALLISER, D. M. *The Age of Elizabeth: England under the later Tudors 1547–1603* (Social and Economic History of England), Longman, 1983.

RAMSAY, G. D. *The English Woollen Industry 1500–1750* (Studies in Economic and Social History), Macmillan, 1982.

THIRSK, JOAN. *Economic Policy and Projects: the Development of a Consumer Society in Early Modern England*, Clarendon Press, 1978.

## Education

CRESSY, DAVID (Ed.). *Education in Tudor and Stuart England* (Documents of Modern History), Edward Arnold, 1975.

CRESSY, DAVID. 'Illiteracy in England 1530–1730', 20 *Historical Journal*, 1977.

CRESSY, DAVID. *Literacy and the Social Order: Reading and Writing in Tudor and Stuart England*, Cambridge University Press, 1980.

MCCONICA, J. K. 'The Social Relations of Tudor Oxford', 27 *Transactions of the Royal Historical Society*, 1977.

O' DAY, ROSEMARY. *Education and Society 1500–1800*, Longman, 1982.

## Law

BAKER, J. H. Introduction to *The Reports of Sir John Spelman* Vol. II, Selden Society, 1978.

BLATCHER, MARGARET. *The Court of King's Bench 1450–1550. A Study in Self Help*, Athlone Press, 1978.

BROOKS, C. W. 'Litigants and Attorneys in the King's Bench and Common Pleas 1560–1640' in BAKER, J. H. (Ed.). *Legal Records and the Historian*, Royal Historical Society, 1978.

COCKBURN, J. S. *A History of English Assizes 1558–1714*, Cambridge University Press, 1972.

HOULBROOKE, RALPH. *Church Courts and the People during the English Reformation 1520–70*, Oxford University Press, 1979.

PREST, WILFRID R. *The Inns of Court under Elizabeth I and the early Stuarts*, Longman, 1972.

## Local Communities

CLARK, PETER. *English Provincial Society from the Reformation to the Revolution: Religion, Politics and Society in Kent 1500–1640*, Harvester Press, 1977.

CLARK, PETER & SLACK, PAUL (Eds). *Crisis and Order in English Towns 1500–1700*, Routledge & Kegan Paul, 1972.

CLARK, PETER & SLACK, PAUL. *English Towns in Transition 1500–1700*, Oxford University Press, 1976.

PALLISER, D. M. 'A Crisis in English Towns? The Case of York 1460–1640', 14 *Northern History*, 1978.
SMITH, A. HASSELL. *County and Court: Government and Politics in Norfolk 1558–1603*, Clarendon Press, 1974.
SPUFFORD, MARGARET. *Contrasting Communities. English Villagers in the Sixteenth and Seventeenth Centuries*, Cambridge University Press, 1974.

## Militia and War

DAVIES, C. S. L. 'The English People and War in the early Sixteenth Century' in DUKE, A. C. & TAMSE, C. A. (Eds). *Britain and the Netherlands* Vol. VI *War and Society*, Martinus Nijhoff, The Hague, 1977.
SMITH, A. HASSELL. 'Militia Rates and Militia Statutes 1558–1633' in CLARK, PETER, SMITH, ALAN G. R, & TYACKE, NICHOLAS (Eds). *The English Commonwealth 1547–1640: Essays in Politics and Society presented to Joel Hurstfield*, Leicester University Press, 1979.

## Miscellaneous

MACFARLANE, ALAN. *Witchcraft in Tudor and Stuart England*, Routledge & Kegan Paul, 1970.
OUTHWAITE, R. B. 'Who bought Crown Lands? The Pattern of Purchases 1589–1603', 44 *Bulletin of the Institute of Historical Research*, 1971.
THOMAS, KEITH. *Religion and the Decline of Magic*. Penguin, 1973.

## Population and Plague

DYER, ALAN D. 'The Influence of Bubonic Plague in England 1500–1667', 22 *Medical History*, 1978.
GOTTFRIED, R. S. 'Population, Plague and the Sweating Sickness: Demographic Movements in late Fifteenth-Century England', 17 *Journal of British Studies*, 1977.
PALLISER, D. M. 'Tawney's Century: Brave New World or Malthusian Trap?', 35 *Economic History Review*, 1982.
*Plague Reconsidered, The* (no editor). *A New Look at its Origins and Effects in Sixteenth and Seventeenth-Century England*. Local Population Studies, 1977
WRIGLEY, E. A. & SCHOFIELD, R. S. *The Population History of England 1541–1871. A Reconstruction*, Edward Arnold, 1981.

## Poverty and Philanthropy

BEIER, A. L. 'Vagrants and the Social Order in Elizabethan England', 64 *Past & Present*, 1974.

BITTLE, WILLIAM G. & LANE, R. TODD. 'Inflation and Philanthropy in England. A Re-assessment of W. K. Jordan's Data', 29 *Economic History Review*, 1976.
POUND, JOHN. *Poverty and Vagrancy in Tudor England* (Seminar Studies in History), Longman, 1971.

# IRELAND AND SCOTLAND IN THE SIXTEENTH CENTURY

BRADSHAW, BRENDAN. 'Cromwellian Reform and the Origins of the Kildare Rebellion 1533–34, 27 *Transactions of the Royal Historical Society*, 1977.
BRADSHAW, BRENDAN. *The Irish Constitutional Revolution of the Sixteenth Century*, Cambridge University Press, 1979.
CANNY, NICHOLAS P. *The Elizabethan Conquest of Ireland: A Pattern Established 1565–76*, Harvester Press, 1976.
ELLIS, STEVEN G. 'Tudor Policy and the Kildare Ascendancy in the Lordship of Ireland 1496–1534', 20 *Irish Historical Studies*, 1977.
ELLIS, STEVEN G. 'Thomas Cromwell and Ireland 1532–40', 23 *Historical Journal*, 1980.
WORMALD, JENNY. *Court, Kirk and Community: Scotland 1470–1625* (The New History of Scotland), Edward Arnold, 1981.

# ELIZABETH I · POLITICS

BARTLETT, KENNETH R. 'The Role of the Marian Exiles' in HASLER, P. W. (Ed.). *The House of Commons 1558–1603* Vol. I Appendix XI, Her Majesty's Stationery Office, 1982.
BRADDOCK, R. C. 'The Rewards of Office-Holding in Elizabethan England', 14 *Journal of British Studies*, 1975.
GRAVES, M. A. R. 'Thomas Norton the Parliament Man: An Elizabethan MP 1559–81', 23 *Historical Journal*, 1980.
JAMES, M .E. 'The Concept of Order and the Northern Rising of 1569', 60 *Past & Present*, 1973.
KITCHING, C. J. 'The Quest for Concealed Lands in the Reign of Elizabeth I', 24 *Transactions of the Royal Historical Society*, 1974.
MACCAFFREY, WALLACE. *Queen Elizabeth and the Making of Policy 1572–88*, Princeton University Press, 1981.
MACCAFFREY, W. T. 'Parliament: the Elizabethan Experience' in GUTH, DELLOYD J. & MCKENNA, JON W. (Eds). *Tudor Rule and Revolution: Essays for G. R. Elton from his American Friends*, Cambridge University Press, 1983.
SMITH, A. G. R. *Servant of the Cecils: Sir Michael Hicks*, Cape, 1977.

THOMAS, DAVID. *'Leases in Reversion on the Crown's Lands 1558–1603'*, 30 *Economic History Review*, 1977.

WERNHAM, R. B. *After the Armada: Elizabethan England and the Struggle for Western Europe 1588–95*, Oxford University Press, 1983.

WILSON, CHARLES. *Queen Elizabeth and the Revolt of the Netherlands*, Macmillan, 1976.

# THE CHURCH OF ENGLAND AND PURITANISM 1558–1640

CLIFFE, J. T. *The Puritan Gentry: The Great Puritan Families of Early Stuart England*, Routledge & Kegan Paul, 1984.

COLLINSON, PATRICK. 'Lectures by Combination: Structures and Characteristics of Church Life in Seventeenth-Century England', 48 *Bulletin of the Institute of Historical Research*, 1975.

COLLINSON, PATRICK. *Archbishop Grindal 1519–83: The Struggle for a Reformed Church*, Cape, 1979.

COLLINSON, PATRICK. *The Religion of Protestants: the Church in English Society 1559–1625*, Clarendon Press, 1982.

COLLINSON, PATRICK. *English Puritanism*, (Pamphlet G.106) Historical Association, 1983.

DENT, C. M. *Protestant Reformers in Elizabethan Oxford*, Oxford University Press, 1983.

GREEN, IAN. 'Career Prospects and Clerical Conformity in the early Stuart Church', 90 *Past & Present*, 1981.

HAIGH, CHRISTOPHER 'Puritan Evangelism in the Reign of Elizabeth I', 92 *English Historical Review*, 1977.

HAIGH, CHRISTOPHER. 'The Recent Historiography of the English Reformation', 25 *Historical Journal*, 1982.

HEAL, FELICITY. *Of Prelates and Princes: a Study of the Economic and Social Position of the Tudor Episcopate*, Cambridge University Press, 1980.

HEAL, FELICITY & O'DAY, ROSEMARY (Eds). *Church and Society in England Henry VIII to James I* (Problems in Focus), Macmillan, 1979.

HUDSON, WINTHROP S. *The Cambridge Connexion and the Elizabethan Settlement of 1559*, Duke University Press, 1980.

JONES, NORMAN L. *Faith by Statute: Parliament and the Settlement of Religion 1559*, Royal Historical Society, 1983.

KAUTZ, ARTHUR P. 'The Selection of Jacobean Bishops' in REINMUTH, HOWARD S. (Ed.). *Early Stuart Studies: Essays in Honor of David Harris Willson*. University of Minnesota Press, 1970.

KENDALL, R. T. *Calvin and English Calvinism to 1649*, Oxford University Press, 1980.

LAKE, PETER. 'Matthew Hutton — A Puritan Bishop?', 64 *History*, 1979.

LAKE, PETER. 'The Significance of the Elizabethan Identification of the Pope as Anti-Christ', 31 *Journal of Ecclesiastical History*, 1980.

LAKE, PETER 'Constitutional Consensus and Puritan Opposition in the 1620s: Thomas Scott and the Spanish Match', 25 *Historical Journal*, 1982.

LAKE, PETER. *Moderate Puritans and the Elizabethan Church*, Cambridge University Press, 1982.

MANNING, R. B. 'The Crisis of Episcopal Authority during the Reign of Elizabeth I', 11 *Journal of British Studies*, 1971.

PLATT, JOHN. 'Eirenical Anglicans at the Synod of Dort' in BAKER, DEREK (Ed.). *Reform and Reformation: England and the Continent c. 1500–c. 1750* (Studies in Church History), Blackwell, 1979.

QUINTRELL, B. W. 'The Royal Hunt and the Puritans 1604–05', 31 *Journal of Ecclesiastical History*, 1980.

RICHARDSON, R. C. *Puritanism in North-West England: A Regional Study of the Diocese of Chester to 1642*, Manchester University Press, 1972.

SCARISBRICK, J. J. *The Reformation and the English People*, Blackwell, 1984.

SEAVER, PAUL. *The Puritan Lectureships 1560–1662*, Oxford University Press, 1970.

SHEILS, W. J. *The Puritans in the Diocese of Peterborough 1558–1610*, Northamptonshire Record Society, 1979.

SHRIVER, FREDERICK. 'Hampton Court Revisited: James I and the Puritans', 33 *Journal of Ecclesiastical History*, 1982.

WHITE, B. R. *The English Separatist Tradition: From the Marian Martyrs to the Pilgrim Fathers*, Oxford University Press, 1971.

WHITE, PETER. 'The Rise of Arminianism Reconsidered', 101 *Past & Present*, 1983.

# ROMAN CATHOLICISM

AVELING, J. C. H. *The Handle and the Axe: the Catholic Recusants in England from Reformation to Emancipation*, Blond & Briggs, 1976.

BOSSY, JOHN. *The English Catholic Community 1570–1850*, Darton, Longman & Todd, 1976.

DURES, ALAN. *English Catholicism 1558–1642: Continuity and Change* (Seminar Studies in History), Longman, 1983.

HAIGH, CHRISTOPHER. 'The Continuity of Catholicism in the English Reformation', 93 *Past & Present*, 1981.

HAIGH, CHRISTOPHER. 'From Monopoly to Minority: Catholicism in Early Modern England', 31 *Transactions of the Royal Historical Society*, 1981.

HIBBARD, CAROLINE M. *Charles I and the Popish Plot*, University of North Carolina Press, 1983.

WIENER, C. Z. 'The Beleagured Isle: a Study of Elizabethan and early Jacobean Anti-Catholicism', 51 *Past & Present*, 1971.

## THE STUART PERIOD

COWARD, BARRY. *The Stuart Age*, Longman, 1980.

CRESSY, DAVID. *Literacy and the Social Order: Reading and Writing in Tudor and Stuart England*, Cambridge University Press, 1980.

CROSS, CLAIRE. *Church and People 1450–1660*, Fontana, 1976.

DYER, ALAN D. 'The Influence of Bubonic Plague in England 1500–1667', 22 *Medical History*, 1978.

EVANS, JOHN T. *Seventeenth-Century Norwich: Politics, Religion and Government 1620–90*, Clarendon Press, 1980.

HOLMES, CLIVE. *Seventeenth-Century Lincolnshire*, History of Lincolnshire Committee for the Society for Lincolnshire History, 1980.

HOWAT, G. M. D. *Stuart and Cromwellian Foreign Policy*, A & C Black, 1974.

JONES, J. R. *Country and Court: England 1658–1714* (The New History of England Vol. 5), Edward Arnold, 1978.

LASLETT, PETER. *The World We Have Lost, further explored*, (3rd edition of *The World We Have Lost*), Methuen, 1983.

PENNINGTON, DONALD & THOMAS, KEITH (Eds). *Puritans and Revolutionaries: Essays in Seventeenth-Century History presented to Christopher Hill*, Clarendon Press, 1978.

SCHWOERER, LOIS. *No Standing Army. The Anti-Army Ideology in Seventeeth–Century England*, Johns Hopkins University Press, 1974.

SMITH, ALAN G. R. *The Emergence of a Nation State: The Commonwealth of England 1529–1660* (The Foundations of Modern Britain), Longman, 1984.

WRIGHTSON, KEITH. *English Society 1580–1680* (Hutchinson Social History of England), Hutchinson, 1982.

WRIGHTSON, KEITH & LEVINE, DAVID. *Poverty and Piety in an English Village: Terling 1525–1700*, Academic Press, 1979.

WRIGLEY, E. A. & SCHOFIELD, R. S. *The Population History of England 1541–1871. A Reconstruction*, Edward Arnold, 1981.

## JAMES I AND CHARLES I

ASHTON, ROBERT. *The English Civil War: Conservatism and Revolution 1603–49*, Weidenfeld & Nicolson, 1978.

ASHTON, ROBERT. *The City and the Court 1603–43*, Cambridge University Press, 1979.

FOSTER, E. R. 'Petitions and the Petition of Right', 14 *Journal of British Studies*, 1974.

GUY, J. A. 'The Origins of the Petition of Right Reconsidered', 25 *Historical Journal*, 1982.

HEINZE, R. W. 'Proclamations and Parliamentary Protest 1539–1610', in GUTH, DELLOYD J. & MCKENNA, JON W.(Eds). *Tudor Rule and Revolution: Essays for G. R. Elton from his American Friends*, Cambridge University Press, 1983.

HILL, CHRISTOPHER. 'Parliament and People in Seventeenth-Century England', 92 *Past & Present*, 1981.

HIRST, DEREK. *The Representative of the People? Voters and Voting in England under the Early Stuarts*, Cambridge University Press, 1975.

HIRST, DEREK. 'Revisionism Revised: The Place of Principle', 92 *Past & Present*, 1981.

JONES, W. J. *Politics and the Bench: the Judges and the Origins of the English Civil War* (Historical Problems. Studies and Documents), Allen & Unwin, 1971.

LEONARD, H. H. 'Distraint of Knighthood. The Last Phase. 1625–41', 63 *History*, 1978.

LOCKYER, ROGER. *Buckingham. The Life and Political Career of George Villiers, first Duke of Buckingham, 1592–1628*, Longman, 1981.

PARRY, GRAHAM. *The Golden Age Restor'd. The Culture of the Stuart Court 1603–42*, Manchester University Press, 1982.

PECK, L. L. 'Problems in Jacobean Administration. Was Henry Howard, Earl of Northampton, a Reformer?', 19 *Historical Journal*, 1976.

PECK, L. L. 'Corruption at the Court of James I: the Undermining of Legitimacy' in MALAMENT, BARBARA C. (Ed.). *After the Reformation: Essays in Honor of J. H. Hexter*, Manchester University Press, 1980.

PECK, L. L. *Northampton: Patronage and Policy at the Court of James I*, Allen & Unwin, 1982.

QUINTRELL, B. W. 'The Making of Charles I's "Book of Orders"' 95 *English Historical Review*, 1980.

RABB, T. K. 'Revisionism Revised: the Role of the Commons', 92 *Past & Present*, 1981.

RUIGH, R. F. *The Parliament of 1624. Politics and Foreign Policy*, Harvard University Press, 1971.

RUSSELL, CONRAD (Ed.). *The Origins of the English Civil War* (Problems in Focus), Macmillan, 1973.

RUSSELL, CONRAD. 'Parliamentary History in Perspective 1604–29', 61 *History*, 1976.

RUSSELL, CONRAD. 'The Parliamentary Career of John Pym 1621–29' in CLARK, PETER, SMITH, ALAN G. R, & TYACKE, NICHOLAS (Eds). *The English Commonwealth 1547–1640: Essays in Politics and Society presented to Joel Hurstfield*, Leicester University Press, 1979.

RUSSELL, CONRAD. *Parliaments and English Politics 1621–29*, Clarendon Press, 1979.

SCHWARZ, M. L. 'James I and the Historians: Toward a Reconsideration', 13 *Journal of British Studies*, 1974.

SEDDON, P. R. 'Household Reforms in the Reign of James I', 53 *Bulletin of the Institute of Historical Research*, 1980.

SHARPE, KEVIN (Ed.). *Faction and Parliament: Essays on Early Stuart History*, Clarendon Press, 1978.

SHARPE, KEVIN. 'Archbishop Laud and the University of Oxford' in LLOYD-JONES, HUGH, PEARL, VALERIE, & WORDEN, BLAIR (Eds). *History and Imagination: Essays in Honour of H. R. Trevor-Roper*, Duckworth, 1981.

SHARPE, KEVIN. 'Faction at the Early Stuart Court', 33 *History Today*, October 1983.

SLACK, PAUL. 'Books of Orders: The Making of English Social Policy 1577–1631', 30 *Transactions of the Royal Historical Society*, 1980.

SMITH. A. G. R. *The Reign of James VI & I* (Problems in Focus), Macmillan, 1973.

SMUTS, R. M. 'The Puritan Followers of Henrietta Maria in the 1630s', 93 *English Historical Review*, 1978.

THOMAS, G. W. 'James I, Equity, and Lord Keeper John Williams', 91 *English Historical Review*, 1976.

WHITE, STEPHEN D. *Sir Edward Coke and the Grievances of the Commonwealth*, Manchester University Press, 1979.

WORMALD, JENNY. 'James VI &I: Two Kings or One?', 68 *History*, 1983.

YOUNG, MICHAEL B. 'Illusions of Grandeur at the Jacobean Court: Cranfield and the Ordnance', 22 *Historical Journal*, 1979.

# THE CIVIL WAR

BRENNER, ROBERT. 'The Civil War Politics of London's Merchant Community', 58 *Past & Present*, 1973.

CLIFTON, ROBIN. 'The Popular Fear of Catholics during the English Revolution', 52 *Past & Present*, 1971.

COPE, ESTHER. 'Compromise in Early Stuart Parliaments: the Case of the Short Parliament of 1640', 9 *Albion*, 1977.

FLETCHER, ANTHONY. *The Outbreak of the English Civil War*, Edward Arnold, 1981.

HILL, CHRISTOPHER. *The World turned Upside Down: Radical Ideas during the English Revolution*, Penguin, 1975.

HOLMES, CLIVE. *The Eastern Association in the English Civil War*, Cambridge University Press, 1974.

HUGHES, ANN. 'Militancy and Localism: Warwickshire Politics and Westminster Politics 1643–47', 31 *Transactions of the Royal Historical Society*, 1981.

HUTTON, RONALD. 'The Worcestershire Clubmen in the English Civil War', 5 *Midland History*, 1979/80.

HUTTON, RONALD. 'The Structure of the Royalist Party 1642–46', 24 *Historical Journal*, 1981.

HUTTON, RONALD. *The Royalist War Effort 1642–46*, Longman, 1981.

KAPLAN, LAWRENCE. 'Steps to War: the Scots and Parliament 1642–43', 9 *Journal of British Studies*, 1970.

KISHLANSKY, MARK. 'The Creation of the New Model Army', 81 *Past & Present*, 1978.

KISHLANSKY, MARK. *The Rise of the New Model Army*, Cambridge University Press, 1979.

MANNING, BRIAN (Ed.). *Politics, Religion, and the English Civil War*, Edward Arnold, 1973.

MORRILL, JOHN. 'The Army Revolt of 1647' in DUKE, A. C. & TAMSE, C. A. (Eds). *Britain and the Netherlands* Vol. VI *War and Society*, Martinus Nijhoff, The Hague, 1977.

MORRILL, JOHN. *The Revolt of the Provinces. Conservatives and Radicals in the English Civil War 1630–50*, Longman, New Edition 1980.

MORRILL, JOHN (Ed.). *Reactions to the English Civil War* (Problems in Focus), Macmillan, 1983.

ROBERTS, CLAYTON. 'The Earl of Bedford and the Coming of the English Revolution', 49 *Journal of Modern History*, 1977.

TOMLINSON, HOWARD (Ed.). *Before the Civil War: Essays on Early Stuart Politics and Government*, Macmillan, 1984.

UNDERDOWN, DAVID. 'The Chalk and the Cheese. Contrasts among the English Clubmen', 85 *Past & Present*, 1979.

WANKLYN, M. D. G. 'Royalist Strategy in the South of England 1642–44', 3 *Southern History*, 1981.

# COMMONWEALTH AND PROTECTORATE

AYLMER, G. E. (Ed.). *The Interregnum. The Quest for Settlement 1646–60* (Problems in Focus), Macmillan, 1972.

BARNARD, TOBY. *The English Republic 1649–60* (Seminar Studies in History), Longman, 1982.

COOK, S. G. 'The Congregational Independents and the Cromwellian Constitutions', 46 *Church History*, 1977.

HILL, CHRISTOPHER. *God's Englishman: Oliver Cromwell and the English Revolution*, Weidenfeld & Nicolson, 1970.

HILL, CHRISTOPHER. *The World Turned Upside Down: Radical Ideas during the English Revolution*, Penguin, 1975.

MASSARELLA, DEREK. 'The Politics of the Army and the Quest for Settlement' in ROOTS, IVAN (Ed.). *'Into Another Mould'. Aspects of the Interregnum* (Exeter Studies in History No. 3), University of Exeter, 1981.

TAFT, BARBARA. '"The Humble Petition of Several Colonels of the Army": Causes, Character and Results of Military Opposition to Cromwell's Protectorate', 42 *Huntington Library Quarterly*, 1978.

UNDERDOWN, DAVID. *Pride's Purge. Politics in the Puritan Revolution*, Clarendon Press, 1971.

UNDERDOWN, DAVID. *Somerset in the Civil War and Interregnum*, David & Charles, 1973.

WEDGWOOD, C. V. *Oliver Cromwell and the Elizabethan Inheritance* (Neale Lecture in English History), Cape, 1970.

WOOLRYCH, AUSTIN. *Commonwealth to Protectorate*, Clarendon Press, 1982.

WORDEN, BLAIR. 'The Bill for a New Representative: the Dissolution of the Long Parliament April 1653', 86 *English Historical Review*, 1971.

WORDEN, BLAIR. *The Rump Parliament 1648–53*, Cambridge University Press, 1974.

# EARLY STUART ENGLAND

## *Education*

CRESSY, DAVID. 'Illiteracy in England 1530–1730', 20 *Historical Journal*, 1977.

O'DAY, ROSEMARY. *Education and Society 1500–1800*, Longman, 1982.

## *Law*

BARNES, T. G. 'Star Chamber Litigants and their Counsel 1596–1641' in BAKER, J. H. (Ed.). *Legal Records and the Historian*, Royal Historical Society, 1978.

BROOKS, CHRISTOPHER & SHARPE, KEVIN. 'History, English Law and the Renaissance', 72 *Past & Present*, 1976.

COCKBURN, J. S. *A History of English Assizes 1558–1714*, Cambridge University Press, 1972.

LEVACK, BRIAN P. *The Civil Lawyers in England 1603–41*, Clarendon Press, 1973.

PAWLISCH, HANS S. 'Sir John Davies, the Ancient Constitution, and Civil Law', 23 *Historical Journal*, 1980.

PREST, WILFRID R. *The Inns of Court under Elizabeth I and the Early Stuarts*, Longman, 1972.

WRIGHTSON, KEITH. 'Two Concepts of Order: Justices, Constables and Jurymen in Seventeenth-Century England' in BREWER,

JOHN & STYLES, JOHN (Eds). *An Ungovernable People: The English and their Law in the Seventeenth and Eighteenth Centuries*, Rutgers University Press, 1980.

## Local Communities

CLARK, PETER. *English Provincial Society from the Reformation to the Revolution: Religion, Politics and Society in Kent 1500–1640*, Harvester Press, 1977.
CLARK, PETER & SLACK, PAUL. *English Towns in Transition 1500–1700*, Oxford University Press, 1976.
FLETCHER, ANTHONY. *A County Community in Peace and War: Sussex 1600–60*, Longman, 1975.
HOLMES, CLIVE. 'The County Community in Stuart Historiography', 19 *Journal of British Studies*, 1980.
MORRILL, JOHN. *Cheshire, 1630–60: County Government and Society during the English Revolution*, Oxford University Press, 1974.
SMITH, A. HASSELL. 'Militia Rates and Militia Statutes 1558-1663' in CLARK, PETER, SMITH, ALAN G. R, & TYACKE, NICHOLAS (Eds). *The English Commonwealth 1547–1640: Essays in Politics and Society presented to Joel Hurstfield*, Leicester University Press, 1979.
SPUFFORD, MARGARET. *Contrasting Communities. English Villagers in the Sixteenth and Seventeenth Centuries*, Cambridge University Press, 1974.

## Poverty

SLACK, PAUL A. 'Vagrants and Vagrancy in England 1598–1664', 27 *Economic History Review*, 1974.

## Science and Medicine

MACDONALD, MICHAEL. *Mystical Bedlam: Madness, Anxiety and Healing in Seventeenth-Century England*, Cambridge University Press, 1982.
SHAPIRO, B. J. 'The Universities and Science in Seventeenth-Century England', 10 *Journal of British Studies*, 1972.
WEBSTER, CHARLES. *The Great Instauration. Science, Medicine and Reform 1626–60*, Duckworth, 1975.

## Society

CLARK, PETER. *The English Alehouse. A Social History 1200–1830*, Longman, 1983.
LANG, R. G. 'Social Origins and Social Aspirations of Jacobean London Merchants', 27 *Economic History Review*, 1974.
SHARP, BUCHANAN. *In Contempt of All Authority: Rural Artisans and Riot in the West of England 1586–1660*, University of California Press, 1980.

STONE, LAWRENCE. *Family and Fortune: Studies in Aristocratic Finance in the Sixteenth and Seventeenth Centuries*, Clarendon Press, 1973.

## Trade and Industry

COLEMAN, D. C. *Industry in Tudor and Stuart England* (Studies in Economic and Social History), Macmillan, 1975.

COLEMAN, D. C. *The Economy of England 1450–1750*, Oxford University Press, 1977.

DAVIS, RALPH. *English Overseas Trade 1500–1700* (Studies in Economic History), Macmillan, 1973.

RAMSAY, G. D. *The English Woollen Industry 1500–1750* (Studies in Economic and Social History), Macmillan, 1982.

THIRSK, JOAN. *Economic Policy and Projects: the Development of a Consumer Society in Early Modern England*, Clarendon Press, 1978.

# CHARLES II

CHANDAMAN, C. D. *The English Public Revenue 1660–88*, Clarendon Press, 1975.

GREEN, I. M. *The Re-establishment of the Church of England 1660–63*, Oxford University Press, 1978.

HABAKKUK, J. 'The Land Settlement and the Restoration of Charles II', 28 *Transactions of the Royal Historical Society*, 1978.

HALEY, K. H. D. ' "No Popery" in the Reign of Charles II' in BROMLEY, J. S. & KOSSMANN, E. H. (Eds). *Britain and the Netherlands* Vol. V *Some Political Mythologies*, Martinus Nijhoff, The Hague, 1975.

JONES, J. R. (Ed.). *The Restored Monarchy 1660–88* (Problems in Focus), Macmillan, 1979.

KENYON, J. P. *The Popish Plot*, Heinemann, 1972.

MILLER, JOHN. *Popery and Politics in England 1660–88*, Cambridge University Press, 1973.

MILLER, JOHN. 'Charles II and his Parliaments', 32 *Transactions of the Royal Historical Society*, 1982.

MILLER, JOHN. 'The Potential for "Absolutism" in Later Stuart England', 69 *History*, 1984.

MILLER, JOHN. *Restoration England: the Reign of Charles II* (Seminar Studies in History), Longman, 1985.

# JAMES II

AVELING, J. C. H. *The Handle and the Axe: the Catholic Recusants in England from Reformation to Emancipation*, Blond & Briggs, 1976.

BENNETT, G. V. 'The Seven Bishops: a Reconsideration' in BAKER, DEREK (Ed.). *Religious Motivation: Biographical and Sociological Problems for the Church Historian* (Studies in Church History), Blackwell, 1978.

CHANDAMAN, C. D. 'The Financial Settlement in the Parliament of 1685' in HEARDER, H. & LOYN, H. R. *British Government and Administration*, University of Wales Press, 1974.

CHILDS, JOHN. *The Army, James II, and the Glorious Revolution*, Manchester University Press, 1980.

GLASSEY, L. *Politics and the Appointment of Justices of the Peace 1675–1720*, Oxford University Press, 1979.

JONES, J. R. (Ed.). *The Restored Monarchy 1660–88* (Problems in Focus), Macmillan, 1979.

MILLER, JOHN. *Popery and Politics in England 1660–88*, Cambridge University Press, 1973.

MILLER, JOHN. 'Catholic Officers in the Later Stuart Army', 88 *English Historical Review*, 1973.

MILLER, JOHN. 'The Militia and the Army in the Reign of James II', 16 *Historical Journal*, 1973.

MILLER, JOHN. *James II: a Study in Kingship*, Wayland, 1978.

MILLER, JOHN. 'The Potential for "Absolutism" in Later Stuart England', 69 *History*, 1984.

# THE GLORIOUS REVOLUTION AND WILLIAM III

FRANKLE, R. J. 'The Formulation of the Declaration of Rights', 17 *Historical Journal*, 1974.

HOSFORD, DAVID. *Nottingham, Nobles and the North: Aspects of the Revolution of 1688*, Archon Books (Hamden, Conn.), 1976.

JONES, J. R. *The Revolution of 1688 in England*, Weidenfeld & Nicolson, 1972.

KENYON, J.P. *Revolution Principles: The Politics of Party 1689–1720*, Cambridge University Press, 1977.

MCINNES, ANGUS. 'When was the English Revolution?', 67 *History*, 1982.

MILLER, JOHN. *The Glorious Revolution* (Seminar Studies in History), Longman, 1983.

REITAN, E. A. 'From Revenue to Civil List 1689–1702', 13 *Historical Journal*, 1970.

ROBERTS, CLAYTON. 'The Constitutional Significance of the Financial Settlement of 1690', 20 *Historical Journal*, 1977.

SCHWOERER, LOIS. *The Declaration of Rights 1689*, Johns Hopkins University Press, 1982.

# QUEEN ANNE

DOWNIE, J. A. *Robert Harley and the Press: Propaganda and Public Opinion in the Age of Swift and Defoe*, Cambridge University Press, 1979.

GREGG, EDWARD. *Queen Anne*, Routledge & Kegan Paul, 1980.

HILL, B. W. 'Oxford, Bolingbroke and the Peace of Utrecht', 16 *Historical Journal*, 1973.

HOLMES, GEOFFREY. *The Trial of Dr. Sacheverell*, Eyre Methuen, 1973.

HOLMES, GEOFFREY. 'The Sacheverell Riots', 72 *Past & Present*, 1976.

HOLMES, GEOFFREY. 'The Electorate and the National Will in the first Age of Party'. Published by the author at the University of Lancaster. 1976.

MCINNES, ANGUS. *Robert Harley, Puritan Politician*, Gollancz, 1970.

SPECK, W. A. *The Struggle in the Constituencies 1701–15*, Macmillan, 1970.

# LATE STUART ENGLAND

COLEMAN, D. C. *Industry in Tudor and Stuart England* (Studies in Economic and Social History), Macmillan, 1975.

COLEMAN, D. C. *The Economy of England 1450–1750*, Oxford University Press, 1977.

CRESSY, DAVID. 'Illiteracy in England 1530–1730', 20 *Historical Journal*, 1977.

DAVIS, RALPH. *English Overseas Trade 1500–1700* (Studies in Economic History), Macmillan, 1973.

DICKSON, P. G. M. 'War Finance 1689–1714' in BROMLEY, J. S. (Ed.). *The New Cambridge Modern History* Vol. VI *The Rise of Great Britain and Russia 1688–1715/25*, Cambridge University Press, 1970.

HOLMES, GEOFFREY. 'The Achievement of Stability: The Social Context of Politics from the 1680s to the Age of Walpole' in CANNON, JOHN (Ed.). *The Whig Ascendancy: Colloquies on Hanoverian England*, Edward Arnold, 1981.

HUNTER, MICHAEL. *Science and Society in Restoration England*, Cambridge University Press, 1981.

*Plague Reconsidered, The* (no editor). *A New Look at its Origins and Effects in Sixteenth and Seventeenth-Century England*, Local Population Studies, 1977.

RAMSAY, G. D. *The English Woollen Industry 1500–1750* (Studies in Economic and Social History), Macmillan, 1982.

STONE, LAWRENCE. 'The Residential Development of the West End of London in the Seventeenth Century' in MALAMENT,

BARBARA C. (Ed.). *After the Reformation: Essays in Honor of J. H. Hexter*, Manchester University Press, 1980.

WESTFALL, RICHARD S. *Never at Rest. A Biography of Isaac Newton*, Cambridge University Press, 1982.

WORDIE, J. R. 'The Chronology of English Enclosure 1500–1914', 36 *Economic History Review*, 1983.


# SEVENTEENTH-CENTURY IRELAND

BARNARD, T. C. 'Planters and Policies in Cromwellian Ireland', 61 *Past & Present*, 1973.

BARNARD, T. C. *Cromwellian Ireland: English Government and Reform in Ireland 1649–60*, Oxford University Press, 1975.

CLARKE, AIDAN. 'Ireland and the General Crisis', 48 *Past & Present*, 1970.


# SEVENTEENTH-CENTURY SCOTLAND

DOW, F. D. *Cromwellian Scotland 1651–60*, John Donald, Edinburgh, 1979.

MITCHISON, ROSALIND. *Lordship to Patronage: Scotland 1603–1745* (The New History of Scotland), Edward Arnold, 1983.

STEVENSON, DAVID. *Revolution and Counter-Revolution in Scotland 1644–51*, Royal Historical Society, 1978.

WORMALD, JENNY. *Court, Kirk and Community: Scotland 1470–1625* (The New History of Scotland), Edward Arnold, 1981.

# Appendix I. English Monarchs

**HOUSE OF YORK**

| | |
|---|---|
| Edward IV | 1461-1483 (in exile 1470-71) |
| Edward V | 1483 (murdered in the Tower) |
| Richard III | 1483-1485 (killed at Bosworth) |

**HOUSE OF TUDOR**

| | |
|---|---|
| Henry VII | 1485-1509 |
| Henry VIII | 1509-1547 |
| Edward VI | 1547-1553 |
| Mary I | 1553-1558 |
| Elizabeth I | 1558-1603 |

**HOUSE OF STUART**

| | |
|---|---|
| James I | 1603-1625 |
| Charles I | 1625-1649 (executed) |
| Charles II | 1649-1685 (in exile until 1660) |
| James II | 1685-1689 (fled the country in 1688) |
| William III & Mary II | 1689-1702 |
| Anne | 1702-1714 |

# Appendix II. English Parliaments

**EDWARD IV**
1461 November-1462 May
1463 April-1465 March
1467 June-1468 June
1470 November-?1471 April
1472 October-1475 March
1478 January-February
1483 January-February

**RICHARD III**
1484 January-February

**HENRY VII**
1485 November-1486 March
1487 November-December
1489 January-1490 February
1491 October-1492 March
1495 October-December
1497 January-March
1504 January-April

**HENRY VIII**
1510 January-February
1512 February-1514 March
1515 February-December
1523 April-August
1529 November-1536 April (the Reformation Parliament)
1536 June-July
1539 April-1540 July
1542 January-1544 March
1545 November-1547 January

**EDWARD VI**
1547 November-1552 April
1553 March

## MARY I
1553 October-December
1554 April-May
1554 November-1555 January
1555 October-December
1558 January-November

## ELIZABETH I
1559 January-May
1563 January-1567 January
1571 April-May
1572 May-1583 April
1584 November-1585 September
1586 October-1587 March
1589 February-March
1593 February-April
1597 October-1598 February
1601 October-December

## JAMES I
1604 March-1611 February
1614 April-June (the Addled Parliament)
1621 January-1622 February
1624 February-1625 March

## CHARLES I
1625 May-August
1626 February-June
1628 March-1629 March
1640 April-May (the Short Parliament)
1640 November-1660 March (the Long Parliament. Purged in
        1648 and expelled in April 1653)

## CIVIL WAR AND INTERREGNUM
1644 January-October (summoned by the King to Oxford)
1653 July-December (the Nominated Assembly, Parliament of
        Saints, Barebones Parliament)
1654 September-1655 January
1656 September-1658 February
1659 January-April
1659 May-1660 March (the recalled Rump)

## CHARLES II
1660 April-December (the Convention)
1661 May-1679 January (the Long Parliament of the Restoration,
        Cavalier Parliament, Pensionary Parliament)

1679 March-July
1680 October-1681 January
1681 March (the Oxford Parliament)

## JAMES II
1685 May-1687 July

## WILLIAM III AND MARY II
1689 January-1690 February (the Convention)
1690 March-1695 October
1695 November-1698 July
1698 August-1700 December
1701 February-November
1701 December-1702 July

## ANNE
1702 August-1705 April
1705 June-1708 April (became in 1707 the first Parliament of
    Great Britain)
1708 July-1710 September
1710 November-1713 August
1713 November-1715 January

(Based on the list given in POWICKE, SIR F. MAURICE & FRYDE, E. B.
*Handbook of British Chronology*, Royal Historical Society, 2nd edition,
1961).

# Index